Reader Series
in Library and Information Science

Published *Readers* in the series are:

Reader in Library Administration. 1969.
Paul Wasserman and Mary Lee Bundy.

Reader in Research Methods for Librarianship. 1970.
Mary Lee Bundy and Paul Wasserman.

Reader in the Academic Library. 1970.
Michael M. Reynolds.

Reader in Library Services and the Computer. 1971.
Louis Kaplan.

Reader in American Library History. 1971.
Michael H. Harris.

Reader in Classification and Descriptive Cataloging. 1972.
Ann F. Painter.

Reader in Classification
and
Descriptive Cataloging

edited by

Ann F. Painter

1972

NCR Microcard Editions

"*Readers in Librarianship and Information Science*
published and distributed by GREENWOOD PRESS,
a Division of Congressional Information Service, Inc.,
Westport, CT 06881."

Copyright © 1972 by The National Cash Register Company
Library of Congress Catalog Card Number: 72-78204
ISBN: 0-910972-13-3

Published by NCR/Microcard Editions,
901 26th Street, N.W.
Washington, D.C. 20037

Printed in the United States of America

Foreword

Unlike many other academic disciplines, librarianship has not yet begun to exploit the contributions of the several disciplines toward the study of its own issues. Yet the literature abounds with material germane to its concerns. Too frequently the task of identifying, correlating, and bringing together material from innumerable sources is burdensome, time consuming or simply impossible. For a field whose stock in trade is organizing knowledge, it is clear that the job of synthesizing the most essential contributions from the elusive sources in which they are contained is overdue. This then is the rationale for the series, *Readers in Library and Information Science.*

The *Readers in Library and Information Science* will include books concerned with various broad aspects of the field's interests. Each volume will be prepared by a recognized student of the topic covered, and the content will embrace material from the many different sources from the traditional literature of librarianship as well as from outside the field in which the most salient contributions have appeared. The objectives of the series will be to bring together in convenient form the key elements required for a current and comprehensive view of the subject matter. In this way it is hoped that the core of knowledge, essential as the intellectual basis for study and understanding, will be drawn into focus and thereby contribute to the furtherance of professional education and professional practice in the field.

Paul Wasserman
Series Editor

Contents

Introduction

I

CLASSIFICATION

II

DESCRIPTIVE CATALOGING

Reader in Classification
and
Descriptive Cataloging

Introduction

American librarians, unlike many of their counterparts in the rest of the world, have always seemed to accept "cataloging and classification" as necessary evils for the organization of collections. At a relatively early stage in the development of libraries, they were endowed with two workable classifications—the Dewey Decimal and the Library of Congress classifications—and one fairly detailed set of rules for descriptive cataloging—C.A. Cutter's *Rules for Dictionary Catalog*. Librarians have been inclined to accept all three as packages and are unconcerned with how and why they work, or do not work, as the case may be. It has only been in recent years that anything concerning the theoretical nature of cataloging and classification has stimulated interest.

The computer, and its accompanying technology, has undoubtedly had some impact on the interest in theoretical structures and philosophies. The traditional has become unworkable because of size, volume and complexity.

Regardless of some increased intellectual and research activity the literature on cataloging and classification, especially the latter, has been sparse. Most professional librarians will admit to a need for new blood with an understanding of, or at least an ability to converse and reason with, the principles and theories of organization. Of course these can be transmitted by word of mouth, as the mysteries of the Library of Congress Classification have been for years, but it has not proven to be very effective. Considerations of principle and theory have been relegated to the advanced seminar level in most schools, way out of reach of the majority of library school students. In many respects it has only been since the incursions of information science to library school curricula that much of the principle and theory of the organization of collections has appeared at all. In few other areas has information science contributed so much to the theoretical base of librarianship.

This particular collection of readings has been assembled with one major objective—to bring to the majority of students some idea of what descriptive cataloging and classification are all about; not the how-to but, rather, the why. These readings are intended to either supplement a basic course in the organization of materials and information (more traditionally labelled cataloging and classification) or to serve as primary readings for seminars in the principles and theory of both. They have indeed been used very successfully in this manner.

As I have indicated, the literature is sparse, and some of it is incomprehensible to most students at any level. The literature of classification is particularly susceptible to these weaknesses. The reader will note that most of the selections in classification come from chapters of books while those of descriptive cataloging come from both the periodical and monographic literature. An attempt has been made to provide a glimpse into the "classics" of both fields, as well as the trend of future literature. The number of selections is of necessity, small. Hopefully the selections are reasonably sound and can offer a stepping-off point for future activities.

The two parts of the readings are tied together not so much by logic—one does not lead to the other—but rather because they are indeed, perhaps unfortunately, still linked in the hearts and minds of the American cataloger. It is hoped that they will stimulate incipient librarians to search more carefully into the theoretical bases of their profession and re-evaluate present methods and procedures.

Philadelphia, Pennsylvania   *A.F.P.*
April 1971

I

CLASSIFICATION

Classification is usually defined by what it does rather than by what it is. Classification is two things: 1) the act or process of arranging, and 2) the act or process of defining. Modern classification theory has developed around the principle of synthesis which in many respects bridges the gap between arrangement and definition. The definition most widely accepted today is that presented by the participants of the Elsinore Conference in 1965: "By classification is meant any method creating relations, generic or other, between individual semantic units, regardless of the degree in hierarchy contained in the systems, and of whether those systems would be applied in connection with traditional or more or less mechanized methods of document searching."

This definition is quite broad. The selections presented here are viewed from a more traditional point of view and hence do not include indexing schemes as classifications. Classification is conceived of basically as a systematic, hierarchical structure of knowledge, primarily enumerative and pragmatic by nature. It bears a strong relationship to indexing and indexing theory and careful analysis shows the transition from one to another.

In order to approach classification in a systematic way the selections have been divided into four sections: historical background and development; principles, theories and philosophies; automatic classification, and research in classification. Hopefully the concepts of each build on the others.

CLASSIFICATION

Historical Background and Development

The classificationist of today is apt to feel that the schemes of the past have little to offer in planning for the future. While it is true such schemes were designed for limited collections, the principles on which they were based are as valid now as ever. (No scheme becomes obsolete.) The contributions of the past merely gain new stature in the light of current analytical techniques. Dewey, Bliss and Ranganathan perhaps represent the three steps in the history and development of classification from the old to the new.

Catalogs and Cataloging

Melvil Dewey

"In arranging books in the classification, as in filling out the scheme, practical useful-ness has been esteemed the most important thing. The effort has been to put each book under the subject where it would be most useful to special students. The con-tent or the real subject of which a book treats, and not the form or the accidental wording of the title, determines its place."

A DECIMAL CLASSIFICATION AND SUBJECT INDEX

It was thought that a description of the plan as in actual use in the Amherst College Library would be its best explanation. It will be seen, however, that its most valuable feature, the classification and subject index, may be adopted, if desired, in connection with very different catalogs and methods. Though the system was devised for cat-aloging and indexing purposes, it was found on trial to be very valuable for numbering and arrang-ing books and pamphlets on the shelves.

The plan of this classification and index was developed early in 1873. It was the result of sev-eral months' study of library economy as set forth in some hundreds of books and pamphlets, and of over fifty personal visits to various American li-braries. In this study, the author became con-vinced that the usefulness of these libraries might be greatly increased without additional expendi-ture. Three years' practical use of the system here explained leads him to believe that it will accom-plish this result; for with its aid the catalogs, shelf lists, indexes, and cross-references essential to this increased usefulness, can be made more eco-nomically than by any other method which he has been able to find.

For the better understanding of the scheme there are appended pages 5 to 8 of the Library Hand-book, giving a brief description of the catalogs; a specimen page of the classification, also of the sub-ject index; the directions for using the subject cat-alog; and the condensed rules for the headings and titles of the cards.

The library is first divided into nine special li-braries, which are called classes. These classes are (1) Philosophy, (2) Theology, (3) Sociology, (4) Philology, (5) Natural Science, (6) Useful Arts, (7) Fine Arts, (8) Literature, and (9) History, and are numbered with the nine digits; thus Class 9 is the Library of History, etc. These special libraries or classes are then considered independently, and each one is separated again into nine special divi-sions of the main subject. These divisions are num-bered from 1 to 9, as were the classes. Thus 59 is the ninth division (Zoölogy) of the fifth class (Natural Science.) A final division is then made by separating each of these divisions into nine sections, which are numbered in the same way with the nine digits. Thus 513 is the third section (Geometry) of the first division (Mathematics) of the fifth class (Natural Science.) This number, giving class, division, and section, is called the classification or class number, and is applied to every book or pamphlet belonging to the library. All the geometries are thus numbered 513; all the mineralogies 549; and so throughout the library, all the books on any given subject bear the num-ber of that subject in the scheme. Where a 0 oc-curs in a class number it has its normal zero power. Thus, a book numbered 510 is Class 5, Division 1, but no section. This signifies that the book treats of the Division 51 (Mathematics) in general, and is not limited to any one section, as is the geom-etry, marked 513. If marked 500, it would indi-cate a treatise on science in general, limited to no division. A zero occurring in the first place would in the same way show that the book is limited to no class. The classification is mainly made by subjects or content regardless of form; but it is found practically useful to make an additional distinction in these general treatises, according to the form of treatment adopted. Thus, in Science we have a large number of books treating of science in general, and so having a 0 for the divi-

SOURCE: Reprinted from *Public Libraries in the United States* (Washington: U.S. Bureau of Education, 1876), pp. 623-643, excerpted and modernized.

sion number. These books are then divided into sections, as are those of the other classes, according to the form they have taken on. We have (1) the philosophy and history of science, (2) scientific compends, (3) dictionaries, (4) essays, (5) periodicals, (6) societies, (7) education, and (8) travels—all having the common subject, Natural Science, but treating it in these varied forms. These form distinctions are introduced here because the number of general works is large, and the numerals allow for this division without extra labor, for the numbers from 501 to 509 would otherwise be unused. They apply only to the general treatises, which, without them, would have a class number ending with two zeros. A dictionary of mathematics is 510, not 503, for every book is assigned to the most specific head that will contain it, so that 503 is limited to dictionaries or cyclopedias of science in general. In the same way a general cyclopaedia or periodical treats of no one class and so is assigned to the Class 0, divided into cyclopaedias, periodicals, etc. No difficulty is found in following the arithmetical law and omitting the initial zero, so these numbers are printed 31, 32, etc., instead of 031, 032, etc.

The selection and arrangement of the thousand headings of the classification cannot be explained in detail for want of space. In all the work, philosophical theory and accuracy have been made to yield to practical usefulness. The impossibility of making a satisfactory classification of all knowledge as preserved in books, has been appreciated from the first, and nothing of the kind attempted. Theoretical harmony and exactness have been repeatedly sacrificed to the practical requirements of the library or to the convenience of the department in the college. As in every scheme, many minor subjects have been put under general heads to which they do not strictly belong. In some cases these headings have been printed in a distinctive type, e. g., 429 SAXON, under English Philology. The rule has been to assign these subjects to the most nearly allied heads, or where it was thought they would be most sought. The only alternative was to omit them altogether. If any such omission occurs it is unintentional, and will be supplied as soon as discovered. Wherever practicable the heads have been so arranged that each subject is preceded and followed by the most nearly allied subjects, and thus the greatest convenience is secured both in the catalogs and on the shelves. Theoretically, the division of every subject into just nine heads is absurd. Practically, it is desirable that the classification be as minute as possible without the use of additional figures; and the decimal principle on which our scheme hinges, allows nine divisions as readily as a less number. This principle has proved wholly satisfactory in practice, though it appears to destroy proper coordination in some places. It has seemed best in our library to use uniformly three figures in the class number. This enables us to classify certain subjects very minutely, giving, for example, an entire section to Chess. But the History of England has only one section, as our scheme is developed, and thus the two might be said to be coordinated. The apparent difficulty in such cases is entirely obviated by the use of a fourth figure, giving nine subsections to any subject of sufficient importance to warrant closer classification. In History, where the classification is made wholly by countries, a fourth figure is added to give a division into periods. As the addition of each figure gives a tenfold division, any desired degree of minuteness may be secured in the classing of special subjects. The apparent lack of coordination arises from the fact that only the first three figures of these more important heads are as yet printed, the fourth figure and the subsections being supplied on the catalogs, in manuscript. Should the growth of any of these subsections warrant it, a fifth figure will be added, for the scheme admits of expansion without limit.

The number of figures used in the class number can be decided according to circumstances in each library. With us three figures seemed best. In smaller libraries two figures would do very well until the growth required further divisions. But it would seem better economy, to save handling the books a second time, to use at least three figures at the first, and in larger libraries four or even more may be desirable.

The arrangement of headings has been sometimes modified to secure a mnemonic aid in numbering and finding books without the index. For instance, the scheme is so arranged that China has always the number 1. In Ancient History, it has the first section, 931: in Modern History, under Asia, it has 951: in Philology, the Chinese language appears as 491. After the same manner the Indian number is 4; Egyptian, 2; English, 2; German, 3; French, 4; Italian, 5; Spanish, 6; European, 4; Asian, 5; African, 6; North American, 7; South American, 8; and so for all the divisions by languages or countries. The Italian, 5, for instance, will be noticed in 35, 55, 450, 755, 850, and 945. This mnemonic principle is specially prominent in Philology and Literature and their divisions, and in the form distinctions used in the first 9 sections of each class. Materials, Methods, or Theory occurring anywhere as a head, bears always the number 1. Dictionaries and Cyclopaedias, 3; Essays, 4; Periodicals, 5; Associations, Institutions, and Societies, 6; Education, 7; Collections, 9. In the numerous cases where several minor heads have been grouped together under the head Other, it always bears the number 9. Wherever practicable, this principle is carried out in subdividing the sections. For instance, the Geology of North America, which bears the number 557, is subdivided by adding the sections of 970 (History of North America). The Geology of Mexico then bears the number 5578: mnemonically, the first 5 is the Science number; the second 5, Geology; and 7, North America; and the 8, Mexico. Any library attendant or reader, after using the scheme a short time, will recognize, at a glance, any catalog or ledger entry, book or pamphlet, marked 5578 as something on the geology of Mexico. Users of the scheme will notice this mnemonic principle in several hundred places in the classification, and will find it of great practical utility in numbering and finding books without the aid of catalog or index, and in determining the character of any book simply from its call number as recorded on the book, on all its catalog and cross reference cards, on the ledger, and in the check box.

In naming the headings, brevity has been secured in many cases at the sacrifice of exactness. It was thought more important to have short, familiar titles for the headings than that the names given should express with fulness and exactness the character of all books cataloged under them. Many subjects, apparently omitted, will be found in the index, assigned, with allied subjects, to a heading which bears the name of the most important only. Reference to this subject index will decide at once any doubtful points.

In arranging books in the classification, as in filling out the scheme, practical usefulness has been esteemed the most important thing. The effort has been to put each book under the subject where it would be most useful to special students. The content or the real subject of which a book treats, and not the form or the accidental wording of the title, determines its place. Following this rule, a philosophy of art is put with Art, not with Philosophy; a history of mathematics, with Mathematics, not with History; for the philosophy and history are simply the form which these books have taken. The true content or subject is art, and mathematics, and to the student of these subjects they are

most useful. The predominant tendency or obvious purpose of the book, usually decides its class number at once; still a book often treats of two or more different subjects, and in such cases it is assigned to the place where it will be most useful, and underneath the class number are written the numbers of any other subjects on which it also treats. These cross references are given both on the book plate and the subject card as well as on the cross reference card. As the cross reference is itself the call number, a reader having any one of the three (book, title, or cross-reference) can instantly find either of the others without the intervention of catalog or index. The call number is given also on the accessions catalog and on the back of the book. The Van Everen printed numbers are used until the book is rebound, when the call number is stamped permanently on the back, for in this system the call number remains the same through all changes of buildings, arrangement, or catalogs.

The necessity of changes in the ordinary system, together with the very great difficulty of tracing all the cross references, renders it quite impracticable to give the call numbers in all places where they are needed. Even where given they must be written temporarily in pencil, in readiness for the changes that are sure to come; for, if printed, a new catalog, with its attendant expense and confusion, becomes necessary as soon as the opening of new rooms, or removal to new quarters, or the growth of the library disarranges the books.

There is a single alternative: to arrange the books regardless of subjects, and even then the numbers must be altered in nearly all changes of buildings or rooms. In our system the book is numbered once for all, and can change that number only by changing its subject matter. Of course mistakes occur as in any system, but when found they are as easily corrected as in any other plan. Certainly there is greater hope that the work will be done well when it is felt that it is not to be done over again in a few years at the longest.

If a book treats of a majority of the sections of any division, it is given the division number instead of the most important section number, with cross-references. Thus, a volume on light, heat, or sound would be classed under the head most fully discussed and referred to from the others; but if the volume treated also of mechanics, hydrostatics, and pneumatics, it would be classed as 530, or general physics, although no mention be made of electricity, magnetism, or molecular physics.

It is one of the marked advantages of the plan

that these cross-references, notes, etc., may be added from time to time, as found convenient. It is necessary at first to find only the predominant tendency of the book, in order to catalog it. If extreme care were taken to avoid mistakes, it might be well to keep books very difficult to class arranged by themselves for a time till read or carefully examined by some one competent to decide their true place. Cross-references are added when they are found necessary. After reading, a volume of sermons may be found to be aimed at the doctrine of evolution, though this fact was not noticed in classing. When it is found, however, the evolution number, 575, is written under the religion-and-science-sermon number, 255, and ever after a reader knows at once by this number the tendency of the volume. It is designed to add these numbers indicating more closely the character of the book as rapidly as possible, and specialists are invited to call the attention of the librarian to every desirable cross reference they notice in their reading. These numbers take but little room, are easily added, and in most cases are valuable.

Collected works, libraries, etc., are either kept together and assigned like individual books to the most specific head that will contain them, or assigned to the most prominent of the various subjects on which they treat, with cross references from the others; or are separated, and the parts classed as independent works. Translations are classed with their originals.

The alphabetical subject index is designed to guide, both in numbering and in finding the books. In numbering, the most specific head that will contain the book having been determined, reference to that head in the index will give the class number to which it should be assigned. In finding books on any given subject, reference to the index will give the number under which they are to be sought on the shelves, in the shelf catalog or in the subject catalog. The index gives after each subject the number of the class to which it is assigned. Most names of countries, towns, animals, plants, minerals, diseases, etc., have been omitted, the aim being to furnish an index of subjects on which books are written, and not a gazetteer or a dictionary of all the nouns in the language. Such subjects will be found as special chapters or sections of books on the subjects given in the index. The names of individuals will be found in the Class List of Biography. Omissions of any of the more general subjects will be supplied when noticed.

In arranging the books on the shelves, the abso-lute location by shelf and book number is wholly abandoned, the relative location by class and book number being one of the most valuable features of the plan. The class number serves also as the location number, and the shelf number in common use is entirely dispensed with. Accompanying the class number is the *book* number, which prevents confusion of different books on the same subject. Thus the first geometry cataloged is marked $513 \cdot 1$, the second $513 \cdot 2$, and so on to any extent, the last number showing how many books the library has on that subject. The books of each section are all together, and arranged by book numbers, and these sections are also arranged in simple numerical order throughout the library. The call number, $513 \cdot 11$, signifies not the eleventh book on shelf 513, or alcove 5, range 1, shelf 3, as in most libraries, but signifies the eleventh book in subject 513, or the eleventh geometry belonging to the library. In finding the book, the printed numbers on the backs are followed, the upper being the class and the lower the book number. The class is found in its numerical order among the classes as the shelf is found in the ordinary system; the book in its numerical order in the class. The shelves are not numbered, as the increase of different departments, the opening of new rooms, and any arrangement of classes to bring the books most circulated nearest to the delivery desk, will bring different class numbers on a given shelf. New books as received are numbered and put into place, in the same way that new titles are added to the card catalog. The single digit occasionally prefixed to the book number, e.g., the 3 in $421 \cdot 3 \cdot 7$, is the nearest height in decimeters of books too large to be put on the regular library shelves, which are only 2½ decimeters apart. The great mass of the library consists of 2-decimeter books, the size numbers of which are omitted. Books from 2½ to 3½ decimeters in height have 3 prefixed to the book number, and are found on the bottom shelf of each range. The larger sizes are prefixed with 4, 5, etc., and are found on the special shelves provided, in order to avoid the great waste of space otherwise occasioned by the relative location. By this use of the size numbers a close economy of space is secured.

Thus all the books on any given subject are found standing together, and no additions or changes ever separate them. Not only are all the books on the subject sought found together, but the most nearly allied subjects precede and follow, they in turn being preceded and followed by other allied subjects as far as practicable. Readers not having access to the shelves find the short titles arranged in the same order on the shelf catalog, and the full titles, imprints, cross-references, notes, etc., in the subject catalog. The uncataloged pamphlets treating of any subject bear the same class number and are arranged on the shelves immediately after the books of each section.

In a library arranged on this plan every specialist has his own special library. If he be a student of science in general, he is sent to class 5; if his department be zoölogy, his library is 59; if his specialty is shells, he finds all the works and references on that subject in library 594. Whether there be a specialist to watch it or not, every subject thus being in a library by itself, shows at once its resources and its wants as no catalog can show them. A catalog cannot be made that will so quickly and thoroughly decide a student's wants as the books themselves. Of course this advantage weighs most in a college or society library, where many persons have access to the shelves, but even in a collection where only the librarians are admitted, the close classification on the shelves will be found of exceeding value. The desirability of such classing is never questioned, only the practicability. With our plan we believe it to be comparatively easy.

In both the authors' catalog and the subject index, brevity has been studied because of the economy, but more because of the much greater ease of reference to a short-title catalog. The custom of giving full titles, etc., under authors, and only references or very brief titles under subjects, has been reversed. A reader seeking a book of a known author, in the vast majority of cases, wants simply the number by which to call for it, and can find it much quicker in a brief-title catalog. In the rare cases where more is needed the class number refers instantly to all these facts on the cards. On the other hand, a reader seeking books on a known subject, needs the full title, imprint, cross references, and notes to enable him to choose the book best suited to his wants.

The subject catalog is a full-title shelf list on cards and is for the use of the public. The shelf list is a short-title subject catalog in book form, made of separate sheets laced into an Emerson binder, and is for official use. We thus have without extra labor both full and short-title subject catalog and shelf lists. The public authors' catalog is a printed volume; the official authors' catalog or index is on cards. As a result, each of the public catalogs is checked by an official catalog; each of the card catalogs by a book catalog; each

of the brief-title catalogs by a full-title catalog—an advantage that will be appreciated by all librarians desiring accuracy in administration and in catalogs.

At the same time the most useful class lists of any subject may be made by simply printing the titles under its class number in the subject or shelf catalog, according as full or brief titles are desired.

The Arabic numerals can be written and found quicker and with less danger of confusion or mistake than any other symbols whatever. The Roman numerals, capitals and small letters, and similar symbols usually found in systems of classification, are entirely discarded, and by the exclusive use of Arabic numerals in their regular order throughout the shelves, classifications, indexes, catalogs, and records, there is secured the greatest accuracy, economy, and convenience. This advantage is specially prominent in comparison with systems where the name of the author or the title must be written in calling for or charging books and in making references.

Some prominent librarians, while admitting the great superiority of the relative location for college and society libraries, have urged with force that in the public library, where so many thousand volumes must be called for, found, and charged, the additional labor and danger of confusion involved in giving the author's name instead of a book number make the system undesirable. But by substituting the book number for the author's name in the relative location we use even fewer figures than in the absolute location by shelves; for every numeral is used from 1 upward without limit, while in the absolute location, where the shelves hold only 25 to 40 volumes, all the numbers remaining, which might be written with only two digits, are not used. As a result, more figures are necessary in the shelf number. When it is considered that the library records are simply a mass of call numbers, and that these numbers are constantly written and printed in catalogs, shelf lists, indexes, etc., it will be seen that a saving of a single figure in the book number is a matter of importance.

As the numbers from 1 to 9 are not used in the regular scheme, it is practicable to effect a further saving by using only the last figure instead of the full class number of the sections where most books are circulated; e.g., in English Literature the number 3 may be used, instead of writing 823 for each novel charged; and as there is no other class number 3 in the scheme, no confusion results . . . .

It would exceed the limits of this brief description to notice all the varied applications of the system. It is hoped that enough have been mentioned to show its wide adaptability to the wants of the librarian and the student.

The system is so flexible that it adapts itself to almost any circumstances. It may be used in any one of its applications without the others, and with a proportionate result. It may be applied to the pamphlets alone, bringing order out of chaos, and solving this vexed and vexing problem, or it may be used for the catalogs, leaving the arrangement on the shelves as before; or it may be applied to the shelves, while the catalog is on the dictionary or any other plan. This application to the shelves may be either with or without the book numbers. If without, the books are arranged on the shelves alphabetically by authors under each class number. For a private collection, or a library where the books are not loaned from the building, this last plan has some marked advantages. The books on any subject, by the same author, always stand side by side whatever the time of their reception; and what is more important, the author and subject being known, the exact place of the book can be found without catalog or index. On the other hand the invaluable shelf list must either be wholly abandoned or kept on cards in order to retain the titles in place, thus sacrificing much of its accuracy and convenience for examining and verifying; and (a much more serious objection) in order to identify the book the author's name and frequently a part of the title must accompany the class number on all the records, catalogs, and references. These objections, with the almost certain confusion of different authors of the same name, or very similar names, make the alphabetical arrangement almost impracticable for a circulating library. The same objections apply with almost the same force to a numerical arrangement based on the alphabet, for the indefiniteness thus introduced becomes a source of confusion in any library where much of the routine work must be done by attendants of little experience . . . .

The claims of the system as in use with us may be summed up as follows: Compared with other systems it is less expensive; more easily understood, remembered, and used; practical rather than theoretical; brief and familiar in its nomenclature; superior to all others in arranging pamphlets, sale duplicates, and notes, and in indexing; susceptible of partial and gradual adoption without confusion; more convenient in keeping statistics and checks for books off the shelves; the most satisfactory adaptation of the card catalog principle to the shelves. It requires less space to shelve the books; uses simpler symbols and fewer of them; can be expanded without limit and without confusion or waste of labor on both catalogs and shelves or in the catalogs alone; checks more thoroughly and conveniently against mistakes; admits more readily numerous cross references; is unchangeable in its call numbers, and so gives them in all places where needed, as given in no other system; in its index affords an answer to the greatest objection to classed catalogs, and is the first satisfactory union of the advantages of the classed and dictionary system.

In this hurriedly prepared account of his plan, the author has doubtless failed to meet many objections which may be raised and which he could easily answer. He would therefore ask the privilege of replying personally to any such objections, where they arise.

In his varied reading, correspondence, and conversation on the subject, the author doubtless received suggestions and gained ideas which it is now impossible for him to acknowledge. Perhaps the most fruitful source of ideas was the Nuovo sistema di catalogo bibiliografico general of Natale Battezzati, of Milan. Certainly he is indebted to this system adopted by the Italian publishers in 1871, though he has copied nothing from it. The plan of the St. Louis Public School Library and that of the Apprentices' Library of New York, which in some respects resemble his own, were not seen till all the essential features were decided upon, though not given to the public. In filling the nine classes of the scheme the inverted Baconian arrangement of the St. Louis Library has been followed. The author has no desire to claim original invention for any part of his system where another has been before him, and would most gladly make specific acknowledgment of every aid and suggestion were it in his power to do so. With these general explanations and acknowledgments he submits the scheme, hoping it may prove as useful to others as it has to himself.

[To illustrate and explain the description of the Amherst College Catalog given in the preceding text, the author has added the following notes embracing specimen pages of the classification and subject index, and a description of the catalogs used, with an explanation of their method and peculiarities.—*Editors.*]

Specimen Pages of Classification

PHILOLOGY

400 Philology.
- 401   Philosophy.
- 402   Compends.
- 403   Dictionaries.
- 404   Essays.
- 405   Periodicals.
- 406   Societies.
- 407   Education.
- 408   Travels.
- 409   History.

410 Comparative.
- 411   Orthography.
- 412   Etymology.
- 413   Dictionaries.
- 414   Phonology.
- 415   Grammar.
- 416   Prosody.
- 417   Inscriptions.
- 418   Texts.
- 419   Hieroglyphics.

420 English.
- 421   Orthography.
- 422   Etymology.
- 423   Dictionaries.
- 424   Synonyms.
- 425   Grammar.
- 426   Prosody.
- 427   Dialects.
- 428   Texts.
- 429   Saxon.

430 German.
- 431   Orthography.
- 432   Etymology.
- 433   Dictionaries.
- 434   Synonyms.
- 435   Grammar.
- 436   Prosody.
- 437   Dialects.
- 438   Texts.
- 439   Dutch and Low German.

440 French.
- 441   Orthography.
- 442   Etymology.
- 443   Dictionaries.
- 444   Synonyms.
- 445   Grammar.
- 446   Prosody.
- 447   Dialects.
- 448   Texts.
- 449   Old French, Provençal.

450 Italian.
- 451   Orthography.
- 452   Etymology.
- 453   Dictionaries.
- 454   Synonyms.
- 455   Grammar.
- 456   Prosody.
- 457   Dialects.
- 458   Texts.
- 459   Romansch and Wallachian.

460 Spanish.
- 461   Orthography.
- 462   Etymology.
- 463   Dictionaries.
- 464   Synonyms.
- 465   Grammar.
- 466   Prosody.
- 467   Dialects.
- 468   Texts.
- 469   Portuguese.

470 Latin.
- 471   Orthography.
- 472   Etymology.
- 473   Dictionaries.
- 474   Synonyms.
- 475   Grammar.
- 476   Prosody.
- 477   Dialects.
- 478   Texts.
- 479   Medieval Latin.

480 Greek.
- 481   Orthography.
- 482   Etymology.
- 483   Dictionaries.
- 484   Synonyms.
- 485   Grammar.
- 486   Prosody.
- 487   Dialects.
- 488   Texts.
- 489   Modern Greek.

490 Other Languages.
- 491   Chinese.
- 492   Egyptian.
- 493   Semitic.
- 494   Indian.
- 495   Iranian.
- 496   Keltic.
- 497   Slavic.
- 498   Scandinavian.
- 499   Other.

NATURAL SCIENCE

500 Natural Science.
- 501   Philosophy.
- 502   Compends.
- 503   Dictionaries.
- 504   Essays.
- 505   Periodicals.
- 506   Societies.
- 507   Education.
- 508   Travels.
- 509   History.

510 Mathematics.
- 511   Arithmetic.
- 512   Algebra.
- 513   Geometry.

514   Trigonometry.
515   Conic sections.
516   Analytical geometry.
517   Calculus.
518   Quaternions.
519   Probabilities.

520 Astronomy.
521   Theoretical.
522   Practical.
523   Descriptive.
524   Maps.
525   Observations.
526   Figure of the earth.
527   Navigation.
528   Almanacs.
529   Chronology.

530 Physics.
531   Mechanics.
532   Hydrostatics.
533   Pneumatics.
534   Heat.
535   Acoustics.
536   Optics.
537   Electricity.
538   Magnetism.
539   Molecular physics.

540 Chemistry.
541   Theoretical.
542   Experimental.
543   Analysis.
544   *Qualitative.*
545   *Quantitative.*
546   Inorganic.
547   Organic.
548   Crystallography.
549   Mineralogy.

550 Geology.
551   Physical geography, meteorology.
552   Lithology.
553   Dynamical geology.
554   Europe.
555   Asia.
556   Africa.

557   North America.
558   South America.
559   Oceanica.

560 Paleontology.
561   Plants.
562   Invertebrates.
563   *Protozoa and Radiates.*
564   *Mollusca.*
565   *Articulates.*
566   Vertebrates.
567   *Fishes.*
568   *Reptiles and Birds.*
569   *Mammals.*

570 Biology.
571   Prehistoric Archaeology.
572   Ethnology.
573   Natural History of Man.
574   Morphologies.
575   Evolution.
576   Embryology.
577   Spontaneous generation.
578   Microscopy.
579   Collectors' manuals.

580 Botany.
581   Physiological.
582   Systematic.
583   Geographical.
584   Europe.
585   Asia.
586   Africa.
587   North America.
588   South America.
589   Oceanica.

590 Zoölogy.
591   Comparative anatomy.
592   Invertebrates.
593   *Protozoa and Radiates.*
594   *Mollusca.*
595   *Articulates.*
596   Vertebrates.
597   *Fishes.*
598   *Reptiles and Birds.*
599   *Mammals.*

Principles and Definitions

Henry Evelyn Bliss

"These five principles, named briefly: subordination, collocation, maximal efficiency, relativity of classification, and alternative location, are basic to the philosophy of classification and to our proposed Bibliographic Classification."

In the *systems* of Science, Education, and Society, the *organizations* (systems) of knowledge, thought, and purpose, established, though incompletely, in a *consensus* of scientists and educators, avail, though imperfectly, for *classifications* of subject matters, and of books or other bibliographic materials, with *a maximal efficiency* relative to various interests and purposes. Such classifications depend principally on valid *subordination* of related *special* subject matters, or subclasses, to the relevant *general* subjects, or classes; and any maximal efficiency depends on purposive and convenient *collocation* of closely related subclasses under the relevant general classes. This *relative* maximal efficiency is complemented by many references to *alternative locations* that avail for different interests or views.

SPECIAL SUBJECTS ARE COMPREHENDED BY GENERAL SUBJECTS

At the International Congress of Physics at Paris in 1900 the eminent scientist, Henri Poincaré, in a distinguished presidential address contrasted with renewed emphasis the intricate, baffling complexity of natural objects in their diverse relations and the intellectual tendency in science and in education to reduce that complexity to relatively simple descriptive statements, comprehensive generalizations, and orderly conceptual systems. He compared this contrast to a kind of conflict, swaying back and forth across the arena of science, between the mental purpose to generalize, and therein to simplify, and on the other hand the mental propensity to differentiate and specify.

The opposition of specialization to simplification recurs in the problems of cataloging and classification for organization of bibliographic resources. But it reduces mainly to the relativity of the special to the general. Special bibliographic subjects, or classes, are related to general bibliographic subjects, or classes; they are logically and inherently related to them, and they may be effectually and practically related to them.

By *bibliographic classes* we mean here classes of books, *documents,* or other bibliographic *materials;* and by *subjects* we mean subjects, or *subject matters,* of study or interest, or *branches* of knowledge and thought. Thus the classification of bibliographic materials is a classification of bibliographic subjects, embodies a structural organization of knowledge and thought, and serves *functional* organizations of knowledge, thought, and purpose. Conversely, a logical organization of knowledge and thought is consistently applicable, with adaptations, to a system of bibliographic classification. Briefly, a bibliographic classification is virtually a classification of knowledge and thought, and, conversely, a classification for knowledge is available for a bibliographic classification. The relation is emphasized here because it has often been denied or distorted by librarian writers.

From this relation two questions arise: How shall we adapt a bibliographic classification to the relevant classification of knowledge; and how special and complicated may a bibliographic system be as a structural organization for the effectual, functional organization of knowledge, thought, and purpose in scientific, education, and humanistic interests? Before offering answers to these questions we should consider the principles that are inherent.

THE FUNDAMENTAL PRINCIPLES OF CLASSIFICATION

The principles that obtain in all classification will first in this section be defined and summarized rather than expounded and discussed.[1] Altogether they are essential to the introduction and comprehension of the Classification expanded in this work.

Classes are correlative to Concepts and to Terms. In the multiplicity, diversity, and complexity of natural objects and their relations we discern that individual *things* and *events* are discrete and that, though they differ in their individualities and specific characteristics, some are similar in certain characteristics and relations; and by these like characteristics we relate them in *classes* and in concepts, in primary learning and in *mental comprehension.* This is the process of *classifying,* of conceiving classes, and of relating them in mental comprehension. It is fundamental to generalization, to simplification, to classification, and to organization of knowledge and thought. A class is denoted by one or more words or terms, which name it, signify it, and mean it. Such *terms or class names* are correlative to their classes and to the correlative concepts.

Classifying and Classification. The verb *classify* thus has two meanings: primarily to relate individuals by their likeness, by a perceptual and conceptual process, that is, to regard them as being in classes with respect to this likeness; and, secondarily, to *relate classes,* in classifications. The term *classification* is also used ambiguously, like so many verbal nouns, sometimes for the process of *classifying* classes, and sometimes for the product, the *classified classes.* Distinct again is the verb *to class,* which means to relate, or refer, or assign, a thing to a relevant class, regarding some characteristic. This is often confused with *classify.* These distinctions should be maintained to avoid confusion in the usage and in the discussions.

Classes are definite, are definable by their like characteristics and relations, real or conceptual, any of which, or any combination of which, common to the class, may be regarded as characteristic; and the class may be defined by the respective terms. The correlative concept of the class is likewise defined.

Terms are definite, as classes are; and they are correlative to the classes as the class names are. They should be distinctive and should be used consistently. A class may, however, be denoted by several *synonymous terms.* The class name may, moreover, be composed of two or three terms together. In different languages the class names differ more or less, though they may be etymologically related.

The Inclusiveness and Totality of Classes. A class comprises all the things that are regarded as

like, that assimilate to the concept of the class, that are defined by its definition and named by its term, or terms.

Classes are distinguished from Groups. A class is *definite,* and it is a *totality;* it is distinct from a *group,* which is *not* definite nor a totality, but *local* and temporary and may be accidental or selective.

Development and Adaptiveness of Classes. New developments, variations, relations, or aspects, not so important as to be regarded as characteristics, may be admitted into a class, and corresponding specifications would modify its definition, but the class so developed or adapted is regarded as remaining the same, as does its class name, or term; it is altered, but not changed into a new and different class.

Real and natural classes exist in real and natural relations, which also have conceptual correlates. The objective realities are correlative to subjective concepts, to conceptual subject matters, to studies, sciences, technologies and arts. Real and natural classes and relations, especially those of natural objects and "kinds" of things, defined by natural, essential, and intrinsic characters, are usually more *stable* and *permanent* than are classes of fabricated things and conceptual classes defined by extrinsic specifications or arbitrarily related to the interests of life and more variable because [they are] subjective; and real classes are usually more *extensively available* to the various interests and purposes. For instance, the class (family) of fishes called Mackerels and their related genera and species are likely to be more permanent and more extensively available, than the class of war vessels called *submarines*, though both, as defined and named, may become extinct or superseded in the course of time.

Division and subclasses. Classes are divisible into two or more subclasses by definite specific characteristics or *specific differences.* These are definite, and the subclasses are defined by putting the respective specific terms into the definitions of the classes. The specific terms that are most distinctive may be added to the class names. This is *specification* and *differentiation.* Subjects, or subject matters, or branches of knowledge, may likewise be subdivided by further specification. This is *specialization*, which is antithetic to *generalization*, both of which will be more expressly defined in a subsequent paragraph. The subclasses, with or without the class, may be spoken of as a classification. This is the simplest case of classification. Usually a classification is composed of many classes and subclasses in relations more or less complex.

Subordination. In division, differentiation, and specification the specific subclasses are derivative from and subordinate to the comprehensive class, but not separated from it. Differentiating table-spoons from teaspoons does not separate them for tables and teas; though so specified, they remain spoons; though logically subordinate, they are comprehended by the general class, spoons. Subordination is distinct from division, though consequent to it; and division is distinct from separation, though separation implies division. The subclasses remain within the *extension* or *comprehension* of the comprehensive class. This relation too has been distorted by librarian authors.

Gradation in *speciality.* The subclass is subordinate to the class, that is, the special class "comes under" the general class, or follows it. This applies also to the subdivisions of subclasses; and so in successive subdivision there is *gradation* in, or by, *speciality,* wherein each term is subordinate to each term that precedes it in the series. We shall return to this principle in relation to scalar classification.

Coördination. Classes, or subclasses, of the same grade, or order, of division are termed coördinate, and the principle of placing them in such order is *coördination.* Subordination and coördination are thus relative to division and gradation. The coördinate subclasses of several coördinate classes may be *coördinated.*

Subclasses of different classes. The coördinate subclasses of a single class are more closely related to one another than they are to the subclasses of another class, whether coördinate or subordinate. This relationship depends on the common derivation. The relation of a subclass to its class is derivative like that of a child to its mother. The subclasses of the one class are like brothers and sisters. To the subclasses of a coördinate class they are like cousins. In these simplified analogies are the rudiments of the principles of *subordination, coördination,* and *collocation.* This last term will be defined in a subsequent paragraph.

Comprehensive classes. Several distinct classes may be comprised in a comprehensive class, the specific characters being disregarded. Individuals of those distinct classes may then be *classed* by their general character, thus be brought into the comprehensive class and under its definition, though they may not exactly fit these. For instance, the comprehensive class, *timepieces,* may be classified so as to comprise all watches, chron-

ometers, and clocks, besides other time recorders, or this last term may name the class. Or otherwise, watches and chronometers, though special classes, may not be distinguished from clocks, and for convenience or simplicity they may even be comprised in the class *clocks,* as comprehensive, and they may be *subsumed* under its class name. This process of extension of a class and comprehension under its term is related to the process of generalization. General and comprehensive classes are usually more adaptive and developmental than specific classes, and they are, therefore, more permanent. This principle, however, does not always apply to the conceptual higher taxonomic *orders* and *classes,* which comprise the *natural genera* and *families* of plants and animals. *Species* in nature are conceptual too, and a large proportion of them are less definite and permanent than genera and families are. These conceptual and variable elements have rendered the classifications of plants and animals, even in the *classificatory sciences* of Systematic Botany and Systematic Zoölogy, less permanent than other customary but *less* systematic classifications of natural kinds.

Generalization and Specialization. Special subject matters, though differentiated and specified, may still be related in their essentials and similar in their general characters. Assimilating them by these to their more comprehensive concepts, or classes, or subjects, is the logical process of *generalization,* which thus proceeds from the special to the general. The opposite procedure from the general to the more and more special is *specialization,* which is thus antithetic to generalization, while specification is antithetic to comprehension, and analysis to synthesis. Specialization and generalization are thus relative terms for related logical processes.

Synthesis is the logical process of mentally, or really, relating special subject matters, or concepts, to comprehensive subjects, or concepts.

Collocation. Synthesis may be purposive in bringing together classes, subclasses, or subjects that are relevant to certain interests and available to the purposes that proceed from them. Such purposive synthesis we have termed *collocation.* The term is derivative from the Latin, whereas *synthesis* is derivative from the Greek. Etymologically they are nearly synonymous, but here we would distinguish collocation as both intrinsic and purposive; synthesis retaining its logical relation to conceptual comprehension.

Systematic classification. A classification is an order of classes and subclasses related by logical

principles and mental interests. If the relations are
not merely logical and structural but effectual and
functional, the classification is *systematic*. In a
system of classification such relations are implied,
not merely the order or structure. The classification may be related to principles that are not
merely logical but effectual, that is, it may be *arbitrary* or *purposive*.

Serial classification and Schedules. A class, with
its subclasses, may be arranged in a column, with
the class name at the *head* and the subclasses
subordinate under it; or the subclasses may be
arranged in a line, following the class name as
heading, and a colon for punctuation, the subclasses being separated by commas. In either case
the classification may be regarded as *linear*, though
in the first case it is *columnar*; and it may be
termed a *serial classification*, or *schedule*.

Tabular classification. A series of two or more
coördinate classes may be arranged in a line as a
horizontal series, and the several subclasses of each
class may be subordinated under the respective
class names, or heads. Otherwise the coördinate
classes may be arranged in a columnar order, or
vertical series, with the subclasses of each class arranged in a linear or horizontal series, following
the class name as head, from the left to the right.
Either order is distinctly two-dimensional, or *tabular.* It may be termed a *tabular classification,* or
table, or *tabulation;* but the last term is functional,
as well as structural, implying that sub-classes are
tabulated. Whether the coördinate classes are to
be in a vertical series or in a horizontal series depends on the purpose and on convenience.

Cross-classification. A specification may be relevant to several classes, thus: Aquatic plants,
Aquatic insects, Aquatic birds, Aquatic mammals.
These may be arranged in a series, whether horizontal or vertical. Other specifications may be relevant to these classes. The logical opposite of
Aquatic is Terrestrial, or Land. So we may have a
second series: Terrestrial plants, insects, birds, and
mammals. Intermediate are the Amphibious, or
Shore, plants, insects, birds, mammals—a third series. A fourth series may specify the Xeric, or
Arid-land, plants, insects, birds, and mammals.
These four series written in four lines are a tabular
classification, thus:

Aquatic plants,	Aquatic insects,
Terrestrial ″	Terrestrial ″
Amphibious ″	Amphibious ″
Xeric ″	Xeric ″

Aquatic birds,	Aquatic mammals
Terrestrial ″	Terrestrial ″
Amphibious ″	Amphibious ″
Xeric ″	Xeric ″

Here we have a *cross-classification* of sixteen
subclasses arranged in four classes, crossed in four
lines by the four specifications that recur in each
of these classes. Instead of using ditto-marks, we
might imply the repetition of the class names by
merely placing them at the heads of the columns.
Moreover the specifications need not be repeated
in all the columns, if they be given in the first column; they would be implied in the other columns,
thus:

	PLANTS	INSECTS	BIRDS	MAMMALS
Aquatic				
Terrestrial				
Amphibious				
Xeric				

Such a tabular cross-classification not only saves
the repetitions, but it provides for tabulating data,
statistical or other, in the spaces in which the respective series intersect.

The four classes might have been arranged vertically in the first column, the four specifications
crossing vertically in the four columns, which they
would head in a horizontal series. In any cross-
classification the classes are treated as coördinate,
and so are the subclasses, whether regarded horizontally or vertically. Moreover, the sixteen subclasses may be regarded as all comprised by a comprehensive class, *Biota,* or Living beings, divided
first by form (morphology) and secondly by habi-
tat (ecology), thus:

BIOTA	AQUATIC	LAND	AMPHIBIOUS	XERIC
Insects				
Birds				
Plants				
Mammals				

Furthermore, other specifications than the eco-
logic might be relevant, or they might be additional or supplementary, for instance, by countries: American, English, French, and Swiss plants,
insects, birds, and mammals; or regarding food:
Carnivorous, parasitic, halophytic plants, insects,
birds, and mammals. From these other cross-classifications could be tabulated. Again relevant to
any of the subclasses above, for instance, Carniv-

orous plants, there might be specifications for countries, e.g, American carnivorous plants. The specifications, however, may not be relevant to all the classes or subclasses. There might not be any European carnivorous plants, or any Amphibious birds in Alpine regions. The cross-classification is not always complete; it need not be.

With such duplex specifications, tabular cross-classifications, though apparently two-dimensional, are virtually of three dimensions, or two extensions, or expansions. The comprehensive class is divided one way and the subclasses are subdivided in another way. But tabular cross-classifications are limited to this, to three dimensional classification. Tabular schedules, however, indenting again and again for subdivisions, may extend beyond the three-dimensional analogy; they may be poly-dimensional. We shall return to this in subsequent pages. Our *Composite Principle* and *Systematic Schedules* involve this extensibility of classification and notation.

Tabular classification may be reduced to a schedule. We have seen that in a tabular classification each horizontal series may also be arranged as a vertical series. The subordination of the doubly specified subclasses to the singly specified subclasses, and of these to their classes, may be shown by inversion and indention, thus:

Mammals	Note: *This example is oversimpli-*
Aquatic	*fied, as would appear on compar-*
American	*ison with most of the schedules in*
English	*the second Part of this volume.*
French	*For instance, in classifying the*
Spanish	*plants in Systematic Botany and*
Land	*again the animals in Systematic*
American, etc.	*Zoölogy economy has led to tabu-*
Amphibious	*lar features in many of the more*
American, etc.	*complicated schedules.*
Xeric	
American, etc.	

This is nearly equivalent to a tabular classification, for each indented series is virtually a column; but the series of secondary subclasses are interposed between the several primary subclasses. Even without indention, the tabular classification may be converted into a schedule, which is virtually three-dimensional, or poly-dimensional. This negates the stricture frequently made that schedules are linear classifications. Serial they indeed are, but, permitting of further subdivision at any place, they are virtually poly-dimensional. If there be a correlative notation, this may take the place of indention, subordination, and even of cross-clas-

sification, as we shall show further on. But, though schedules of classification may thus be virtually poly-dimensional, the arrangement of the things classified, for instance, books on shelves, or pamphlets in boxes or files, is really linear, and to this the stricture does indeed apply. In a limited way, however, even linear arrangements on shelves may be disposed in tiers so as to become two-dimensional like tabular classifications, and a three-dimensional arrangement is attainable by placing one tier of shelves at right angles to another tier of shelves. Thus related subjects may be brought into near proximity.

Branches and ramifications. Two or more subclasses may be regarded as branches. This is the customary term in speaking of subjects, or subject matters, as branches of science or of study. If the class is divided into only two sub classes, the branching is termed *dichotomy*—the term of the ancient Greek logicians. Each branch, or each branching, may be termed *dichotomous.* Further branching is termed *ramification.* Many ramifications may cross in complex relations. It is often impossible to reduce these to tabular classifications or to schedules. Some of the branches may be dichotomous, while other may not. Classification may thus become *complex* difficult to reduce to a system. With such complications we shall have to deal in the details of bibliographic classification. The metaphor of ramification extends into the metaphor of the "tree of knowledge."

Scalar series (or classification). If a class is logically divided into two subclasses, one of which is specified as *not* having the character of the other, e.g., Books, *not* bound, this negative subclass may be disregarded; and so in a successive gradation of dichotomous subdivisions, each with a negative subclass, all these negative subclasses may be discarded, e.g., Books *not* in the English language, *not* on England, *not* on the North Country, *not* recent, etc.; and we may retain only the positive and significant terms: Recent, bound books on the North Country of England. This process of successive dichotomy, discarding the negative alternatives, called by the olden logicians *abscissio infiniti* (cutting off the infinite, or insignificant), results in a series of subordinations of single subclasses, or a series of specifications. If this series of subclasses is shown in a tabular form or in the equivalent form of a schedule, the subordinations being indicated by indentions, each a space farther in than its predecessor, the resulting series is analogous to a *stair* or *ladder,* and hence it has been called a *Scalar series* or classification. It is closely related to analysis, and to specialization; also to definition of the last specific positive class by *all* of its specifications. A scalar series may also be formed by single subclasses chosen from successive grades of more than two coördinate subclasses. (By Ranganathan termed a Chain of Classes).

The series of sciences that form the backbone, so regarded, of the System of Science, may be considered as virtually a scalar series of successive subordinations of more and more special sciences, combined with several coördinate and derivative studies grouped under them.

Natural classifications. Systems in which most of the classes and relations are real and natural are more stable and permanent than conceptual classes and relations, so natural classifications are likely to be more stable and permanent than those in which the classes and relations are *selected* and arranged with some subjective interest or purpose, but not consistently with the logical and natural relations. Such are called arbitrary, or "artificial", classifications. But even natural and scientific classifications have conceptual elements in them. They should conform as closely as possible to the classifications of natural objects and relations that are established in the consensus of scientists and educators in the organization of knowledge and thought. Such comprehensive classifications are available and adaptable to many interests and purposes. They are not only more available to the several divergent interests and purposes, and more efficient in serving them; but in their general classes they are more stable and permanent, because they are more comprehensive, adaptive, and developmental. Moreover in their special details they tend to become more stable as the relevant theories become better verified and as the knowledge comprised in them becomes more definitely organized. This stability depends on the constancy of the order of nature, on the reality of the relations comprised, and on the correlation of the knowledge to the verified realities. . . .

The term *bibliographic classification* has still broader usage, as bibliographies, special or general, may well be classified, and many of them are well classified. They, of course, may well be classified better. A bibliography, moreover, may be on cards, and they may be classified. On the other hand, a classified subject catalog may be in book form. Furthermore a union catalog may have a classified subject counterpart. Union catalogs are bibliographic too. All these considerations justify the extension of the term *bibliographic classification*. Still another consideration, a classification *for* books may be applied to a classification *of* books; or conversely, a classification *of* books depends on a classification *for* books, that is, a bibliographic classification. It is consistent to maintain this distinction. We should *not* speak of a classification *of* books on the shelves as a bibliographic classification, nor should we so term a classified subject catalog on cards, which would depend on a bibliographic classification. Thus there are four correlates: (1) a classification of knowledge in books, etc.; (2) a classification of books, etc., in conformity to that classification of knowledge; (3) a schedule, or system of classification, on cards or in a book, for maintaining that classification of books, etc., that is, a classification *for* libraries, etc., or a bibliographic classification; (4) a shelf list, or a subject catalog, corresponding to that classification of books, etc., and serving to make it available to users . . . .

A bibliographic classification, whether in a book or on cards, whether *for* books, etc., in libraries, or for subject catalogs, or for documentation, is in the form of a serial schedule, not in a tabular form. Though it may be equivalent to a tabular classification, two-dimensional, or poly-dimensional, it is reduced to the serial or linear form of a schedule. Its *expansion* in the second dimension and in the third, and so on, is represented by subordinate series of divisions and subdivisions, or sections and subsections, whether these be indented or not; if not indented, the subordination, or expansion, is represented by suffixed factors in the *correlative notation.* Thus the division and subdivision of subject matter is represented in serial schedules. Yet the conversion of ramifying subject matters into serial order of cards in catalogs or books on shelves is only partly effective. The branches that extend from any subject are interposed as divisions, or subordinate series, between the main subject and its *other branches;* and where there are several of these, some may be at considerable distance from the main subject and the farthest removed may indeed be nearer *another* subject. It is this condition of serial classification that is often spoken of as a stricture; and it is because of probable inconvenience and inefficiency in use that the logical principle of subordination needs to be complemented by the effectual or practical principle of *collocation* for convenience and for *maximal* efficiency in service, to the effect that the subjects most likely to be needed in proximity should be placed as near to one another as is feasible under the conditions of relatively permanent subordination and collocation.

The *symbols of a bibliographic notation* are usually the letters of the alphabet and the Arabic numerals, correlated to the classification in the conventional order. The series of symbols is termed the *base* of the notation; their number is by analogy termed, the *length of the base*. The series of letters furnishes a much longer base than the series of digits. So the literal base avails for a larger number of main classes. In a bibliographic classification of general scope the number of major subjects that should have distinctive class marks is more than ten and nearly twenty-five. (But this is a matter of *apportionment*.) The square of the length of base, or its area, or its first expansion, into its second dimension, is again much greater for a literal base than for a numerical base, in the ratio of 676 to 100. Again there is need for more than 100 subjects of secondary importance, including sciences, sub-sciences, histories, nations, languages, literatures, and arts. The *second expansion* of the literal base into its *third dimension* provides a *capacity* for minor subjects, specifications, subdivisions, details, aspects, topics, etc., that suffices for most *requirements* and in this capacity is greatly superior to a numerical notation; for a thousand divisions may prove inadequate, and so may ten thousand subdivisions, many of which might not be applicable.

THE PRINCIPLES ON WHICH THIS SYSTEM IS BASED

The principles and definitions summarized in the preceding pages are generally applicable to bibliographical classification and therefore to this System, which is based on such principles more definitely than other classifications that have been criticised for the lack of such grounding. But now the principles that are especially characteristic of this System will be briefly described.

The System is comprehensive, or general, in its bibliographic scope and purposes; it comprises, or comprehends, all the branches of knowledge, all the main subjects of interest and study, all the bibliographic classes. Moreover it is comprehensive of the most important of the several views in which the interrelated subjects may be regarded.

The Point of View of this System is the *central* view of *humanity in nature*, whether subjectively or objectively regarded. This combines the so-called "naturalistic view" with the "humanistic

view." They are closely related and complementary, the latter depending on the former. Considering knowledge as a unitary system of interrelated branches,[2] human life, mind, knowledge and thought, the "humanities," objectively regarded in the broadest sense, are related to human nature and this to biological and physical nature, regarded comprehensively. Thus the system is comprehensive of natural science and the philosophy of nature and of human life, comprising also religion, theology, ethics, and aesthetics—all the sciences of nature and all the studies of humanity. This system of knowledge and thought may be *organized* and *systemized* about the central point of view of *humanity in nature*.

Comprehensive and coherent, this system is mainly consistent with the systems of science and education established in the *consensus* of scientists and educators and embodied, though imperfectly, in their institutions, *curricula*, and programs.[3] As developed in this work it has been adapted to the purposes of bibliographic classification . . . .

Subordination is the dominant principle of this classification, secondary only to its comprehensiveness. Special subjects are subordinated throughout these classes to the relevant general subjects; *derivative* studies and *applied sciences* are related to their *fundamental* sciences; and all these are successively subordinated in *gradation by speciality*. Subordination is important not only for special subjects but for general subjects. For instance, Zoölogy is subordinated to Biology, and coördinated with Botany. These relations are shown by indention in the synopsis, though not in the serial schedules, where it is not necessary to show them, nor is it feasible.

Coördination is related to subordination, and the two principles are combined in the serial schedules, whether the subordination is shown by indention or not, whether the notation shows it or not. Thus, Religion, Political Science, and Economics are coördinate Main Classes, but all three are subordinate to the Main Class [of] Social Sciences, to which also Sociology, a fundamental science, is subordinated and is there coördinate with Political Science. In another view Sociology is a general science comprehensive of the whole class of Social Sciences and both Political Science and Economics are subordinate to that general science, as Botany and Zoölogy are subordinate to Biology. In a more general survey Sociology, with all the Social Sciences, is subordinate to Anthropology, and this to Zoölogy, and this to Biology, which is related to the Biological Sciences as

Sociology is to the Social Sciences. Again Biological Science is coördinate with the class of Physical Sciences, and both these classes are subordinate to the class of Natural Sciences. The relations of Psychology to Anthropology, and of Religion to Sociology and to Psychology, and of Philology to Sociology, Psychology, and Anthropology are less simple and clear. But from all the relations noticed above we may abstract and apply the principle of successive subordination and *gradation by Speciality.*

Collocation of closely related special subjects, whether they are coördinate subclasses of a single class or coördinate under several coördinate classes, or subordinate to closely related classes, however related, locating them as near together as the conditions allow—this effectual or practical principle, which we have named *collocation,* is carried out in this system as consistently as can be under the conditions, and wherever the potential convenience or serviceability is discerned. Research and Reference may thus the more conveniently pass from the general subject to the special subjects comprised under it, or conversely, from a special subject to closely related special subjects nearby on the shelves, and to the general subject that comprises these special subjects and precedes them on the shelves. The shelf labels should indicate some of these relations not only by the notation but by *see also* references. Similar convenience and efficiency may be effectuated in subject catalogs, in collocating cards directly—not indirectly as by means of cross-references in alphabetical subject catalogs. The classified cards are thus a more direct means of collocating the subject matters in books, etc., though less direct than actual access to the classified books. Users should be informed of these facilities, Reference librarians and readers' advisers should be trained for competence in these services, and so should catalogers and classifiers. Synthesis and collocation thus facilitate reference and research, also selection of books by readers and grouping them by librarians for whatever purposes. This is "how classification works," to use Dr. Kelley's phrase,[4] and how librarians and readers may work the more efficiently by means of classification. This is the principle of *Collocation* for convenience and efficiency in service. It is virtually a kind of applied synthesis. It is effectual in this system wherever it is feasible.

Adaptation of logical order to practical uses and to convenience through collocation, together with adaptation to different views and various purposes,

are principles that pervade this system. *Alternative locations* are accordingly provided throughout the schedules, and also *alternative methods* of classifying the complex subject matters relative to the several languages and literatures, for which special auxiliary schedules are available. Besides these indicated and available *alternatives,* there are many *see also references,* which would serve not only for subject cataloging but for use of "shelf list" catalogs and for research at the shelves. The alternative locations are not only for important major subjects, such as Theology, and for sub-sciences, such as Bacteriology, Mineralogy, Paleontology, and Biochemistry, but for special subjects everywhere throughout the schedules; for instance, Ecological Variation, Spectroscopy, and Education in Hygiene, or "Health Education," often, as in the last instance, involving synonymous terms. For special subject bibliography, Biography, Periodicals, Pamphlets, Documents, etc., there are alternatives either to sub-classify them specially throughout the system, or else to keep them unitary under major classes or divisions. These alternatives are termed *systematic alternatives,* as distinct from the *indicated* alternatives and alternative *methods* defined above. This principle of Adaptation by Alternatives is most distinctive of this system. It renders the schedules somewhat more complicated but that is compensated by the enhanced *adaptability.*

The Composite Principle, or principle of Composite, or Complex, Classification and Notation, is also a main feature of this Classification, in which it is developed more consistently and more economically than in other systems that have in their several ways applied it. This economy is effected mainly through the brevity and comparative simplicity of the notation. In Systematic Auxiliary Schedules, which provide for sub-classification by *form,* or *format,* by language, by country, or nation, by historical period, or other recurrent specification, relation, aspect, or sub-division of the subject, the correlative notations are so apportioned and economized that usually one letter, or figure, suffixed to the class mark, suffices for the composite specification. Sometimes, however, suffixes of two or even three letters, or figures, or letters and figures, are requisite for more minute or more complex specification.

Extensive Specification by the Composite Principle. A subject may be specified as related to another subject, and the notations of the two subjects may be combined. The simplest instance is CB for Physical Chemistry, where C is for Chemistry and B is the mark of the class Physics. Women in Journalism might be placed under Journalism, YV, as YVYQW. This composite result is similar to Dewey's "Number bilding." If adopted as a principle, it economizes, because such composite subjects would need no entry in the schedule. Moreover the interest and the order might be inverted in the alternative QWYVV. In either case the middle letter Y is intermediary. A lower-case y might be preferred. But for really important subjects, such as Psychology of Childhood, IV, (Psychology being I and Childhood QV) a distinct section, collocated in the schedule is still better, and the mark may be shorter as IV is shorter than IYQV.

The Efficiency of the Classification depends on its consistent application of the principles outlined in the preceding paragraphs: its comprehension of all the general subjects and the most important alternative views in which these may be regarded, more especially in *alternative locations* and *alternative methods;* its *inclusion* and *subordination* of all requisite special subjects under the relevant general subjects, and its *collocation* of the most closely related subjects, whether coördinate or subordinate, whether general or special; its coherence and *consistency,* yet its *adaptation* to different but consistent views, and to effectual and practical bibliographic purposes; its *expansibility* for further specification, its extensibility in *composite subclassification* for recurrent specifications by means of *systematic auxiliary Schedules;* its comparatively short and simple notation,

and its complete alphabetic index to all its terms and their synonyms by means of its notation. Thus the system is efficient in service, whether in classification of books or in classified subject catalogs.

The efficiency so attained is *maximal,* that is, it approaches to the highest efficiency attainable under the conditions.[5] This is not, of course, the *maximum* efficiency of 100 *percent.* No classification, no subject catalog, no special bibliography is so efficient as that in serving the various purposes. Nor will any of these indicate *all* the resources of a library on a given subject; still less will any classified union catalog or subject bibliography cite all the resources of all the libraries and collections comprised by it. A classification does not bring all the resources on a subject together on the shelves of a library, nor does any subject catalog bring them all together on a table; nor does a subject bibliography. But a classification, a classified subject catalog, or a classified subject bibliography may have a structural efficiency on which such maximal functional efficiency will largely depend.

Systemization is a term that epitomizes most of the foregoing principles. In classification of books on the shelves, or in a classified subject-catalog, or in a bibliography classified by subjects, or in a classified bibliography of bibliographies, a *system*, structural and functional, organizes subject matters for the subject approach in libraries. This systemization is fundamentally logical and scientific, but in development of its organization, it becomes methodic, effectual, and functional.

NOTES

[1] For more adequate exposition and discussion of these principles the author's prior volumes on *The Organization of Knowledge* may be consulted. The second of these has recently, March, 1939, been revised in a second edition, published by the H. W. Wilson Company. For a different purpose a fuller restatement was contributed in an extended paper on "Theoretic Principles of Bibliographic Classification," presented at the XIV Conference of the International Federation for Documentation, at Oxford, in September, 1938, and published in the *Transactions.*

[2] Henry Evelyn Bliss, *The Organization of Knowledge and the System of the Sciences,* by the author, pp. 73, 166-8, 237, 299, 410.

[3] This consensus has been defined in the author's preceding books: *Ibid.,* pp. 16, 301, 397; *A System of Bibliographic Classification*, pp. 42, 138, 292.

[4] Grace O. Kelley, *The Classification of Books,* p. 83–A study that shows how classification doesn't work in certain other systems.

[5] Henry Evelyn Bliss, *The Organization of Knowledge in Libraries* (———: H. W. Wilson Co.), 2nd ed 1939, pp 35, 103-104.

Historical Background of Classification

Leo E. LaMontagne

"American library classification, according to a tradition of long standing, began in 1870 with the system devised by William Torrey Harris for the library of the St. Louis public schools. Harris, a Hegelian, is said to have derived his classification from Francis Bacon's divisions of knowledge. It is a sad commentary on librarians as historians that this myth and the assumption of a previous state of bibliographic chaos has so long survived. Classifications grow, they are not created. . . ."

During the last quarter of a century so much has been written about the failure of classification and individual classification systems that I feel more obituarist than historian for a day. I am confident, however, that . . .[this is not] a defunct process.

The story of library classification is a long one. Man's attempts to classify, to introduce order into the arrangement of his books and of the records describing them, have been many and varied. From the "brick books" of Assyria and Babylonia and the papyri of Ancient Egypt, to the books and microfilms of the present, many systems of classification have been devised. Cicero's dictum, "Ordo est maxime qui memoriae lumen affert," has indeed been followed and there has been no limit to man's ingenuity in devising methods to create that order. And library classification is but a part of a larger process of classification which goes back to the dawn of man's thinking. For man uses classification in all his affairs as unwittingly as Molière's M. Jourdain used prose.

American library classification, according to a tradition of long standing, began in 1870 with the system devised by William Torrey Harris for the library of the St. Louis public schools. Harris, a Hegelian, is said to have derived his classification from Francis Bacon's divisions of knowledge. It is a sad commentary on librarians as historians that this myth and the assumption of a previous state of bibliographic chaos has so long survived. Classifications grow, they are not created; each succeeding system-maker, philosopher, scientist or librarian, draws from his predecessors, and there are no long gaps in their development. Like the culture of which it forms a part, American classification was both derivative and original.

American library classification can be conveniently divided into prehistoric and historic eras. It is with the former that this paper will be chiefly concerned, even at the risk of my being classed with the German scientist who began a treatise on the snakes of Ireland with the cautious, "Strictly speaking, of course, there are no snakes in Ireland."

One of the earliest American essays in the classification of knowledge was made by the Reverend Samuel Johnson, first president of King's College, now Columbia University, New York. Johnson's essay was first published anonymously in *The Present State of the Republick of Letters* for May, 1731. It had been forwarded to the journal by "P. N.," who wrote, "I make bold to send you here a Scheme for a general Partition of the Sciences, drawn up by a friend of mine, which seems to me very well calculated to give the Youth a good general notion of the Nature, Order and Use of the Sciences. . . ." Two centuries ago, in 1752, a third revision contained in the *Noetica* left the presses of B. Franklin and D. Hall in Philadelphia.

Johnson found that all parts of Learning could be reduced to two, "Philology, or the Study of Words and other Signs, and Philosophy, or the Study of Things signified by them." This division of knowledge has a long history and goes back at least to Marcus Terentius Varro, contemporary and friend of Cicero. The tradition was continued by Martianus Capella, Magnus Aurelius Cassiodorus, the Spanish bishop, Isidore of Seville, the Englishmen Bede and Alcuin, and many others. During the Middle Ages it formed the basis of the *trivium* (Artes or Scientiae Sermocinales) and the *quadrivium* (Disciplinas or Scientiae Reales) which determined the preparatory work of medieval stu-

SOURCE: Reprinted from M. Tauber, ed., *The Subject Analysis of Library Materials* (New York: Columbia University, School of Library Service, 1953), pp. 16–27, by permission of the editor.

dents leading to the universities. In the hands of Konrad Gesner of Zurich it received its classic form as a bibliographic classification in the twenty-one divisions of his *Pandectarium* (1548).

The immediate source of Johnson's classification was probably the Reverend Thomas Bray and his parochial libraries. Like Bacon, Bray first divided knowledge on the basis of its source into Divine and Human. He then cautiously subdivided human knowledge into the sciences concerned with (1) Things and (2) Words, and made subdivisions under each. The "Register" of books which Bray sent to Trinity Parish, New York, in 1698 contains his complete classification.

Johnson subdivided Philology into (1) General, or common to all kinds of speaking (Grammar and Rhetoric), and (2) Special, or particular kinds of speaking or writing (Oratory, History and Poetry, including Criticism). He divided Philosophy into the sciences of bodies and the sciences of spirits. The first contained mathematics, natural history, mechanics, geology, and astronomy; the second, noetics, or logic, pneumatology, theology, ethics, economics, and politics.

When Thomas Clap, rector of Yale College, assisted by Tutor Worthington, compiled the first published catalog of the Yale Library, he adopted Johnson's classification as the basis of its arrangement. Clap made several changes to adapt the classification to the educational needs of his students and added many subdivisions.

Johnson's division of philosophy into the sciences of bodies and the sciences of spirits carries us to a classification devised by Augustus Brevoort Woodward, who was graduated from King's College in 1793. Woodward, a friend and correspondent of Jefferson, began his study of classification while still a student, but it was not until 1816 that his work was published. He made an incredible survey of historic classifications and then developed two systems, one of knowledge as man sees it, and the other as a being superior to man views it. Woodward's classifications were based upon the dualism of mind and matter, and his main divisions were: (1) Hylica: The sciences dealing with matter, (2) Hylennoeica: The sciences dealing with matter and mind, and (3) Ennoeica: Those concerned with mind.

Woodward's essay represented a significant advance and it is unfortunate that his fondness for Greek nomenclature destined his classification to oblivion. Roswell Park continued Woodward's theory in his *Pantology*, which he hoped would serve as a "model for libraries" by bringing together books relating to the same subjects, whether in the catalogs or on the shelves. Strangely enough, although he had criticized Woodward for using Greek terminology, Park followed the same practice. He divided knowledge into four provinces: (1) Psychonomy, including the law of mind, or intellectual sciences, (2) Ethnology, or the study of nations, geographically and historically, (3) Physiconomy, or the laws of the material world, and (4) Technology, or the study of the arts which relate to material objects.

One of the most prominent early American classifiers was Thomas Jefferson, third President of the United States, who seems to have been responsible for introducing the divisions of knowledge of Francis Bacon into this country around 1770. To a mind like Jefferson's, encyclopedic in its interests, practical and methodical in all things, the problem of classification must have come early. Jefferson made two separate ventures in the classification of knowledge, the first for the selection and arrangement of his own books, the second in connection with his plans for the reorganization of the College of William and Mary and the organization of the University of Virginia. They reveal a strange dualism in Jefferson, the classifier, which resulted in the creation of classifications so different that they might well have been the products of different minds.

As a book collector, Jefferson early in life adopted Bacon's classification, with some of d'Alembert's modifications, made a few changes of his own, and was content with the system for life. To Jefferson, as to many others, Bacon's system was, as Flint said, ". . . a comprehensive and attractive, sketch of the intellectual world, indicating in a striking way, difficult to forget, not only what provinces had been acquired by the human mind, but where and in what manner new conquests were still to be made." Jefferson, the educational philosopher, was not so easily satisfied, and his contributions in this area are more original and closer to today's thought.

Jefferson's classification was based upon d'Alembert's modifications of the divisions of knowledge used by Bacon in the *Advancement of Knowledge* (1605) and the *De Augmentis Scientiarum* (1623). Bacon's first division of knowledge was by source: sacred theology revealed to man by God and human knowledge acquired by man's unaided powers. Next come the divisions based upon the faculties of the minds. ". . . from these three fountains, Memory, Imagination, and Reason, flow these three emanations, History, Poesy, and Philosophy; and there can be no others." Bacon's subdivisions were many, and unfortunately they were rarely, if ever, given correctly. His Poesy is restricted to feigned history, and verse as a character of style is found in Philosophy. The chief divisions of History are Nature and Man; of Philosophy, God, Nature, and Man.

D'Alembert adopted Bacon's main plan but made many variations in preparing his classification for the *Encyclopédie ou Dictionnaire raisonné des sciences des arts et des métiers* (1751-1765). He rejected Bacon's primary division of knowledge into Divine and Human and followed the sequence History, Science, and Poetry. D'Alembert expanded the scope of Poetry by including in it the Fine Arts, which Bacon had classed in Philosophy with the sciences of the Human Body. In both History and Philosophy his main divisions were God, Man, and Nature. In brief, this was the tradition followed by Jefferson and many American librarians.

Jefferson's views of the importance of classification in library management and his main divisions are recorded in a letter written to James Ogilvie in January, 1806:

> . . . The key [to the library at Monticello] is at present in the hands of Mr. Dinsmore, at the place, who on sight of this letter will consider you as at all times authorized to have access to the library & to take from it any books you please. I will only ask the favor of you to keep a piece of paper on one of the tables of the room, & to note on it the books you have occasion to take out, and to blot it out when returned. The object in this is that should I want a book at any time when at home, I may know where it is. The arrangement is as follows: 1. Antient history. 2. Modern do. 3. Physics. 4. Nat. Hist. proper. 5. Technical arts. 6. Ethics. 7. Jurisprudence. 8. Mathematics. 9. Gardening, architecture, sculpture, painting, music, poetry. 10. Oratory. 11. Criticism. 12. Polygraphical. You will find this on a paper nailed up somewhere in the library. The arrangement begins behind the partition door leading out of the Bookroom into the Cabinet, & proceeds from left to right round the room; Then entering the Cabinet it begins at the eastern angle, & goes round that room. The presses not having sufficed to contain the whole, the latter part of the polygraphics was put into the kind of closet at the first entrance of the book-room. As after using a book, you may be at a loss in returning it to it's exact place, & they cannot be found again when misplaced, it will be better to leave them on a table in the room. My familiarity with their places will enable me to replace them readily . . . .

One of the best early library classifications of the Bacon-d'Alembert tradition is that contained in the 1789 *Catalogue* of Benjamin Franklin's Library Company of Philadelphia. The classification which reached Philadelphia from London or Dublin may have played an important part in perpetuating Bacon in American libraries. Zachariah Poulson was Librarian of the Company at the time. Three years before Jefferson's Chapters were installed in the Library of Congress a variant of the Philadelphia scheme formed the basis of the arrangement of the 1812 *Catalogue of the Library of Congress*.

Another early American follower of Bacon was Thaddeus Mason Harris, Librarian of Harvard (1791-1793), who compiled a catalog for a small and cheap library adapted to the taste and circumstance of common readers. He listed the 276 entries, some 700 volumes in all, worth perhaps $1500 in the money of the period, in the order of Bacon and d'Alembert in 23 subdivisions. His classification is a far better one than many which followed.

It was Harris who proved that, unlike old soldiers, old librarians do not even fade away, and we have as authority Nathaniel Hawthorne. In 1856, while he was American Consul in Liverpool, Hawthorne told of meeting Dr. Harris in the Boston Athenaeum. One evening a friend told Hawthorne that Harris had died and Hawthorne was incredulous, for he had seen the old librarian that very day. Hawthorne mounted the steps of the Athenaeum the following day, thinking within himself: "Well, I shall never see old Doctor Harris again!" He opened the door of the reading room and to his astonishment saw Harris seated in his accustomed chair reading a newspaper which must have contained his obituary. For weeks after, Hawthorne continued to see Dr. Harris as frequently as before his death, regarding the "venerable defunct no more than any other of the old fogies who basked before the fire and dozed over the newspapers."

Brunet's classification entered Harvard (and for practical purposes the United States) in 1830, when the Library of the College published another in its list of catalogs. When William P. Curtis of the St. Louis Mercantile Library prepared the first catalog of that institution in 1850 he chose the Harvard catalog of 1830 for his model and adopted Brunet for the classified section. Four years later the influence of the St. Louis catalog carried Brunet to the west coast, to the San Francisco Mercantile Library, only six years after Captain John B. Montgomery of the U.S.S. *Portsmouth* had raised the American flag in the plaza which now bears the name of his ship. Within a quarter of a century after its introduction Brunet's system had spread from Cambridge, Massachusetts, to San Francisco and from Salem, Massachusetts, to Richmond, Virginia. From then on it was Bacon *versus* Brunet in American libraries.

This classification has a long history and was variously known as the System of the Paris Booksellers, the French System, or, more simply, the Brunet. It was Jacques-Charles Brunet who gave the classification its classic form and the name by which it is commonly known today. In this form it played an important role in the classification of bibliographies and libraries in Europe and in this country.

Brunet was born in Paris on November 2, 1780, son of Thomas Brunet, a man of peasant stock who had left a home "chargé d'enfants" in Morigny, Normandy to seek his fortune in Paris. The elder Brunet tried many occupations before finally settling into the book trade. Jacques-Charles received a good elementary education, but when he was about twelve the effect of the French Revolution on his father's business forced him to leave school to help in his father's shop. Brunet's interest was in books, not business, as his father soon found out. In 1810 he published his *Manuel du libraire et de l'amateur de livres* (3 vols. in 8) and he was an octagenarian when the fifth and last edition was published (1860-1865, 6 tomes in 12 parts). It is interesting to note that the first four editions brought Brunet 400,000 francs, an unheard-of sum for such a profession.

The paternity of Brunet's classification has long been disputed but there seems to be little doubt that it was published for the first time in 1678 in Jean Garnier's *Systema bibliothecae collegii parisiensis Societatis Jesu.* A year later a slightly different version appeared in the *Catalogus bibliothecae Thuanae,* the work of Ismael Boulliau. Garnier provided four main divisions—Theology, Philosophy, History, and Jurisprudence—and Boulliau five—Theology, Jurisprudence, History, Philosophy, and Belles-Lettres. There are many likenesses and many differences between the two systems, disclosing that each man had drawn from common patterns of organization and adapted them to his presumed needs. Succeeding bibliographers modified and improved the system.

Brunet's *Table méthodique en forme de catalogue raisonné* consisted of five main classes—Theology, Jurisprudence, Sciences and Arts, Belles-Lettres, and History—and there were over six two-column pages of subdivisions in the early editions. In brief this was the system that Benjamin Peirce, librarian of Harvard College, introduced into the United States. He added a sixth class for works relating to America which contained added entries for books classified in American History, Voyages and Travels, Politics, etc. and made other changes to adapt the system to the needs of an American library.

Brunet drove Bacon from the Library Company of Philadelphia during the librarianship of George Campbell. Campbell, librarian of the venerable institution from 1806 to 1829, adopted the grand divisions of Religion, Jurisprudence, Sciences and Arts, Belles-Lettres, and History, prefaced them with a division for Bibliography, and made many subdivisions to provide for the 44,000 volumes to which Benjamin Franklin's library had grown. A successor of Campbell, Lloyd Smith, revised and expanded the classification and provided it with a notation which is still used to frighten library science students. Smith described his system as early as the 1853 Convention of Librarians. Published in 1882, it is usually considered one of the contributions of the historic period.

Seth Hastings Grant, who played a prominent part in the Librarians' Convention of 1853 and acted as its secretary, introduced Brunet into the Mercantile Library of New York in 1850. Grant modified the historic system and provided the following main divisions: Theology, Mental and Moral Science, Political Science, History and Geography, Mathematics, Natural Sciences, Medical Science, Technology, and Encyclopedic. Grant's work later became associated with the name of Frederic B. Perkins, who revised the system and published it in 1881; and it thus became one of the systems usually described in the historic period of classification.

Although the future of American classification has been determined with the strange inevitability of a Greek drama, it is interesting to pause briefly at this point and ask, "What would American library classification be today if the men of the historic period had followed more modern trends?" Consider for the moment the work of J. Peter Lesley which was published in 1862.

Lesley, geologist and clergyman, became secretary and librarian of the American Philosophical Society in 1858. He thought that a reasonable arrangement of every collection of minerals, or of books, in the hands of man was "a call of the soul to be obeyed." He developed and applied in the Library of the Society a classification which is far closer to today's theories of organization than most existing systems.

Lesley divided knowledge into eight main divisions progressing "from the universal to the special, from the abstract to the concrete, from the inorganic to the organic and from matter to mind." These divisions were: (1) General Science, (2) the Mathematical Sciences, (3) the Inorganic Sciences, (4) the Organic Sciences, (5) the Historical Sciences, (6) the Social Sciences, (7) the Spiritual Sciences, and (8) Personal Science, or Biography. Within each class he observed two rules, which he termed the Law of Space and the Law of Time. Whenever possible, books were arranged in each of the divisions and subdivisions geographically in a sequence proceeding, like that of history, from the East westward. In all other sections the books were arranged chronologically. Lesley disregarded size in shelving except in the case of very large books. Although he knew that this practice might be a fatal defect to those who were more disposed to please the eye than assist the brain, he was confident that working scholars would soon be cured of undue estheticism in externals.

The final battle in the conflict between Bacon and Brunet for the dominance of American library classification was fought in the St. Louis Mercantile Library in 1857. William P. Curtis, who had adopted Brunet in 1850, was succeeded by Edward William Johnston, a man of strong convictions and a Baconian of long standing. Johnston evicted Brunet and installed the divisions of knowledge which Baron Verulam had developed over two and a quarter centuries earlier. The decision was final, determined the course of American classification from 1870 to the present, and extended its influence to the world at large.

Johnston was born in 1799 at Cherry Grove, later Longwood, a mile east of Farmville in Prince Edward County, Virginia. He was the son of Judge Peter Johnston and Mary Wood Johnston, daughter of Col. Valentine and Lucy (Henry) Johnston, a sister of Patrick Henry. Another son was the Confederate general, Joseph Eggleston Johnston. Edward William devoted his life to journalism and library work. After his death in St. Louis on December 9, 1867, the *New Orleans Crescent* summarized his scholarship: "If men could bequeath their knowledge, as they do their material property, to posterity the heir of Edward William Johnston would be possessed of a rich legacy indeed." Johnston did bequeath part of his knowledge, but the nature of the bequest and its influence have long been unknown.

In 1835 the trustees of the College of South Carolina (University of South Carolina) created a new position—secretary of the board of trustees and librarian—and appointed Johnston to fill it. Within a year he had devised a system of classification and compiled a catalog of the library's books. He then went to New York and applied the same classification to the collections of the Mercantile Library Association there. Years of journalism followed, until in 1857 he entered the service of the St. Louis Mercantile Library. Within five months he had compiled a catalog of the library, which numbered nearly 15,000 volumes at the time. The classed catalog filled over 550 pages and the Index nearly 250.

The classification Johnston applied in St. Louis differed greatly from his first essay at the College of South Carolina. Older, and for many years separated from library work, his last classification lacks the cogency and logic of his first. History is improved by the transfer of Natural History to Philosophy, thus bringing the content of these divisions closer to the history and natural sciences of the day. The contents of Philosophy, however, which once contained six branches—Moral Philosophy, Theology, Grammar, the Art of Government, the Mathematical Sciences, and the Art of Healing, which included the biological sciences—now comprised Theology, Jurisprudence, the Social Sciences, Metaphysics and Ideology, Physics, the Art of Healing, Military Science, Particular Arts, Education, and Language and Literature. It is obvious that Johnston attempted, with poor success, to merge Bacon and Brunet in this division. The third division, Poetry, including the Fine Arts, and the fourth, Polygraphs, remained unchanged.

We have now come to 1870 and the historic period, to William Torrey Harris, the follower of Hegel, who inverted Bacon and created American classification. Harris left Yale in his junior year when he became convinced that the College had little more to teach him and went West to teach the new subject of shorthand. In 1858 he was appointed a teacher in the St. Louis public school system and remained there as teacher, principal, assistant superintendent, and superintendent until 1880.

Harris was led to attempt the compilation of a classed catalog for the school library by the practical success of the classification contained in the "Catalogue of that excellent collection, the St. Louis Mercantile Library." He adopted the general plan of the classification applied by Edward William Johnston in 1858, inverted the order of the main classes, made additions and changes, and reorganized Science or Philosophy, the class in which he found Johnston's work unsatisfactory. The oft-quoted inversion is a terminological *tour de force*, for the main divisions had long been drained of their Baconian meaning.

It is interesting to contemplate what American classification might have become had Harris, the Hegelian, followed his master, of whose work Flint wrote:

> Whatever be the faults of Hegel's *Encyclopaedia*–although they be even "thick as dust in vacant chambers"–this glory, I think, cannot fairly be denied to it, that there for the first time, appeared a system of such a character and scope, so vast in its range of conception, so rich in suggestion and doctrine, and so skilfully constructed, as to present to the mind something like what a Science of the Sciences ought to be.[1]

Forgotten or unknown were Lesley and others who were trying to develop classifications adapted to the knowledge of the time, and not simply to readjust historic, outmoded patterns of organization.

A year after the publication of Harris' work in 1870, Jacob Schwartz was faced with the problem of finding a classification for the Apprentices' Library of New York. In the long history of library classifications few schemes exhibit more ingenuity than the Combined System he developed. Schwartz studied the various classifications in use at the time and concluded that "... the only thing that classifiers from Aristotle to Messrs. Cutter and Perkins are agreed upon is ... to disagree." His system represented an attempt to translate the principles of the alphabetico-classed catalog to the arrangement of books on the shelves. Schwartz divided human knowledge into three main classes—History, Literature, and Science—and subdivided each into departments, classes, and subclasses. He then devised a somewhat intricate "Alphabetical Table of Author Numbers" to provide book numbers in each of the four divisions of his subclasses. Schwartz maintained that his pioneer effort of combining the three fundamental forms of shelf arrangement influenced directly or indirectly all succeeding systems. He is one of the three classification makers mentioned by Dewey in his "Aknowlejments" of the first edition of his Decimal Classification. Ironically, Schwartz is criticized for his failure to achieve the systematic classification he sought to avoid.

We now reach the year 1876 and the Decimal Classification devised by Melvil Dewey. At this point it has long been customary among historians to advert briefly to La Croix du Maine and Nathaniel Shurtleff and their decimal systems. It

has been traditional to cite, but not quote, the former and to misinterpret the latter. La Croix du Maine's proposal to Henri III of France in 1583 "pour dresser une bibliothèque parfaite et accomplie de tous points" in 100 "buffets" of 100 volumes each actually required 107 "buffets." The classification, which ran from Almighty God in "buffet" one to the End of the World in "buffet" 107, comprised seven "orders":

1 - 17	Religion
18 - 41	Arts and Sciences
42 - 62	Description of the Universe
63 - 72	Mankind
73 - 81	Nobility ("hommes illustres en guerre")
82 - 96	Works of God (Natural History) and
97 - 107	Memoirs

Shurtleff's plan for the Boston Public Library, on the contrary, involved shelving and not classification, for he thought that the purposes of libraries were so different that a common classification was impossible. His decimal shelving plan (1852) was adaptable to any classification.

Dewey's interest in classification, like that of Judge Woodward, was awakened during his college years. And while decimal classification was not uncommon in American libraries—it was used in Amherst in Dewey's time—it was Dewey's destiny to attach the notation to a classification based in the main upon W. T. Harris' reorganization of Edward William Johnston's pioneer work and to spread its influence throughout the world. And so it came about that the Universal Decimal Classification begun in Brussels in 1895 carried Francis Bacon back to the Old World.

Charles A. Cutter began his work in classification in the Boston Athenaeum shortly after the first conference of the ALA in 1876. He foresaw the continuing growth of the library and knew that each change in the shelving of books entailed the changing of "shelf marks"—a long and expensive process. Cutter therefore decided to abandon fixed location and to adopt a method which would allow books to be moved without changing "the marks on the catalogues."

Cutter was attracted first to the "Amherst decimal plan" because it was simple and symmetrical, but soon decided that the decimal notation would not afford the close classification he thought necessary. He then developed a system using both letters and figures which he tried out in the town library in Winchester, Massachusetts before applying it in the Athenaeum. The system was a success, but Cutter was not satisfied and began to develop a scheme he called the Expansive because it was designed in seven schedules of increasing fulness which could be applied to collections ranging in size from a village library to a national library of a million volumes. The first six expansions were published between 1891 and 1893. After Cutter's death in 1893 several parts of the seventh expansion were published, but they were inferior to the work Cutter himself had developed or revised.

Cutter sought to devise not a classification of knowledge but a logical and practical method for the arrangement of books. He knew, however, that a work of permanent value could be achieved only by a classifier who based his system upon a classification of knowledge. Cutter chose to follow the "evolutionary idea throughout," but his interpretation of evolution was far different from that of J. Peter Lesley. His main divisions were: General Works, Philosophical Sciences, Historical Sciences, Social Sciences, Natural Sciences, Useful and Fine Arts, and Literature and Language.

In the fall of 1897 the Library of Congress moved from the cramped quarters in the Capitol it had occupied for nearly a century to the new building which the persistence of Librarian Spofford had brought into being. John Russell Young succeeded Spofford as librarian, James Christian Meinich Hanson was chief of the new Catalogue Department, and Charles Martel was his first assistant and chief classifier. One of the first problems faced by the new administration was classification.

The system in use was based upon that which had come to the Library in the spring of 1815 with Jefferson's books. Succeeding librarians had modified and expanded it and by 1897 the scheme contained over 10,000 subdivisions within the Jeffersonian framework of forty-four chapters. There were three possibilities: first, to reconstruct the old Jeffersonian arrangement, second, to adopt an existing classification—Dewey or Cutter—and third, to devise an "eclectic" system adapted to the collections and needs of the Library. After three years of quest and experiment, which produced Class Z, Bibliography and Library Science, Herbert Putnam, who had become Librarian of Congress in 1899, made the decision; and in the closing days of 1900 the Library began to develop its "new" classification.

The purpose of the Library, the composition of its collections, open shelves, and a classed catalog were the assumptions upon which the classification was constructed. The structure of the Library of Congress Classification reflects the sharp dichotomy of Otto Hartwig's division of all knowledge into Geistes-und Naturwissenschaften. In classes B-P are the Humanistic Disciplines and the Social Sciences, followed by Q-V, Science and Technology. At the head of these broad groups is Class A for Polygraphy, and following them is the experimental Class Z, Bibliography and Library Science, the index or key to the whole. The first schedule, Class E-F, was published in January, 1901.

Five years later, at the 1905 Conference of the American Library Association in Portland, Oregon, Putnam summarized the problem and its solution.

> How excellent a service if the national library could adopt a classification which would become universally current! We have had visions of such a one. They have passed. We long considered existing systems, in the hope that one of these might be adopted by us, if that could be seen to have a clear prospect of general adoption. We considered long, but felt obliged to conclude that no existing system likely to be generally current would serve our purpose without modifications which would defeat the very purpose of uniformity—that is, identical call numbers. We have proceeded to construct a system of our own, and have thus added one more crime to the calendar, and further confusion.

It is perhaps beyond the responsibilities of a historian for a day to turn moralist and make certain observations upon his findings. I find it difficult to refrain, but shall limit myself to two generalizations. The first is that librarians rarely learn from experience. The history of any old library recapitulates the history of all—experiments with classed or author catalogs: if classed, with this or that system of classification. A better name for experiment in library science might be institutional vacillation or abulia. Ernest A. Savage, long-time chief librarian of Edinburgh Public Libraries, wrote:

> The truth is that the chief processes in library adminstration undergo periodical occultations. They emerge again the brighter for their eclipse, and shine upon us for a time, and fade again into obscurity. We lose ideas, regain them, fight against them, yield to them, and forget them once more.[2]

The reason, however, is not that librarians are any less capable than other humans of learning from the past. It is rather that the past of librarianship remains unrecorded. Its antiquities are, as Francis Bacon said, ". . . *tanquam tabula naufragii*," "remnants of history which have casually escaped the shipwreck of time." Much could be done here in the United States to salvage these remnants and turn them into history.

The second generalization concerns the theoretically desirable and the practically possible. It is curious that many librarians who in everyday life live within their budgets, dwell in modest homes, and drive low-priced cars will be satisfied only with mansions and Cadillacs in matters of classification. Morris Cohen's statement that ". . . the confusion between practicality of empirical classifications (to be tested by their applicability) and the absoluteness of division based on logical principles, is perhaps the most fruitful source of philosophic error,"[3] applies *a fortiori* to librarians. It is time for a return to Jeffersonian realism—to the realization that classification is an instrument or tool to assist in the management of libraries. It is not an end in itself—an *objet d'art* of high intellectualization.

NOTES

[1] Robert Flint, *Philosophy as Scientia Scientiarium* . . . (Edinburgh and London, 1904), p. 157.

[2] John L. Thornton, *The Chronology of Librarianship.* Introduction by Ernest A. Savage (London: Grafton and Co., 1941), p. x.

[3] Morris R. Cohen, *A Preface to Logic* (New York: Henry Holt and Co., Inc., 1944), p. 77.

CLASSIFICATION

Principles, Theories, and Philosophies

The philosophies are as many and varied as the individuals themselves. They run the gamut from the simplistic to the highly complex, yet fundamentally they are founded on logic and progress through mathematics. They are concerned with order and organization for retrieval and hence bear similar characteristics. While the principle and theory may seem to many nebulous and often remote, in this day of rapidly changing functions in classification, it is requisite to understand such precepts as hierarchy, synthesis, enumeration and facets in order to truly determine what many have asked: "Is classification dead?"

Classification: Theoretical and Practical

Ernest Cushing Richardson

"Classification is, in its simplest statement, the putting together of like things, or more fully described, it is the arranging of things according to likeness and unlikeness . . . . The need of adjusting theoretical classification to practical conditions is not peculiar to the classification of books, but is characteristic of the treatment of all complex concrete things."

THE NATURE OF CLASSIFICATION

Classification may also be expressed as the sorting and grouping of things. It is convenient sometimes, to speak of "likeness and unlikeness," but really in classification it is "likeness" which rules, while "unlikeness" is merely what is left over when likeness has been defined. The "putting together of like things" is, therefore, the fullest and most exact form of the definition.

So simple an act as the putting away of a handful of change in one's purse contains the gist of a process through which every thing and every thought in the universe has come into being—the paper money is put in one compartment, the coin in another, and then, perhaps, the coin is subdivided again by putting the gold, silver, nickel or copper each in a separate compartment. If the money is to be counted, it will probably be laid on a table, in groups of paper, gold, silver, etc., these groups arranged according to value into one and two-cent pieces copper; three and five nickel; ten, twenty-five, fifty and one dollar silver; and so on with gold and paper. Into each group will be put all the pieces of like material and like value. The money in this act is fully classified, its pieces have all been put together according to likeness, first according to material and then according to value.

This is a mechanical example of what actually goes on in every process of classification whether of ideas or things. It represents also the real order of arrangement of things in the universe—a series of groups and groups of groups arranged according to degree of likeness from the simplest to the most complex. What this process leads to will be discussed under the order of the sciences, but the process is the same all along the line.

The object at which classification aims is in every case order or system and its result is called a system. It starts facing a disorderly mass, and aims to reduce this to an orderly whole.

If this is classification, what then is a thing?

A *thing* as subject for classification is whatever is; that is to say, whatever has separate existence. Whether its substance is matter or motion or spirit is indifferent. If it is, it may be classified, and if it can be classified it must be that it is. That is the whole of it. Identity, sameness, and thing-ness are one and the same thing. The characteristic of a thing is that it is itself. It is *a* and it is not *b*. It is discrete, separate and, in short, subject to definition.

Ideas are, therefore, the subjects of classification just as much as anything else, not only because they have a material as well as a spiritual substance, but because they are individual separate things existing in a certain place at a certain time in a certain definable nature.

Things, therefore, as the subject of classification include the things in man and the things outside. The things outside include in turn the things which make man (nature and environment) and the things which man makes, or art. Things, therefore, include nature, ideas and art. Of these man has to do only with ideas and art. The things of nature are already classified, but this classification according to nature may be rearranged by man, and this is art, whether it is plowing or breeding, the making of houses, paintings or books, or yet the reorganization of a man's ideas in education.

Ideas themselves are, therefore, of two sorts, corresponding with the two kinds of outer things, nature and art. One kind is facing nature and the other is facing art, but the operation with either sort is one of classification. Classification of ideas on the one hand facing nature is knowledge, and when carried to perfection is called science. The classification of ideas, on the other hand, into

SOURCE: Reprinted from Ernest Cushing Richardson, *Classification: Theoretical and Practical* (Hamden, Conn.: Shoestring Press, 1964), pp. 1-7 and 23-42, by permission of the publisher.

a group which never yet has had any likeness in the outer world, but may have, and is intended to have, is art. The true classification of the ideas of things that have been—in short, the classification of the sciences—is simply the order of nature paralleled. The classification into new ideas or art is by this same token not an imitation of nature, and is endless in possible variety.

It is must be remembered in this connection that from the standpoint of the individual, i.e., the standpoint of knowledge, everything is an outside thing to a man save his own ideas (and perhaps even the major part of his own ideas). Everybody's ideas save his own and all art, even his own if represented in outer things, is "nature." His business is first to get within himself exact ideas of these things and, second, to classify these exact ideas into a series which shall itself be an exact idea of the order of outer things. As a race and as an individual, man gets his ideas helter-skelter. When he starts to think, they are a disorderly mass, a chaos of ideas which he must reduce to order by classification. The final goal of his effort is exact ideas of everything that is, arranged according to the real order of things in the universe; the idea, in short, of the whole of things, a whole which includes ideas and art as well as nature. The process to that end is classification, or the putting together according to likeness.

What then again is likeness?

Likeness, as the ground of the putting together of things in classification, is, in brief terms, interchangeability—the state in which some portion or element of any two things is such that it can be taken from one and put in the other and *vice versa* without changing the real character of each. A homely example of this is the Waltham watch. Take two machine-made watches of the better type—they are so nearly alike in all their details that any part of one may be exchanged for the like part of the other, or *vice versa*, and both watches will still go as before. They are alike in all essential parts.

Likeness is to be distinguished from identity or sameness, on the one hand, and from similarity or resemblance on the other. Note, therefore, in the case of the watch, that the pieces exchanged are not "the same" or "identical," but "like" pieces, and note, also, that a variation of the most trifling kind might stop both watches. The pieces must, on the other hand, be less than the "same" piece; otherwise only one watch could be kept going at a time. Likeness, therefore, is neither identity nor mere resemblance.

Likeness thus, on the one hand, is less than identity or sameness. One might possibly call identity "absolute likeness," i.e., likeness in every conceivable respect, including the position of each of its smallest parts in space, but this is forcing language. In this state it is the same substance. Absolute likeness, or likeness complete in every respect, including position in space, is not to be distinguished from thingness itself, and is better called identity, or sameness.

Likeness might perhaps be described as identity in kind but not in substance. Like things are of the same kind, but not the same substance, and here is where a mistake is oftenest made. We say loosely that two gold pieces are made from the same substance. They are not—they are made of like substances, or the same kind of substance; but every molecule of gold is a separate thing by itself, and perhaps even every atom and every ion of it. Like things are not the same but equal, and perhaps the fundamental law of the determination of likeness might be described as the law that things equal to the same things are equal to one another. Likeness is, therefore, less than identity.

Likeness, on the other hand, is more than resemblance or similarity. These latter may be well described as partial likeness. Things are more or less alike according to the amount which they have in common, i. e., the amount which can be taken from the one and put in the other without material disturbance. It is a mere question of subtraction or better, of algebraic substitution. The difference, therefore, between likeness and resemblance is the difference between exactly alike, very much alike, and more or less alike.

We mean thus ordinarily by likeness or exact likeness, such degrees of likeness that no test or experiment which we can apply will reveal any condition under which one cannot be substituted for the other. We do not exhaust likeness even in this, since even the minutest atom, which can be substituted for any other atom of the same kind in every known chemical compound is supposed to resemble its other atoms not as shot does shot, but as two grains of sand, each with its own individualities.

KINDS OF CLASSIFICATION

Classification being the putting of things together according to likeness, there may be as many kinds of classification as there are kinds of likeness.

Likeness may be in respect of mass or weight; it

may be likeness of form or shape (i.e., all circles, crosses, etc., together), likeness of color (black and white marbles or children in a school), likeness in size (e. g., grenadier regiments), in hardness (your lead pencils), in brittleness (table ware), in elasticity (golf balls), in conductivity (insulators). It may be in transparency, specific gravity, radiating power, or what not.

The likeness may be one of position in space (geographical), or position in time (chronological), or of origin (genetic), or of power (dynamic).

The series in likeness which is formed may be in respect of quality (better or worse), quantity (more or less), extent or duration (longer or shorter), position (near or far).

In every case a series is formed by taking from many things what is common to each and letting the more like follow the less like, or *vice versa*.

Where the likeness is one which is essential, which resides in the very character of the thing itself, the classification is called natural or logical classification; and this is, in fact, a classification according to the total amount of likeness. Classification according to some single mark of likeness is partial classification, while arrangement according to some accidental feature is artificial classification—the most familiar example of this being the alphabetical classification. Partial and artificial are often not distinguished.

The commonest kinds of classification are:

1. *The Logical Classification*, or classification according to degree of likeness from most complex to the simplest. This is to be regarded as forming one face of what is known as Natural Classification and of which evolution is the opposite face. Each regards all elements of real likeness, but the logical leads the series along the path of the real order of things back from the most complex to the simplest, from the now back to the beginning of things, whereas evolution leads it forward over the same ground.
2. *Geometrical Classification* is classification according to the order of position in space. It is founded on the fact that every atom of the universe at a given instant of time has a definite geometrical position with reference to every other atom. Its commonest form is the geographical, which arranges together all men, horses, cats, dogs, trees, etc., in given geometrical position on the earth's surface.
3. *Chronological Classification*, or classification according to position in time, is founded on the fact that at every successive instant of time every atom in the universe has a changed position with reference to every other atom. It groups together all things extant at a given time. e. g., all men born on a certain day. Its commonest example is a table of dates.
4. *Genetic Classification* is the grouping according to likeness of origin and is seen every day in family history.
5. *Historical Classification* combines the chronological, the geographical and the genetic ideas and arranges (1) according to position in space, (2) according to order in time, (3) according to the order of genesis.

    This, carried to its highest power, results in:
6. *Evolutionary Classification* or classification according to the order of likeness from the simplest to the most complex. This is, as has been said, the complement of logical classification and both are faces of the one "natural" order.

    To these familiar general forms should perhaps be added:
7. *Dynamic Classification*, or classification according to the order of power.
8. *Alphabetical Classification*, or classification according to the letters of names—one of the commonest of artificial classifications, and
9. *Mathematical Classification*, or classification according to the order of numerical symbols—the prince of artificial classifications and servant of all the natural classifications.

LAWS OR PRINCIPLES OF CLASSIFICATION

A *law* is simply the way in which things are in the habit of acting. It may be defined as the like action of like things under like circumstances. Any given law is simply the historical fact that certain things under certain circumstances act in a certain way. The idea of law is that things having always acted in this way may be expected to act in this way in the future, although there is no guarantee of this because some other "law" may come in to modify.

A law is distinguished from an hypothesis or theory simply by the number of times that a given thing has been known to happen. If like things under like circumstances are seen to act in like fashion two or more times we affirm an hypothesis. Care is then taken to note exactly, when it happens again, whether the resulting action is still like those before noticed. When experiments have been carried to every conceivable extent, it becomes a law. The shades of meaning between hypothesis, theory, law and principle are such that one cannot quarrel much with the interchange of bordering ones, although one must try and stop short of the interchange of hypothesis and law and principle.

Among the chief principles or laws which have to be taken into account in classification are:

The law of likeness. Likeness is the universal principle of the order of things. Things are either already put together according to likeness in nature or they are put together by man in his mind or in outer material. Things arranged according to likeness without the aid of man are *nature*. Ideas arranged according to likeness are *knowledge*. Outer things arranged by man according to likeness are *art*. In every case the true likeness is the one which determines order.

In nature or outer things unmodified by man this principle of likeness reigns in mathematics in the law that things like the same thing are like one another; in physics according to the law that like masses attract in like manner. The most familiar example of this is a pair of scales where if the masses in each pan are equal they are equally attracted by the earth. If they are unlike in mass, the amount which constitutes likeness balances, but the remainder of mass is also attracted and, having no counterpoise, approaches the earth.

The law reigns again in nature in the magnetic and electric laws that like quantities attract (or repel) equally. It reigns again in the law of chemical affinity according to which like atoms attract more strongly than unlike and the more complex a molecule the more unstable it is.

The principle of likeness in living things takes the form of the law of genesis, or that like begets like, and the complementary law of homology that that real likeness among things indicates common ancestry.

Among ideas likeness is the foundation of all thought and every variation of the act of thought can be summed up according to Bain into likeness, unlikeness and retentiveness, or, according to Spencer, into likeness, unlikeness and integration. Likeness is so the essence of all human thought, that literally there is no smallest act of the human mind which cannot be analyzed into just this operation of distinguishing like and unlike and either holding to or rejecting. Likeness, in particular, is the foundation of that systematic thought carried to its ultimate which we call logic.

And what is true of science is also true of art,

that every artistic impression is merely a classification of presentations of likeness and unlikeness. What we see in a landscape can be resolved into terms of contrast of light and shade.

Indeed, the law of likeness carries itself into the active personality as well, for here it is that character resolves itself simply into choice, the classification of things into like and dislike and the integration of the like. Action itself is choice, or the classification according to like and unlike.

In the field of sociology, enlarging from the sphere of individual character to the nature of men as a whole, it may be said that all social relations, economic and political, are founded according to the latest opinion upon the fact of likeness, or, if you choose, the consciousness of likeness, the "consciousness of kind," as Mr. Giddings says.

Likeness is, therefore, characteristic of all things and its law may be expressed as the law that all things in the universe are organized according to their likeness. Many if not most laws are, so to speak, sub-laws of this, and among those especially interesting in our task are: (a) The law that things like the same things are like each other; (b) The law that like draws like; (c) The law that like begets like, and (d) The law that true likeness points to a common ancestry.

The second general principle useful for our task is *the historical law* that the progress of things in space and time is also in general a genetic progress in complexity.

The law of evolution adds to the law of history the observation that the law of historical progress from the simple to the complex holds good of all things which tend toward continued existence. In the general use of the word it is a complex including the ideas, (1) of logical progress in complexity, (2) progress in space and time corresponding with progress in complexity so that the order of complexity is also the order of appearance in time, (3) the genesis of the more from the less complex, (4) growth in complexity the conditions of life, and (5) degeneration, which is the complement to evolution proper and adds the fact that wherever things are not growing in complexity they are proceeding toward dissolution. The net result of the law is the doctrine that in the long run those things which are constantly growing in complexity continue to have existence, while others perish.

These laws or principles are, as you see, simply a sort of resumé of what went before as they are the foundation of what is to follow.

BOOK CLASSIFICATION AN ART

The aim of this paper has been described as practical. By this is meant that it aims chiefly to suggest certain adjustments or adaptations of the strictly logical order which are made necessary in the matter of book classification by the fact that we are dealing not with ideas but with concrete things.

This need of adjusting theoretical classification to practical conditions is not peculiar to the classification of books, but is characteristic of the treatment of all complex concrete things. It is sometimes said that the classification of books differs radically from classification as used in science in that many books are made up in such way as to cover a great variety of subjects, e. g., periodicals, books of essays, etc. It is true that books are complex, but for that matter so are things in the universe. The crust of the earth, for example, is made up not merely of seventy different elements, but of seventy times seventy combinations of these elements massed in every imaginable sort of form. A book could hardly be more complex as to subjects than a lump of rock may be as to elements. The classification of books is like classification of specimens in a museum: Each is an art; neither is theoretically exact. If we attempt to rearrange things strictly according to likeness with scientific exactness, we have to vaporize them so that the elements may be brought together. This is precisely what the chemist does, and what he does with molecules we can do pretty well with ideas so long as they remain in that more or less volatile condition where we call them "thoughts." We cannot, however, do this so well where the ideas have been crystallized into books. Even among ideas, vaporizing them so as to recrystalize according to their real likeness is a painful task, and few enough men have mental heat or enthusiasm sufficient to do it very often or very perfectly. They prefer to let their ideas stay in the original mixed masses in which they first cooled, and in the order in which they then happened to be. This is what is generally though falsely called conservatism when applied to thoughts. It is in reality intellectual petrification. Books, on the other hand, are real petrifications, or rather planets in an advanced stage of evolution, where the mass of ideas has passed out of the fluid into a solid unchanging state. They do not therefore, however, differ "radically" from other complex masses in the matter of their classification. All masses alike, whether books or stones, are conditioned in the attempt to arrange them in space according to their likeness by the fact of their complexity, and need to be adjusted accordingly. But this does not, however, make the theoretical order of less value. On the contrary, this ideal order is in the end the only one which can serve as a real basis without ending in a chaos of self-contradictions. The librarian can no more afford to ignore the question of the real scientific order in arranging his books than the professor of mineralogy in arranging his specimens. It is identically the same thing. I wish I could say that the average librarian had the same scientific attitude towards his problem that the average professor of minerology has towards his. The fact is, that the practical modifications which complex concrete things call for in their actual classification in space are similar for all masses. The classification of books is, however, in some respects the best example of this— so much so, in fact, that if there were a philosopher here present I would commend to him the study of book classification as being as valuable to him as I have urged that theoretical classification is important to you.

The main fact about the classification of books is in brief the fact that it is an art, not science. The classification or order of things is nature and is not a human creation. The classification or order of ideas follows the order of this classification of things and is science. The classification of books, on the other hand, is an art—a human creation for a human end. The order of sciences is its backbone, but in the adjustment of books in this order there are many practical accommodations to be made, determined by not merely complexity of material but by the end in view.

This classification of books deals, as we have said, with concrete objects, not with ideas. Its end, too, is not a scientific law, but a rule; not the discovery of how things are done, but the formulation of a decree as to how they shall be done. The end of ends in scientific study is, properly, a scientific law suited to produce in a man the exact knowledge of what is. The end of ends in the rules of art is to produce in concrete substance something which never yet has been, suited to a certain purpose. If you say that in this statement the analogy with other complex things falls through, I say that it is of no great importance if it does come to an end at this point, and yet the fact is that the mineralogist who arranges his specimens with strict reference to illustrating the real order of things does face nearly the same artistic problem. Suppose, e. g., a vein of gold embedded in quartz. In a metallurgical collection it could be arranged according to its metal; in a collection illustrating, e. g., the strength of materials, it might be arranged as quartz. This is the chief book classification problem in a nutshell—the arranging of complex material with a view to its practical end. The main factor is the end sought. The adjustment of material depends on this end.

In describing this paper as practical, therefore, it is intended to imply not a systematic technical treatise, but only the treatment of the practical modifications of the theoretical order called for by the fact that we are here treating complex material with reference to a practical end. No attempt will be made here to give a survey of the history of classification, or a history of that discussion of its individual points and problems of which our American library history is full, not yet in any sense will the attempt be made to give detailed description of technique. This is the ordinary commonplace of library school routine. You are doubtless referred in your classes to Kephart's bibliography in the World's Fair papers, to the introductions of the Dewey and Cutter systems, as well as to the pages of the library periodicals, and in particular to the index to the *Library Journal*, not to mention the treatises of Maire and Graesel and the like. When these papers are printed they will have something of the nature of a historical sketch with outlines of various systems both theoretical and practical; but for the brief treatment of this lecture the historical and technical must be largely disclaimed. Even what I have called the practical aim of this paper is, therefore, in a way, theoretical; but it is the theory of an art, not the theory of a science. In short, it is method, and as has been said, its aim is to distinguish the difference between book classification and theoretical classification.

BOOK CLASSIFICATION AND CARD CLASSIFICATION

The first step in this process of differentiation is evidently to explain what it is here intended to include under book classification. In speaking of the classification of books here, then, it will be understood that both the classification of the material books on the shelves and the analytical classification of the contents of these books in catalogs and bibliographies will be included. Although there are some differences between the two kinds which will, from point to point, be

noted, the principles and practical difficulties of these two forms of book classification are substantially the same. The chief difference lies in the fact that the card classification can be carried nearer to scientific completeness than that of books on the shelves, for it is not conditioned by the paper and binding, and the analysis can, therefore, be carried further. The librarian who analyzes his books in this way approaches nearer to the chemist who vaporizes his material and yet he never reaches his point. He is rather like a mineralogist, who is so situated that he cannot apply the blow-pipe and must get as pure a lump of ore as may be by breaking. It is only the author who uses the contents of books to make new books, breaking up the very ideas in the alembic of his own mind, who is the scientist of books. He alone makes the book-atoms free to take their affinities. Nevertheless, as has been said, the difference between shelf classification and analytical card classification is considerable in this respect and is like the difference between big rough lumps of mixed ores and smaller purer specimens which can be arranged with greater exactness.

But whatever differences there may be between these kinds they are alike as to (1) the object that they have in view and (2) the different ways in which the classification can be carried out.

THE OBJECTS AND IMPORTANCE OF BOOK CLASSIFICATION

If we come down to the real fact why we put books or cards together according to subjects in a library, we find that it is to get together those books or cards which will be most used together. The object is a practical one just as the object of the library itself is a practical one. Libraries are not gotten together as a museum to exhibit what we have called the fossils of knowledge. It is a machine got together to instill that knowledge into men's minds. The books are collected for use; they are administered for use; they are arranged for use; and it is use which is the motive of classification.

The putting of the most-used books together saves, in the first place, actual labor on the part of users and librarian in assembling any given mass of material for use. No catalog can take its place. It is sometimes said that the bibliography, or catalog, serves as well or better, but suppose the user or librarian does get bibliographical references to all the things that he wants in a classified catalog. The work then has only begun. Somebody must either go from one point to another and examine the different books where they stand on the shelves, or else some one must go to each point and bring together in a class temporarily the things wanted. In an unclassified library the books are thus classified over again every time a man wants to use them. It is a labor-saving device to assemble them in classes once for all instead. It is sometimes objected to this that no classification actually does get all the material that a man wants together, and that a man wants to use it from various points of view at different times. This is entirely true, but what of it? It is aside from the point. One might just as well refuse to pick up pound nuggets in gold mining, if he should have the good luck to find them, on the ground that there were still gold dust to be gotten by panning. Any roughed-out group of books is a positive and great gain to economy in bibliographical search and promotes economy in the actual use by bringing the books together in space and thus saving innumerable steps on the part of the man who goes to the shelves to consult them. The actual advantage to science which comes from having books closely classified, through this economy of labor in the work of research must be, even in our present hardly fully developed usage, hundreds of years annually to the highest of all skilled labor-- that of the highly-trained expert scholar. When you put it down as a cold, concrete fact, that good classification in any group may save in a few years the research work of a man for a century, it begins to be a very practical matter. The saving of actual dollars in administration (*for a given efficiency*) must figure out as equally great. I believe the statement will stand the most careful examination, that in a large scholarly library, doubling the entire delivery and reference force would not give the efficiency to an unclassified library of even a barely tolerable classification. A prime advantage of having most used books in classes together, therefore, is the fact that the rough bulk of material so gathered together saves a vast amount of bibliographical work and a vast amount of work in actual gathering together and use of material.

A second and great advantage of having the most used books together in the classes in which they are used together is, that they furnish in this way an incentive to the user to get a full view of his material. This is a matter of the utmost value. Men are naturally lazy. They are too little inclined anyway to exhaust material, and when you add to this also the fact that the scientific man is generally also extremely ignorant of books, you open a vast field of profit in a method of setting out before a man so that he can get at it with the

least trouble a large amount of his material. In looking over much material, too, he is pretty sure also to be tempted by references to look up other material (such as articles in proceedings of academies) not grouped in the class; at least, he is more likely to than if his only resource was chasing up bibliographical references apart from his books. Men not librarians are almost invariably surprised to find how much material has been written on their subject. It very often happens that they find that work on which they have been wasting much time has already been done by some one else, and it is of the utmost importance that they should discover this at the earliest date in order that they may turn their attention as soon as possible to more profitable channels. This end is greatly promoted by the simple fact of having the material grouped together so that men can glance over it and get their eye on what has really been done. On the other hand, as a guide especially to men in looking over the field to see beforehand what fields are still comparatively unworked, this classification of books becomes of still greater importance to the progress of knowledge.

And what is true of trained scientific research, I take it, is still more true of popular work. On the one hand, there is a great economy to the librarian who has to help in school work, essay work, club work, etc., in his task of hunting up references, and, on the other hand, where there is access to shelves especially there is the greatest educational advantage in the actual incentive to the reader to read or at least, what is of almost greater importance, browse through books in order to pick out certain things. The "average reader" will hardly study even a classed catalog and is utterly at sea with an alphabetical list or an unclassified library. If, however, he can look over the shelves in a classified library he is surprised to find how much there is that is interesting, he learns to get facts that he wants more readily, and in the end saves much time for himself and for the librarian, while at the same time he gets far better cultivation in the same time than he could possibly have thought of getting in an unclassified library.

And besides this economy of time and labor there is a third advantage in classification, by no means to be despised, in the fact of the psychological or mnemonic training of those who, through seeing books arranged in certain classes, get in the habit of running over these categories in their minds and associating their own ideas in these classes. Men who are bound to make up such pigeon-holes for themselves—otherwise there is no thought at all—they must make up for themselves some sort of schedules in which to associate their ideas together. The nearer these schedules approximate the real order of things, of course, the better it is— the more retentive the memory, the more intense the developed power of attention —but they must have the schedules, and any well-thought-out system of classes is better than the rubbish heap of odd boxes which serves men in lieu of pigeon-holes.

The object of classification is thus economy and increased efficiency in the use of books. "Use" is the watchword of book-classification as "truth" or "true order" is of theoretical classification. Any variation whatever from the scientific order is permissible if so be it promote this end of use. The motive of the whole process is "getting together the books most used together."

But just here is a snag on which many have split, including the whole school of the go-as-you-please librarians who consider it very practical to make every petty little adjustment to temporary needs that they happen to think of when they think of it. It is also one which we must keep in mind in saying what we do most earnestly say, that any well-worked-out system is better than no system. The fact is, that while it is true that any system is better than no system, and even the artificial schedules of mnemonic subjects are a vast improvement over the common go-as-you-please schedule which every one makes up for himself, nevertheless, it is true that the nearer classification gets, as a rule, to the real order of things, the more fully it serves the purpose of getting together the books that will be most used together, and especially of getting the ideas together which belong together. Thus those nearest right serve the purpose of use best. The nearer, too, the classification is to the real order of things the longer it will serve men's needs before breaking down. Men will surely cling for sound reason to a familiar and well-established order just as long as they can and will not lightly give it up for a new one, but there must come a time for every system when, as of late in botany, the system long clung to must be given up because the new one has been clearly established as the real order.

Passing now to—

THE KINDS OF BOOK CLASSIFICATION

We have already spoken in the first lecture of the theoretical kinds of classification. The kinds of book classification are the same, but they have more concrete applications, combinations and

variations. It will be worth while to note some of those which are more familiar in ordinary use. You have seen in use, e. g., (a) *the natural or logical classification*—books arranged in series according to degree of likeness, the ordinary form to which we refer in the use of the word. You have seen that classification arranged forward in an evolutionary form from simple to complex and also backward in the strictly logical form from the complex to the simple. You have seen the Baconian and the inverted Baconian.

You have seen also (b) the purely artificial *alphabetical system* where books are arranged strictly by author throughout the library as used to be the case in the New York State Library under an earlier administration.

I am not sure that I have ever seen (c) a strictly *alphabetical subject arrangement*, but we have often seen large subdivisions of a system arranged chiefly alphabetically by subjects. In fact, almost all classifications have this element in them, as they usually reach sooner or later the point of arranging in the order of the "person biographed," and here it becomes a strict alphabetical classification by subjects.

In the same way again (d) the strictly *chronological* by periods throughout a whole library may not be exclusively applied anywhere, but it enters into almost all classification and is a legitimate principle in its place. This principle, like all others, is sometimes carried to excess, but it is hard to think of a system where at certain points the recognition of dates and periods is not a practical advantage.

(e) This is still more true of *geographical classification*, which is still a favorite notion with many as a semi-universal principle. While this again may not be absolutely in use as an exclusive first principle, in many libraries there is a strong tendency to urge it as at least one of a few primary principles and to arrange, for example, things under Europe, History, Geology, Mining, Agriculture, etc., rather than under Geology, Agriculture, etc., with geographical subdivisions. As a subordinate principle it is, of course, in use in substantially every practical library system.

(f) The primary *division* of all books *by size* into three classes—folios and over, quartos, octavos and under—is one of the commonest of the older classifications, and even today we are obliged, for reasons of space, to observe it in a sense, though, as a principle of classification it has practically gone out, and in libraries the principle of the "dummy" has taken its place.

Another artificial principle of arrangement which

we have met is (g) the *arrangement by color*. This is ordinarily an *ex post facto* principle, and the colors are applied to the classes rather than the classes made an induction from the color. In this form it is common enough, e. g., green books may be books on Greece, red books on France, etc. One can imagine a man arranging books in a private library on the strict principle of color for the sake of artistic effect, but I have never actually quite met it, although I fancy almost everybody makes some concession to harmony of color in a library with colored bindings not otherwise classified.

This classification by color differs somewhat from the principle of (h) *classification according to binding*. There are said to be known instances in which the principle of placing the best bindings nearest the door in a comprehensive series from the best bound to the worst was the actual ruling principle of the classification—and a most excellent principle it was in a library which, like one of these that I knew, was perhaps more suited to be looked at than looked into.

You have, of course, heard also of the theological library where the ruling principle was (i) *orthodoxy*—the separation of the sound from the unsound, the sheep from the goats. What a chance, by the way, for the application here of the "mnemonic binding"—say, white, sheep; and black, goat; or blue, orthodoxy, and yellow, heterodoxy. This, indeed, is one of the earliest classifications of Christian theology. The ante-Nicene fathers divided their books into those "received" and "not received" and else "orthodox" and "heretical."

(j) The *form* principle of classification is also sometimes practically a universal first principle. It is used, in fact, in all systems where, e. g., all encyclopaedias are picked out from the other books in their subjects, and it becomes a prime principle in the case of those libraries which put together all encyclopaedias, including such as those of medicine, political economy and the special sciences in a department of encyclopaedias. The same thing is true in the matter of periodicals.

An example of what may be called (k) *classification by literary value* is the putting together of select books in a reading-room. Another possible distinction is (l) classification according to *interest*. This usually has the utilitarian purpose of saving steps, but is illustrated by the putting out on special shelves of the latest books and the putting of fiction and biography and, in general, the most used books nearest the delivery desk. The

principle of (m) *linguistic classification* is also much used. In the popular library this is liable to be a fundamental principle, books being arranged first of all according to language throughout, etc. This principle always comes in, too, at the point where we separate an author's works into editions and translations. (n) The classification which is *chronological by books* may arrange either in the order of their publication or of their accession to the library.

This list of kinds of book classifications in actual use might be extended still further: (o) *breadth* of book sometimes governs location, as in the case of oblong folios; (p) *thickness* even, in the case of broadsides and pamphlets generally. There is hardly a characteristic imaginable which may not modify the grouping on shelves at least: (q) *weight* (as in the case of inscriptions), (r) *fragility* (as in the case of papyri), (s) *financial value* (in the case of rare books), etc., etc. All these principles are not only in use but are legitimately in use, for it is the useful purpose which determines, and if in any case the most useful service which classification can perform for its users is, say, to separate the orthodox and unorthodox, then this becomes legitimately the prime principle, and after it, but only after it, the logical, historical, etc., principles may come. It is clear, therefore, that the kind of classification to be used—judged by its leading principle—depends on the kind of use to which it is to be put.

This gives us a clue in the case of the special libraries, but what of the general libraries? What is the prime principle for them, and is there any order of subordination in the application of the secondary principles? With so many principles in actual use as dominating principles, is there any way of deciding when doctors disagree? I say yes. When doctors disagree we let some principle decide. In this case, as the first lecture tried to show, the fundamental law is the law of likeness. The order which dominates is the one which takes into account the greatest number of points of likeness, and in the use of subordinate principles the order of sequence in use depends on the same law. The true order, according to total points of likeness as here interpreted (whether interpretation is just or not each must judge for himself) is as follows: (1) The *logical order*, or order of likeness of contents following the order of real things from the complex to the simple. This, which is the inverted evolutionary order, is on the whole better practically as well than the evolutionary, or the order from the simple to the complex, because the most complex books containing the greatest variety of subjects should precede instead of follow their inclusive sub-divisions in the book classification. Nevertheless, in subordinate parts, the evolutionary (or, what is identical, the "historical") order is often the more useful. (2) The *geographical order* or classification according to the position of things in space includes all kinds of things, though each at only a single instant of time. (3) *Chronological classification by subjects* indicates the position of only a single thing in space, though showing it at different instants of time. This exhausts the "natural" order. (4) The *alphabetical* now follows, taking up an artificial series at the point where the natural stops. It may be alphabetical by subjects or alphabetical by authors. (5) To this should be added, and ordinarily only after we have gotten past the alphabetical by subjects and the alphabetical by authors, a second artificial form, the *linguistic*. (6) Finally we have the *chronological by books* (not subjects), or the arrangement by dates or dates of first edition, of the works of any individual author in his particular language. This should only come in as a rule after others have been exhausted.

This I take to be the true sequence of principles as applied to a classification for any general library—logical, geographical, chronological by subjects, alphabetical, linguistic, chronological by books; e. g., History (logical or natural); France (geographical); the Revolution (chronological); Carlyle (alphabetical); French translation (linguistic); 1865 (chronological by books). Note that by chronological is here meant not the chronological by accession, which is a very common usage at this stage, but chronological by date of publication, which is a very different thing. The accession sequence only comes in where there are two books of the same date and hardly deserves to be called a "principle." We have here, thus, no less than six distinct principles of classification, all legitimately used in one system and all in use in most approved systems.

LIKENESS BETWEEN THEORETICAL CLASSIFICATION AND BOOK CLASSIFICATION

Having defined thus the object and kinds of book classification, we return again to the prime object of the paper, which is to call attention to the differences between theoretical and practical classification and the adjustments of the former necessary in the latter. We must not forget, how-

ever, that the two things are essentially the same, and that the principles which guide in forming as well as the actual sequence of the theoretical order are to be regarded as the normal, which hold except as they have to be modified by practical conditions.

Attention was called in the introduction to the first lecture to the meaning and laws as well as to the kinds of classification, universally considered. The same considerations as to the real nature of the act and the laws which govern the process hold in the formation and application of a practical book classification. Among these the chief thing to be kept in mind is the fact that the arrangement of your books as a whole and in detail is a discrimination of likeness and an arranging of the books according to likeness or unlikeness from the most complex to the simplest. There is no definition that was there given or law there defined which does not hold equally well for your book classification *as principles*, however much the application of them may consist of exceptions, and the quintessence of the whole is the *law of likeness* itself—especially the law of sequence from the like to the like-and-unlike, or *vice versa*. The principle of likeness and of sequence through the more to the less alike governs the whole process of practical classification; the order of the classes in the making of schedules; the preparing of notation, the plan of arranging the books on the shelves or the cards in their cases, and the actual practice of assigning of books to their places. It may be said, therefore, that theoretical and practical classification are absolutely alike in their principles, however radically they may differ in their application to concrete things.

DIFFERENCES BETWEEN THEORETICAL CLASSIFICATION AND BOOK CLASSIFICATION

These differences may be roughly summed up as differences which come to light in making the schedules, in making a notation, in arranging cards, in locating books on shelves, in the practical work of assigning books to their classes. Under each of these classes variations arise, chiefly from the nature of the material and circumstances and the intended use.

1. Making the Schedules: The basis of the schedules for book classification is, of course, the order and divisions of the sciences. It has already been said that in general the closer a classification can get to the true order of the sciences and the closer it can keep to it the better the system will be and the longer it will last. True as this is, it is nevertheless also true that there are many adjustments of the pure order of the sciences useful and even necessary in making the classes in book classification, and that the too wooden insistence on having the schedules follow the order of the sciences will often miss the real spirit of classification and result in putting books where a delicate common sense would not put them. In short, the common-sense adaptation is often at bottom the more scientific.

(A) *Modification by Circumstances*: If you wish this expressed in technical terms, I should say "variations arising from environment."

For most librarians the making of a classification is merely a selection of one already made. They make their schedules thus wholesale. An important question in the selection of such a ready-made system of classification for any individual library is the question whether that system is actually much used. After all that I have said about conservatism and the petrification of ideas, I shall not be misunderstood in saying that the first principle in the construction (or choice) of a classification is a true conservatism. The very fact that a large number of people do think already in certain schedules, that large amounts of actual material have already been arranged in these schedules, is in itself a reason for wise conservatism. This, you will note carefully, is especially true when the general spirit of the prevailing classification is not directly contradictory to the natural order. The great gain to librarians trained in one set of schedules or to users similarly trained, in being able, in passing from one library to another, to use the same system, is obvious. In cases, therefore, where the main classes do not overlap and contradict one another, and especially when the variations are merely matters of geographical order or personal taste, the giving up of a practical system actually in use for one ideally better is to be deprecated, except when the new is so markedly better that it is likely to command general use. For this reason the Dewey Decimal Classification, from the very fact of its wide use, will probably endure long after some of the systems now rising, which have more pretension to follow the true order of the sciences, are dead (though having said this much it should be said also that the tenacity of the Dewey Classification is due even more to a certain versatility and hospitality towards adjustments within

its limits). It is for this reason, too, together with the other very important circumstance that they are more fully worked out than others, that librarians generally, even those who, like the writer, have a special system better adapted, as they think, to their own libraries, always advise other librarians to "take Dewey or Cutter" rather than their own. What is true of a general system is true also of its parts, and one must take into account in any attempt to make a system, e. g., the conventional divisions of economics or philosophy and the Hagenbachian divisions of theology. The fact that men are in the habit of looking for things under certain heads is quite reason enough for a strict conservatism when there is question of changing to some other order.

(B) *Variation Arising from the Nature of Books*: The order of things and the corresponding order of sciences follow naturally in their statement the order of progress from the simple to the complex, from the like to the like-and-unlike, from the less various, therefore, to the more various, from the less to the more inclusive.

The classification of books, on the other hand, does not, in the first instance, follow the historical order or order of complexity, but the inverse evolutionary order, the more to the less inclusive, the unlike to the like. It follows thus rather the order in which the human mind proceeds in tracing out the order of things than the natural order of things itself. If we were following the order from the less to the more inclusive we would place, say, first treatises on individual animals, then treatises on a class of animals, then treatises on all animals, then on all living things, then on all things living and lifeless. This would be most awkward in practical classification, where we are accustomed to the idea that the whole should precede the parts. The awkwardness comes perhaps partly as the result of habit. Certainly it would look queer enough (although the matter is not wholly unprecedented) to put encyclopaedias, essays and periodicals at the end rather than at the beginning of each class. It seems like standing a tree on its branches. But the reason for the queerness lies fundamentally in the fact of the composite character of books like encyclopaedias, which makes them "more complex" than any part and puts them logically after rather than before. In an inverted evolutionary order, however, this comes out right. While, therefore, it is of no very great practical importance in this matter whether we write backwards or forwards, provided we get all the letters in their proper order, and while either method or a mixed method is proved to be practical in use, nevertheless at present writing I incline to prefer an order of theology, anthropology, biology, hylology, rather than hylology, biology, anthropology and theology, but in this I do not feel very dogmatic.

(C) *Differences Arising from Intended Use*: Again, the practical classification of books is conditioned by the kind of use which is to be made of the books. The kind of classification, e. g., which is needed in a free public library is not necessarily the same in its details as that which is suited to a university library, although the general outline may be the same. The chief differences regard (1) the adjustment of building, (2) the principles of subdivision, (3) the question of degree and proportion in sub-division.

(1) Adjustment to Building: The general order in which the main classes are to be placed with reference to one another in a library may not be so much determined by their natural relation as by the shape of the library building and by the rule that the most used books are to be placed nearest the delivery desk. Most public libraries keep fiction nearest the door. One famous library already mentioned and not wholly without its counterpart in others, classified its books so that the best bound ones should come nearest the door. This was correct. This being the chief use, the books were placed where they would be most used. According to the law of use the books should be arranged from the most to the least used. In a reference library, therefore, where the reading room is at the top of the building, as will be the case in the New York Public Library, there most used classes should be nearest the top, and where, as is generally the case, the reading room is at the bottom, there they should be nearest the bottom. In case it happens to be a stack after Mr. Winsor's favorite scheme, exemplified in the Cambridge Public Library, where delivery desk is at the middle of three floors, then most used classes should be on the middle floor. In all circulating libraries the most used classes should be nearest the door. In an agricultural college, therefore, Agriculture should be nearest the desk, and in medical, theological, engineering, etc., schools, the same law should prevail. In the Massachusetts Historical Society Library, Massachusetts history, and in the New Jersey Historical Society Library, New Jersey history would be nearest the desk. As a matter of actual practice, something like this is

actually done even when the notation follows a different order. It is regarded as a small matter whether main divisions follow the notation order or not. It is this practice, by the way, which tends to remove the chief practical objection to the D. C. by allowing the 400s and the 800s to be put side by side.

(2) The Principles of Subdivision: This question of the 400s and 800s in the D. C. is a good illustration of a possible modification of the scientific order by the law of putting together the books most used together. In some libraries "Language" and "Literature" are main classes and books are arranged under each in the order of languages. In other libraries "Language and literature" is one class divided by languages and then under each language again divided into "Philology and literature." This latter, rather than the D. C. method, is usually preferred in a college library according to the law of the most used, since a "department" generally is linguistic and the same professor handles both language and literature. This is typical of all branches in a college library where the department generally rules—and departments (strange as it may seem) by no means strictly follow the real order and divisions of the sciences. In each case, whichever order is finally pitched on, the ground of choice is, rightly, less the "real order" than the order in which the books are used together.

(3) The Question of Degree and Proportion in Subdivision: This question is, in brief, the burning question of close or broad classification; or at least the question which once was burning—the question, in other words, whether classification distinctions shall be carried beyond the limit even of the minutest subdivision of the sciences or shall be limited to the most general schedules. The controlling law in the matter is the principle of usefulness and the general rule is "the greater the number of different books the closer the classification." So long as there is only a shelf-full or two, a class subdivision is of little importance; when there are a hundred or two shelf-fulls it becomes a matter of great importance. It follows, therefore, that every library feels this need of minute classification in its specialties and can be satisfied with broad classes in the rest. Thus the Halle Library devotes about one-third of all its schedules to a very minute subdivision of Law. In the same way we at Princeton wish to use three times as many prime schedules for New Jersey history as we do for the history of any

other state, and fifty times as many for the United States as for Holland. The library of a zoölogical museum really needs to follow the scientific subdivisions of animal classes to the very farthest sub-class, but it may arrange such botanical works as it happens to have in a very few classes. The proportion in subdivision, therefore, depends on the kind of books that the use of the library calls for. That this proportion would be, in a general classification, a pretty hard thing to judge, is witnessed by Dr. Wire's complaint against the Decimal Classification—that it gives one-hundred places each to philosophy and theology where they should be joined in one! There are still, probably, as many books on theology in existence as on all the other sciences put together, and for a universal system surely one tenth of the schedules is none too many.

The question of degree of subdivision is really included in what has been said. No general scheme of classification has ever been carried out in all its parts to the minuteness with which these parts have been carried out in special libraries. I doubt if one-hundred thousand schedules would do this. As a rule, the best general systems carry to about ten thousand places, and the question over which dispute has raged so violently may fairly be said to reduce itself to a question between one hundred, one thousand and ten thousand.

I hope that we are now agreed on close classification, but for fear that we may not all be fully persuaded, a word or two more on the matter. The practical use of the broad classification is simply to help a man who wants a specific book and has access to the books to go somewhat more quickly to that specific book in a broad class by beginning the alphabetical arrangement by authors earlier.

But this help would be a greater one still if the whole library were arranged alphabetically, and this I take to be the inevitable logical end of a refusal to carry close classification to a somewhat extreme degree of minuteness. As a matter of logic, too, if the broad classifier is consistent he must not even arrange by authors under one of his broad classes (for that is making alphabetical classes) but must leave helter-skelter. In reality the broad classifier is as close as the closest and differs merely in insisting that the logical subdivision according to likeness shall be abandoned for an artificial division according to name, size, color, or what-not, at an earlier stage than his "close" adversary. For my own part, I see no good scientific reason and, indeed, no practical reason, why, even for a small number of books, it is not better to have the most minute logical subdivision, providing there is a good index to the classification and the author index to books. All the books of a given subject are together just the same in the close as in the broad, and at least in the cases where you are after the more specific subject you make a great gain through getting the greater bulk of material together at once; whereas, on the other hand, if you are referring to a specific book, the reference from catalog to this book is just as specific, and there is no loss. The rule of this matter seems to me to be to carry classification to the last degree of real natural likeness and as much farther in the various artificial forms as the special conditions of the library require, but the "broad" classifier will, if he thinks it more useful, properly increase or diminish the natural sub-divisions according to the special needs of his library.

Library Classification as a Discipline

S. R. Ranganathan

"I have a feeling that abstract classification will make better progress if it marches hand in hand with mathematics. Library classification is essentially a problem in mapping or transformation."

This International Study Conference will have an able and diverse panel of experts from different lands to delve into the value for information retrieval of the fascinating discipline of library classification. It is a discipline with a charming field of theory and a vast field of application. Within a single generation the design of classification has marched from the workshop stage to the laboratory stage, and the hit-or-miss method has given place to a scientific method based on normative principles, canons,[1] postulates, and empirical tests.

SCIENTIFIC METHOD IN CLASSIFICATION

The first point I should like to make is that the development of the discipline of library classification has already entered into the spiral of scientific method. The cycle implied in the spiral was first completed by W. C. Berwick Sayers as early as 1918, when he set forth the first draft of a set of canons of classification, which H. E. Bliss reexamined later. After distinguishing work in the idea plane, verbal plane, and notational plane, canons for each of the planes have been separated out and amplified by myself. In addition to normative principles special to classification, there are the Five Laws[2] governing every branch of library science and principles of an even more general nature, such as the need for economy and impartiality, common to any context. I have also enunciated principles for securing helpful sequence, devices for securing hospitality[3] in array,[4] and devices for securing hospitality in chain.[5] The first set of this group pertains to the idea plane; while the last two sets pertain to the notational plane. Further, we have found that an analytico-synthetic[6] scheme of classification implies a few postulates. The Colon Classification, for example, has been so far seen to imply twenty-one postulates.

The stage has thus been set for the systematic design of schemes of classification. The spiral of scientific method visualizes that systematic pursuit. It recognizes the normative principles at the zenith, schemes of classification at the nadir, empirical devices and postulates leading up to the zenith, and derived devices and postulates leading down from it. In this process 'Observation of Literary Warrant' is of vital importance. We owe to Wyndham Hulme the crisp term 'literary warrant' to denote the quantity of expressed and embodied knowledge in any given field, waiting to be organized. Ever since J. Mills brought it to my knowledge in 1954 I have been enjoying the economy it brings in thought and expression. An implication of such a systematic pursuit is that a set of normative principles, in the form of stated canons of classification and principles for securing a more or less helpful sequence, should be adhered to. Different schemes of classification, within the limits set by the normative principles, should be designed only in accordance with a self-consistent and sufficient set of postulates and devices applicable to the idea plane and notational plane, stated explicitly by the designer concerned.

Analytico-synthetic Classification: The development of the discipline of library classification, so briefly summarized above, has led us to replace the traditional enumerative classification,[7] suited to the relatively finite and lethargic universe of knowledge, finding embodiment in books, by the analytico-synthetic classification needed to face the challenge of the infinite, ever-growing, and turbulent universe of knowledge embodied in microdocuments.[8] Analytico-synthetic classification calls for coordinated work in the idea plane, the verbal plane, and the notational plane. Of these, work on the verbal plane has to be done by each linguistic group according to certain prescribed standards. An international conference,

SOURCE: Reprinted from the International Study Conference on Classification for Information Retrieval, Dorking, England, 1957, *Proceedings* (New York: Pergamon for ASLIB, 1957), pp. 3-13, by permission of ASLIB.

on the other hand, can deal fully with the idea and the notational planes.

Analytico-synthetic classification is so called because it starts with the analysis in the idea plane of the main idea embodied in a document into facets[9] corresponding to certain basic fundamental categories.[10] The Colon Classification is based on the five fundamental categories—time, space, energy, matter, and personality. Whatever categories are adopted, the classification then translates the name of the isolate[11] term in each facet into its isolate number according to the schedules of the scheme in use, and finally synthesizes in the notational plane the isolate numbers into a class number.

The schedule of an enumerative scheme is essentially a hugh monolithic one of class numbers; whereas in an analytico-synthetic scheme, we have several short schedules of isolate numbers. For example, in the Colon Classification, we have about two hundred such schedules occupying only as many pages; whereas the number of class numbers which can be synthesized out of them is of the order of ten. Classification by an analytico-synthetic scheme has been compared to the work of an apothecary compounding a mixture according to any given prescription. The thought content of the document gives the prescription. The short schedules give the ingredients. The connecting symbols and the digits[12] for relations correspond to the adhesives and other materials used to bind all the ingredients into a state of consistency and stability.

Examples: To illustrate the way in which isolates are compounded to form a specific subject in this type of classification three examples are given below. The Colon Classification is used for demonstration, but its role is only that of a "guinea-pig."

Consider the subject: "Diseases of rice plants in Madras in 1957." Analysis in the idea plane gives the following result:

FUNDAMENTAL CATEGORY OR FACET	ISOLATE TERM	ISOLATE NUMBER	CONNECTING SYMBOL
Time	1957	N57	.
Space	Madras	441	:
Energy	Diseases	4	:
Matter	nil	nil	;
Personality	Rice	381	,
Basic subject	Agriculture	J	

The postulates of the classification provide that

the fundamental categories should be synthesized in a sequence which is the reverse of the one occurring above and that the connecting symbol may be omitted for the personality facet immediately following the basic subject number in certain cases, this being one of them. The resulting class number for the subject is J381:4.441.N57.

Next consider the subject: "Stem diseases of rice plants in the deltas of Madras during the wet season of 1957." Here analysis in the idea plane gives the following result, omitting the column of connecting symbols, which are the same for the different fundamental categories as shown in the preceding section:

FACET	ISOLATE TERM	ISOLATE NUMBER
Second level time	Wet season	p5
First level time	1957	N57
Second level space	Deltas	137
First level space	Madras	441
Energy	Diseases	4
Second level personality	Stem	4
First level personality	Rice	381
Basic subject	Agriculture	J

The synthesized class number for the subject is J381,4:4.441.137.N57.p5.

Here is a still more specialized document: "Biological cure of virus disease of the stems of rice plants in the deltas of Madras in the wet season of 1957." The synthesized class number for this is J381,4:423:6(G).441.137.N57.p5. Four blocks can be recognized in this class number:

1. J381,4:4, which is called the first round,[13]
2. 23:6, which is the second round,
3. (G), which is the third round, and
4. 441.137.N57.p5, which is the space-time mesh.

There is nothing new in the first round and in the space-time mesh. In the second round, 23 denotes Virus and is the personality facet in that round, and 6 denotes Cure and is the energy facet. In the third round (G) denotes Biological means (of cure) and is the personality facet in that round. There is no matter facet in any of these rounds and no energy facet in the third round. Though these statements have been made for the notational plane, they all hold good quite independently in the idea plane and they can be worded to suit that plane.

POSTULATES

Work in recent years has shown that there is an advantage in working out the ideas in the idea plane and the notational plane independently of each other, though help may be drawn from their reciprocal influence. It has also been found that it is helpful to clear thinking and further development if a scheme of classification can be based on a system of explicitly stated postulates which lay bare the unexpressed assumptions implied in thinking. The postulates [usually] can be separated into those concerning the idea plane and those concerning the notational plane.

Postulates for the Idea Plane: Those belonging to the idea plane are universal–that is they should be respected by any analytico-synthetic scheme of classification. Here is the substance of a sample of postulates in the Colon Classification:

1. Any class is either a basic class[14] capable of forming a subject by itself (e.g., agriculture), or an integration of a basic class with any number of isolates which are not capable of forming subjects by themselves–i.e., unless integrated with a basic class. Examples of such isolates in the above examples are disease, cure, biological means, Madras, deltas, 1957, or wet season. A third type of class is formed by the integration of two or more classes, each of which forms a phase[15] of an overall class: e.g., J381:4:60gF "Cure of crop diseases as influenced by chemical technology," where "Cure of crop diseases" is the first or the basic phase, "Chemical technology" is the second phase, and the phase relation[16] is "Influenced by," denoted by the digits 0g.
2. Any facet or isolate is a manifestation of one or more of the five fundamental categories–personality, matter, energy, space, time. These are mentioned here in the descending sequence of concreteness. In each round the facets should be assembled in this sequence. As a result, documents will be arranged on the shelves and entered in catalogs in a helpful sequence.
3. Energy facet may repeat itself more than once in a subject. The sequence of such energy facets will be determined by the nature of the subject. In other words, the Gestalt of the energy facets of a subject is more or less unique as far as our present-day way of thinking goes. For example, Cure can come only after Disease. Method of administering the means of cure, which may be an energy facet of a still later round, can come only after Cure.
4. Any energy isolate can start a new round of isolates. For example, after the energy isolate

Disease, we have the second round consisting of the personality isolate Virus and the energy isolate Cure. Again after Cure, we have the third round consisting of the personality isolate Biological means; this may be followed by the energy isolate Administration (of the means). After Administration we may have still another round, the fourth, with perhaps the Instrument used for administration as the personality isolate in it, and the Material of which the instrument is made as the matter isolate in that round.
5. Space and time isolates can occur ordinarily only after the last round.
6. Personality and matter isolates may occur more than once in the same round. They will occur in consecutive facets, for personality first and for matter next. Each such facet is called a level[13] of the fundamental category concerned. The sequence of levels will be determined uniquely by the nature of the subject, as the present-day way of thinking goes.
7. The isolates in a facet may be formed on the basis of one or more characteristics.[17] The isolates formed on the basis of one characteristic form an array; the totality of characteristics belonging to one facet is called a train[18] of characteristics.

Such postulates are not based on any metaphysical system at all. The only reasons for their choice are that they aid in the analysis in the idea plane in a more or less objective way, that they lead to a more or less helpful sequence among the known classes of knowledge, and that they are of use in finding a more or less helpful place for a newly emerging class among the already existing classes.

Postulates for the Notational Plane: The postulates belonging to the notational plane will vary with the scheme of classification. Here is a sample of postulates implied in Colon Classification:

1. A mixture of five species of digits will be used– *viz.* roman lower case, roman caps, arabic numerals, punctuation marks and arrows, and circular brackets.
2. In each of the first three species of digits, the last digit will generally be used as an octavizing[19] digit and not to represent any isolate by itself.
3. In each of the first three species of digits, the first digit may have to be reserved for representing the comprehension of all the isolates represented by the other digits of the species.

4. The roman lower case will be used to represent enumerated common isolates and as first digits of the chronological numbers of the second level.
5. Roman caps will be used as first digits for certain main class numbers and for chronological numbers of the first level.
6. Arabic numerals will be used as the first digits for enumerated special isolates and for certain main classes.
7. The part of an isolate number given by subject device will be enclosed in round brackets.
8. The sequence of the ordinal values of the various digits is fixed by another postulate. Any roman lower case has anteriorizing value.[20]

These postulates are framed in the light of experience and are found to implement in the notational plane the findings in the idea plane and in particular to give to each newly emerging class the place given to it in the idea plane, with hardly any need to change any of the already existing class numbers.

Stability in Postulates: Scientific method demands that any scheme of classification should be based on an explicitly stated set of postulates, such as those enumerated above. The designers of classification schemes should respect another implication of the discipline of scientific method. It is that we should not change an accepted set of normative principles lightheartedly. They should be changed only if overwhelming factors arising out of unexpected changes in the way of reaction of the human mind or in the social purposes of classification compel change. Changes in literary warrant alone will not call for a change in normative principles. The exigencies in the work of a particular designer should not be taken to be sufficient reason to force a change.

The position is different in respect to notational devices. To implement in the notational plane all the findings of the analysis of documents in the idea plane, there is bound to be need now and then to forge new notational devices. In fact, it is the difference in notational devices that distinguishes one scheme from another in most cases. Change in notational devices may imply also change in the postulates made for regulating work in the notational plane.

Perhaps the postulates pertaining to the idea plane come midway between the overall normative principles on the one side and the devices and postulates pertaining to the notational plane on the other. They are dependent less on the design of classification than on the happenings in the universe of knowledge in respect to its development and structure. New factors, calling for a change in the postulates for the idea plane, are not likely to occur frequently. However, sufficient work has not yet been done in the subject for a coherent set of postulates to have taken shape.

WHAT IS A NEW CLASSIFICATION

In the light of what has been stated above, a scheme of classification is new if and only if it is either based on a new set of normative principles (which is rare), or on a new set of postulates and devices (which is recurrent). For example, the Decimal Classification and the Library of Congress Classification are new relatively to each other, because D.C. uses the decimal-fraction device and L.C. uses the gap-device, but not because their sequences of basic classes or of isolates in facets are different. Again, D.C. and the Expansive Classification are not new relatively to each other because they both conform to the same normative principles and devices, and mere variation in the enumerated sequences or the use of Arabic numerals instead of Roman capitals does not amount to essential difference. The D.C. and the Colon Classification are new relatively to each other because D.C. does not use facet device nor conform to the Canon of Mixed Notation, whereas C.C. does both. For this reason D.C. and Universal Decimal Classification are also new relatively to each other, in spite of U.D.C.'s having adopted D.C. as its core and fettered itself thereby.

It may be repeated again that a new scheme is not created merely by either changing the species of digits used for the notation or by repermuting the sequences of the basic classes or the isolates in a facet, or by changing the sequence of facets. Nevertheless, such changes in some cases may lead to improvement in a scheme though not amounting to a new scheme. So also, it must provide additional facets and additional arrays within a facet form in ever-continuing processes of improving a scheme, if it is to keep pace with the development in the universe of knowledge as recorded by literary warrant. Some improvement in a scheme is also possible with the aid of exegetics—that is by a new interpretation of the normative principles, postulates, and devices brought to light as possible interpretations by newly developing literary warrant. Scientific method would welcome this way of exploiting the resilience of existing normative principles, postulates, and devices. In fact, this should be exhausted before venturing to change the principles, postulates, and devices, as is the practice in the applications of scientific method in the development of all other disciplines.

WORK TO BE DONE

Whatever be the scheme of classification devised, much will be gained if some of the problems mentioned below are examined and settled once and for all. The results can then be adapted by any scheme using its own notation.

Many of the difficulties now met with in the classification of the natural sciences and their applications will stand solved if a comprehensive schedule is worked out for properties of materials. This should include mensurational properties such as length, area, volume, and other indications of size and shapes of all possible varieties; physical properties such as weight, density, state of matter, elasticities of diverse kinds, viscosity, capillarity, acoustic, and vibrational properties; thermal properties of various kinds such as conduction, critical points, specific heat, etc.; radiational properties including colour, permeability to hard rays; electrical, and magnetic properties of all kinds; isotopic properties, radioactivity, etc.; chemical properties including those of physical chemistry such as solubility, osmotic pressure, etc.; stereochemistry, atomic weight, valency, chemical affinity, etc.; and biological properties. In C.C. the isolate numbers in these cases will begin with a small roman. Of the twenty-three digits (excluding i, l, and o) a should be reserved for denoting disjunctive treatment of several properties and z should be reserved as an octavizing digit. The remaining twenty-one digits may be allocated somewhat as follows: b and c for mensurational properties; d to m for physical properties; n to v for chemical properties; and w to y for biological properties. The second order array of each of these can use the entire base except the first zone.[21] About twelve hundred physical properties can then be individualized by isolate numbers with two significant digits; and if we set apart z as an octavizing digit, the number of physical properties that can be represented with two significant digits will be about two thousand. Similar hospitality can be found for the other classes of properties. The work in the notational plane is thus already completed to receive them. What has to be done is to enumerate and group them in a helpful sequence. This is work to be done in the idea plane. I mention this as a sample

of routine work to be done in the design of classification schemes. If this work is completed in the idea plane, any scheme can fit up the notation according to its notational system. I hope it is possible for this Conference to set up an organization for completing this work in the idea plane at an early date.

Similar work has also to be done on the schedule of posteriorizing common isolates of value correlated to the humanities and social sciences.

Three years ago I attempted to construct a schedule of posteriorizing common isolates of Energy. At that time the difficulties in the notational plane had not been solved to the extent to which they are now. There was not sufficient clarity in the idea plane either. It is my feeling that the time will become ripe to take up this work only after we complete the schedules for properties and values.

To meet the pressure from industry in the least wasteful way—that is, to avoid doing something temporarily from time to time and undoing it equally often—in addition to the schedule of common isolates of properties, we should also work out the schedule for materials, semi-commodities, commodities, and services of all kinds. These are innumerable but the large base given by mixed notation, including packet notation,[22] makes the notational plane quite hospitable for these innumerable isolates. The immediate piece of work to be done systematically is in the idea plane. That is to make a list of all kinds of materials, semi-commodities, commodities, and services, to check up if they are within the notational limit of, say, ten millions; to form them into filiatory[23] subgroups and groups; and to arrange the groups, the subgroups, and the materials, etc., in a filiatory sequence. If this is done any scheme can fit it with its own notation. I very much hope that this Conference can bring about an organization to complete this task as quickly as possible.

If the tasks indicated above are completed the number of special isolates to be scheduled for the various facets of the various basic classes will be comparatively few; and each such schedule will also be comparatively short; many of them may not have more than a dozen isolates each. These can be built with ease as and when need arises if they are not already done in current editions of the schemes.

The most baffling subject area from the point of view of classification design is organic chemistry including biochemistry. The rate of growth of literature is immense in this area. It is also basic for industry. But this factor does not baffle classification. It is the Personality facet of this subject that baffles. The isolates in that facet are the organic substances including biosubstances. Their number is bewilderingly large. The real trouble is in getting the substances thrown into sought groups and subgroups and into a helpful filiatory sequence to the satisfaction of the specialists in the various applied and pure fields. Can this be done?

MACHINERY FOR RETRIEVAL

Machinery, extending from the simple slotted card operated by a knitting needle on to a super-electronic machine, can also be used for retrieval. The design of such machinery falls within the province of the engineer except in the case of the simple punched card. Machinery can do the work at great speed; but it is more costly, and it requires a vast quantity of minimum turnout to become economical. It is for the management specialist to decide on the wisdom of its installation in a particular place after investigating the economics involving the cost of setting up, maintenance, replacement due to obsolescence, extent of use, and all the other relevant factors. The classificationist and the engineer should collaborate in regard to the machinery. It is only from this angle that I can say a few words on the subject. All the steps in classification from facet analysis to translation of isolate ideas into isolate numbers should be done by a classifier before the coding of numbers for the machinery. The only step in classification not needed by the machinery is that of arranging the facets in a preferred sequence and synthesizing the isolate numbers and the basic class number into the class number. The classificationist should take into account the special needs of the engineer, if any, in designing the isolate numbers and the basic numbers. This is a problem in which this Conference may arrive at some useful results by collaboration between the classificationist members and the engineer members. Reciprocally, the engineer too should see to it that his demands do not unduly curtail the freedom of the classificationist in his classification design, for it also has to serve certain other purposes in library service, such as:

1. the arrangement of documents and their main entries which need a synthesized class number for each document and not merely the basic and the isolate numbers pertaining to it;

2. the very work of classifying which can be done with greater ease and precision with the aid of the concepts of the five fundamental categories, phases, rounds, levels, and zones;
3. the reference service to readers, the most vital and delicate part of which is to work with the reader and find out in a systematic way the different facets in the topic of his interest at the moment and the isolates in each of them; and also display before him a helpful panorama of documents and their entries; and
4. possibly also disclosing fallow regions in the universe of knowledge awaiting cultivation. One way this has been happening is the formation of possible synthesized class numbers on which no document exists.

The sphere in which mutual accommodation and understanding is needed is that of notation. For the engineer would prefer as short a base as possible for the notation to minimize the cost and the complication in the machinery involved in reducing the numbers to his preferred binary scale; and he has no need for seminal, alphabetical, or scheduled mnemonics or for expressiveness in the numbers. On the other hand, the classificationist is in need of all the freedom which a mixed notation can give; he has to make his base of notation as long as possible to make the synthesized class number as short as possible; and to enable him to give the greatest possible autonomy to the classifier—and this is necessary to minimize reference back to him—autonomy in dealing with the ever-turbulent universe of knowledge throwing forth at all times and in all facets either newer or sharper isolates, the classificationist has to exploit all three kinds of mnemonics to the maximum extent. To give mental ease for the reference librarian, the classificationist has also to make class numbers as fully expressive of the make-up of the thought-units as possible.

THE FUTURE

I believe that we have had enough discussion on the issue of special v. universal classification. It is time that we agreed upon universal classification. In the past this issue was clouded by the absence of a sufficiently advanced discipline of library classification, with a clear separation of work in the idea, verbal, and notational planes, with a dynamic approach based on helpful normative principles, postulates, and devices, and provision for watching the flow of literary warrant and carrying the schedules to greater depths. I think that we have now made sufficient progress in these matters to clear that cloud. Secondly, the Canon of Local Variation removes the resistance given by individual libraries or groups of libraries to the adoption of a universal classification. The frivolous plea, born of ignorance due to lack of actual experience of classifying and put up now and again by garrulous "committee men," should no longer mislead people into beliefs such as "the school library needs a special simple classification," or "the rural library needs a special simple classification." It should carry no weight if it is remembered and put across to the lay management that in such simple libraries the books are simple and call only for simple class numbers even though the universal scheme has the potentiality for depth classification of specialized books. The method of osmosis[24] has set at rest the equally faulty plea for resisting reclassification as an impracticable task.

The answer to the question "What is a new scheme?" deserves careful study. If it is really understood the illusion of creating a special classification by a rearrangement of isolates or by a change in the species of digits used will disappear. All those who have the urge to work in the field of a special classification will have sufficient opportunity within a universal scheme. Those who have the influence to get money provided for this kind of work—and they will have an integrated personality—will be putting their weight on the right side if they do not fritter away their energies and resources on *de novo* special schemes.

This appeal does not imply freezing of original work in library classification. There is endless opportunity for original work in solving the unsolved problems in the idea plane as well as the notational plane, which crop up from time to time. There is endless opportunity also in constructing or adding to schedules of isolates in the special fields of knowledge in the light of newly developing literary warrant. This kind of constructive work is a continuing process as the development of knowledge itself is a continuing process.

Apart from working with literary warrant as the concrete basis there is also scope and need for theoretical research in library classification. There is need for making intellectual experiments in library classification. This can be done by varying the postulates, by introducing new postulates, by dropping some postulates, or by varying the devices used. Classification-design based on different postulates and devices without direct or immediate correlation to literary warrant is Abstract Clas-

sification. For this kind of work on abstract classification there is a rich precedent in the development of mathematics as an abstract tool. It is developed both to meet actual demand from fields of application and freely without any immediately visible opportunity for application. To illustrate, there are many kinds of algebras designed by varying the axioms and the postulates. Similarly, there are many geometries and calculuses built on a purely abstract basis. But sooner or later the developments in the physical, biological, and the social sciences have found them to be just the tools needed. But for the development of statistical calculus by Karl Pearson and his coworkers as an abstract discipline, the social sciences could not have entered the spiral of scientific method and enriched themselves at the rate at which they are now doing for the good of humanity.

My belief is that the time has now come for the advance guard in the field of library classification to go on inventing several new schemes of abstract classification. Sooner or later they will meet a concrete want created by newly developing literary warrant. My plea is that there should be provision for the periodical mutual stimulus of persons engaged in abstract classification through the media of periodicals on the subject and through conferences of the present kind. My appeal is that universities should provide chairs for classification, so that abstract classification may be developed ostensibly for the pure joy of it, but in reality to prepare the ground for making the organization of the new kind of recorded nascent thought of the future efficient, without the need to fumble about after it has accumulated to a great mass.

I have a feeling that abstract classification will make better progress if it marches hand in hand with mathematics. Library classification is essentially a problem in mapping or transformation. It maps a multi-dimensional space on a uni-dimensional one. It transforms a pattern of n dimensions into a pattern of one dimension. But this kind of transformation is needed in many sectors of knowledge. They all get their common method developed in association with mathematics. Then each discipline works out its own version of this transformation. The discipline of management, for example, has developed Linear Programming. Its basic problem is but a version of "The basic problem in classification." An alliance of mathematics and abstract classification will, I am sure, lead to mutual enrichment in a similar way.

Research in the discipline of library classification can contribute not a little to the productivity drive and to the conservation and maximal use of the research-potential of humanity. Industry, the great foundations, and governments should provide finance for research. Society should spare a sufficient number of able persons for research in this subject also. Universities should maintain chairs and research fellowships in the subject.

The field for cultivation is vast and never ending. There is need for systematic research, as a continuing process, to keep library classification abreast of the literary warrant getting newly created by the never-ending new formations in the universe of knowledge. There is also scope for research in the fundamentals and the tools of classification design as much as in any other traditional discipline. Abstract classification is a new territory for development. Its development is necessary to prepare library classification to meet unexpected, sudden developments in the universe of knowledge, like the one in nuclear physics and engineering taking rapid strides in our own days. May the fields in the territory of library classification be forever kept in active cultivation!

GLOSSARY

D. J. Campbell

[1] Canon: a principle regulating practice in a given subject.

[2] Five Laws of Library Science:
  i. Books are for use.
  ii. Every reader his book.
  iii. Every book its reader.
  iv. Save the time of the reader.
  v. A library is a growing organism.

[3] Hospitality: the quality of a notation which permits insertion of new classes in their appropriate place in a classification—flexibility.

[4] Array: the set of mutually exclusive coordinate subclasses totally exhaustive of a class, derived by its division according to some one characteristic.

[5] Chain: a hierarchy of subclasses of decreasing extension and increasing intension derived by successive division.

[6] Analytico-Synthetic Classification: a classification which represents a subject by analysing it into its fundamental constituents (isolates) and synthesizing a class number for the subject out of the isolate numbers linked by appropriate connecting digits.

[7] Enumerative Classification: a classification made up by enumerating separately all the subjects to be included, e.g., the Library of Congress Classification.

[8] Microdocuments: Communications, usually short, on specialized topics (e.g., articles and papers in periodicals and symposia, separates, pamphlets, news-cuttings) as opposed to macrodocuments (e.g., books, treatises).

[9] Facet: the totality of the subclasses of a basic class corresponding to a single fundamental category and based on a coherent set of characteristics not leading to an organ or a constituent of the typical entity of the universe classified.

[10] Category: a form or class of concepts, varying from subject to subject, into which isolates can be grouped, e.g., matter or material, energy or action, organ, property, space, time. Ranganathan postulates five fundamental categories: Personality, Matter, Energy, Space, and Time. Personality covers "manifestations of wholeness," for example, chemical compounds, plants, and animals, and parts of them, languages, and religions: the other fundamental categories are attributes of Personality.

[11] Isolate: a single component ("ingredient") of a compound subject; also a generic term to denote isolate idea, isolate term, and isolate number, these being the manifestations of an isolate in the idea plane, the verbal plane, and the notational plane.

[12] Digit: includes letters (capital and lower case), punctuation marks, and any other symbols used in notation.

[13] Level and Round: originally, only one appearance of each category was allowed for in a class number; rounds and levels were introduced to allow more than one appearance of each. With Ranganathan's fundamental categories, any Energy facet can introduce a new round of Personality, Matter, and Energy facets, but Space and Time can only appear in the last round. Personality, Matter, Space, and Time can appear more than once in a round, these appearances being levels.

[14] Basic Class: a main class, i.e., a member of the first order array of the universe of knowledge, or a canonical or traditional subclass of a main class.

[15] Phase: any one of two or more classes brought into relation to one another in a document. Each phase will contain one and only one basic class with or without isolates attached to it.

[16] Phase Relations: the relations between phases. Ranganathan has recognized several kinds, e.g., 'influenced by,' and 'adapted to' (bias phase).

[17] Characteristic: the attribute forming the basis of division in classification. Language, form, and period are common characteristics in the classification of literature.

[18] Train of Characteristics: the successive characteristics used to derive a chain of isolates.

[19] Octavizing Digit, Octave Device: originally so called because with decimal notation only the numbers 1–8 were assigned to subjects, 9 being the octavizing digit, which could be subdivided 91–98, 991–998, etc. All these numbers were thus made available for one array. Clearly this can be extended to letters, z (or the last letter of any other alphabet) becoming the octavizing digit. The octave device thus provides hospitality in array.

[20] Anteriorizing Value: a digit is said to have anteriorizing value if its addition to a class number causes the resulting number to precede the original number.

[21] Zone: a region in an array which can be used to accommodate some particular set of isolates. Usually the sets of isolates in the different regions are formed on the basis of different characteristics.

[22] Packet Notation: normally the use of a special connecting symbol—in Colon a bracket—to divide an isolate number by a number drawn from another schedule; such a digit can also be used as an octavizing digit to extend the hospitality of an array.

[23] Filiatory: in hierarchical sequence, or in a sequence determined by the affinity between coordinate classes or between co-ordinate isolates, as the case may be.

[24] Osmosis, Method of: the classification, by a newly adopted scheme, of all literature received after a given date, and the reclassification of such older literature as is still in active use, as and when returned after use.

Classification

John Sharp

"We have thus isolated two separate things which logic can do for us. Firstly, it can help us to argue more rationally, to be surer of the validity of the way in which we draw conclusions from evidence we have. Secondly, it helps us in the process of the formation of classes. . . . Physical grouping is not the real, essential classification: it is only an illustration of it. The essence of classification consists of the fact that certain things are thought of as related in certain ways to one another."

Classification as it has been expounded over the past fifty years in textbooks written for students of librarianship is not an easy subject. This is due in no small measure to the fact that the theory is based on the principles of classification which derive from logic, and it is exceedingly difficult to reconcile what is taken as it stands out of the context of logic with what we try to do when we apply classification for bibliographical purposes. Logical principles are undoubtedly very helpful, but though differences are stressed between classifications of "knowledge" and classifications of "books" the limitations of logic are seldom recognized.

Logic can be said to be the study of the validity of inference or, more simply but perhaps more crudely, the soundness of argument. It concerns itself with the ways in which conclusions can be drawn from premises, and it is limited to just this, for the truth of the premises, that is whether what the premises assert bear any relationship to actual fact, does not affect the soundness of the argument based on the premises. Thus the validity of the argument is the point at issue, not the truth of the premises, nor indeed of the conclusions. Logic has done its work when it has established that if a premise is true then the conclusion must be true.

Logic is concerned with making statements about things. It affirms or denies one thing of another, and the unit which it uses to do this is the proposition. The simplest proposition consists of two terms joined by the 'copula'. One term is the subject of the proposition, i.e., that about which the affirmation or denial is made; and the other is the predicate, i.e., that which is affirmed or denied of the subject. The copula is the present tense of the verb "to be." Any simple statement such as "All metals are conductors" is a proposition and in fact the definition of a proposition is "anything that can significantly be said to be true or false."

One very important type of argument used in logic is what is known as the "syllogism." The definition given by Luce will serve: "A syllogism is a triad of connected propositions, so related that one of them, called the Conclusion, necessarily follows from the other two, which are called the Premises."[1] If we use the proposition "All metals are conductors" and another proposition "All copper alloys are metals," we have two premises from which we can draw the conclusion "All copper alloys are conductors." We have inferred the conclusion from what is stated in the premises. This particular form of argument is introduced here as it serves to show clearly how logic uses classification for its purposes. If we imagine a class of things which are metals and a class of things which are conductors of electricity, we can easily imagine, from the first premise, that the former class is entirely included in the latter. We can also see from the second premise, that the class of things which are copper alloys is entirely included in the class of things which are metals. This means that the class "copper alloys" is entirely included in the class "conductors" and it can therefore be asserted that "All copper alloys are conductors." This is one of several kinds of logical relation between classes, i.e., inclusion, partial inclusion, exclusion and coincidence, which can be displayed diagrammatically by the use of Euler circles. Stebbing[2] gives a clear and concise account of their mode of application.

It is clear that relationships between classes serve logic's particular purpose, i.e., they enable us to affirm or deny a predicate of a subject by

SOURCE: Reprinted from John Sharp, *Some Fundamentals of Information Retrieval* (London: André Deutsch, 1965), pp. 20-47, by permission of the publisher.

virtue of the one being included in, partially included in, excluded from, or coincident with the other. Indeed it may be said that Aristotelean logic, with its concentration on the subject-predicate relationship is a study of the relationships between classes. However, the last century has seen the development of another kind of logic, which pursues the same objectives, but which introduces the principles of mathematics. Because this logic uses symbols in a way similar to that in which algebra uses them (not exactly the same way, be it noted), it has become known as "symbolic logic" and is considered to comprise a set of calculi, including the calculus of classes, which treat the subject more widely and more rigorously.

An important aspect of the treatment of classes becomes explicit in the calculus of classes for it introduces the idea of operations on classes in addition to dealing with relationships. This can hardly be considered to have been dealt with even implicitly in traditional logic. Cohen and Nagel sum up the two concepts: "The difference between operations upon classes and relations between classes is this: operations upon classes yield classes; the assertions of relations between classes are propositions, not classes."[3] In other words logical operations on classes define new classes and the relationships between classes represent statements, or propositions. In books on symbolic logic, the two are treated quite separately, e.g., in Lee,[4] where separate chapters are devoted to the two principles.

Diagrams are used for illustrating operations in a fashion similar to that used for illustrating relationships, and the type used is usually the circles devised by the English logician John Venn. The operations concerned are those of conjunction disjunction and negation, which are sometimes spoken of as logical multiplication, logical addition and logical subtraction. Thus if we have a class of red things and a class of square things, multiplication will give us the "logical product," a new class of things which are both red and square. Addition will give us the "logical sum," a new class of things which are either red or square and subtraction will give us the 'logical difference', a new class of things which are red, but specifically not square. To distinguish between relationships as we have illustrated them with Euler circles, and operations as illustrated by Venn diagrams, we should think of the two concepts in the following way. In the case of relationships, if we take a particular area, we have a class which we have already defined and we can say certain things about

that class according to its being included in, partially included in or excluded from another class as shown by the areas. In the case of operations, a particular area defines what the class is, according to what that area is made up of, i.e., according to which classes are associated to form that area.

We have thus isolated two separate things which logic can do for us. Firstly, it can help us to argue more rationally, to be surer of the validity of the way in which we draw conclusions from evidence which we have. Secondly, it helps us in the process of the formation of classes. Now those who have introduced the principles of classification which derive from logic into the field of bibliographical classification have assumed that when logic talks of genus, species, etc. and relations between classes, it is concerned with arrangement between classes. The idea seems to be given some support in textbooks of logic, because these often mention classification in the fields of botany and zoology, but the purpose of this type of classification coincides exactly with logic's own purpose, that is it tries to provide new knowledge by drawing conclusions from what is already known or thought to be known. It is not interested in the physical arrangement of specimens, but the intellectual process of deducing what is not already known from observations of relationships between classes. Wolf makes this clear when he states "Classification is a method of science, it is a way of knowing or regarding things. It is primarily an intellectual activity, not a physical activity. The classification may be exemplified or illustrated by the grouping of objects in a museum for instance. But the physical grouping is not the real, essential classification: it is only an illustration of it. The essence of classification consists in the fact that certain things are thought of as related in certain ways to one another."[5]

There is more of this in Wolf, and other textbooks on the subject provide no ground for believing that logicians have ever intended to convey the idea that the concept of relationship means anything other than class inclusion for the purpose of inference. As far as the making of classes is concerned, as was stated above, traditional logic has not concerned itself with logical operations as has the newer symbolic logic, but it would not be true to say that it has never been concerned with class making, for "definition" has received some attention and inasmuch as definition has been considered to be the same as connotation it is the same as class making, for connotation means the sum of the attributes which determine a class, and the eligibility or otherwise of things for membership in the class is decided by it. Indeed it might be argued that definition is an important aspect of classification in the context of traditional logic, for it is treated as part and parcel of it, and even more significant is the fact that of the five predictables, the one we know as "species" was known in the doctrine of Aristotle as "definition," until the substitution was made by the Greek philosopher Porphyry.

Now the point of all this is that the two things which we have discussed, i.e., class making and logical relationships do not provide us with a complete basis for bibliographical classification. Class making we must have of course because we have to assign the subjects of documents to classes to which they properly belong, but it is not always possible to create classes by logical principles. By no stretch of the imagination can the main classes of general classification schemes such as Dewey be said to be derived from a genus by any principle belonging to logic, and while logical division can be recognised at particular points in such schemes, this nonlogical division is much in evidence, even down to the most specific level. So that logic, though it can provide for class making by rigorous methods for its own purposes, cannot provide us with a universal method for generating classes which will give us an hierarchical arrangement of the subject matter of even a comparatively narrow field. And when we have our classes, even though they may be the result of perfect logical division, logic has nothing to offer us in the way of determining the order in which those classes shall be arranged. If we take the class "engineering" and divide it into the various species of engineering such as hydraulic, mechanical, electrical, aeronautical, etc., criteria other than logical ones must determine that order. The logical relationship of class inclusion has determined that the species shall be so located as to be shown to be subordinate to the genus, but this is as far as it goes. We are left with the need to provide an overall arrangement of classes, taking into account this one type of relationship which logic determines for us, and it is the principle of arrangement between classes which marks off bibliographical classification from classification in logic. Metcalfe sums up the difference thus: "Classification in logic is not classifying or classing in the wool classing or book classifying senses; it is not the examination of individuals for their distribution over already established classes. The word is made up of the Latin word for class, which is ours, and the Latin word

for making, and originally it meant simply the making or setting up of classes; in logic it means this, and may also mean an arrangement of classes, but although this use of the name is recognised in logic, logic is hardly interested in class arrangement."[6]

It is the arrangement of the multitude of classes with which we are faced when we classify a subject field for bibliographical purposes which gives such classification its value, for it is the relative position of things on such a "map" which serves both purposes (a) of finding a particular subject by its being known to be located in a particular area of the scheme and (b) of grouping together those subjects which the user will find it advantageous to have at one position. The idea of the significance of the relative position of classes was recognised by Wright when he said of classification: "It also has the ability to indicate meaning through position when there is no brief individual name for a subject."[7] Relative position is the fundamental question whether a subject has a brief individual name or not, but Wright did appreciate that bibliographical classification should observe this principle. Obviously, for providing for the placing of an unnamed subject in any scheme of things or for the converse process of implying the nature of such a subject by its position something more than mere class making and class naming is required and only classification with a clear display of relative position between classes can do this. If we are to argue the pros and cons of classification in the bibliographical sense we must be careful not to invoke definitions and principles from logic and quote them as though their context is that of bibliographical classification, for classification in logic is not synonymous with classification in the bibliographical field.

It is not surprising that there should arise out of this the controversial issue of whether classification schemes should follow a "natural order" or "the order of the sciences." When logic, which provides a useful method, leaves a large part of the problem or arrangement still to be settled, it is understandable that philosophers should seek an order for the overall scheme of things and the classification schemes such as that of Francis Bacon resulted from such inquiries. Scientists have sought such order in narrower fields, for their purposes also can be furthered by the discovery of such order, and it is easy to see the wisdom of this by reference to very modern books in the field of zoology, botany, etc. Such a book is *The algae* by Chapman,[8] the very first chapter of which is entitled 'Classification'. Classification pervades the whole of this book and its purpose is clearly to further understanding of the book's subject and to provide a basis for the discovery of new knowledge. Further evidence of the application of classification in this way is the report on a recent conference sponsored by ASLIB at which people concerned with the natural sciences discussed it from this point of view.[9]

The inevitable result of these approaches to the problem by philosophers and scientists seeking tools for their own trades has been that those interested in problems of bibliographical classification have argued for or against "natural order" in bibliographical schemes. On the one hand, we have those such as Richardson[10] who argue strongly in favour of trying to make bibliographical schemes follow the order of the sciences and on the other those such as Hulme[11] who take the opposite view, while Bliss[12] based his scheme on the "scientific and education concensus," that is the arrangement which conformed most closely to the views of experts in their respective fields. The Library of Congress, though its scheme in outline owes something to the *Expansive classification* of Charles Ammi Cutter,[13] adopted the procedure of arranging the books which comprised its stock in that order which suited them best from the point of view of the actual usage of books, and the order is therefore empirically derived. More recently the theories of faceted classification have introduced the principle of "preferred order" among categories, which again provides for the adoption of an order which best suits the purpose in hand, and while Ranganathan bases his theories on the "five fundamental categories" of Personality, Matter, Energy, Space and Time, the idea of "natural order" finds no place in his writings.

It is probably true to say that as far as the natural sciences are concerned some following of the order recognized there is inevitable. In many other cases the order within limited areas is easily ascertained. In the field of hydraulic engineering for instance, the arrangement of physical things such as Pipework, Closures, Valves, Butterfly valves in that order is self–determining. In the field of information retrieval in special fields however, the issue is frequently nothing like so clear-cut.

Classification in the sense in which it is used in logic is much nearer to the idea of definition or description and it might more properly be considered in relation to the alternative method of dealing with subjects for the purposes of informa-

tion retrieval. It is probable that classificatory principles can be useful for the purpose of subject designation and we might well consider this kind of classification as being subject "specification" rather than subject classification. By specification we mean here the accurate, unambiguous and consistent designation of a subject without reference to its relative position in a classification scheme. It seems paradoxical that Ranganathan, whose disciples pay so much attention to "helpful order" and whose principles underlie so much current thinking on the formulation of bibliographical classification schemes, should have defined library classification as: " . . . the translation of the name of the subject of a book into a preferred artificial language of ordinal numbers, and the individualisation of the several books dealing with the same specific subject by means of a further set of ordinal numbers which represent some features of the book other than their thought content. The first of these ordinal numbers is called the Class Number of the book. The second ordinal number is called its Book Number." Ranganathan also says: "Library classification means the reduction of subjects and books to ordinal numbers for specific purposes."[14] This sort of definition is nearer to subject specification than to subject classification and there is perhaps not so much paradox as there seems to be, for it may well be that the theories which Ranganathan has propounded have more useful application in subject specifying than they have in the now accepted form (at least by some in Great Britain and elsewhere) of faceted classification with chain index.

The principles of bibliographical classification which have formed the basis of the syllabus for examination by the Library Association in Great Britain for many years are those expounded in textbooks such as Phillips[15] and Sayers.[16, 17] The theories put forward here are those derived from Aristotelean logic and though their effect is more limited than librarians have conceded, they still have much value. In these works the process of classification-making is described as being one of division, that is the breaking down of the field to be classified, according to rules whose purpose is to ensure a systematic procedure and a resulting scheme which satisfies recognised criteria. These criteria are seen at their most formal in the "canons" of Sayers, which he first propounded in 1907, but which he later modified, and which are currently regarded as of little value, particularly as the methods of analysis of a subject field now available are so much more rigorous. The well-known "Five Predicables" are the basis of such division, and Phillips states that "The principles laid down in the Predicables govern all classification, for all division proceeds by the addition of differences to the genera."[18]   The Five Predicables are as follows:

Genus	A class of things which is capable of division into two or more sub-groups, which are called "Species."
Species	Groups resulting from the division of a genus, each of which may itself become a genus subject to further division.
Difference	An attribute, which, when used to qualify a genus produces a species.
Property	A quality possessed by each species of a genus but which is not peculiar to the members of that genus. Though not essential to the definition of the species, the possession of a property is inherent in the nature of a species.
Accident	A quality which may or may not be possessed by any species of a genus. It is not necessary to the definition of a species, and its existence cannot be inferred by the definition. It can, however, be used, in practice, as a difference.

We might illustrate the application of these principles by a simple example. The class of things called "military aeroplanes" might be divided in many different ways, but we can demonstrate the principle well enough by a crude breakdown on the principles of "purpose," "number of engines" and "wing position." These latter are called the "characteristics" of division and are the bases by which the "differences" are derived. We begin with the "summum genus" that is the all-inclusive class, which in this case is "military aeroplanes," and by application of the characteristic "purpose" we might derive the differences "fighting," "bombing" and "transport." Each of these added to the genus "military aeroplanes" gives us a species of the genus. Thus we have "military aeroplanes," plus "fighting" which gives us the species of "fighters," and similarly we have the species "bombers" and "transport aircraft." Each of these species now becomes a genus which is subject to further division and on applying the characteristic "number of engines" we arrive at the species "single–engined fighters," "twin–engined bombers," etc. Applying the third characteristic, wing position, we arrive at the "infima species" as far as this crude classification goes, i.e., the final species to be derived, and we have species such as twin–engined mid-wing bombers," etc.

It is essential that one characteristic only be used at each step of the division and this must be exhausted before another is introduced. The next characteristic is then used to divide the species so derived to form sub-species, and all the resulting classes are then mutually exclusive. The nonobservance of this rule produces collateral classes, i.e., classes of the same order, which are not mutually exclusive, resulting in the possibility of assigning a subject to any of several alternative places in the scheme. If, at the first step of division in this breakdown, we had derived species by both characteristics "purpose" and "number of engines," we would have had "fighters" and "single-engined aircraft" as collateral species. Obviously, a classifier would then have doubt about whether he should place a document on "single-engined fighters" in one place or the other. This is the fault known as "cross-division."

This classification fails to meet some of the requirements of an ideal classification. Among others, it does not necessarily "modulate" as it should, for we might argue that the characteristic "type of propulsion" should have been interpolated between "purpose" and "number of engines," to give us "jet–propelled," "propeller-driven," etc., before dividing by number of engines. It is also certainly not exhaustive, i.e., it does not include every species of every genus, as is obvious from the omission of "reconnaissance aeroplanes" under "types." The contravention of either of these two rules could result in the impossibility of properly placing items in the scheme for which there is no specific provision. We could not, for instance, classify "jet-propelled fighters," or "reconnaissance aeroplanes." This could be serious in an "enumerative" scheme, but both eventualities could be provided for by proper provision for expansion, which is a problem both of schedule arrangement and of notation. Such modifications can more readily be incorporated in faceted schemes because of the greater inherent flexibility.

Of the five predicables, two have not so far been mentioned in this breakdown. A "property" of this class of aircraft might be its being subject to the effect of drag. This is an attribute which is possessed by all members of the class, but which is not peculiar to it, in that birds also have this property. Examples of "accidents" are "serviceable," "unserviceable," "armed," "unarmed," etc. Properties and accidents are equally eligible for use as differences for the purposes of practical classification.

These principles of division have now been

largely abandoned in favour of the newer techniques of classification-making, but familiarity with them is a great advantage from the point of view of clear thinking about classification and indexing, and though their limitations are severe, it is a mistake to consider that they cannot usefully complement other principles. Whatever else they might be, and however limited, they are certainly not invalid.

The newer techniques of "facet analysis," propounded by Ranganathan, provide a more easily applied procedure for the making of schedules, and they have the advantage that the material is first collected and then marshalled in the way best suited to the purpose in hand. Thus every aspect to be dealt with, as far as is known up to the point of compiling the schedules, is in evidence, and the classification maker is not in the difficult position of having to anticipate every requirement by spontaneously thinking of every potential need, as he must if he uses the traditional processes.

The technique is briefly as follows. The literature which is to be classified is examined and all the significant terms which it uses are listed. The terms are then examined to determine how they might best be grouped according to their similarities, thus providing a number of "facets" consisting of terms denoting similar kinds of concept. Thus we might have a list of materials forming a "materials" facet, another forming a "processes" facet and so on. Each term in such a facet is called a "focus." This part of the process is called "facet analysis" and a very powerful process it can be for many different purposes, and not just for the formulation of faceted classification schemes of the form usually referred to by this expression.

If we were to examine the literature comprising an aeronautical library, we should discover terms such as Delta, Fighters, Ailerons, Landing, Lift, Rectangular, Drag, Control, Wings, Elliptical, Bombers, Elevators, Lateral, Stability, Repair, Transport Aeroplanes, Twin-Engined, Low-Wing, Single-Engined, Longitudinal, Swept-Forward, High-Wing, Take-Off, Climbing, Design, Mid-Wing, Diving, Three-Engined, Maintenance, Sweptback, Tailplanes, Unswept, Directional, Rudders, Triangular, Fuselages, etc. We can readily recognise terms which belong to the same family, or "facet." Obviously Delta, Rectangular, Elliptical, Triangular are "planforms," i.e., the shapes of wings, tailplanes, etc., Maintenance, Design, are "operations," and Lateral, Longitudinal, Directional signify "axes" with regard to control, stability, etc. Marshalling all the terms into facets would result

in an arrangement of this kind:

Types of aircraft		No. of engines		Wing position	
Ac	Fighters	Cd	Single-engined	Ec	High-wing
Ad	Bombers	Cf	Twin-engined	Ee	Mid-wing
Ae	Transport	Ch	Three-engined	Eg	Low-wing

Parts of aircraft		Control surfaces		Planforms	
Gd	Tailplanes	Gm	Ailerons	Je	Delta
Gf	Wings	Gp	Elevators	Jg	Rectangular
Gj	Fuselages	Gt	Rudders	Jh	Elliptical
				Jm	Triangular

Position determined relative to an axis		Aerodynamic problems		Flying operations	
Jq	Swept-back	Kd	Control	Lb	Landing
Js	Swept-forward	Kf	Stability	Lg	Take-off
Jv	Unswept			Lm	Climbing
				Lp	Diving

Forces		Axes		Operations	
Mb	Lift	Pd	Lateral	Tb	Design
Mf	Drag	Pf	Longitudinal	Tf	Maintenance
		Ph	Directional	Tj	Repair

It is clear that some of these groups could be combined, for there is a relationship between planforms and axial positions such as "swept-back," etc. Control surfaces also belong with other parts of aircraft. Proper marshalling of the terms will produce an arrangement free from "cross division" for with facet analysis the fault is virtually impossible.

Having sorted the terms in this way, a decision must be made regarding the order in which the facets shall be arranged. Once this "preferred order" is determined, terms derived from the facets are always cited in that order, or rather the notational elements representing the terms are so cited, in order to provide compound class numbers to stand for complex subjects.

We will concern ourselves henceforward with the first three facets listed above. It can be seen at once that the facets are named by what we called the "characteristic" when discussing enumerative classifications formed by the process of division, and indeed with facet analysis we have discovered what the characteristic is in each case by empirically grouping families of terms and recognising the feature which they have in common, e.g., "delta," "rectangular," etc., are all recognised as being "planforms" and "planform" is therefore the characteristic of division. In classifying with a faceted classification scheme we select those elements representing the various concepts which go to make up the compound subject and synthesize them to form a compound class number. If we took the first facet above and set its terms down in a horizontal array, then took the second facet and qualified each of the existing terms with each of the terms from this new facet, and finally repeated the process with the third facet, we should be left with a classification. The end result of Classification making by facet analysis is exactly the same as that from division on the classical principles, if we take all the terms produced and form an enumerative schedule in this way.

The really significant difference, apart from the fact that facet analysis relieves the classification maker of the necessity to be omniscient in order to anticipate every characteristic of division, is that a class number can be synthesized from only some of the terms available to the classifier, whereas an enumerative scheme predetermines what class numbers shall exist by the choice of the order of characteristics. If a characteristic has been used at some high level in the hierarchy, it cannot be ignored when we are concerned with differences derived at a lower level, but in a faceted scheme we are not committed to such ready-made numbers. Thus, if we wished to classify low-wing, twin-engined military aeroplanes, using the above classification, we could not find a single place for the subject in the enumerative schedules but should have to use one or all of the subdivisions for aeroplanes with the attributes under the three types of aeroplanes, "fighter," "bomber" and "transport," i.e., Ac Cf Eg, Ad Cf Eg and Ae Cf Eg. With the faceted schedules left as they are, as they are found in so-called 'faceted classifications', we do not have this problem, for we can take the terms from the second and third facets and ignore the first, which gives us the one place Df Eg. Now, on the face of it, this seems to be an undoubted advantage, and it does facilitate the placing of a subject at a point determined solely by the attributes which it possesses, without its being forced unnaturally into a position depending to some extent upon extraneous attributes. This supposed advantage is, however, a delusion, for faceted classifications are bedeviled by the fundamental problem of "what you put in and what you leave out," which is the crux of the whole matter as far as the argument on "conventional" versus "nonconventional" systems is concerned.

One other point ought to be clarified before we leave the principles of classification. The textbooks dealing with classification as based on the classical principles are at pains to expound the methods of Aristotelean logic, but they do not explain the limitations of its "genus" and "species" principle as far as classifications of knowledge or bibliographical classifications are concerned. This limitation is severe because we cannot go further than dividing a "thing" into its "species" or "kinds" and are unable to introduce "processes" or even "parts" of things. The statement by Phillips, which is quoted above is left unqualified. It must be qualified to permit classification of the kind required for classifying information. For instance, it is impossible to provide for a class of information on "the design of single-engined fighter aeroplanes," because this is not a "species" of single-engined fighter aeroplanes, and "design" is not a legitimate "difference" for the derivation of this spurious species. Similarly, no part is a species of the whole from which it is derived. The fuselage of a fighter is not a species of fighter. It is the different kinds of fighter which are species, i.e., delta–winged fighters, single-seat fighters, etc. Metcalfe contends that classifications of information need not suffer from this, because information is divided into species of information by subject, and it is information which we are classifying, not the subject of that information.[19] This seems to be begging the question, but the point is really academic anyway, because we can achieve our objective without the niceties of Aristotelean logic, and the principles of faceted classification provide one way of doing this.

There is a tendency to reject classification as something which has served its purpose well enough in the past but which has nothing to offer for the solution of current problems. It is a pity, however, that a little trouble is not taken by those who so frequently resurrect it, to understand the elementary principles concerned, for we should then be spared the sort of illustration of so-called classification which is exemplified in the proceedings of a recent American symposium.[20] Here a schedule of but ten terms is shown, with only two steps of division, but the classification maker has managed to create cross-division at both steps. The most elementary knowledge of the principles of faceted classification, or of the older logical methods would have avoided this.

We might also have a more rational system of terminology in the field of information retrieval if note were taken of some of the older principles. We have, for instance, in the United States, the reference to coding for all attributes other than the name by which a subject is known, this is called "generic encoding." The confusion which arises from this is typified by the example which Jahoda gives to demonstrate how provision can be made for "generic searching."[21] He cites the case of propylene, which, with hierarchical notation might be dealt with thus:

Hydrocarbon	1
Unsaturated compound	14
Mono olefin	143
C_3 Mono olefin	1435

Without hierarchical notation it would be "generically encoded" with the descriptors "hydrocarbon," "mono olefin" and "C_3 compounds." Now if we talk of anything being generic, we must presuppose class inclusion and this implies that the classification scheme is "enumerative" or that there is a preferred order of facets which produces this same enumerative arrangement. In many subject fields there is an obvious enumerative arrangement, and classification by chemical composition is a case in point.

It might be argued that if we regard the classification as consisting of schedules of faceted terms, without presupposing a particular hierarchy it is possible to imagine many different hierarchies formed by the arrangement of the facets in different orders. It could then be said that each term would find itself representing a genus in one of such hierarchies. This argument is rather pointless, however, for acceptance of the principle would mean that every coding, except that for the term which ordinarily represents the subject, would be "generic" coding. It is surely better to reserve the expression for those codings which represent what are generally recognised as being truly including classes as are "hydrocarbon" and "mono olefin." This kind of term is the only one which has in the past, in the context of bibliographical classification, been regarded as generic and it seems to be a retrograde step to have extended its meaning to include all terms except that which specifically represents the subject being coded. The preservation of the proper meaning of the term would clarify the position, because its use is now so wide as to be virtually meaningless. It is still useful to be able to regard hierarchical notation as providing for easy generic encoding where classification is used in retrieval systems, and even the very recent newcomer to the retrieval field, the "thesaurus," preserves the idea, at least by implication, in that its use of the principle of instructing the user to post a document to another term also when a given term is assigned admits of coding by the including

class of the assigned term, but requires no action as far as other kinds of term are concerned.

In many cases the encoding which is referred to as 'generic' is coding a thing by an attribute which it possesses, by a process applied to it, etc., and while such coding is not just desirable, but often essential for meeting the requirements of particular retrieval systems, it should not be called by this name. A thing coded may legitimately be regarded as a species of several classes and generic encoding need not be tied to the hierarchical coding of a fixed classification scheme, but the use of the term "generic" should be confined to those cases where there is a clear case for it. Subjects are sometimes deliberately split up into elemental terms so that a group of such terms together form a description of a subject in order to provide for retrieval by citation of one or more of the concepts when the overall subject coded is not the actual subject of search and these are commonly referred to as "semantic factors." This seems to be a perfectly reasonable name for such concepts, and we should do better to think more often in terms of searching by 'semantic factors' rather than by 'generic codes' for we should then concern ourselves with subject specification rather than subject classification, which comes into the picture only when we make provision for retrieving information on a subject, when a search is made, by naming a class of which the subject can reasonably be regarded as a species.

When we have completed the making of schedules for a bibliographic classification scheme we are left with the need to provide two important auxiliary devices. The first of these is a notation, and the second is an alphabetical index to the schedules. The purpose of notation is to "mechanize" the arranging of things classified by the schedules. The word "mechanize" is used, not in the sense of the application of machines to do a job, but in the sense which the Shorter Oxford English Dictionary ascribes to the word "mechanical" when it equates it with "automatic," the relevant definition of the latter being "not accompanied by volition or consciousness." Once the order of terms in the schedules is determined this order is fixed by attaching to the terms symbols which have easily recognised ordinal value, of which arabic numerals and the letters of the alphabet are the best known. When documents, or records of documents, which bear elements of the notation are handled, their arrangement is easy because of this recognized order, and finding or filing them is an 'automatic' of 'mechanical' process. The absence of notation would necessitate the reclassification of every document each time it had to be returned to the file, assuming that the documents were filed in a classified sequence.

There is an excellent illustration of the value of notation in a letter written by Thomas Jefferson to his friend James Ogilvie[22] who had been granted the use of the library at Monticello, Jefferson's home at Charlottesville:

> As after using a book, you may be at a loss in returning it to its exact place, and they cannot be found again when misplaced, it will be better to leave them on a table in the room. My familiarity with their places will enable me to replace them readily.

Jefferson had arranged the books on his shelves according to a classification scheme of his own, and if after he had done this he had assigned a notation to the scheme, then the return of the books to their rightful places would have been a "mechanical" process for Ogilvie and there would have been no need for Jefferson's fears that his orderly arrangement would be upset.

Notation is a fairly complex subject, but it is purely subordinate to the classification itself and it must meet the demands which the scheme makes on it. A classification scheme must not be modified to the slightest extent to suit the notation for notation is the servant of classification and any concessions to it may mar the quality of the scheme. Consequently, the demands of a complex scheme on its notation can be very severe, for there are several different kinds of difficulty which can arise. Two of these are the limitation of the number of collateral species which can be catered for by a hierarchical notation of limited base length (the base of decimal notation is 10, *i.e.*, the 10 digits 0—9) and the problem of interpolating new subjects both in "chain" (i.e., vertically) and in "array" (i.e., horizontally). An example of the former type of interpolation is that of introducing the division of aeroplanes by type of propulsion before division by number of engines.

There is also the general problem of the desirability or otherwise of having a notation which is hierarchical, or one which is purely ordinal. The former type preserves the order of the schedules, which is the main purpose of notation, but it also reflects the hierarchy of the schedules, so that we recognise from the structure of a particular class number what other classes are subordinate to it and exactly how far we need go along the linear array of books, catalogue cards, etc., before we have exhausted the class and all its divisions. It is also apparent what other classes are collateral with it, and what is its containing class. Thus we know that if we have selected the class number 3.43 that only numbers consisting of this number and additional digits will be subordinate classes, that all other numbers differing from it only in the second place after the point, i.e., 3.42, 3.44, etc., will represent collateral classes and that the class is itself a species of the class represented by 3.4.

The notation shown in the faceted arrangement shown before is also hierarchical in that the structure of the schedules is reflected by a synthesized class symbol such as Ac Cd Gf Je Kd—Control of delta-winged, single-engined fighters. Difficulty would be experienced with these particular schedules in some sections however, because, though they serve to show the process of facet analysis, they have not been completely rationalized. The terms in the facets "Planform" and "position determined relative to an axis" for instance, are not entirely mutually exclusive, but this is a problem of the connotation of terms and consequent difficulty in facet analysis. There is no fault as far as the hierarchical nature of the notation goes.

With a purely ordinal notation the order of the schedules is preserved for all purposes, but no attempt is made to show hierarchy and we might, for instance, with these faceted schedules, have spread the three letters A, B, C, each subdivided by the whole of the alphabet, or as many letters as necessary, over the whole breakdown. This might have shown "wings of fighters" as collateral with "twin—engined fighters" notationally. There is some contention that hierarchical notation is unnecessary, but it does have the advantage of delimiting the area of search on shelves and in catalogs and indexes, and if "chain indexing" procedure is used, it simplifies the process of making index entries so that much of this work can be transferred from the indexer to clerical labor.

A lengthy discourse on this complex problem of notation would be out of place here, but a simple explanation of the subject is to be found in the book by Palmer and Wells[23] and an excellent and exhaustive treatise by Coates is to be found in the Proceedings of the Dorking Conference.[24] This latter paper shows how virtually every contingency can be met, though some concessions have to be made. There is no point in arguing the case against classification on the grounds of notational problems unless these are insurmountable. The trouble is often that notation and classification are taken to be one and the same thing. On the contrary, a classification scheme must stand or fall on its merits as such. If it stands, then notation must be made to serve it properly.

In special libraries in Great Britain, where the classified catalog has been much used, particularly that based on the Universal Decimal Classification, there has been a tendency to neglect the alphabetical index in favor of the classified file. This seems to stem from the idea that a classified catalog is self-sufficient and that the user should be sufficiently conversant with the classification scheme to find his way about the catalog without reference to an index. In the nature of things, however, any comprehensive scheme, whatever its quality, can hardly be assimilated in all its ramifications by anyone, apart perhaps from a cataloger whose sole activity is maintaining the catalog and index. If this is admitted, it does not detract from the arguments of the protagonists of the classified catalog that useful collocation of related subjects is brought about and that this is no less useful on account of the need for an alphabetical index to point out the location of the appropriate area of the scheme. In theory we should have the best of both worlds—specific reference through an alphabetical index, and generic survey by the proper display of related subjects.

Alphabetical indexes to classified catalogs range from the simplest affairs which cover only the broadest heads, being nothing more than, or even less than, the index to the classification schedules themselves, to elaborate structures of the 'chain index' variety. It is necessary for retrieval of specific information from classified files of moderate to great complexity to provide an index of commensurate specificity. This is not difficult if subjects are easily designated in spite of their being minute divisions of the subject field concerned, provided that such subjects are not compounds of a number of significant subject elements. An example of this type of index is that compiled for the ASLIB Cranfield Research Project, where the specific subject was taken as entry word and qualification made when necessary by quoting the immediate superordinate class or classes as far as was necessary to distinguish the various contexts of the indexed subject.[25]

For the purpose of retrieval systems for the kind of information with which we are concerned in this book, i.e., that which is 'multi-topical', only one kind of index for the classified catalog is of real interest to us, and that is the 'chain index' developed by Ranganathan. 'Chain procedure' is a perfectly simple method and provides for entry under each of the terms of the complex subject in a rigidly controlled way. The indexing of the subject mentioned above 'Control of delta–winged, single-engined fighters', which would take the class symbol Ac Cd Gf Je Kd would be carried out as follows. The terms represented by the notational elements are set down in the reverse order of the class symbol, in order to provide the basic entry, and the full class symbol is cited as the relevant point at which to consult the classified file for this compound subject:

CONTROL: DELTA: WINGS:
   SINGLE-ENGINED: FIGHTERS   Ac Cd Gf Je Kd

Further entries are made by progressively deleting the first term and the corresponding notational element (*i.e.*, the last):

DELTA: WINGS: SINGLE-
   ENGINED: FIGHTERS   Ac Cd Gf Je
WINGS: SINGLE-ENGINED:
   FIGHTERS   Ac Cd Gf
SINGLE-ENGINED: FIGHTERS   Ac Cd
FIGHTERS   Ac

Thus the entry for this compound subject will be found whatever term is selected as entry word to the chain index, the theory being that all the entries in the classified file which are subordinate to that at which entry is actually made should be searched, and the distance necessary to search down is obviously greater the broader the heading chosen for consultation of the chain index. It is apparent also that this searching will have to be done at many different points in the classified file, for the term chosen for entry to the chain index is likely to be shown to be used in different combinations with other terms and many or all of these combinations may be relevant. A useful account of the principles of chain indexing is that by Mills.[26]

This chapter has been devoted to as brief a summary as possible of classification and its relationship to the problems of documentation.

NOTES

[1] A. A. Luce, *Teach yourself logic,* (London: EUP, 1958), p. 83.

[2] L. S. Stebbing, *A modern elementary logic,* 5th edition, (London: Methuen, 1952), pp. 24-26.

[3] M. R. Cohen, and E. Nagel, *An introduction to logic* (paperback edition of the first part of *An Introduction to logic and scientific method*, 1934), (London: Routledge, 1963), p. 123.

[4] H. N. Lee, *Symbolic logic: an introductory textbook for non-mathematicians,* (London: Routledge, 1962), pp. 62-91.

[5] A. Wolf, *Textbook of logic,* 2nd edition, (London: Allen and Unwin, 1938), p. 172.

[6] J. Metcalfe, *Information indexing and subject cataloguing: alphabetical: classified: co-ordinate: mechanical,* (New York: Scarecrow Press, 1957), p. 297.

[7] W. E. Wright, The subject approach to knowledge: historical aspects and purposes. In *The subject analysis of library materials*, edited by M. F. Tauber, (New York: School of Library Service, Columbia University, 1953), p. 10.

[8] V. J. Chapman, *The algae,* (London: Macmillan, 1962).

[9] Classification: an interdisciplinary problem. Proceedings of an ASLIB Conference, London, 6th April 1962. *ASLIB Proceedings*, Vol. 14, No. 8, August 1962, pp. 222-262.

[10] E. C. Richardson, *Classification, theoretical and practical*, 3rd edition, (New York: H. W. Wilson, 1930).

[11] E. W. Hulme, The principles of book classification. *Library Association Record*, Vol. 13, 1911, pp. 354-8, 389-94, 444-9; Vol. 14, 1912, pp. 39-46, 174-81, 216, 21. (Association of Assistant Librarians, Reprint No. 1, London, 1950).

[12] H. E. Bliss, *A bibliographic classification*, 4 vols., (New York: H. W. Wilson, 1940-53).

[13] C. A. Cutter, *Expansive classification*, Boston, 1891-3.

[14] S. R. Ranganathan, *Elements of library classification,* edited by B. I. Palmer, 2nd edition, (London: Association of Assistant Librarians, 1959), p. 2.

[15] W. H. Phillips, *A primer of book classification*, 5th edition, (London: Association of Assistant Librarians, 1961).

[16] W. C. B. Sayers, *An introduction to library classification*, 9th edition, (London: Grafton, 1954).

[17] ———. *A manual of classification for librarians and bibliographers*, 3rd edition, (London: Grafton, 1955).

[18] Phillips, *op. cit.*, p. 13.

[19] Metcalfe, *op. cit.*, pp. 30-31.

[20] B. E. Holm, The information problem in industry. In *Proceedings of the EJC engineering information symposium*, 17th January 1962. (New York: Engineers Joint Council, 1962), p. 10, Fig. 6.

[21] G. Jahoda, *Correlative indexing systems for the control of research records.* Columbia University, D.L.S. thesis, 1960. University Microfilms. Mic 60-3082, p. 47.

[22] Thomas Jefferson, Letter to James Ogilvie, dated Washington, January 31st 1806.

[23] B. I. Palmer, and A. J. Wells, *The fundamentals of library classification*, (London: Allen and Unwin, 1951), pp. 60-75.

[24] E. J. Coates, Notation in classification. In *Proceedings of the International Study Conference on Classification for Information Retrieval* held at Dorking 13th-17th May 1957. (London: ASLIB 1957), pp. 51-64.

[25] ASLIB Cranfield Research Project. *Alphabetical Index for the Universal Decimal Classification*, Cranfield, 1960.

[26] J. Mills, Chain indexing and the classified catalogue. *Library Association Record*, Vol. 57, No. 4, April 1955, pp. 141-148.

Classification: Current Functions and Applications to the Subject Analysis of Materials

Jesse H. Shera

"There are seven properties that inhere in traditional library classification, and their mere enumeration suffices to suggest the limitations upon book classification which they impose: linearity, inclusiveness, significance of terms, arrangement of terms significantly, meaningful differences between terms, uniqueness of the arrangement of terms, and infinite hospitality."

TRADITIONAL LIBRARY CLASSIFICATION— PROPERTIES AND DEFINITIONS

The theory of library classification from the days of Melvil Dewey has been predicated upon the implicit assumption that it is possible to arrange books in a way that would make their substantive content apparent to the user. The traditional library classification is a bibliographic mechanism derived from contemporaneous opinion about the organization of knowledge expressed in terms appropriate to the description of the subject content of books. More precisely, a traditional library classification may be provisionally defined as a list of terms intended to describe the subject content of books, arranged in a logical order, which, when applied to books, results in their arrangement on the shelves according to the logical principles that inhere in the schematism.

But such a definition is only superficially adequate, for more careful scrutiny of the process of book classification reveals that there are certain properties common to all traditional library classifications, and through the identification of these properties it should be possible to arrive at a more meaningful definition of library classification that may help to clarify our thinking about its limitations and possibilities. There are seven properties that inhere in the traditional library classification, and their mere enumeration suffices to suggest the limitations upon book classification which they impose.

The first property, that of *linearity*, is dictated by the physical form of the book and the characteristics of library architecture. In effect, a library is one continuous shelf of books, and each particular book represents a specific point in that line. It must follow, therefore, that any classification that can be applied to such an assemblage of units must necessarily exhibit a linear sequence of its terms.

Second, a classification must be *inclusive*, in that it must encompass within its limits the totality of knowledge within the universe of its concern. It must include not only every book, but every use of books. This has nothing to do with length—a simple dichotomy is inclusive. For example, the dichotomy "human = non-human" may not be a very useful classification, but by encompassing everything within its limits it does meet the test of inclusiveness.

Third, the terms of the classification must not only be descriptive of the content of books, they must be meaningful to both the classifier and the user. The term is the verbal correlate of the class for which it stands, and if it is meaningless the classification loses all value. This property of *significance of terms* by its very emphasis upon specificity and uniqueness of interpretation is something that few, if any, branches of knowledge are prepared to meet.

Fourth, the *arrangement of the terms must have significance* for, or be meaningful to, the user as well as the classifier or the very purpose of the classification is defeated. It is obvious that the arrangement of a classification must vary as the needs of users vary. There is not, and probably can never be, a common denominator that will meet the requirements of all. Perhaps no other property of library classification so eloquently denies the possibility of universality toward which Dewey, Cutter, Bliss, and their contemporaries were striving.

The fifth property of classification derives from

SOURCE: Reprinted from M. Tauber, ed., *The Subject Analysis of Library Materials* (New York: Columbia University, School of Library Service, 1953), pp. 29-42, by permission of the editor.

the principle of differentiation in the classification, and since classification implies the determination of successive differences, as well as the recognition of likeness, it must follow that the *differences between the terms must be meaningful.*

The sixth property of library classification, *uniqueness of the arrangement of terms*, is closely related to the property of significance of arrangement. This insistence upon one, and only one, possible place for each subject in the schematism does not deny the possibliity of differing points of view in the treatment of any specific subject, but it does decree that identical subjects observed from identical points of view must coalesce into one, and only one, class.

The seventh property is best described by Ranganathan's phrase, *infinite hospitality*, by which he means that a classification must provide a specific place for every constituent part of its universe, tangible or intangible, real or imaginary, existent or nonexistent, in the past, present, and future. Provision must be made for such diverse concepts as the Philosopher's Stone, the $\sqrt{-1}$, or the reality of the absolute.

Finally, one should add that the traditional library classification is usually, though by definition not necessarily, supplemented by a *notation system* which is a convenient and economical array of symbols capable of a unique and necessary arrangement which, when applied to the terms of the classification result in the ordering of the schematism. This notation, while it is a thing apart from the classification itself, and is not to be confused with it, serves two purposes: (1) as a convenient shorthand technique for indicating the terms of the classification, and (2) as a key to the organization and structure of the classification schedules without which the classification could not be interpreted except by constant reference to the schedules themselves. Notation follows classification, not the reverse; Dewey's great failure lay in his forcing of an organization of knowledge into a preconceived and rigid notational pattern.

From these seven properties of a bibliothecal classification it is possible to derive a more precise definition—

The traditional library classification is a list of terms which are specifically and significantly different each from the other, capable of describing the subject content of books, inclusive of all knowledge, infinitely hospitable, in an arrangement that is linear, unique, and meaningful, and which when applied to books, usually, though not necessarily, through the medium of a notation, results in their arrangement on the shelves according to the logical principles that inhere in the schematism.

Yet this very definition is eloquent testimony to the truth of Jevons' protest that library classification is "a logical absurdity."[1]

THE LIMITATIONS OF LIBRARY CLASSIFICATION

From the seven properties of library classification arise four limitations of traditional library classification that devastatingly discredit it as an adequate instrument for the subject interpretation of books. These limitations are not an inherent part of the classification process as a potential instrument of bibliographic organization, but are imposed by the conflict between the nature of the book as a physical entity and its properties as a record of human thought and experience.

The first of these limitations is inextricably associated with the property of *linearity* in bibliothecal classification. A classification that is linear must perforce be uni-dimensional. Yet the relationships among books are multi-dimensional and cannot be represented as the projection of a straight line, or by the position of a specific point, i.e., a particular book, on that line. Thus the classifier is compelled to select a single relationship from all the possible relationships which any given title might have to its fellows, and to disregard the remainder, however important these may be to the users of the collection. The property of linearity, therefore, imposes upon the classifier the impossible task of reconciling that which is irreconcilable. But often this limitation on linearity is concealed by a mathematical or alphabetical notation which in itself is linear, and hence obscures the absence of linearity in the schedules. This confusion between the classification and the notation has resulted in much muddled thinking about the true nature of the classification process and accounts for the prevalent error of employing the notation merely as a locational device with little relationship to a useful arrangement.

The second limitation is that of *inconsistency of organization*, for no book classification can be made consistent throughout with respect to its principles of differentiation. In the biological sciences the principle of organization may follow closely the familiar genera and species for the classification of natural phenomena; in the geography and travel section the principle may be spatially derived from either natural or political boundaries or a combination of both; in the history section both space and time are the bases of differentiation; in philosophy the order may be dictated by schools of philosophic thought; in literature by literary form with little regard to subject content; and in the generalia classes the principle of subject arrangement is completely disregarded. A book classification, then, cannot be a continuous hierarchy of progression from general to specific, but is a series of independent and self-contained orders, loosely assembled into a kind of pseudo-hierarchy by a grand design.

Third, there is the limitation of *inherent incompleteness* which is the product of the striving for infinite hospitality; for if a book classification is to provide for all knowledge, past, present, or future, one must presuppose either a static universe or the ability to predict all future knowledge.

The final limitation is that of *complexity*, for a book classification that could achieve the objectives implicit in the above definition would be so intricate that it would collapse of its own weight. Already there is ample evidence that this is happening in the large and unwieldy collections of research libraries.

The history of library classification, then, has been the narrative of a pursuit of impossible goals, and its pages are strewn with the wreckage of those who either were blissfully unaware of the dangers by which their paths were beset, or who hoped to circumvent them through mere modification of previous schematisms or simple tinkering with notation. Today the essential failure of traditional library classifications is no more real than it was three quarters of a century ago, but it has become more apparent because of the increasing bulk and complexity of the materials that libraries are being called upon to service, and the growing specialization of the demands that librarians are being asked to meet.

THE BREAK WITH TRADITION

The first real break with tradition came at the turn of the present century when Paul Otlet and Henri LaFontaine determined to establish at Brussels a world bibliographic and documentation center, and began their search for an adequate bibliographic instrument that would effectively organize for subject accessibility the mass of diverse materials that they planned to catalogue. Not too unnaturally they turned to Dewey for their basic scheme, but they soon became aware that the decimal system had two major weaknesses for the

task which they imposed upon it: (1) being a general classification, it lacked sufficient detail for the adequate analysis of a vast agglomeration of highly specialized materials, and (2) it lacked adequate provision for displaying the variety of relationships inherent in this body of accumulated record. To correct the former the schedules were expanded to such an extent that the symbols in the notation, in many areas, exceeded the economic maximum. To introduce dimensions into a linear arrangement certain "signs of association" were devised to combine related parts of the schedules in a variety of ways. But again, the remedy served more to complicate than to clarify. Admittedly the editors of the UDC were, at least dimly, aware of the limitations of a book classification, but they never effectively attacked the problems that such limitations raised, with the result that the Brussels classification merely perpetuated in an exaggerated form the weaknesses of the parent scheme, and their innovations were palliative rather than remedial.

A second major advance toward a possible solution to the problem of library classification came when S. R. Ranganathan developed the philosophic orientation of his colon scheme. That he was fully aware of the limitations that inhere in any classification of bibliographic units is evident to anyone who has read with care his *Prolegomena*. But even he fell victim to many of the dangers that had dogged the footsteps of his predecessors. Nevertheless he was successful in devising a system of completely interchangeable parts that would admit of almost unlimited collocation of related subjects or points of view. These relationships he later categorized into the five fundamentals of Time, Space, Energy or Action, Matter, and Personality. His great contribution to classification, and the one that is far in advance of the thinking of his contemporaries, is his implicit rejection of the physical book as the constituent unit in classification and his substitution of the thought- or subject-unit. The distinctive property of the Colon Classification, then, is its emphasis upon the basic ways in which a subject may be characterized and its attempt to ignore the traditional hierarchical grouping of such characteristics. That he achieved only partial success was due to two errors: (1) like the editors of the UDC, he attempted to represent all possible relationships within the universe of knowledge and this led him into increasing complexity; and (2) his too hasty adoption of the decimal notation of Dewey and the UDC prevented any real escape from the shackles of the hierarchy. But these weaknesses do not minimize the magnitude of his contribution. He was striking at the most fundamental problems of library classification in ways that they had never been attacked before, and his still remains the most fertile mind that has yet addressed itself to the problems of bibliographic organization. One cannot but regret that, on this side of the Atlantic at least, unthinking librarians have been content to dismiss his work with the verdict that Thomas Carlyle wrote against seventeenth-century England—"Grand unintelligibility!"

OTHER ATTEMPTS TO IMPROVE LIBRARY CLASSIFICATION

The limitations inherent in traditional library classifications existed, of course, from the beginning, but their importance became intensified by a variety of influences. The sheer bulk of the materials to be classified itself became a complicating factor. The increasing importance to scholarship of the journal literature greatly intensified the problem of subject accessibility in ways that traditional library classifications were powerless to meet. This impotence derived mainly from the peculiarities of the journal as a physical embodiment of the records of scholarship. The great proliferation of highly specialized research reports and monographs multiplied the complexities of subject arrangement in geometrical progression. Growing specialization in the uses of recorded information placed a burden upon traditional library classification that earlier generations of library classifiers could not have foreseen. In short, traditional library classification had not only reached and passed the point of diminishing returns, it was seriously threatened by the internal collapse of its own intricate structure.

Responses to these new demands followed one of two major approaches. At first, and quite naturally, the assumption was made that subject accessibility could be improved by the refinement of existing schematisms or the invention of new schematisms that, in general, followed traditional patterns. This process of adaptation is so familiar to any one who has examined even a limited number of the specialized classifications used in special libraries that examples need not be presented here. In practice this meant little more than the addition of new terms to existing schedules, the rearrangement of terms into different relationships or contiguities, and the expansion of the notation accordingly. In some instances new schematisms were created *ad hoc* either from an examination of the literature or after consultation with subject specialists, or both. But whatever technique was adopted the underlying theory remained the same as it had been ever since that memorable Sunday in the Amherst chapel when Melvil Dewey first awakened to the beauties of the decimal system.

A second avenue of approach to the problems of library classification was opened when a substantial number of non-librarians began to think seriously about the need for improving existing methods for bibliographic organization. During, and in the wake of, the Second World War there came an unprecedented era of technical advance, and the scientists and technicians, in a variety of fields, suddenly awoke to the realization that if their efficiency was to be fostered, the bibliographic organization of their materials must be improved. They rejected most of the precepts and experience of the librarians, and attacked the problem of classification from an entirely different philosophic orientation. The limitations of the present discussion preclude the possibility of considering more than a very limited number of these attempts, but enough may be said to indicate that, though they achieved varying degrees of success, taken together they present an accumulation of experience that merits more intensive examination and study than is possible here.

Story prepared for the Department of Defense a classification based on the principle of gradation by generality rather than the Comteau principle of gradation by speciality and the filiation of the sciences. This inversion was predicated on the assumption that "entry" into the schematism would be through specific terms, and that increasing generality would be achieved through downward progression. Though such a scheme may have possessed certain operational advantages, it was still hierarchical; and a hierarchy is no less a hierarchy for being "up-side-down."

The Standard Aeronautical Indexing System was advanced as a monumental undertaking that would be a classification to end all classification, and in its fabrication a great variety of subject specialists were employed. Its underlying principle was "the need to know," a schematism based upon areas of interest. For example, if an aeronautical expedition were planned for the Arctic, the classification, it was hoped, would bring together all the necessary elements in terms of their abilities to withstand subzero temperatures. The classification was composed of only three levels: some fifty major, and fairly obvious, classes, with twenty-five to thirty subheads under each, and finally long listings of specific terms. As a library classification its success can hardly be characterized as conspicuous, but it has survived as a system for dissemination of reports because of its effectiveness as an instrument for identifying fields of interest.

A much more scholarly approach to the problems of subject access to bibliographic materials has been taken by Sanford Larkey's Medical Indexing Project at the Welch Medical Library of [The] Johns Hopkins University. In an attempt to explore the possibilities of machine coding of medical bibliography and at the same time to gain some insight into the problems involved in classifying medical materials, the research staff of this project has been classifying the subject headings used in the more important medical bibliographies. The terms thus derived were classified along certain axes to discover the scattering of materials among synonymous or nearly synonymous headings, the burial of material under obsolete terminology, and the accumulation of material requiring new terminology. From early attempts at classification developed a plan for sorting the terminology by categories based on certain common characteristics which might, or might not, agree with more traditional classes, or, in some cases, cut sharply across them. Though classification was but one part of the work of the entire project, certainly every student of bibliographic classification will await the final results with eagerness.

Finally, one should mention in passing the experimentation in the analysis of concepts carried out in the preparation of the Cross-cultural Index formerly at Yale University but now known as The Human Relations Area File Inc., and the *Syntopicon* of the University of Chicago. The latter is an alphabetico-chronological listing, by generic terms, of the philosophical concepts contained in the great philosophical writings of the Western World.

Whatever the values and shortcomings of the several attempts at specialized bibliographic classification, enough experience has already been gained to make possible the formulation of certain axiomatic principles respecting the classification of bibliographic materials.

1. Classification, either explicitly or implicitly, lies at the foundation of, and must be the point of departure from which begins, every attempt to analyze the subject content of bibliographic materials. This is as true for the alphabetic index as for the elaborate numerical schedule.
2. The Aristotelian concept of the hierarchy must be rejected as a basic principle of classification, if classification is to adapt itself to constantly changing needs, uses, and points of view. This is so because a hierarchy, of whatever structural design, implies a specific philosophical orientation, and the crystallization of a hierarchical structure into a particular orientation precludes, or does violence to, all others.
3. Human wisdom grows not only through the discovery of new facts but also through the reorganization and reorientation of familiar phenomena into new and quite unfamiliar patterns and relationships. Thus an excessive formalization of the structuring of knowledge may become a real barrier to improvement in the intellectual processes of society. The structuring of knowledge, therefore, must be sufficiently flexible to prevent an undue restraint upon that which to the traditionalist may appear "impracticable," "outlandish," or "absurd."
4. Bibliographic classification must be completely independent of physical objects (books), for no arrangement of such objects can reveal the complex of relationships that may exist among the many separate thought-units that make up the subject content of these books.
5. Librarians must, therefore, reject the traditional concept of librarianship as involving only the custody of books and their arrangement on library shelves in favor of a larger dedication to stewardship over the ideas the books contain.
6. This implies, then, that the unit of thought, rather than the book, manuscript, pamphlet, report, or journal, is the material with which bibliographic classification is concerned.

SYMBOLIC LOGIC AND THE NEW APPROACH TO BIBLIOGRAPHIC CLASSIFICATION

Implicit in these principles is an entirely new approach to the problems of the subject analysis of library materials, an approach that begins with Leibnitz's conviction that the processes of logical analysis and synthesis can be greatly facilitated by the substitution of compact and appropriate ideograms for the phonograms of ordinary language. This superiority of ideograms to phonograms had already been demonstrated in mathematics, especially in algebra, and the developments which he envisaged for science in general have coincided to a a remarkable extent with the logical analysis now achieved in the exact sciences, and which are now beginning to appear in certain of the social sciences. His prophetic insight thus laid the foundation for a method of reasoning that is today known by such terms as "mathematical logic," "exact logic," or, most commonly, "symbolic logic." But it was not until the renaissance in logical studies which occurred in the first half of the nineteenth century, that Augustus DeMorgan laid the foundation for the theory of relations and George Boole revived the Leibnitzean doctrine that the processes of logic might be both generalized and expedited if appropriate symbolic conventions were made.

Boole's great contribution, however, and the one which laid the foundations for the development of Boole-Schroeder algebra, was his ability to demonstrate that the methods of mathematics are not only applicable to the study of quantities, but to any ordered realm of knowledge whatever, and particularly to the relationships between classes and between propositions. This view that the study of logic was the study of *types of order* was a complete revolution against the old Aristotelian logic that had dominated men's minds for centuries. The limitations of the present discussion preclude the possibility of tracing the evolution of this new system of reasoning, but perhaps enough can be said, concerning its basic principles, to indicate its relevance to the subject organization of graphic materials.

Reduced to its simplest terms the method of reasoning devised by Boole and Schroeder and later expanded by Bertrand Russell and Alfred North Whitehead is nothing more than a symbolic language that is capable of manipulating the relationships of ideas as algebra can manipulate the relationships of numbers. By means of symbolic signs large masses of complex concepts can be related to each other in easy algebraic terms; and these terms, expressed as equations, can be arranged and rearranged, simplified and expanded, and the results, upon retranslation into English, can reveal new forms or relationships and disclose inconsistencies. Moreover, this new science of pattern or order is a binary algebra in that it is limited to two, and only two, values, i.e., 0 and 1, true and nontrue, or, more colloquially, "yes" and "no." It is further limited by being restricted to only three relations, "and," "or," and "not."

The values inherent in this new approach to the problems of reasoning became conspicuous when it was understood that the binary principle was coincident with the behavior of an electrical or mechanical impulse, and that it was therefore possible to construct digital calculators capable of manipulating large masses of information expressed in the algebraic terms of symbolic logic. Not only could these machines be made to process intricate mathematical problems of quantitative measurement in pure research, but through proper codification they could be useful instruments for the determination of relationships and internal consistencies of classes of propositions peculiar to practical problems of management in business and industry. Having thus established the

utility of these machines for the manipulation of large masses of intricate information, their application to the problems of the subject analysis of bibliographic data becomes a relatively simple step.

If any specific area of knowledge can be analysed into its constituent concepts, expressed in a standardized and consistent terminology, so that the totality of these concepts may be represented by these terms or their truth functions (i.e., their logical combinations and relationships) it follows that symbolic logic can make an important contribution to the organization of and searching for information in that field. The *depth* of the analysis of the field, i.e., the extent of the intension or extension of the terms used to express the constituent thought units will depend upon a variety of factors: the nature of the field itself, the degree of standardization of its terminology, the structure of the literature of the field, and the needs of the users of that literature. The level of analysis, then, will certainly vary from field to field, and will probably vary within the same field during different periods of time, for the characteristics of the field will themselves shift as the constituent elements that make up the total pattern of the field and its records become altered through their own interaction.

In an earlier paragraph the statement was made that symbolic logic is restricted to but two values, 0 and 1, and the relations or "operators"—"and," "or," and "not," but these limitations of all complex thought units of the field to logical sums or logical products, i.e., the truth functions, of their constituent simple thought units does not invalidate its utility as an instrument for the organization and location of information. A simple illustration should make this clear. Let it be assumed that field "Q" is analyzed into its constituent thought units a, b, c, etc. then the logical relationships that can be expressed are

a
not a
a and b
a or b (rejects everything that is not a and not b)

The magnitude of a, b, and c, can be any order appropriate to the particular situation and the logical relations of addition and negation will still allow for adequate subject access, because it is in these relationships that literature searches are made, (i.e., the searcher is interested in "this" and "this and/or this," but "not that." Literature searching, shorn of its superstructure of complexities, reduces to a simple dichotomous process of acceptance and rejection. Or, as D. J. Urquhart has so dramatically stated it, the problem of bibliographic organization is "how little to read."

THE VALUES OF AND THE PROBLEMS RAISED BY THIS NEW APPROACH TO BIBLIOGRAPHIC ORGANIZATION

The values of this new approach to bibliographic classification as an instrument for the analysis and organization of literature is at once apparent when it is reexamined with respect to the limitations inherent in the traditional book classifications as they are generally employed in libraries. Since the analysis of literature in terms of its constituent thought units dissociates content from the physical object (book) the limitation of *linearity* cannot apply. Nor does the limitation of *inconsistency of organization* apply because it is a conceptual, rather than a book, classification and hence inconsistencies due to the physical nature of books do not have to be introduced into the system. Further, by denial of the principle of a universal classification and insistence upon individual and separate schematisms for each field, or segment of a field, of knowledge, internal consistency throughout any given scheme can be maintained. The limitation of *inherent incompleteness* is avoided and the system becomes *infinitely hospitable* because it is a referential, rather than a hierarchical structure, and thus can be expanded at any point without doing violence to an underlying hierarchy. Finally it escapes *complexity* by being utilitarian and practicable rather than theoretical and hence is as simple as the field to which it relates and the purposes or objectives for which it is created. Its approach is pragmatic rather than absolute.

The latent possibilities in this conceptual approach to the problems of bibliographic analysis are evident from the amount of work that has already been done upon it. Either directly or indirectly it underlies such schemes as Calvin E. Mooers' Zatocoding,[2] the Coordinate Indexing of Taube and Thompson,[3] Holmstrom's experiments,[4] the Samain system,[5] Vickery's Connective Index,[6] and the work of Casey and Perry on punched card techniques for the classification of scientific data for quick reference.[7]

But however promising this new approach appears to be, a great many problems must still be solved before its full value for bibliographic purposes can be realized. Of all these perhaps the most basic is the standardization of terminology, a goal that is still very far from realization, even in the most specialized fields. This is a problem that can only be solved by the discipline itself, but librarians would be well advised to assume a position of leadership in emphasizing its importance and urging its solution.

Of perhaps equal importance is the need for far more basic research into the uses of literature, and in the effectiveness of existing bibliographic aids in the promotion of such use. The present writer has repeatedly urged this as a major research area for our graduate schools of librarianship but as yet singularly little is being done about it. One of the most encouraging recent developments is the study now being formulated by the John Crerar Library of the utility of its classified catalog as a bibliographic key to its rich scientific materials. Also the New York Public Library has become interested in a more critical examination of the subject catalog in its Reference Department. Together these studies, especially if they can be properly coordinated, should yield extremely valuable data that should make hypothetical discussions such as this more practicable and realistic in the future. Finally, it should be mentioned that for the past two years the Library of Congress has had a special committee working on the task of improving its dictionary catalogs, a study that should have professional importance far beyond its own marble halls.

The technical improvement of machines for the manipulation of bibliographic data is, of course, an ever-present problem, but it is one that so excites the imagination, not only of the librarian-bibliographer but also of the electronics engineer, that little urging is necessary to stimulate activity here. Furthermore, it must be emphasized that this new approach to bibliographic organization is not inherently machine-centered, or even machine-oriented. Machines have dramatized the problem, but binary classification can, with equal effectiveness, be applied to techniques of manual manipulation, and some experimentation here is under way by W. E. Batton in England,[8] and under the direction of Mortimer Taube at the Atomic Energy Commission. Such developments make this new approach applicable to even the smallest bibliographic installations, just as the machines promise greater and more effective subject access to the large research collections.

IMPLICATIONS OF THE NEW APPROACH FOR TRADITIONAL LIBRARY OPERATIONS

We have this afternoon indulged ourselves in the luxury of much theoretical speculation, and it now seems appropriate to ask its meaning for traditional library operations, especially for our present system of stack classification and the work of the subject cataloger. A few conclusions seem, to the present writer, to be reasonably obvious:

1. Traditional book classification has been convicted by the ample testimony of its own inadequacy. As a bibliographic device it falls between two stools; it is too complex for the general public library and it is completely inadequate to the demands of the large research collection. The concept of a universal library classification is not only a pretty illusion, it is a contradiction in terms. There can be no universal library classification because there is no universal library user. Only professional timidity and inertia and the costs of conversion have enabled traditional stack classification to survive. Had librarians thought seriously about the problem, instead of accepting uncritically the schematisms of Dewey and the Library of Congress, they would have long ago anticipated the present procedure of the John Crerar Library and arranged their research book stocks in a simple chronological sequence.

2. For small public libraries or the branches and "popular" collections of larger systems, the shelf arrangement should follow a practice similar to that of the Detroit branches which arrange books in large categories according to "reader interest," the titles being shelved under such headings as "Current Affairs," "Family Life," "The Arts," and "People and Places," with appropriate subordinate groups.[9] Further evidence of the trend of current thought on the problem of shelf classification is the adoption by the Harvard College Library of a very drastically modified and simplified version of the Dewey scheme for the new Lamont undergraduate collection.[10] Admittedly these schemes are not original in conception, but

they are symptomatic of a growing awareness on the part of librarians that traditional library classifications are not successfully meeting the the needs of users.

3. The possibilities of adapting machine techniques to bibliographic organization will permit extensive centralization of bibliographic operations, and this will in turn increase the coverage and effectiveness of the entire bibliographic system. Through the bibliographic centers that these machines will make not only possible but mandatory, the libraries of the country can have available to them an integrated network of subject bibliography that could bring when necessary the entire bibliographic resources of the nation to bear upon any specific problem at any particular time and place. Further, the operation of such a system would not limit its benefits to the world of scholarship, but would make them available to all users of graphic records and at all levels of use.

4. The extension of these new ideas in bibliographic classification to manual, as well as to mechanical and electronic, manipulation will effectively answer the criticism that such methods are applicable only to the most elaborate and expensive installations, and will make their benefits available for use in small, and especially the small but highly specialized libraries.

5. Finally, these new techniques for the organization of bibliographic materials are in no sense a substitute for the human intelligence; they cannot do our thinking for us; and they do not prognosticate an era of technologic unemployment for the subject cataloger and the classifier. Neither do they imply the deterioration of librarianship into a mechanized automatism. On the contrary, by opening up vital new areas for research into the theory of bibliographic organization, into the effectiveness of existing library processes, and into the subject analyses of our graphic records and the use that is made of them, librarianship can be raised to a higher level of intellectuality and a new and greater substance. For the cataloger of the future philosophy may well become Biou Kubpratus—the "Pilot of Life."

NOTES

[1] W. Stanley Jevons, *The Principles of Science* (London: Macmillan, 1887), p. 715.

[2] Calvin E. Mooers, *The Theory of Digital Handling of Non-numerical Information and Its Implications for Machine Economics* (Boston: The Zator Company, 1950).

———, *Zatocoding Applied to Mechanical Organization of Knowledge* (Boston: The Zator Company, 1951). See also *American Documentation* II, (Winter, January 1951), pp. 20–32.

[3] Mortimer Taube and Alberto F. Thompson, *The Coordinate Indexing of Scientific Fields*. Unpublished paper read before the symposium on mechanical aids to chemical documentation of the Division of Chemical Literature of the American Chemical Society, Sept. 4, 1951.

[4] J. E. Holstrom, *Records and Research in Engineering and Industrial Science*, (2nd ed.; London: Chapman & Hall, 1947).

[5] J. Samain, *A New Approach to Classification and Selection of Documents and References by Perforated Cards* (Royal Society, RSSICR Document No. 57, 1948).

[6] B. C. Vickery, "The Structure of a Connective Index." *Journal of Documentation*, VI (September 1950), pp. 140–51.

[7] Robert S. Casey and James W. Perry, *Punched Cards, Their Application to Science and Industry* (New York: Reinhold, 1951).

[8] W. E. Batton, "A Punched Card System of Indexing to Meet Special Requirements," in A.S.L.I.B., *Report of 22d Conference*, 1947, pp. 37–39.

Also: B. DeGorter, "The Indexing of British Patents on Plastics," Royal Society Scientific Information Conference 21 June–2 July 1948. *Report and Papers Submitted* (London: Royal Society, 1948), pp. 685–89.

[9] Ruth Rutzen, "Shelving for Readers," *Library Journal* LXXVII (March 15, 1952), pp. 478–482.

[10] Richard O. Pautzsch, "The Classification Scheme for the Lamont Library," *Harvard Library Bulletin* IV (Winter 1950), pp. 126–127.

Harvard College Library, *Classification Scheme of the Lamont Library* (Cambridge: Harvard College Library, 1950).

The Nature and Purpose of Classification

W. C. Berwick Sayers

> *" . . . the whole object of library classification is to secure an arrangement which will be useful to our readers with the smallest complication of search or other effort for them or for ourselves. It is a technique involving the systematic grouping of books by subject . . . ."*

From the day when a man first assembled books of any kind or form, men have been interested in the ways of arranging them. It is merely a part of the divine instinct that 'order is Heaven's first law'; for arrangement, or classification as we call it, lies at the base of every well-managed life and occupation. As we shall see later, the clay tablets which formed the books of the library of the Assyrian, Assur-ban-i-pal, were placed on their shelves in a considered order; and in the record of libraries throughout the ages, wherever we have any details of them, we have also evidences of the preoccupation of their librarians with this question. It is one of much interest and is simple in its basic essentials, but in the course of years has assumed a complexity which is perhaps in part the outcome of the general tendency of men to seek scientific or philosophical reasons for the processes they employ, but is also due to the rapid increase annually in the number of newly published documents. The classification of libraries may be briefly defined as: *The arrangement of books on shelves or the systematic arrangement of catalogs and similar tools in the manner which is most useful to those who read*. Classification, then, is a tool for a very simple but infinitely important purpose. If, however, a preliminary definition is easy, its full explanation and application are not so; but it is essential from the outset that we keep clearly in mind the fact that the whole object of library classification is to secure an arrangement which will be useful to our readers with the smallest complication of search or other effort for them or for ourselves. It is a technique involving the systematic grouping of books by subject and is designed to expedite the full use of the knowledge stored in the books and other material housed by the library.

In this chapter we shall consider classification in the widest sense of the word and its function in our everyday activities as a prelude to the study of the need for bibliographical classification. Every classical reader knows that the word 'class' in our sense has the same meaning that was given it in Ancient Rome, when the effective nobility were arranged in six orders or ranks according to their real or supposed qualities of blood or wealth. These were the *classes* of the population as distinct from the lower orders. A *classis*, then, was made up of a number of persons having a certain quality in common. So, in our studies, a class consists of a number of things which are alike in some particular or have some quality in common by which they may be sorted out from other things and which at the same time makes their own unity. It may safely be assumed from the outset that everything in the universe is a member of some class. We can test this readily if we consider any of the common things of life—plants, animals, men, houses, streets, stones, stars, clothes and so forth. The mere mention of any one of these brings to the mind not a single object but a whole series of things which have the common name. Such a name is a *class* name.

We cannot reason, even in the simplest manner, unless we possess the power of being able to classify things; indeed we cannot live at all. A Wellsian picture is easily conjured up of an inhabitant of another planet, who possesses every human faculty but has had no human experience, who finds himself set down suddenly on one of our country roads. The world he has come from has none of the features of this; everything therefore before and around him is new. He walks along the road and the first object of consequence that he notices is a tree. He sees that it has a perpendicular trunk covered by a corrugated substance, that it branches off above his

SOURCE: Reprinted from W. C. Berwick Sayers, *A Manual of Classification for Librarians*, 4th ed. (London: André Deutsch, 1967), pp. 25-31, by permission of the publisher.

head, and that on these branches are rustling extremities which we call leaves. With no knowledge to aid, his eyes do not awaken in his mind memories of something like it seen elsewhere which will tell him what it is. He proceeds to experiment; he feels the trunk, and finds it solid; he plucks a leaf, somewhat surprised to find that it is easily detachable; greatly daring, he tastes the leaf, and finds it has a sweet, acid, not pleasant or unpleasant, flavour. He goes on his way, and meets another such object, but different in shape—in an accidental particular—and he repeats the experiments he made with the first tree. His impressions of the solidity of the trunk, the detachability and flavour of the leaf are repeated. He is on the way to classification; he decides that this second thing must have a definite *likeness* to the first thing. Repeated experiments with other trees strengthen and confirm this inference. So, by gradual and sometimes painful processes, he arrives at the notion that there is a group of things every member of which is like every other in all essential particulars. If he lives long enough he may learn from man that the group has a name, Trees; but in any case he has formed an idea to which he will attach some label or name of his own in order to distinguish it. This is classification, in a broad sense.

It becomes more advanced classification when from repeated experiences he learns that, while all trees resemble one another in their main characteristics, some trees have darker leaves than others, some have oval leaves, others bifurcate or double leaves, some have smooth edges, some are serrated or tooth-edged; and his recognition of these differences enables him to make groups within the greater group of trees; to separate mentally the pine tree from oak, the alder from elder and birch from beech; and later he may find that fir, larch and cedar very closely resemble the pine, although they have differences, but differences not nearly so marked as the difference between the oak and pine. Later still, if his observations are continued, he will discover that even the pine tree has several kinds, the Weymouth, the Norwegian, the Italian Stone Pine, and so on. When he has reached this stage, he has coordinated a series of observations by the use of memory—and subordinated subclasses to their parent class—in such a way that the sight of one pine tree calls into his mind the characteristics of all pines as distinct from other kinds of tree. He can *classify* them.

We doubt if a man would survive for twenty-four hours if he were entirely without this power

of classifying. Imagine a man in a London street, who beheld a car knock down and injure another man and yet was unable to infer from the incident that any other car would behave similarly in similar circumstances—who could not recognize that any swift-rolling vehicle (and 'swift-rolling vehicle' constitutes a *class* of things) was a dangerous thing with which to collide! From a single incident of this kind a man with classifying power but without experience might make the error, but a second would teach him to avoid it and the first would make him cautious. But the man without the power to classify objects would be unable to relate one car to another; experience would be of no use to him; he would probably walk quite carelessly in front of any car he saw. The example may seem ridiculous enough, but were we deprived of classifying power the circumstances might be precisely as suggested.

'Classification made the ape a man' stated E. C. Richardson, meaning that it is the ability to distinguish the likenesses and differences existing between things which is peculiar to man—the higher reasoning power. However, we may be underestimating the mental powers of birds and animals, if we suggest that they are without reason. For example, the lower animals certainly have the power of distinguishing two classes of things; those that are eatable and those that are not. The beaver in his architecture shows a power which may be instinct but is very like reason. So, too, the eagle in choosing a nesting place on great heights, usually over precipices, must in some way be aware that precipices are inaccessible. Yet it is probable that animals and birds have no consciousness of the reasons which underlie their actions and in this respect man alone may be preeminent; in any case these powers which seem to be merely rudimentary in animals are developed in a man to a high degree; they are so even in the uneducated man; and on these considerations may rest the validity of Richardson's saying.

All this may enable us to reach another useful definition of classification. It is that exercise of the powers of perception and reason which enables us to assemble things in an order of likeness, and to separate them according to an order of unlikeness. There is rather more in this than may appear on the surface. The definition means not merely the grouping of things which resemble one another, but the arrangement within each group of its components according to their degrees of resemblance. To take a rough unscientific example, which will, however, illustrate our point sufficiently. A group of dogs will contain, perhaps, many kinds of dog—greyhounds, foxhounds, wolfhounds, terriers, Irish terriers, and Scotch terriers. All these have the general resemblance which is implied by their common name—dogs. But all hounds are more like other hounds than they are like terriers; all terriers more like other terriers then they are like hounds. So these would form subclasses within the class, dogs; but, again, a bull terrier is more like a mastiff than it is like a hound; and this relationship too must be shown in our arranging of the class. Classification, then, is not only the general grouping of things for location or identification purposes; it is also their arrangement in some sort of logical order so that the *relationships of the things may be ascertained*. Here we have a vital principle in classification theory: It is one that must be constantly borne in mind.

Enough has been said to emphasise the truth that man's universe is so great and complex that on first appearance it is a chaos, a tangle of things to which he has no clue and of such extent that he can obtain no grasp of it unless he provides himself with some sort of map. This map of things is a convenient expression for a scheme of classification. The whole universe of thought and objects must be put into some order by the mind and that order must be recorded. Not only the whole universe, which means everything; even the single sciences are far too extensive for our comprehension until we have made some sort of map of their territories. Much of the study of man has been of what may be called a classificatory kind; that is to say, it has been concerned with observing and recording the apparatus, structure, habits and purposes of things with a view to their accurate description; so that we may name them adequately and understand them. Indeed Thomas Carlyle once said, with much justice, that the greater part of knowledge consists in the giving of right names to things. Such study and research reveals the various likenesses which things have, and by these the things tend to be assembled into classes. By likeness, we mean the quality or qualities in things which enable them to be substituted for each other, as for example, the cartridges in a particular type of machine gun, the cards used in a catalogue, or pennies. Each of these represents the companions in its class to a high degree. It is clear that there must be many ways in which things are alike; the likenesses stressed in a particular classification will be those which best serve the purpose of the maker of that classification.

Richardson asserts, without qualification, that 'the things in nature are already classified', and from this we may infer that what man has to do is only to trace out the order of that classification and to record it. We shall see in succeeding chapters that the history of book classification shows that librarians have a tendency to return continually, with some fascination, to the idea that the classification of knowledge—the accurate mapping out of ideas and objects in the world around us—is the essential basis of a book classification. That there are differences between the book classification and the knowledge classification is obvious to simple perception, but the resemblance between them is even greater. Thus it can be seen that the ideas of Richardson, Bliss, and others, and the current interest of some members of our profession in the philosophical theory of levels of integration within the universe, are all attempts to ensure that a book classification will be both helpful and durable by corresponding closely to a scientific organization of knowledge. There are not wanting those who declare that there is no order in nature apart from the human mind that conceives it, yet this is surely a vain speculation of Berkeleyan sort which declares that things only exist in as much as the human mind perceives them. More valid perhaps are those objections which suggest that the natural order is too complex for any man's classificatory map to suit us all, that the order of nature defies the classifier because it is never static, or that book classification in particular presents many examples of items which cut across orthodox subject disciplines. Yet, when all such objections have been considered, we can at least say that nature offers man some clues concerning the organization of the multiplicity of objects which surround him. We do know, for example, that in the natural world animals with a backbone form one group and those without another; that plants with flowers are one group and flowerless plants another; that some birds live mainly in the water and that some are exclusively land creatures, and so the process may be extended. The mere recognition of such likenesses and differences as these is an act of classification and the commonness of the process is patent. It may be well, however, to say that while classification is necessary to knowledge, it is only a method of approaching it. Much of the difficulty that is found in classifying (and this is especially true of book classification) arises from a want of knowledge either of the subjects we are endeavouring to arrange or of the use that will be made of the completed arrangement. We cannot classify an object or idea without knowing at least some of its qualities, and we cannot classify accurately or with any degree of finality without knowing a great many of its qualities. We could not, for example, classify dogs without knowing what dogs are, and still less could we subdivide them into their many species. Observation must first tell us the main characteristics of dogs: and having some view of these the classifying process is to arrange them. In like manner, we cannot classify books by subjects unless we know what they are about. That seems trite enough when thus stated; but the statement is not at all unnecessary.

Our rough definition of classification as the arrangement of things according to their degree of likeness has served to lead up to a much more extended and now classic definition. It was first enunciated by Huxley, has been modified by Jevons and added to by Jast:

> By the classification of any series of objects is meant the actual or ideal arrangement together of those which are like and the separation of those which are unlike; the purpose of this arrangement being, primarily, to facilitate the operations of the mind in clearly conceiving and retaining in the memory the characters of the objects in question, and the recording of them that they may be conveniently and quickly referred to; and secondarily, to disclose the correlations or laws of union or properties and circumstances.

This can be explained more simply perhaps. Classification is primarily a mental operation. When we say we arrange things we mean that we place them in an order which corresponds with an idea or series of ideas in our minds; we could not arrange things in an order which did not thus exist in our thought. To do this we have mental pictures of the things we are to arrange. That is *ideal* arrangement, indeed this mental process is the true meaning of the term classification. *Actual* arrangement is the placing in order of objects that we can see or touch, such as botanical specimens, or coins, or, of course, books. We may anticipate later chapters here by stating that one of the main problems in bibliographical classification lies in the fact that an actual arrangement of tangible objects is involved. A book may have links with more than one subject field, but it can have only one place in a scheme of classification designed for the arrangement on the library shelves.

To return to our present theme, it will be seen, we think, that the classifier is concerned not only with external things, the manifestations of the natural universe; he has a whole universe within himself—of emotions, thoughts, percepts, concepts, ideas—which he must also reduce to order. Some of man's thought is really external to himself, having been derived from others; his thoughts for example, on current happenings are too often merely the reflection of the leading article in the newspaper he reads; but for most useful purposes we may regard them as his own. This subjective, intangible matter is equally to be controlled and set in order. Man cannot communicate his opinions or knowledge readily unless the ideas represented are first arranged in his own mind. So the definition might read 'Classification is the arrangement of things themselves or of our mental picture of things'. This gives us a valuable point for consideration, which may be put in the form of a question: 'What is the material of classification?' The reply is—everything. We can classify not only tangible objective things; we can also arrange impressions, ideas, notions; we can and must arrange things which exist, have existed, or may exist. Thus classification clarifies thought, advances investigation, shows gaps in the sequence of knowledge and promotes discovery; revealing, as it should, the relationships of things, it enables a more or less complete survey of knowledge to be made.

In many ways a classification, when committed to paper, can be compared to a map. Its task is to provide for the field of knowledge or part of it, as comprehensive and clear a statement as the cartographer is able to make of a territory of the earth. For just as a map makes clear the relationship between place and place so a classification strives to show the relationship of each branch of knowledge with other branches. Likewise just as the map may stress physical, geological, meteorological, economic, or other features, the features stressed by a classification must be determined by the purpose for which it is made and the needs of those it is designed to serve. Yet, in a sense, a classification is more complex than a map. The globe of the earth is, as it were, fixed; the countries may change hands indeed but they do not change position; while in a classification topics may grow or diminish in importance. They may abandon their relationships with certain subject fields and forge new links with others. In short, the problem of organizing them is complicated by the fact that knowledge is in a constant state of flux.

Decimal Clasification and Relativ Index

Melvil Dewey

> *"Utility has not been sacrificed in order to force subjects on the 'decimal procrustean bed'. Decimals have been uzed as servants, not as masters. When subjects ar combined or separated into just 10 heds, it has been from no necesity of the skeme, but becauz it seemd most useful. . . ."*

Simpler spelings ar strongly recommended for jeneral adoption by both American and English filolojic associations, including nearly all prominent skolars in English now living.

The speling of this introduction has many more changes than we recommend for jeneral use at once. For convenient reference we hav included in 'Simpler speling reazons and rules' the famus 12 words adopted in 1898 by the National Education Association for all its official printing and correspondence, and adopted later by hundreds of periodicals, colejes and normal skools; also the 30 words, as a better tipical list with which to begin simpler speling; also the S.S.B. rules, from which one shud select those which most appeal to him; also the 10 joint rules of American and English filolojists, and selections from rules of U.S. Geographic Board. From these one may choose chanjes he is willing to make, knowing how ampl authority is behind them. We recommend that each one convinst of the importance begin with a few of these chanjes, ading others from time to time as he and his correspondents becum familiar with the new forms. That it 'looks queer' is admittedly the only argument left to objectors. This introduction is speld to show how it wil look if practicaly all these recommendations ar uzed. Sum with specialy strong vizual prejudis wil hav attention distracted from the matter to the speling but if with an open mind they wil try to concentrate on the meaning, they wil be surprized to find how quikly the new forms wil cease to annoy. Then if they continue reading them they wil soon be surprized to find that the old absurd common speling wil annoy. There ar comparatively few simpler spelings in Tables or Index but we decided to show in Introduction how extreme chanjes wud look.

Orijin and growth: The plan of this Classification

and Index was developt erly in 1873, the result of long study of library economy as found in hundreds of books and pamflets, and in over 50 personal visits to libraries. This study convinst me that usefulness of libraries myt be greatly increast without aded expense. Only a fraction of the servis posibl cud be got from them without clasification, catalogs, indexes and other aids to tel librarians and readers what they containd on any givn subject yet, by methods then uzed, this cud be dun satisfactorily only at a cost so great as to be prohibitiv to all but a few welthy libraries. With rare exceptions, libraries wer growing rapidly. Catalogs, made at great cost soon became antiquated. Methods uzed involvd frequent rearranjement, renumbering and remarking of books, and of necessity remarking of catalogs and indexes, as the only escape from a confuzion that seriusly cripled usefulness. In this costly repetition, work of previus librarians was larjly lost. The great need was a sistem which wud enable each to stand on the sholders of his predecesors, and fully utilize their labors; which wud make work dun today permanent, instead of sumthing to be superseded in so few years as not to be worth doing in the best way; which wud supply the best applyances, insted of leaving yung librarians not only to lern how to work, but to make all their own tools.

Practical use for 54 years proves that this sistem wil accomplish this result; for with its aid catalogs, shelflists, indexes and references, essential to this increast usefulness, can be made faster and cheaper than by any method not having its essential features, and, when dun, they ar better and vastly more permanent. Practical utility and economy ar its keynotes and no theoretic refinement has been allowd to modify the skeme, if it wud detract from usefulness or ad to cost.

Notation: We devised and experimented with

SOURCE: Reprinted from Melvil Dewey, *Decimal Clasification and Relativ Index*, 12th ed. (Lake Placid, N.Y.: Forest Press, 1927), pp. 9-21, by permission of Forest Press, Inc., owner of the copyright.

several notations by means of numbers, letters, and combined numbers and letters, with bases of 26, 35, 50, 100 and 150, yet none seemd good enuf to warrant publishing details, except that here printed, based on simpl arabic numerals with their uzual decimal powers. International adoption of this sistem is larjly becauz no one ever complains that any clasification is too simpl, while there is constant complaint of complexity. Decimal simplicity has so commended itself that many think of it as the only form, tho obviusly it wud be just as much a 'relativ index sistem' if the clasification wer wholly markt by letters or other simbols.

The Subject Index is the simplest application of a, b, c, the simbols next in simplicity to 1, 2, 3. This use of the simplest 2 sets of simbols known, with their common meanings, has givn our notation its worldwide reputation as the simplest yet devized.

Best known decimal form: Decimal form means simply that heds ar groupt and numbered with common arithmetic figures uzed decimaly. This, the only decimal form thus far carefuly elaborated and publisht, is commonly spoken of as if it wer the only posible form of our orijinal plan; tho obviusly an infinit variety of 'relativ index sistems' in decimal form *cud* be made by filling the outline with different heds, or with the same heds in different order.

To make out new heds involvs labor and cost vastly beyond the dreams of any person who has not tryd exactly this work. Time actualy spent on tables here printed, by varius committees and individuals, totals hundreds of years and has cost an immense sum. Uniform and urjent advice of the experienst is to adopt a poorer skeme alredy made rather than undertake so herculean a labor. When dun, the maker may posibly be better suited with it, but few if any others wil be. It is wizer for anyone whose time is of value, to uze it in sumthing more practicaly useful to himself and his library than in trying to construct a 'satisfactory' skeme of clasification. No one yet ever wholly suited himself or anyone else, and probably no one ever wil. By adopting this alredy workt out he saves much time and money, and gains the immense advantaj of uzing a sistem in common with thousands of others, so that he may utilize their labors and investigations and share with them economies of cooperation.

Relativ Subject Index: This alfabetic Index, the most important feature of the sistem, consists of

hedings gatherd from a great variety of sources, as uzers of the sistem hav found them desirabl in 54 years experience. After all these efforts, many new heds ar aded in each new edition.

The Index gyds in both numbering and finding books. In assyning numbers, the most specific hed that wil contain the book having been determind, reference to that hed in Index givs proper clas number. Conversely, in finding books on any givn subject, reference to Index givs number under which they ar found on shelvs, in shelflist, or in clast catalog. When any new subject cums up, interline it and its sinonims in Index, with clas number decided on, so clasifyer may be uniform with himself in future work.

The Index givs similar or sinonimous words, and the same words in different connections, so any intelijent person wil surely get the ryt number. A reader wishing to know sumthing of the tarif looks under T, and, at a glance, finds 337 as its number. This gyds him to shelvs, to all books and pamflets, to shelf catalog, to clast subject catalog on cards, to clast record of loans, and, in short, in simple numeric order, thruout the whole library to *anything* bearing on his subject. If he turns to Tables, he sees that it means clas 3, Sociology; division 3, Economics; section 7, Protection and free trade; but the number alone is enuf to clas the book or find it, for either clasifyer or reader. If he had lookt under P for protection, or F for free trade, or D for duties, or C for customs, or under any other leading word relating to his subject, he wud have been referd to 337, or sum one of its subdivisions.

Had he lookt for 'railroad' he wud hav found after it 22 separate entries, each preceded by a word or fraze indicating the faze of the subject in the skeme. A book on railroads may treat of the desirability of government ownership, control, etc., and then is clearly a question of social syence; or it may be a practical handbook for an employee explaining business methods or railroading, running trains, handling freight, etc., when it is clearly one of the useful arts. The clasifyer knows to which of these heds his book belongs, and the reader knows in which of its fazes he wishes to examin the subject. Moreover, 3 and 6 beginning the numbers clearly indicate caracter of each clas.

But even if significance of these figures is entirely disregarded, no confuzion results, for, on consulting the numbers in catalog, in skeme, or on shelvs the difference is clearly seen. In other cases, it is more useful to keep books on the same subject together, thos treated from different standpoints. A glance at the Index tels either reader or clasifyer which plan has been adopted.

All topics in blakface typ in Index ar further divided in Tables, where one may see the subheds. This saves reprinting all these subdivisions, which wud increase Index bulk many-fold; e.g., if one having a book on 'prison labor' looks in the Index for 'Convict labor' or 'Prison contracts', he finds at once its special number 331.51; but if, on the other hand he thinks to look only for jeneral subject 'Labor', he finds in blackface typ the entry 'Labor, political economy, 331', and turning to Tables he finds under 331 the subdivision '331.51, Convict labor', the exact topic in hand.

The greatest objection to a clast catalog has always been the difficulty in knowing just where to clas a book and just where to look for it when again wanted. Different librarians, or the same librarian at different times, clast the same or similar books in widely different places. Where one man did all the work for many years, there was a degree of uniformity; but even then there was danjer of looking at the same book at different times from different viewpoints, thus cauzing confuzion. When the daily pres is ful of one faze of a subject, tendency is strong to clas all books on this subject from current viewpoint; and next year, if a different side of this same subject is before the public, there is same tendency to clas books from new viewpoint, thereby separating similar books and bringing together books on different fazes. But fortunately, practical usefulness does not require that the ideas of this or that one be followd, but only that books of same caracter be always put in same place, and that there be sum means of knowing redily what that place is. The Relativ Index, with its cach-words, was desynd and is found in use to meet both these requirements, for it insures that books on same faze of any subject cuming before the clasifyers shal be assynd to same place, and that any reader seeking these books shal be referd instantly to that place. If this is dun, all requirements of a good clasification ar fild. If it is not dun, the sistem is a failure; for the only real test of any skeme is its helpfulness to its uzers.

Sum prominent opponents of clast catalogs admit that the Relativ Subject Index, in deciding where to clas a book at first and where to look for it ever afterwards, has removed their strongest objections. Certainly it wud be imposibl to make an Index more compact or eazier of reference.

This Index allows a great part of the work of clasifying to be dun in advance by experts in larj central libraries with ampl resources, thus securing,

at a mere fraction of uzual cost, better and more uniform results than wud be posibl to the ordinary clasifyer and reducing labor to much narrower limits than ever before.

To these thousands of subjects hav been carefully assynd their individual numbers, many of them after long consideration and consultation with specialists. No one person is lerned enuf to clas wizely books on all subjects and syences; but botanists can assyn all botanic subjects to the ryt number, mathematicians all mathematical topics, and thus the Index wil in time becum as accurate as the best skolarship of the day can make it. Even if the decision reacht is not always wizest, all practical purposes ar servd, becauz, as each clasifyer copies the number from same Index, all books on that subject ar together; and, as each reader gets his number from this same Index, he goes directly to the book he seeks.

What Relativ Index includes: The Index, containing 43,000 entries and constantly being enlarjd by ading new subjects, aims to include all topics exprest or implyd in Tables, together with every corresponding sinonim likely to be sought, but does not include most names of cuntries, towns, animals, plants etc. except when mentioned in Tables; e.g. it can not enumerate all species of trilobites, but when clasifyer has found from proper reference books that Remopleurides is a trilobite, the Index sends him to 565.393, and he can clas his monograf on that subject.

Tables: The essential complement of the Subject Index is the Tables of Clasification, so mapt out as to show in 4 ways—i.e., by size of typ, face of typ, indention, and number of figures prefixt—each subject's rank in the Clasification.

The field of knowlej is divided into 9 main clases numberd 1 to 9, and cyclopedias, periodicals etc. so jeneral as to belong to *none* of these clases ar markt 0 (naught) and form a 10th clas; e.g., clas 1 is library of Filosofy; clas 5, library of Syence; clas 9, History, etc. These special clases or libraries ar then considerd independently, and each is separated again into 9 special divisions of the main subject, numbered 1 to 9, as wer the clases, jeneral works belonging to *no* division having 0 for their division number. Thus 59 is division 9 (Zoolojy) of clas 5 (Syence). A 3d division is then made by separating each of these divisions into 10 sections, numbered in same way with 0 and the 9 dijits; and this decimal subdivision is repeated, til it secures as many subsections as may be needed in any topic. Thus 513 is section 3 (Jeometry) of division 1 (Mathematics) of clas 5 (Pure syence). This number, giving clas, division, section and sub-section, if any, is cald the clas number, and is applyd to every book and pamflet belonging to the library. All jeometries ar thus numberd 513, all mineralojies 549, and so thruout the library all books on any givn subject bear the number of that subject in this skeme.

Where 0 occurs before the decimal point in a clas number, it has its normal zero value. Thus a book numbered 510 is clas 5, division 1, but *no* section; i.e., treats of division 51 (Mathematics) in jeneral, and is limited to no 1 section, as is jeometry, markt 513. 500 indicates a treatis on syence in jeneral, limited to no division. 0 occurring in the 1st place wud in the same way show that the book was limited to no clas; e.g., a jeneral cyclopedia which treats of all 9 clases.

With the same 'jeneral' sense, 0 is often uzed to indicate chanje in caracter of subdivision, meaning in this case 'basis of subdivision chanjes at this point', i.e., figure (or figures) following 0 apply to what precedes *in jeneral*, e.g., 505 indicates syence in *jeneral* treated in the form of a periodical. In history, clasification is by cuntries (i.e., *jeografic*) and as minute jeografic divisions ar needed for travels, gyd books, and varius other uses, the figures 1–9 ar jenerally uzed for jeografic subdivisions and again for further jeografic subdivisions, as far as needed, and 0 followd by another figure for time division, i.e., the figures before the 0 in-dicate the locality as a whole, while figures after the 0 indicate the special time at which the history of the locality is being considered; e.g., 942.06, consisting of 942 (*jeografic* division) and 06 (*time* division), means history of England in *jeneral* in time of the Stuarts, while 942.6 and 942.7 mean respectively history of eastern England and history of Essex co., to which the same time division may be aded, giving 942.606 and 942.6706 as the history of those localities under the Stuarts. As any subdivision may, by ading figures 1–9, be givn 9 further subdivisions, any desired degree of mi-nuteness may be secured in clasing special subjects.

Coordination: Theoreticly division of every sub-ject into just 9 parts is absurd. Practicaly it is de-sirabl to clas as minutely as posibl, without use of aded figures; and decimals, on which our skeme hinjes, allow 9 divisions as redily as fewer. This has proved wholy satisfactory in practis, tho ap-parently destroying proper coordination in sum places.

Where more than 9 divisions ar needed the diffi-culty is commonly obviated by grouping on singl numbers the subjects most closely allyd, or by assyning 1-8 specificly to most important subjects and grouping minor subjects on 9 as 'Other.' Since any of these groups may be further subdivided for specific topics as needed, provision is thus made for an unlimited number of subjects.

As in every skeme, many minor subjects ar under jeneral heds to which they do not strictly belong. In sum cases, these heds ar printed in distinctiv typ; e.g., 829 Anglo-Saxon, under English litera-ture. The rule has been to assyn these subjects to the most nearly allyd heds, or where it was tho't they wud be most useful. The only alternativ was to omit them altogether. If any such omission occurs, it wil be supplyd as soon as discoverd, for we intend to provide in the Tables a place for every known topic.

New subjects: A new topic is always closely related to sum existing hed. If there is no blank number availabl it is combined with the hed nearest allyd, and, when important enuf, distinct provision for the new cumr is made by ading another decimal. The sistem is thus capabl of unlimited expansion, and can never break down for lak of room for growth.

Choice and arranjement of heds: Detaild explana-tion of selection and arranjement of the many thousand heds wud be tedius; but everywhere filosofic theory and accuracy hav yielded to prac-tical usefulness. The imposibility of making a satisfactory clasification of all knowlej as preserved in books, has been appreciated from the first, and theoretic harmony and exactness hav been re-peatedly sacrificed to practical requirements.

Sequence of allyd subjects: Wherever practicabl, heds hav been so arranjed that each subject is pre-ceded and followd by most nearly allyd subjects, and thus aded convenience is secured both in clast catalogs and on shelvs; e.g., Bilding (690) follows Mekanic trades (680) at end of Useful arts, and Arkitecture follows at beginning of Fine arts.

Students of Biolojy (570) find fossil life or Paleontolojy (560) before, and vejetabl life or Botany (580) after, this followd in turn by animal life or Zoolojy (590), ending with Mammals (599); while Useful arts (600) begin with human Anat-omy (611) under Medicin, thus giving a regular growth from fossil plant thru vejetabl and animal kingdoms to living man.

Cachtitles: In naming hedings, strict accuracy has often been sacrificed to brevity, for short familiar titles ar more important than that terms chosen shud express fully and exactly caracter of all books clast under them. Many subjects, apparently omitted, wil be found in the Index, assynd, with allyd subjects, to a hed which bears the name of the most important only. Reference to the Index wil decide at once most doutful points.

Form distinctions: The clasification is mainly by *subject* or *content* regardless of form but an aded form distinction for jeneral treatises is found practicaly useful.

Thus, in Syence there ar many compends, dictionaries, essays, periodicals and socyeties, treating of Syence in jeneral, and so having 0 for the division figure, but treating it under different forms, and therefore divided into sections according to this form: 501 for filosofy or theories of Syence, 502 for compends, 503 for dictionaries, etc. This treatment is as nearly as practicable, uniform in all clases. Creasy's[6] '15 decisiv battles' is 904, the 1st figure being 9, becauz the book is clearly history; the 2d figure 0, becauz limited to *no* division of clas 9; and the 3d figure 4, becauz the book is a colection of essays.

The 10 main clases ar regularly divided by form, e.g., 809, history of literature in jeneral. For divisions, sections or subsections having *enuf* jeneral material to make such division advizabl, form numbers, preceded by 0, may be uzed (e.g., 820.9, history of English literature; 821.09, history of English poetry), except when 0 and the following number hav been otherwize assynd, e.g., 821.04 English liric poetry, *not* essays on English poetry; 942.05 England in time of the Tudors, *not* a periodical on English history. A history of English literature is 820.9, not 809, becauz every book belongs to the *most specific hed* that wil contain it; so 809 is limited to histories of literature in jeneral. Books treating of many clases, such as jeneral cyclopedias or periodicals, go in clas 0 and ar then divided by form into cyclopedias, periodicals, socyeties or newspapers.

Do not confuze form number 07, meaning 'methods of study or teaching', with number for same subject under 375, which is for its value as a means of education, or for its curiculum place.

These form distinctions ar introduced at the beginning of the clas becauz the number of jeneral works is larj, and these 1st numerals wud otherwize be unuzed.

Form divisions always hav the same set of numbers, preceded by 0, i.e., 1 filosofy, theories etc. 2 compends, outlines; 3 dictionaries, cyclopedias; 4 essays, lectures, letters etc.; 5 periodicals, magazines etc.; 6 socyeties, associations, transactions, reports etc.; 7 education, study, teaching, training etc.; 8 poligrafy, colections etc.; 9 history. Thus a periodical on a subject has the subject number followed by 05; e.g., a periodical on public helth, 614.05.

But if the number alredy ends in 0, 0 is not repeated before form-division figures; e.g., a zoolojic magazine is 590.5, not 590.05.

As in close subdivision, wish for nemonic correspondence has never outweighd any claim of greater usefulness. In many cases choice between numbers was hardly perceptibl: e.g., whether in filolojy order shud be French, Spanish, Italian, or French, Italian, Spanish. In such cases nemonic numbers wer givn preference, and 54 years use has proved this wizest. Great gain, beside eaz of remembering, results from this *uniform* use of same numbers with same meaning whenever similar division is made. Wherever division by languajes or cuntries is made, it follows filolojy or history numbers, and in Tables, the note 'Divided like 900' fully takes the place of reprinting all history subdivisions. This saving justifys use of these numbers in sum cases, even where a sumwhat different order myt seem more nearly fitted to the special case; e.g., in 342, constitutional history of Canada (342.71) and Australia (342.94) next that of England (342.42) wud be better than our order, which separates them both from England and from each other. Stil by following the uzual 'procrustean' numbers, many topics can be subdivided minutely without further study, by simply applying history or languaj subdivisions. A singl ilustration of the astonishing power this principl givs wil suffice, tho thousands myt be givn: 016 is 'Bibliografy of special subjects, divided like main clasification', therefore by aid of tables under 581, 016.58197472 redily translates itself to all uzers into 'Bibliografy of flora of Albany co., N Y'. While these 12 figures myt never be uzed, if a specialist wishes minute division, it is redy to his hand, conforms to Index, and wil be clearly understood by anyone familiar with our plan. A specialist wud in such cases probably adopt a contraction for his long number, and uze in ful only the minute divisions. . . .

Decimalism: Utility has not been sacrificed in order to force subjects on the 'decimal procrustean bed'. *Decimals hav been uzed as servants, not as masters.* When subjects ar combined or separated into just 10 heds, it has been from no necesity of the skeme, but becauz it seemd most useful, all things considerd. In many cases there wer orijinaly only 3 to 7 heds insted of 10; but uzualy, during years of testing before publication, it proved advizabl to divide sum of these heds, as it took no aded space or labor. On the other hand, there wer cases where more than 10 heds seemd more natural; and, as any number up to 100 is provided for by ading one decimal, this was dun in most cases. As only 1000 sections wer first printed, it was often necesary to put 2 or more closely allyd topics together under the same number, as must stil be dun whenever a library limits number of figures uzed to 3; but during 54 years use subdivisions hav multiplyd, til now nearly every topic has its own special number. The skeme givs us for each topic, as it wer, a case of 9 pijeonholes, with a larj space at the top; and we uze them as every practical business man uzes such pijenholes about his desk. If, as in 220, there ar les than 9 main topics, it is often convenient to uze the extra spaces for subdivisions. Thus we keep separate, under Old Testament, historic, poetic, and profetic books; and under New Testament, the Gospels, Epistls and Apocalips. Spaces ar there, and it is convenient to uze them for jeneral works on those groups—a reason that experience proves a good anser to the charj of lak of coordination, tho indention and typ in Tables make that charj baseless. Then in 280, having more than 9 topics, if we ar uzing only 3 figures we put Congregational in same space with Presby-

terian, and small denominations together in the last box, just as a business man puts his papers in his pijeonholes. If he insisted on having a different case made to order for each use, it wud cost over twice as much; he cud not group them together or interchanje them, and they wud not fit offis shelvs.

There has been perverse misapprehension of this feature, and critics oftenest stumbl over 'procrustean 10'. In fact, this is an element of usefulness. A railroad also has the fault that it is procrustean in its path and in its times. It can not cum to yur door nor wait yur convenience, as does the automobile; it can not go to the fields for its loads of produce; it can not turn out for obstacles; but *becauz it is procrustean* it can do its larj-scale work much better and quicker and cheaper. The paralel cud be fairly extended to many other cases, but any tho'tful mind wil recognize that the economy and eaz of working the Decimal sistem ar larjly dependent on its being procrustean. To this we owe much of the great simplicity of the Relativ Index, many nemonic correspondences, and the useful 0 to indicate form and period divisions. Our intersecting lines of space and time in History, etc., of languaj and form in Filolojy and Literature, and scores of similar advantajes, depend wholy on 'procrustean 10', or else on sum other number equaly procrustean, but lacking the advantajes of exact correspondence to our arithmetic.

Classification as an Indexing Device

Jack Mills

> *"The first Aslib-Cranfield Project seemed to indicate that arrangement (a vital feature of classification "systems") is relatively unimportant compared with the number and specificity of the individual classes established. But whilst it is true that class definition is the crux of indexing, it should be recognized that the establishment of classes and the subsequent arrangement of these classes is a continuum: Arrangement is simply one way of facilitating the adjustment of the size and nature of the classes to be recognized."*

A major theme of the Dorking Conference was the problem of making classifications for pre-coordinate classified indexes. This theme had four major strands: The Conference considered methods of arriving at class descriptions for documents; of systematically arranging these descriptions in a single sequence in a pre-coordinate index; of providing for retrieval (mainly via the A/Z index) of the "distributed relatives" implied by strictly limiting the number of entries in the classified file; and of providing a code or notation for the rapid locating of particular classes, once their position in the sequence had been determined.

The evidence of the Aslib-Cranfield Project, which commenced soon after Dorking, suggested strongly that differences between "systems" as such were relatively unimportant compared with the size of vocabulary and with error and inconsistency on the part of the indexers and searchers. In the test, four different systems performed at much the same level and this suggested that what determined retrieval was the nature of the classes recognized by a system, rather than its file arrangement[1]–i.e., the way they were linked together by the system (the second and third problem above).

Theoretically, we can distinguish clearly between the act of deriving or defining classes and the act of arranging these. Failure to make this distinction underlies the failure to recognize how similar may be quite differently arranged systems (e.g., a classified index and an alphabetical subject catalog) so far as the classes recognized in the indexing are concerned.

But in fact these two actions form a continuum; arrangement is simply one way of facilitating the adjustment of the size and nature of classes to be recognized, and it is this operation which is crucial.

The essence of indexing for information retrieval is the assignment of the information "quanta" in the store to classes, variously described: requests for information are then couched in terms of these classes and search is made in those classes which have the greatest probability (according to the rules for prediction implied by the choice of descriptions) of containing the relevant documents. If the result of the first search fails to satisfy (by providing either too much or too little) different classes are then examined—either smaller classes included in the ones already examined, or larger ones which include the first, or simply classes associated in some way with the first. The function of arrangement is to provide an order which is helpful in indicating further connections and so enabling the class definitions to be varied and adjusted.

A class definition may consist of one term or several terms standing in particular relations to each other. Adjustment of a definition in order to meet search requirements may be made by expanding it or by narrowing it. In searching, if we assume that the index language allows it, adjustment is made in two ways.

Firstly, by moving up or down the one or more hierarchies in which each term stands, e.g., in an Aerodynamics collection, from Cone to Body of revolution, or *vice-versa*. Or, from Jet stream to Flow elements (which includes vortices, waves, etc.) *and* to Winds, under Atmospheric phenom-

SOURCE: Reprinted from the International Study Conference on Classification Research, Elsinore, Denmark, 1964, *Proceedings* (Copenhagen: Munksgaard for FID/CR Committee on Classification Research, 1965), pp. 428-441, by permission of the author and the publisher.

ena (which includes gusts, air currents, etc.). The most drastic expansion of a term possible is to disregard its hierarchy entirely, which is tantamount to accepting the whole category implied by the term. If Cone and its hierarchy is dropped from a search prescription this means that any shape will be accepted—or no shape at all. At this point, reduction in specificity (the hierarchical level at which a concept is recognized) becomes the same thing as a reduction in exhaustivity—i.e., the concept is simply not recognized. A useful penultimate stage here is to accept the name of the category itself as a comprehensive class covering the category as a whole, but nothing more—e.g., Shapes or Flow elements.

Secondly, by adjusting the relations between the terms. This may take the form of inserting an explicit relation, where none was given—i.e., a "role" (or its "relational operator" equivalent) is inserted; or, a further category may be introduced—i.e., a further term is coordinated with an existing one. This constitutes an adjustment of relation in that, by implication, the absence of a specified relation is equivalent to the acceptance of all unstated relations; e.g., to omit a specification of flow velocity from an index description in aerodynamics would imply that *any* speed would be accepted. To now demand coordination with Supersonic, say, would restrict the relation. The addition of terms from other categories like this is analogous to moving down a hierarchy; e.g., moving from Grain to Storage of grain constitutes a pseudo-hierarchy and is analogous to moving from Grain to Wheat. It may be noted that a chain includes both hierarchical and pseudo-hierarchical sequences. Both these last two moves would narrow the class. But acceptance of other categories in a logical sum relation would widen it; this is seen in the confounding of word forms—e.g., Magnesium alloys $\times$ (Heating + Heated + Heat) where the metal may be associated with the process, the condition, or the property.

Facilities for expanding and contracting classes in search programmes as indicated above depend on specificity in indexing. If Arc welding has not been recognized specifically in the index language we cannot refine the class Welding in order to examine Arc welding alone. Specificity here includes the use of roles; e.g., if, when indexing the subject "The value of sugar beet tops as fertilizer," we do not distinguish the beet as an *agent* (and not a patient, or thing acted on) a later search cannot be refined to exclude documents on fertilizer *for* sugar beet.

The Aslib-Cranfield Project is at present investi-

gating the devices by which an index language can control class definition. These devices are surprisingly few in the final analysis. They fall fairly obviously into two groups: firstly, *recall devices*—those which, applied to any existing class, increase the size of the class in terms of the documents responding to the definition; e.g., if the class Bakelite is expanded by hierarchical linkage to include all Phenolic resins more documents are retrieved; secondly, *relevance devices*—those which, applied to any existing class, decrease its size; e.g., if we coordinate Bakelite with Extrusion we exclude those documents on Bakelite which do not refer specifically to this operation.

To the recall devices referred to above (hierarchical linkage, and confounding word forms) may be added the confounding of synonyms or near synonyms (in which, for the purposes of the document collection concerned, there is a mutual inclusion relation, *e.g.*, Hovercraft includes Ground Effect Machines and Ground Effect Machine includes Hovercraft). Generally speaking, the use of a hierarchy as a device implies the use of synonym control—i.e., a particular concept, however it is referred to in the natural language, should end up in the particular class it represents; but in a postcoordinate system care is needed to recognize those synonyms which emerge only after coordination—and an element of pre-coordination (in classification schedules, or thesaurus, etc.) is necessary for this; e.g., a Ground effect vehicle is a synonym for Air cushion machine, although there is no synonymity between the individual constituent terms.

To the relevance devices referred to above—role indicators and coordination (and, in searching, descent in a hierarchy)—may be added two more important devices, the need for which is generally associated with exhaustive indexing. These are firstly, links or interfixing. At the most generalized level this is the need to mark off clearly the different themes of a document, when the index description of a document ceases to be simply an integrated statement of the document's single general theme (which implies a relation of logical product between all constituent terms) and includes description of subsidiary themes (which collectively are related to the general theme as a logical sum); e.g., abcde + bfgh + cdij, where abcde is the general theme of the paper and bfgh and cdij are subsidiary themes.

Secondly, the weighting of the concepts in the indexing description according to their relative importance in the document concerned. When searching, this device allows a sort of figure of merit to be attached to the documents which match the search prescription and this is obviously very useful in a situation of high recall. According to his needs, whether they are for everything on the subject or simply a selection, the searcher will accept a wide range of weights or only the highest.

This attempt to go beyond systems as such in order to evaluate the contribution of indexing performance (as measured by recall and relevance ratios) made by the individual weapons in the indexer's armoury has led to certain difficulties in deciding the exact scope of classification as an indexing instrument; this paper discusses some possible ways of measuring its contribution and some implications this may have for our view of classification in information retrieval.

The first obvious lesson drawn from an attempt to isolate the constituent devices which go to make up our "systems" is that the latter really are different aggregates or syntheses of the same few devices. It is only the mixture which varies.

The second is that some systems are richer in their armory than others, i.e., it is not simply a question of different balances being struck and of all systems arriving at the same set of classes by different routes but of some systems having an absolute superiority in range in that they utilize all the devices open to some other system *plus* a few more. For example, some post-coordinate systems have no interfixing or links, no roles, and very little hierarchy in that the system provides only poor facilities for hierarchical expansion or contraction of classes; this may be the result of lack of specificity in its vocabulary, a method of posting (i.e., relating index descriptions to document addresses) which makes hierarchical searching difficult, or a degree of selectivity in those hierarchical relations it *does* recognize which seriously impairs this device (as in many thesauri and subject heading lists).

Thirdly, that the classified index, observing specific entry, whether using a conventional system like UDC, mixing enumeration and synthesis, or a completely faceted one, is the richest system we know, in that it uses every known device for establishing classes except bibliographical coupling and statistical association. Even the latter is observed after a fashion in that the establishment of particular categories or facets within a larger class, or the recognition of "phase relations" reflects directly those useful associations which have been established in the literature.

But "classification" in this sense of a highly organized *system* cannot be measured as a *device* at the same level as coordination, weighting, etc. Many of the classes established in a conventional classified index are the result of simple coordination and as such retrieve much the same material as their equivalent class arrived at by post-coordination—only their arrangement is different. Similarly, one term qualified by another term drawn from an Agents facet (e.g., Fertilizers—*use of* Beet Tops) constitutes the same class as that produced by two terms coordinated, with a role indicator introducing one of them.

In traditional library classification it is well established that any relationship may be used to establish subclasses of a given class. In the sense that library classification deals with classes of documents, and that documents on any aspect whatsoever of a subject x can be regarded as belonging to some subclass of "Documents on x," then Extrusion of plastics is just as much a subclass of Plastics as Bakelite.

But recognition of this is of little or no use until the further step is taken of organizing these subclasses according to their particular relations, in terms of subject content, to the class x.

Historically, two major stages can be observed in presenting such an organization of subclasses. Examples of the first stage can be found in UDC, e.g.:

533.6	Aerodynamics
533.69	Aircraft elements, Aerofoils
533.692	Wing sections (diamond, wedge, etc.)
533.693	Complete wings, Planforms
533.694	High-lift devices. Controls
533.695	Interference between parts
533.696	Bodies, spheres, cylinders, etc.
533.697	Internal aerodynamics: intakes, nozzles, etc.

This is a fairly indiscriminate mixture, combining subclasses in the strict sense of kinds of a thing (e.g., a wedge wing is a kind of aerofoil) and subclasses in the looser sense covering the products of coordination with other categories (what Ranganathan has called lamination) e.g., Interference is a flow process. Nozzle is a mechanical device associated with a particular boundary condition, and so on.

In faceted classification (the second major stage) these other relationships are systematized so that all terms standing in the same relation to the original class are marshalled together to constitute a category or facet of that class; so all the Properties of whatever concept comprises the original class are assembled together, all the Operations, all the Agents of those Operations, and so on. So far as they lend themselves to the process, the members within each category are organized in a hierarchy and their relationship within the category is one of a thing and its kinds—kinds of properties of x, kinds of operations on x, kinds of agents of the operations on x. Hierarchical linkage is established between the terms of a category, not between individual terms from different categories or between the terms of a category and the original class. In collections on Aeronautics or Plastics, for example, such individual subclasses as Blunt body heat transfer or Extrusion of Bakelite may occur equally as subclasses in a classified index, as subject headings in an alphabetical subject catalogue, or as the product of coordination in any post-cocodinate system. The distinctive contribution of the modern classified index, however, is that it establishes and displays comprehensively and systematically connections between these classes at two fundamental levels. Firstly, it gathers together all these subclasses into categories, so that Extrusion appears as one member of the Operation facet under Plastics, or Aerodynamic heating, for example, appears as a member of a category of Thermodynamic processes under Fluid dynamics; secondly, it organizes the terms within each category into hierarchies, as when Heat transfer is regarded as one of a number of thermodynamic processes, and Cooling as a species of Heat transfer processes and Ablation cooling as a species of Cooling. At both levels, the classified index contrasts with other systems, such as thesauri and subject heading lists, which indicate only a selection (often very restricted) of the connections which exist between a class and its categories, and between the different terms within a category.

For purposes of measurement, these two processes (of subordinating to a class the categories relating to it, and within these categories, establishing hierarchical relations) must be clearly distinguished. The effect on recall and relevance of moving from Plastics to Extrusion of plastics, or vice-versa cannot be attributed to hierarchical linkage—it is simple coordination. But as soon as we pursue the hierarchical relations of one term, and fill out each step or level by including terms coordinate with each other we produce a comprehensive category whereby the full scope of the particular relationship is displayed (i.e., the full range of Operations on plastics is now seen)—and these different operations are displayed systematically in hierarchical form.

Although such terms as "hierarchical classification" and "generic search" (to say nothing of "specific") are well established, their exact con-

notation is open to dispute. It was pointed out above that the association of a class such as Lift on a delta wing with Delta wing, or of Storage of cereals with Cereals, although not a hierarchical one, nevertheless might lead to a helpful arrangement because it reflects, at one remove, so to speak, the relation of a thing to its kind. That is to say, it is obviously useful on some occasions to recognize the first as one member of a category of Kinds of aerodynamic load on delta wing, or the second as one of a category of Operations in cereal husbandry. The helpfulness is not a reflection of some vague associative factor (fluctuating in value from one collection to another) between Lift and Delta wing, or between Storage and Cereal, but in the relatively precise, ubiquitous and fundamental relation of a thing and its kinds.

In traditional logical division, this relation has been equated with that of genus/species in its logical (i.e., in its nonbiological) sense. It is sometimes argued that this relation (genus/species) holds only in those cases where the differentiating characteristics are intrinsic, permanent or "fundamental," reflecting the old Aristotelian distinction between difference, property and accident. So turbulent and laminar flow are true species of flow, as are Subsonic, Supersonic, etc. (since they reflect the important compressibility effects attaching to flow). But flow characteristics determined by body shape (conical flow, wedge flow, cylindrical flow, etc.) are doubtfully so.

In taxonomy, distinguishing characteristics which are applied successively often have an irreversible order of application, each successive difference or complex of differences implying the preceding ones; this produces such well-known hierarchies as Vertebrate—Mammal—Rodent—Rabbit, etc. In library classification literary warrant demands recognition of multiple characteristics which do not enjoy this invariable citation order, e.g., it is equally logical in some contexts to think of Aircraft—Passenger—Supersonic or Aircraft—Supersonic—Passenger, although the distinction by speed is far more significant aerodynamically speaking.

Although such distinction (between more or less "fundamental" characteristics) may be significant when deciding citation order, or in choosing between common and differential facets when designing a classification, they do not affect the underlying argument for treating the use of the general relation of Thing/Kind itself as a fundamental indexing device, whatever principle is used to characterize these kinds.

The importance of hierarchical linkage is that it provides an automatic relevance network based on the inclusion relation. It does not require mathematical techniques to disclose the fact that separated boundary layer flow is a kind of boundary layer flow and that documents on the latter are likely to have *some* degree of relevance (possibly a high one) to questions on the former.

There is a similar automatic connection reflected in the Whole/Part relation and this is often regarded as hierarchical. It may be noted that in the alphabetical subject catalogue, which seeks *direct* entry by ignoring implied "class" terms as leading terms, both Thing/Kind and Whole/Part relations are vetoed in subject heading construction as constituting entry under a more general head, e.g., Wheat (*not* Cereals–Wheat), or Wing (not Aircraft–Wing). But other relations are allowed, e.g., Cereals–Storage.

Measuring the performance of hierarchical linkage: The central function of classification in its narrow sense of hierarchical linkage is that it provides a clear and helpful mechanism for expanding (and contracting) classes according to a fundamental relation–that of a thing and its kinds. How helpful this adjustment is in a given situation can only be assessed by determining the degree to which the expansion of a class (effected by examining the containing classes at different hierarchical levels) increases recall and decreases relevance.

This assumes, of course, a test collection and a set of questions to be put to it, where it is known just what documents are relevant to each question. Such a test situation is described elsewhere.

The simplest situation is demonstrated by the following example:

a	Experimental wind tunnel methods for investigating flow
ab	Visualization methods
aba	Using smoke, vapours, etc. (3)
abaa	Vapour screen (1)
abab	Fog (1)
abac	Wood smoke (1)
abad	Oil smoke (1)
abb	Using coatings, flows, etc. (3)
abba	Oil flow (1)
abbb	Oil film (1)
abbc	China clay (1)
abbd	Phosphorescent lacques (1)
abbe	Ink flow (1)
abc	Using spectrum (3)
abca	X-ray spectrography (1)
abd	Using Stroboscope (3)
abe	Using photography. Photorecording (3)
abea	Drum camera (1)
abeb	Photomultiplier (1)

abec	Television (1)
abed	Motion picture (2)
abeda	High speed (1)
abee	Schlieren (2)
abeea	Spark (1)
abeeb	Photomultiplier (1)
abef	Interferometry (2)
abefa	Fringe shift (1)
abefb	Interferential strioscopy (1)
	etc.

The full hierarchy provides twenty-eight classes.

The first reduction, replacing the terms marked (1) by a *see* reference to their immediate containing head (e.g. Drum camera *see* Photography) leaves ten classes.

The second reduction, similarly replacing terms marked (2), which now include those originally marked (1), by *see* references to their containing heads, leaves seven classes.

The third reduction similarly replacing terms marked (3), leaves two classes.

In this way figures are obtainable to show the exact effect of moving, say, from the quite specific class Interferential strioscopy to Interferometry in general, then to Photographic methods in general and then to Visualization methods in general, and so on.

It will be noted that by the second reduction there is no separate class left for Schlieren photography, whilst a distinct class is retained for Stroboscope. Yet in this subject field Schlieren photography is a decidedly more important class than stroboscopic. This suggests that reduction by pure hierarchical criteria may be unsatisfactory. When we reflect that the choice of terms within categories and the choice of the categories themselves is ultimately a matter of literary warrant it is reasonable to assume that reduction of classes hierarchically should not be a rigid process, but should take note of the weight of literature in the different classes so that Schlieren photography, for example, might be retained although all other subclasses at that level were removed and incorporated in the containing class.

The above example stresses the primary function of hierarchy as a recall device whereby the index vocabulary is systematically reduced and the scope of each remaining class is consequently widened (hence the greater recall). In practice, however, by varying search programmes, hierarchical linkage allows movement in both directions–to greater relevance by refining class definition or to greater recall by coarsening class definition. If specific indexing is assumed (i.e., each document, or document-theme, is assigned to its most specific class), a search may be made in a number of different directions through the hierarchy. For example, a searcher commencing at x may find the amount of material there unexpectedly excessive and so decide to search a narrower class. This may be done, of course, independently of hierarchy, by adding a qualifier or two (e.g., moving from Photorecording to Photorecording in high speed wind tunnels). But it may also be done by moving down the hierarchy (e.g., to Schlieren tests).

Such a decision implies that the links established by the hierarchy are permissive, not obligatory, and that the searcher selects from a comprehensive hierarchy just those routes he considers likely to be fruitful. It is not certain whether figures produced for a number of such searches would be useful in the sense of allowing firm generalizations to be drawn since much will depend on the subject field (and on the choice of pathways in searches 4 and 5). But the following illustrates the basic routes which might be followed (in the following a, aa, etc. are terms in hierarchical relation):

```
a
aa
   aaa
   etc.
ab
   aba
   abb
   abc
   etc.
ac
ad
```

If a request is made for ab the following programmes might be followed:

1. Terms and species–i.e. ab + aba, abb . . . abz.

2. Superordinate–i.e., ab + a (but excluding other subclasses of a; this is how 'generic' search is popularly interpreted in general library practice where a might represent a general treatise on the subject of which ab is a subclass).

3. Generic–i.e., a + aa + aaa, aab . . . aaz + ab + aba, abb . . . abz + ac + aca, abc . . . acz + aza, azb . . . azz (this is how 'generic' search is normally interpreted in machine systems and is analogous to search (1) where the content of class ab is taken to include the individually specified subclasses aba, abb, ace . . .).

4. Coordinate–i.e., a selection of the more likely classes coordinate with ab–say, ab + aa + ad; e.g., in a category of three dimensional shapes a search for spheroid can be extended generically by searching under Body of Revolution, or by examining all the different kinds of Body of Revolution (Sphere, Hemisphere, Ogive, Cone, etc.). But some of the latter will be more closely connected to spheroid

than others (e.g., Sphere) and an intermediate search, stopping well short of examing *every* species can be made. It is true, of course, that a 'closer connection' between several subclasses implies the possibility of an intermediate step of division being inserted. But we have to stop somewhere.

5. Subordinate–i.e., a selection of the more likely subclasses of ab–abb + abn, say.

A category may contain several hierarchies (constituting subfacets, or arrays as Ranganathan calls them); e.g., Wing may be characterized by shape (to give delta wing, etc.) by dimension (to give Thin wing, etc.) and so on. A request for material on a Thin delta wing, implies in a precoordinate index the subordination of one characteristic to the other i.e.

either	*or*
Wing	Wing
Delta	Thin
Thin	Delta

Without this subordination (with its analogue in post-coordinate system, of couse, of the logical product of Thin and Delta and Wing), complete specificity in searching would be impossible. Clearly, the precise effect on recall and relevance will differ according to what citation order is used (although the first and last steps–Thin delta wing and Wing will be constant), and it is possible that the figures for this, when correlated with term frequency counts, might give some assistance in determining citation orders. But despite the work done in the last decade or so on the problem of citation order it should be remembered that its importance is bound up to a large extent with the assumption that a precoordinate classified index provides one entry only for a document or document-theme and that "distributed relatives" are retrieved via the A/Z subject index. This method is now generally recognized to be very restrictive, and it is to be tolerated only on grounds of economy (in a large printed bibliography, for example).

If the central claim of post-coordinate systems is that they allow equally direct access from any term within a compound subject description, then pre-coordinate systems should try to meet the challenge by minimizing the occurrence of the distributed relative by the adoption as far as possible of multiple entry (i.e., entry under Wing-Delta-Thin and Wing-Thin-Delta). However, multiple-entry can rarely be pursued indefinitely, and so citation order remains a serious problem in discussions on classification systems.

It has already been noted that hierarchical relations exist within a category and not between one category and another. This theoretical point must be strictly observed in measuring hierarchical performance. For example, in UDC we find the following:

533.6.071	Wind tunnels
533.6.071.1	Construction, Working Section, Vanes, etc.
533.6.071.2	Walls
533.6.071.3	Apparatus
533.6.071.31	Visualization methods

It would appear reasonable from the above to move from Visualization methods to Wind tunnels as the ultimate containing class—and indeed it is reasonable. But Visualization methods as a class does not constitute a kind of wind tunnel, its highest containing class in this context would be Wind tunnel test methods. To move from Visualization methods in wind tunnels to Wind tunnels is a reduction in exhaustivity, not in specificity. From the point of view of hierarchy as a principle for reducing vocabulary this has one minor but useful implication in the making of schedules, which is that the index language should at least provide for the naming of each category *per se*. For example, in a very restricted classification of aeronautics a distinction should at least be drawn between a class Wind tunnel, its physical *parts*, and the *operations* associated with it. If no specific class were recognized for Visualization methods, the broader containing class Wind tunnel test methods would at least exclude material not relating to *methods*—the relevance ratio should be higher than if search were now made under *everything* appertaining to wind tunnel. Similarly, in the same restricted classification, even if Delta wing or Thin wing specifically were not recognized (given a discrete class each) recognition might be made of Wing *planforms*, and Wing *dimensions* as being a more accurate containing class than Wing in general.

However, although it is necessary, for purposes of measuring discrete indexing devices, to distinguish hierarchical relations in this way, it is also necessary to see what further vocabulary reduction is possible by interpreting "classification" in the wider sense implied by the example above from UDC, where classes from numerous different categories stand directly under a containing head. This implies a further measurement; having measured the effect of moving, say, from a specific kind of Visualization test (e.g., Interferometry) right up to Wind tunnel test methods in general, the class Wind tunnel is now expanded to include the total contents of each of its categories in turn. Now, a search for, say, Visualization methods draws in everything on Wind tunnels.

Another problem in expanding a class hierarchically is caused by the different contexts in which the same term might occur. For example, in an aerodynamics collection the term Dust appears in at least two quite distinct hierarchies; under Ground effect phenomena it constitutes one of a class of soil or surface constituents, along with loose gravel, sand, etc. which have particular effect on, and are affected by, airjets or streams near to the ground, (as from a helicopter or a ground effect machine). Under Roughness elements it constitutes one of a class of quite different elements, including surface protuberances, pimples, insects, and so on which disturbs the smooth flow over an aerofoil. If Dust were considered solely as a member of one hierarchy (e.g., of soil elements) its relations in the second hierarchy would be quite obscured, and any recall/relevance figure based on moving up the former hierarchy for a request on dust as a roughness element would be very misleading.

This implies that multiple hierarchical links shall be taken into account when assessing the improved recall obtained by hierarchy. A further implication is that it would be most unwise, in a post-coordinate system, to assume that the programming of a generic search can be done by treating each term in isolation and assuming one set of hierarchical relations is sufficient. *All* the hierarchies to which a term belongs must be considered.

This situation is also relevant to the question of common *versus* differential facets. The tendency to push analysis further and further towards the former is one of the features distinguishing modern faceted classification from the older semi-enumerative classification, in which the same term might find itself enumerated anew in many different contexts. The dangers of both processes should be recognized. The function of hierarchy in a category or facet is to allow the controlled expansion of class definitions. If the class mates drawn in by this expansion prove too remote by virtue of the comprehensiveness ('commonness') of the category the relevance ratio is likely to suffer seriously.

NOTE

[1] C. W. Cleverdon and J. Mills, "The testing of index language devices," *Aslib Proc.*, 3:4, April 1963, pp. 106-130.

The Future of Generalized Systems of Classification

Phyllis A. Richmond

"The future of generalized classification depends in large part upon man's ingenuity. So far there has been no limit to the capabilities of the human mind, and there seems, therefore, to be no justification for the view that classification as a way of organizing knowledge is dead . . . ."

It is fashionable at present to dismiss the future development of *generalized* classification as if there could be no such thing—as if no synthesis were ever possible again because no one can see any unifying factor or factors in the proliferation of subjects with which we have to deal. This is equivalent to saying that the sky is less blue because the blind man does not see it. There will be new generalized classification systems in the future for the simple reason that we have to have them. And anything we have to have sooner or later is found.

George Gaylord Simpson, the vertebrate paleontologist, points out that classification in zoology has proceeded alternately by stages of analysis and synthesis, carried out by men who might be categorized as "lumpers" and "splitters."[1] In library classification, by analogy, the older systematizers, Dewey, Bliss and others, would be "lumpers." Those who make faceted classifications and special subject analysis systems of all kinds are "splitters." When the "splitters" have finished analyzing the new alignment of parts that make up the sum total of human knowledge—an analysis which must be performed if we are to make any use at all of the mechanical and electronic aids now available to us—there is no reason to believe that a new synthesis cannot or will not be made. It is historically true that the impasse of one age is solved in the next, or the one after the next. The only fault, a very human one present in every generation, is that impatient men grow hopeless or even antagonistic because they cannot see the solution in their own lifetimes.

In classification, as in any other discipline, one must lay groundwork for future development. Even if it is possible to be clairvoyant to the extent of predicting correctly what form future development must take, it is still necessary to take steps to get there. An Einstein, for instance, will hit upon "some great unifying idea from which one can deduce consequences that can ultimately be bought into agreement . . . with observed and measurable phenomena."[2] But even an Einstein does not build on nothing. He takes account of all the abortive, inconclusive, tentative, incomplete, or even rejected solutions of his predecessors. Thus fortified with knowledge of the major blind alleys, at least, he can lay out his course. It is the duty of those now working in classification to discover and explore all possible approaches so that valuable negative as well as positive evidence will be available for the ultimate synthesizer.

This is not to say that all current work in classification will be fruitless or that things will necessarily proceed so slowly that a synthesis is impossible before the end of the century. It is to say that avenues not yet considered must be explored and that work already begun must be carried much further. Ideas, no matter how bizarre, deserve consideration, because, with any research, we never know exactly where we are heading. Nor do we know which line of development will bear the ultimate prize.

Essentially classification is the process of taking identifiable entities and relating them in one way or another to each other. These items may be anything the mind distinguishes as an entity in itself. Since the mind is rather free in coalescing raw material of all types into entities, this means that anything "thinkable" is classifiable.

Past syntheses almost exclusively have been constructed in a dendritic pattern—an inverted tree—from general to specific. The tree has been delineated as a plane figure and treated as if division were the only method of construction. Many of

SOURCE: Reprinted from *College and Research Libraries*, 24 (September, 1963), pp. 395-401, by permission of the publisher, the American Library Association.

the writers who look with horror upon classification as a tool for organizing knowledge see only this type of deductive system and identify all classification with it.

A different approach is to build new generalized classification systems from collections of particulars, gathered by observation, ordered by reasoned criteria, and formed by induction into generalities as an ascending scale. These generalities can then be tested through hypothesis and deduction, and finally conclusions derived from the process, which, when tested and verified by further observation, will provide a solid basis for a more accurate representation of the world in which we live. This is essentially the scientific method, defined in very simple terms. Note that the main classes which will result from such a process are not predicted or predictable in advance.

Such a system, however, does not present a perfect picture of knowledge because it, too, usually ends in a dendritic pattern, although sometimes the net results are expressed in chains or even in chains made up from intermediary matrix or lattice analysis patterns. Something vital has been left out. This is a study of the very nature of the material to be described. In the final analysis, it is this nature which will determine the system of classification. Any system which ignores actual makeup of individual subjects, with all their ramifications, is doomed from the start.

The universe we live in is apparently open and genuinely infinite, both infinitely big and infinitely small. Data, laws, methods, theories in all fields are partially and imperfectly known. On one hand, the possibility of discovery seems unending. On the other hand, the use of creative imagination appears limitless. While the idea of progress as a fundamental pervading force has been somewhat shaken as an accepted philosophic view in the last two decades, there is no corresponding diminution in either creativity or discovery, both of which are highly individualistic matters and probably not related to progress as an ideal.

It is the job of classification to show the waxing and waning of ideals as well as ideas, since the spirit of the times, its *Zeitgeist*, adds dimension to any aspect of the sum total of human knowledge. For reasons not entirely clear, this *Zeitgeist* has usually been ignored, especially in classification involving the sciences, medicine and technology, although it exists in these areas just as much as in the humanities. The totality of the intellectual atmosphere in each era determines to a large extent what shall be accomplished in that era. This totality, which is a dimension external to the individual, can be both narrow, representing the sum total of knowledge in a given field of research, or it can be broad, reflecting the generally held attitudes, motivation, philosophical outlook, mores, and such of a period of time.

There is also an internal factor which adds dimension to classification. This is the individual's own world outlook, his *Weltanschauung*, which affects his personal motivation, intuitive capacity, and imagination. This results from learning, influence of other people, inspiration, and experience. It is a process of accretion, that is to say, lifetime learning added up, and of inner maturation. The long process of growing up as a part of being alive is most noticeable in research in the humanities, where outstanding work is almost never done by young men.

The addition of further dimensions to the material to be classified greatly broadens the base of classification. The necessity for describing a body of knowledge with no known boundaries, which is the real work of classification, calls for a type of description which also can have no boundaries. In a discussion of the future of physics, Albert Einstein wrote:

> The belief in an external world independent of the perceiving subject is the basis of all natural science. Since, however, sense perception only gives information of this external world or of "physical reality" indirectly, we can only grasp the latter by speculative means. It follows from this that our notions of physical reality can never be final. We must always be ready to change these notions—that is to say, the axiomatic substructure of physics—in order to do justice to perceived facts in the most logically perfect way. Actually a glance at the development of physics shows that it has undergone far-reaching changes in the course of time.[3]

This is true of all subjects, and it is this truth that has made all classifications obsolete over a period of time. So far as generalized classification is concerned, we have not even discovered most of the main categories, to say nothing of the thousands of related categories which must exist. At best, our classifications are an approximation, and subject to constant revision as new information becomes available.

Does this mean that all classification is a waste of time, since it can never be finished? The answer is "yes" only if by classification we mean a process of assigning a fixed and relatively unalterable "address" to each categorical item. An ideal classification should be entirely flexible. Until all research and scholarly efforts cease, there will be no way of avoiding major alterations in subject organization, and, in fact, there should be no question of having anything but constant change. In making systems, provision for this change should be all the way through as required, not just at marginal spots where it will be the least upsetting. As the Indian classification theorist, Ranganathan, has ably put it:

> A classificatory language must be nimble enough to keep step with the field of knowledge. Its expectation of life is determined by the degree of its self-perpetuating quality, i.e., by the smallness of the dependence of the classifier on the classificationist [maker of the classification] to seize the correct class numbers of the new formations. The degree of its self-perpetuating quality is determined by the notational devices with which it is armed.[4]

In other words, the classification must be flexible enough to cope with unlimited additions to itself, and it must not be defeated by the notation used with it.

The notation used in a classification is an extremely important feature. Most notations are inadequate and actually strangle the classification system in the process of trying to reflect its internal structure. Something that will break this stranglehold and at the same time will broaden the class structure by freeing it from dependence upon limited criteria is a must for the future. It may even prove advisable to avoid notation in a classification or to use a random number system, with no effort to reflect the structure.

Classification is and must be a mirror of the intellectual as well as the external world it seeks to represent. If this combined world is a reality of four or five or more dimensions, the classification must have four or more dimensions, with some kind of spatial representation for visualization purposes.

Such a spatial representation is a *sine qua non* of adequate symbolic description of anything approaching reality. To use a letter-number string can be unwieldy as well as distorting. What this spatial representation should be—a fraction, lattice, or matrix in depth, or something better—cannot now be determined. The forms suggested seem too rigid. One needs a spatial "notation" that is more amorphous.

Such a spatial representation is needed for another reason. The human mind can cross subject boundary lines without much difficulty. Ideas in one field are applied or adapted to another with comparative ease. It is commonplace for new *area* studies to be set up in academic circles by drawing upon specialists from several fields to bring their different backgrounds to bear on a set of problems common to all of them. Thus we have new programs in space research, brain research, biomedical engineering, non-Western civilization and so on, all inter-departmental affairs. Old geographic divisions are replaced by new ones: Sub-Saharan Africa, Southwest Asia, Middle America. The late Robert C. Binkley, in teaching history, broke down the vertical stream of time applied to political-geographic regions (England since 1485) into horizontal units (all of Europe in December 1587). The next step logically is to realize that there is no reason for not treating space and time as a unit because that is exactly what they are.

Space time is a dimension common to everything. Even the apparent "here and now" of contemporary science has retrospective features. For example, scientists never cease to remind us that, so far as they are concerned, the printed announcement of new research is already out of date on the day it appears. This means that even as the announcement is read, it is describing something already in retrospect. This has significance—and not just in priority struggles. Even if a new generalized classification system is no more than an ephemeral conglomeration, it has to take into account the space-time factor.

Other dimensions are the *Zeitgeist* and *Weltanschauung* mentioned earlier. Just as no scholar or creative artist functions in a vacuum, so no output, be it a scientific discovery or a piece of poetry or a musical composition, comes from a void.[5] All of them have antecedents, and sooner or later most also have descendents. There are branches of scholarship which specialize in locating and studying connections and relationships among things which apparently have sprung up *de novo*. A classification which only describes a limited number of qualities pertaining to entities and which deliberately stultifies itself because it must fit into a preconceived code of very limited proportions has small chance of lasting. First a classification must be free to cross subject boundary lines as freely as our minds cross them. Then the notation, if there is one, must be so free that the classification can expand into infinity in any direction.

Another point to be considered in the future development of generalized classification, in addition to taking a clear look at the nature of the material to be classified and making a flexible system while freeing this system from dependence upon notation, is the need to be able to show *relationships* between elements of a classification system in a completely unhampered way. This is extremely difficult. Up to now, few classification schemes, no matter how well designed or modified, have been able to show area relationships or cross-connections between subjects which pertain to two or more fields simultaneously. The only solutions attempted have been to enter such things in each related spot as a recognition of each separate emphasis, or to lock the codes for the individual related topics together in a linear chain or a series of more or less connected chains.

In this respect, a system which can build its own class descriptions, as with Uniterms, has advantages. With present trends in research tending more and more to break down existing barriers between subjects, and the content of individual fields being realigned in consequence of this, the barriers between subjects, as classically outlined, are a positive menace. If growth continues to be nonlinear, in the mathematical sense,[6] and expansion continues in revised patterns, added freedom to cross boundaries in all directions is a vital necessity.

A further point is related to the preceding ones. In a classification, it is not only the basic categorical concept that is significant, but also the modification thereof. The multidimensional quality of knowledge is no less complex than the multidimensional descriptive possibilities for each individual item in a classification schedule. Even the descriptive terms themselves can be permuted to widen the scope of the system. A class is by nature an exclusive generalization. It is also inclusive, and in this respect covers considerable variety, according to its criteria. There are as many potential classification entities as there are terms applicable to the description of an element. A classification element, in turn, is only a temporary convenience, since it is potentially a class in itself, in the light of later knowledge. It may also be eliminated in the same light. A classification system, on the other hand, may never be fully described in the terse terms of a classification schedule. Actually, the traditional classification systems have been made by arbitrarily selecting some descriptive factors and deliberately ignoring the rest. Indexes to the systems pick up some of the alternatives, but only in a hit-or-miss fashion. The faceted classifications, by their very nature, attempt to allow for a multitude of possible descriptive factors.

In sorting out the multidescriptive possibilities for classification elements, the *criteria* of the classification system are important. In the past, these criteria have been unwritten as a rule; in fact, it appears that in most cases they have been intuitively assigned. Sometimes the intuition has been quite realistic, judging by the state of knowledge at the time the systems were made. The science sections in the Dewey Classification, for instance, with the emphasis on paleontology, fit American science in the later 19th century like a shoe. Unfortunately, the creature wearing the shoe turned out to be a millipede—a situation with which Dewey's successors were never able to cope. Ranganathan has departed from intuitive practices to the extent of trying to spell out the criteria for each class. Others are carrying the process farther, but as yet there is no general agreement on what these criteria should be or even on how they should be reached.[7]

The criteria of classification might serve as mental diffraction gratings. Something is needed to split concepts systematically the way such gratings work with rays of light or other rays. It would seem that current research on descriptor language[8] is a fine beginning, but only a beginning. The argumentative leap which produces a generalization from a collection of particulars must be made and its nature noted. No attempt to do this has come at all, perhaps because of lack of awareness among classification makers that such a leap exists. Those who work with machines may be more alert to this possibility.

The advent of the giant calculating machine has inspired documentalists to see if a use cannot be made of it to organize the tremendous body of knowledge which threatens to overwhelm us with the products of our own brains. Success both in the reduction of mathematical calculations and in handling huge masses of factual data in business has led to considerable experimentation with such machines for literature searching and information retrieval. Three features, among others, stand out as a net result of this endeavor.

First, those concerned with the organization of knowledge, in attempt to make use of the machines, have tended to pay more attention to the capability of the machine than to the needs of the person using the knowledge or of the internal makeup of the knowledge itself. Early meetings between "hardware" men and librarians were unproductive because the librarians asked "What can you do?" and the engineers said "What do you want done?" Neither side understood the answers given by the other. Machines with positive talent in searching certain kinds of data were designed, but their effort was negated by the erroneous assumption that input was a simple matter, suitable for untrained clerks. After a succession of failures, the realization dawned that input is the major key to successful output. Here again, there was no rapport between the "hardware" men and librarians, who could have predicted this result. A productive combination of vast experience with classification and subject analysis on one side and brilliant inventiveness of the other has not been realized because of lack of communication between the two groups. This gap has existed because there was no common frame of reference between the two until the "hardware" men tried out their systems and in the process made the same mistakes that the librarians had made fifty years ago. It is to the lasting shame of the catalog librarians that so few of them have made any attempt to mechanize the experienced approach which they alone possess.

The second feature is one that gives a false sense of capability to the machine. On the surface, finding a piece of factual data in a mass of other factual data appears not unlike finding a box of rotary switches in a warehouse full of electronic supplies. The joker here is that the warehouse is a selective situation, limited to a homogeneous collection of highly specialized items, and serving a small segment of the total buying public. If a collection of information has the equivalent qualities, homogeneity and limited access, then the machine solution to the problem of information retrieval looks pretty good. However, under such restricted circumstances, practically anything, including a hierarchical classification of the most rigid type, works well. The difficulty comes when the collection becomes heterogeneous.

Even given the same special situation, if the information to be retrieved is theoretical instead of factual—an idea, a line of thought, an argument for or against a point, a suggestion for future research—the machine falls even flatter on its transistorized face than the old classification. The classification at least has some way of indicating relationships and can give a hint to where to look for an answer. The machine is an all-or-nothing proposition.

The third factor is a temptation which came with the machine. The very success with mathematics, the relatively easy manner in which a computer can be programmed to deal with a formula, the facility with which symbolic logic can be handled, all suggested that the thing to do was to find a mathematical model, or a series of mathematical models, to express the essence of organization of knowledge. Fit the data to the model and the model to the machine and the problem of information retrieval was as good as solved. Unfortunately this was equivalent to putting the cart before the horse, as even the most elementary grasp of the scientific method should have warned. Quantification—the formula for the law, the shorthand for an accepted generalization—is usually the last step, not the first, in the whole process of organization. Even when one begins with a great unifying idea, subject to verification by later observation, quantification comes slowly. For information retrieval, the mathematical model, to be satisfactory, has to wait until answers are found to questions that have not yet been asked.

There are many questions to be asked and answered before new generalized classification systems of any stature can be expected. A few of the basic ones have been raised in this study: How do we represent a multidimensional reality, presuming such exists, on paper? How do we cross departmental lines in subject fields with a classification system the way the human mind crosses them? How do we show relationships between parts of a system in a completely unhampered way? How do we indicate the multidimensional descriptive possibilities for each individual item being classified? How do we orient our criteria for classification in such a way that concepts may be diffracted into elements in a systematic fashion? Should we dispense with notation altogether? If not, can we use something more graphic than a notation made up of letters and numbers? Is it possible to get better spatial perception into our classification systems? It would be convenient to replace the plane and linear by something with depth, perhaps analogous to proper motion and radial velocity in astronomy. Can we avoid the pitfall of adapting our classification systems to the capability of the computer instead of vice versa? Can we make a machine that will handle the infinite variety that composes the sum total of human knowledge? Will our final classification synthesis be capable of being represented by mathematical models?

The lines of development to be pursued in the future make it imperative that we also ask questions pertaining to methodology: Where can classification borrow ideas, techniques, and philosophic approaches from other disciplines? Do we have to stoop to some degree of fantasy in our classification composition before we can conquer with cold, hard facts? In other words, how much creative imagination can we put into a classification system without losing touch with reality? Is it possible that we have made a mistake in tending to view classification as a science rather than a art? Is some combination of the two, perhaps achieving the *rapprochement* between science and the humanities that has eluded us, the ultimate answer?

The future of generalized classification depends in large part upon man's ingenuity. So far, there has been no limit to the capabilities of the human mind, and there seems, therefore, to be no justi-fication for the view that classification as a way or organizing knowledge is dead merely because the philosophic approaches used so far have led to blind alleys. It is time to look for new approaches.

ACKNOWLEDGEMENT

The author is grateful to Mrs. Pauline Atherton, American Institute of Physics, and Gertrude Oellrich, Rutgers University, for reading and commenting upon this article in manuscript.

NOTES

[1] George Gaylord Simpson, "The Principles of Classification and a Classification of Mammals," *Bulletin of the American Museum of Natural History*. **LXXXV**: 22–24, October 1945.

[2] Morris R. Cohen, *American Thought, a Critical Sketch* (Glencoe, Illinois: Free Press, 1954), p. 81.

[3] Albert Einstein, *The World as I See It* (New York: Covici, Friede, 1934), p. 60.

[4] S. R. Ranganathan, "Self-Perpetuating Scheme of Classification," *Journal of Documentation*, **IV**: 240, March 1949.

[5] John Livingston Lowes, *The Road to Xanadu* (New York: Vintage Books, 1959) is an interesting example.

[6] Ladis D. Kovach, "Life Can Be So Nonlinear," *American Scientist*, **XLVIII**: 218–25, June 1960.

[7] For a summary of the work of the English Classification Research Group, see D. J. Foskett, "The Classification Research Group, 1952–1962," *Libri*, **XII**: 127–38, 1962.

[8] B. C. Vickery, *On Retrieval System Theory* (London: Butterworths, 1961), pp. 23–55.

Modern Classification Theory

Ann F. Painter

*"Classification schemes fall into two major groups depending upon their purpose:
1) traditional, deductive, systematic, hierarchical classification, and 2) nontraditional,
inductive, syndetic classification. All classification theory is modern in a sense being
a child of the twentieth century at least in relation to bibliographic materials."*

There are many different groups of people today who are quite concerned about the state of health of classification. First of all the practitioner involved with the acquisition, arrangement, maintenance and retrieval of an ever increasing volume and complexity of materials and information. Secondly, the planner, or perhaps better named the theoretician, who is immediately involved with the problems not necessarily tied to the actual operating system. Classification theory to each of these groups has a distinct and important meaning. There is the general feeling among both camps to reject classification as something which has served its purpose in the past but has become obsolete and has little to offer for the solution of current problems. This attitude seems a little extreme and is not supported by evidence either actual or experimental in the area of classification theory.

In a sense all classification theory is modern being a child of the twentieth century at least in relation to bibliographic materials, and most classification still concerns itself with the bibliographic unit. One of the difficulties in dealing with modern classification theory is that it is in a transitory period in which the traditional classifications and their principles are the ones with which we are operating primarily and only just now beginning to analyze and understand as opposed to the newer classifications which are still developing and hence their theories have not yet jelled. Experimentally it is moving toward concept classification. This is what makes classification theory such a fertile ground for research and development and an exciting challenging field for librarian and information scientist.

This paper cannot hope to provide an in-depth study of classification theory. Its intent is rather to explore, based on a personal definition of classification, some of the theory on which the traditional and transitory schemes are founded; and, to indicate through some description of current research the directions of future theory. There will be no attempt to describe the individual natures of existing schemes or their applications, but rather to illustrate the principles on which they operate.

As I have indicated the base of this discussion will be a rather personalized definition of classification. There are almost as many definitions as there are classificationists. The definitions themselves provide a ready access to the theories expounded.

One of the more traditional definitions of classification is expressed by Sayers in his *Manual of Classification:*[1] Classification of libraries is the arrangement of books on shelves or the systematic arrangement of catalogues and similar tools in the manner which is most useful to those who read. It is that exercise of powers of perception and reason which enables us to assemble things in order of likeness and separate according to order of unlikeness. Phyllis Richmond, whose paper is above, in a recent conference in discussing classification research, broadens the definition: classification (as an activity) consists of methods for analysis, description, and organization of the information content of documents. A class is a group of persons, things, qualities, ideas having common characteristics and capable of being recognized as an entity or concept. A classification system is a structural arrangement of classes in some helpful order, with relationships between classes clearly defined or delineated. The structure may be in Euclidean or hyperspace, and in the form of hierarchy, lattice, trees, maze, a net, or any other kind of ordered system.

Ranganathan refers to analysis, description, and organization as the "idea plane, the verbal plane,

SOURCE: Reprinted from the Preconference on Subject Analysis of Materials and Information, Atlantic City, N.J., 1969, *Proceedings* (New York: Columbia University, School of Library Service, 1971?), by permission of the publisher.

and the notational plane."[2] Classification is "the uncovering of the thought content of a written or expressed unit of thought. A method by which a written or expressed unit of thought is exhaustively analyzed in terms of entirety rather than in terms of parts."[3] A. P. Srivastava points out that there are two kinds of classification, natural (one that exhibits inherent properties of things classified and depends on homology and likeness resides in the structure and function of the entities classified) and artificial (based on analogy and external likeness).[4]

Jesse Shera in 1959 in an institute at the University of Illinois quotes as one of the best, somewhat modified, the definition of William Randall. "A list of terms which are specifically different from each other, used to describe subject content of graphic records, inclusive of all knowledge defined by the limits of the scheme, infinitely hospitable with regard to significant differences among the concepts, with an arrangement that is linear, unique and meaningful to the user, and which, when applied to graphic records, results in the arrangement of the record themselves."[5] One of the best essays on classification theory appears in John R. Sharp's *Some Fundamentals of Information Retrieval*. He provides the following definition: "Classification in the sense in which it is used in logic is nearer to the idea of definition or description. . . . It is probable that classification principles can be useful for the purpose of subject designation and we might well consider this kind of classification as subject specification rather than classification. By specification we mean accurate, unambiguous and consistent designation of a subject without reference to its relative position in the scheme.[6]

And finally, two definitions have been supplied by two major gatherings of classification experts, one at Dorking, England 1957 and the other at Elsinore, Denmark 1964. The Dorking consensus contains many of the elements referred to in other definitions: "Traditional classification has been concerned with the construction of hierarchies of terms—chains of classes and coordinate arrays. Modern information retrieval techniques also necessitate the combination of terms to express complex subjects. . . . All intellectual organization is classification and that such things as alphabetical indexing or numerical arrays are species of classification."[7] Elsinore Conference defines classification: "By classification is meant any method creating relations, generic or other, between individual semantic units, regardless of the degree in

hierarchy contained in the systems, and of whether those systems would be applied in connection with traditional or more or less mechanized methods of document searching."[8]

Classification is thus often defined by what it does rather by what it is. Simply condensed, it is two things: 1) the act or process of arranging, and 2) the act or process of defining. Modern classification theory has developed out of these two and the transition between them and is essentially based on the principle of synthesis. If one were to select a theme for modern classification, I think there is little doubt that it is "Synthesis." The purpose of belaboring so many definitions has been to show these several variations and orientations as well as to pinpoint several of the major theories. In addition, assuming the role of the true librarian as a reader's advisor, these excerpts will lead the leader in classification into some of the best, concise discussion of classification theory.

Classification schemes and the theories on which they are based fall into two major groups depending upon their purpose: 1) traditional, deductive, systematic, hierarchical classification, and 2) nontraditional, inductive, syndetic classification. Into the first fall such schemes as Library of Congress, Dewey Decimal, Cutter Expansive and to a certain extent the Universal Decimal Classification and Bliss Bibliographic Classification. Into the second falls Universal Decimal, Ranganathan's Colon Classification, and the various faceted schemes developed by the British classificationists, and perhaps to some limited extent the Thesaural structures of modern indexing systems. The specific aspects of both traditional and nontraditional classifications which constitute the principal theories are: the idea of a universal and general classification, a set and predetermined order of classes, the scheme of order (hierarchy), the determination of classes, the internal order of classes, notation, and the hospitality or flexibility of classification.

Traditional classifications like DC and LC are concerned with the organization of all knowledge rather than a particular part. They thus acknowledge the idea of a universal, general classification as did many of their predecessors such as Aristotle, Plato, Brunet, Bacon, Harris, Cutter, Bliss, etc. The theory of the organization of this knowledge also assumes that there exists a universal order of nature, that the schematization of such order is hierarchical (genus-species, class-subclass, general-specific), that the principle of separation or categorization lies in likeness and unlikeness, and that these similarities and dissimilarities constitute the primary nature of the items classified.[9] The schemes which resulted were not for the most part used for book classification, this was a requisite superimposed by the bibliographers and librarians of the nineteenth century. The library schemes were thus based on the concept of one location for each bibliographic item.

The older ideas of book classification which are still manifested in DC, LC and Cutter owe a great deal to the principles of logicians. They generally start with knowledge in totality and describe each division exhaustively before going on to the next, hence the enumerative nature particularly of LC where everything is outlined in its proper place whenever it is needed regardless of duplication instead of providing auxiliary tables. Taube demonstrates several ways of determining classes:[10]

1. product of two classes
2. sum of two classes
3. inclusion of two classes

In library classifications there is a set of main classes with all subclasses included in only one main class and this principle is extended on down with each sub-subclass included in only one subclass.

Logic may be defined as the study of the validity of inference, a concern with the ways in which conclusions are drawn from premises. There are several kinds of logical relations between classes—inclusion, partial inclusion, exclusion, and coincidence. The last century has seen new logic based on mathematics, symbolic logic. It pursues the same objectives and introduces the idea of operations on classes. Such operations yield classes. The assertions of relations between classes are propositions and not classes. The relations between classes may be diagrammatically represented by Euler circles, the operations on classes by Venn diagrams.[11]

Despite the assumed "logic," class making and logical relations do not always provide a suitable foundation for classification. This is particularly evident in DC where the determination of classes or their order or both have little to do with logic. De Grolier at the Elsinore Conference points out that no one theory explains what is to be done and no conceptual framework is sufficiently sophisticated and comprehensive to be a base of classification practice. Logic can in many instances provide substantial guidelines for class de-

termination even though they are not universally applicable. Schemes developed on the basis of a set of main classes as shown by Taube have proven fairly effective for ordering and arranging bibliographic units which can physically be put in only one place. They also go far toward maintaining a very rigid hierarchy moving from general to specific following a systematic and deductive logic.

While logical class determination is often difficult to achieve, the ordering of classes and subclasses makes considerably more sense. There are several principles of ordering which can be followed, the natural order of the sciences as advocated by Richardson, consensus as proposed by Bliss, the order of actual usage found in LC, preferred order as in faceted schemes, or one of the several presented by Ranganathan which are almost taken for granted in parts of all schemes, i.e., chronological, geographical, customary, evolutionary, alphabetical, complexity. These are not necessarily rigid and may vary from class to class, subclass to subclass; they may not be used at all as a careful application of this concept to either LC or DC will reveal. The closest to standardized usage either achieves appears in the use of supplementary tables.

In summary therefore, traditional classifications still in use today are based on a "logical" hierarchy which follows rigid principles of division and subdivision, in which each class and subclass is arbitrarily determined and exhaustively detailed. The schemes are enumerative in nature.

Notation, or the alphabetic, numerical, alpha-numerical coding of classes theoretically should not determine the order or content of classes. It is merely a shorthand designation. Traditional classifications have not been very good about observing this principle. One of the greatest contributions to modern classification has been the decimal idea. That every grouping can be divided into ten and only ten parts. As has become increasingly evident in DC and will become so as LC increases its use of the decimal concept, the assumption is hopelessly invalid, and notation and classification determination rule each other to the ill-fortune of the scheme. The newer classifications have retained the decimal principle but through other techniques have alleviated some of the difficulties.

The last principle in considering the traditional classifications is that of hospitality or flexibility, the ability to accommodate new knowledge, the ability to detail rather specifically subject content. Since the schemes are intended to cover all knowledge it should logically follow that they must accommodate new knowledge in its appropriate logical sequence. Anyone who has attempted to work on this assumption with both LC and DC has seen the problems involved particularly in recent years. Theoretically however, the decimal principle provides infinite flexibility for the insertion of new knowledge and is the major attraction not only of the traditional schemes but in many of the newer ones. Phyllis Richmond points out an interesting condition about the LC system: "It (LC) is a pragmatic, functional system that is widely used with considerable consumer satisfaction. It is not logical; it is not scientifically or probabilistically built; it has little to do with language or linguistics other than to provide the best classification of these subjects extant; in organization it sprawls in all directions; it violates all the postulates, principles and laws that are considered important in classification making; in some areas relationships are shown in hierarchies, but throughout most of the schedules nothing seems to be next to anything for any particular reason. . . . Why does it work?"[12]

The above principles are the major theories on which the traditional classifications of DC, LC, Cutter, Bliss and UDC are based. Since they are still very much in vogue today and will be in the foreseeable future, the theories constitute modern classification theory. However, there is a theory inherent in even the earliest form of the Dewey Decimal system which acts as a bridge to the truly modern theories, and another in Bliss which does as well. The former theory is that of synthesis, the use of supplementary or auxiliary tables (in Dewey's case form divisions) to extend the capabilities of the classification in depth and specificity when and if it is called for. DC has maintained the relative degree, admittedly minimal, for most of the twentieth century, but has added the area divisions to it. The idea was conceived even if not as completely employed. Bliss[13] in his Bibliographic Classification recognized that knowledge is diffuse and that man's interests are unpredictable and it is impossible to anticipate or provide for new subjects. One may only enumerate existing subjects in light of consensus (current agreement of experts). Consensus is a rather interesting idea and one which has become in a way basic to the development of modern schemes. Bliss' answer to the problem was to remake the classification every generation or so. This answer becomes increasingly impractical and modern classificationists have forsaken it but have maintained the prin-

ciple of consensus. Bliss also provided for alternate locations negating the theory of one place/ one book. This is another of the foundation stones of current operational and experimental classifications.

The second major group of classifications are characterized as being nontraditional, inductive, and syndetic. For the most part they do not acknowledge the concept or practicality of a universal, general classification of all knowledge. The overall framework of UDC and also of Colon indeed do embody all of knowledge yet the schedules themselves are made up of small units carefully detailed and synthesized and then loosely combined. There is much more concern for the specialized collection of knowledge in the newer schemes. The arbitrariness in determination of major classes is very similar to that of the traditional schemes and hence will not be elaborated again at this point. Ranganathan[14] does, however, describe the process of class formation in four parts: Dissection—subdivisions are mutually exclusive (flower-non-flower); Denudation—progressive decrease in extension of a class—classes are subordinate to one another—a chain; Lamination—subdivision by indicating one division within—attach an isolate or facet to a class; Loose-assemblage—overlapping of altogether different classes.

It is the theory of arrangement or ordering of subclasses which has probably created the most significant contribution to modern classification. S. R. Ranganathan in his Colon Classification introduced the concept of facets which he defines as trains of characteristics. Literature for instance would have four facets: language, form, author, and work characteristics. Other major classes would have different and varying numbers of facets. While Ranganathan was theoretically concerned with a formal ordering of subclasses and in fact postulates such orders as chronological, canonical, geographical, etc., his real contribution, at least to Western classification theory has been the principle of faceting. The faceting principles used today are essentially those developed by the British Classification Research Group which was organized in London in 1952 to discuss the principles of classification.

The success of the faceting principle is founded on the idea of synthesis or inductive logic, rather than deductive. Vickery defines faceted classification as a schedule of standard terms to be used in the subject description of documents. The terms are first grouped into homogenous subject fields. Each field is then divided into facets and the terms in each facet *may* then be arranged in a hierarchy. For the most part the faceting technique is used with material which is first collected and then arranged in an order best suited to the purpose at hand. Thus the strict hierarchy of the traditional schemes is almost totally lacking. Faceting is only partly analogous to traditional rules of logical division and differs in three ways: the strictness of the rules applied, the lack of a rigid schedule, and the freedom from the rigidity of the genus-species relationship.[15] For those less familiar with the faceting idea B. C. Vickery's *Faceted Classification* is recommended.[16]

The idea of starting with the material to be organized is a relatively new one, although Bliss implied something of it in his consensus theory. Classification is therefore no longer concerned with the overall logical framework of all knowledge but only in the fabric if the smaller parts built up or synthesized in to varying kinds of wholes. This is the principle on which the thesaurus indexing structure is also based. The primary aim of the thesaurus structure is not really classification but rather subject specification, as Sharp has indicated. Most thesauri are derived from terms in the literature organized group by group in a broadening hierarchy. Similar in some respects but quite different from the faceting concept.

The concept of synthesis is not solely the realm of the faceted schemes. The Universal Decimal Classification has employed the technique since the early twentieth century. It is an expansion of Dewey's idea of auxiliary tables however rather than faceting, but there is some provision for definition of multiple subjects by combining classification groups. This same characteristic has been incorporated into the seventeenth edition of DC with less facility of use because there are no connecting symbols provided, as in UDC, to show the relationship of classes.

In summary faceted classification is based on a synthesizing technique which makes use of arbitrarily determined main categories subdivided into mutually exclusive facets (characteristics) which are not controlled by a rigid hierarchy. Classification is accomplished by taking the various parts and typing them together with connecting symbols to represent an idea or concept.

The notation is such systems while not simplified in any sense of the word does at least separate itself almost exclusively from the scheme itself and hence some of the rigidity of classification is lost. Even in UDC which is a traditionally based notation, the reliance on combination of smaller units rather than the strict enumeration of hierarchical levels alleviates the problem of the notation controlling the schedule construction. Most of the non-traditional schemes make use of all combinations of alphabetic, numeric, and symbolic characters.

Therefore, in regard to the hospitality or flexibility of the syndetic schemes, it is almost self apparent that they must of necessity be more useful than the traditional. Any subject, concept or class may be expressed without restraint, new knowledge need not fit into a rigid hierarchical structure and hence there is always room. This statement is somewhat fiction since even the syndetic have a loose hierarchical framework which present the same constraints for adaptation as the traditional schemes, but the problems are definitely decreased as the hierarchy is eliminated at the lower and more specific levels.

It should also be pointed out that while I have painted an almost blissful (no pun intended) picture of the capabilities of the syndetic scheme, they have been used primarily in fields where the terminology is fairly well defined and already controlled, science and technology. As a result the techniques, efficiency and effectiveness have not really been proven and indeed many of the problems not yet uncovered. There is something to be said for the logical arrangement of the traditional classifications even if their logic does not agree with our logic.

Current experimental research in classification theory falls mainly into three categories: 1) deductive, or those concerned with logic and mathematics, thesauri and Boolean algebra techniques which often appear more intuitive than logical; 2) inductive, or those concerned with scientific and probability methods including counting word frequencies), faceting and the automatic classification experiments of Borko and Maron, and 3) linguistic, those concerned with semantic and syntactical analyses, artificial languages. De Grolier points out that four influences have directed the level and intensity of research in classification. These appear to be fairly much the same influences that get blamed for all research: developing technology, growth in the number and complexity of materials, developments in the sciences of mathematics and logic, and mechanical translation.

Since several of these areas will be covered much more extensively in other papers, I shall not go into detail but rather try to show the overall direction and its impact on traditional and nontraditional classification theory. Most of the current experimental research is aimed at a highly detailed level of subject specification which most librarians associate with indexing. While it is not completely being done by computer most of the interest and perhaps value is being derived from trying to find out what, how and why a computer can contribute to the organization, storage and retrieval of information. Borko who has been working with automatic classification does not claim it as a substitute for traditional classification. It is not used to devise detailed specialized classification schedules. On the other hand, some of the current indexing schemes and their accompanying research imply although they do not specifically state an intention of avoiding classification. A half-way house on this route has been the development and extension of use of the thesaurus structure which is part classification, part-indexing in approach. The tendency therefore seems to be to work at both ends, classification and indexing, down toward the middle.

Farradane in Britain has been working on relations between concepts in compound subjects. There is work underway by NATO into the basis for a new general classification. "Most of the work on the theoretical foundations of the first stage are based on the Integrative Level Theory. The aim is to establish a basis for recognizing the 'uniquely definable place' for every entity which need then to be set down and notated only once in the scheme."[17] Common recurring patterns are emerging and their existence should be considered significant.

In 1964 a conference held in Washington, D.C.

indicated a strong interest in statistical association techniques and their use in indexing, classification and thesaurus building. Statistical association (oversimplified, the counting of words, their frequency of appearance in differing contexts and with different words) has supported if not initiated research in automatic classification. An extension of this plus added sophistication partially related to linguistic studies has been work in the Theory of Clumping at the Cambridge Language Research Unit in England.

The Elsinore Conference concluded with possible areas for classification research: study of mutual interrelationships between thought and language, the linguistic study of terminology, the construction of controlled vocabularies, the study of various methods for embodying analytical relations given by context, analysis and evaluation of functional relationship between the various components of systems, and the study of behavioral processes. Specific studies should explore the use of universally applicable categories, the domains of application and conditions for the use of integrative levels, and the formal (mathematical and logical) foundations of classification among others.

The most direct impact of this research on classification theory will be an expansion in our knowledge of what classification is and does, which form of classification (traditional, hierarchical, enumerative or non-traditional, faceted, syndetic) can best fulfill our needs. Also of importance will be the determination of the role that the computer and other mechanical equipment will play in the development of schemes.

NOTES

[1] W. C. Berwick Sayers, *A manual of classification for librarians.* 4th ed. Rev. by A. Maltby. (London: Deutsch, 1967), p. 25.

[2] Phyllis Richmond, Transformation and organization of information content: aspects of recent research in the art and science of classification. Paper presented at the FID Conference, Washington, D.C., 1965. p. 3.

[3] Pauline Atherton, Ranganathan's classification ideas: an analytico-synthetic discussion. *Library Resources and Technical Services* 9: 463–473 (Fall 1965), p. 463.

[4] A. P. Srivastava, *Theory of knowledge classification in libraries.* (New Delhi: Lakshmi, 1964), 206 p.

[5] University of Illinois, Graduate School of Library Science. The role of classification in the modern American library. Papers presented at an institute, November 1959. (Champaign: 1960), p. 121.

[6] John R. Sharp, *Some fundamentals of information retrieval.* (New York: London House & Maxwell, 1965), p. 28.

[7] University of Illinois, p. 37.

[8] *International Study Conference on Classification Research.* 2d. 1964. Elsinore, Denmark. Edited by Pauline Atherton. (Copenhagen: Munksgaard, 1965), p. 544.

[9] University of Illinois, p. 120.

[10] *Ibid.* pp. 38–39.

[11] Sharp, pp. 20–21.

[12] Richmond, p. 35.

[13] B. I. Palmer, and A. J. Wells. *The fundamentals of library classification.* (London: Allen & Unwin, 1951), p. 13.

[14] Atherton, p. 468.

[15] B. C. Vickery, *Faceted classification.* (London: Aslib, 1960), p. 12.

[16] *Ibid.*

[17] Classification Research Group. Minutes. *Journal of Documentation* 4: 278 (December 1968).

Faceted Classification Schemes

Brian C. Vickery

"These systems use the principle of concept coordination: the subject matter of a text is represented by the coordination, combination or synthesis of two or more symbols, each of which represents an independent conceptual term. Instead of trying to construct, from above, one vast tree of knowledge, facet analysis starts from below. It first groups terms encountered in a given field into categories: substance, state, property, reaction, operation, device, and so on, and then arranges the terms with each category into a classificatory map."

INTRODUCTION TO FACETED CLASSIFICATION

Basic Characteristics: The systems to be described here are classifications in special subject fields, constructed according to the techniques of facet analysis.

These systems use the principle of concept coordination: the subject matter of a text is represented by the coordination, combination or synthesis of two or more symbols, each of which represents an independent conceptual term.

The terms used have previously been sorted into groups, and within each group they are hierarchically arranged. The distinctive contributions of the system are the techniques by which this sorting is achieved. Facet analysis is essentially a technique of vocabulary control—a method of controlling the kind and level of term that is admitted into the system vocabulary.

Faceted classifications have primarily been used in pre-coordinated retrieval systems based on the card catalog in conventional (item entry) form. For this purpose, notations have been fitted to the schemes, and various methods have been tried of arranging both the notational headings and the verbal indexes to them. This is the other distinctive contribution of the system.

Historical Background: From this brief description, the historical origins of faceted classification will probably be clear.

The use of classification for information storage and retrieval is traditional. The occurrence of groups of terms that we can recognize as homogeneous facets was not unknown even in the older general schemes of book classification, but this was not the result of a conscious technique, and inconsistencies abound. The Universal Decimal Classification, as Jack Mills showed in an earlier seminar,[1] was the first general scheme to display any real degree of faceted structure; and even there much inconsistency remained.

It was of course Ranganathan who, at first intuitively and later intellectually, developed the technique of facet analysis in the Colon Classification; and all subsequent workers in this field owe a great deal to his work, which he has already described in a previous seminar.[2]

Despite the existence of the Universal Decimal Classification and Colon, there has been a continuing demand for special schemes of classification, designed for particular groups of users and adapted to their needs. (The claimed advantages of such schemes will be considered later). In response to this demand, a group of librarians in London began to discuss the problems of constructing special schemes, and these discussions led to a considerable volume of work.

The Classification Research Group was formed in 1952. Its aim was to discuss the principles and practice of classification, unhampered by allegiance to any particular published scheme. The Group's composition has fluctuated, but there has always been a "hard core" of about a dozen regular members. Those who have most actively contributed to the literature of the subject are Jean (Binns) Aitchison, D. J. Campbell, Eric Coates, Jason Farradane, Douglas Foskett, Barbara Kyle, Derek Langridge, Jack Mills, Bernard Palmer, Jack Wells and myself. Robert Fairthorne and Cyril Cleverdon have often attended meetings, although their main interests have lain in other directions.

SOURCE: Reprinted from Brian C. Vickery, *Faceted Classification Schemes* (New Brunswick: Rutgers State University, Graduate School of Library Service, 1966), pp. 30–39, 40, 42, 45–46, 50, by permission of the publisher.

From 1952 to 1960, the Group concentrated on the theme considered in this seminar—the construction and use of special schemes of classification. During the last few years, it has turned its attention to the relation between special and general classifications, and to the problems of constructing a new general classification. The Group was responsible for interesting the Science Research Fund of NATO in the problem, and NATO has given a grant to the Library Association, London, to study the project. An international conference has been held, and exploratory work has been undertaken. . . .

Significance of the System: The importance of facet analysis is made evident by its growing influence. This is shown in three ways.

First, its impact on the older general schemes. The Universal Decimal Classification in its early days displayed some faceted structure. Schedules revised or newly developed during the last decade have been consciously constructed in this mold. It is most significant that the British Standards Institution chose a member of the Classification Research Group, Jack Mills, to prepare its recent Guide to the Universal Decimal Classification.

Second, its use in the construction of special schemes. Both in the United Kingdom, and increasingly in Europe, members of the Classification Research Group are consulted by institutions needing new classifications; and a number of schemes have been commissioned in this way. Favorable reports on their use have been received.

Third, the potential importance of facet analysis is suggested by the way in which systems based on other principles have developed. Coordinate indexing, although perhaps not as novel as has sometimes been claimed, entered its modern phase of development during the 1950's. At first the virtues of an unstructured, unconstrained vocabulary of indexing terms were extolled, but as document collections grew in size, the need for vocabulary control was recognized. In some quarters the pendulum swung to the opposite extreme (for example, the complexity structured code used at Western Reserve University). If a vocabulary is to be controlled, principles and techniques of control are needed. Facet analysis offers a set of principles and techniques that have now been applied in a variety of subject fields, and these have been shown to be workable and useful. It is potentially of considerable value to all prospective designers of retrieval systems in special fields.

Speaking at the Rutgers seminar, Calvin Mooers commented: "One of the first things that the work of the Classification Research Group represents is a revolt from a channeling, a very respected channeling. They had worked with the Universal Decimal Classification. Their work took off from the Universal Decimal Classification, explored and expanded in certain new directions.

"One thing that the Classification Research Group developed was the desire to impart a concentrated focus to a method of classifications. They looked at particular jobs at hand, a particular company or a particular library, and they decided—and I believe quite rightly—that to do full justice to what they wished to do intellectually with the subject matter they should not have to provide detail for material which would never appear in that library, but should focus narrowly upon that which was at hand. This is also characteristic of developments in the U.S.A. during the same period.

"Another aspect of the revolt from the Universal Decimal Classification was in the actual method of construction of whole classification systems. The Classification Research Group does not depend upon authority from the big book. They start out by looking at a collection and make a classification appropriate to the collection.

"Part of the impact of the work of the Classification Research Group is evidenced, I think, by some collateral work. In particular, I noticed in reading the first paper in this series, by Jack Mills on the Universal Decimal Classification,[3] that it is quite clear that people, Jack Mills in particular but also others working on the Universal Decimal Classification, are kept on their mettle by the work of the Classification Research Group. Indeed, Jack Mills uses a fair amount of Classification Research Group terminology. In short, in the various classification developments there is a flow of ideas and a cross-fertilization, one from the other, and a stimulation.

"Facet provides an analytical tool; that is, the idea of facet allows you to peel the onion of an idea. Ranganathan approached this and, of course, Ranganathan developed it in part from suggestions which lay in the Universal Decimal Classification. The Classification Research Group felt free to introduce a new symbolism; that is, to depart from the decimal. All this is exciting whether we agree with them or not."

Alan Rees commented: "In very brief summary we might say that faceted schemes are analytico-synthetic rather than enumerative. They precoordinate rather than postcoordinate. They operate at the present time with manual rather than mechanized searches and are, in American parlance, mission-oriented rather than discipline-oriented. What we mean by that is that they are designed for user groups whose interests cut across the traditional fields. We are very much aware in terms of indexing and abstracting services and in information centers of the concept of mission-oriented services as opposed to discipline-oriented services.

"I do not think that any of us at this seminar is in a position to make an evaluation of facet analysis. Apart from the very thorny problem of test and evaluation, we are faced with a lack of operational experience. We just do not know how these faceted schemes actually work in terms of operational practice. Facet analysis is almost unknown in the U.S. and, to the best of my knowledge, is not taught in any of the library schools.

"I think that if we learned anything from Cranfield,[4] it is that an indexing language is not a retrieval system in itself but is one component, and a complex one at that, in a total retrieval system. It is now obvious that the indexing language is significant in determining the performance of a retrieval system, not only as a result of the actual intellectual arrangement of indexing but also very significantly on the output side. It is very significant in question analysis and definition. So my point in this connection is simply that one cannot tear a classification scheme or an indexing language out of the context of a total retrieval system.

"There are three main purposes of a classification scheme or, indeed, of any indexing language. The first is, in my opinion at least, to normalize the language of the documents on the one hand and the language of the questions on the other; i.e., to bring document language into coincidence with question language. Two, to serve as a useful device to the indexer in the intellectual task of characterizing the subject contents of the document; i.e., to display synonyms, hierarchical and other relationships, to facilitate intelligent selection of terms by the indexer. Three—and here is the one that is usually overlooked—to provide a tool in the searcher in analyzing and defining questions put to the file. In this connection it should again

display alternate terminologies, synonymous terminologies, related terminology and association pathways which can be utilized in expanding on the words of a question. One can search only for the words of a question, and a good indexing language can materially assist in defining underlying requirements of the questioner because the question is, after all, only a formalized representation of a need.

"So we come back to the idea that a good indexing language or a classification scheme should provide a useful tool for the questioner to define what his question really is. People come to retrieval systems and to libraries because they do not know what they want. If they did know what they wanted with any great precision, the chances are they would not want to go to the library. So you have to provide, by means of an indexing language, not only a retrieval tool but a conceptual tool to define what a person really wants to know.

"Now, in general, my feeling is that facet analysis is more useful as an accurate, flexible and logically-based indexing rationale rather than a successful searching tool. In other words, it serves purpose two rather better than purpose three."

Major Claims for the Method: Special faceted schemes may be compared in usefulness either with general classifications such as the Universal Decimal Classification, or with less structured systems based on verbal indexing, or with more structured schemes such as that of the Western Reserve University. In general it is claimed that faceted schemes are no less efficient in retrieval than other systems, and that, in addition, they offer the following advantages:

(i)   Relative to general classifications such as The Universal Decimal Classification, they can bring conveniently together all the aspects of a special field of knowledge, aspects that may be scattered in the Universal Decimal Classification. They can itemize the concepts in that field in more detail, yet with shorter notational symbols. They can provide for more flexible combinations of terms. Being locally produced, they can be more readily altered in response to change in local interests.
(ii) Relative to less structured systems, facet analysis produces a vocabulary that can be used more consistently both in indexing and in formulating search questions; and the facet hierarchies make it easier to conduct generic searches.
(iii) Relative to more structured systems such as the Western Reserve University system, faceted schemes are easier and less costly to construct and use in indexing and search, and there is as

yet no evidence that the greater complexity introduced by the Western Reserve University system improves retrieval.

In short, it is claimed that the degree of structure in a faceted vocabulary is nearer the optimum than that provided by other systems.

Major Disadvantages of the Method: There are of course disadvantages to faceted schemes to be set against these claims.

(i)   Relative to published general schemes such as the Universal Decimal Classification, they require more effort to intitiate – the schedules must be constructed and "debugged." Since they cover a restricted subject field, they cannot as readily incorporate marginal topics that become of interest.

(ii) Relative to less structured systems, they are again more arduous to construct. The use of notational symbols instead of natural language may lengthen both the indexing and searching processes. They cannot so simply introduce new indexing terms.

(iii) Relative to more structured systems, they cannot provide such flexible facilities for generic search.

In general, being intermediate in degree of structure, faceted schemes introduce more constraints than verbal indexes but have fewer search facilities than more structured codes.

Fields of Application: Faceted classification schemes are tools for use by human indexers, and their application is not restricted to any particular material forms of recorded information.

Since each is a special scheme, its application is restricted to the interests of a relatively homogeneous user group. Some idea of the width of field that can be covered is given by the titles of some faceted schemes currently in use: Engineering; Aeronautical and allied subjects; Occupational safety and health; Pharmaceutical industry; Diamond technology; Music. The Colon Classification may be regarded as a set of special schemes in a variety of fields, in some of which it has been developed in detail, e.g., Agriculture and Management.

Up to now, faceted schemes have typically been applied to the indexing of documents at the "article" level, such as journal papers, research reports, patents, and trade literature.

Faceted schemes have up to now mainly been used in precoordinated card catalog systems, but there is not inherent reason why they should be so restricted. A vocabulary of faceted hierarchies can be (and has been) used in a post-coordinate

fashion. The notational symbolisms of existing schemes are designed for human search, but with suitable coding a faceted vocabulary would be equally adaptable to machine search.

Aids in Initiation and Operation: To operate a faceted scheme it is necessary to have available (1) a faceted schedule of indexing terms, usually fitted out with a notation or code; (2) an alphabetical index to these terms; and (3) a set of rules indicating how the schedule is to be used. A few examples of these tools are publicly available.

English Electric Company. A faceted subject classification for engineering. 3rd edition. Cambridge Rd., Whetstone, Leics. England, English Electric Co., Ltd., 1961.

D. Langridge. Classifications of enterprise activities. London, British Institute of Management, 1956.

E. J. Coates. British Catalogue of Music Classification. London, British National Bibliography, 1960.

D. J. Foskett. London Education Classification. In Education Libraries Bulletin, Supplement 6, 1963.

Occupational Safety and Health Information Centre. Guide to the card service and classification scheme. Geneva, International Labour Office, 1960.

Since each scheme is designed for a particular group of users, these tools must themselves be constructed. This is done with the aid of (1) a detailed knowledge of user interests, (2) existing glossaries, subject heading lists, systematic manuals, and collections of literature such as indexes or abstracts in the field.

Classification, Traditional and Faceted: Classification has been used in bibliography and documentation since libraries first began. In what ways do faceted classifications differ from traditional schemes?

Traditional classification starts from above with an "original universe" of knowledge, which it divides and subdivides to construct a single vast classificatory tree. Each item of knowledge, each topic or each text, must be located at a single point in the tree structure. It is this feature that has led to criticism of traditional classification as "a rigidly specified network of pathways leading to rigidly grouped collections of items." (J. W. Perry).

In the practice of classification, the "original universe" at the top of the family tree, the subject field to be divided, is one of the so-called "main classes" or traditional disciplines. In theory, the process of division is logical; i.e., each genus is differentiated into species by means of a particular characteristic of division, each class term is divided in only one way; and all the subdivisions of any one class are true species of the parent genus. In every classification there are fields where this logical division is present. But division is not always logical. For example, consider the first array obtained by subdividing Physical Chemistry in the Colon Classification:

1. Chemical combination and action
2. Solution
3. Mixture
4. Thermochemistry
5. Photochemistry
6. Electrochemistry
7. Magnetochemistry
8. Stereochemistry

By no stretch of the imagination can these terms be regarded as having been derived from Physical Chemistry by a single characteristic. Classes 2 and 3 are molecular assemblies; classes 4 to 7 are relations between chemical reactions and forms of energy; class 1 is the chemical reaction itself; and class 8 is the spatial aspect of chemical structure.

Although these terms are not all collateral species of a genus Physical Chemistry, they can be sorted into groups, each of which has been defferentiated on the basis of a single characteristic. This sorting was called by Ranganathan "facet analysis." Thus Alcohol is a kind of chemical *substance*, Liquid is a *state* of that substance, Votatility is a *property* of it, Combustion is a *reaction* of it, Analysis an *operation* performed on it, and Burette a *device* for carrying out an operation. The six emphasized words are *categories* into which chemical terms can be sorted.

Instead of trying to construct, from above, one vast tree of knowledge, facet analysis starts from below. It first groups terms encountered in a given field into categories: substance, state, property, reaction, operation, device, and so on, and then arranges the terms with each category into a classificatory map.

Categories in Classification: The first explicit use of categories in classification was made by Ranganathan. His Colon Classification exhibited from the start a division of classes into facets or categories. For example, in his main class, Medicine, before starting a family tree subdivision, Ranganathan first formed two groups of terms; *organ* (e.g., femur, diaphragm, blood, eye, tooth) and *problem* (e.g., morphology, physiology,

disease, hygiene). A subject such as 'Diseases of the femur' was expressed by linking together terms from the two groups, FEMUR–DISEASE. Ranganathan also found the need to introduce other groups of terms to express the *symptoms* of disease, (e.g., fever, inflammation), its *agents* (e.g., virus, bacteria, poison) and its *handling* (e.g., surgery, diet, nursing, therapy). He was thus able to form compound headings of the type FEMUR–MARROW INFLAMATION (OSTEOMYELITIS)–PHARMACO-THERAPY. The *drugs* used in pharmacotherapy formed yet another group, enabling Ranganathan to cope with the subject FEMUR–OSTEOMYELITIS–THERAPY–STREPTOMYCIN. The Colon Classification, by dividing its terms into categories or facets and making notational provision for linking facets together, was thus able to bring together terms in a coordinate relationship to designate a complex idea.

However, many years before Colon, provision for forming compound subject headings (and even the use of categories) had come into classification. Cutter in his Expansive Classification introduced 'common subdivisions' for literary form, and the 'local list' for geographical specifications, both of which could be applied to numbers from the main scheme. Brown's Subject Classification included form, geographical, language and date divisions. His 'categorical tables' also listed many other 'common standpoints.' Thus he could link the categorical term Classification (.89) to the main schedule term Cuttlefish (F237) to give F237.89. Two main terms could also be combined; e.g., F237E026, Cuttlefish respiration.

Dewey and later editors of the Decimal Classification extended such synthetic devices. To the form, geographical and language divisions, they added "view point." Certain class numbers were divisible directly by the main tables; e.g., 016 Bibliography, or 658.9 Specific Industries. Others could be linked by the "relation" symbol, 0001. The Universal Decimal Classification used several relation symbols to combine terms, in particular the colon. Thus the subject "The influence of fertilizers on the vitamin content of wheat" could be represented as 631.8:577. 16:633.11.

Categories were first introduced into classification in the guise of 'composite' schedules. Thus Dewey divided Chemistry into Physical, Practical, Analytical and Systematic, splitting up the field by categories such as *problem*, *operation*, *analysis* and *substance*. The U.D.C., in its breakdown of the Chemistry schedule into categories, went much further than Dewey. The "analytical numbers" 54.01/09 comprise general *properties* of and *operations* on chemical substances: the numbers 54-1 to 54-94 are *states* of the substance: the analyticals applicable to 541.12 Chemical Mechanics refer to the *phase* condition of the substances: those applicable to 541.18 Colloids refer to *properties* and *operations*; in 542 four categories can be recognized— *laboratories*, *apparatus*, *operations* and chemical *processes*; and so on.

The Value of Facet Analysis: Facet analysis offers advantages to the maker of classifications, to the classifier, and to the user.

1. The classificationist. To the maker of classifications, the prior analysis of his material into facets is a most valuable intellectual aid. Every classification must start with a medley of terms derived from the literature and from glossaries. It is his job to organize them in such a way as to display correctly the most useful relations between them. Many terms are only apparently simple; they are in fact compound concepts. For example, a Colorimeter is a Color:Analysis:Instrument; a Haemometer is a Blood:Flow:Measurement: Instrument; Nephrosclerosis is Kidney: Hardening, and so on. If such compound terms are put into the classification unanalyzed, relations will be concealed; e.g., the links between Haemometer and Flow, or between Nephrosclerosis and Kidney, will not be made.

It is in the "factoring" of such terms that the conceptual categories which we call facets be so usefully applied. They aid clear thinking, reveal discrepancies in our analysis, and point the way to omissions in our schedules. For example, in analyzing a glossary of Soil Science, we come across a number of terms such as Cohesion, Consistence, Porosity. If, instead of just "finding a place" for them we first identify them as being terms in a *property* facet, we are reminded (a) that there are a number of other physical properties of soil which we have not yet put into our schedules; and (b) that there are many other physical properties of matter which, though not yet of interest in Soil Science, may eventually prove to be important. Our schedules can be so designed that they can later incorporate any of these properties.

2. The classifier. The product of facet analysis is a set of schedules in which the terms are first grouped into more or less clearly defined facets,

and then, within each facet, arranged in a class (generic) order. The classifier using these schedules is aided because the structure of each subject field is displayed. He can see what sort of terms he must choose to describe a compound subject. Each facet is relatively short and can be scanned as a whole to pick out the right term. The classifier finds it easier to spot the compound terms in a title and to "factor" them appropriately. Lastly, if he is making a classified catalog he is given definite rules as to the order in which the facets are to be cited.

These advantages hold with equal force if we are indexing either alphabetically or by a mechanical selection or coordinate indexing technique. The prior analysis of a subject into its simple term is equally necessary in all these processes. To have our terms displayed in the form of a faceted classification is equally helpful.

3. The user. Some users (they are rare) approach the catalog by consciously trying to formulate a query in the terms appropriate to the catalog. They want to know its structure and its terminology. Faceted schedules aid them exactly as they aid the classifier.

The more common user, however, does not take such a wide view. He starts with a "keyword" such as SOLVENTS, and with this key tries to unlock the secrets of the catalog. The word is hardly ever the full compound subject. It is either one term of the compound, or it is related to one such term (and often is a term broader than that specifically sought). This key will only unlock the catalog if it either (a) itself provides access to the compound subject sought, or (b) directs the user in some way to a more specific term which will give access to the subject. These objects are attained most readily if the index is based upon generic relations which are clearly displayed in faceted schedules.

WORDS AND CONCEPTS

In analyzing retrieval, I have described a transition from keywords extracted from text to standard descriptors that may be assigned to texts. A faceted classification is a controlled and structured vocabulary of descriptors.

At the Rutgers seminar, Calvin Mooers drew a clear distinction between words and concepts. He regards his descriptors as "controlled verbal symbols, but not words. They are merely symbols for concepts . . . . For indexing it may be useful to standardize on certain symbols to represent concepts, and these symbols may be alphabetical words. Yet one can easily discover concepts that are essentially non-verbal yet exceedingly important."

Mooers further commented: "In the description of faceted classification, the emphasis is upon verbal words, terms; and this is in contrast to the approach epitomized by J. C. Gardin in which the emphasis, at least the emphasis that Gardin tries to make, is upon concepts. In other words, Gardin approaches the matter of classification by looking for the idea first and then looking for the symbol which might be used to clothe it. In constructing a faceted scheme, as has been repeatedly mentioned in one form or another, you collect terminology from dictionaries, thesauri, and then try to organize a terminology. You collect words. You use terms. As I see it, only as an after-the-fact matter do you come around to the fact that these words epitomize conceptual entities. There are confusions inherent in basing your work at the terminological level rather than trying to truly go to the conceptual level."

It is true that a descriptor is only a symbol for a concept. It is also true that there are concepts for which we do not have a simple word-representation. It is even true that there are words that represent nothing. But if a word means anything, it too is a symbol for a concept (that is what "meaning" means). The crux of the matter is that words in general use do not form as controlled and structured a vocabulary as do descriptors. The difference between words in general and descriptors is one of degree—the degree of control and structure—not one of kind. Both are symbols representing concepts.

Texts are mainly composed of words. What does it mean, to handle them purely at the symbolic or terminological level? It means simply to extract words from texts, and to express no relations between the extracted words that are not explicitly present in the text. KWIC indexing and automatic statistical indexing are purely at the terminological level. But the moment any implicit relation between words is displayed in the retrieval system, the indexer has moved to the conceptual level. The symbols "rats" and "mice" do not reveal any relation between the corresponding concepts. The indexer will only make an entry "Rats, see also Mice" if he considers the concepts that the symbols represent. The structure introduced into a controlled vocabulary is revealed only by conceptual analysis.

Facet analysis is one form of this conceptual analysis. It begins, as Mooers rightly emphasizes, by collecting terminology. The collected terms form the raw material of analysis. Each term is then examined: what concept does it represent? in what conceptual category should this concept be included? what are the class relations between this concept and other concepts included in the same category? The resulting faceted schedule is a conceptual scheme, a structure in which terminologically expressed concepts have been organized. These concepts already have, for the most part, "symbols which might be used to clothe them"—the verbal terms first collected. The position of each concept in the facet structure is made evident by assigning to it a notational symbol as well as its verbal symbol.

Classificationist, classifier and user must start with words, for these are the usual symbols in which concepts are clothed. But the construction of a faceted scheme the classing of a text, and the formulation of a search question all involve conceptual analysis.

Faceted classification schemes are, as their name implies, (a) classification schemes and (b) based upon facet analysis. . . .

Construction of the Classificaton Schedule: The feature that most distinguishes a special faceted scheme from a general one is the structure of its classification schedule and its mode of construction.

The framework of a general classification is a list of traditional disciplines chosen as "main classes." The framework of the Universal Decimal Classification is, of course, those fields of knowledge and their subdivisions chosen by Dewey at Amherst College in the nineteenth century. The framework of Colon is a not dissimilar group of disciplines, to which a number of newly emerging fields has been added. Each discipline forms the boundary of a main class, and it is this main class that is submitted to facet analysis. . . .

Facet analysis is therefore partly analogous to the traditional rules of logical division on which classification has always been based. The result, however, differs from traditional classification in three ways. First, in the strictness with which the rules are applied: In the analysis performed in order to construct a scheme, every distinctive logical category should be isolated, every new characteristic of division should be clearly formulated, every new relation should be recognized, even though at a later stage it may be possible and advisable to present a less refined analysis. Second, a faceted classification differs from the traditional in that the categories so distinguished are not locked into rigid, enumerative schedules but are left free to combine with each other in the fullest freedom, so that every type of relation between terms and between subjects may be expressed. Third, from the theoretical point of view, faceted classification breaks free from the restriction of traditional classification to the hierarchical, genus-species relation. By combining terms in compound subjects it introduces new logical relations between them, thus better reflecting the complexity of knowledge. . . .

Structuring each facet: Once facets have been identified, the next step is to amplify and structure each of them. The literature so far examined may, for example, have mentioned only a few terms in a particular facet, say, facet 28, Properties of materials; whereas, it is known that users are interested in a wide variety of properties. Texts comprehensively covering the properties of materials are examined to discover other terms that might fall in this group.

It is helpful at this stage to construct a hierarchical order for the terms collected within each facet. Even if no well-developed classificatory tree results, the procedure helps to coalesce synonyms, to eliminate terms that have found their way into the wrong facet, and to indicate where extra terms should be inserted. There are times when a term is considered to be complex, better represented as a combination of terms from two facets. For example, the term switchboards in one scheme is represented as the combination Switchgear: Indicating devices; Sherardising as Impregnation: Zinc; the Schlieren method as Fluid flow: Visible: Photography; and Photolysis as Decomposition: Light.

The result of these operations is a set of structured facets, not unlike, for example, the set of generic charts at the back of the ASTIA Thesaurus.

NOTES

[1] Rutgers Series for the Intellectual Organization of Information. Susan Artandi, ed., (New Brunswick, N. J.: Graduate School of Library Service, Rutgers, the State University, 1964), Volume I. The Universal Decimal Classification by Jack Mills.

[2] *Ibid.* Volume IV. The Colon Classification by S. R. Ranganathan. 1965.

[3] Thesaurus of ASTIA Descriptors. 2nd ed., (Arlington, Va.: Armed Services Technical Information Agency, 1962)

CLASSIFICATION

Automatic Classification

Automatic classification research and the techniques developed from it have brought to bear several factors not heretofore considered as elements of classification. Linguistic and semantic analysis and interpretation have been used to determine relationships of concepts not founded on one man's preconceived notions of the map of knowledge. The techniques are interesting ones ranging from mere tabulation to rather sophisticated syntactical analysis and of course manipulated almost solely by computer. The potential is great and research is needed. Perhaps the greatest barrier lies not in the technology but rather in the complex nature of language itself.

Research in Automatic Generation of Classification Systems

Harold Borko

"Up to this point the criterion for correct classification has been the human classifier, but this is not necessarily the best criterion. We know that humans are not perfectly reliable, and therefore, it is not possible to predict human classification with perfect accuracy. . . . Automatic document classification procedures should be evaluated on how efficiently they retrieve information and not on how well they can match the imperfect human classifier."

This paper is concerned with the organization of information, in the form of documents, for efficient storage and retrieval. By documents we mean books, technical reports, articles, memoranda, letters, photographs, data facts, etc.—all forms of memory file organization ranging from documents in a library to data in a real-time command-and-control system. Therefore, the implications of this work are applicable to a field broader than the concerns of the ordinary library.

In actual practice, most of the information retrieval research has been concerned with document files because the most highly organized collection of documents in existence today is the library, and in doing research on methods of organizing information, one must compare the adequacy of proposed new techniques with existing library methods. Procedures which will improve information storage and retrieval in a library will probably be sufficiently powerful to help improve other methods of file organization.

PURPOSES OF DOCUMENT CLASSIFICATION

The reason for maintaining a collection of documents is to have an available store of information and to be able to retrieve desired information rapidly and with confidence. The value of classification is that it increases efficiency in locating this desired information. If we tried to locate a book on a particular subject in a library that did not use any system of classification, we would have to spend a long time reading the titles and authors of several thousand books before we could find the one for which we were looking. If we knew the author, and the books were arranged alphabetically by author, we could locate the book quickly. On the other hand, if we didn't know the author, but knew the subject content of the book, we would want the books arranged by subject category in order to search the file efficiently. Finally, if all we knew was that the book we sought was a big black one which we could recognize, we would like the files arranged by color. The point being made is that there are various ways of organizing a file, and whether or not a particular method of file organization is efficient depends upon search strategy. Furthermore, no one method of file organization would be equally efficient for all search questions. This is an important, if obvious, point and one which is often overlooked.

The central theoretical problem of classification as a method of organizing documents is that only one principle at a time can be utilized for gathering items together. This principle can be alphabetic arrangement by author, color coding based on the binding of the book, subject classification, or any other scheme—as long as only one principle is used at a time.

Since a document collection is a store of information, it is usually desirable to organize this store according to subject matter. By establishing clearly demarcated groups, or classes, of documents on related topics, the number of documents to be scanned can be reduced to reasonable proportions. This, in essence, is the purpose of classification.

Based upon the data in the document-term matrix, one can compute the degree of association among the terms as a function of their occurrence in the same set of documents. A measure of this

SOURCE: Reprinted from AFIPS Conference, *Proceedings*, 1964, Vol. 25: Spring Joint Computer Conference (New York: Spartan Press for AFIPS, 1964), pp. 529–535, by permission of the author.

association is the correlation coefficient. This is a decimal number which varies from +1.000 to −1.000. A + 1.000 would mean a perfect correlation, namely, that every time word X occurred, word Y appeared in the same document; a zero correlation would indicate no relationship; and a negative correlation would mean that if the word X occurs in a document, then word Y is not likely to occur.

The formula for computing the correlation coefficient is as follows:

$$r_{xy} = \frac{N\Sigma XY - (\Sigma X)(\Sigma Y)}{\sqrt{[N\Sigma X^2 - (\Sigma X)^2][N\Sigma Y^2 - (\Sigma Y)^2]}}$$

By applying this formula and computing the correlation between each of the ninety words with every other word (a total of approximately 4000 correlations), one creates the term-term correlation matrix (Table 1). This matrix expresses selected words in a sample of documents.

These statistical procedures, preparatory to the factor analysis, are important in demonstrating a method for translating a conglomeration of words and documents into a set of vectors which can be processed mathematically. Factor analysis, when applied to the correlation matrix, enables one to determine the basic underlying variables which account for the relations among the words as expressed in the vectors. It enables us to mathematically determine which words are related and form a set; these sets, in turn, are interpreted as classification categories for grouping the original sample of documents.

In the experiment just described, the original ninety-column matrix was reduced to ten vectors which accounted for 62 percent of the total, and it is assumed most all of the common, variance. These vectors were then rotated mathematically to achieve a simpler and more meaningful structure of the hyperspace. They were then interpreted by the investigator as ten classification categories into which the original sample of 618 psychological reports could be grouped—and by implication, all psychological literature.

To illustrate how the factors were interpreted, let us examine the words which had significant loadings on the first factor.

TERM #	WORD	FACTOR LOADING
33	girls	.74
10	boys	.73
70	school	.30
2	achievement	.20
63	reading	.18

There were only five words with significant loading. It is fairly obvious that the concept underlying these terms deals with the achievement of boys and girls in school; consequently, this factor was interpreted as academic achievement of boys and girls in school; consequently, in a like manner. These included factors named experimental psychology and community organization, school guidance and counseling, clinical psychology and psychotherapy, etc.

Thus, we have arrived at answers to two [important] questions: How many classes should be established, and what shall be a measure of similarity? The application of factor analysis enables one to determine the number of categories which should be established in order to adequately describe a given sample of documents. Furthermore, it provides a statistical technique, or principle, for measuring the similarity of content based upon the co-occurrence of key content terms.

There are many questions still to be answered before one can decide on the usefulness of this technique for classification. These questions include:

1. Are the categories stable; do they hold from one sample of psychological literature to another?
2. Are the categories valid; can all documents be reasonably classified into these categories?
3. Are the categories useful; do they lend themselves to automated document classification?
4. Is the technique a general one; can it be applied to documents other than psychological reports?

Before reviewing the studies designed to answer

TABLE 1

A Portion of the Correlation Matrix

	ABILITY	ACHIEVEMENT	ACTIVITY	ANALYSIS	ANXIETY
Ability		.272	−.028	.048	.080
Achievement	.272		−.026	−.041	.119
Activity	−.028	−.026		−.002	−.025
Analysis	.048	−.041	−.002		.030
Anxiety	.080	.119	−.025	.030	

these questions, it would be well to first examine some other mathematical techniques for deriving classification schedules.

Clump Theory—Parker-Rhodes and Needham: At the Cambridge Language Research Unit in England, Parker-Rhodes was also interested in classification theory and a mathematical basis for forming classes of documents. Interestingly, he considered the use of factor analysis but rejected it on two grounds, one theoretical and the other practical. From a theoretical point of view, Parker-Rhodes claimed that "the statistical type of technique has its place only after we have discovered whatever classification there may be. For then it is up to the statistician to say how nearly the properties of particular elements of the universe are inferable from a statement of the classes to which each belongs. . . . This is quite a different enterprise from that of finding the classes themselves."[1] On the practical side, factor analysis is rejected as being incapable of handling "really large universes."

Having decided to avoid the statistical concept of determining the probability of class membership, Parker-Rhodes restructured the problem in terms of locating clumps "in a Boolean lattice representing all possible subsets of the universe." Within a Boolean lattice there are many ways of defining clumps, and in fact, many different clumps are defined. Without getting involved in details, it can be broadly stated that "members of a clump must be more like each other, and less like non-members, than elements of the universe picked at random."[2] Thus, we see the relationship between the theory of clumps and the theory of classification. The method used for locating clumps within the lattice remains to be worked out. Initial procedures for clumping are described by Needham.[3] Research aimed at improving and testing these procedures is still going on. However, even now these techniques have been applied to a 346 X 346 matrix which is beyond the capabilities of presently available factor analysis programs.

Latent Class Analysis—Baker: The similarity between document classification and the problems inherent in the analysis of sociological questionnaire data was recognized by Baker. He then proposed an information retrieval system based upon Lazarsfeld's latent class analysis.[4] As Baker points out, "The raw data of documents, the presence or absence of key words, is amenable to latent class analysis without modification of either the analy-

sis or the data. The latent classes and the ordering ratios yielded by the analysis provide the basis for a straightforward means of classification and retrieval of documents."[5]

The latent class model assumes that the population—that is, the number of documents in the sample—can be divided into a number of mutually exclusive classes. Usually the number of classes is determined by the investigator, although it is conceivable that this parameter can be determined mathematically. One starts by selecting the key words which characterize each class of documents. Then latent class analysis is used to compute the probability that a document having a certain pattern of key words belongs to a given class.

Baker gives the following example: Let us assume that we have one thousand documents in our file. We are interested in classifying these documents into two classes—those dealing with computer automated instruction and those not directly related to this topic. We select as the key words in our search request the following:

1. computer.
2. automated.
3. teaching.
4. devices.

Each of the one thousand documents are then analyzed to determine whether they contain one or more of the four terms. Sixteen (2) response patterns are possible, ranging from ++++ to 0000.[6] A χ^2 test enables one to estimate the latent structure from the observed data. Having obtained a latent structure which fits, one can compute an ordering ratio, which is the probability that a document having a given word pattern belongs to a particular latent class. For example, a document with all four key words present has a probability of .998 of belonging to class 1, i.e., it is concerned with computer automated instruction.

Table 2 shows the relationships between the response pattern, expected frequencies, and ordering ratios of the one thousand documents analyzed, in terms of their latent class structure.

The table readily reveals the applicability of latent class analysis for information retrieval. This application is still in the theoretical and experimental stages. It has yet to be tested with empirical data from actual files.

AUTOMATED DOCUMENT CLASSIFICATION

The preceding discussions of factor analysis, clump theory, and latent class analysis all dealt

TABLE 2

Expected Frequency of Response and the Ordering Ratios Based Upon the Estimated Latent Structure

RESPONSE PATTERN	EXPECTED FREQUENCY		TOTAL FITTED	ORDERING RATIOS	
	CLASS 1	CLASS 2		CLASS 1	CLASS 2
++++	158.76	.24	159.00	.998	.002
+++0	105.84	2.16	108.00	.980	.020
++0+	68.04	.96	69.00	.986	.014
+0++	68.04	2.16	70.20	.969	.031
0+++	17.64	.56	18.20	.969	.031
++00	45.36	8.78	54.14	.838	.162
+0+0	45.36	19.44	64.80	.700	.300
0++0	11.76	5.04	16.80	.700	.300
+00+	29.16	8.60	37.76	.772	.218
0+0+	7.56	2.39	9.95	.768	.232
00++	7.56	5.04	12.60	.600	.400
+000	19.44	77.76	97.20	.200	.800
0+00	5.04	20.16	25.20	.200	.800
00+0	5.04	45.36	50.40	.100	.900
000+	3.32	20.16	23.48	.142	.858
0000	2.16	181.20	183.36	.012	.988

with methods for devising empirically based classification categories. These and other researchers have been investigating mathematical methods for deriving classification categories because of their belief that empirical classification systems will provide a more efficient means for the classification and the retrieval of information than the traditional methods of document classification. This belief has been subjected to scientific tests and evaluations.

In a study by Borko and Bernick,[7] an attempt was made to test the hypothesis that a classification system derived by factor analysis provides the best possible basis for automatic document classification and would result in more accurate automatic classification of documents than would be possible using more traditional classification categories. Maron,[8] in pursuing his interests in automatic indexing and classification, worked with 405 abstracts of computer literature which had been published in the *IRE Transactions on Electronic Computers*, Volume EC-8. In essence, Maron proposed a set of thirty-two subject categories which he felt were logically descriptive of the computer abstracts. Then he selected ninety clue words in such a manner that they would be good predictors of his thirty-two categories. The 405 documents were divided into two groups— 260 abstracts made up the experimental group and the remaining 145 comprised the validation group. Maron classified all 405 documents into the 32 categories. Working with the documents of the experimental group only, he computed the value of the terms in the Bayesian prediction equations. He then used this formula to automatically classify the documents into their categories. Auto-matic document classification was correct in 84.5 percent of the cases in the experimental group and in 51.8 percent of the cases in the validation group.

Borko and Bernick decided to test the hypothesis that a higher percentage of correct classifications could be made using the same set of documents if a factor analytically-derived classification system were used instead of Maron's logically derived categories. However, their results were approximately the same as those obtained by Maron. Because of the nature of the experimental design used, it was impossible to determine whether the difficulty lay in the mathematically derived classification system or whether the factor score method used to predict correct document classification was not as effective as the Bayesian prediction equation.

Another series of experiments were designed and executed.[9] It was concluded from this series that, while there was no significant difference between the predictive efficiency of Bayesian and factor score methods, automatic document classification is enhanced by the use of a factor-analytically derived classification schedule. Approximately 55 percent of the documents were automatically and correctly classified. While this 55 percent current automatic classification of the documents is statistically very significant, it will have little practical significance until greater accuracy can be demonstrated.

Up to this point the criterion for correct classification has been the human classifier, but this is not necessarily the best criterion. We know that humans are not perfectly reliable, and therefore, it is not possible to predict human classification with perfect accuracy. The ultimate criterion of the usefulness of any indexing and classification system is whether it retrieves relevant information in response to a search request. Automatic document classification procedures should be evaluated on how efficiently they retrieve information and not on how well they can match the imperfect human classifier. This is a much more difficult problem, but research is already under way to evaluate the retrieval effectiveness of automatic document classification. As work progresses on the evaluation and improvement of techniques for automatic document indexing and classification, it can be anticipated that the bottleneck which now exists between the collection and the processing of documents will be eliminated and automated storage and retrieval systems will become possible.

NOTES

[1] A. F. Parker-Rhodes, *Contributions to the Theory of Clumps.* M. L. 138. (Cambridge, England: Cambridge Language Research Unit, 1961), March, p. 4.

[2] *Ibid*, p. 9.

[3] R. M. Needham, *The Theory of Clumps, II.* M. L. 139 (Cambridge, England: Cambridge Language Research Unit, 1961), March.

[4] F. B. Baker, Information Retrieval Based Upon Latent Class Analysis. *Journal of the Association of Computing Machinery*, 9:512-521, Oct. 1962, No. 4.

[5] *Ibid*, p. 520.

[6] H. Borko, The Construction of an Empirically Based Mathematically Derived Classification System. *Proceedings of the Joint Computer Conference*, San Francisco, May 1-3, 1961, 21:279-289. (Also available as SDC document SP-585.)

[7] H. Borko and M. Bernick, Automatic Document Classification. *JACM*, Vol. 10, No. 2., April 1963. (Also available as TM-771.)

[8] M. E. Maron, Automatic Indexing: An Experimental Inquiry. *JACM*, 8:407-417, No. 3, July 1961.

[9] H. Borko and M. Bernick, Automatic Document Classification, Part II—Additional Experiments. *JACM*, 11:No. 2, April 1964. (Also available as TM-771/001/00.)

Classification and Mechanical Selection

J. Farradane

"The following brief summary of a few main lines of research is given as background to the main purpose of this paper, which is to make comparisons between the different approaches, eliminate those which can be shown to be blind alleys, and finally, to show that classification principles are essential to the fulfillment of the aims of mechanical selection."

The needs of information retrieval, especially in the scientific field, have posed a number of problems, not yet adequately solved, in the fine analysis of subject matter, its organization into a form in which it can be examined or scanned by some systematic principles and from different viewpoints, and in the reassemblage of requisite parts to yield not only possible references but also the information content required. It was long ago clear that bibliographic classification, as hitherto known to librarians (e.g., Library of Congress, Dewey, UDC, Bliss systems), is quite incapable of dealing with the degree of detail required, the flexibility needed, or the unpredictable complexity of a given inquiry. The problem in science, especially, for example, in physics or organic chemistry, has also been that of dealing with rapidly expanding areas of knowledge. Efforts to cope with the problems have taken different paths in different countries, according to their assessments of the problems. There has been little contact between these approaches, and agreement on any basic principles has therefore not hitherto been attempted. The following brief summary of a few main lines of research is given as a background to the main purpose of this paper, which is to make comparisons between the different approaches, eliminate those which can be shown to be blind alleys, and, finally, to show that classification principles are essential to the fulfilment of the aims of mechanized selection.

In Europe, and in France in particular, the task appears to have been seen largely as one of notation only, and Cordonnier, de Grolier, and others have put forward new ideas, such as syllabic notations, for coping with detail or complexity together with brevity in notation. Notation is, however, but a systematization of already ordered material; it cannot by itself, however ingenious it may be, contribute to the analysis or ordering of knowledge, and can be of value only as a step in the scanning problem. Without previous formulation of accepted principles of order in knowledge, it remains sterile.

The Colon Classification developed by Ranganathan in India represents a radically new departure (even though small, unconscious, indications of such an approach can be discerned in older systems of library classification). The method is still intended, by its author, principally for use in book classification. In previous systems the necessity of coordinating concepts, instead of expecting to find them all by processes of subdivision, received only small attention. In Colon, this need becomes the dominating principle. Shortened schedules with the older type of subdivision remain, but all complex subjects are dealt with by groupings of similar concepts into categories of substantives, or facets, between which relations exist by implication. This gives a great advance in flexibility of analysis, and organization by a preferred order of facets gives a reproducible system capable of well-ordered notation. These categories of substantives are, however, often ambiguous in nature, the implied relations do not always seem to have the flexibility required above all in scientific work, and the notation (retaining decimal subdivision in each facet) shows little advance on that of earlier systems. Various other newer proposed systems show trends, often unrecognized as such, towards the incorporation of elementary facet structure.

In England, the Classification Research Group, endeavouring to investigate basic principles, has reached considerable agreement[1] that the principle of using facets, in a preferred order, is the

SOURCE: Reprinted from the International Study Conference on Classification for Information Retrieval, Dorking, England, 1957, *Proceedings* (New York: Pergamon for ASLIB, 1957), pp. 65–69, by permission of ASLIB.

best so far available, but has concluded that much greater freedom in selection and order of facets is required than in Colon, and that the facets cannot be tied to any universal set of categories of substantives.

The present author considers that the establishment of facet structure by categories of substantives is inadequate, since the relations between concepts are not made explicit. He considers it essential to analyse subjects by the relations between concepts, and has endeavoured to show,[2] on a basis of the experimental psychology of thinking, that a limited small number of categories of relations exists, and that these relations have their own 'natural' preferred order. Facet grouping by relational equivalence can thereby likewise be produced as desired. The system can also be used, and perhaps finds more immediate application, in that halfway stage to classification—an indexing system.

In the United States of America the failure of older classifications has led (as it appears to us in England) to a rejection of classification for information retrieval, in favour, initially, of the correlation of concepts by mechanical methods, using punched cards or equivalent means. In the majority of its forms, mechanical selection has been concerned with simple or complex forms of the mere correlation of terms by juxtaposition, or sorting together, whether by Batten, Zator, IBM, or other types of card. Earlier one-to-one correspondence of punched holes and concepts was replaced by ingenious methods of multiple punching, by which much greater freedom of notation becomes possible. The complexity of correlated terms has led to the replacement of hand sorting by various automatic, mechanical, and electronic sorting machines. It should be remarked that many developments of such methods, such as Sphinxo or Uniterm, remain only methods of undefined correlation of terms, and do not offer logical or classificatory principles.

The inadequacy of this mechanical approach was, however, soon felt in practice. The difficulties were, for example, due to the occurrence of synonyms, to loss of material not indexed directly under the term sought but under a cognate term or a class term of higher order, and to selection of unwanted material, owing to the multiple relations by which concepts can be connected. This has led chiefly to three types of approach intended to improve searching. The simplest is one resembling the facet principle, by creating varied categories of substantives in terms of notational guides or 'role indicator encoding'. Thus, for example, in the recent Battelle system, concepts in a chemical process are grouped under such categories as 'effector', 'effected', 'data', 'starting material', 'process', 'absence', 'relation of', etc. These are notational additions to the notation for the substance or process, etc., concerned, and complicate the notation considerably. If regarded as facets, many of these 'indicators' are ambiguous or redundant and unsuitable as index terms. Moreover, many of the difficulties mentioned above are not obviated.

The second approach has been an attempt to apply what is called linguistic analysis or semantic factoring. This might seem to be a sort of rethinking of classificatory principles, but, all unrealized, it contains long-discarded fallacies. The idea that a given concept can be expressed by the mere conjunction of terms found by analysis of that concept into different aspects of its meaning (e.g., 'thermometer' into 'heat' and 'measure') is logically absurd, even if ambiguities of meaning of such complexes were not all too easily producible by erroneous relational implications, e.g., 'measure'. It also depends greatly upon the language employed, since words, or their apparent equivalent in other languages, may vary greatly in shades of meaning or emphasis in different situations.

The third approach is that in which it is thought that ideas from symbolic logic (the propositional calculus) or from Boolean algebra (the calculus of classes) can be applied to information retrieval. For this purpose only the simplest operations of complementing, intersecting, and joining have been tried. Two grave logical faults have constantly been committed in such applications. The calculus of classes applies to classes, but most concepts which have to be dealt with in information retrieval are not class terms, but single concepts, and hence these methods, even in their simplest form, are not applicable.[3] The intersection of two classes undoubtedly yields entities having the characteristics of both classes, and these entities are still class terms, never single concepts; these entities sometimes yield ambiguities when, as often happens, they are read as ordinary language, e.g. 'fish' and 'food' intersection gives 'fish which are food', but not 'food for fish'. When one or both initial terms are not classes, but single concepts (however complex), the result of intersection is logically meaningless, and only a correlation of terms is achieved. Since the relations between such correlated terms are not specified, even the supposition of a definite meaning is absent. The second logical fault arises when methods borrowed from propositional calculus are applied. This calculus deals with statements or propositions (not classes or single concepts) and concerns the accuracy of deductions made from two or more propositions. Its rules and manipulations, which have resemblances to parts of the calculus of classes, cannot apply to single concepts. Furthermore, the relations between propositions are of a nature quite different from those implied (or intended) between correlated concepts, or between class terms used as single concepts (as in simple correlative selection). Another fault is the idea of using a negation term, e.g., 'not a' or 'a'', as the full complement of 'a'; this is not necessarily true in logical systems, even though it is assumed in Boolean algebra, since alternative elements may exist. For example, melting processes and nonmelting processes together do not allow for glass softening processes. In Taube's writings, these logical faults (and others) constantly appear. In Perry's work, all three of the above errors of correlation, semantic factoring, and logical systems have been applied, alone or in combination.

It may be noted that where the notation or punching system used for mechanical selection has been contrived with an attempt to show some degree of order, as in classification, the methods of deriving such order have been very empirical, using only some obvious generical relations, or groupings showing apparent class similarities. Developed ideas in classification have not been applied to mechanical selection, though Bernier[4] has made suggestions for correlative indexes which contain some resemblances to Ranganathan's chain indexing methods and to simple facet structure (without preferred order).

It has become clear that the difficulties of mechanical selection are due to the lack of a pertinent and correct logical structure. The problems of logical structure in the ordering of concepts therefore require consideration as a separate study; they will not be solved by uncritical experimentation with systems inapplicable to it. Furthermore, the use of sorting or selecting machines based on principles originally required for, e.g., the treatment of statistical records or commercial data, is likely to involve its own train of difficulties. What is required is a satisfactory logical system to which principles of mechanical selection can be matched, after which a machine can be devised to perform the requisite tasks.

This study of the logical ordering of knowledge in terms of concepts is an essential part of classification. Classification is here definable as the study or practice of ordered structure in knowledge; the problems of notation are separate and ancillary, but secondary, to the question of structure. Classification does not nowadays imply merely the setting up of classes (on the empirical basis of existing data), followed by varying degrees of subdivision; the faults of this method have been obvious in many older library classifications, and include the cardinal defect that the subdivisions are often in mixed relational dependence on the main term, which is a logical error, and that the subdivisions, owing to notational difficulties, are only too frequently not even uniformly members of the same class or sub-class; in a small special classification, where the intended order can be grasped by inspection, this may not matter; but in a general classification, especially for use with mechanical selection, it is inadmissible. Such difficulties, whether recognized in fundamental terms or not, rightly led to the rejection of 'classification' by many serious workers in information retrieval. The setting up of 'main classes' with subdivisions is derived by the application or earlier philosophic concepts. We have seen, however, that all newer attempts have in one way or another involved the idea of expressing *relations between concepts*, for which the known logical relations are no substitute. The generic or class relation is clearly not the only relation which may occur, and this has tacitly been recognized, in several older classifications, by the use of various auxiliary schedules. It is clear that information retrieval is never intended to produce groupings of unrelated concepts.

The underlying principle of facet structure is that of relations between concepts. As pointed out earlier, the approach to facets through categories of substantives yields only relations by implication, though the results may be satisfactory since the intuitive thinking involved will usually be unconsciously rational. The present author's approach through categories of relations should, if correctly based, provide a more positively testable system. The relations involved are quite different from those of formal or symbolic logic, and are hence very unfamiliar in appearance. It is important to note, however, that both methods of deriving facet order have usually been found to provide the same analysis of a given complex subject. The problems of order within a facet, and of notation, require further study.

Machines so far used for correlative selection

have mostly been of the type capable of selecting terms from any position, and are not suited to the search of classified material. The use of a structure of facets in a fixed preferred order makes possible the use of simpler sorting machines. Such straightforward sorting machines are cheaper to construct. Notational problems for machine sorting are also simpler than for the usual needs of library classification (where brevity is desirable), since the machines can cope easily with long, simple notations—much more easily than with complex shorter notations containing different species of indexing marks and special symbols: a strictly logical breakdown in classification order is more easily achieved when the length of notation is not a drawback. When the relations between concepts are made obvious and explicit, the task of information retrieval is immensely simplified. In correlative searching, as hitherto carried out, what is retrieved (via the notational marks) has been references to papers where the required concepts occur, and such papers may or may not contain the required information. With relational facet structure it will be possible to retrieve (again via the notation) the actual information content.

The value of classification in facet order is not to be found only in providing order. It gives greater precision to detail, to any desired degree, tends to prevent ambiguous correlations and erroneous permutations of concepts, and enables related concepts to be found, the latter being a form of browsing in ideas which is of the greatest value. It also enables searches to be made in only the relevant sections of an index (instead of the whole set of cards), which greatly reduces the time of search. It can likewise aid the task of 'sorting-in' new material into an index. Finally, classification is essential as the basis for good notation, which clearly must reflect, and not run counter to, the logical principles of the ordered structure. Since the magnitude of the tasks of information retrieval today inevitably call for mechano-electronic methods, the problem before us is therefore to find how classification and mechanical selection can be applied together. In their fusion the way will be opened for fruitful advances.

NOTES

[1] B. C. Vickery: 'The need for a faceted classification as the basis for all methods of information retrieval.' UNESCO (IACDocTerPAS) Report, Ref. 320/5515, Paris, 26th May 1955.

[2] J. Farradane: 'The Psychology of Classification,' *J. Doc.*, 11: 187–201, 1955.

[3] Y. Bar-Hillel: 'A Logician's reaction to recent theorizing on information search systems,' *Amer. Doc.*, 8: 103–122, 1957.

[4] C. L. Bernier: 'Correlative Indexes. I. Alphabetical correlative indexes,' *Amer. Doc.*, 7: 283–288, 1956.

CLASSIFICATION

Research in Classification

Classification research has been for a number of years centered primarily in Europe with a major exception being Mr. Ranganathan in India. For some reason it has not been popular in the United States. Such research has provided the major tools or devices in the development of new and very different classification schemes—some very traditional, some very nonconventional. A great deal of what has been done has been tested and proven workable; some is still highly experimental. There is still a very definite lack of classification research in all parts of the world and a multitude of questions still remain unanswered.

Some Aspects of Basic Research in Classification

Phyllis A. Richmond

"Basic research in classification covers many areas and problems. As with the development of modern mathematics in the nineteenth century, the chief impediment to advancement is not thinking in terms of new ideas, but unthinking or breaking free of old concepts."

In recent years, basic research in classification has taken the form of questioning some of the accepted axioms of the subject. Traditionally, classification has meant a process of division and subdivision, proceeding from general to particular, until specific units of considerable concreteness are reached. This produces a rigid set of classes and class relationships. The classes are displayed in tables, arranged to show a hierarchy or family tree of relationships, often called a tree of knowledge. It is possible, however, by using a broader definition of classification,[1] to introduce a different approach, utilizing the scientific method and working from particular to general. The specific unit is accepted as the basic element of the system, and classes are formed by grouping units which are similar. The classification is created by building upwards, by putting individual parts together to form a whole (synthesis). The net result is a flexible set of classes and class relationships, displayed through block patterns rather than by the more familiar hierarchy or tree diagram.

The new, analytic types of classification are being developed in recognition of the fact that, as Shera points out, every book is a complex creation composed of a larger number of related patterns which reflect the multidimensional nature of knowledge.[2] In the analytic classifications, it is recognized that every relationship of a single classification element is vitally necessary for the eventual retrieval of information. The classification must at once be as broad and as fine as possible. This is extremely difficult to achieve.

The purpose of this nontraditional classification is twofold: to escape from the procedure of classifying something in one place and in one place only (pigeon-holeing), and to permit approach to information from any angle which may be perti-nent.[3] Various analytic methods are utilized.[4] These produce a compound classification composed of elemental parts, each of which is made available for searching purposes because it can be indexed separately. In this paper, the term "faceted" shall be applied throughout to denote any classification which is compounded of parts, each of which in turn is built up by assigning individual items to more general, related categories.

Probably the chief motivating factor behind the new approach to classification has been the tremendous growth of scientific literature during the past century. This growth, which is still taking place at an exponential rate, has necessitated a new approach to the cataloging or storage process, simply because traditional methods cannot cope with either the deluge of material or the forms in which it is presented.

The traditional method of analyzing material for purposes of storage and retrieval has been in the form of a general information system tailored to suit books. Its catalog is in unit card form, alphabetically arranged, with a standardized method of entry and a standardized set of descriptive terms. For all practical purposes, the alphabetical or dictionary arrangement of the catalog has limited use of the classification to providing a classified shelf list—that is, it supplies a code number necessary for placing each book on the shelf with others on the same subject. Classification is made a tool for achieving consistent, fixed location of like material. On the other hand, realization that a classified shelf list leaves something to be desired in the way of subject analysis has forced catalogers to add subject entries to the card catalog, each corresponding to one of the major topics covered by the book and chosen from a standardized subject heading list containing a mixture of terms gath-

SOURCE: Reprinted from *Library Resources and Technical Services*, 4 (Spring, 1960), pp. 139–147, by permission of the publisher, the American Library Association.

ered through literary warrant.[5] Throughout this whole cataloging process, the physical book, not its contents, has been the primary bibliographic target.

Therefore, one of the first questions raised in reassessing the value of classification was whether the the cataloging procedure was directed towards the right target. In other words, should the primary bibliographic target be the book *per se* or its contents? If the book is a monograph on a homogeneous subject, the system of shelf classification, supplemented by subject headings, is usually adequate. On the other hand, if the book represents a cross-fertilization among subject fields or if it is a collection of papers, possibly on one central theme, but from many points of view representing many different fields, and if the information in it is to be sought from all these subject angles, then it is impossible to present its true subject coverage without either a multiple-classification approach or a much deeper subject analysis than can be made with standard methods.

The fact that journal articles and reports, rather than monographs, are now the most important sources of *new information* in many fields has led to the development of different cataloging systems. These are subject-oriented and are based on the idea that it is the *content* of the book, article or report which is of prime significance, not the book, article or report in itself. In many of these new systems, notably in Uniterms, cataloging methods involving standardized form of entry and description have been eliminated completely, and classification, if present at all, has been made subservient to the subject analysis (by words) process.

The revised fundamental concept, that one should bring out the full scope of the book or article, has had some far-reaching consequences upon the development of modern classification. In the attempt to present more than a cursory indication of the content of a book, a special system was devised almost thirty years ago by S. R. Ranganathan, who was influenced by Berwick Sayers and Henry E. Bliss.[6] The canons of classification, as enumerated by Ranganathan, led him to the conclusion that it is possible in every subject to analyze knowledge into five basic categories: personality, matter, energy, space, and time. Others using Ranganathan's pattern have not limited themselves so strictly, and have added more categories as the individual subjects demanded.[7]

In any case, the main categories are converted into the links or *facets* of the classification. The facets themselves may represent the fundamental categories directly or in combination, and they are made up of elements, called "foci" in Ranganathan's schedules. Then a notation is assigned, and the whole is riveted together in a predetermined order with special connective symbols (originally colons, hence the name "Colon Classification"). The necessity of distinguishing between the whole and its parts and of using the elemental material of a single category more than once in describing a title has led to the adoption of the idea of different "levels" and "rounds" of classification. The need for indicating what influences what or is influenced by what, and the form in which the material is presented, has resulted in the addition of special indicators for relations, and the "common isolate" for an expanded system of form division. Other problems, such as what to do with a classic (any work that attracts other works about itself) have produced ingenious solutions, but the complexities involved in some of these, as well as the difficulties of trying to divide everything into five basic categories, have complicated the Colon Classification almost to the point of no return.[8] It is possible that some of these devices could be eliminated by a careful reworking of the schedules.

Other classificationists have followed Ranganathan, with wide modifications.[9] The approach to subject analysis inherent in faceted classification has been promoted by recognition of the fundamental element or "isolate"[10] as the basis for this type of classification. These isolates, the atoms for the facet (itself the equivalent to the molecule), are the building blocks from which the classification is made. It has also led to the realization that there are two ways in which expansion in any classification takes place: horizontally, called classification in *array*, and vertically, called classification in *chain*.[11] A method and a notation are sought whereby unlimited additions may be made in both directions without impairing the pattern of the system as a whole. So far, this has proved relatively easy for classification in chain, but quite an obstacle for classification in array. Some improved way of indicating *relationships* between concepts contained in facets is also sought, since, as Farradane points out, these are often of greater significance than the concepts themselves.[12] It has even been suggested that alphabetical indexes may be made more pertinent through classification. In this case, the analytic process is used to make the index more exhaustive and to cut down on scattering of related material.[13]

The notation used in classification has been re-examined in the process of creating analytic classification.[14] It is recognized that many conventional classifications have been unnecessarily limited by their notations. Is it necessary, for example, to try to pour all knowledge into the ten or twenty-six categories that can be represented by the Hindu-Arabic numerals 0-9, or the Roman letters A-Z? Must the elaboration under each be limited to multiples of the original base of the notation, as in Dewey, Universal Decimal, or Bliss? Standard letters and numbers are too limited to satisfy the requirements of analytic classifications. A larger base of operations is needed. Various suggestions have been made for enlarging the capacity of classification systems, either by adding symbols as purely ordinal numbers or by using a number system with a larger base.[15] In faceted classifications, the necessity of employing sign-posts to signal the introduction of a new facet, or to divide components of a facet, or to indicate relationships, has resulted in the adoption of a special series of letters or marks or punctuation signs or other devices, each with its own peculiar meaning, position and purpose. The Colon Classification now utilizes a system of about seventy digits for all purposes. These numbers are an odd mixture, which makes them more difficult to understand and use than would be the case if some logical and uniform numbering system were required. The notation problem is another which requires adequate solution before an ideal classification can be constructed.

The single book which treats of many subjects or of one subject from many viewpoints has been mentioned. The multidimensional nature of knowledge itself presents another problem. There are some subjects which refuse to be compartmentalized.[16] Classification of material in interdisciplinary or area studies and of topics which cover several categories simultaneously is very difficult. Auxiliary tables and the analytic process were designed to solve this problem. Multiplane classification and dual classification numbers have been suggested as solutions.[17] Since the current tendency in all areas of knowledge is to realign old fields into new fields, and to rearrange the basic academic classification of knowledge, solution to this problem is imperative.

A more fundamental question related to the realignment of fields of knowledge is whether a full hierarchy in classification is necessary.[18] Would it be possible to classify without hierarchical arrangement? We are so accustomed to thinking in terms of a tree of knowledge that it is difficult even to consider an alternative. Nevertheless, with analytic classification, it is possible to classify in several nonhierarchical forms. These have been described figuratively as a series of related classification maps, or as a ball made up of layers and layers of connecting material, or as an interlocking network in depth, a lattice or a plexus of classification chains, or even, perhaps in despair, as a maze.[19]

A further question may be raised: if a classification does not necessarily have to be hierarchical in arrangement, does it have to be logical? The Dewey, Universal Decimal and Bliss classifications are made primarily by logical division, which is mirrored to some extent in their notations. The Library of Congress classification, in contrast, is definitely nonlogical and the notation is largely ordinal. This classification functions as well, if not better, than the others. A nonlogical classification has the great advantage of flexibility, since one may add to it rather freely without upsetting the whole pattern. The fact that the Library of Congress classification is displayed in an almost random fashion, after some initial form divisions in each main class, does not seem to be a disadvantage in its operation. In a nonconventional classification, the elements of each category may be expressed either in a logical or a nonlogical manner. The advantage of variability, rather than the display of relationships, is the chief motivation for choosing a nonlogical arrangement.

In addition to the traditional and the faceted classifications, there is a third type emerging from the subject approach to knowledge. This kind, which is, as yet, still uncertain, ill-defined and has no distinctive name, is based on utilization of the concept, the class, or even the actual word representing these ideas, as the fundamental element. The element itself is analyzed and fitted into the larger scale of things by relating it to more generic terms. This type of classification is represented in at least three forms: a specialized system of words (sometimes called "keywords" or "descriptors"), hierarchical definition, and semantic factoring.

The simplest example of the first form is the original Uniterms system, in which compound terms are reduced to their elementary components, and these matched (or "correlated") at will to construct new relationships. Various types of correlative indexes have been devised, all stemming from the same principle, but with different methods for determining index words.[20] This kind of word utilization, however, has developed problems arising from the peculiar nature of living language, and it has been necessary to turn to linguistics in order to try to find a way of dealing with words and their meaning(s) in a satisfactory manner. Classification was originally excluded as a means of indicating precise meaning, but recently there has been reconsideration of its values in this respect.[21]

In addition, the analysis of word indexing systems on a classification basis has begun to be extended to subject headings. Various investigations have been made of the concealed classification in the "see also" reference structure of these headings.[22] Here classification has proved more useful in determining relationships than in making the meaning of words more explicit.

A method of solving the ambiguity problem and at the same time indicating relationships is through hierarchical definition.[23] Hierarchical definition is a method of classifying words based on two principles. The first principle is that a word without context lacks precise meaning, and therefore, to be perfectly clear, it should carry some or all of its family tree around with it. This tree may be supplied by ordinary classification, but with this difference: the classification is limited to the contents of a major category, so that there would be a separate classification supplying definitions for each word, thus creating a classification chain for each word. These definition chains may be made by the standard method of division or by building up from elemental terms. The second principle in hierarchical definition is that the searcher should be led from the specific term of his choice to more general terms, so that if he enters an information system with a narrow or very specific subject in mind, he may be led to broader subjects related to his own and of value to him.[24] If hierarchical definition is used for the facets of a faceted classification, the definitions in each facet may be drawn from a separate subject classification—each subject may be classified separately.[25] There is no reason to limit subjects to those currently contained in existing classifications—one may branch out and away from academic listings, along the line of the Detroit Public Library's Reader Interest Arrangement, for example.[26] In the case of hierarchical definition for an analytic classification, the possibility of altering or revising the basic isolates in a single category without upsetting the whole system is a desirable feature. Hierarchical definition may also be used without notation in subject heading terms to tighten up the connective structure, and in correlative indexing to give more accurate meaning to index terms.

A third and much more advanced solution lies in the approach known as semantic factoring. In this process, as in the case of hierarchical definition, it is recognized that a word without context or amplification is likely to be ambiguous, and that to be sure of pinpoint precision in definition, some ways of providing context must be found. This is done by analyzing words into their basic concepts, and a classification of concepts and their relationships is created as the raw material for definition. The generic concepts (semantic factors), which are the isolates of the system, are linked together, as in the facets of a faceted classification, to form a compound classification for the original term. Thus, the resulting code word is very similar to the notationalized content of a facet, both being the reconstruction of a concept through an analytic process. As with facets, every factor in the compound term is subject to indexing link by link (chain indexing). A mixed notation is utilized. The whole classification number or code word also forms a "machine language word," and it and its component parts may be used for machine literature searching.[27] Classification is basic to this system, but the analysis is somewhat different from that of systems designed solely for classification purposes.

It may be noted that in all of the analytic classification approaches, the visualization of the patterns of knowledge cannot be shown as a tree, the standard division diagram, because the classification terms, such as the compound evaluations produced by faceting or semantic factoring, simply cannot be represented in this way. Probably the best way to visualize such analyses is as a lattice or multidimensional network.[28] Finally, it is necessary to point out that Vickery has emphasized and reemphasized with great persuasiveness the essential classification features of all subject approaches to the problems involved in analyzing information for storage and retrieval.[29]

In all forms of classification, but particularly in the nonconventional ones, language is an extremely important factor. The introduction of linguistics into classification has opened up a major area for research. One of the great weaknesses of the storage process is the necessity for describing a subject in language that is constantly changing. Material very often has to be cataloged long before the language in its field has crystallized and become stable, which means that, while a standard classification may be acceptable temporarily because its very nature gives the new material a definite place in relation to what has gone before, the *index* to this classification, the subject headings, and any classification whose links are composed of elements expressed in words almost certainly will be inadequate as to terminology and rarely will be in the final language of the field except in old and relatively unchanging areas.[30] Since the terminology is always changing and ambiguity does occur, even in classification, it is necessary to find some adequate means of dealing with constant change.

Some attempts have been made to analyze subject terminology linguistically, without particular regard to *meaning*, as is current practice in some portions of linguistics. The bits and parts of words produced are converted into a new kind of language, sometimes by a process resembling classification.[31] The tendency to ignore meaning as a primary target, which is decried by some linguists, lessens the value of these contributions to the subject analysis of bibliographic material, where results are not much use without meaning.

In some respects, the linguistic approach to subject analysis appears, philosophically speaking, diametrically opposed to the classification one. Actually, the two are almost inseparably intertwined: one cannot make a satisfactory classification without an alphabetical index based on words, and one cannot convey the precise meaning of words in any general information system without some kind of analysis based on classification. The possibility of considering classification as a language has not been overlooked.[32] This provides another intersection for classification and linguistics, particularly as manifested in mechanical translation.

One of the more interesting recent developments in library classification (though not called such) is the Detroit Public Library's Reader Interest Arrangement.[33] In this system, books are classified as usual with the Dewey Decimal Classification. Then, however, chosen ones are given a location symbol corresponding to one of the major categories into which the book fits, according to the dictates of reader interest. In other words, the rigidity of one-place, one-number classification is overcome by *physically* moving the book to shelves of related subjects where it might also have been classified. This is applied multiplane classification. Traditionally, the dictionary catalog has required books to have a fixed classification and a fixed location. With the classified catalog, the location is fixed, but the classification is mobile. With the Detroit system, the formal Dewey classification is fixed, but the "Reader Interest Arrangement" classification is mobile and the book is mobile. Ideally, both book and classification should be mobile. This could be done either by making the classification number solely a string of location symbols, as the content of the book suggests—a multiplane classification in linear style—or by developing some more sophisticated classification by means of an analytic process adapted to such a situation. The Detroit system and its classification possibilities deserve serious consideration, both as a means of escaping the limitations imposed by the dictionary catalog and as a potential method of surmounting the confines of hierarchical classification.

There are other areas deserving more study. The success of the subject approach in many of the present mechanical selection systems is deceptive. In most cases, the material handled has been extremely explicit and finite, and limited to a narrow subject. When one comes to the realm of ideas, as in pure research in science, or generally in less exact areas such as the humanities, the requirements are quite different and new methods must be devised to meet them. In many fields, for instance, notably in history and the humanities, the factual data are far less important in a research contribution than the argument or reasoning about them. Up to this point, the present methods of subject analysis have been able to do little with this type of information. Classification, by supplying a frame of reference, is probably in the best position to handle intangible or developing ideas, but even here there must be fuller recognition of the problem before really satisfactory solutions are to be found.

Basic research in classification covers many areas and problems, some of which have been discussed in this paper. As with the development of modern mathematics in the nineteenth century, the chief impediment to advancement is not thinking in terms of new ideas, but *un*-thinking or breaking free of old concepts. Once this has been accomplished, it is possible to approach the subject from angles which offer interesting opportunities for further study. It is too soon to know which viewpoints will be the most productive, and much too soon to tell which will ultimately yield new general classification systems. Suffice it to say that there is now enough interest in basic research in classification to make the future look very promising.

NOTES

[1] *Classification*: An orderly method of grouping things according to their salient characteristics of properties. The thing classified is a concept (an idea, an inference) or a complex of concepts, which is an accepted subjective representation of a real, but not necessarily observable, unit. The groups (or categories) are arranged systematically according to definite criteria, so that the relationships among them or derivation of one group from another are clearly indicated. A unique designation or verbalization is applied to each category. A notation, preferably either one which mirrors the internal structure of the classification or which reflects the constitution of its elemental concepts, may be applied.

[2] J. H. Shera, "Pattern, Structure and Conceptualization in Classification." *Proceedings of the International Study Conference on Classification for Information Retrieval Held at Beatrice Webb House, Dorking, England, 13th-17th May 1957* London. ASLIB, 1957. (Hereafter referred to as *Dorking Papers*) p. 21.

[3] B. C. Vickery, "Developments in Subject Indexing," *Journal of Documentation*, 11:7. March 1955. Vickery's ideas are elaborated in his book, *Classification and Indexing in Science*. London, Butterworths Scientific Publications, 1958.

J. E. L. Farradane, "A Scientific Theory of Classification and Indexing and Its Practical Applications." *Journal of Documentation*, 6:84-85. June 1950.

J. H. Shera, *Dorking Papers*. p. 20.

Eric de Grolier, *Théorie et pratique des classifications documentaires*. (Paris: Union française des organismes de documentation, 1956), p. 345.

"Concluding Survey." *Dorking Papers*. p. 82.

[4] "Conclusions and Recommendations." *Dorking Papers*. p. 111.

[5] *Literary warrant*: 1) The justification for putting a given term in a schedule because published material exists on that subject. 2) The justification for using a certain principle of division in facet analysis because it appears in the literature. (Definitions by J. Mills, courtesy of B. C. Vickery.)

[6] S. R. Ranganathan, *Prolegomena to Library Classification*. (Madras: Madras Library Association, 1937), pp. xiv-xvi.

_____ "Library Classification as a Discipline." *Dorking Papers. p. 3.*

[7] See, for example: B. C. Vickery, *Classification and Indexing in Science*. pp. 34, 85, 87.

[8] S. R. Ranganathan, *Colon Classification*. 5th ed. (Madras: Madras Library Assoc., 1957), v. 1. "Basic Classification."

[9] See B. L. Palmer and A. J. Wells, *The Fundamentals of Library Classification*. (London: Allen & Unwin, 1951), pp. 42-52, 82-100.

J. H. Shera and Margaret Egan, *The Classified Catalog*. Chicago, ALA, 1956. Appendix A., pp. 104-121.

D. J. Foskett, "Occupational Safety and Health Documents Classification Scheme." *Dorking Papers*. Appendix I. pp. 115-136.

B. C. Vickery, *Classification and Indexing in Science*. Appendix B. pp. 146-162. "Classification Research Group Bulletin no. 5." *Journal of Documentation*, 15:39-57. March 1959.

The classification of Brisch is somewhat similar. Cf. Barbara Kyle, "E. G. Brisch: Something New in Classification." *Special Libraries*, 47:100-105. March 1956.

[10] *Isolate*: An item of knowledge . . . which is an object or class of objects, a process or class of processes, or an abstract term or class of terms, which is clearly and, *at its own level of complexity*, uniquely definable, as far as may be possible. Cf. J. E. L. Farradane, "A Scientific Theory of Classification and Indexing and Its Practical Applications." *Journal of Documentation*, 6:87. June 1950.

[11] S. R. Ranganathan, *Prolegomena*. Canons 8-11 (array), pp. 40-58; Canons 12-13 (chain), pp. 59-61; also pp. 99-119.

J. E. L. Farradane, "A Scientific Theory of Classification and Indexing: Further Considerations." *Journal of Documentation*, 8:88-89. June 1952.

S. R. Ranganathan, "Self-Perpetuating Scheme of Classification." *Journal of Documentation*, 4:227. March 1949.

[12] J. E. L. Farradane, "The Psychology of Classification." *Journal of Documentation*, 11:187-201. December 1955.

[13] B. C. Vickery, *Classification and Indexing in Science*. pp. 103-109.

[14] Charles Bishop, "An Integrated Approach to the Documentation Problem." *American Documentation*, 4:56. Spring 1953.

J. E. Daily, "Subject Headings and the Theory of Classification." *American Documentation*, 8:269-270. October 1957.

E. J. Coates, "Notation in Classification." *Dorking Papers*, pp. 51-64.

B. I. Palmer and A. J. Wells, *Fundamentals of Library Classification*, pp. 60-75.

J. E. L. Farradane, "A Scientific Theory of Classification and Indexing: Further Considerations." *Journal of Documentation*, 8:74. June 1952.

B. C. Vickery, "Notational Symbols in Classification." *Journal of Documentation*, 8:14-32. March 1952; 12:73-87. June 1956; 13:72-77. June 1957; 14:1-11. March 1958; 15:12-16. March 1959.

B. C. Vickery, *Classification and Indexing in Science*. pp. 48-74.

[15] B. L. Palmer and A. J. Wells, *Fundamentals of Library Classification*, p. 70.

P. A. Richmond, "A Simple Mnemonic Large-Base Number System for Notational Purposes." *Journal of Documentation*, 14:208-211. December 1958.

Transformation and Organization of Information Content: Aspects of Recent Research in the Art and Science of Classification

Phyllis A. Richmond

"No classification system of any kind will be outstandingly successful until some of the fundamental questions underlying the making of classifications are answered."

Classification research is directed towards making classification systems which accurately represent the current state of human knowledge, and also towards developing more efficient ways of applying such classification. Considerable research of both types has been undertaken during the past five years. This will not be described here since it is fairly easy to find in the literature. The purpose of this study is to indicate the significance of current research and to try to put this into some perspective. Unless otherwise indicated, attention will be devoted primarily to the type of research that attempts to make better classification systems, the work of the classificationist, rather than to that aimed at better application of classification schemes, the work of the classifier. The views presented here escape few of the pitfalls of oversimplification, but they are a synthesis made in the interest of noting trends and future possibilities wherever possible.

DEFINITIONS

For the purposes of this study, a *class* shall be defined as a group of persons, things, qualities, ideas, and such, having common characteristics, a common *name*, and capable of being recognized as an entity or concept. This is not the same as a mathematical class, such as the class of all numbers divisible by nineteen, which is recognizable but not nameable. The stipulation that the class be both recognizable and nameable is made to ensure easy communication of the entity or concept of the class from person to person.

A *classification system* shall be defined as a structural arrangement of classes in some helpful order, with the relationships between classes clearly defined or delineated. The structure may be in Euclidean or hyperspace, and in the form of a hierarchy, a lattice, a tree, a maze, a net or any other kind of *ordered* system.

Classification (as an activity) shall be defined as methods for the analysis, description and organization of the information content of documents, using "document" in its broadest sense to mean any kind of graphic record. Methods may be applied singly or in a multiple approach as necessary to present a comprehensive and comprehensible picture, in concise form, of the sum total of recorded knowledge. They may be utilized by either the classificationist or the classifier.

Science. Since there are two major definitions of the word "science" in English and both are used, it will be necessary to differentiate between them. The first definition is "science is an organized body of knowledge." This is equivalent to the German "Wissenschaft," and is used in such areas as social science, library science, linguistic science and the romantic "theology, queen of the sciences."[1] Ranganathan, the classificationist, usually uses science in this sense, treating logic, mathematics and natural philosophy as one *science*. The second definition considers science as a body of knowledge "dealing with material phenomena and based mainly on observation, experiment and induction."[2] This is the German "Naturwissenschaft," and it is in this restricted sense that the term is used in this study. It will thus *exclude* logic, mathematics, linguistics and such.

SCOPE

The classification research to be discussed is a selection of that produced within the last five years except where earlier work was particularly apro-

SOURCE: Reprinted from the Congress of International Federation for Documentation, 1965, *Proceedings* (Washington: National Academy of Sciences, 1965), pp. 87–106, by permission of the publisher.

pos. Discussion is limited to material in English because interpretation of the terminological nuances is difficult in one's native tongue and almost impossible in other languages unless one is a good linguist. A deliberate choice has been made among material available in print, near-print and typescript, with print being first choice whenever possible because of its availability and reliability as compared with the other two.

The problems involved in classification will be approached from several different angles and the same basic data will be treated from various viewpoints. By the end of the study, some of the topics will have been seen in several guises. Two major themes will run throughout: the basic premises of S. R. Ranganathan in classification theory, and Colin Cherry's insights about human communication.

The methods used in classification: Analysis, description and organization, fit into what Ranganathan has called the idea plane, the verbal plane and the notational plane.[3] The idea plane comprises raw material, the units of information, that make up the sum total of human knowledge and belief, as well as the categorization of this totality, based on meaning and expressed in words, gestures, sounds, pictures, and so forth, which are interpretable at the pragmatic level by humans in the same cultural milieu. The choice of words in natural or meta-language takes place on the verbal plane. The notational plane is concerned with the codification of the products of the first two planes. This tripartite distinction classification is highly significant and will be referred to again and again throughout this study.

Classification research, in recent years, has branched out in several directions, notably by adopting the methodology and outlook of three disciplines: *deduction*, including logic and mathematics, *induction*, including scientific and probability methods, and *language*, including linguistics. These three disciplines are often treated philosophically under the general heading *logic*. They are mutually overlapping to a considerable degree. It is difficult, for instance, to say where mathematical logic leaves off and the mathematical school of Logicism begins, or whether structural linguistics is nominalism in mathematics or formalistic mathematical linguistics; and probability is treated both as mathematics and as science. Allowing for the fact that all of the types of methodology used in classification have a tendency to shade into each other at one point or another, attempt will be made here to stress the differences between them

rather than the similarities. All of the work discussed as deduction belongs in the idea plane, as well as much of that considered as induction. Most, but not all, of the work in language belongs to the verbal plane. The notational plane received much attention in the 1950's and it has reached a higher degree of refinement than the other two. Momentarily it is of lesser interest in a discussion of trends.

DEDUCTIVE METHODS

The first area of classification research, and the traditional one, is that of deduction. Deduction in classification is best known through the classical method of logical division. Three of the major bibliographic classification systems are based on this method: the Dewey Decimal Classification, the Universal Decimal Classification and the Bliss Bibliographic Classification. All of these systems, in spite of uneven growth and imperfections in logical organization, limited notation and two-plane representation, are very much alive and functioning, though Bliss is not kept up-to-date as are the others. The Universal Decimal Classification has some faceting features similar to the Colon Classification, but, to Dr. Ranganathan's distress, these are not well-developed.[4] All three systems are universal in scope, and, for their purpose, unlikely to be displaced during the next few decades, though the Library of Congress Classification has been making inroads in Dewey territory in academic libraries, and the scientific and technical parts of the Universal Decimal Classification may supplant Dewey in some special libraries. All three are hierarchical systems, and, in theory at least, similar in their basic pattern to the inverted tree structures produced by biological classification.

Deductive logic in various forms has always been clearly allied to classification. In recent years, symbolic logic has been utilized for the organization of information through several systems which are rationalized via Boolean algebra. Since they have some classification features, they will be considered here, although perhaps, technically speaking, they should be regarded as independent. Various forms of coordinate indexing, whereby the user makes up his own searching unit by combining terms selected from an authorized list, are the most popular of such systems. The searching unit may or may not be a class. It is interesting in these systems to see the way in which classification has been introduced into lists of indexing terms. The *Thesaurus of Engineering Terms*, of the Engineers Joint Council, is an example. Most of the terms have relationships with other terms in the list, indicated by direct cross-references for synonyms, by references to broader or narrower terms for words in hierarchical relationship to one another, or by indirect cross-references, called "related terms." In some cases, the related term is used to redefine the headword, thus turning it into a homograph.[5] The relationships among the broader and narrower terms can be traced through the list and the resulting classification illustrated by diagrams based on hierarchy. In some parts of the system, these diagrams look like parts of cubes in outline, triangles or diamonds in flying V's, and so forth.[6] Whether these scraps of lattice structure or what remains to be seen. It might be desirable to rework the diagrams into trees of the type used by Gerard Salton of the Harvard Computation Laboratory. With trees, it might be possible to compare the class structure in the *Thesaurus* with that of a modern faceted classification such as the English Electric scheme.[7]

The *Subject Authority List* of the American Petroleum Institute's Information Retrieval Project avoids the complexities of the engineering thesaurus by the simple expedient of adding two more lists to its thesaurus. The first pulls together the hierarchy of broader and narrower terms, giving some context and definition to individual terms; the second gives cross references and scope notes. The latter probably contains a concealed classification as in standard subject heading cross-references, but the omission of "related terms" at least ensures that a headword should only have a single semantic interpretation.[8]

Classification features have been added by visual means in some thesauri in order to show relationships between terms—in other words, to throw in some of the family tree in order to make meanings clearer. This is done with lists in the American Petroleum Institute opus mentioned, and the *Thesaurus of ASTIA Descriptors*,[9] and with arrowgraphs in the *EURATOM-Thesaurus*.[10] The arrowgraphs per se may not be intended to be a classification system, but the effect is to make it possible to create both classification in array and in chain, starting at any point.

In other context, Lauren Doyle has developed an association or semantic road map. These maps have a definite structural order, in this case a hierarchy, and its classes are named.[11] It is more definitely a classification system than the arrowgraphs. John Melton and Jessica Melton have worked out an association diagram showing the relationships which can be developed starting from a single word,

which is like a one-family arrowgraph.[12] All these visual aids are used to indicate the meaning of words or word combinations.

Word combinations, as in coordinate indexing, work well when the document collections are not too large,[13] and where limited, homogeneous subject fields are involved.[14] The need for a homogeneous field can be seen quite easily by taking any thesaurus and picking out words which have alternate meanings in other subjects. Calvin Mooers' insistence upon definitions for every descriptor (to which no one has paid any attention) is well taken.[15] Undefined terms offer a field day for misinterpretations and guarantee retrieval of non-pertinent material. Both Robert A. Fairthorne and Mooers have commented upon the unsuitability of Boolean algebra as a logical base for any but static systems, and Donald Hillman has demonstrated this view in an almost textbook example of deductive reasoning.[16] The logical argument holds regardless of the size of the collection or its homogeneity.

Both Fairthorne and Mooers have suggested other kinds of mathematics as alternatives to Boolean algebra.[17] The methodology of deduction is a necessary part of all mathematics, but applications vary. There are three major schools of thought operating in the borderline area between mathematics and philosophy known as *foundations of mathematics*. All of them make use of the same rigorous techniques of reasoning for purposes which Hempel calls "theoretical juice extraction."[18] These schools are Logicism, Intuitionism and Formalism.

Logicism, which treats mathematics as reducible to logic and is exemplified in the work of Russell, Whitehead, Frege, Church and Carnap,[19] includes axiomatics, logical inference, mathematical proof, validity, and, of course, traditional deductive procedure.[20] Boolean algebra is a part of this field. Logicism recognizes universals or abstract entities existing independently of the mind and holds that classes are discovered. Those documentalists who hope to discover new knowledge in the process of putting elements together to create classes follow this school. The application of logicistically-based systems, such as coordinate indexing, has not been a great improvement over the forms of classification made by logical division, so that, in recent years, some attention has been paid to the other two schools.

The Intuitionist school, which is exemplified in the work of Brouwer, Heyting, Poincaré, and Weyl, holds that there are universals or abstract entities, but they are mind-made. Classes are invented. Deduction is regarded as an accidental feature of mathematics. In the view of this school, mathematics, "a product of the activity of the fallible human mind, . . . is based upon a fundamental intuition of some process or principle which is not capable of deduction from tautologies and is therefore synthetic in character."[21] Classification, in this view, would be a synthetic process. Evert Beth's semantic constructions, with trees as illustration, suggest a possible approach.[22] The Intuitionist school rejects the law of the excluded middle—that is, rejects the idea that everything must be true or not-true (the either-or situation). There are many instances in classification where relationships seem more intuitive than logical. These turn up in particular with the limited classifications made among thesaurus terms. A more disciplined and rigorous approach through pure mathematics would appear to be highly advantageous.

One possibility is the retrieval theory of Donald Hillman, which is based on Vincent Giuliano and Paul Jones' association measure technique for determining synonymy, on Mooers' rejection of Boolean algebra as a basis for *dynamic* retrieval systems, and on Fairthorne's perception of the need for dual algebras of the Brouwerian type for composition of the free distributive lattices needed to handle a constantly growing system. Hillman's method derives genera of ordered components from terms taken from documents and develops these, through algebras of closed and open sets of a topological space, into two types of free distributive lattices which describe all possible retrieval operations.[23] Whether these lattices can be further developed into a viable classification system remains to be seen, but application could lead to a nonprobabilistic method of constructing classes automatically from words in documents.

The third school, Formalism, represented by Hilbert, von Neumann, Curry and (indirectly) Gödel, emphasizes proofs of consistency, and the manipulation of notations by means of syntactical rules, which, unlike symbols or notations, are "quite significant and intelligible."[24] Max Black points out that the appearance of Formalism as an "exhibition of structure by the employment of symbols meaningless in isolation, is to suggest analogies with the manner in which the structure of concrete systems—can be represented by diagrams (family trees, maps)."[25] The Formalist "ideal elements" are not finite or concrete, but symbols of indeterminate reference. A system's *framework*, not its representation or content, is stressed. Whether the

analysis of the framework of deductive systems will have value for classification is not yet apparent. It would appear unlikely that any formal structure which does not emphasize semantic content could be functional in an information transmission situation, yet the statistical theory of communication is built on such an assumption.[26]

Formalism, carried to the point of Nelson Goodman's nominalism—no classes, no abstract entities, only a world of individuals—appears a little hard to apply, although, in the interests of clarity, a similar approach has been adopted for structural linguistics by Zellig Harris and Noam Chomsky.[27] Jessica Melton has suggested that structural linguistics, in turn, has definite value for classification.[28] Nominalism may be used as justification for the initiation of classification-making in the verbal plane instead of the idea plane—that is, starting with words as the finite embodiment of ideas. This aspect will be discussed later.

The possibility of the application of Formalism to classification more directly has been demonstrated in experiments using statistical treatment of index terms as a means of making "automatic classification" systems, where the meaning of words is not considered and the resultant "classes" in many cases cannot be named or identified.[29] The theoretical background of the method is Formalism, though the technique is experimental and lacks the rigor of pure mathematics.

This flight into the stratosphere of foundations of mathematics has been made to indicate some of the underlying trends and explorations in current classification research. On a more mundane plane, a mathematical analysis of concept recognition has been developed by Robert Ledley and James Wilson in a very interesting paper which may have far-reaching consequences.[30] Two methods of deductive reasoning are used: one is a rigorous, logical inference pattern; the other is based on *mathematical* induction using recursive transformations. (*Mathematical* induction should not be confused with inductive *reasoning*, which is a different procedure entirely.)[31] The pair of methods are advanced as a valid argument for production of the minimum attributes necessary for recognizing a concept.

Another development that may have interesting consequences for classification is the making of mathematical models for retrieval systems. In some of these, the input sections would have some bearing upon classification.[32] In connection with such models, it should be remembered that a model, mathematical or other, does not have to fit phenomena, but it does have to provide an analogous situation.[33] So far, there have been no models strictly for classification and possibly the subject cannot be formalized to the extent that mathematics accomplishes. However, just as it is convenient to have a formula to wrap up observations in science, so it also would be handy to have a formula or set of formulas for classification. Ranganathan has been working in this direction to some degree. He has also suggested an alternative possibility which is to develop a parallel discipline of *abstract classification*.[34] Such activity would take cognizance of the peculiar nature of classification as a subject in itself, not as an adjunct to logic or mathematics or linguistics, but as a subject in its own right, worthy of a methodology and a rationale developed to fit its own sphere of interest. Work in this direction may yet prove the most promising. The value of probability methods in particular for classification research may very well be that they point out directions for possible abstraction.

On the other hand, it may turn out to be that deductive methods, logical or mathematical, apply more directly to the sphere of the classifier rather than the classificationist. Certainly it seems reasonable to expect that some kind of concept recognition, once that concept has been conceived, or some kind of model for representing a functioning classification system, or some kind of a rigorous method for deriving dependent classes in an existent classification scheme are not beyond the possibility of achievement. Deductive reasoning may seem limited as compared with inductive reasoning for *creation* of a classification system, but it seems a sound way of proceeding in the application of a system.

INDUCTIVE METHODS

Compared with deductive methods, induction[35] is more nebulous; it cannot be nailed down so nicely into logical and reasonably precise generalities. Comparatively speaking, it looks like a leap into the dark. Recent reconsideration of the sources of *a priori* assumptions from which deduction proceeds has removed some of the certainty from that method, but the step-wise argument from hypothesis to proof cannot but be admired. The inductive method in classification builds systems from particulars to generals by accretion, by sorting into mutually exclusive groups according to various criteria, by combining terms into compound subjects, by distinguishing characteristics and noting multiple relationships, and so on. As

with scientific method, it is often mixed with deduction so that the pure Baconian example of Salomon's House is rejected in classification as in other fields.[36] In any case, there is in induction a mental leap from a group of individuals to the whole and the filling in of detail is done after the fact, if at all.[37] More likely, the conclusion is confirmed with additional examples, always with the knowledge that the next case may be the contrary example that upsets the whole and brings down part or all of the edifice. The Michelson-Morley experiment was such an example in physical science.

Classification research has produced two kinds of systems from inductive principles. One is the Colon Classification and its offspring, the faceted classifications. The other is a generic type, which, for lack of a better name, will be called experimental classification The former is a combination of scientific, deductive and intuitive methods, the latter of scientific, probabilistic and intuitive methods.

The Colon Classification principles have best been described by its creator, S. R. Ranganathan, in several works, two of which cover recent advances.[38] During the past decade, several difficult points have been cleared up. The most notable has been the clear differentiation of the idea, verbal and notational planes—a most significant advance because with it one may now end some of the talking at cross-purposes which has characterized discussions of classification systems. The terminology of the Colon system has been improved and the notation greatly extended by the introduction of the ideas of sector and zone, permitting depth classification on a greater scale than possible before.

In connection with explanation of the foundations of his classification system, Ranganathan uses the terms "postulate," "law" and "principle" synonymously. It is very important to grasp this point because it is not the more common usage of these terms, and, even more important, it means that all are regarded as assumptions or working hypotheses which may be altered at will, if classification problems show that alteration is needed. In other words, there is no hard and fast rule that says the postulates, laws, and principles are inviolate. They are based, not on the idea of being self-evident as are axioms, since self-evidence is such a subjective matter, nor on consensus, which is only a statistical subjectivity, but on the criterion of helpfulness *to the system*. (Note: to the *system*, not the user. The assumption is that if the system is sound it will serve the user.) If certain postulates, laws and principles make the system more logical, easier or more efficient to operate than other postulates, laws and principles, they are considered helpful. If not, they should be replaced by better ones. The problem is, "Who decides?" Currently, the postulates, laws and principles are based on intuition. Eventually someone will develop a formal argument for each one. Dr. Ranganathan has deliberately avoided this because he feels that it is more important to make a functional system, then clear up philosophical problems.[39] This pragmatic approach is not unknown in other fields.

Since many of the basic assumptions and some of the practices of the Colon Classification are being rediscovered annually by documentalists who have not read Ranganathan's work, one should not scoff at his intuitive method. After all, what is intuition? One may argue that a scientific discovery is an intuition universally accepted. The axioms or basic premises of practically all reasoning are intuitively derived. Sooner or later one comes down to some fundamental assumption that cannot be proven. One cannot get the human being entirely out of things. With regard to communication, Colin Cherry regards the recipient as an inseparable part of the communication chain: signal, transmission, receiver. Without all three there is no communication between human beings. The precursory events (discovered by hindsight) and rediscovery of the various assumptions and basic premises of the Colon Classification suggest that perhaps there may be a collective subconscious which, under certain circumstances, makes communication of the "obvious" possible. Or perhaps there is a universal subconscious learning pattern in a given era or common unvoiced environmental factors in a cultural climate for a given period. Is a discovery, then, an intuition that has "arrived"? Success with axiomatic systems in pure mathematics, ones that start off as abstraction and much later turn out to have practical applications, suggests that intuition cannot be shrugged off as totally irrelevant. Psychological research will undoubtedly cast more light on the matter, and this light cannot but help classificationists.

The principles relating to *facet* sequence in the Ranganathan system are essentially axiomatic, while those concerning *isolate* sequence are, with two exceptions, permissive and subject to the vagaries of probability.[40] As to the postulates, laws, and principles, since these are assumptions, the question becomes one of which axioms can be denied or altered. The Classification Research Group,

for example, did not accept the limit of five fundamental categories (the first five postulates), and so by adding more, produced faceted classification of a different sort.[41] They also identified their fundamental categories with basic classes, a practice deplored by Ranganathan as too rigid, since he has now decided that the idea of basic classes should come at the end of the creation of a classification system, using provisional main classes in the interim.[42]

In the Colon Classification, the former centralized position of the faceting procedure has been de-emphasized during the past few years and the system has been undergoing change to make its design more fully analytico-synthetic.[43] This should tighten up the organization. One may comment at this point that such connectors as links and role indicators look rather raw and unfinished beside Ranganathan's facet and phase relations. J.E.L. Farradane's emphasis on relationships in classification and Jean Perreault's exhaustive listing of "relators" carry the idea beyond Ranganathan.[44]

The influence of Ranganathan's ideas has been widespread. The Classification Research Group in London has studied and discussed them with interesting results. Members of the Group for several years have been experimenting with faceted classification schemes, and comparing learning experiences in the process. After several years of such work, the Group has come to realize the necessity for having some generalized pattern into which specialized subject schemes will fit. It has proved necessary to return to the idea of a general classification system because individual subject schemes, no matter how exhaustive, do not function well in a vacuum and sooner or later have to be related to other subjects in other schemes. Theory of integrative levels has been discussed as a possible unification factor in construction of a general classification.[45] This theory is easier to apply to scientific fields than to the humanities and social sciences, though with modification it might be made to apply, especially if it were part of a broader procedure based on consideration of the informative capacity of a class and the enumeration of factors which make up the intellectual leap characteristic of inductive method.[46]

The publications of members of the Classification Research Group have been most impressive.[47] Their books and papers cover many aspects of classification and represent many viewpoints, for, while the Group members are in fundamental agreement with the principles originally given in 1955,[48] there has been wide variation in individual interpretation.

Currently discussions of the Group follow several paths. Fine points of facet procedure continue to be treated in detail. Other matters include discussion of the necessity of close relation between schedule terminology and that used in subject fields, the treatment of compound terms, the purpose of notation, further thoughts about the theory of integrative levels, and classification of geology. Recently a preliminary draft edition of a faceted classification of library science has been circulated for comment.[49]

Perhaps the most interesting feature of the proposed scheme is the extent to which data processing equipment and techniques, including computers, have been made an integral part of library science. This is certainly the modern trend and is producing something of a revolution in operational patterns. It is forcing systems analysis to a degree unknown since the turn of the century. The status of classification has risen in the process because it is more amenable to mechanization than most other input procedures.

Both faceted and hierarchical classification systems can be used with computers. Western Reserve University's semantic factoring procedure, a form of faceting, is mechanized, and Malcom Rigby and associates at the American Meteorological Society have mechanized part of the Universal Decimal Classification.[50] An interesting compiler language has been developed at the RAND Corporation. This language, IPL-V (Information Processing Language 5),[51] looks like a reasonable possibility for both making and searching classification systems by computer. It is especially designed to handle sequences of lists. If one thinks of the classes and subclasses of a hierarchy, as well as the foci, chains and arrays of faceted classification, as sequences to be searched as lists and sublists of given categorical headings, then such a programming language might be very useful. IPL-V has an "available space listing" feature which might be helpful to the classificationist who must know where there are free areas for new material in his mechanized system. IPL-V also seems a likely bet for man-machine interaction via a console. It has a series of J process commands which could be used for searching by means of classification to locate a desired area of interest. The disadvantage to searching by IPL-V is that one has to start at the beginning of a series of sequences; one cannot drop in the middle. It is like using a classification schedule as compared with an index.

Computerized classification systems have been rather slow in coming. One would have expected that a pre-coded subject analysis system, such as the Universal Decimal Classification, would be chosen in preference to index terms. Perhaps the slowness is a result of the interaction of bibliographic classification and the user, both the user at input and the user at output. A classification system *must* function successfully for the user at input and for the most part this has happened. Since the classifier knew where he had put things, he did not feel pressed to make great changes in his methods. It is gratifying, but not necessary in a closed stack situation or vital in an open stack one, for a classification to function successfully for a user at output.

However, with open stacks the user at output has not been able to follow classification patterns and prefers not to be always asking for help. Dissatisfaction of the user at this point has been one of the chief reasons for the development of experimental classifications. These form the other major school of classification research whose work is founded on inductive method. Unlike the hierarchical and faceted classification systems, which have large bodies of theory attached to them, the experimental types have a minimum of theoretical background, at least so far as classification is concerned.

The outstanding feature of many experimental classification systems is the use of probability methods. "Probability" is used here as Carnap's probability$_1$ (degree of confirmation) because there is no possibility of having definite numbers of terms or occurrences to ensure a sound base for probability$_2$ (frequency of occurrence),[52] unless one goes individual document by individual document in every case. All of the probability methods introduced into classification involve some kind of counting and their use may be attributed to the availability of the digital computer. The computer has been applied in bibliographic classification as "automatic" classification, in biological classification as "numerical taxonomy," and in linguistic classification as "computational" or "mathematical" linguistics. A part of the interest in interpretation of phenomena by probability methods is the ability to deal with masses of data for purposes of induction by "enumeration."[53] The inconclusiveness whereby results may be incompletely valid or capable of being overthrown by further data merely adds to the attractiveness of probability methods. Scientists may not like things that cannot be nailed down fairly exactly, but to humanists, who perennially deal, not with black or white but with myriad shades of gray, probability looks like reality.

There are several different kinds of experimental classification procedures. There are types based on word frequency, with the words selected by computer with very little editing either before or afterwards.[54] It is more common to use them for alphabetical indexing than for classification. There are kinds based on selection of co-occurring words in a single document—the words being considered as linked.[55] These are also used primarily in indexing since the combinations are not necessarily classes. There are types based on computer selection of words in juxtaposition, weighted according to formula, and producing a list of classes which may also be an embryonic classification scheme.[56] Some of these are made from complete texts, some from abstracts, and some from titles. In the case of titles, it is not known how much additional text is needed for satisfactory results since experimentation so far gives conflicting answers.[57] None of these experimental procedures produces classification in the more formal sense, meaning a finished system that can be used to classify documents. The kinds of experimental systems that do this are considerably more sophisticated.

There are four main types of experimental classification systems based on probability methods, all of which have been designed or used with small samples in very specific subject fields (Fig. A). The initial experimental work was reported by M. E. Maron of the RAND Corporation in 1961 as "automatic indexing."[58] Maron selected some classes, divided documents in his test collection according to these classes, selected a group of representative index terms ("clue words") from the documents, and identified the class categories by means of these terms, using a Beyesian formula. He then worked backwards by taking a group of new documents in his selected categories, picked out the index terms by computer, and then applied the results of his earlier statistical method to assign the new documents to the correct classes. This, of course, is classic scientific method as used, for example, to demonstrate the relationship of a specific causal factor (pathogenic microorganism) to a specific disease entity. The same experimental method, with multiple discriminant functions as the distinguishing criterion, has been used by J. H. Williams of IBM.[59] In both cases the classification recovered at the end was the same as that at the beginning, and in both cases the method of identifying the classes with terms taken directly from the documents was reasonably successful. This type of automatic classification can be used by the classifier, but not by the classificationist,

A

list word frequencies (machine)
select index terms from list (man)
search documents for these index terms & record occurrence per document (machine)
treat results to create groups of weighted terms (man-machine)
 —data matrix (doc.-term)
 —correlation matrix (term-term) for word pairs
 —factor analysis, etc.
terms in group list constitute a class name classes (man)

B

select class categories (man)
divide docs. according to these categories (man)
select index terms from these documents & calculate frequency (machine)
select index terms from this list (man)
identify index terms with categories via data matrix (category-term) & calculate prediction value of each term for its categories (attribute numbers) (man-machine)
search documents for selected index terms, assign attribute numbers, rank, identify category (machine)
a class is identified by the first item of a group of ranked index terms pertaining to a document

C

select keywords from authoritative list & put into some order (man)
search documents for THESE keywords only (machine)
make keyword pattern for each doc. by indicating presence or absence of these keywords in fixed order (machine)
treat pattern to yield "ordering ratio" (fixed probability listing for each combination of words) for each pattern (man-machine)
 —matrices (several in series)
 —latent class analysis
a class consists of an indefinite-sized group of keywords in a fixed pattern

D

select index terms from document (man)
treat to create groups or clumps (man-machine)
 —data matrix (doc.-term)
 —co-occurrence matrix (term-term) for word pairs
 —algorithm for group formation
terms in group membership (clump) constitute a class; one term may occur in several groups

FIGURE 1.   Four types of "automatic classification." All classify specific (not general) subject matter.

since it assumes that a ready-made classification system exists to start with. Further experimentation will reveal which of many available statistical techniques is the most effective. At least two now function within the framework of this method. Truly automatic application *of an established classification system* is possible under the circumstances established by Maron and Williams.

A second form of experimental classification was that of Harold Borko and associates at the System Development Corporation. In this system, first a machine listing of words with their frequencies was derived from a set of test documents; human beings then selected index terms from this list and the documents were searched again for the frequency of occurrence of these terms in individual documents; the results were treated with two successive matrices to yield data and correlation figures; then factor analysis was applied to create groups of weighted terms, which constituted classes.[60] At the end, these groups were named by human beings. The method has been successfully applied in all contexts tried except one.[61] In the case that failed, the end products were not recognizable as classes, even though, as in prior cases, the selection of index terms was made by the same people who evaluated the results. The failure suggests the presence of an unsuspected variable somewhere in the conditions of the experiment.

The third type of experimental classification is somewhat different from the preceding two. Frank B. Baker, of the University of Wisconsin, has described a theoretical system for classifying documents according to their content. In this case, which had not been tried on a collection of documents at the time of reporting, keywords were selected by a human being from a subject authority list that was assumed to exist. Such a list could have been a classification schedule. Documents were to be searched by machine for these terms only, and a pattern established for each document, according to the presence or absence of the terms. The proportion of documents with joint occurrence of individual terms was determined with a series of matrices, and latent class analysis was used to fit results into structural categories. For each response pattern, an "ordering ratio" was assigned, this being the probability that a given pattern of index terms was "generated by a document of a particular latent class."[62] This ordering ratio was also used as the accession indicator. In Baker's system, a class was a group of index terms in a fixed pattern. If such terms had been taken from a faceted classification schedule, his ordering ratio might possibly correspond to the citation order for the facets, although this has not been suggested. The end-products of the system might or might not be nameable, depending on the original source of the terms. In the example given, they were not. Even if the result was a group of classes, the only relationship between classes was that determined by the weighting which put them into a single chain. Equal weightings could open up an array at any point, but then the chain would close in again with the next class as a single descendant from each member of that array. One might suggest that, under certain very special circumstances, Baker's method could produce the first stage in the formation of a classification system. It might recover classes if it began with class components from a classification schedule, though this is highly conjectural.

The fourth and last type of experimental classification, also called "automatic," was that of Roger Needham and Karen Sparck Jones of Cambridge University. In this system, index terms were selected from documents by human effort. A test set of documents was examined for frequency of occurrence of these selected terms, which were then treated in a data matrix and a co-occurrence matrix. The results were put into "clumps" or groups by computer, using a special statistical algorithm.[63] Terms in a clump were considered to be a class, but since the clumps are not recognizable or nameable as classes, perhaps automatic "aggregation" would be a more accurate name for the result. As classes, the clumps give the impression of artificiality. The work of the Dales in Texas is similar, except the co-occurrence formulas are different.[64] In their case, the clumps could be roughly divided into two classes because these classes were the two from which all the terms were selected in the first place. It is possible that if the terms had been selected as broadly as in the Cambridge experiment, this polarization would not have taken place.

The method of initial input of the fourth type of experimental classification was not radically different from that used in the other three, and the Cambridge results are similar to the reported Baker conclusions and to the Borko-Atherton experiment that failed. It would be interesting, as with the Baker proposal, to see what this fourth experimental procedure could do by starting with the multiple hierarchy of a formal faceted or enumerative classification scheme as input, rather than with a freer multiple hierarchy or lattice *built from words*, which Needham and Sparck Jones tried and rejected for good reasons. The comparative success of Maron and Williams suggests very strongly that a probabilistic system that starts with selected classes from an existing classification ends with a classification, while one that starts with selected words without a classification ends with aggregates of words that do not form a classification system. So far, the process of applying statistical techniques to nonpreclassified words does not classify them into anything similar to that produced by a human classificationist. Donald Hillman gives the philosophic background for the formation of concept-classes by similarity, and points out, with the aid of Nelson Goodman, that concept-class formation can only take place by similarity means under certain favorable circumstances and therefore does not occur in every case. Goodman's difficulties are not resolved "by claiming that the process of concept-formation is statistical in nature and by proposing statistical similarity-measures."[65] This comment applies to classification-making rather than to classification-assigning. The latter is always subject to variation in practice, due to human fallibility, and statistical methods may be an improvement on manual methods.[66] Similar variation in classification-making is unacceptable because it would make it impossible to achieve any kind of consistency.

Actually, in two and one half out of four of the experimental methods described, the resultant "classes" appear to be aggregates and do not fit our definition of the word "class." The fact that new material, when grouped in a pattern identical with old material, can readily be added to the collection still does not make a classification. In some of the experimental systems, such as Baker's, any new material that does not match the old is ignored or rejected. In others, new material requires recalculation of the basis for the whole system, a matter, however, of no great consequence when a computer is used. It is a moot question as to whether an unrecognizable "class" conveys any information as a class, a problem which will be discussed later in connection with

language. There is also a question as to whether a handful of genuine classes, even if formed by statistical means, constitutes a classification system in the absence of any relational network other than a rank order. Ranking does not even have the flexibility of a hierarchy.

It is extremely difficult to escape the human factor in classification. As with medicine, the field at best is part art and part science. For example, even the most successful procedures in "automatic" classification involve the psychological factor of recognition. Essentially these methods arrange material into classes that were initially set up by human selection. The results have to be recognizable by humans to be usable. No method produces classes without human intervention. As Colin Cherry points out, "recognition implies a classification of the recognizable object into an existing class; but the setting up of a new class is a creative act."[67] The clumping procedures, involving statistical similarity measures, set up what would be in effect new classes, since the results to date are not recognizable and cannot be identified with existing classes, or named. The question here becomes one of whether the new classes bear any relation to the way in which human experience, both internal and external, is organized in the existing cultural milieu.

This is partly a matter of psychology. In the past, application of the principles of psychology to classification has been conspicuous by its absence. Farradane has been almost alone in pointing out the potential value of psychology to classification.[68] Recently, *association* has come in for some attention, but from a statistical viewpoint rather than a psychological one.[69] The carryover value of psychological discoveries to classification would be great even if one limits application to ones which Berelson and Steiner accept as scientifically established.[70] These parts of psychology include, to name a few of the more obvious: transfer of training, symbolized and verbalized thought process, discrimination between named things, constancy of fundamental vocabulary, concept formation with and without recognition of principles involved, strategy of concept formation, concreteness of concepts, identification of concepts, similarity of connotations among similar cultures, use of insight in new situations, methods of problem solving, and significance of clues. All of these factors certainly apply to classification, and offer possible alternatives to approach via probabilistic methods.

In summary, inductive procedures, both scientific and probabilistic, are still in their infancy in classification research. Since the faceted procedures began much earlier, they have been carried farther and applied more broadly than experimental ones. Psychological factors have hardly been touched. Probabilistic methods applied to classification *making* may, as in the sciences, point out likely directions for discovering what occurs, and for this purpose they are admirable. It is unlikely that they can ever mirror what actually happens. This is like mathematics which can give a model or formula for an occurrence, but the model or formula is a means of description, not an occurrence in itself. Less concise language can be equally descriptive and is usually the first approach to any explanation as well as the last resort when nothing else works.

LANGUAGE

The third major factor in modern classification is language, particularly as exemplified in linguistics.[71] It is safe to say that any discoveries, any advances made in linguistics will aid classification. Anything that makes our means of communication clearer cannot help but make better classification procedures possible.[72] As in other disciplines, there are many schools of thought in linguistics and these will not be discussed here. The branches receiving most attention in relation to classification seem to be structural linguistics, which is similar in approach to Formalism in mathematics and attempts to get down to bedrock by studying language structure without concern for the meaning conveyed by words and word patterns, and computational linguistics, which uses probability methods to arrive at word groupings which may turn out to be meaningful as classes.[73] Little has been done in relation to semantics, although application of the Carnap-Bar-Hillel theory of inductive probability in semantics may have value as a means of conveying the end products of a classification scheme.[74]

Semantics, if defined as theories of meaning in relation to specific usage in specific settings,[75] becomes a psychological matter, and this, for classification, is probably what it should be. "Information," says Cherry, "in most, if not all of its connotations seems to rest in the notion of *selection power*."[76] The selection is a matter of recognition, in the psychological sense. This in turn, depends on recognizing a learned cultural pattern. Recall may be tied mechanically to recognition, but recognition comes first.

One may consider the matter from the point of view of statistical communication theory as outlined by Colin Cherry. Cherry has emphasized that communication theory is not information theory and also is not concerned with the content of its messages, only with their transmission intact. It is time to recognize a similar distinction between the information content of a classification system and the means of conveying that information. Ranganathan has made a beginning recognizing three planes is classification: the idea, the verbal and the notational. Philosophers may argue that the idea and verbal planes are intermixed to such a degree that neither can be differentiated with a sufficient margin of safety. Or, in layman's language, one idea in words is worth an infinity in the head. However, Ranganathan's differentiation may be combined with Cherry's views on transmission. Only the idea plane cannot be a carrier. With the idea plane as the message and the verbal-notational planes as carriers, one may achieve results of the type reached by Maron and Williams. Similarly, it should prove possible to extract classes from notation, provided the notation has been assigned to such classes in some prior commitment. The late H. P. Luhn thought that his statistical system would leave the idea content of information intact, but this has proved to be only partly true because of the syntactical necessities of language.[77] The thing that is not possible under statistical communication theory is to get classes from words merely by sending the message. The words must have interpretation possibilities for the recipient or he may be justified in regarding the message as garbled in transmission, Clifford J. Mahoney has pointed out the inverse relation between "semantic information" (information-bearing properties of messages) and signal information (the message itself), where a gain in signal information may mean a loss in semantic information.[78]

Getting the message through is only part of the problem. A class concept may be written by means other than words in phonetic form with letter notation. The mode of expression is a matter of notation since the verbal plane is oral, not written. For example, the ideographs of Chinese represent words, but began as stylized pictures of the ideas behind them. A formula is a good representation of the idea plane, but many times cannot be verbalized briefly or expressed in a written word or two. Ranganathan's verbal plane does not require that the representation of ideas be expressed in any particular written form, only that it be expressed in the general vocabulary of a language. One may bypass the old argument as to whether an idea is an idea before it is named by simply saying that, for classification, an idea without a name cannot be communicated sufficiently well to be classified.

Making a classification system from words is a great challenge. Figuring the workings of the mind from language is somewhat like trying to separate substance from shadow. It is still possible that, in terms of ultimate reality, we may decide in favor of the shadows. As mentioned previously, in connection with deductive methods and experimental classification systems, alphabetically-arranged index lists and thesauri have developed classification features, both recognized and un-recognized.[79] If one accepts Tefko Saracevic's definition of index term as "a word or string of words connoting a concept and denoting a class,"[80] then any processing of words, either singly or in combination, is fair game for consideration on Ranganathan's verbal plane, since words all represent something on the idea plane. However, one of the most fascinating problems in modern linguistics is the high semantic significance of words which do not connote a concept or denote a class. These can totally alter the meaning of a statement as Chomsky and Salton have shown.[81] For classification purposes, they can throw a verbalization into one of several classes in the idea plane. Even worse, homonyms which are also homographs are completely ambiguous for purposes of classification, unless treated in context. The synonym also is a classification-wrecker, and the metaphor is by no means confined to literature.

The most promising approaches to classification through linguistics, either directly or indirectly, therefore, are not those which deal with words by a single means such as thesaurus-making, word-counting and clumping, or term pairing and binding, but those which employ a systems approach. Currently there are two major projects of this type, with the delightful names of SMART and SYNTOL.

The SMART system, primarily linguistic in origin and orientation, but with some classification features, was developed at the Computation Laboratory at Harvard University by Gerard Salton and associates.[82] In this system, the classification is derived from a series of tree structures of various types which indicate relationships between class concepts. The class concepts, in turn, are normalized terms taken from either a null thesaurus (where concept classes are in one-to-one correspondence with word stems) or from a general Harris thesaurus (where concept classes are mapped many to many). These concept thesauri are the mechanized equivalent of a subject authority list and concepts themselves equivalent to subject headings. In the mechanized system the matching of words from documents to standardized concepts is accomplished automatically, except for totally new words, while with the subject authority list it is always done in the human brain.

Such classification as exists in the SMART system is constructed from relationships between concepts as shown by trees. This is an inductive type, but based on linguistic rather than statistical analysis. As with statistical types, this form of analysis has not yet been linked up into an overall classification system, but is a collection of hierarchies of a few levels each. Scattering of hierarchies is a weakness of all systems which begin with words, so that none are yet more than rudimentary classification *systems*. The SMART system, with its trees, appears to be in a better position for development into a full scale classification scheme than statistical types, which have nothing to build on after the first level or two. There is no logical reason why SMART could not be developed into an analytico-synthetic system.

Although the SMART system has only been tried with a very small sample in a highly specialized field, the possibilities of multiple subject analysis have been well exploited. Gerard Salton, project director, has realized and has demonstrated with a combination of methods that a multiple approach to subject analysis produces greater opportunities for retrieval than any single method. This is in accordance with library experience. Salton's battery of dictionaries, thesauri, classification trees and such is equivalent to the six files libraries use for processing input (classification schedule, shelf list precedent-record, subject heading list, subject authority precedent-record, National Union Catalog, official entry file). With computers, the problem in both the SMART and ordinary library systems is to get adequate core storage and fast, random access to handle the look-up, which requires concurrent usage of all these files. If the SMART system can develop a full scale general classification scheme from its tree structures, this might replace both the classification schedule and the subject heading list in library usage.

The second systems approach, SYNTOL developed by Jean-Claud Gardin and associates at the Centre National de la Recherche Scientifique, goes even farther than SMART by constructing an information system that includes classification, subject analysis based on words, and entry as it is understood in library cataloging. SYNTOL is the only mechanized system that covers the full range of processing for input as is now performed in libraries. The purpose behind SYNTOL was to develop a "general program in the field of automatic documentation, independent, to a certain extent of the content of documents, the kinds of classification or indexing systems, searching methods, etc."[83] The system was to be one with broad applications, not just limited to science and technology as has been the case with so many nonconventional forms. It was also designed to have the depth of subject analysis that Ranganathan is now building into the Colon Classification.

The analytic part of SYNTOL consists of four parts: Abstract, Catalog, Source, the two latter corresponding to entry and descriptive cataloging, and Content, which is divided into two parts, a PARADIGMATIC (patterned) part, which may be any formal classification system, and a SYNTAGMATIC part, which is a word-input system with relationships indicated in order to retain syntactical and semantic values. The syntagmatic part has low level classification built into its word relationships, as with many other systems which start with words. So far the input analysis is performed by human beings, but the output is in machine-readable form and the system is designed for mechanized retrieval. A clearly written *and detailed* description of SYNTOL in English is badly needed.

There are several studies in linguistics which may influence future classification research. The most interesting of these is the Cambridge University doctoral dissertation of Karen Sparck Jones, *Synonymy and Semantic Classification*.[84] In this work, a logical argument has been made for using synonymy as a basis for classification, and a method was devised whereby rows of synonymous terms could be derived from the *Oxford English Dictionary* according to similarity of use patterns. Various rows were made from the same starting base, according to semantic interpretation of *word usage*. The problem then was to group these rows. The methodology of the theory of

clumps, which has been mentioned above in connection with probabilistic experimental classification, was used. Ambiguity among synonymous choices was overcome by means of proximity measurements. It should be emphasized that the research was intended for improvement of machine translation, not for information retrieval, and the multiple-word rows were intended to give some flexibility in translation, not to produce precision-made classes. Within this framework, the project results were satisfactory, at least from an intuitive point of view since there was no way of testing the achievement in a practical situation.

The results from a classification point of view left something to be desired. In the only example shown in which groups are given a headword, the name of the headword has been selected from terms in the sets of rows.[85] The conditions of the study in part made the terms in each row interchangeable, so that one word could stand for a row. By the time this was accomplished, the grouping of rows became a pair or trio of related words.[86] Since these final words were not interchangeable, choosing one of them as the class designation does not seem appropriate. Sometimes the words in rows were considered as close relatives which could be used to define each other.[87] With such rows, one would need an inclusive class designation for each row and another for the group of rows as a whole (the clump). The qualities which made up the classes might have been inherent in each individual row-meaning according to the various use situations, but they are not indicated and cannot be reached ex post facto by intuitive means. The clumping procedure which grouped rows did not identify the common denominator which put specific rows together. The point here can be seen more readily if nonsense words are substituted for synonymous terms. The statistical procedures of clumping will make groups just as easily from nonsense words in rows.

In a way, this study of synonymy is an attempt to give account of the semantics of a language, on a very small scale, by specifying all the senses of each word expressing the same concept, together with a method for combining them into larger units, but without specifying the mode of combination in such a way that the larger units have meaning. It would be interesting to see the Sparck Jones thesis carried further by some means other than application of the theory of clumps. There is no reason, for example, for not looking deeper into the synonymous terms, collected as she collected them, and trying to build a classification system from the added evidence of the sample dictionary sentences which she used to show that her synonyms were indeed synonyms. Evidence as to *why* they were synonyms might better indicate the class each row represented as well as the relationship between rows. The mathematical techniques of the Formalist and Intuitionist Schools offer alternatives and possibly more productive methods of reaching several levels of nameable classes from the linguistic analytic processes utilized. A tree procedure might help bring out relationships between rows.

The chief problem in natural language seems to be ambiguity, which has been tackled by both the Salten and the Sparck Jones experiments. Ambiguity is less apt to occur in scientific texts, provided these are segregated from general material. The difficulties are so great in fields where a literary approach to scholarly writing is valued that they seem almost insurmountable. In a field like philosophy, where reasoning upon facts, not facts in themselves, is paramount, word occurrence, juxtaposition and frequency will not catch the argument. In fields where ambiguity is deliberately cultivated, such as some kinds of poetry and the literary prose, as well as in propaganda, classification by internal context can be quite problematic. Language problems in a single subject are minor compared with those which come up when the entire range of knowledge has to be considered. In this respect, the current tendency to break down old lines between subject fields and realign them into new ones makes even the definition of a subject field more and more difficult. On the positive side, the type of computer searching that turns up new words is probably the best way of keeping up with a terminology that is constantly changing, and the type of processing that can relate these new words to old concepts or that can point to a change in meaning of an existing word by revealing a relationship with *different* old concepts, promises to be a major factor in updating class descriptions in any classification system that is created more or less automatically. A terminological updating service could be used with any kind of classification.

LIBRARY OF CONGRESS CLASSIFICATION

In a discussion of classification research, the Library of Congress system does not fit any of the categories described. It is a pragmatic, functional system that is widely used with considerable consumer satisfaction.[88] It is not logical; it is not scientifically or probabilistically built; it has little to do with language or linguistics other than to provide the best classification of these subjects extant; in organization it sprawls in all directions; it violates all the postulates, principles and laws that are considered important in classification making; in some areas relationships are shown in hierarchies, but throughout most of the schedules nothing seems to be next to anything for any particular reason; yet it grows steadily without any serious signs of stress. Why does it work? Its broad and apparently unlimited hospitality is certainly one factor. Another, which will show up better if a unified index to the classification is ever compiled, is its diffuseness: if a subject fits into six categories, it is put into six categories. Whether it would be possible to make a mathematical model analogous to this classification is a matter of conjecture. It certainly would be a challenge, and might throw some light on the reasons why this anomaly is so successful. The method in the madness, if it can be discovered, might well be applied to other kinds of classification making.

CONCLUSION

User satisfaction with the Library of Congress Classification adds up to the obvious conclusion that the problems of classification are infinitely complex. Each of the various research methods discussed here lights up another facet of the complexity. One may safely say that the work of the past few years has been largely exploratory rather than definitive. It has outlined problems more distinctly, but it has not solved any of them.

No classification system of any kind will be outstandingly successful until some of the fundamental questions underlying the making of classifications are answered. These problems are:

1. the place and nature of intuition in human thinking and understanding. This is first a psychological problem and then a philosophic one. We need to know more about how the brain works.
2. the nature of the full cycle of communication from person to person in terms of semantic content or meaning, particularly over irregular or lengthy periods of time. This is also a psychological question first and then a linguistics one, perhaps even a historical one.

3. the nature of self-evidence. It may be possible to build adequate classification systems on an axiomatic basis alone, or there may be no such thing as self-evidence to serve as a basis for axiomatic ramifications of this question have not been recognized in many experimental classification situations where self-evidence governs the initial input. This is partly a psychological and partly a philosophic problem.
4. the nature of mathematical models needed to describe a total world of interrelated subject fields, not one of which may ever safely be considered static. This is a problem of mathematics.
5. the nature of meaning and how it is contained in words. This is a linguistics problem.
6. the degree to which inductive methods, scientific and probabilistic, can be applied to a field as amorphous as classification. How much is science and how much is art?[89] How much depends on creative intuition? This is a practical problem which

probably cannot be solved until there are answers to the preceding five.

The experimental classifications and those based on linguistics have been instrumental in turning up these questions in the form and emphasis listed above. So long as the intuitive approach was the sole means of deriving classes, these questions were either academic or they were discussed in other forms, as attitude/interest motivation of the user or notational organization. With further experimentation, we may expect to turn up more of these fundamental questions. Ultimately, greater clarification of its foundations should benefit classification both in its theoretical and practical aspects.

NOTES

[1]C. Singer, *A Short History of Science to the Nineteenth Century.* (Oxford: Clarendon, 1946), p. 126.

[2]*Concise Oxford Dictionary of Current English.* 3d ed. (Oxford: Clarendon, 1940).

[3]S. R. Ranganathan, "Design of Depth Classification: Methodology," *Prolegomena to Library Classification.* 2d ed. (London: Library Association, 1957); *Library Science with a Slant to Documentation,* 1:1, Mar. 1965, pp. 1–42; "Colon Classification: Paper presented for the Rutgers Seminars on Systems for the Intellectual Organization of Information," 1964. MS, 1961, published by Rutgers University Graduate School of Library Service, 1965. *See also* A. Neelameghan, "New Developments in Library Classification in India," *Classification Research; Proceedings of the Second International Study Conference held at . . . Elsinore, Denmark . . . 1964.* (Copenhagen: Munksgaard, 1965), pp. 503-523. (Conference hereafter referred to as Elsinore Conference 1964).

[4]*See* his comments in *Prolegomena,* 2d ed., passim. *See also* D. J. Foskett, *Classification and Indexing in the Social Sciences.* (Washington: Butterworths, 1963), pp. 63-66; Eric de Grolier, *A Study of General Categories Applicable to Classification and Coding in Documentation.* (Paris: UNESCO, 1962), pp. 18-42; B. Kyle, "The Universal Decimal Classification. A Study of the Present Position &c.," *UNESCO Bulletin for Libraries,* 15:2, Mar./Apr. 1961, pp. 53-96; B. C. Vickery, "The Universal Decimal Classification and Technical Information Indexing," *UNESCO Bull. Libs.,* 15:3, May/June 1961, pp. 126-138, 147.

[5]Engineers Joint Council. *Thesaurus of Engineering Terms.* (New York: 1964) see APPRAISALS (p. 15), BLOW-OUTS (p. 26). CABLES (p. 32), CLASSIFICATION (p. 42), CONTAINMENT (p. 53), HISTORY (p. 125), LANGUAGES (p. 146), etc.

[6]*Ibid.,* pp. 214-215, 218, 223, 278-279.

[7]G. Salton, "Manipulation of Trees in Information Retrieval," *Communications of the Association for Computing Machinery,* 5:2, Feb. 1962, pp. 103-114; J. Binns and D. Bagley, *English Electric. A Faceted Subject Classification for Engineering.* 3d ed. (Whetstone, Eng.: English Electric Company, 1960).

[8]American Petroleum Institute. Information Retrieval Project. *Subject Authority List, January 1964.* (New York: 1964).

[9]U. S. Defense Documentation Center. Document Processing Division. *Thesaurus of ASTIA Descriptors.* 2d ed. (Arlington, Va.: 1962), pp. A-1 to A-80.

[10]European Atomic Energy Community–EURATOM. *EURATOM-Thesaurus; Keywords Used with EURATOM's Nuclear Energy Development Project.* (Brussels: Directorate "Dissemination of Information," Center for Information and Documentation CID, 1964), pp. 35-79; L. Rolling, "The role of graphic display of concept relationships in indexing and retrieval vocabularies," Elsinore Conference 1964, pp. 295-320.

[11]L. B. Doyle, "Semantic Road Maps for Literature Searchers," *Journal of the Association for Computing Machinery,* 8:4, Oct. 1961, pp. 553-578; "Indexing and Abstracting by Association," *American Documentation,* 13:4, Oct. 1962, pp. 378-390; "Some Compromises between Word Grouping and Document Grouping," System Development Corp. *Report* SP-1481 (March 1964); "Is Automatic Classification a Reasonable Application of Statistical Analysis of Text?" System Devel. Corp. *Report* SP-1753 (August 1964).

[12]John and Jessica Melton, "The Semantic Code: Predetermined Relevancy," *Information Retrieval in Action.* (Cleveland: Press of Western Reserve University, 1963), pp. 180-181.

[13]*Centralization and Documentation; Final Report to the National Science Foundation.* (Cambridge, Mass.: A. D. Little, Inc., 1963) (C-64469), p. 12.

[14]A. Rees, "Why are Information Centers Successful?" American Documentation Institute. *Proceedings.* 1: Parameters of Information Science, Annual Meeting, Philadelphia, October 5-8, 1964. p. 175.

[15]C. N. Mooers, "The Indexing Language of an Information Retrieval System," *Information Retrieval Today; Papers Presented at the Institute Conducted by the Library School and the Center for Continuation Study, University of*

Minnesota, September 19-22, 1962. (Minneapolis: Center for Continuation Study, University of Minnesota, 1963), pp. 21-36.

[16] R. A. Fairthorne, "Delegation of Classification," *American Documentation*, v. 9, no. 3, July 1958, pp. 159-164; also in his *Towards Information Retrieval*. (London: Butterworths, 1961), pp. 124-134; other comments in *Towards Information Retrieval*, pp. 6-8, 59-61, 144; C. N. Mooers, "From the Point of View of Mathematical etc. Techniques," *Toward Information Retrieval*, pp. xxi-xxii; D. Hillman. "Two Models for Retrieval System Design," *American Documentation*, 15:3, July 1964, pp. 217-225.

[17] Mooers, comment in Fairthorne, *Towards Information Retrieval*, pp. xxi-xii; Fairthorne, *Towards Information Retrieval*, pp. 124-134.

[18] C. G. Hempel, "On the Nature of Mathematical Truth," *Philosophy of Mathematics; Selected Readings*, ed. Paul Benecerraf and Hilary Putnam. (Englewood Cliffs, N. J.: Prentice-Hall, 1964), p. 379.

[19] R. Carnap, "The Logicist Foundations of Mathematics," *Philosophy of Mathematics*, p. 31.

[20] E. W. Beth, *The Foundations of Mathematics*. (Amsterdam: North Holland, 1959), pp. x-xi.

[21] M. Black, *The Nature of Mathematics; a Critical Study*. (Patterson, N. J.: Littlefield, Adams, 1959), pp. 171-172.

[22] E. W. Beth, *Foundations of Mathematics*, pp. 444-461.

[23] D. J. Hillman, "Mathematical Classification Techniques for Non-Static Document Collections, with Particular Reference to the Problem of Relevance," Elsinore Conference 1964, pp. 177-209; "On Concept-Formation and Relevance," American Documentation Institute, *Proceedings*, 1, 1964, pp. 23-29.

[24] W. V. Quine, "On What There Is," *Philosophy of Mathematics*, p. 193.

[25] U. Black, *Nature of Mathematics*, p. 161.

[26] C. Cherry, *On Human Communication; a Review, a Survey, and a Criticism*. (New York: Science Editions, John Wiley, 1961). Passim.

[27] Z. S. Harris, "Linguistic Transformations for Information Retrieval," *Proceedings of the International Conference on Scientific Information, Washington, D. C., November 16-21, 1958*. (Washington: National Academy of Sciences–National Research Council, 1959) vol. 2, pp. 937-950; N. Chomsky, "Logical Structures in Language," *American Documentation*, 8:4, October 1957, pp. 284-291; *Syntactic Structures*. (The Hague: Mouton, 1964) (Janua Linguarum, no. 4); N. Goodman, "A World of Individuals," *Philosophy of Mathematics*, pp. 197-210.

[28] J. Melton, "A Use for the Techniques of Structural Linguistics in Documentation Research," Elsinore Conference 1964, pp. 466-480.

[29] *See for example* F. B. Baker, "Information Retrieval Based on Latent Class Analysis," *J. ACM*, 9:4, October 1962, pp. 512-521; H. Borko, "The Construction of an Empirically Based Mathematically Derived Classification System," *Proceedings of the Spring Joint Computer Conference 1962*, vol. 21, pp. 279-289; Borko and M. Bernick, "Automatic Document Classification," *J. ACM*, 10:2, Apr. 1963, pp. 151-162, 11:2, Apr. 1964, pp. 138-151; Borko and Bernick, "Toward Establishment of a Computer Based Classification System for Scientific Documentation," System Development Corp., *SDC Technical Memorandum TM-1763*, February 1964; Borko, "Research in Computer Based Classification Systems," Elsinore Conference 1964, pp. 220-257; R. M. Needham and K. S. Jones, "Keywords and Clumps. Recent Work on Information Retrieval at the Cambridge Language Research Unit," *Journal of Documentation*, 20:1, March 1964, pp. 5-15; A. G. Dale and N. Dale, "Some Clumping Experiments for Associative Document Retrieval," *American Document*, 16:1, January 1965, pp. 5-9; D. R. Swanson, "Searching Natural Language Text by Computer," *Science*, 132:3434, October 21, 1960, pp. 1099-1104.

[30] R. S. Ledley and J. B. Wilson, "Concept Analysis by Syntax Processing," American Document Institute, *Proceedings*, vol. 1, 1964, pp. 1-8.

[31] For the difference, see S. F. Barker, *Philosophy of Mathematics*. (Englewood Cliffs, N. J.: Prentice-Hall, 1964), pp. 58-59, 75; M. Black, *Critical Thinking; and Introduction to Logic and Scientific Method*. 2d ed. (New York: Prentice-Hall, 1952), pp. 291-299. Philosophers such as Black use the term "inference" synonymously with "deduction" (*cf. Critical Thinking*, p. 442), and this is how it is used by Ledley and Wilson.

[32] Some examples: R. A. Fairthorne, "Algebraic Representation of Storage and Retrieval Languages," *Towards Information Retrieval*, pp. 151-169; also in *Proc. International Conf. on Sci. Information*, vol. 2, pp. 1313-1326; C. Mooers, "The mathematical Theory of Language Symbols," *Proc. International Conf. on Sci. Information*, vol. 2, pp. 1327-1364; C. J. Maloney, "Abstract Theory of Retrieval Coding," *ibid.*, vol. 2, pp. 1365-1382; "Semantic Information," *American Documentation*, 13:3, July 1962, pp. 276-287; G. Salton, "Some Hierarchical Models for Automatic Document Retrieval," *American Documentation*, 14:3, July 1963, pp. 213-222; P. E. Jones, "Research on a Linear Network Model and Analog Device for Associative Retrieval," *Automation and Scientific Communication: Short Papers Communicated to the Theme Sessions of the 26th Annual Meeting of the American Documentation Institute of Chicago . . . 1963*, pp. 211-212; H. J. Podell, "CITIS: a Generalized Mathematical Model for a Centralized Integrated Technical Information System, from a Resource Allocation Point of View," American Document Institute, *Proceedings*, vol. 1, 1964, pp. 155-172; also B. C. Vickery, *On Retrieval System Theory*. (London: Butterworths, 1961), pp. 58-78; G. W. King, "The Automation of Library Systems," *Libraries and Automation; Proceedings of the Conference on Libraries and Automation Held at Airlie Foundation, Warrenton, Va., May 26-30, 1963*. (Washington: Library of Congress, 1964), pp. 233-242.

[33] M. Hesse, "The Role of Models in Scientific Theory," *Philosophical Problems of Natural Science*, ed. Dudley Shapere. (New York: Macmillan, 1965), pp. 102-109; S. Toulmin, *The Philosophy of Science, an Introduction*. (New York: Harper & Row, 1960) (TB 513), pp. 38-39, 165.

[34] Ranganathan, *Prolegomena*, 2d ed., pp. 451-457.

[35] The unabridged Webster (3d ed.) defines induction as (1) "an instance of reasoning from a part to a whole, from particulars to generals, or from the individual to the universal. (2) a process of mathematical demonstration in which

the general validity of a law is inferred from its validity in particular cases by proving that if the law holds in a certain case it must hold in the next and therefore in succeeding cases." Stephen F. Barker describes scientific induction as "reasoning in which a conclusion is inferred which expresses an empirical conjecture going beyond what the data say; and therefore we cannot know a priori that if the data are true, the conclusion will be true, too. . . . At best, all that one can say is that the data support and confirm the conclusion, not that they absolutely guarantee its truth," *Philosophy of Mathematics*, pp. 6-7.

[36] F. Bacon, *New Atlantis*, ed. G. C. Moore Smith. (Cambridge: University Press, 1938), pp. 34-46.

[37] W. Whewell, *Novum Organon Renovatus, Being the Second Part of the Philosophy of the Inductive Sciences*. 3d ed. (London: John W. Parker, 1858), Book 2, Chap. 5, p. 88, Chap. 6, p. 114.

[38] Ranganathan, *Prolegomena*, 2d ed.; "Colon Classification [Rutgers Seminar]."

[39] _____ , "Colon Classification [Rutgers Seminar] ," and personal correspondence.

[40] _____ , "Colon Classification [Rutgers Seminar]," pt. G. K.

[41] "The Need for a Faceted Classification as the Basis of All Methods of Information Retrieval," *Proceedings of the International Study Conference on Classification for Information Retrieval Held at Beatrice Webb House, Dorking, England, 13th-17th May 1957*, (London: ASLIB, 1957), p. 145.

[42] Ranganathan. "Design of Depth Classification: Methodology," *Lib. Sci.*, 1:1, pp. 11-15; "Colon Classification [Rutgers Seminar]," pt. D83.

[43] _____ , "Colon Classification [Rutgers Seminar]," pt. B77; "Library Classification through a Century," *Lib. Sci.*, 2:1, March 1965, p. 14 (Presidential Address, International Study Conference on Classification, Elsinore 1964).

[44] J. E. L. Farradane, "A Scientific Theory of Classification and Indexing and its Practical Applications," *J. Doc.*, 6:2, June 1950, pp. 83-99; "A Scientific Theory of Classification and Indexing; Further Considerations," *J. Doc.*, 8:2, June 1952, pp. 73-92; "Fundamental Fallacies and New Needs in Classification," *The Sayers Memorial Volume; Essays in Librarianship in Memory of William Charles Berwick Seyers*, ed. D. J. Foskett and B. I. Palmer. (London: Library Association, 1961), pp. 120-135; J. Perreault, "Categories and realtors: a new scheme," *Revue internationale de la documentation*, 32:4, November, 1965, pp. 136-144.

[45] D. J. Foskett, "Classification and Integrative Levels," *Sayers Memorial Volume*, pp. 136-150; E. J. Coates, "CRG Proposals for a New General Classification," *Some Problems of a General Classification Scheme; Report of a Conference Held in London, June 1963*. (London: Library Association, 1964), pp. 38-45; P. A. Richmond, "Contribution Toward a New Generalized Theory of Classification," Elsinore Conference 1964, pp. 39-54; Classification Research Group, "Bulletin no. 8," *J. Doc.*, 20:3, September 1964, pp. 146-169.

[46] P. A. Richmond, "Contribution Toward a New Generalized Theory of Classification," Elsinore Conference 1964, pp. 39-54.

[47] *See* "Bibliography of Papers on Classification and Allied Subjects," *J. Doc.*, 12:4, December 1956, pp. 227-230; "Articles, Papers, and Other Writings by Members of the Classification Research Group," *J. Doc.*, 17:3, September 1961, pp. 169-172; "Bibliography of Writings by Members of the Classification Research Group," *J. Doc.*, 20:3, September 1964, pp. 166-169.

[48] *Proceedings of International Study Conference . . . Dorking*, pp. 137-147.

[49] Classification Research Group, *A Classification of Library Science; Preliminary Draft Edition*. (London: ASLIB, 1965).

[50] J. Melton, *Note of the Compatibility of Two Information Systems, Colon Classification and Western Reserve University (Encoded Telegraphic Abstracts) and the Feasibility of Interchanging Their Notations*. (Cleveland: Center for Documentation and Communication Research, Western Reserve University, 1960). AFOSR TN-60-261; M. Rigby, *Mechanization of the UDC, Final report on Pilot Project to Further Explore Possibilities for Mechanization of Universal Decimal Classification (UDC) Schedules*. (Washington: American Meteorological Society, 1964). (NSF GN-131); "Experiments in Mechanized Control of Meteorological and Geoastrophysical Literature and the UDC schedules in these fields," *Rev. Int. Doc.*, 31:3, August 1964, pp. 101-106; "Standardization for Classification in Computerized Documentation Systems," Elsinore Conference 1964, pp. 524-539; R. R. Freeman, "Computers and Classification Systems," *J. Doc.*, 20:3, September 1964, pp. 137-145.

[51] A. Newell and F. M. Tonge, "An Introduction to Information Processing Language V," *Comm. ACM*, 3:4, April 1960, pp. 205-211. A programmer's manual is available. User comment (by Robert Strom) may be found in M. M. Kochen, *Some Problems in Information Science*. (New York: Scarecrow Press, 1965), pp. 113-116.

[52] R. Carnap, "Probability and Inductive Logic," *Philos. Problems of Nat. Sci.*, p. 68. Examples: probability $_1$ – there is a probability that the word "information" may be used in this paper; probability $_2$ – the probability of drawing an ace of diamonds at random is 1 in 52.

[53] W. D. Salmon, *Logic*. (Englewood Cliffs, N. J.: Prentice-Hall, 1964), p. 55-56.

[54] H. P. Luhn, "A Statistical Approach to Mechanized Encoding and Searching of Literary Information," *IBM Journal of Research and Development*, 1:4, October 1957, pp. 309-317, For a full description of all kinds of automatic input procedures, see M. P. Stevens, *Automatic Indexing: a State of the Art Report*. (Washington: Govt. Print. Off., 1965) (National Bureau of Standards Monograph, 91).

[55] J. C. Costello, Jr., "Storage and Retrieval of Chemical Research and Patent Information by Links and Roles in duPont," *American Documentation*, 12:2, April 1961, pp. 111-120.

[56] D. R. Swanson, "Searching Natural Language Text by Computer," *Science*, 132:3434, October 21, 1960, pp. 1099-1104; A. R. Meetham, "Probalistic Pairs and Groups of Words in a Text," *Language and Speech*, 7:2, April/June 1964, pp. 98-106; D. V. Black, "Automatic Classification and Indexing for Libraries?" *Library Resources & Technical Services*, 9:1, winter 1965, p. 50.

[57] C. Montgomery and D. R. Swanson, "Machine-Like Indexing by People," *American Document*, 13:4, October

1962, pp. 359-366; J. O'Connor, "Correlation of Indexing Headings and Title Words in Three Medical Indexing Systems," *Amer. Documentation*, 15:2, April 1964, pp. 96-104; M. J. Ruhl, "Chemical Documents and Their Titles: Human Concept Indexing vs. KWIC-Machine Indexing," *American Documentation*, 15:2, April 1964, pp. 136-141.

[58] M. E. Maron, "Automatic Indexing: An Experimental Inquiry," *J. ACM*, 8:3, April 1961, pp. 404-417. Once the ranking keyword (which identifies a class) has been found, documents can be selected for this word alone, as if by a code, rather than by recalculating the relation of keyword to humanly selected concept with every document.

[59] J. H. Williams, *Results of Classifying Documents with Multiple Discriminant Functions*. (Rockville, Md.: Federal Systems Division, International Business Machines Corp., 1965).

[60] H. Borko, "Construction of an Empirically Based Mathematically Derived Classification System," *Proc. Spring Jt. Computer Conf. 1962*, vol. 21, pp. 279-289; Borko and Bernick, "Automatic Document Classification," *J. ACM*, 10:2, April 1963, pp. 151-162, 11:2, April 1964, pp. 138-151; Borko and Bernick, "Toward Establishment of a Computer Based Classification System for Scientific Documentation," *SDC Technical Memorandum* TM-1763, February 1964; Borko, "Research in Computer Based Classification Systems," Elsinore Conference 1964, pp. 220-257.

[61] P. Atherton and H. Borko, *A Test of the Factor-analytically Derived Automated Classification Method Applied to Descriptions of Work and Search Requests of Nuclear Physicists*. (New York: American Institute of Physics, 1965). AIP/DRP 65-1 (also System Development Corp. SDC/SP 1905L).

[62] Baker, "Information Retrieval Based on Latent Class Analysis," *J. ACM*, 9:4, October 1962, pp. 512-521.

[63] Needham and K. S. Jones, "Keywords and Clumps," *J. Doc.*, vol. 20, March 1964, p. 5-15.

[64] A. G. Dale and N. Dale, "Some Clumping Experiments for Associative Document Retrieval," *American Documentation*, 16:1, January 1965, pp. 5-9.

[65] Hillman, "Two Models for Retrieval System Design," *American Documentation*, 15:3, July 1964, pp. 28-30.

[66] Borko, "Toward the Establishment of a Computer Based Classification System for Scientific Documentation," System Development Corp., *Technical Memorandum* TM-1763, pp. 33-37.

[67] Cherry, *On Human Communication*, p. 269.

[68] J. E. L. Farradane, "The Psychology of Classification," *J. Doc.*, 11:4, Dec. 1955, pp. 187-201; "Relational Indexing and Classification in the Light of Recent Experimental Work in Psychology," *Information Storage and Retrieval*, vol. 1, no. 1, January/Mar. 1963, pp. 3-11.

[69] L. B. Doyle, "Indexing and Abstracting by Association," *American Documentation*, 13:4, October 1962, pp. 378-390; G. Salton, "Associative Document Retrieval Techniques Using Bibliographic Information," *J. ACM*, 10:4, October 1963, pp. 440-457.

[70] B. Berelson and G. A. Steiner, *Human Behavior; an Inventory of Scientific Findings*. New York, Harcourt, Brace & World, 1964, pp. 160-161, 188-208.

[71] The unabridged Webster (3d ed.) defines linguistics as "the study of human speech in its various aspects (as the units, nature, structure, and modification of language, languages, or a language including esp. such factors as phonetics, phonology, morphology, accent, syntax, semantics, general or philosophical grammar, and the relation between writing and speech)."

[72] *Cf* W. Alston, *Philosophy of Language*. (Englewood Cliffs, N. J.: Prentice-Hall, 1964; C. K. Ogden and I. A. Richards, *The Meaning of Meaning*. (New York: Harcourt, Brace & World, 1938); Cherry, *On Human Communication*, pp. 66-120, 217-255; J. R. Pierce, *Symbols, Signals and Noise: the Nature and Process of Communication*. (New York: Harper & Row, 1965) (TB 574) pp. 107-124.

[73] Some of the projects reported to the American Council of Learned Societies are of possible future interest for classification research. Cf. "Computerized Research in the Humanities: a Survey," *ACLS Newsletter*. 16:5, May 1965, pp. 13-24, 28. .

[74] Y. Bar-Hillel and R. Carnap, "Semantic Information," *British Journal for the Philosophy of Science*, 4:14, August 1953, pp. 147-157.

[75] Cherry, *On Human Communication*, p. 241.

[76] *Ibid.*, p. 242.

[77] Luhn, "Statistical Approach to Mechanized Encoding and Searching of Literary Information," *IBM J. Res. Devel.*, 1:4, October 1957, p. 317. Statistical methods may alter idea content. The significance of word order for semantics is diccussed in Chomsky, "Logical Structures in Language," *American Documentation*, 8:4, October 1957, pp. 284-291, and in his *Syntactic Structures*.

[78] Maloney, "Semantic Information," *American Documentation*, 13:3, July 1962, pp. 276-287.

[79] *Cf*. S. C. Bradford, *Documentation*. Washington, Public Affairs Press. 1950. p. 51; B. Sayers, "Classification," *Library Trends*, vol. 2, 1953, p. 239; B. C. Vickery, "Recent Developments in Subject Indexing," *J. Doc.*, 11:1, March 1955, pp. 1-11; V. W. Clapp, "Subject Controls—Nature and Levels of Controls," *American Document*, 3:1, January 1952, pp. 11-14; G. Scheerer, "The Subject Catalog Examined," *Library Quarterly*, 17:3, July 1957, pp. 191-194; P. A. Richmond, "Cats: an Example of Concealed Classification in Subject Headings," *Lib. Resources & Tech. Serv.*, 3:2, spring 1959, pp. 102-112. Also J. Pettee, *Subject Headings; the History and Theory of the Alphabetical Subject Approach in Books*. (New York: H. W. Wilson, 1946), pp. 3-4, 57-60, 73-80.

[80] T. Saracevic, "The Comparative Systems Laboratory at Western Reserve University: Progress Report on Operational Procedures," *American Documentation Inst.*, *Proceedings*, vol. 1, 1964, p. 249.

[81] Chomsky, "Logical Structures in Languages," *American Documentation*, 8:4, October 1957, pp. 284-291; *Syntactic Structures*, passim; G. Salton, "Automatic Phrase Matching," Harvard University Computation Laboratory, *Information Storage and Retrieval. Scientific Report No. ISR-8 to the National Science Foundation*. (Cambridge, Mass.: 1964), pt. V.

[82] Harvard Univ. Computation Lab., *Sci. Rept.* ISR-8, 1964, Chap. 1, 2, 4, 5, 7, 8, 10.

[83] J. C. Gardin, *SYNTOL*. (New Brunswick, N. J.: Graduate School of Library Service, Rutgers the State University, 1965) (Rutgers Series on Systems for the Intellectual Organization of Information, vol. 2). This book is very poorly written and does not do justice to the SYNTOL system.

[84] K. S. Jones, *Synonymy and Semantic Classification, Ph.D. Thesis, University of Cambridge, 1964.* (Under the name K. S. Needham). (Cambridge: Cambridge Language Research Unit, 1964) (M.L. 170).

[85] *Ibid.*, Chap. 6, pp. 21-22.

[86] Thus the samples on pp. 21-22 of Chapter 6 could be reduced to "groups" of two or three terms: staging, production, performance; activity, briskness (based on individual occurrence in rows and then on frequency of occurrence).

[87] The thesis tends to oscillate between these two poles. Cf. Chap. 8 where words are considered replaceable within a class of uses, and Chap. 5, where words are grouped in semantic fields consisting of sets of closely related words. In the former case, the class of uses, if it is a class, should be namable. In the latter case, the closely related word sets should be recognizable as a class and namable.

[88] R. S. Angell, "On the Future of the Library of Congress Classification," Elsinore Conference 1964, pp. 101–112. At last count, the Library of Congress was well into the classification of its 14th million books. (*Annual Report of the Librarian of Congress, 1963/64*). In documentation literature, it is not unusual to find serious proposals to replace this "outmoded" functional general classification system with silly little mechanized schemes that have only been tried on 100-1000 documents in a highly specific subject field!

[89] L. B. Doyle, "Expanding the Editing Function in Language Data Processing," *Comm. ACM*, 8: 4, April 1965, pp. 238–243. Doyle's views could apply to much more than language data processing.

II

DESCRIPTIVE CATALOGING

The concepts of cataloging normally refer to all of the functions which surround the processing of a book or other material. They have traditionally been divided into descriptive cataloging and subject cataloging. Today cataloging is almost exclusively reserved for descriptive cataloging, or those functions concerned with the bibliographical identification of materials and information. American cataloging rules are based on the rules originally laid down by C. A. Cutter in his *Rules for a Dictionary Catalog.* Keyed to the book, overburdened (according to some) by unnecessary detail, and challenged by new forms, new types of information needs and demands both intellectual and technological, descriptive cataloging is a sleeping giant. Rules set a hundred years ago are being adapted to suit individual needs and inconsistency has set in. New standards and guidelines have appeared for the newer forms, or at least some of them, yet these conflict with the "official" prescriptions.

One of the greatest problems faced by today's cataloger is the challenge presented by the theoretical versus the practical, the official stand as opposed to that used operationally. There is often a gap of some twenty years between the two. Probably more than with classification, descriptive cataloging suffers from the secure attitude of "we've always done it this way and it works."

The following selection again reflects both an historical and present-day approach. It is divided into five sections: historical background and development; principles, theories and philosophies; standards; the catalog, and application and automation.

DESCRIPTIVE CATALOGING

Historical Background and Development

Present-day codes are firmly based on those of the past. This has been one of the problems encountered by librarians dealing with new materials and information needs. C. A. Cutter is perhaps the "father" of library codes in the United States but many of his ideas are directly attributable to his predecessors, such as Panizzi at the British Museum. One of Cutter's contributions, which some have cursed and others blessed, is that of the concept of corporate authorship.

Familiarity with the past is perhaps not quite so vital an issue with descriptive cataloging as with classification. As a result there is little, if any, attempt to record this history for posterity.

Development of the Catalog and Cataloging Codes

Ruth French Strout

"From the beginning, humankind has shown itself notably unable to act upon lessons it should have learned from history; perhaps the best we can expect is an increased ability to take the far view and to examine the present with the same scrutiny with which we regard the past."

It would, I believe, be a customary procedure to start with a definition of the subject. At first thought, "catalog" would seem to be a simple enough word to define; yet the major component of the word involves one of the oldest and most discussed definitions in the entire history of words.

The word "catalog" is the Greek phrase *kata logos. Kata* means "by" or "according to"–the puzzle lies in the word *logos.* A variety of meanings have been attributed to the word, and in historical and philosophical thought much attention has been attached to it, especially since one of the writers of the New Testament begins his discourse with the startling statement "In the beginning was *logos.*"[1] Philologists and philosophers are still finding difficulty in arriving at a definition, for *logos* seems sometimes to mean simply "word," sometimes "order," and at other times "reason." Therefore, is a catalog a work in which the contents are arranged in a *reasonable* way, according to a set *plan*, or merely *word by word*? I am sure that advocates may be found for each point of view. If . . . we should reach that nearly impossible situation of agreement upon the mere definition of "catalog," many of the problems would thereby be resolved, since a definition of the meaning of "catalog" becomes, for practical considerations, identical with the definition of its purpose. If we could reach some decisions about the purposes of catalogs or if we could know simply for whom we were making them, we would have gone far indeed toward solving the problems which await us.

Knowledge of the historical development of an institution or concept helps to clarify it. In certain fields what has gone on in the past is held to be so important that the very solution of a problem is considered synonymous with the discovery and recognition of its source. We cannot go to this extreme in dealing with problems in cataloging; nevertheless, a survey of origins and manner of development may make it easier to evaluate present usages; it may, by furnishing better perspective, help to free us from some of the bonds of tradition.

Many past practices now seem ridiculous; there was a time when it seemed important to arrange books in a catalog according to the color of their bindings; there were periods when it was the accepted procedure to enter authors under their forenames; at another time the most pressing question to come before an international congress of librarians was whether an added-entry card should give as full detail as the main card. It sometimes seems difficult to see how librarians of the past could have been so unimaginative and shortsighted; it seems that, if only they had scrutinized their procedures in the light of need, use, and expediency, they could not have helped arriving at some of the simple solutions we have found. If we remember that the people who instituted these practices were intelligent and serious scholars who seemed not at all ridiculous in their time, it may turn us to thinking anew about the usages which we take for granted and which may some day look equally ridiculous to another age. We may be so blinded by such firmly established customs as, for instance, the principle of the main entry, that we are incapable of seeing some utterly simple alternatives which might quickly resolve our problems and which will some day look so easy and obvious that our descendants will in turn look upon us as unseeing and unimaginative.

When one considers how difficult it is to answer

SOURCE: Reprinted from Ruth French Strout, *Toward a Better Cataloging Code* (Chicago: University of Chicago Press, 1957), pp. 4–25, by permission of the author and the publisher. Copyright © 1957 by the University of Chicago Press.

such questions as the present purpose and use of catalogs in a situation which is immediately at hand, it becomes obvious how nearly impossible it is to make any statements about catalogs of far-gone centuries, not only as to what uses they were put, but even to determine which of the surviving fragments were actually catalogs and which were mere inventory lists or even just bookcase labels.

One of the oldest lists of books of which we have knowledge occurs on a Sumerian tablet[2] found at Nippur and dated about 2000 B.C. Sixty-two titles are recorded on this tablet; 24 are titles of currently known literary works. What purpose the list served, there is no way of knowing, and its use may have borne no resemblance to that of a catalog.

Here and there throughout ancient periods there are fragmentary remains that might possibly be relics of catalogs or some sort of book listings, but, in regard to most of these, this is about as definite a statement as can be made.

It is only reasonable to assume that Egyptian libraries developed earlier than Babylonian; yet there are many more remnants of early records from Babylonia than from Egypt. This is probably due to the fact that the Babylonians incised their written records upon clay tablets which were then fired, while the Egyptians wrote on papyrus, a material which is far from everlasting even when buried in the parched sands of the desert.

Among the famous Amarna tablets of 1400 B.C. there are some references to books. This collection of clay tablets, excavated in Egypt and addressed to the king and queen of Egypt, were written in the Babylonian language. Among the tablets are fragments of small plaques on which are written the names of the king and queen, together with the title of a book. These may have been ownership or identification tags which were attached to books or to cases which held books, but there is no basis for claiming anything like catalog entries for them.

On tablets dated about a century later than this, excavated in the capital city of the Hittites, there is what may be the earliest evidence of the use of a colophon to convey bibliographical information. These tablets bear subscripts which identify the number of the tablet in a series, its title, and often the name of the scribe.[3]

Some six hundred years later, in about 650 B.C., in the city of Nineveh, which was then at its apex, we again come upon the use of the colophon. Of the approximately twenty thousand tablets[4] which were excavated there from the library or archives of the Assyrian king, Ashurbanipal, many bear quite elaborate colophons, in which are recorded title (which in antiquity is often synonymous with the opening lines), the tablet—or volume—number, the first words of the following tablet, the name of the owner of the original if the tablet had been copied from an older one, as well as the name of the scribe who copied it, and, finally, a stamp showing that the work belonged to the king. In the search for evidences of ancient catalogs, this is one of the most frustrating periods to study, for, with all the care which was taken to preserve order and authenticity in the library at Nineveh, it seems so likely that some sort of catalog existed, yet all we have is this reasonable assumption. Indeed, we are forced to leave pre-Greek antiquity with literally nothing more than assumptions.

There is, of course, the well-known catalog of books carved on the walls of the temple at Edfu in Egypt, but this inscription is of a much later period than that of which we have been speaking; and, actually, even before the erection of this temple in the third and second centuries B.C., the source of civilization had made its way from the Middle East to Greece.

Throughout Greek literature there are references to book collections; in the earlier periods, to the collections of individuals, later to the libraries of schools and even to libraries built by public subscription. In the period following Alexander, when the most active centers of Greek civilization were to be found outside Greece, the two famous libraries of Alexandria and Pergamum developed into the greatest libraries of antiquity. In such libraries as these there must have been some kind of catalog, but no remnants have survived about which there is any certainty. In much later writings there is mention of the "Pinakes" of the Pergamene scholars,[5] but no fragments, or even a quotation from them, have survived. Calimachus, one of the scholars of Alexandria, compiled his Pinakes in about 250 B.C. A few quotations from these have been cited by other writers, so that we do have a slight knowledge of these lists.[6] They are generally assumed to have been a catalog of the Alexandrian library; yet this claim is not made by the ancients. The work may have been a library catalog, or it may have been a bibliography of Greek literature. Whichever the case, Callimachus recorded the number of lines in each work as well as the opening words; however, no sort of imprint is given, the scribe is never mentioned or the date of copying—at least no mention is made of these items in the quotations which are extant. This, added to the fact that biographical data on the authors are included in the entries, tends to strengthen the belief that the Pinakes of Callimachus were a bibliographical work rather than a list of holdings. They may, of course, have been written to serve both purposes, and in either case they do offer some insight into the Alexandrian scholar's conception of entry and choice of bibliographic detail. Ancient quotations from the lists themselves, as well as comments about them, seem to make possible the following generalizations on the cataloging or bibliographical procedures of the period: a few very general categories were considered a sufficient subject approach to the literature of the time; the scholar, after going to the general subject in which he was interested, was accustomed to look next for the author—title was secondary; it was considered important to record the opening words of a book and its length by number of lines. The arrangement of entries differed, being at times classified, at times chronological, and in other instances alphabetical. In regard to the latter, there is evidence from inscriptions that the Greeks never arrived at a strictly alphabetical arrangement. There are a few instances in which lists of names are grouped by initial letter, but nowhere is there an alphabetical arrangement based on any letter following the first one. This probably indicates, among other things, that their lists never approached the length to which we are accustomed.

The scholarship of this period was what might be called "encyclopedic" rather than creative. It was a time of gathering, compiling, and organizing the works of previous generations. Some creative writing went on, to be sure—Callimachus himself was a poet—but the bulk of productivity was in the editorial field. An age with such interests would seem likely to produce catalogs; of course, one might say that dictionaries, encyclopedias, anthologies, and collections of excerpts—all developments of this age—do partake essentially of the nature of catalogs. Even if there were no catalogs as such, these Alexandrian "reference" publications exerted considerable influence on Roman and Byzantine scholarship and played an important part both in the preservation of learning and in establishing precedents for the future avenues of approach to collected knowledge.

It may be that the most significant contribution which the Greeks made to cataloging was the use of the author of a work for its entry. There is no doubt that our whole concept of author entry first came with the Greeks; it never once appeared in any work which has survived from the earlier civilizations of the East. Even today in the Orient the traditional entry for a book is its title, and whenever, under the influence of modern librarianship, a book in an oriental library is entered under author, it is considered a very progressive and "Western" thing to do; older Chinese and Japanese books continue to be entered under title. How basic this difference is between East and West was brought rather vividly to my attention not long ago when a Japanese librarian expressed his opinion that the principle of author entry is concomitant with democracy, since it rests upon belief in the importance of the individual.

When, in the search for catalogs, we come to the Romans, there is even less available information than among the Greeks. There is the well-known story from later writings that Crates, a scholar from Pergamum, made a trip to Rome and, because of an injury suffered while he was there, was forced to stay for a rather long period of convalescence.[7] During this time he is reported to have been very active conversationally and thereby to have whipped up a good deal of interest in libraries among the Romans. If it is true that libraries were started in Rome under the influence of Crates, they undoubtedly took on the cataloging methods of the library at Pergamum, all of which is of little help, of course, since nothing remains of the Pergamene catalog. From other sources which mention Roman libraries there is evidence only that there was some way of finding a designated book when it was requested, probably through some kind of fixed location. About the middle of the second century after Christ, Marcus Aurelius related how, in the midst of a discussion, he and his friends dispatched a servant to the library to get a copy of a certain one of Cato's speeches.[8] He added that the servant went first to the library of Apollo, but was unsuccessful in obtaining the book there, so he went then to the library of Tiberius, where he got the book. Another Latin author two centuries later mentioned that a certain book to which he was referring was to be found on the sixth case in the Ulpian library.[9]

Scholarship in late Roman times was, in general, occupied with the same kind of pursuits, if not of quite the same quality, as those which had occupied the scholars of the Alexandrian age. There were anthologies, digests, commentaries, paraphrases, textbooks of rhetoric, and encyclopedias.

Again it appeared to be an age in which library catalogs would be much needed and in which there would be great interest in compiling them; however, either catalogs had not been developed as tools of research, or, if they did exist, the vagaries of late fate have seen fit to save for us not one fragment of them or even one reference to their existence.

In 529 [A.D.], when the life of Greece and Rome came to an end officially and one must look rather to Constantinople as the center of learning, we find nothing more to add to the history of cataloging. The same kind of activity occupied the scholars of this period, the same re-working of the literature of the past. We know that there were church and monastery libraries throughout the eastern empire and the imperial library in Constantinople, but about catalogs we have no information.

The same year in which the aging glory of Greece and Rome was put to rest saw the humble birth of literary activity among a new people, for the most part unlettered and in uncouth and primitive surroundings. This new and lowly beginning had no scholarly motivation—it may have been that Benedict thought his monks at Monte Cassino ought to be kept busy, so he set them to copying manuscripts. There was no demand for books, and knowledge was not sought in any way which would require the use of catalogs, but in this un-pretentious way a system was set up through which the monastery became the sole keeper, manufacturer, and finally cataloger of books through long and uninterested centuries.

One of the earliest listings of the holdings of a medieval library is dated two hundred years later, in the eighth century. It is written on the final flyleaf of a book[10] and consists of only a list of brief titles with authors appended to a few of them. There is no observable order in the arrange-ment, neither classified nor alphabetical. In no way can the list be called a catalog with any meaning which we attach to the term. It more probably served as an inventory record and per-haps represented the shelf arrangement, which might well have been made according to size or acquisition or both, but no location symbols ac-company the titles. Although it was the custom of the time to bind together a number of works into one volume, this list quite obviously gives only the title of the first item in each volume, a further indication of its being an inventory. This list is typical of most of the so-called catalogs of the several following centuries—the briefest sort of inventories recorded in the most casual places.

Two libraries from the ninth century might be mentioned as having produced catalogs more out-standing than those of the general run. One was the library at Reichenau in Germany, which com-piled several catalogs between 822 and 842.[11] One of these catalogs includes a gift enumeration; another lists only the valuable books; but all of them give the several works contained in each volume, as well as the number of volumes or rolls in which each work was contained. Only one maintains any order in its arrangement (this is, strangely enough, the earliest of the lists), an order for the most part classified, yet all the works of an author are kept together. Sample categories are *Works of St. Augustine (De opusculis S. Augus-tini), Lives of the Fathers (De vita patrum),* and *Dictionaries (De libris glossarum).*

The other ninth-century catalog[12] to which I refer is from the Benedictine house of St. Requier, compiled in 831. It likewise gives the contents of volumes and records the number of volumes to a work. It used author entries, but in no discernible order. The chief interest in this list is that the compiler stated the reason for its composition, namely, an accounting of the library was re-quested by Louis le Debonnaire. Even without this evidence, one might reasonably assume that all the library lists of the period were inventory records—from their nature they could not pos-sibly have served any purpose except mere count. Furthermore, we have the compiler's word that the St. Requier inventory contained only 246 volumes, and it would, of course, be quite un-realistic to expect libraries of this size to feel any need for catalogs.

As simple and as uninformative as these in-ventories from Reichenau and St. Requier are, they stand out not only as the superior lists of the ninth century but superior throughout a number of centuries, both preceding and subse-quent. From the time when the Greco-Roman civilization came to an end in the sixth century, there is little evidence of the existence of book lists until the eighth century; then came the im-provements of the ninth century, and after that no development in the quality of lists for sev-eral hundred years.

By the tenth century, libraries had grown con-siderably in size. A catalog from Bobbio[13] in Italy records nearly seven hundred volumes, and one from Lorsch[14] in Germany, nearly six hun-dred; but even Bobbio and Lorsch, which were among the most famous and largest libraries of the time, produced no catalogs which were in any way improvements over the naive ninth-century inventories. The comparative excellence of the ninth-century records may have been due to the upsurge of interest in books which came about under the influence of Charlemagne and his immediate successors; for, as you recall, Alcuin and other scholars in the employ of the Frankish kings spread abroad great enthusiasm for producing and possessing books, as well as for improving their quality in both format and contents.

Throughout the eleventh and twelfth centuries no improvement is seen in library lists—rather, even retrogression. Some of them occasionally record the contents of volumes, and at times it seems as if an order of arrangement is being observed. Whenever there is subject arrangement, it is very broad, often-times using only two categories, "Biblical" and "Humanistic."[15]

A twelfth-century inventory from the monastery of St. Peter at Salzburg[16] gives in a few instances the opening words of a work; however, this seems not to have been done in the interests of fuller cataloging but only in cases where the librarian was not able to determine either author or title. In general, noticeably less information is recorded in the lists of the eleventh and twelfth centuries than in those of the ninth.

Neither did the thirteenth century bring anything new in the way of entries. A list from the library of Glastonbury Abbey, dated 1247.[17] added some unusual descriptions in designating books variously as "useless" (*inutiles*), "legible" (*legibles*), "old" (*vetusti*), and "good" (*bon*). In earlier lists the beauty of a volume had been mentioned or its unusual size or the fact that it was a treasure (*praegrandis*); but the Glastonbury characterizations are of a different sort. The easiest explanation is that they pertained to the physical condition of the books; but whether they were used as an aid in identification for inventory or to help the reader by pointing out which books could be easily read is impossible to state.

Toward the end of the thirteenth century someone whose identity is not known started a project which might well be considered a milestone in the history of catalogs. This was the compilation of the Registrum librorum Angliae,[18] a union list of holdings of English monastery libraries in which, in a quite modern way, each library was assigned a number for coding purposes. The Registrum was never finished. There are evidences of later attempts to compile continuations of it, although no finished version has survived—in fact, quite surely never existed. The catalog of John Boston of Bury[19] of about 1410 seems to have been conceived as a continuation and revision of the Registrum, since the code numbers assigned to the participating libraries are identical with those used in the earlier catalog.

The fourteenth century brought some improvements, and a few lists of this peroid might rightly be called shelf lists. One from Christ Church, Canterbury,[20] compiled during the first part of the century, is arranged by numbered sections of the library, subdivided by numbered shelves, thus observing a fixed location to the extent that each book was designated for a certain shelf. There is no improvement in entries here, but there is an overall attempt to list the contents of volumes, although with such lack of clarity that it is frequently impossible to determine with which work one volume ends and the next begins.

A list from Exeter Cathedral,[21] bearing the date 1327, records the opening words of each volume and gives its price. This document is part of a general inventory, which also included the vestments and treasures of the cathedral. The fact that this, one of the superior lists of the period, was prepared as an inventory strengthens the belief that none of the lists compiled thus far were intended to serve what we consider catalog purposes.

Fifty years later, in 1372, a list from the Augustinian friars in York[22] pursues a more truly classified arrangement than occurs earlier, in that it separates the writings of an author when the subjects of his works so dictate, a practice which was a rather radical departure from custom. Another bit of progress is seen here in that the opening words of the second leaf of each volume are given, certainly a much surer means of identification than the customary opening words of the book.

The outstanding list of the fourteenth century is from St. Martin's Priory[23] at Dover, dated 1389; in fact, it may be the first of the lists which could be justly designated a catalog. It is divided into three sections; the first is a listing by call number, a number representing fixed location even to the placing of the individual volume. The entries in this section include short title, the number of the page in the book on which the call number was recorded, and the first words of the text on that page, as well as the number of pages in the book and the number of works contained in the volume. The second section of the catalog, likewise arranged by call number, gives the contents of each volume, with the paging and opening words for each work included. The third part is a landmark in the development of cataloging: a catalog of analytical entries and an alphabetical listing, but with entries of the usual medieval type, some under author, others under title followed by author, with still other entries beginning with such words as "book" (*liber*), "part" (*pars*), or "*codex*," obviously with no importance attached to the entry word.

This is also the century which saw the beginning of college libraries, but that did not mean any advanced contributions to the development of cataloging. The earliest lists from college libraries revert, for some reason, to the primitive inventories of the preceding centuries. This condition may possibly be explained by pointing to the fact that their book collections were very sparse. It was not at all unusual for a college library at this time to have less than one hundred books. A catalog from Trinity Hall, Cambridge,[24] dated 1394, contains entries such as "one small Bible" (*unam Bibliam param*), "a large and beautiful concordance of the Bible" (*liber concordantiarum Bibliae magnus et pulcher*), or "another concordance of the Bible, less beautiful but portable" (*alius liber concordantiarum Bibliae pulcher minor et portabilis*). Entries such as these under the Latin equivalents of "one" and "another" would seem to us completely useless for students and but little better for the librarian, even when only checking his inventory.

Fifteenth-century catalogs brought few innovations; there was no improvement in entry form; there was some reference to location symbols; but shelf numbering had still not become a common procedure. Probably the only new practice to appear in this century was the use of cross-references. In both the fifteenth-century catalogs in which I found these, there seems to be an attempt to make them serve the purpose of analytical entries. In the catalog compiled in 1410-12 by Amplonius Ratnick de Berka[25] the cross-references are not in themselves entries but are merely appended to a sort of contents note pointing out in what other place in the library a certain item might be found, with wording such as "which seek in the 96th volume of theology" (*quas require in 96 volume theologie*). These are cross-references in a most undeveloped and primitive state, but they are a beginning, and they make their appearance here in a catalog which is otherwise undistinguished, especially in its feeling for entries which are typically of this sort: "a book of Plate" (*item liber Platonis*) or "a rare and good volume in which the following writings are included" (*item volumen rarum et bonum, in qou infrascripta continentur*).

In the catalog of St. Augustine's Abbey, Canterbury,[26] compiled about eighty years later, cross-references appear again. Here they also serve as analytics, but there is an important difference, for in this catalog they reach the status of entries. A typical example of one of these references is "The Meditations of Bernard, not here because it is above in the Bible [which was given by] W. Wylmynton" (*Meditaciones Bernardi non hic quia supra in Biblia W. Wylmynton*).

Toward the close of the century the German bibliographer and librarian, Johann Tritheim, stands out as having taken an important step in the development of cataloging. He compiled a bibliography in chronological order, which was unusual enough for his time, but—what holds chief interest for us—he appended to this an alphabetical author index.[27] It is difficult to understand why such a simple and useful device had not always been used, yet it took centuries of compiling book lists to reach this degree of accomplishment.

As the sixteenth century opens, our attention is drawn to the catalog of Syon Monastery, Isleworth, England.[28] Here, about thirty years after Tritheim, appears a classified catalog which also included an alphabetical author index. From this time on, the practice became more usual but by no means universal.

The other catalog of the sixteenth century to which I shall draw attention is that of the Priory of Bretton in Yorkshire, dated 1558.[29] It is a small catalog with the casual forms of entry characteristic of medieval catalogs, but included within the entries are the names of editors and translators, a practice which seems not to have appeared earlier.

The history of cataloging in the sixteenth century would not have much to show in the way of progress if it had been forced to depend solely upon librarians and library catalogs. Following the precedent set by Tritheim before the turn of the century, bibliographers rather than librarians continued to take the lead in raising cataloging from the low level which it had consistently maintained throughout the medieval centuries. One of the first names which comes to mind in this connection is that of Konrad Gesner of Zurich. With the publication of his author bibliography in 1545[30] and the subject index in 1548,[31] a new standard of excellence was set.

In the matter of entries, it is true that he continued to use the forenames of authors in accordance with the tradition of his time, but he did recognize the possible inconvenience caused by this practice and prefixed to his bibliography an alphabetical list of authors in which the names were inverted. Furthermore, the main listing includes cross-references from the main forms and spellings of names to the accepted entry form. It is unprecedented for such aids to be given the reader as "Thobias: vide Tobias," and it seems practically modern to find Gesner's use of merely the word *see* in contrast to the quaint and involved directions given by earlier cross-references. Gesner, the bibliographer and naturalist, included in his *Pandectarum* instructions for the arrangement of books in a library, and he conceived of his system of classification for library as well as for bibliographical purposes. He even suggested that libraries use copies of his bibliographies as their catalogs by inserting call numbers beside entries which represented their holdings, thus providing themselves with both an author and a subject catalog. This proposal, I remind you, was made in 1548.

Twelve years later, Florian Trefler, a Benedictine monk, published at Augsburg a treatise on the keeping of a library.[32] He commented in his Introduction on the difficulty of finding information in libraries in which books were not kept in any discernible order and where the material was not cataloged. (After studying a few medieval catalogs one has the conviction that Trefler was indeed speaking from experience.) He devised a scheme of classification and call numbers quite advanced for his time, in spite of the fact that one unit in the call number was made to represent the color of the binding. He advocated a five-part catalog which consisted of an alphabetical author catalog, a shelf list, a classified index to analytics, an alphabetical index to the classified index, and, finally, a list of books which, for various reasons, were not kept with the main collection. Catalogs made according to Trefler's plan would have been far ahead of their time, indeed. He had a comprehension of the value of providing more than one means of access to a book, something wholly unknown in his day. In another way, too, Trefler showed himself progressive, i.e., in following Gesner's suggestion for the use of the *Pandectarum* as a library catalog. Trefler recommended that a checked copy of it be used as one section of his proposed plan for a catalog, namely, the subject index to analytical entries. Whenever we wonder at how long it took for certain simple cataloging ideas to catch on, such as the alphabetical index, let us remember that it has been

four hundred years since the suggestion was first made that printed bibliographies be substituted for catalogs or sections of catalogs and that it still seems too daring and radical a thing to try.

Thirty-five years after Trefler, once more significant contributions came from outside the field of cataloging. In 1595 Andrew Maunsell, an English bookseller, compiled his *Catalogue of English Printed Books* and in the Preface stated his rules for entry. He advocated the entry of personal names under surnames rather than Christian names, noting that this was contrary to the usage set up by Gesner. His rule for the entry of anonymous works runs like this: "I have placed them either upon the titles they be entitled by, or else upon the matter they entreate of, and sometimes upon both, for the easier finding of them." Other regulations call for including in the entry translator, printer or for whom printed, date, and number of volume. He also set up the principle of uniform entry for the Bible and insisted that one should be able to find a book under the author's surname, the subject, and the translator, all three. These were radical and sudden advances in the development of cataloging, and one cannot help noticing that they came from the bookseller rather than the librarian, something not unknown in our own time and our own country.

The political, social, and intellectual movements of the sixteenth century brought wide, sweeping, and at times even violent changes for libraries. These are well known to you: the impact which printing made on book collections, the destruction of monasteries, the rise of princely and municipal libraries, and the growth of universities. When attempting to interpret catalogs in relation to their times, one certainly comes to an impasse before the conflicting situation which prevailed during this century. It was an age of book-burning and wholesale destruction of libraries, and yet it was this age which produced the first cataloging codes.

On the one hand, we find the foregoing situation, which was confusing enough; on the other, there is the fact that at this time, when scholarship was entering upon a period of great activity motivated by such significant world movements as the Renaissance, the Reformation, and the dawn of scientific experimentation, library catalogs were still in a primitive state, completely inadequate for what must have been the demands of the age. It is unthinkable that the kinds of catalogs which we have been examining could ever have served as usable tools for the type of scholar that the period produced, for this was, you recall, the age of Scaliger, Galileo, Grotius, Descartes, Bacon, and Kepler. If we are to learn from history, a study of the sixteenth century should certainly put us on the alert. Here in the midst of an enthusiasm for scholarships and intellectual activity which has not often, if ever, been equaled, library catalogs did not at all rise to the occasion. Rather it fell upon the scholars themselves both to originate the ideas and to make the initial attempts toward providing some kind of index to the world's learning. It devolved upon them and the booksellers to point out to the libraries the potentialities of library catalogs. Even after the way had been pointed out, it was by no means followed by the majority of catalogers. The great and seemingly obvious improvements in cataloging which appeared in Maunsell's code were neither immediately nor universally adopted by librarians and bibliographers; for instance, the practice of using Christian names as entries survived for many years, even in the listings in which there were column after column of entries under "Johann." The use of forename for the entry word was, of course, a carry-over from times when there was no system of surnames, but the appalling thing is that for century after century catalogs and bibliographies remained so immured by this tradition that they failed to become aware of the change in custom. (One cannot help wondering which of our intrenched procedures, now so completely taken for granted, will some day look quite as ridiculous as this, and for which there must be as simple an answer as the use of the surname. It may well be that the conglomeration of entries under "U.S." in our catalogs will someday look not only as stupid but as easily obviated as their entries under "John.")

At the beginning of the seventeenth century Sir Thomas Bodley appeared as an important figure on the cataloging scene. An English diplomat, retired from foreign service, he offered to undertake the building-up of the Oxford University Library, which had been destroyed some fifty years before. After his offer had been gratefully accepted, he appointed Thomas James as his librarian, but he himself retained complete supervision, even to dictating the most minute cataloging procedures.[33] The practices which Bodley instituted hold interest not only because they were progressive but also because Bodley approached them as a user of the catalog for the purpose of carrying on his acquisitions program. Once more we find the layman user of the library assuming initiative and responsibility for what the catalog should contain.

Bodley's code included, among other regulations, insistence upon a classified arrangement with an alphabetical author index arranged by surname, although James preferred a completely alphabetical catalog. He insisted upon the inclusion of analytical entries. On this point Bodley was very vehement, and yet James, the librarian, seems to have attached little importance to them and frequently failed to carry out Bodley's wish. Bodley entered noblemen under their family names and insisted, over the objection of the librarian, on using as entry form the inflected cases of the names of Greek and Latin authors rather than the nominative when they so occurred on the title page.

During the century several discourses on librarianship were published in which one can find evidence of progressive attitudes toward catalogs. In France, Gabriel Naudé stressed the importance of catalogs as a means of finding books and of identifying them bibliographically;[34] he recommended the compilation of a divided catalog, with one section for subjects and the other for authors. He also suggested a shelf arrangement which would allow for expansion.

A few years later (1650) in England John Dury's treatise made some of the same suggestions; it also favored the printing of yearly supplements to catalogs, recommended selective cataloging, and even suggested a method of dealing with unwanted gifts.[35]

Toward the close of the seventeenth century an incident occurred through which we are able to gain some insight into what were considered the major cataloging problems of the time. In 1697 the curators of the Bodleian requested from the staff of that library any suggestions they might have for its improvement. In answer to this request, one member of the staff, Humphrey Wanley, included with his suggestions an account of the questions which he thought needed to be solved before a new catalog could be attempted. Some of these questions were whether the catalog should be classified or alphabetical; whether titles and dates of books should be recorded in the language of the book; whether the size of a book should be recorded; whether author and title analytics should be included; whether the name of the publisher should be included in the imprint; whether there should be mention of the fact that a book lacks place or date; whether the first or best edition of a book should be so indicated; or whether a book's rarity or costliness should be noted. Wanley made no mention of any problem concerning entry, although this whole area was still in a very undeveloped state.[36]

In the same year Frederic Rostgaard published in Paris his discourse on a new method for setting up a library catalog.[37] Rostgaard's rules call for a subject arrangement subdivided at once chronologically and by size of volume. He states it as his purpose to organize the catalog in such a way that authors who treat of the same subject and all the editions of the same work are always found together. This he proposed to achieve by means of a printed catalog, with the spread of two facing pages divided into four parallel columns, each column to contain books·of a certain size, arranged so that the books of various sizes which had been published on a certain subject within the same year would come directly opposite each other in the parallel columns. His rules also provide for a secondary arrangement under the chronological order, whereby books which treat of a subject *in toto* are entered before those which treat of it in part. Rostgaard worked out a model catalog in which he actually achieved this strangely complicated arrangement— and more clearly, too, than one might expect.

He gives directions for an alphabetical index of subjects and authors to be placed at the end of the catalog, with authors entered by surname; works bound together are to have separate entries; the word order of titles as found on the title page is to be preserved, and authors' names are to be supplied for anonymous works when known. His final suggestion is that his rules not be followed when it seems best to arrange things differently. As an example he shows where one might wish to violate his basic chronological order in the case of translations if one preferred to enter, first, the books containing the original text, then those containing the original plus the translation, and, finally, the translations alone.

There is an almost modern note in Rostgaard's attitude toward the catalog. The intricate organization for which his code provides seems never to have had wide following, but his influence must have been felt on the Continent as that of Maunsell and the librarians of the Bodleian was in England.

By the beginning of the eighteenth century, catalogs were at last looked upon as finding lists rather than inventories. During this century they were sometimes classified and sometimes alphabetical; indexes were considered useful, though by no means necessary; some catalogs were still divided according to the size of books; authors were now always entered under surname and were often arranged chronologically; the wording of the title page had assumed a certain degree of prestige and was now being transcribed literally and without being paraphrased; imprints were included; "bound-with" notes were used; cross-references were quite common; and some analytical entries were used in most catalogs.

This state of things did not undergo much change throughout the century—it was as if a plateau had been reached in the development of cataloging principles. The reason could not have been that catalogs were now sufficient for the scholarship and research of the time, for this is the age which saw the beginning of specialized research, a new systematization of the sciences, and an attempt at organized international scholarly co-operation. There was scholarly activity on all sides, and the size of libraries increased tremendously. It may have been because libraries were so busy with their growing collections that they now ceased to philosophize about what catalogs ought to be or to experiment with new forms. Whatever the reason, these conditions prevailed throughout the century.

The only noticeable innovations came from the library activities of the new French government. During the Revolution, after the newly formed government had confiscated libraries throughout the country, it set up directions for their reorganization. In 1791 the government sent out to these libraries instructions for cataloging their collections.[38] Here we have the first instance of a national code. It was a paragon of brevity and practical simplicity. In the first place, the libraries were directed to use card catalogs—as far as I know, the first appearance in history of the card catalog—introduced, I feel sure, not because someone thought it would be the best or even a convenient form but because, with wartime shortages, it was a practical way of getting available materials on which to make the catalogs, since playing cards were to be used for the purpose. The added suggestion was included in the instructions that aces and deuces might well be reserved for the longest titles. There was no fuss and bother or philosophizing in this code. The title page was to be transcribed on the card and the author's surname underlined for the filing word. If there was no author, the key word in the title was to be underlined. A collation was added which was to include number of volumes, size, a statement of illustration, the material of which the book was made, the kind of type, any missing pages, and a description of the binding if it was outstanding in any way. There are here a number of procedures which have remained to the present, so that this code, coming as it did at the end of the eighteenth century, makes a rather easy steppingstone to the extensive cataloging developments of the next century.

During the first part of the nineteenth century, the Rev. Thomas Hartwell Horne published both a classification scheme and a code of cataloging rules in England.[39] He compiled a classified catalog for the library of Queen's College, Cambridge, and also submitted a scheme to the British Museum. The catalog of Queen's College was printed in 1827, but the catalog suggested for the British Museum never materialized, although a number of years and a sizable sum of money were spent on it. Horne's code was not revolutionary in most ways. I mention it chiefly because of its insistence that a book ought not to be limited to a single subject entry or to a single place in a scheme of classification. Not only was this a novel idea at the time, but it took many years for it to become a commonly accepted principle. Even yet it is not universally accepted, especially in the compilation of classified catalogs.

This was a period of much argument over the relative virtues of classified and dictionary catalogs not only among librarians but among readers and scholars in general and even in reports to the House of Commons. Feelings ran very high on the subject, and rather emotional arguments came forth on both sides of the issue, from the statement that classified catalogs and indexes were not needed because living librarians were better than subject catalogs to the opinion that any intelligent man who was sufficiently interested in a subject to want to consult material on it could just as well use author entries as subject, for he would, of course, know the names of all the authors who had written in his field.[40]

As one might infer from these arguments, the eighteenth- and nineteenth-century discussions in regard to classified versus alphabetical catalogs do not have much to offer librarians today. The very terms did not carry the same meaning then as now, and the type of catalog which we call classified, as well as what is now designated as a dictionary catalog, were at that time both completely unknown concepts. There would, in fact, be almost no common ground on which

to discuss any phase of librarianship dealing with subject approach. The subject heading had not yet evolved as an entity, but was still almost completely identified with the title, and added entries in the classified catalog were all but unheard of.

At the height of the frustration resulting from wasted time and money in abortive attempts to produce a satisfactory catalog for the British Museum and when arguments were most heated over this question and that, there appeared a figure at the Museum with strong convictions and the power to persuade. Anthony Panizzi, a lawyer by profession, a political refugee from Italy, was appointed extra-assistant librarian in 1831.[41] I need not remind you that this incident proved to be of great significance for the future of both British and American cataloging.

In 1836 a select committee was appointed by the House of Commons "to inquire into the condition, management, and affairs of the British Museum." One of the "affairs" which the committee undertook to examine was the state of catalogs and cataloging in the Museum library. During the hearings witnesses came forward in great numbers to testify for and against the current catalogs, some to speak in favor of an alphabetical catalog, others for a classified catalog, many becoming actually vehement about this or that sort of entry, even over the question of whether a complete title should be used in a certain case or only a catchword title. Surely, such great interest in the minutiae of cataloging has never been displayed at any other time by scholar, reader, and government. Panizzi figured prominently in the hearings and again and again was able to persuade the examiners to accept his views.

The next year he was appointed Keeper of the Printed Books.[42] In 1839, after hearings during which the trustees of the British Museum examined Panizzi's proposals in detail, although they insisted upon an untimely publication of the catalog, he was able to exact from them official approval of his proposed code, and the now famous 91 Rules went into effect.[43] In many instances his code vested great authority in the title page; for example, if an author used his forename only in a book, this was used as the entry even if the complete name was known; when the author of an anonymous work became known, his name was still not used as the entry but was merely inserted after the title; pseudonymous publications also were entered under the author's feigned name, although the actual name might be known. However, in other instances Panizzi directed that research was to be expended, if necessary, in order to establish certain forms of name for entry; for example, a nobleman was always to be entered under his family surname, even though all his writings had been published under his title.

Another characteristic of Panizzi's code was the occasional use of form headings as main entry; universities and learned societies were entered under the general heading ACADEMIES; the entries for magazines, newspapers, and annuals were under the heading PERIODICAL PUBLICATIONS; almanacs and calendars, under EPHEMERIDES; missals, prayer-books, and liturgies, under LITURGIES; anonymous dictionaries, under DICTIONARIES; likewise with anonymous encyclopedias and catalogs, under their respective form headings. Here seems to be an indication that the concept of subject entry as it exists today had not then been separated from that of main entry, a tendency which seems to be indicated again in Panizzi's rule for anonymous works in general. For these the preferred entry was the name of a person if one were mentioned in the title; second choice, the name of an organization, provided that there was one in the title; or, lacking these, the name of a place. If the title contained neither person, organization, nor place, then entry was made finally, when no other choice presented itself, under the first word of the title. A title entry was thus never *chosen* but was resorted to only when all else failed. In this procedure there seems to be a very conscious attempt to arrive at a main entry which is at the same time a subject entry, and still not depart from the authority of the title page; in fact, during one of the hearings Panizzi made the statement that those who want to find a book by subject "can obtain this information (as far as it can be obtained from a title-page which is all that can be expected in a catalogue)."[44]

By 1847 a further investigation of the British Museum was deemed necessary, and the Crown appointed the Commission To Inquire into the Constitution and Government of the British Museum. Many witnesses were again called in, among them Thomas Carlyle. He told of his search through the catalog, as he described it, through those things which you do not know anything about, and which you have no business to know anything about. If you cannot find the book in the catalogue, they will not attempt to seek it. . . . Like a haberdasher requiring me, if I went into his shop and asked for a yard of green ribbon, to tell him in what drawer the ribbon was lying. . . . I am not a catalogue-maker, and I have not turned my mind particularly to it. I merely understand that it is a work which ought to be done by a man of order; and that a man of order will arrange a catalogue properly, and a man of disorder will not do so . . . will not arrange the huge mass of jungle that he has to arrange.[45]

One witness attacked the entry of learned societies under the heading ACADEMIES and was thereupon questioned in great detail how he thought this or that society should be entered, what different classes of societies should be entered in different ways, and even which words from specific titles should be chosen as the entry word. When the witness stated that he was in favor of the rule which would enter anonymous works under the first substantive in the title, he was asked thereupon to apply this rule to the title *Is It Well with You?* and the title *Ye Must Be Born Again.*[46] Though such sections of the hearing make fascinating reading, they do not get us quickly on with our subject.

Panizzi's training as a lawyer doubtless put him in good stead. He pleaded his case brilliantly and, as would be the custom in a court of law, dealt with exact evidence to prove his points. As one illustration of this, I mention that well-known episode which involved John Payne Collier, the Shakespearean critic. When Collier was called before the commission as a witness, he criticized the 91 Rules most vehemently, stating that Panizzi with his many rules and too careful cataloging was not only delaying the production of a catalog but was making a useless tool of it and referred to the work as "Mr. Panizzi's interminable catalogue."[47] Collier tried his hand at cataloging twenty-five books according to the system which he was advocating, and then Panizzi appeared before the commission, using the results of Collier's cataloging as a basis for the defense of his own 91 Rules. Needless to say, the barrister Panizzi presented his case in a manner which was rather devastating for Collier.

A perusal of only this one day's hearing is enlightening in a number of ways. First of all, it leaves us with no doubt that we have now arrived at "modern" cataloging, for all the problems are here and, with them, many of the same answers, too. A number of the solutions suggested are exactly the ones which have been brought forward recently as quite radical ways by which we might streamline these old-fashioned catalogs of ours. The question of whether the catalog should be anything more than a finding list was discussed a hundred years ago quite as seriously as today, and it sounds anachronistic when, in the hearing of March 9, 1849, the Earl of Ellesmere, chairman of the day, puts the following question: "Have you ever heard it proposed that each book should be catalogued under the form of name appearing on the title without any regard to uniformity and without regard to the different forms of name adopted by an author, or arising from the different languages in which works by the same author may be printed?"[48]

Now, at the halfway point in the nineteenth century, developments in cataloging in the United States begin to warrant our attention. Up to this time American cataloging was still following the same general pattern that had characterized European cataloging during the preceding century. For example, of the three catalogs which Harvard printed, one had been divided into three alphabets according to the *size* of books, all three contained the briefest of entries, and none provided much in the way of subject approach. However, in 1850, with the acceptance of Charles C. Jewett's code for the catalog of the Smithsonian Institution,[49] it would not be far wrong to say that cataloging in this country first came to maturity. The unprecedented and still unparalleled interest and activity in cataloging which had flared and flourished at the British Museum for well over a decade now could not help having its effect on American librarians.

In the Preface to his code Jewett acknowledged his debt to Panizzi, and he departed in only a few instances from the precepts of the 91 Rules, instances in which can be seen the basis for some of the entry principles which have come to be entrenched in American usage. Jewett extended the principle of the corporate author further than Panizzi had and entered all corporate bodies directly under their names without the use of any intervening form headings. He specifically established "U.S." as the author of public documents issued by particular departments, bureaus, or committees. While he followed the letter of Panizzi's law for the entry of noblemen, he very openly questioned the propriety of the rule and gave examples of instances in which he thought it did not achieve the most desirable form of entry. He also differed from Panizzi in the entry of pseudonymous works and established the practice of entering a book under the real name of its author, regardless of what name appeared in the book itself, "if," as he said, "he be known to have published any edition under his own name or to have avowed

the authorship." Another departure of major importance that he made from the 91 Rules was concerned with the entry of anonymous works which he entered under the first word of the title rather than under some catchword contained in the title. In no case did he provide for the entry of an anonymous work under a form heading as Panizzi had done; in fact, in the matter of form headings he departed from Panizzi completely and made no use of them at all for main entry. All these emendations proved to be significant and pertinent to the later development of cataloging in this country.

In regard to the concept of subject entry, Jewett not only did not go beyond Panizzi but showed rather that he had even less awareness of it. The only provision he made for subject at all was a cross-reference from the subject of a biography and "from any word in the title of an anonymous work, under which one would be likely to seek for the work in an alphabetical catalogue."[50]

Jewett spelled out in detail his theory of what purpose a code should serve: "The rules for cataloging must be stringent, and should meet, as far as possible, all difficulties of detail. Nothing, as far as can be avoided, should be left to the individual taste or judgment of the cataloger."[51] In view of this theory, it is interesting to observe that Jewett's rule book is a slim little pamphlet containing thirty-three regulations.

When Charles Cutter published his *Rules for a Printed Dictionary Catalogue* in 1876, he gave further support to those principles on which Jewett had been at variance with Panizzi. He entered authors who used pseudonyms under their real names and questioned the wisdom of Panizzi's rule for noblemen. He made no use of form headings for main entry but rather transferred this type of heading to the area of subjects, a procedure which, although now taken quite for granted, might, for functional purposes, not be able to survive too great scrutiny. The closest we have ever come again to the use of form headings for main entry is in the practice introduced by the Library of Congress of using form *sub*headings such as *Laws, statutes, etc., Treaties, etc.,* or *Selections.* It must be admitted that the principle makes for rather good organization, and it does not seem quite idle to wonder whether it was totally unquestioned progress on the part of Jewett and Cutter to disregard Panizzi in this respect. Cutter, like Jewett, entered anonymous works under the first word of the title, with an interesting exception, however, in the case of anonymous biographies, which he entered not under the first word of the title but under the subject. With him this procedure was certainly not a matter of having failed to define the concept of subject entry, as was probably the case with earlier catalogers; it must rather come down to the simple fact that he felt free to make main entry under subject when he thought common sense dictated it.

Cutter strengthened the concept that catalogs not only should point the way to an individual publication but should also assemble and organize literary units. While this was not an entirely new principle, since Maunsell in 1595 had used the heading "Bible" to assemble its various versions and translations, Panizzi in 1841 had strengthened it as a concept by introducing corporate and government entries, and Jewett had given it still further support by his use of real names rather than pseudonyms, yet it was Cutter who actually stated it as a formal principle: "In regard to the author entry it must be remembered that the object is not merely to facilitate the finding of a given book by the author's name. If this were all, it might have been better to make the entry under . . . the form of name mentioned in the title, but we have also . . . [that other object] to provide for [of showing what the library has under a given author]."[52]

Sixty-three years ago, in Cobb Hall on the University of Chicago campus, at a meeting of the World's Library Congress which was being held in connection with the World's Fair, William Coolidge Lane of Harvard gave a report on the state of cataloging. First he enumerated those points in regard to a library catalog which he considered had been settled and, second, those on which there was still no general consensus. The following are a few of the items on which he considered that agreement had been reached: (1) most works should be entered by subject as well as by author or title; (2) the author's name if possible should be given in the vernacular; (3) on the author card the author's name and bibliographic detail should be given in full, but the title in brief; on subject cards the title should be given in full, but the author's name and bibliographic details in brief; (4) in transcribing titles the words and spelling of the title page should be strictly adhered to, with any deviations indicated by brackets; (5) periodicals should be entered by title except those society publications which bear the name "Bulletin," "Proceedings," or "Journal." Then some of the points on which he said that opinion was still divided were: (1) the

form of the catalog, whether it should be printed, loose-leaf, or on cards, or a combination of these; whether it should be a dictionary or a divided catalog and, in the latter case, whether the subject section should be alphabetical or classified; (2) the question of the entry of pseudonyms; (3) the entry of English noblemen; (4) the entry of societies and institutions (the present distinction between them had not yet been devised).[53]

After he had delivered his report, Mr. Lane proposed three questions which he thought called for discussion: (1) Should libraries go to the effort of seeking out the full names of authors for entry? (2) Should scientific and art subjects, as well as historical and descriptive material, be put under place, or should they be subdivided by place? (3) Are the days of the subject catalog ended in favor of the use of subject bibliographies?[54] The subsequent discussion was, as always, partly to the point and partly not, partly far seeing and partly nïave. and in many places picturesque. On the question of using the author's full name for purposes of identification, one librarian said he thought that the author's residence was the most important item to use for identification, giving as evidence the fact that he knew three William Sanders, one living in London, England, another in London, Ontario, and the third in Washington. At this Mr. Dewey quipped, "Your Ontario man may move to London or Washington."

In 1904 another international meeting was held, this time in St. Louis in connection with the Louisiana Purchase Exposition, and Mr. Lane again reported on "Present Tendencies of Cataloguing Practice."[55] One gathers from this report that during the interlude of eleven years since the Columbian Exposition the compilation of subject catalogs had become an accepted procedure and that card catalogs had won out over the other forms. In fact, there was already concern over the size to which card catalogs might grow, and Mr. Lane was suggesting a solution which has lately been brought up again as something new, viz., printing up sections of card catalogs in order to reduce their too great bulk. He also mentioned that many codes had come into being mostly for the purpose of simplifying procedures and in this connection expressed the regret that "codes become longer, the oftener they are revised." Mr. Lane concluded his report by enumerating the questions which in his opinion should be the concern of the profession: (1) how to establish a just relation between subject catalog and bibliography; (2) how to improve subject catalogs; (3) which form of subject catalog is best; (4) what should be the attitude toward putting into the catalog analytical entries from periodicals and society transactions; (5) how to make the best possible use of printed cards from the Library of Congress, and how to extend the work on similar lines; (6) how to obtain inter-national uniformity; (7) how to get foreign govern-ments to print catalog cards; and (8) how far librarians should go in keeping on file cards for books in other libraries.

During the years between the appearance of the 91 Rules and the year 1900, cataloging codes had become very numerous. To mention only a few of them, there were in England, in addition to the revised editions of the British Museum rules, the Bodleian and Cambridge codes; in the United States, there were Jewett and Cutter, and Linder-felt's *Eclectic Card Catalog Rules,* Dewey's simpli-fied rules, and rules for the Library of Congress; in Germany, Dziatzko's *Instruction* of 1886, the basis of the Prussian code. There were codes in Belgium, the Scandinavian countries, France, Italy, the Netherlands, Spain, Switzerland, and the Vati-can. Hundreds of libraries had their own individ-ual rules.

Considering the great number of codes in use at the turn of the century, there were relatively few points of disagreement among them in regard to basic principles. There was universal agreement on entry under author, although there was not always agreement on what constituted an author, for the codes of Germany, Austria, Switzerland, Spain, and the Netherlands differed from the others in maintaining that authorship can be only a personal thing, and hence they did not, in general, treat the names of organizations as potential main entries. In the case of joint authors, there was agreement among the codes that entry should be under the first-named author, but there was a great variety of opinion as to how many authors' names might be included in the main entry at the same time.

We have noted that, from the beginning, there had been disagreement in regard to which part or form of personal names should be used for entry—the forename, the surname, the title, the possessive case, or the nominative. By 1900 there was still a great variety of differing opinion on the entry of compound names, on the entry of names begin-ning with prefixes, and the names of noblemen and royalty. In this area it was not even possible for Americans and British to arrive at agreement when they were co-operating on the formulation of the Anglo-American code. During the three-score years which elapsed between Panizzi's rules and our 1908 code there can be observed a gradual tendency toward giving less weight to the author-ity of the title page and placing more reliance on information gained from sources outside the book itself.

An attempt to summarize in brief form the find-ings from this excursion through catalogs and cata-loging codes of the past might lead to something like this:

Modern library cataloging has been little influ-enced by ancient cataloging. Whatever develop-ments there may have been in the compilation of catalogs in antiquity, no remains of them survived. There was no carry-over into the Middle Ages, for during that period cataloging as we conceive it did not even exist; neither did the Renaissance turn up anything about cataloging from classical periods except the barest and most conjectural evidence. Therefore, with the exception of the fact that the Greeks taught us to refer to books by their authors, it is not far wrong to maintain that the art, the technique, of cataloging is a completely modern development.

Cataloging throughout the Middle Ages was limited to casual and unorganized inventory lists, the earliest examples of which come from the eighth century. The thirteenth century produced an attempt at a union list of holdings for English libraries; in the fourteenth century the idea of lo-cation symbols made its appearance, as well as more complete identification of editions, and entries for more than the first work in a volume; in the fifteenth century cross-references appeared and the compilation of a bibliography and, of special importance to our subject, an index to the bibliography. The sixteenth century produced a catalog which made mention of editors and trans-lators and bibliographies in which, for the first time, attention was paid to the entry word; this century also brought the first use of entry under surname, and the principle of uniform entry for the anonymous classic. The seventeenth century brought an increased interest in catalogs, as well as treatises on how they ought to be made; it was a time of garnering past accomplishments rather than inventing new devices. The eighteenth cen-tury pursued a similar course, with the one ex-ception in its last decade of the use of card cata-logs by the French government. The nineteenth century was characterized by a keen interest in catalogs and greatly increased demands on the part of library users. Many of the great modern cata-logs appeared during this century in Germany, France, England, and the United States.

The development of the concept of entry, the idea that significance attaches to the *entry word* because it in itself constitutes a means of approach to books and information, while a concept so basic today that in every kind of listing we accept it without recognizing it, is nevertheless, a relatively recent notion. Actually, the first time any manifestation of this sense of entry seemed to appear was in 1545 in the work of Konrad Gesner. It was developed further a half-century later in the code of Andrew Maunsell, but the idea had not yet been apprehended by the majority of librarians. Even Thomas Bodley showed that he did not have a complete comprehension of the principle.

Once the general concept of entry was recognized, as it seemed to have finally been during the eighteenth century, there followed the question as to what factor in the book should constitute the entry. There was the ancient oriental tradition of title, the Western tradition of author, and then the modern notion that something should be done about *subject.*

The principle of *added* entry—the idea that there might be more than one way of finding a book in a catalog—made its first appearance in the form of indexes to catalogs, a device which seems to have been used for the first time by Johann Tritheim in 1494 and also appeared shortly thereafter in the catalog of Syon Monastery in England. The system was followed by subsequent bibliographers and codifiers—Gesner, Trefler, Maunsell, Bodley, Rostgaard, and Horne. By the beginning of the nineteenth century, librarians were well aware of the advantage of making a book available through more than one approach, but by no means did they always see their way clear to accomplishing this.

When the dictionary form of catalog was used, the added-entry function was performed by cross-references rather than by indexes. Bodley, Panizzi, Jewett, and the Library Association of the United Kingdom (1883) included in their codes definite rules for the use of cross-references to accomplish the added-entry purpose. However, by 1876 in this country, when Cutter published his code, he was already taking for granted the use of actual added entries.

The need for analytical and "bound-with" entries was recognized in the fifteenth century by the librarian of St. Augustine's Abbey in Canterbury; he met the need by the use of cross-references. Two hundred years later both Bodley and Rostgaard included in their rules the regulation that actual analytical entries be made, but, by the very nature of their instructions, they made it evident that this was far from a customary practice. At the end of the seventeenth century Wanley posed it as one of the problems to be faced in the compilation of catalogs, and at the middle of the twentieth century the question is still with us.

As one looks back over the development of cataloging codes, beginning with the rules of Trefler in 1560, one becomes impressed with the fact that throughout history codes seem always to have envisaged catalogs which were far better than their contemporary catalogs ever were—more complete, more progressive, and better organized. Examined from the perspective of history, codes have not been a statement of the usages of their day but rather the very means through which progress has come. If it is true that codes become the unintentioned pioneers, the forerunners of future practices, then the responsibility which is upon us is heavy indeed.

NOTES

[1] *The New Testament in the Original Greek,* revised by Brooke Foss Westcott and Fenton John Anthony Hort (New York: Macmillan Co., 1926), p. 187.

[2] S. N. Kramer, *From the Tablets of Summer* (Indian Hills, Colo.: Falcon's Wing Press, 1956), pp. 254-58.

[3] A translation of one of these colophons is given by Fritz Milkau, *Geschichte der Bibliotheken im alten Orient* (Leipzig: Otto Harrassowitz, 1935), p. 55.

[4] British Museum, Department of Egyptian and Assyrian Antiquities, *Catalogue of the Cuneiform Tablets in the Kouyunjik Collection,* ed. Carl Bezold (London, 1899).

[5] Dionysius of Halicarnassus, *De Deinarcho* i. 11; Athenaeus *336E.*

[6] Athenaeus 70B, 244A, 252C, 585B, 669E; Diogenes Laertius viii. 86; Suidas *Callimachus.*

[7] Suetonius *De illustribus grammaticis* 2.

[8] *Ad Frontonem* iv. 5.

[9] Vospiscus *Tacitus.* viii. 1.

[10] St. Augustine's *De trinitate* (MS Laud. Misc. 126 in the Bodleian Library); a facsimile of this flyleaf is reproduced by E. A. Lowe in *Speculum,* III (1928), facing 6.

[11] Printed in Gustav Becker, *Catalogi bibliothecarum antiqui* (Bonn: Max Cohen, 1885), pp. 4 ff.

[12] Printed in Becker (*ibid.,* pp. 24 ff.); in Edward Edwards, *Memoirs of Libraries* (London: Trübner & Co., 1859), I,

297-302; and recorded in Theodor Gottlieb, *Ueber mittelalterliche Bibliotheken* (Leipzig: Otto Harrassowitz, 1890), No. 402.

[13] Printed in Becker, *op. cit.*, pp. 64 *ff.*

[14] *Ibid.*, pp. 82 ff.

[15] "Libri alii sunt diviae auctoritatis tam ueteris testamenti quam novi alli humane" in catalog of 1158 from Prüfüning, printed in Becker, *ob. cit.*, p. 209.

[16] Gottlieb, *op. cit.*, No. 178; printed in Becker, *op. cit.*, pp. 233 ff.

[17] Gottlieb, *op. cit.*, No. 471. A portion of this list is printed in D. M. Norris, *A History of Cataloguing and Cataloguing Methods, 1100–1850* (London: Grafton & Co., 1939), pp. 26–30.

[18] A. Savage, "Notes on the Early Monastic Libraries of Scotland," *Edinburgh Bibliographical Society Publications* (1930), facing p. 1, prints a facsimile of one leaf.

[19] John Boston of Bury, *Catalogus scriptorum ecclesiae;* printed in part by Thomas Tanner, *Bibliotheca Britannico-Hibernica* (London: G. Bowyer, 1748), pp. xvii-xliii; M. R. James, *The List of Libraries Prefixed to the Catalogue of John Boston and the Kindred Documents* ("British Society of Franciscan Studies," Vol. X; "Collectanea Franciscana," Vol. II [Manchester: Manchester Universtiy Press, 1922]), pp. 37-60.

[20] Gottlieb, *op. cit.*, No. 451; printed in Edwards, *op. cit.*, I, 122 ff.; and in M. R. James, *The Ancient Libraries of Canterbury and Dover* (Cambridge: At the University Press, 1903), pp. 13 ff.

[21] Printed in George Oliver, *Lives of the Bishops of Exeter* (Exeter: W. Roberts, 1861), Appendix III, p. 301.

[22] Gottlieb, *op. cit.*, No. 512; printed in Norris, *op. cit.*, pp. 47-52.

[23] Gottlieb, *op. cit.*, No. 457; Parts I and II and a specimen of Part III are printed in James, *The Ancient Libraries of Canterbury and Dover,* pp. 407 ff. A translation of the Introduction to this catalog is printed in J. W. Clark, *The Care of Books* (Cambridge: At the University Press, 1902), pp. 188 ff.

[24] Printed in *Antiquarian Communications* (Cambridge, 1864), II, 73.

[25] Printed in Paul Lehmann, *Mittelalterliche Bibliothekskataloge Deutschlands und der Schweiz* (Munich: C. H. Beck, 1928), II, 5-95.

[26] Gottlieb, *op. cit.*, No. 453; printed in James, *Ancient Libraries of Canterbury and Dover,* pp. 172-406.

[27] A facsimile of two pages from his *Liber de scriptoribus ecclesiasticis* is in Theodore Besterman, *The Beginnings of Systematic Bibliography* (London: Oxford University Press, 1935), Pl. II.

[28] Printed in Mary Bateson (ed.), *Catalogue of the Library of Syon Monastery, Isleworth* (Cambridge: At the University Press, 1898).

[29] Printed in Joseph Hunter, *Catalogue of the Library of the Priory of Bretton in Yorkshire* ("English Monastic Libraries," No. 1 [London: J. B. Nichols & Son, 1831]).

[30] *Bibliotheca universalis* (Zurich: Christophorus Froschoverus, 1545).

[31] *Pandectarum sive partitionum universalium* (Zurich: Christophorus Froschoverus, 1548).

[32] Florian Trefler, *Methodus exhibens per varios indices, et classes subinde, quorumlibet librorum, cuiuslibet bibliothecae, breve, facilem, imitabilem ordinationem* (Augsburg: Phillippum Ulhardum, 1560).

[33] G. W. Wheeler (ed.), *Letters of Sir Thomas Bodley to Thomas James, First Keeper of the Bodleian Library* (Oxford: Clarendon Press, 1926).

[34] Gabriel Naudé, *Avis pour dresser une bibliotheca* (Paris: F. Targa, 1627).

[35] John Dury, *The Reformed Librairie-Keeper* ("Literature of Libraries in the Seventeenth and Eighteenth Centuries," Vol. II [Chicago: McClurg, 1906]).

[36] *Bodleian Quarterly Record,* I Oxford: Bodleian Library, 1914), 106.

[37] Frederic Rostgaard, *Project d'une nouvelle methode pour dresser le catalogue d'une bibliothèque* (2d ed.; Paris, 1698).

[38] *Instruction pour procéder à la confection du catalogue de chacune des bibliothèques sur lesquelles les Directoires ont dû ou doivent incessamment apposer les scellés* (Paris: Imprimerie nationale, 1791); a later version, "Le Précis de l'instruction de 15 mai 1791," in France, Convention nationale, Comité d'instruction publique, *Procès-verbaux du comité d'instruction publique, publiés et annotés pàr M. J. Guillaume* (Paris: Imprimerie nationale, 1894), Vol. II.

[39] Cambridge University, Queen's College Library, *A Catalogue . . . Methodically Arranged* (London, 1827).

[40] Edward Edwards, *A Letter to Benjamin Hawes* (London: Wilson, 1836), p. 30.

[41] Great Britain, Parliament, House of Commons, *Report from the Select Committee on British Museum* (1836), Question 4767.

[42] Louis Fagan, *The Life of Sir Anthony Panizzi* (London: Remington & Co., 1880), I, 134.

[43] Great Britain, Parliament, House of Commons, *Report of the Commissioners Appointed To Inquire into the Constitution and Government of the British Museum* (London, 1850), Questions 2954-65.

[44] *Ibid.*, Question 9869.

[45] *Ibid.*, Questions 4361-4506.

[46] *Ibid.*, Questions 6435-37.

[47] *Ibid.*, Question 5066.

[48] *Ibid.*, Question 7338.

[49] Charles C. Jewett, *Smithsonian Report on the Construction of Catalogues of Libraries, and of a General Catalogue and Their Publication by Means of Separate, Stereotyped Titles, with Rules and Examples* (Washington: Smithsonian Institution, 1852).

[50] *Ibid.*, p. 47.

[51] *Ibid.*, p. 6.

[52] U. S. Bureau of Education, *Public Libraries in the United States* (Washington, 1876) (Special Report, Part II: "Rules for a Printed Dictionary Catalogue," by Charles A. Cutter).

[53] American Library Association, *Papers. Prepared for the World's Library Congress Held at the Columbian Exposition* (Washington: Government Printing Office, 1896), pp. 835-49.

[54] *Library Journal,* XVIII (September, 1893), 75 ff.

[55] American Library Association, *Papers and Proceedings of the Twenty-sixth General Meeting of the American Library Association Held at St. Louis, Mo., October 17-22, 1904,* pp. 134 ff.

Library Catalogs

Charles A. Cutter

"A catalog is designed to answer certain questions about a library, and that is the best which answers the most questions with the least trouble to the asker."

WHAT KIND OF CATALOG

It is fortunate for those who have the use of a library if their number is so small and their character so high that they can be admitted to the shelves and select their books on actual examination. As that is often not the case, a catalog becomes necessary, and, even when it is the case, if the books are numerous there must be some sort of guide to insure the quick finding of any particular book. The librarian can furnish some assistance, but his memory, upon which he can rely for books in general use, is of no avail for those which are sometimes wanted very much, although not wanted often. And a librarian without a catalog would be utterly overpowered by the demands arising with a large circulation. In a library used entirely for desultory reading, like most private circulating libraries, and many town libraries, the catalog may be very simple; as soon as the books begin to be used for study it must become more elaborate. The latter is alone worth considering, for of the few difficulties of the simpler plan the greater part will be found in the more complex.

The catalog may, however, for reasons of economy, decline to answer certain classes of inquiries with very little practical loss of utility, and different libraries may properly make different selections of questions to be answered. There are two sets of probable inquiries, the first asking what books the library contains; the second relating to the character of the books. Of the first set the most common and the most important—those which a catalog must answer or be an imperfect guide—are these:

1st. Has the library such a book by a certain author?
Have you Bell on the Brain?
Have you John Brent, by Theodore Winthrop?
2d. What books by a certain author has it?
What other books by Winthrop have you?
3d. Has it a book with a given title?
Have you John Brent?
4th. Has it a certain book on a given subject?
Have you a pamphlet on the bull-frog, by Professor—I've forgotten his name?
5th. What books has it on a given subject?
Have you anything on glaciers? What have you on philosophy? I wish to see all the books.
6th. What books has it in a certain class of literature? What plays have you? What poems?
7th. What books have you in certain languages?
What French books have you? How well provided are you with German literature?

Similar questions may be asked with reference to certain other classes, but they are of less importance.

The enumeration of the systems that have been devised to answer these questions would be as long as Polonius's list of plays. We may have a catalog of authors or of subjects, or both, or of authors with a subject-index, or of subjects with an author index, and each of these may be divided into two varieties by the presence or absence of title-entries, and lists of kinds of literature introduce another source of variation.[1]

Now, as it is evident that a subject catalog by itself can answer the first and third questions (have you a book by a certain author or with a certain title) only when the book has an unmistakable subject by which it can readily be found, and even then answers in a roundabout way, and as it cannot answer the second (what books have you by a certain author) at all unless one knows the subjects of all that writer's books, this kind of catalog may be at once rejected. And as an author catalogue by itself cannot answer the third, fourth, fifth, and sixth questions, (for how many persons will look through a list of 20,000 or even of 1,000 titles to see if there is among them a book with a given title or on a given subject?) this kind of catalog is equally unsatisfactory. An author-

SOURCE: Reprinted from *Public Libraries in the United States* (Washington: U.S. Bureau of Education, 1876), pp. 526–555 excerpted and modernized.

and-title catalog with a subjective index, or an author catalogue with a title-and subject index, or a subject catalogue with an author-and-title index, answers the first four questions; and if it contains lists of classes of literature, (as fiction, poetry, German literature) it answers all seven. The chief difference between them is this: in the first a book is entered in full once under the author and once briefly under the title; and then appears briefly in the index under as many subjects as the book may treat of. In the third the book is entered in full under as many subjects as it treats of, and appears only twice briefly in the index, once under the author's name and once under the title.

There is yet another—the author-, subject-, title-, and form-catalog—which answers all the seven questions. In this the full entires are made both under author and subject and form, and perhaps under title. They will differ a little, it may be, because under author should be given all the bibliographical description of the book, and special pains taken to identify the author, whereas under the subject these details can be omitted or abridged, and their place taken by greater fullness of title, or notes designed to show how the book handles its topic. And the author entry would give in full the contents of collections of essays, whereas in the subject entry only those of the contents would be mentioned which concern that particular subject. The entry under the title would be very brief, and might for economy of room be reduced to a mere reference. But setting these minor variations aside, the distinguishing characteristic of this catalog, which makes it superior to the others, is that the inquirer finds under subject as well as under author a sufficiently full title, and the details which show him whether the book is old or new, in what language it is printed, and where and when, whether it is compendious or voluminous, portable or not. For these facts, often of great importance to him in choosing his book, he does not have to turn to another part of the catalog. Now, such turning, although it is a slight matter for a single book, becomes intolerably wearisome after a few repetitions, and most people would rather go away without the information which they want than take the trouble to search it out at such an expense of time and perseverance. Indeed, it is impossible to compare titles so widely separated. While one is looking for and at a tenth he forgets the first five or six. And the loss of time, which can be borne when one is using a single printed

volume, would be utterly unendurable with the complete catalog of a large library, especially if in manuscript.

The method upon which the author and title parts of the catalog shall be made is tolerably well settled except in regard to some details. But in regard to the subject part there is no such agreement. Two great principles of arrangement dispute precedence, the logical and the alphabetical, and the adherents of the latter are divided as they prefer class or specific entry.

Among the logically arranged (classed or classified) catalogs there is a difference, according as they are more or less minutely subdivided. The larger the collection of titles the greater need of division. For it is plain that if a hundred thousand titles are divided into only sixty or seventy classes, some of the larger divisions will contain several thousand, all of which the impatient reader must look through to find what he wants. Generally an attempt is made to bring all books under a strictly philosophical system of classes, with divisions and subdivisions, arranged according to their scientific relations. It is a very attractive plan. The maker enjoys forming his system, and the student fancies he shall learn the philosophy of the universe while engaged in the simple occupation of hunting for a book. And there are more real advantages. One who is pursuing any general course of study finds brought together in one part of the catalog most of the books that he needs. He sees not merely books on the particular topic in which he is interested, but in the immediate neighborhood works on related topics, suggesting to him courses of investigation which he might otherwise overlook. He finds it an assistance to have all these works spread out before him, so that he can take a general survey of the ground before he chooses his route; and as he comes back day after day to his particular part of the catalog he becomes familiar with it, turns to it at once, and uses it with ease. The same is true of the numerous classes who are not making any investigation or pursuing any definite source of study, but are merely comprised of desultory readers. Their choice of books is usually made from certain kinds of literature or classes of subjects. Some like poetry or essays or plays; others like religious works or philosophical works or scientific works, not caring about the particular subject of the book so much as whether it be well written and interesting. To these persons it is a convenience that their favorite kind of reading should all be contained in one or two parts of the catalog, and freed from the confusing admixture of titles of a different sort. An alphabetical list of specific subjects is to them little more suggestive than an alphabetical list of authors. It is true that by following up all the references of a dictionary catalog under Theology, for example, a man may construct for himself a list of the theological literature in the library; but to do this requires time and a mental effort, and it is the characteristic of the desultory reader that he is averse to mental effort. What is wanted by him and by the busy man when now and then he has the same object, is to find the titles from which he would select brought together within the compass of a few pages; few, that is, in comparison with the whole catalog. It may be 500 pages, but 500 pages are better than 10,000. The classed catalog is better suited also than any other to exhibit the richness of the library in particular departments.

It is true that no system of classification can bring together all related works. The arrangement that suits one man's investigations is a hinderance to another's; and in the act of bringing into juxtaposition subjects that have many points of resemblance, the classifier separates them from those with which they have fewer characteristics in common. But this very statement shows that the majority of general inquirers will be assisted by good classification, and only a minority disappointed. For the more points of likeness any two subjects have, the more chance is there that many men will be interested in both at once; and the more they differ, the greater is the improbability that any one will wish to study them together.

On the other hand, there are some disadvantages. A large part of the public are not pursuing general investigations. They want to find a particular book or a particular subject quickly; and the necessity of mastering a complex system before using the catalog is an unwelcome delay or an absolute bar to its use. Its advocates think that this difficulty may be in great measure removed by prefixing to the catalog a full and clearly printed scheme of classification. "Any one at all familiar with systems," they say, "can, in nine cases out of ten, see at a glance where his subject occurs in the scheme. An ignorant man will be puzzled by any arrangement. His untrained eye cannot find words in a dictionary or names in a directory, so that this plan is no worse for him than another." But experience shows that even to the scholar this difficulty, which comes at the very outset of each man's search in the catalog, and recurs every time he consults it until he becomes familiar with

its plan, this necessity of generally looking twice to find one thing, and often not finding it readily, is undeniably irksome, and produces a feeling of distaste out of all proportion to the real trouble occasioned. And it unfortunately happens that in most schemes of classification yet constructed these difficulties attach to some very common subjects. There are certain questions which a man expects to find difficult of investigation. He does not think ill of a catalog which delays or even disappoints him in regard to these; but when, for some very simple thing, with which he is familiar, he has to hunt, to hesitate, and to lose time, he is provoked.

Besides, the difficulty is not merely in mastering the system, but in applying it, which, in many departments of science, demands considerably more knowledge than most men have. Suppose one wants to find something about the badger; in a minutely subdivided catalog it might be found under Science, division Natural History, subdivision Zoölogy, group Vertebrates, class Mammals, subclass Monodelphia, setion Carnivora, and so on, or under some other hierarchy of classes. A man may want a book on the badger without being much of a naturalist, but he could hardly find it in such a catalog unless a naturalist should help him.

It is this which has made these catalogs so unpopular, and the unpopularity is increased by the want of agreement among classifiers, which prevents any system becoming common enough to be known to everybody and to seem the only natural one. And the occasional vagaries of otherwise excellent catalogs have had their influence in bringing classification into disrepute. It would take the average man some time to get accustomed to look for the Rollo books under Art, and Mother Goose's Melodies under Prose Fiction, where they belong in a system now before me. Nor is it likely that many men would at first think of looking for railroad reports under **Commercial Arts**, or cookbooks under **Productive Arts**, or navigation under **Engineering**, however proper such subordination may be. The fact is that the action of the mind in outlining a system and fitting books into it is very different from that of inquiring where, in a system already formed by another, a given topic will be treated. It is hard, apparently, for the system makers to put themselves in the place of the public; otherwise they would have adopted more frequently than they have done the simple remedy which will almost remove all these difficulties—an alphabetical index of the subjects treated in the classed catalog. By that an inquirer is referred in an instant to the exact part of the catalog where he will find the topic he wants. The catalog of the Mercantile Library Company of Philadelphia (1850) has such an index, also the Newark Library Association (1857), and the California State Law Library (1870). Beyond these I cannot recall one. . . .

The alphabetical index not occurring to or not pleasing those who were dissatisfied with classification, they adopted the alphabetical catalog, and, naturally enough, in its extreme form, the dictionary plan, in which the attempt to subordinate individuals to classes, and classes to one another, is abandoned, and the subjects, special or general, are arranged like the words in a lexicon. Thus, if a book treats of natural history, it is put under that heading; if it treats of zoölogy alone, that word is the rubric; if it is confined to mammals, it will be found under Mammals; and, finally, if one is looking for a treatise on the elephant, he need not know whether that animal is a mammal; he need not even be sure that it is an animal; he has merely to be sufficiently acquainted with his alphabet to find the word Elephant, under which will appear all the separate works that the library contains on that subject. Nothing, one would think, can be more simple, easy to explain, easy and expeditious to use than this. No matter what he wants he will find it at once, *provided* (1) that the library has a book on just that subject, and (2) that it has been entered under the very word which he is thinking of. If these conditions are not fulfilled, however, there is more trouble. If (1) the library has no book or article sufficiently important to be cataloged on that topic, he must look (*a*) in some more comprehensive work in which he will find it treated, (as the history of Assyrian art is related in the histories of Art,) in which case he will get no help whatever from any dictionary catalog yet made, in finding the general work, but must trust to his own knowledge of the subject and of ordinary classification to guide him to the including class; or (*b*) there may be something to his purpose in less general works, (as books on Iron bridges or Suspension bridges might be better than nothing to a man who was studying the larger subject Bridges,) but in this case also he will very seldom get any assistance from dictionary catalogs, and must rely entirely upon his previous knowledge of the possible branches of his subject. If (2) the books which the library has are entered under some other word than the one which is in his head, (under Development, or Evolution, or Origin of species, or Species, when he is thinking of Darwinism,)

nine tenths of the dictionary catalogs will again fail him; he must rack his brain to recall all the synonymous names of his topic. And even in those which relieve him of this trouble by giving cross-references, he must look twice, first for his own word, and then for the word to which he is referred from that.

The plan is undeniably convenient, but its advocates have in general so entirely overlooked these defects that they have made no attempt to remedy them. A minority have had recourse to cross-references, which almost remove evil No. 2; but evil No. 1 generally remains untouched. . . .

That any of these systems, well carried out, will attain the end of a catalog, can easily be shown. First, the dictionary catalog, not as it exists in any example, but as one might be if there were plenty of time to make it and no need of economy in printing. (1) A man asks for a book by the author's name. He finds it in the alphabetical place of that name. That he may not fail to get it by a disagreement as to who is its author, references have been made from pseudonyms, editors' names, when prominent, translators' names, especially for poetical translation, and from any other names under which it is likely that any one will remember it. (2) He wants to know what works we have by a particular author. He finds them all enumerated under the author's name, with a note of the more important parts of books written by that author in other men's works or in collections of memoirs, in the publications of societies, and perhaps even in periodical literature. (3) He asks for a book by its title; he finds a reference under the first word not an article, or under the word which indicates the subject, or from some prominent and memorable word; if it is a novel, he finds a full entry. (4) He asks for a book on a certain subject; he finds it under that name of the subject with which he is familiar, or he finds there a reference to the synonymous[2] word, which, for reasons, the cataloger has preferred as a heading. And if it is a general subject, he finds references to all the subordinate subjects treated. If, for instance, the subject is Middlesex County, he finds a reference to the name of every town in that county which occurs in the catalog. He will also find references to subjects which illustrate the one he is looking up; and in certain cases he will find references to the subjects which include his. These last references will, however, in general, be left to his knowledge and intelligence. They are necessary to the completeness of the system, but they are not, in a majority of cases, of such practical use as to pay for their uniform insertion. As he may, however, want to study the relations of his subject to others, and to follow it up through all possible ramifications, he will find at the end of the catalog a scheme of classification, in which every heading in the catalog is included and set down in its proper place. (5) and lastly, he asks for a book in some form of literature, (as an encyclopaedia, a book of enigmas, or one in the Hungarian language,) and he finds, under these names, lists of all in the library.

It is objected to the dictionary catalog, and with much truth, that it gives no help to the man who wishes to glance quickly over all the literature on a comprehensive subject, including the books on its various branches, and that it treats the desultory reader as badly. It seems to me, however, that the objection is sometimes a little overstated, or too much is made of it. The inquirer above mentioned will find the general works under the general head, and with them a number of cross-references, perhaps five, perhaps fifty. If his needs oblige him to look them all up, his case is indeed pitiable. But how often would that happen? Generally, he will run his eye over the references, find two or three in which he is interested, look them up, and get reading enough for one day at least; and this will be the easier if the references are classified, as they ought to be when they are numerous. But it is useless to deny that here is the weak point of the dictionary catalog. Here is an evil which it tries, not unsuccessfully, to reduce to a minimum, but can never do away with altogether. Mr. Schwartz gets over the difficulty by adding a classed catalog to a dictionary—a perfect but a somewhat expensive remedy. That the cost is not justified by the gain in a library where the public have access to the shelves, and the books are their own classed catalog, better than any that the librarian can make, is undoubted. How it is in town and city libraries, where the public do not go beyond the delivery room, their librarians must say.

In the alphabetico-classed catalogs, the first two questions are answered in the author part, where will be found an entry of the book; the third in the same part, by a reference to the author; the fourth in the subject part, by an entry either under the subject asked for or under some including subject, to which a reference will be found from the subject asked for; the fifth in the same part, generally under the very class asked for, synonyms not being very troublesome here, and kinds of literature not being generally included in larger classes.

In the Schwartz system the first three questions are answered, in Part 2, (the dictionary part;) the fifth in Part 1, (the classed part;) the fourth is partly answered in Part 2, if there are any books about that particular subject; but for full information, to find not only the books devoted to that subject but those which treat of it in part and those which treat of similar subjects, one must turn to Part 1, guided to the right place there either by a reference found alphabetically in the other part or by the study of the scheme of classification prefixed. So that either of the systems answers all the questions if it be well carried out. Which answers the most usual questions quickest, and reserves its difficulties for the rare questions?

There remain one or two points to be considered, the fullness of the catalog, the insertion of biographical data, of contents, of analysis, and of notes. As to fulness, the general rule is, the larger the library the more elaborate the catalog. Travelers who need no guide in a grove would be lost without one in a forest. As there are more chances of similarity between the various objects, there is need of more detail to distinguish them. Names must be given in full, dates inserted in references, divisions made under more subjects; more exactness and more system sre required in the selection of subject headings, and in their interconnection by references. So that the difficulty of making the catalog and its bulk increase in faster ratio than the size of the library. For a very small-town library, especially if it be poor, a very brief, cheap list may suffice. If it would cost $20 to add imprints, for example, it would be better to spend the money in books, for the questions which imprints are designed to answer would occur so seldom that it would not pay to answer them. A printed catalog need not be so full while the library is small as it must be afterwards, because as its library grows it can be reprinted with the necessary additional details. But a card-catalog should be made as full at the start as it is ever to be, otherwise there will be no uniformity between its different parts, and the task of filling out the first defective entries will be troublesome, and nothing gained after all.

The ideal catalog would give under every subject its complete bibliography, not only mentioning all the monographs on that subject, but all works which in any way illustrate it, including all parts of books, magazine articles, and the best encyclopaedias that treat of it; in short, the catalog would lay out just that course of reading which a man who thoroughly studied the subject, with a view not only to learn it, but to master the history of its treatment by others, would be obliged to pass through.

PRINTED OR MANUSCRIPT?

Whether or not the catalog should be printed depends in large measure upon circumstances.

The advantages of a printed catalog are briefly:

1. That it is in less danger of partial or total destruction than a manuscript volume or drawers of cards. To be sure the destruction of any part of a catalog is very unlikely except by fire, and if the library should be burned, the catalog generally might as well be. It would indeed be of use in replacing the library, and if it had been carefully made, it would help the making of a new catalog, even if the library should be only partially replaced. The research and thought that go to the making of a catalog are considerable, and it would be a pity if all were lost. This reason, however, is not of much weight, as the circumstances under which it would apply are not likely to arise.

2. That it can be consulted out of the library. This reason has always some force. How much it has in any given case depends on the character of the library and of those who use it. In the case of college libraries, for instance, it is very weak. Both professors and students usually live near the library or go near it several times a day in their attendance on lectures and recitations. Besides, they must go or send to the library to get the book after they have discovered by the catalog that it is there. For town and city libraries, especially in large cities, where the hurry of modern life makes it important to save every moment, the printed catalog has a greater chance of usefulness at home; and yet it is doubtful if its use there very often saves trouble. What the general feeling is on this point may be gathered in some degree from the very limited sale of catalogs. In nine libraries which have published them within the past few years the sale has averaged 265 copies each.

3. That it can be consulted in other libraries. Here again much depends upon the size of the library and the character of the catalog. Those of the Library of Congress, of the Boston Public Library (especially its late Class-list History), of the Mercantile Library of San Francisco, are continually consulted in other libraries, but an ordinary catalog of a small town library is not likely to be of use in any other town. And it may always fairly be questioned by trustees how far the bene-

fit to any other library is a justification for incurring the expense of printing.

4. That it is easier to read than the best manuscript volume, and very much easier to consult. A card presents to the eye only one title at a time, whereas a printed catalog generally has all an author's works on a single page. Time and patience are lost in turning over cards, and it is not easy either to find the particular title that is wanted or to compare different titles and make a selection. It is difficult also to pick one's way among the confusing series of names like Godefried, Godefroi, Godofredus, and Gottfried, or among the Allens, the Williamses, or the John Smiths. Here again everything depends on the hurry or impatience of those who consult the catalog. If that is so great that a very slight impediment will cause them to give up the search altogether or never undertake a search after having failed once, printing is necessary; but in college and country libraries this can hardly be the case.

5. That several persons can consult it at once. In the case of much used libraries this is decisive. At Lawrence, fifty copies are in constant use in the delivery room. To make fifty copies of a manuscript catalog and to renew them as often as they wore out, would be more expensive than to print. A card catalog, to be sure, can be so arranged in drawers as to admit of simultaneous consultation. At Harvard College Library forty-eight persons could use the cards at once, provided none of them wanted to see the same part of the catalog. Indeed, by taking out the drawers, which is allowed, 335 persons could be accommodated at once if their wants happened to be spread evenly through the alphabet. Of course that would never be the case. Certain drawers are often in request, others not at all; but I believe little practical inconvenience arises, because people do not often wish to consult a catalog long at a time. One moves away as another comes up.

The disadvantages of a printed catalog are:

1. That it is costly, and, if full and accurate, very costly.

2. That a mistake once made is made forever; whereas in a card catalog a mistake in name or in classification or in copying the title can be corrected at any time. (On the other hand the order of a printed catalog is fixed, but in a card catalog order is easily disturbed, and a card misplaced is a book lost.)

3. It is out of date before it is published. As it cannot contain the newest books, the very ones

most sought for, fresh supplements are continually needed, each of which causes an additional loss of time and patience to consulters. The average man will not look in over four places for a book. A few, very persevering or driven by a great need, will go as far as five or six. It becomes necessary, therefore, if the catalog is to be of any use, to print consolidated supplements every five years, and that is expensive. The Boston Public Library reprints the whole catalog of some particular class, as fiction or history, every two or three years. The Library of Congress has printed annual supplements, and reprints its whole catalog from time to time. But it is not everyone that can afford to do this. The card catalog has no such difficulty. Additions can always be made without disturbing the alphabetic order, and the titles of new books can be inserted on the very day on which they are received.

If the library is too poor to keep up with current literature (to say nothing of supplying gaps in the past) it seems very extravagant for it to spend any money on type, paper, and press work. But if the library is not as much used as it ought to be, it may be worthwhile (since a library so far as it is unused is useless) to increase the call for books by printing and circulating a catalog—in short, to advertise. It is true that the parallel here suggested is not exact. The increase of business which is profitable to the merchant brings in no money to the free public library, but it may prevent the money already spent in books being a loss, as it certainly is while the books lie idle on the shelves. It may be well, however, for a library committee to consider whether there are not other means to increase their circulation—an occasional lecture from some competent person on the benefits and the best methods of reading; words in season from the ministers and the schoolteachers; and the addition to the library of attractive books, especially

if lists of additions, no matter how brief, be published from time to time.

It may be asked why printing the catalog should always be spoken of as a source of expense, and why the printers' bills cannot be paid by selling copies. Because, however much the inconvenience of having no catalog may have been felt, however loud the demand for one may have been, when the work is ready for delivery very few persons can be found who are ready pay for it. Similarly, if a town library should charge for the loan of its books anything like what it costs to buy them, store them, and keep them in order, it would almost annihilate its circulation; it would certainly cut it off from those who need it most. People may be willing collectively to vote the money in town meeting, but they will not pay individually for either books or catalog.

In conclusion, a printed catalog is a great convenience. If there is money specially intended for printing, or if money can be obtained for this purpose, without diminishing the funds for the purchase of books, by all means print. But if the printing is going to stop or seriously diminish the purchase of books, try the card catalog. See if you can educate your people to use that, and to get fully as much good from it as they would from printed pages. Or combine with the cards one of the cheaper forms of printed catalogs. This will accomplish many of the purposes of the more expensive catalogs, so many that its deficiencies will hardly be noticed. But if the library has any prospect of growth it ought to be accompanied by a properly made card catalog.

To turn from the smaller to the larger libraries. In 1873 the examining committee of the Boston Public Library writes:

> We have long passed the period when it was possible to print in one alphabet, upon any intelligible system, the titles of all the books contained in our libraries.

NOTES

1. *Author-catalog.* One in which the entries are arranged alphabetically according to the names of the authors, (a dictionary of authors.) 2. *Title-catalog.* One in which the entries are arranged alphabetically according to some word of the title, especially the first, (a dictionary of titles.) 3. *Subject-catalog.* One in which the entries are arranged according to the subjects of the books, either alphabetically by the words selected to denote those subjects (dictionary arrangement) or philosophically according to the scientific relations of the subjects, (logical, classed, or classified arrangement, the subjects being formed into classes.) 4. *Form-catalog.* One in which the entries are arranged according to the forms of literature and the languages in which the books are written, whether alphabetically or according to the relations of the forms to one another. 5. ——— (?) *catalog.* One in which the entries are made according to the kind of people for whom the books are designed. To this belong the classes "Juvenile literature" and "Sunday-school books," which include works on various subjects and in various forms, and often have a subclassification by subjects. Either of the first two, or of the second two when not classed, or a combination of two or more of them, is a *dictionary* catalog. The third, or the last three together, when logically arranged, forms a *classified* catalog. The fourth is often

published in a single or with two or three classes, or in combination with the fifth, (the unnamed catalog,) as a class-list of "Novels," or of "Drama and Poetry," or of "Fiction and Juveniles."

[2] The dictionary catalog is sometimes reproached with the trouble arising from synonyms, as if it alone was affected by those difficulties. But the alphabetico-classed catalog is in the same plight; it has a subject which must be called either Natural Philosophy or Physics. Which will it choose? Ethics and Moral Philosophy, Religion and Theology, (Practical,) Military art and War, Art and Fine arts, Sanitary science and Hygiene are synonyms as troublesome to it as to the dictionary. These are in its main alphabet; but its difficulties do not stop here. Every one of the synonyms which plague the dictionary cataloguer must appear somewhere in the alphabetico-classed; if not in the main alphabet of classes, then among the branches and sections, and the same doubt will arise as to the selection. It must be confessed, however, that though the occasions for doubt are as frequent the doubt will not be so troublesome, at least among the subdivisions, because the separation of subjects in a secondary alphabet cannot be great.

Rules for a Dictionary Catalog

Charles A. Cutter

GENERAL REMARKS

No code of cataloging could be adopted in all points by everyone, because the libraries for study and the libraries for reading have different objects, and those which combine the two do so in different proportions. Again, the preparation of a catalog must vary as it is to be manuscript or printed, and, if the latter, as it is to be merely an index to the library, giving in the shortest possible compass clues by which the public can find books, or is to attempt to furnish more information on various points, or finally is to be made with a certain regard to what may be called style. Without pretending to exactness, we may divide dictionary catalogs into short-title, medium-title, and full-title or bibliographic; typical examples of the three being, 1°, the Boston Mercantile (1869) or the Cincinnati Public (1871); 2°, the Boston Public (1861 and 1866), the Boston Athenaeum (1874–82); 3°, the catalog now in the making by the Library of Congress. To avoid the constant repetition of such phrases as "the full catalog of a large library" and "a concise finding-list," I shall use the three words Short, Medium, and Full as proper names, with the preliminary caution that the Short family are not all of the same size, that there is more than one Medium, and that Full may be Fuller and Fullest. Short, if single-columned, is generally a title-a-liner; if printed in double columns, it allows the title occasionally to exceed one line, but not, if possible, two; Medium does not limit itself in this way, but it seldom exceeds four lines, and gets many titles into a single line. Full usually fills three or four lines and often takes six or seven for a title.

The number of the following rules is not owing to any complexity of system, but to the number of widely varying cases to which a few simple principles have to be applied. They are especially designed for Medium, but may easily be adapted to Short by excision and marginal notes. The almost universal practice of printing the shelf-numbers or the class-numbers renders some of them unnecessary for town and city libraries.

OBJECTS.*

1. To enable a person to find a book of which either
   (A) the author
   (B) the title
   (C) the subject
   } is known.
2. To show what the library has
   (D) by a given author
   (E) on a given subject
   (F) in a given kind of literature.
3. To assist in the choice of a book
   (G) as to its edition (bibliographically).
   (H) as to its character (literary or topical).

MEANS.

1. Author-entry with the necessary references (for A and D).
2. Title-entry or title-reference (for B).
3. Subject-entry, cross-references, and classed subject-table (for C and E).
4. Form-entry and language-entry (for F).
5. Giving edition and imprint, with notes when necessary (for G).
6. Notes (for H).

REASONS FOR CHOICE.

Among the several possible methods of attaining the OBJECTS, other things being equal, choose that entry

(1) That will probably be first looked under by the class of people who use the library;

(2) That is consistent with other entries, so that one principle can cover all;

(3) That will mass entries least in places where it is difficult to so arrange them that they can be readily found, as under names of nations and cities.

This applies very slightly to entries under first words, because it is easy and sufficient to arrange them by the alphabet.

Note to second edition. This statement of Objects and Means has been criticized; but as it has also been frequently quoted, usually without change or credit, in the preface of catalogs and elsewhere, I suppose it has on the whole been approved.

SOURCE: Reprinted from *Special Report on Public Libraries*, Part 2, 4th ed. (Washington: U.S. Bureau of Education, 1904), pp. 11–12.

DESCRIPTIVE CATALOGING

Principles, Theories, and Philosophies

Most of the principles of cataloging have been handed down to present-day librarians from early booksellers of 16th and 17th century Europe who needed to devise a system of selling books to a public generally unable to visit the shop and who did not want to purchase a "pig in a poke." Booksellers developed fairly detailed descriptions and put them in a catalog in order to accommodate this need. When libraries sought guidelines for cataloging their stock they naturally turned to the bookseller for assistance. At the same time, the librarian sought the same functions for their catalogs. A careful study of the codes and the history of codes will reveal many of these characteristics.

Librarians have not been ignorant of the changing needs of bibliographical description of the trade. Unfortunately they have been very slow to do anything about them. These few selections will reflect the growing concern over the past thirty years along with the latest reflection of recommended practice in the International Conference on Cataloging Principles.

The Bibliographical Function of the Library

Pierce Butler

> *"Bibliography is the systematic process by which civilized man finds his way about in the world of books that he has created. A catalog is a bibliography of the books in a particular collection. Accordingly the practice of cataloging must conform to bibliographical principles."*

Nobody loves a cataloger. Catalogers are the pariahs, the untouchables, in the caste system of librarianship. Everyone seems to loathe or pity them. Their fellow workers regard them as psychotic or subnormal, grubbers in detail, dabblers in trifles, sticklers for convention, idolaters of conformity, dull, obstinate people, literal-minded and humorless. Library boards deplore the cost of cataloging and cherish a stubborn conviction that any business man could reduce it overnight to microscopic dimensions. Administrators and executives defend catalogers—insincerely—in public, and bully them in private. The order department resents the divergence of library entries from those that appear in booksellers' catalogs. The reference room begrudges the catalog room its working tools and ridicules its misuse of the terms "research" and "authority." The circulation staff scolds ceaselessly because every accession is not completely processed within thirty-nine minutes after its arrival. And readers of every race, creed, age, and sex complain to Heaven and to each other, whenever a book is not listed under the nickname that they happen to use for it. Thus from every direction, always, and by everybody, catalogers are an abused people. But possibly they themselves are not altogether blameless for their present lowly position in the library world. One reason why they are not respected may be that they are not fully conscious of their own diginity. Perhaps they are misunderstood because they do not fully understand themselves and their office.

Yet it would be unfair to single out catalogers and berate them for these failings when so many other library workers are liable to the same indictment. Librarians at large are the world's most thorough-going empiricists. They are so intent on getting things done that they dislike any interruption for theoretical discussion. Generations of intelligent, industrious, and devoted workers have been content to enter librarianship as a going concern, adopt prevailing practices, and devise a working solution for each new problem as it arises. But inevitably under such a pragmatic regimen librarians have been singularly helpless against adverse criticism and unable to justify their procedures—simply because they have never bothered to think about the principles that make those procedures necessary. But lately—within the past thirty years—librarians have made a new departure; they have become more self-conscious and are beginning to develop a theoretical scholarship whereby they can orient and explain their present and future activities. This new professional scholarship, however, will never be either recondite or esoteric for it must consist largely of simple but systematic common sense—recognitions, correlations, and interpretations of things already well known to every working librarian. These limitations certainly apply to the survey of the bibliographical function of the library.

The definition of the library as a source of information, recreation and inspiration has long been generally accepted. It is, no doubt, and adequate statement of what the library does for the individual reader. But culture is more than an aggregate of individual activities. Those activities coalesce into a larger organic unity—civilization—that transcends the membership, the interest, and the life span of any particular community or generation. Accordingly, to define the cultural status and function of the library one must make a different approach and use a different terminology. But since we are here concerned not with all the functions of the library, but only with one of them, we may thus summarize a more extensive inquiry that is reported elsewhere.[1]

A library is a collection of books that has been

SOURCE: Reprinted from *Journal of Cataloging and Classification*, 9 (March, 1953), pp. 3–11, by permission of the publisher, the American Library Association.

selected and organized with reference to its content and the intellectual needs of the community. As such it performs scholarly, economic, and bibliographical functions.

The scholarly function of the library consists in its presentation of all forms of literature—scientific, technological, and humanistic, factual and fictional—not only separately, but in a synthetic unity. The library takes over where the school leaves off, fills in its omissions, and keeps the public mind continuously progressive. The library likewise supplements the activities of the press by making out-of-print literature just as much alive as current publications. And the library also acts as a corrective to the intellectual fragmentation imposed upon us by our vocational and avocational specializations; it enables each citizen, if he will, to be not merely a scientist, a technician, of a humanist, but, to a reasonable degree, all of them.

The library also performs distinctly economic functions by making available to everybody the books that are too few, too expensive, and too bulky to permit anyone to possess private copies of all the publications he will need in the course of his lifetime.

The third, the bibliographical function, is implicit in the definition of the library. A library, as we have previously remarked, is a collection of books that have been selected and organized in reference to their content and the community. Now, the selection and the organization of books are both distinctly bibliographical processes. More than that they are of such a character that they cannot be performed on a large scale by laymen. A professional scholar always knows far more than any librarian about the literature of his specialty, but he also knows far less about all the other subject literatures. But the library must contain not only a selection from all literature, but it must be a microcosm of the larger intellectual universe, on the scale required by the community it serves. It must likewise consist of books that are interrelated across subject boundaries. Hence a librarian by virtue of his encyclopedic attitude can perform the bibliographical function of book selection in a way that subject specialists, however numerous and however cooperative, cannot.

The importance of this bibliographical principle appears perhaps most clearly in those cases where it has not been observed, as has happened in some of the most characteristic trends of American librarianship. Most of our libraries are new. Their book stocks have been artificially assembled instead of being geologically deposited by successive generations of bookmen, as was so often the case in the older European libraries. But in their hasty and artificial assemblage of new book stocks American librarians have usually shirked their distinctive responsibility. Instead of doing the work themselves, they have called in subject specialists to do it for them. They have done this, not only in educational institutions where tradition subordinates the librarian to the teacher, but also in the great municipal libraries where he is autonomous. Consequently, by European standards, the ordinary American library is more a motley conglomeration of special collections than a self-contained organic unit.

Again, the same distortion occurs in those "standard lists" that have been compiled for various evaluative purposes. Of these the "Shaw list," one of the earliest, though by no means one of the worst, may be taken as typical. That surely will always furnish amusement to any librarian who is anything of a bookman and not merely an administrator. This list is ridiculous for two reasons: The selections were made by subject specialists, and these selections were submitted to the mumbo jumbo of statistical manipulation in a vain attempt to solve a purely qualitative problem by a purely quantitative method—the problem being, of course, to distinguish between good books and bad books by college library standards.

In our preliminary survey of a field which we can view, as it were, from the outside—dispassionately and without antecedent personal prejudices, we may have discovered certain principles that will be of service to us when we turn to discuss a field in which you all have such a deep personal interest. In the two examples of book selection which we have cited, things that appear very plain to us outsiders seem to be obscure to those who are immersed in the details of the problem. Perhaps, then, we are all afflicted with a similar impairment of our vision when we look at our own activities. Again, procedures that were theoretically unsound led, not to the end desired, but to something quite different. And may it not be that some of the cataloger's frustrations are of the same origin? If so, it would appear that theory is just as practically important for him as operative skill. And, best of all, we can generalize from these examples freely and even recklessly. Behind every human activity is a purpose—an attempt to attain a particular value; no process can be justified except by reference to its purpose; any practice or custom is meaningless until its cultural value is plainly recognized. Let us endeavor, then, to keep all these principles clearly in mind as we turn to our examination of the second bibliographical function of the library—book organization.

The general purpose of library organization is to make the content of its book stock accessible for use, and this involves at least two major facilities: (1) a means whereby any particular book in the collection may be located; and (2) a means whereby all the books in the collection having a common content may be identified. We librarians, of course, are accustomed to call the standard process for meeting the first requirement "cataloging" and the second "classifying." But in practice both processes involve two separate operations: a systematic arrangement of the books in the stacks, and the provision of an index to that arrangement.

These two operations supplement each other. A library could be perfectly cataloged by stack arrangement alone, if the books were shelved in an alphabetical sequence of their authors or titles; any particular volume in the collection could thus be located. Again, a library could be perfectly classified by stack arrangement alone, if the books were shelved in a logical sequence of their subject content; all the volumes in the collection concerning a particular matter could be identified. And in either case the preparation of an index to the system would be wasted labor. But for ordinary use a library must be both cataloged and classified. Sometimes the reader wants a particular book, sometimes books about a particular subject. However, since the principles that rule these processes are incompatible with each other, only one of them can be used in the actual stack arrangement. Hence, the other can be only virtually presented in the index which we call a catalog.[2] And here we have a demonstration of the ambiguity of the terms catalog, cataloging, and cataloger; at times the reference is to the organization of books by their authors or some other discriminant, at times to the index of this organization, and at times to the manufacture of that index. Now the ambiguity of this term leads too many people to take it in its last meaning only, so that they conceive the cataloger as merely a sort of clerk who writes out the individual index entries and files them. Actually, despite all subdivisions of labor, a cataloger is a professional expert who organizes the book stock of the library in accordance with various incompatible principles. Though he may never shelve a single volume with his own hands he controls every detail of the stack room. And, even more miraculously, he enables one arrangement to produce the effects of all the others.

Now catalogers at large are only vaguely aware of the functional significance of their office. Certainly they have not thought enough about the matter to be coherently and plausibly articulate when a real necessity for that arises. If they are accused of being slow, fussy, and extravagant workers, all they can ordinarily say is that the library would be useless if people could not find what is in it. But that is no valid rejoinder to the standing indictment against them. Their most virulent critics would agree with every word in this general statement. What these critics object to is not the end that catalogers seek but the means they adopt to attain it. If catalogers are to win the professional respect that is due them, they must learn to justify, explicitly and realistically, every detail in their bibliographical operations.

Bibliography is the systematic process by which civilized man finds his way about in the world of books that he has created. A catalog is a bibliography of the books in a particular collection. Accordingly the practice of cataloging must conform to bibliographical principles. These stem from two major sources: the characteristics of the book and the characteristics of the reader. In general terms, then, the cataloger is a specialist in applied sociology and applied psychology within narrowly defined limits. He studies the customs that civilization has developed in connection with books and the intellectual routines to which civilizied people are habituated. Consider, for instance, the various ways in which books are labelled; in a modern printed volume it is on a title page, in a medieval manuscript it was in a colophon at the end of the text. These are good examples of what we mean by custom. Again consider the various ways in which books are divided into categories today by different people; for general readers it is by authors, for professional scholars by subject matters, for collectors by editions, and for wholesalers and distributors of books by publishers. These are good examples of what we mean by intellectual habit. Moreover, such customs and habits appear, not only in conspicuous matters like those just mentioned, but likewise in all sorts of minor bibliographical details.

Accordingly the cataloger has to select out of

all the characteristics of the book that he might notice, those that custom makes most important, and out of all of the ways in which a human mind might work, those that most people ordinarily follow. Hence the cataloger is a research worker in the field of custom and habit. When he consults biographical dictionaries and encyclopedias—obviously secondary literature by ordinary academic standards—his procedure is just as valid, just as scholarly, just as scientific, if you will, as that of the historian perusing original medieval charters, or that of a chemist in his laboratory.

In much the same way the catalogers' acceptance of British Museum or Library of Congress entries as authoritative is eminently justifiable. It is not merely the case of a worker in a smaller institution deferring to his opposite number in a great one. The cataloger knows perfectly well that the persons responsible for any Library of Congress entry are probably no more capable than he is—and possibly less so. But he also knows that because Library of Congress cards are used so widely, they must exert a powerful influence toward confirming present bibliographical customs and habits or establishing new ones. As such he must regard them, within reasonable limits, as authorities on normal usage.

But the task of the cataloger is not merely straightforward research in bibliographical customs and habits, for it is complicated by many circumstances. Of these only three will here be mentioned. The first is the fact that the bibliographical organization at which the cataloger labors is a cooperative enterprise and—despite our addiction to recataloging on the least provocation—presumably a permanent one. What each cataloger does must, therefore, harmonize with what his fellow workers are doing, and the work of all must also harmonize with what their successors, as yet unborn, will do in the distant future. Now these things are possible only if all catalogers, today and tomorrow, observe strictly a code of uniform practice.

A second modifying circumstance is the fact that frequently the cataloger faces an array of possible procedures each of which would be just as good as any of the others. This situation arises particularly in the matter of subject headings, where the wealth of the English language in synonyms is overwhelming. In every such case the cataloger must select one of the alternatives arbitrarily and, once his choice is made, he must stick to it, if the library index is to be uniform and permanent. Thus emerges the principle of consistency which is so often referred to by catalogers with awe, and by other library workers with derision. This principle should not be described by either side in poetical terms—as a "jewel" or as a "bugbear of little minds"—but in those of stark practicality. The cataloger must be consistent, not because he is a logician, or because he is opinionated, but simply because he is a realist.

A third consideration that complicates the task of the cataloger is the principle of historicity. Here, as in every other human activity, what should be done today is largely prescribed by what was done yesterday, last week, and ten years ago. This is inevitable, for culture must be cumulative. Unless each generation can start with what its predecessors have already accomplished, civilization would be impossible. But a heritage often imposes a burden as well as a benefit. In librarianship, no less than in family life, the sins of the fathers are visited upon the children. In establishing routines which have become historic the founders of our profession sometimes made errors. To err is human not only because of the original sin in us but because the universe is so bewildering, so enigmatic, and so ironic.

If man could leap directly from intention to execution, human life would be vastly more simple than it is. But purpose is not identical with process. To know what we want does not give us knowledge of how to attain it. In pursuit of the noblest ends men are constantly adopting means that lead them to what they least desire. The impractical idealist is always a dangerous citizen just because he is so single-minded, so logical, and so energetic. Fanaticism always possesses a force that common sense usually lacks. Hence the eccentric often rises to dominance over normal people. This is why history records so many patriots who became tyrants as soon as they attained power. No doubt Julius Caesar and Napoleon and Mussolini—not to mention their latter-day successors—started their careers with the loftiest motives. But man, however intelligent, cannot operate in a realm of pure emotional inspiration. Every act he performs must occur in a specific cultural complex; its effect is modified by the things that surround it, and it radiates an influence upon them, often of a most unexpected character. This is why human progress is more often achieved by trial and error than by deliberate planning—by reformation rather than by revolution.

Now all this may seem like an excursus into

world politics, but it is not. Librarianship is a typical segment of human activity in its highest cultural development. Therefore, anyone who studies librarianship systematically must discover principles that prevail in every other reach of civilization. Accordingly a thorough-going philosophy of librarianship would be a philosophy of universal application. And in exactly the same way, library history is a typical segment of general history. Every trend and movement in the great world has its replica on a much smaller scale in the little world of librarianship. We, too, have had our dictator, and we still suffer from his tyrannies although, happily, they never involved, even at their worst, human cruelty, carnage, or slaughter, such as we commonly associate with the term "dictator."

Our dictator was, of course, Melvil Dewey. He was a typical great man. History records debits as well as credits against him. Generally speaking, the good he wrought came chiefly in the area of classification; the evils in the fields adjacent to it, particularly in cataloging. Dewey was inspired. He believed intensely, and, with him, to believe was to act and to compel other people to act with him. Gifted with talents approaching genius, he was equally proficient in politics, propaganda, and personal advancement. From the first he wanted to promote librarianship in every direction—a noble ambition surely. But as he rose in the library world and gained dominance over it, he lost touch with realities. When a new whimsy struck him—and his mind teemed with whimsies—he pursued it with fanatical zeal and tried to regiment his library empire into conformity with it. Sometimes, as in the case of simplified spelling, he failed to do so. But on occasion Napoleon likewise met with irresistible opposition to his favorite projects. Usually, however, Dewey got what he wanted. And in so doing, whether his success was well or ill advised, he infused a historic force into librarianship that still is potent. In many instances that force is beneficial, but in some others it is baneful. But whether we deplore or admire it, we should recognize its purely historical character and not try to ascribe it to a different origin.

Thus, for example, it is solely because Melvil Dewey was a tyrant that catalogers today in describing a book use the metric system. Functionally that is preposterous. If there is any reason at all for noting the measurement, it is to give the person using the catalog an approximate idea of the size of the volume. For this the metric measurement fails utterly. To most readers and even to some catalogers twenty centimeters means nothing, eight inches everything. Accordingly, if a cataloger is under fire in defense of his profession, and the metric system becomes an issue he will make a great mistake if he tries to justify it as "scientific," or, more subtly, as "internationally intelligible." The only effective response is a citation of its historical origin and force: use of the metric system has become so traditional in cataloging, that the disturbance and cost of a return to the English standard would be prohibitive. Here, as always, remember that a good case can be lost by a bad argument.

And exactly the same course should be followed when objections are raised to the cataloger's peculiar system in transcribing book titles. The name of a book, like the name of its author, is a proper noun. Consequently literary people and printers capitalize all the principal words in it. Catalogers do not; they capitalize only the first one. But this is not, as is commonly said, to avoid constant use of the shift key on the typewriter. That is a recent rationalization of the practice. Actually, all the early typewriters had double keyboards, and, as a matter of fact, the rule even antedated them; it was adopted while catalog entries were still hand-written. The real and sole origin of our practice was the mysterious workings of the late Mr. Dewey's mentality, and we might as well admit it.

In this connection I should like to mention a project which I have long cherished, namely, to persuade librarians to establish a professional Thanksgiving Day on which they could celebrate each year their gratitude because Melvil Dewey never turned his attention to the order of the letters in the alphabet. If he had done so, he surely would have undertaken to reform it. The sequence A B C D . . . is obviously irrational. Any manual of phonetics would have given him a more scientific classification; first, the vowels in their order of pronunciation from the throat to the lips A E I O U, then the sonants, or semivowels, and finally the mutes—labial, lingual, and palatal. But, happily, this matter somehow escaped Dewey's notice.

But please understand me. In speaking thus somewhat lightly of Mr. Dewey's marginal activities I would not in the least degree seem to disparage the greatness of his accomplishments in his two central interests—classification and library education.

In library education, however, we are still paying

a price for the benefits we have received from him. Dewey conceived the librarian as exclusively a technician. Therefore, the curriculum he set up was one of vocational training rather than of professional education. And such was the power of the man, that the plan he drew still persists in every library school in the country—and most strongly in the courses on cataloging.

Librarianship is a unique profession. It is not education, it is not communication, it is not social service, although in some particulars it resembles all of these. Its scholarship has many facets, technological, scientific, and humanistic; but Dewey could see only one of them—the technical. His ideal library school graduate was, therefore, a person who on being hired and assigned any job whatever in a library could hang up his hat and sit down to work just as fast and just as effectively as any departmental veteran. But such universal proficiency is impossible. To acquire it would necessitate, not one year of schooling, but many; and only dullards would submit to such meticulous drilling. Library activities are highly diversified, and here, as always, one man's meat is another man's poison. Every professional candidate can and should follow the bent of his own temperament. Just as some scholars are born to be librarians, so some librarians are born to be scientists, some technicians, and some humanists, some practitioners, some teachers, some investigators, some administrators, some reference workers, some rare book men, and some catalogers. Hence, the primary purpose of library education cannot be to train each candidate in the routines of the specialty which he will follow. On the contrary, the primary task of the library school might be paradoxically described as just the opposite—to give each candidate such a knowledge and understanding of the specialities which he will not follow, that he can see his own in perspective with them. Actually, of course, the goal of library education is even broader than that. It is not merely to enable the graduate to see the library as a whole, but to see it as an essential component of civilization. In other words, the major responsibility of our library schools is to provide what we might call a "general education" in librarianship. The other responsibility, though it is called minor here, is scarcely less important. This is to provide advanced courses in all the various library disciplines so as to provide each student with a secondary "special education" for the particular career which he expects to follow.

Now in many areas these schools have lately freed themselves from the thrall of Melvil Dewey's technological assumptions, but, least of all, one may venture to assert, in the teaching of cataloging. There the emphasis is on practice almost to the exclusion of principle, as if the purpose of the instruction were to turn out catalogers. It is not that so much as it is the production of library workers of every sort who can live and work on reasonable terms with catalogers. To achieve that every library school should have a general as well as a special course in cataloging: the first, prescribed to all students, would deal with principles, the second, building on that, with their implications in practice.

Such general education in librarianship is undoubtedly what you, as catalogers, most desire. Indeed your own actions prove this plainly. When you hire a young graduate for your own department, you always give preference to an intelligent attitude toward librarianship as a whole, and cataloging in particular, over mere operative skill in the routines of the latter. Similarly, the one thing you most long for in the other divisions of the library is a realistic comprehension of the problems that you face and the conditions under which you must solve them. You know, none better, that if such an understanding prevailed, you could work more cheerfully and sleep more soundly, for you would no longer have to repel at short notice and with inadequate weapons, frequent guerrilla attacks and crafty diplomatic offensives from other departments of the library.

Accordingly, with seemly deference as an outsider, I venture to put to you certain questions and ask you to give prayerful consideration to them. Cannot this influential organization of catalogers make a definite contribution toward the development of such a general education in librarianship? Would it not be well if you enlarged the scope of your activities? Could you not profitably alternate your yearly discussions between (a) cataloging problems that arise outside of the catalog room and (b) those that arise within it, like the one to which the present session is devoted? More particularly, could you not in common council formulate a schedule of what every library worker should know about cataloging—not merely enumerating the facts, but in each case explaining them theoretically?

Certainly, if you could see your way to do this, without neglecting your other responsibilities as specialists, you would confer a great benefit, not only upon yourselves, but upon every other member of our noble profession.

NOTES

[1] Here I immodestly refer to an essay of my own on "The Cultural Function of the Library," which appears in the current issue (the April, 1952 number) of the *Library Quarterly*.

[2] For practical reasons we American librarians always shelve our books by classification and let the index serve as a catalog. In many of the older European libraries, however, a much more complicated procedure survives: Books are shelved in their accession order so that both catalog and classification exist only in index form.

The Crisis in Cataloging

Andrew D. Osborn

> *"More and more rules and definitions are being worked out constantly, until at the present time it begins to appear that classicism is taking full control. Thus it is that cataloging has become elaborate, highly technical, a skill too often existing in and for itself."*

A wise German librarian has linked the library administrator and the cataloger as working for the common aim of economy in work and cost coupled with better utilization of a library's resources. This aim, he thinks, is expressed in various kinds of cooperative work, of pooling interests, and of setting standards. It is to be developed prudently, he says, with the objectives setting limitations in such a way that more values will not be destroyed than are created.[1]

This ideal he set out in a chapter entitled "Tasks for the future." There was a time, and not so very far back, when the library administrator and the cataloger worked side by side. In the more immediate past, however, the two have become separated, so that their closer collaboration does need to be set down as a task for the future, the immediate future at that. Many new problems of administration have served to busy the administrator, and most catalogers have had more work than enough, with the result that administrators have come to know less and less of cataloging, and catalogers have come to know less and less about general library administration. The situation now is that the administrator will be forced to pay more attention to cataloging because it has become a major problem field. Neither the administrator alone nor the cataloger alone can solve the many problems. Collaboration is essential, and to this end administrators must know more of cataloging and catalogers must know more of administration.

This is not to say that administrators must be catalogers, although it is true that there is a great need for catalogers who are administrators. The administrator does need to know enough of cataloging from the inside to be able to control the destiny of his catalog department wisely. Thus it would appear that, if the internship is to be looked on as a possible element in the training of a library administrator, then one excellent way of exploiting the internship would be to have the prospective administrator spend a year in a good catalog department. Another way for prospective administrators to study the problems to be found in a catalog department is to take the second-year course in cataloging in library schools where that course is treated as a seminar devoted to problems of catalog department administration and not merely as an advanced course in cataloging techniques, as, for example, the cataloging of rare books. Library schools should be encouraged to plan such a course with administration uppermost in mind, and administrators should be urged to take it.

It seems a little odd to be saying such things when as far back as 1915 Dr. Bishop put the matter in classic form in his address to the Albany Library School entitled *Cataloging as an asset.* "The cataloger," he said, "must be an administrator if he is to meet the needs of the future: and the administrator can not afford to be ignorant of these problems of cataloging, which must be solved."[2] And again: "If you are to administer libraries, you must know libraries, you must be able to work your machine, you must have practical knowledge of its parts. Nothing in the craft should be foreign to you, least of all the art of cataloging."[3]

Cataloging is an art, and as an art it is technical. Its basic rules are actually rather few and simple, and, in so far as the rules are kept few and simple, it is a delightful art to practice. That is admittedly the romanticist point of view. A period of romanticism tends to be followed by a period of classicism with its subservience to rules, and this is what has been happening to cataloging. More and more rules and definitions are being worked out constantly, until at the present time it begins to appear that classicism is taking full control. Thus it is that cataloging has become elaborate, highly technical, a skill too often existing in and for itself.

SOURCE: Reprinted from *Library Quarterly*, 11 (October, 1941), pp. 393–411 by permission of the author and the publisher. Copyright ©1941 by the University of Chicago Press.

This is the kind of cataloging that the administrator finds himself out of touch with, at a loss to comprehend, and without sufficient depth of understanding to guide it to safer and surer paths. Cataloging does not need to call for so much sheer craftsmanship. In point of fact, the less the cataloger is a craftsman pure and simple, the more room there is for him to be just an excellent librarian.

Much of library science and library administration is not at all scientific. Over a period of years good administrators have developed a body of sound practice, and this it is that can be called library science. Perhaps there has been a minimum of theory and a maximum of common sense in developing this body of sound practice, and it may be that there are certain losses in minimizing the role of theory.

THE LEGALIST THEORY OF CATALOGING

Actually there are a number of theories of cataloging more or less vaguely in application today. The principal ones might be characterized as the legalistic, the perfectionistic, the bibliographic, and the pragmatic.

The dominant one is probably the legalistic. According to it, there must be rules and definitions to govern every point that arises; there must be an authority to settle questions at issue. So the reviser sits in judgment on the cataloger, and the head cataloger is the supreme court for his particular library. Many of the decisions handed down are purely arbitrary, partly because many of the points at issue are simply a matter of taste or judgment.

On the face of it, this seems too arbitrary to be true, but it is precisely the way things are done. Here are a few examples from everyday practice. The cataloger says in the collation that the book contains a portrait. The reviser changes the collation because she says it is not a portrait, the reason being that it is not the picture of anyone named or determinable; or it is the picture of the author's wife standing in front of the great pyramid, and so the reviser rules that it is to be taken as a picture of the pyramid instead of as a portrait; or it is the picture of a native in a book on ethnology, the native being taken as an object of study rather than as an individual, apparently; or a hundred and one other nice distinctions. Here is another case in point. Thomas Thompson writes a book of short stories entitled *Lancashire Lather.* The setting is a barber's shop, and the frontispiece de-

picts a barber. The cataloger enters in the collation *front. (port.).* There is no question but that it is the portrait of a real person attired as a barber; but it might be an actor dressed up to represent a barber; at any rate, it does not say "Tom Smith," who could be verified as this particular Lancashire barber. Accordingly the reviser, with much justification, changes the collation from *front. (port.)* to mere *front.*

It requires definite skill to determine when a portrait is not a portrait. The cataloger must pass on caricatures, likenesses on coins and medals, effigies from tombs, pictures of mummies, spirit photographs, and a host of other difficult situations. And then, of course, there is the group portrait to add to the problem. How many people are needed to make a group? For example, in the autobiography of a distinguished English lawyer, the frontispiece shows him in his wig and gown attended by various flunkies in front and behind. Since it is a picture of three or four people, the cataloger enters in the collation *front. (group port.)* The reviser changes the collation to *front. (port.)* on the ground that the flunkies do not count and that the intention is to provide merely a portrait of the author in an appropriate setting.

This kind of procedure is part and parcel of the daily conduct of catalog departments. Examples could be multiplied to show that there is the greatest of confusion in catalogers' minds as to what a facsimile, a map, or many another seemingly innocent thing might be when they begin to take on some of their varied forms. The cataloger takes time debating the question; the reviser takes still more time; and the head cataloger may be called on for a final decision. Debate, discussion, and decision eat up a surprising amount of time. Hence the demand in some quarters for a cataloging code that will define or rule on all debatable points.

Some catalogers are so impressed by this legalistic theory of cataloging that they are ready to maintain that a fully developed body of definitions, rules, decisions, and precedents will result in decreasing the cost of cataloging. The argument is that if everything has been covered in the code of laws then there will be no more debates, no more wasted time. If there are "57 varieties" of facsimile, they must all be differentiated. Some kinds would be called facsimiles on the catalog card and others would not. It would not matter if the word *facsim.* in the collation stood ambiguously for any of the valid kinds of facsimile. The decisions are not concerned with that kind of knowledge. The decision is simply to determine whether in this particular instance the general term *facsim.* has been used legitimately or not in the collation.

Thus the classical tendency in cataloging tends to push on to the final phase of classicism—the phase that leads to decline, the valuing of rules and definitions for their own sake. In this way cataloging can become an end in itself, and the cataloger can become a craftsman instead of a librarian. Such cataloging does not ask whether the close definition of a facsimile results in economy of work and cost coupled with better utilization of a library's resources. The systematic determination of out-of-the-way, unusual, or exceptional points, the attempt to rationalize vague, ambiguous, and highly diverse concepts—these result in a theory and practice of cataloging neither economical nor particularly effective.

The weakest point in the legalistic theory is its treatment of matters that must be left indefinite. The proposed revision of the A. L. A. cataloging code has been worked out from a legalistic point of view. Where it has failed most signally, in the light of its own theory, is in the rules that result in a choice of entry. In the old code such rules (e.g., in the treatment of collections under editor or under title and in the treatment of government and other publications under personal or corporate name) led to great difficulty. They were probably the hardest rules in the whole code to apply. The proposed revision has not improved the situation in the slightest, simply because matters of taste and judgment are too intangible to operate well in cataloging or other codes.

A second serious defect in a legalistic approach to cataloging is that, once it is decided to formulate rules and decisions for all points, the process must go on indefinitely. When in the future a point arises not covered in the past, the cataloger cannot use judgment to settle the matter but must set a complicated decision-giving apparatus in motion. Time and attention must be given to settling an infinite variety of small details such as the scholastics of the Middle Ages might have delighted in debating.

A final weakness worth emphasizing is that codification tends to obscure reasons and principles. Much of the original meaning and intention has been lost from the 1908 code. As a result the approach to cataloging becomes less and less a matter of comprehending principles and more and more a matter of the mere learning of arbitrary rules and definitions. Thus elements of catalog-

ing practice that were introduced for historical reasons come to be accepted and perpetuated without any understanding of why the rule was made. For example, there was sound reason for introducing the cataloging form known as hanging indention. That reason no longer exists, yet the form carries on and receives new emphasis in the proposed new code. Survivals of this kind tend to make the teaching and the practice of cataloging mere techniques.

Since the proposed revision of the A. L. A. Cataloging code has the weaknesses of the legalistic point of view, it is accordingly to be deprecated strongly. The dignity of cataloging as an art calling for the display of intelligence and sound judgment is something that stands in sharp contrast to a tendency that would so define and regulate that catalogers would need little more enterprise than good clerks.

PERFECTIONISM

Since the legalistic approach to cataloging is the principal danger to be watched at present, there is little need to discuss the perfectionistic and bibliographic approaches in detail.

The perfectionist cataloger is guided by the compelling desire to catalog a book in all respects so well that the job will be done once and for all. In 1935 the Library of Congress promulgated a definition of cataloging along such lines. Every detail on the catalog card is verified according to some authority, nothing has been omitted, and all users of the library now and in the future must be satisfied with the product.

The error behind the perfectionist theory is that so far no cataloger has succeeded in doing work that would last indefinitely. Invariably one generation of catalogers does over the work of its predecessors. This fact is clear from the history of older libraries. The library of Harvard University has had a dozen or more catalogs since 1764.

Obviously there is much to be said for a theory of cataloging which will not be rapidly outmoded. Ways and means must be found to make cataloging products endure. Yet recataloging proceeds apace in many a library, while classification, subject headings, and other details are constantly subject to change with the lapse of time. Tastes and needs change continually, and with them go the elements in cataloging that are based on taste or the needs of the time.

The perfectionist cataloger has been overwhelmed by the enormous masses of material constantly flowing into twentieth-century libraries. As a result many libraries have accumulated considerable arrearages of cataloging, material has sometimes been temporarily processed, records may be made inadequately or temporarily with the expectation that the work will be done over more fully at a later date, and all the time the cost of cataloging increases. Perhaps even more disconcerting is the fact that if there were time and opportunity, owing to less pressure from the current work, much good work could be done polishing up what has been accomplished in the past and planning for the future.

So the judgment on perfectionism must be that, although efficient technical work is to be desired in cataloging, perfectionism is not necessary to such work. The time element is the great foe of perfectionism. Catalogs cannot be created at one stroke; they contain many inconsistencies and imperfections. Many of these inconsistencies and imperfections hurt no one but the perfectionist.

BIBLIOGRAPHICAL CATALOGING

The relationship between cataloging and bibliography has been a difficult one to define. The two have many points of contact and many elements in common. Their history has been intertwined in many respects.

The bibliographical theory of cataloging attempts to make cataloging into a branch of descriptive bibliography. The collation and the bibliographical notes are much affected. They become detailed to a degree. This detail is right and proper in its own place; it does harm when it is applied to everyday cataloging. For example, much processed material is being produced and cataloged today. How much of it needs to be collated in the detailed way that the printed book is? It is not at all uncommon, when bibliographical details are overemphasized, for the collation to become a meaningless conglomeration of terms which puzzle even the most experienced cataloger.

Descriptive notes, such as "Head and tail pieces," "Title vignette," "Illustrated lining-papers," tend to fill up the catalog card without serving any real library or bibliographic function. Some of these formal descriptive notes are fortunately passing into disuse, and more could do so without loss. Examples of notes that are drifting from use are "Plates printed on both sides," "Title in red and black," and "Reprinted in part from various periodicals," the latter being for a volume of poems.

Kaiser's criterion of cataloging reads: the minimum of cost and effort in conformity with the best use of the library. It is from the practical point of view that the problem of bibliographic cataloging must be approached. The card catalog is at best a barrier between the reader and the book. "To the books themselves!" must be the motto for as much as possible.

The ordinary book and the rare book commonly need little bibliographic description; the one because it is ordinary, the other because there are printed bibliographies to provide much of the description. It is an intermediate type of book, the one that belongs in a local collection or a highly developed special collection, that may call for more detailed work from time to time. Such books are not treated as ordinary holdings and are not so likely to be listed in readily available and well-known bibliographies.

THE PRAGMATIC THEORY

Many libraries have for long been conducting their cataloging along purely practical lines. Rules hold and decisions are made only to the extent that seems desirable from a practical point of view. As a consequence nothing is pushed to an extreme, and hence the rules and definitions have no opportunity to become ends in themselves.

The quality of cataloging in such libraries is satisfactory, because it has been developed with the practical needs of the library constantly in mind. The legalistic cataloger would not approve of its standards because they have not been defined to any very great extent; the perfectionist cataloger would dislike the omissions and the failure to check enough authorities; while the bibliographical cataloger would think the job only half-done.

It is difficult to systematize cataloging according to the pragmatic theory. In the first place, standards and practices need to be set for a number of types of library. Where the legalistic code is likely to set one standard, ignoring the needs of certain types of libraries, or leading to a degree of standardization whether wisely or not, the pragmatic emphasizes the differing needs of various types of library. The school library, the special library, the popular public library, the reference library, the college library, and the university library—all these have differing requirements, and to standardize their cataloging would result in much harm. There have been standardizing tendencies: the A. L. A. cataloging code, the use of Library of Congress cards, the development of union catalogs, and the teaching of cataloging in

library schools. Some but not all of this standardization has been good. For example, all types
of libraries can and should use Library of Congress
cards—not necessarily all available Library of Congress cards, but still some; yet this does not mean
that such libraries should adopt any more Library
of Congress standards than are right and proper
for their particular type of institution.

The forgotten man of cataloging is the college
library. The last annual report of the Library of
Congress showed that the principal user of Library
of Congress cards is the college library. One-half
the cards sold by the Card Division go to college
libraries. But the A. L. A. cataloging code of 1908
was made without regard to college libraries. It
was made for "larger libraries of a scholarly character,"[4] and there was not a single representative
of the college library on the editorial committee.
The college library has found it expedient to use
Library of Congress cards and to follow the
A. L. A. cataloging code. There are many college
libraries but relatively few large, scholarly libraries.
More attention should be paid to the needs of
these many libraries, and they should more frequently express their requirements.

The A. L. A. *List of subject headings* presents
an interesting study from this point of view. It
was one of the very few tools worked out for the
medium-sized library. The effectiveness of that
list and the satisfaction which everyone who used
it had from it seem to indicate that the medium-
sized library may have an important stabilizing
role in cataloging practice. The A. L. A. *List of
subject headings* is dead and should never be
brought back to life, but its significance should
not be forgotten. Perhaps more tools should be
worked out with the interests of the medium-
sized library at heart; perhaps this type of library
should be willing to take on more responsibility
and leadership in cataloging councils.

Rules specially worked out for large scholarly
libraries did not result in plain sailing for those libraries. The biggest of them—the Library of Congress—steadily lost ground, acquiring annually
some thirty thousand more books than could be
cataloged on this basis. When the cumulative
effect began to be felt, the Library of Congress
had amassed several million uncataloged books.
The cataloging system had plainly broken down.
At present the old rules need simplification, not
amplification, if the Library of Congress is to
carry on. In other words, a practical set of cataloging rules must be drawn up for such a library.
The day of the legalistic, perfectionistic, or biblio-

graphic cataloger is over; the day of the pragmatic
cataloger has begun.

If this is true for the Library of Congress, it
must apply likewise to the other large scholarly
libraries of the country. No regular library need
calls for more detailed cataloging than that done
at the Library of Congress. Other libraries, then,
should simplify their cataloging and should adopt
the practical point of view. Consequently, the
new cataloging code ought to be drawn up from
that standpoint.

Generalizing, and passing over many minor matters, a pragmatic approach to cataloging and to
the catalog code would result in the following developments:

1. All cataloging practices would be meaningful, so
that libraries where certain factors were present or
absent would know whether they needed to adopt a
given practice. For example, hanging indention would
not be prescribed unless it was clearly understood for
what use hanging indention is intended. It would be
the function of the catalog code to make known such
reasons or lack of reasons, so that libraries could determine whether to follow the particular rule or not.

2. Three distinct and approved grades of cataloging
would be followed in the code and in many libraries.
These would be standard, simplified, and detailed cataloging. The classes of books which would be treated
according to these methods should be specified. Standard cataloging would be less detailed in many respects than the 1908 code or the Library of Congress
formerly required.

3. In addition, self-cataloging methods must be put
in good standing and exploited. This would apply in
some measure to city directories, college catalogs,
documents, large duplicate sets on open shelves, pamphlets and other ephemeral material arranged by subject, special collections of recreational reading, telephone books, and items in vertical files. Some or all
of these practices are being used in one way or
another; their use should increase.

4. Rules for cataloging would be relatively few and
simple, partly because they would not attempt to
cover exceptional and unusual cases. Revisions of the
catalog code would thereafter result in slight change,
so that whole classes of material would not have to
be recatalogued.

5. The quality of the work would be high for anything regarded as essential. Nonessentials would be
given little attention or passed over.

6. Catalogers would be trained to use their judgment, not to expect a rule or a precedent to guide
them at all turns. It is hard to do intelligent work if
that work has to be all by rule of thumb. If catalogers are called on to use judgment, the work will
again become more interesting.

7. Unwritten rules and practices would be subject
to the same pragmatic scrutiny. Some catalogers, for
example, think that the sequence of subject headings
in the tracing should follow certain requirements.
Attention to such a detail is completely valueless except where printed or mimeographed cards are con-

cerned, and even there its value is doubtful.

8. The interpretation of any point will follow practical lines. If certain illustrations were intentionally included in a book as portraits, whether they are caricatures, representations on coins, or effigies on tombs, they can be recorded in the collation as portraits. This is the natural thing to do. Much artificiality has resulted from ignoring natural and obvious methods of procedure.

9. The cataloging of serial documents and non-documents should be reviewed to see to what extent this class of material needs cataloging. Should superior indexes be provided instead for government publications? Should the *Union list of serials* serve as the catalog for such serials as it covers?

ORGANIZATION OF THE CATALOG DEPARTMENT

Catalogers and library administrators are thus faced with many and difficult cataloging problems of a technical nature. Organizational questions are equally pressing however. Far too little attention has been given in library literature to the organization of catalog departments, while in actual practice physical conditions have controlled matters to an undesirable extent.

Large or small divisions and sections are followed in some libraries. In others small groups of catalogers are under the control of revisers. Again the work may be done by units consisting of an experienced and a junior cataloger. Some catalogers do their own typing, ordering Library of Congress cards, or filing, while in other libraries special people are set aside to do such work. Some libraries are organized to catalog for others, as is the case with school libraries in Chicago and Los Angeles or with departmental and branch libraries. These are some of the many organizational patterns in use today.

Many catalog departments pay too little attention to the flow of material and hence tend to be organized less advantageously. The catalog department of any size will have to be streamlined in the future. Material that can move rapidly should be segregated from other books that move at an average or at a slow rate. Fiction, second copies, other editions, books to be stored directly in deposit libraries—these and others can be treated with considerable rapidity. Rare books and difficult cataloging of one kind or another may move very slowly. If the various types go along together, there are two dangers. One is that the slower books will obstruct the general flow, and the other is that if a cataloger pays special attention to getting the faster books along the others may be slighted either through setting

them aside to be done when time permits or through treating them in the same way that an easy book might be treated.

Many popular libraries have for years streamlined their cataloging departments. It is not difficult to do if the types of cataloging are easily determinable, as, for instance, if second copies in considerable number keep coming into the catalog department as intentionally purchased duplicates. It is in the larger catalog departments where there may be many gifts and exchanges as well as purchased books that streamlining has been slow in developing. This may be partly due to the fact that such a department would need more central administration to take care of the decisions involved and to direct the flow of work.

It has commonly been stated that the three essential departments of a library are reference, circulation, and cataloging. In some school, branch, and departmental libraries the catalog department has been eliminated. More catalog departments ought to disappear in the near future. Cataloging can and should be supplied as a service in many libraries. It is possible that the development of regional deposit libraries will provide the means and the accommodation for regional cataloging centers. Neighboring libraries of a common type can at least share the work or concentrate it in one particular place.

This question is related to the further one regarding the future of official catalogs. Large libraries are finding official catalogs an increasing burden. It may cost the very large library ten thousand dollars a year to maintain such a catalog. If the building were designed so that all users of the library were conveniently brought together, then an official catalog would be unnecessary, provided the pressure on the public catalog were not too great. Money is better expended on service than on duplicating records. If library buildings can be designed so that an official catalog becomes unnecessary, the organization of a catalog department will be a simpler thing to control. As official catalogs have grown it has become increasingly hard to operate catalog departments efficiently. A layout that was close to ideal in the beginning may in the course of time result in situations far from ideal, owing to the growth of the official catalog as well as of the staff and its duties.

Mention of service, which is a basic factor in library work, brings up the need for considering the concentration of trained librarians who are working behind the scenes in catalog departments, while at the same time student assistants, untrained help, or insufficient professional help may be working with the readers. This is a major problem of organization, namely, how to make that concentration of trained people more generally useful throughout the library.

THE SITUATION AS REGARDS CLASSIFICATION

The many problems confronting catalogers and library administrators are not confined to cataloging proper; they are both significant and numerous in the field of classification. The complicating factor in classification is that the theoretical literature on the subject is in a state of confusion. This is in no small measure due to the emphasis that certain writers place on the classification of knowledge and on bibliographic classification. German philosophers and scientists delighted in drawing up schemes for the classification of knowledge all through the nineteenth century. Such schemes had some slight value but were too much on the order of intellectual pastimes. As a practical matter library classification is far removed from any such schemes.

Bibliographic classification has been worked out and successfully applied in such an undertaking as the enormous card bibliography developed by the Brussels Institute for Documentation. Miss Mann successfully applied bibliographic classification in the classifed catalog at the Engineering Societies Library in New York. On the books, however, she used relatively simple Dewey numbers. This example of the Engineering Societies Library shows clearly the difference between the two types of classification. Bibliographic classification is unsuited to the classification of books in workaday libraries; that classification must be governed by practical requirements.

In its application classification calls for a high degree of good judgment. Classification can be a game. It is good fun to build up long numbers, to put books in precise but out-of-the-way classes, to debate academic niceties. Such classification hurts a library. The classifier with good judgment will not waste time arguing which alternative is the better; the case will be decided pragmatically, according to the wording of the title, for example. There must be the realization that some books have one precise class, while fully as many again could go equally well in one of a number of places.

Reclassification raises problems of two kinds. The daily question of reclassifying an odd book or two is one, while the reclassification of a whole library is another. As regards the former, it requires constant administrative pressure to prevent much reclassification. Relocation is, of course, a separate matter, as the relocation of a book from the reference room to the stacks. Much reclassification is purely academic in nature. A cataloger or a professor thinks that a book would be better in some other class. This kind of reclassification must be resisted as much as possible, and all the more so if the book concerned shows every evidence of not having been used in many a year.

Decisions to reclassify a whole library should be arrived at only after clearly realizing that the old classification scheme was ineffective to a high degree. Many libraries are using poor classification schemes, usually homemade ones. As long as those schemes work there is no real reason why they should be given up. Classification schemes age very rapidly. Both Dewey and the Library of Congress scheme have suffered the ravages of time. That situation will be aggravated with the further passage of time. Total reclassification of a library is terribly expensive. Partial reclassification may be a desirable compromise. Less used books may be left according to the old scheme, so that the new classification will represent a live collection of books; or some main classes which are unsatisfactory can be changed, leaving unchanged those that were satisfactory.

Suitability of a particular scheme to the type of library is a matter of importance. Modification of a standard scheme may be a solution. At the least, great caution is necessary before reclassifying a whole library. Some libraries have made serious mistakes by adopting the Library of Congress classification; it is not true that it is necessarily the best scheme for a college library. Perhaps the situation as regards classification and reclassification can be summarized by saying that the golden age of classification is over.

THE SITUATION AS REGARDS SUBJECT HEADING

If it is necessary to say that the literature on classification is in a state of confusion, it is equally necessary to say that the literature on subject heading is almost nonexistent. At most, it would be only a slight exaggeration to say that Cutter's *Rules for a dictionary catalog,* the fourth and final edition of which appeared in 1904, provides the latest word on the theory and practice of subject heading. Cutter's work was that of the pioneer.

He saw a new day dawning with the printing of Library of Congress cards, but neither he nor anyone else has been a guide through this era of printed cards.

Even the best of cataloging instructors admit they do not know how to teach subject heading properly. The theory, practice, and needs are all ill defined. For such reasons it is better to say less rather than more about subject headings here.

In part the trouble springs from the use of words, since words can be local, obsolescent, or technical, or they can stand for vague, ambiguous, or emergent concepts, or they can even be lacking for some ideas or relations of ideas. In part the trouble comes from trying to make a science of subject heading when it is necessarily an art. Some subject heading has no other dignity than the mere expression of opinion; much of it has to be based on judgment, in which experience counts greatly; some has to be precise. In part the trouble comes from differentiating insufficiently between the needs of different types of libraries. Here the compelling dictionary-catalog idea has been a handicap.

The principle of the dictionary catalog is to provide a record that will make for a maximum of self-help on the part of readers. This means that the catalog must be adapted to the needs of varying institutions. It also means that the maximum of self-help can be obtained only as long as the catalog does not become too complex. Many dictionary catalogs are becoming too complex and are accordingly defeating the ends for which they were created. That is why there are signs of the decline of the dictionary catalog, as would be indicated by the possibly unfortunate trend toward a divided author and subject catalog and by the search for substitutes for the dictionary catalog.

WHAT THE LIBRARY ADMINISTRATOR NEEDS TO KNOW

These, then, are the things the library administrator needs to know about cataloging and these are the pressing problems which confront cataloger and administrator alike. It is not that the library administrator needs to be a technician, though some knowledge of cataloging technique is desirable. It is rather that he must know the nature of present-day cataloging problems if he would be in a position to help in their solution and to supply a certain amount of leadership and direction.

A crisis has been reached in cataloging history.

The system that shaped up about the year 1900 showed ominous signs of falling apart in 1940. In the Library of Congress the system actually broke down, and what happens in that library as far as cataloging is concerned affects libraries throughout the country while the Library of Congress holds the key position that it does.

Excellent work was done between 1900 and 1940. Praise and appreciation can properly be expressed for the accomplishments of those four decades. Perhaps at the same time there is a certain satisfaction in realizing that the giants of those days did not solve all the problems, leaving little if anything for their successors to accomplish. This problem field known as cataloging is still a challenge to clear thinking and sound judgment.

The foremost problem confronting library administrators has been set down as the cost of cataloging. Elements contributing to that problem are questions as to what theory of cataloging to follow, how to work out a satisfactory cataloging code, how best to organize a catalog department, what classification scheme should be used, and how it should be applied. These and many other questions of greater or less significance are what the library administrator must know about and be prepared to tackle in collaboration with catalogers.

Cataloging policies and practices are about to be set for another generation. Whether the people of the 1980's will say librarians and catalogers of today had as much understanding and ability as can now be attested for the people of the early 1900's depends on the success of the deliberations of the 1940's.

It is important to say that the awareness of these problems is not to be taken as one generation criticizing another. I have cataloged through twenty of the forty years that made up the era which I believe has now come to an end. In 1920 there was enough remaining of the original inspiration to make itself felt and appreciated. Nevertheless, there were clear signs that the picture was rapidly changing. Pressure of work was in no small measure responsible, resulting as it inevitably did in systematization and standardization to an unwelcome degree.

Those of us who see ourselves bridging the two eras have an added responsibility. We know and respect what was good in the past. We honor the traditions in which to greater or less extent we participated. And for such reasons our leadership in charting new courses should and can be so much the wiser.

NOTES

[1] Rudolf Kaiser, in Fritz Milau, *Handbuch der Bibliothekswissenschaft, II* (Leipzig: 1933), p. 318.

[2] W. W. Bishop, *Cataloging as an asset: an address to the New York State Library School, May 1, 1915* (Baltimore: 1916), p. 8.

[3] *Ibid.,* p. 22.

[4] *Catalog rules* (Chicago: American Library Association, 1908), p. viii.

Tradition and Principle in Library Cataloging

Hugh A. Chaplin

"If, as I think we must agree, a tendency on the part of catalogers to cling to tradition and to established practices has hindered the development of a new cataloging code based on logical principles, is it possible to discern what a code might be like?"

The growth of libraries from mere handfuls of books to their present almost uncontrollable size has resulted inevitably in an ever increasing dependence on catalogs of various kinds, and in an increasing complexity of cataloging systems. When large collections of books first became common—collections such as that which was accumulated in the British Museum in the eighteenth and early nineteenth centuries—it became necessary to make codes of cataloging rules. These were originally designed for a single library, but as the interdependence of libraries increased, national codes, even international codes, were produced. International codes were at first confined within the boundaries of the use of a single language; now we aspire to producing them in a wider field. At the same time, increasing variety in the modes of presentation of published material and in the interests and approaches of library users has tended to produce new situations for which the old catalog codes were not adequate. They have tended to become obsolete, and in the absence of authoritative guidance from the accepted codes *ad hoc* decisions have had to be made to deal with new situations. These have tended to be inconsistent and not to follow any guiding principle; hence arises the recurring demand for new and up-to-date codes.

Such was the background of the production in 1949 of the *A.L.A. Cataloging Rules for Author and Title Entries,* an event which took place just over forty years after the publication of the code which these rules replaced—the 1908 Anglo-American Rules. Similar periods had elapsed before that time between the appearance of earlier codes of epoch-making importance—Cutter's *Rules for a Dictionary Catalog,* of which the first edition was published in 1876, and, before that, Panizzi's ninety-one rules for the British Museum, drafted in 1839.

We are now on the eve of the publication of an entirely new revision of the Anglo-American code—only seventeen years after the last revision. The explanation of this shorter interval may be found partly in a statement which appears in the preface to the 1949 code—that when the 1908 rules were examined by the revising committee, it was found that "the basic rules were on the whole satisfactory" and that "expansion was needed rather than change." In fact, as catalogers amongst us will remember, the main difference between the two codes lay very largely in the addition of numerous further categories of material for which special rules were provided. The new code was a codification of *ad hoc* decisions which had been made in the interim rather than a rethinking of principles. The length and complexity of the new code—224 pages of rules for entry, without any descriptive rules—caused some dismay, and it was not long before the code was subjected to a devastating analysis by Seymour Lubetzky, whose influence on subsequent developments has been profound. His exposure of the absence of logical structure in the code extended also to its earlier form—the 1908 rules—and stimulated a demand on both sides of the Atlantic for a new code of a simpler and more logical nature.

Meanwhile, dissatisfaction with older cataloging codes and a new interest in cataloging principles was not confined to the English-speaking world. In Germany, several projects for radical revision of the prevailing code, the *"Prussian Instructions",* had been adopted or were under consideration; thorough revisions of cataloging rules were in progress in France, Italy, the Soviet Union and elsewhere; and references to cataloging principles appear frequently in the literature of the period. For example, a symposium entitled *Cataloguing Principles and Practice* was published in London in 1954; in India, Ranganathan published in 1955 his work *Heading and Canons,* which was a study of

SOURCE: Reprinted from Hugh A. Chaplin, *Tradition and Principle in Library Cataloging* (Toronto: University of Toronto, School of Library Science, 1966), pp. 5–24 excerpted, by permission of the publisher.

five major cataloging codes in the light of principles which he himself had developed in earlier works on cataloging. In 1954 the International Federation of Library Associations appointed a "Working Group on the Co-ordination of Cataloging Principles," so initiating a process which led to the holding of an "International Conference on Cataloguing Principles" seven years later.

During all these discussions on *principles* reference was frequently made to the varying *traditions* embodied in existing cataloging codes. The International Conference on Cataloguing Principles was in fact mainly an attempt to reconcile these traditions and to create a coherent system which would give due weight to what was best in each of them. The document entitled *Statement of Principles* which was produced by that conference was not, I think I can safely say, a statement of general principles of catalog construction at all; it was rather a set of general rules blending various traditions and designed to provide a basis for international uniformity in cataloging.

After this attempt to review tradition in the light of certain only partially understood principles of cataloging, the question still remained: Are tradition and principle really in direct conflict in this field? One of the most acute participants in the 1961 conference, Akos Domanovszky of Hungary, had published shortly before it met an article[1] on principles of cataloging in which he put this question very sharply. The chief cause, he said, of the unsatisfactory nature of our cataloging rules was that they were rooted in practice; they harked back to older codes of rules—in short, they rested mainly on traditional, not on rational foundations. He gave two examples. The first was the traditional German rule for cataloging anonymous books which had been worked out in the nineteenth century and which was, and is, still followed in many German libraries. The other was entry under corporate authors, as practiced in the Anglo-American world. Domanovszky pointed out that, in the first place, the German rules for cataloging anonymous books, by which the entry-word is chosen from the title by applying a complicated grammatical formula, were adopted in spite of the fact that entry under the first word of the title was a system which already existed and had, in fact, been powerfully advocated in England by Panizzi—although he had been obliged to bow to an adverse decision by the Trustees of the British Museum and to create a rule somewhat similar to the German one. Few people, even in Germany, would now dissent from Domanovszky's

judgment that the Prussian rule was a concession to a tradition which was already out of date when the rule was formulated. Both the Prussian and the British Museum rules for cataloging anonymous books represent, in fact, an uneasy compromise between the old tradition that an anonymous work would be found in the catalog under a word which would suggest the subject or character of the book and the principle (firmly championed by Panizzi) that, if any certainty or consistency was to be achieved, cataloging must be based on the actual wording of title pages.

There will probably be a good deal less agreement with Domanovszky's other example of the triumph of tradition over principle: his contention that the whole concept of corporate authorship is based on a rationalization by Jewett of something he found in Panizzi's rules—the entry of the publications of academies under the name of the publishing institution—and that this concept has led catalogers along a false trail. But we will return to this question later....

We must first consider what the principles of catalog construction are. These must emerge, I think, from a description of the essential characteristics of a catalog, in terms of its function and the means by which this function can be performed. Here is my attempt at such a description:

> A catalog is a record of the contents of a collection, so designed as to facilitate the finding of any particular item in the collection, or of items having particular characteristics. An item may be a single object or a group of related objects. In the latter case the single objects constituting the group may also be regarded as items. The catalog contains a separate record, known as an "entry," for each item. To provide rapid access to any required item, each entry must specify an item by reference to a recognized scheme of characteristics; the characteristics must be presented in the entry in a recognized order; and entries must be ordered among themselves by applying a recognized system of arrangement to the characteristics appearing first, or in a conspicuous position, in each entry. Since each successive characteristic in the entry will assign the item to a subclass of the class denoted by the preceding characteristic, the arrangement of characteristics within the entry may be designed to facilitate access to classes and subclasses of items as well as to single items. Each entry must include enough characteristics to distinguish the item to which it refers from all other items and (if the collection itself is appropriately organized) to show the location of the item in the collection. Only one system of classes can be presented by a catalog which consists of one entry for each item; a catalog may, however, make use of several systems simultaneously either by multiplying the entries for an item, or by providing index-entries (i.e., entries directing the user to the characteristic standing first in an entry from another characteristic of the same item).

Index-entries may either be arranged in a separate sequence from the main series of entries in the catalog or, if expressed in terms or symbols of the same kind as those used in the main series, may be intercalated in it.

This rather long and dry statement is intended to be a description which can be applied to catalogs of all kinds. As you will have noticed, it implies that every catalog is a classified set of entries—that is to say, that all cataloging is a form of classification; and I have no doubt that this is so. Even when the purpose of a catalog is to give rapid access to individual items, it can work only by means of specifications which, in fact, assign items to classes, even if these are such relatively meaningless classes as the class of documents whose titles begin with the letter A. Such a catalog will be efficient if the leading characteristic of the entry (otherwise known as the heading) is one which will specify with a single term the smallest possible class of items. It is the attempt to do this that is one of the distinguishing features of an alphabetical catalog.

This outline of the structure of a catalog may seem unduly abstract and to have little relation to practical matters. Is it linked with the practical problems that we know as catalogers? The link is to be found in one word deliberately introduced into the description—the work "recognized." The scheme of characteristics (by which I mean the different aspects of a book—author, title, imprint and so on—which are recorded in a catalog, the order in which the characteristics appear in the entry, the system by which the entries are arranged among themselves—these, I said, must be "recognized." The term means, of course, known and accepted by the user of the catalog as the basis of what he expects to find in it. It contains the implication that the catalog is a means of communication and that to fulfil this function it must be composed in a language that its users understand. Such a language can, of course, be a purely conventional one agreed upon in advance between the makers and the users of the catalog. This is the case, for instance, if a catalog is arranged by the artificial notation of a classification system which has to be known in advance by the users of the catalog. But usually the relation between the users and the maker of the catalog is not close enough for this sort of previous agreement. The cataloger must make some general assumptions about the people who are going to use his catalog and what they will expect to find in it. It is in the process of designing a means of communication

between the cataloger and the user, who is a person unknown to him, that tradition comes into the picture.

But the word *tradition,* used in relation to cataloging, may mean two different things, which I will call user's tradition and cataloger's tradition. The expectations of a person about to look up something in a library catalog are determined by a tradition—a set of concepts in his mind which he has derived from many sources: from his past education, from the books he has read, from his previous experience of reference books—bibliographies, dictionaries, encyclopedias, directories, and, of course, library catalogs, including perhaps the one that he is dealing with at the moment. To take account of this tradition, of these established expectations of the user, is itself one of the basic principles of cataloging. We must remember that this tradition is something which varies from person to person; no two people come with precisely the same expectations, the same ideas, the same backgrounds in their minds. It is also something which changes with the passage of time—the readers of today have a different background from the readers of fifty years ago. It follows, therefore, that no one single set of rules will suit all libraries and all users, and also that every cataloging code must from time to time be revised so as to take into account the needs of the user of the present day.

There is also, as I have said, a cataloger's tradition. This is something quite different; it consists of all those rules and customs which are followed by catalogers because they ensure stability; they enable the cataloger to feel that he or she is doing the right thing; they make sure that one particular set of users' expectations will be, in fact, fulfilled. They are very important to the cataloger, particularly when the cataloger is adding entries to large catalogs of long-established collections. But these, the cataloger's shibboleths and established practices, are the traditions to which Domanovszky's strictures are rightly applied. If they are allowed to dominate the making of catalogs, they will, in course of time, undermine the efficiency of the catalog as a means of communication. It is true, as is often argued, that the cataloger's tradition, the cataloger's rules, are one of the factors which form the expectations of the users. But they are only one of a number of factors, and if they are allowed to dominate the situation this will lead to unfortunate results. I suggest, therefore, that revisers of cataloging codes must bear several things in mind. They must adapt their rules to development and change in the user's tradition, the expectations of people using the catalog, and where this would be hindered by their own habits, their own tradition, the cataloger's tradition must be disregarded. They must also do their best to ensure that any new rules which they create conform to the general logical principles of the construction of catalogs. The difficulty is that the expectations of the users of catalogs are inconsistent and variable, while the rules must conform to a system. The solution is to make general rules, which conform to generally prevalent expectations. Exceptions can be made, but only for important and clearly definable categories of material. Minor variations—the odd isolated case where some people will expect a variation from the normal—and the expectations of a minority of users—the specialists who have their own special vocabularies and ways of approaching literature—must not be allowed to disturb the general pattern. They can be taken care of in the catalog, if necessary, by additional entries and references. . . .

Our code then must take account of two conflicting traditions. One of these—the tradition that a book should be described in terms derived from itself—is primarily a cataloger's tradition, although fortunately it has had some influence both on readers and on publishers. The other, older tradition which regards a book as a vehicle for a work, and assumes that a work will be known to readers by a name that is independent of particular title pages, is still a powerful influence on users' expectations. The cataloger must base himself on those expectations, but must also subject them to systematic treatment which will produce consistent and predictable results. The solution of this problem, I would suggest, is that the cataloger, while taking full advantage of the fact that for the majority of books the title page can supply the leading elements of the entry, should define as closely as possible the main categories of books to which this use of the title page does not apply. These will include not only those works which are differently described on the title pages of different editions, but also those which, because of the remoteness of their origin from the time and place to which the catalog belongs—books of ancient literature, books belonging to remote civilizations such as China—or because of their exceptional fame or notoriety, are better known to the user of the catalog by reference to them in other works than by direct acquaintance with the books themselves. . . .

We cannot assume, therefore, that the traditional author entry is a sound foundation on which to build the whole structure of a modern catalog. In an increasing number of large and important libraries the predominant classes of items are periodicals, series of reports issued by research institutions and other kinds of corporate bodies, proceedings of conferences and symposia, accounts of work done by teams rather than by individuals, and those numerous documents composed by unnamed officials or hammered out by committees of legislators, by means of which a network of impersonal "authorities" regulate many aspects of our lives. In such libraries the cataloging of "one work, one author" books is of minor importance; and even in the large general libraries for which our principal codes are designed its relative importance is diminishing. For books containing more than one work and for books of multiple and collective authorship a strong consistent tradition, either among users or among catalogers, is lacking. Rather we find a number of separate traditions which group themselves into two main streams emphasizing two opposing principles. One of these regards the title as the primary characteristic of any work which is not closely associated with a particular person as author; the other tradition refuses this status to the title except in the last resort, and prefers the name of a person (even a person only obscurely associated with the work) or the name of an institution or association, or even of an inanimate object, which stands in some relation to the work which may be analogous to authorship, but may in fact be quite dissimilar—for example, the relation of being the subject of the book or the source from which information in the book has been derived. . . .

The Paris Conference attempted a compromise between these two traditions. Its *Statement of Principles* carefully avoids the term "corporate author," and merely states that in certain circumstances a main entry may be made under the name of a corporate body. Its recommendations represent a close approximation to the Russian position, which, while not objecting to the term "corporate author," is based, as some of its advocates have made clear, not on an abstract theory of authorship but on the need to "characterize" a work in a convenient way. The main principle laid down at Paris was that a work should be entered under a corporate body "if, by its nature, it represents the result of the collective thought or activity of the body"; this is supplemented by approval of entry under the corporate body if its name is an essential part of the title of the publication, provided that the publication contains some account of the activities of the body. This proviso is not only a concession to the authorship theory, it is also an attempt to deal with the problem of serials. It does not succeed, however, in disposing of the difficulty presented by the cataloging of serials under a theory of corporate authorship. The difficulty is this: If authorship is the deciding factor, main entries for different serials with titles which (apart from the name of the body concerned) are identical will have to be split between entry under title and entry under the corporate author. The choice will depend on the contents of the publication, the character of which may not be indicated in references to it, and in which material of corporate authorship may be mixed with other material in an unpredictable proportion.

If time permitted, it would be possible to look at a number of other cases of conflict between tradition and principle in catalog construction. One that I should have liked to consider in some detail is the reappearance in the new Anglo-American code of special rules for special kinds of material. For example, there is a whole section of rules on legal materials, another on religious materials, in which you will find the problem of collections and the question of traditional titles for what are called anonymous classics receiving, just because the material is defined as legal or religious, solutions which are different from the general solution in the main part of the code. This, I think, is an example of the general principles of the code being upset by the intrusion of a special kind of tradition—the tradition of the specialist librarian who has worked out a particular way of dealing with the sort of material in which he is primarily interested. It has had sufficient influence over the Revision Committee to persuade them to adopt solutions for this sort of material which differ from those they have found correct in general.

The brief survey I have made of some of the main problems raised by the cataloging of books which do not conform to the general type—works of multiple authorship and publications emanating from corporate bodies—has led me to certain conclusions which I should like to summarize.

First, whether we like it or not, any cataloging code must be based on the expectations of the user. These, it is true, are partly determined by his experience of catalogs or by what we tell him about the catalog. But to a greater extent they are determined by what he has learnt from his wider experience to associate with the books and classes of books he is seeking.

Secondly, we must recognize that the structure of the catalog cannot be based on one kind of association only—the association of an individual author with his intellectual or artistic work. Many books are not works in this sense. Different kinds of books will be associated with different characteristics—with the author, the title, some distinctive part of the title, a traditional name, a corporate body which is connected with the book as a publisher or sponsor or in some other way.

It has been said among those responsible for preparing the new Anglo-American code that although it is not perfect it will be the best code obtainable now, but that it will still need revision. Perhaps this future revision could take as its starting point an effort to define the kinds of books with which each of these characteristics is most likely to be associated, and to build the rules around these definitions and not around the conception that the whole catalog is based on the question, "Who is the author of this book?" In this way we may avoid trying to force into the author and title mould headings which we are bound to use but which are neither authors nor titles.

NOTE

[1] Akos Domanovszky, "Einiges über die Grundsätze der Titelaufnahme," *Libri,* X (1960), pp. 205-54.

Design for a Code

Seymour Lubetsky

"It is apparent that a rationalization of our cataloging will require not a revision of any particular rules, but a complete reconstruction of our code in accordance with deliberately adopted objectives which should define the aim of our rules, and well considered principles . . . ."

OBJECTIVES AND IMPLICATIONS

The objectives implicit in our rules for entry are two. The first objective is to enable the user of the catalog to determine readily whether or not the library has the book he wants. The catalog is constantly searched by many readers and members of the staff, and the quicker this information can be found the better the catalog. The second objective is to reveal to the user of the catalog, under one form of the author's name, what works the library has by a given author and what editions or translations of a given work. Many users of the library, particularly scholars and students, require this information which otherwise might have to be gathered laboriously from various parts of the catalog. Other users are thus enabled conveniently to select the edition or translation of a work which will best suit their purposes, or to find related works of the author, or to identify a work whose title was vaguely or inaccurately cited, or to find a work which was not cataloged separately. This information also helps the classifer to arrange the books systematically under a given subject—first by author, then by title, and last by edition and translation.

The need for the second objective arises from the fact that the works of any author may be issued under different names as a result of a change, translation, transliteration, or even misprint of the author's name, and the editions of a work may be issued under different titles for similar reasons, and could, therefore, otherwise be separated in the catalog. The cataloger is thus required, in recording a work, to establish the identity of the author and the relationships of the work. This has proved to be costly, and the provisions designed to implement this objective have also served to complicate our rules. For these reasons, some librarians have been inclined to challenge the second objective and to limit cataloging to the first objective—to showing whether or not a given book is in the library. This report assumes that the second objective will continue to be recognized as important to the integrity and effectiveness of the catalog, and that it will be followed in the future to the extent that a library may find it reasonable and feasible. To discard a useful objective which can often be carried out without material difficulty because its unqualified application would lead us into serious difficulties is to abdicate the role of administrative policy, which must in the application of all principles and rules determine the point of diminishing returns and the limits of the library's ability to cope with the task.

Both these objectives were staunchly defended by Panizzi before the Royal Commission in 1849 and have since been pursued in the Anglo-American cataloging rules. But the objectives are inherently in conflict, and the conflict is reflected in the vicissitudes of our rules. Thus we may find that, on the one hand, Panizzi decried the entry of a work "under a title of nobility or dignity, or the mere form of name as it appears on the title-page," because this might disperse "the works of many noblemen and most prelates in different parts of the catalog"; on the other hand, he deprecated the entry (by one of the witnesses before the Commission) of a given work under its editor's name "Utterson, Edward Vernon," because "the preface by the editor is signed E. V. U., and there is no other indication on the book of the editor's name." In the latter case, then, Panizzi seemed unperturbed about the possible dispersal of Utterson's works, but concerned primarily with facilitating the location of the particular work, which would probably be looked for under the initials under which it was published. Panizzi's rules pro-

SOURCE: Reprinted from Seymour Lubetsky, *Cataloging Rules and Principles* (Washington: Library of Congress, 1953), pp. 36–55 excerpted.

viding for the entry of a book under the author's initials if so issued (rule XXXII), or under the pseudonym used by the author (rule XLI), or under the title of the book if anonymously published, even when its author is known to the cataloger (rule XXXIX), were aimed at the first objective—to facilitate the location of these books, which are bound to be so cited and looked for, even though the works of many authors would thus be dispersed. But his rules providing for the entry of translations under the vernacular form of the author's name (rule X), of noblemen and church dignitaries under their family names (rules XIV, XV), and of authors who changed their names under their original names (rule XI) were designed in accordance with the second objective—which is to bring the works of these authors together, even though the location of many books which are bound to be cited and looked for under the names given in the books would thus be made more difficult. The A. L. A. rules are logically more consistent when they provide for entry under the author's name of works published under his initials, pseudonyms, or without his name; but in so doing they sacrifice more of the time and convenience of all those who will look for these works under the initials or pseudonyms given on the works, or under their titles if anonymously published—that is, they sacrifice the first objective to the second.

We are then confronted, at the beginning, with the question of whether and how the two conflicting objectives might be reconciled. The answer appears to lie in the fact that while the second objective requires that the works of an author should all be entered under one form of the author's name, it does not dictate any particular form; whereas the first objective requires that the books should be entered under that form of the author's name under which he is bound to be cited and looked for most frequently by the users of the catalog. That form is generally the one which appears in the author's works, unless he is best known under another form of name.

BIBLIOGRAPHIC CONDITIONS AND PRINCIPLES

Having considered the objectives at which we should aim in cataloging and their implications, let us now turn to examine the material for which our principles and rules are to be designed and note the conditions encountered.

Basic conditions and principles: The prevailing type of material which is found in a library and is recorded in its catalog is the book; and the most important characteristic of the book, for the purposes of cataloging, is the fact that it is provided with a prominent identification tag in the form of a title page. The cataloger can thus anticipate how a particular book will normally be cited and looked for and provide for it accordingly. The title page generally includes the name of the author and the title of the book, sometimes only the title of the book, and occasionally only the name of the author. The name of the author and the title of the book are therefore the most important clues by which the book will be identified when cited, and by which it will be looked for in the catalog or called for in the library. The principles and rules for the entry of books must consequently be based on these two elements, and will apply similarly to other materials identified by an author, or title, or both.

It is interesting to note that, at the hearings before the Royal Commission on Panizzi's rules in 1849, one of the witnesses, a diligent user of the British Museum library and a severe critic of its catalog of that time, postulated that the difficulty in finding books in the British Museum catalog could have been obviated by "following the simple plan of their being put under the author's name, or where you cannot do that under the name of the work." He went on to explain, "If you take any work, there is the title-page. If they will describe the books in the catalogue by the title-page any reader will find what is wanted." Panizzi demonstrated that this simple plan was not always sufficient; but Cutter, in his first discussion of cataloging principles in the article on "The New Catalogue of Harvard College Library" mentioned before, maintained that

> although bibliographers are not agreed upon all the details . . . yet almost all the rules may be reduced to two great principles: first that books shall be cataloged under the name of the author, or (in the case of collections) the editor, or the body responsible for their publication; second, that, if this is not known, the first word in the title not an article or a preposition shall be taken for the heading.

These "two great principles" concern themselves with the elemental bibliographic conditions of a book and thus provide the core around which a logical and practical pattern for a cataloging code could be evolved . . . .

Another very important consideration that should be borne in mind in designing and evaluating our principles and rules of entry is the fact that the introduction and general use of printed and otherwise manufactured catalog cards has given the main entry a new significance: It has become also the "unit" card—that is, copies of the main entry are overtyped with the title of the book, the name of the series, the subject headings assigned to the book, the name of the editor or translator, etc., and are used as title, series, subject, and other added entries. Thus, when the main or unit entry is made under the author's name, the entries under a given title, series, subject heading, editor, translator, etc., will automatically be subarranged in the catalog first by the name of the author and then by the title of the book. Obviously, this is a more logical and useful arrangement than the one that would result from entering all works under their titles, in which case the entries under the various added headings would automatically be subarranged by the titles of the books. Cutter's "two great principles," therefore, remain as valid as they have always been.

Preliminary Official Report

I.F.L.A. International Conference on Cataloguing Principles, Paris, 1961.

"The aim of the conference . . . was to reach agreement on basic principles governing the choice and form of entry in the alphabetical catalog of authors and titles."

INTRODUCTION

The International Conference on Cataloguing Principles, sponsored by I.F.L.A. with the aid of a grant from the Council on Library Resources, was held at the UNESCO Conference Building, Paris, from 9th-18th October 1961.

The aim of the Conference, as laid down by the Preliminary Meeting held in London in July 1959, was "to reach agreement on basic principles governing the choice and form of entry in the alphabetical catalog of authors and titles." With this aim in view, library associations and other interested organizations in all countries with which contact could be established were asked to form national committees for the purpose of appointing and instructing delegates. A number of international organizations were also invited to participate in the Conference. Working Papers, on subjects suggested by the Preliminary Meeting, were prepared and circulated for study and comment, and a draft Statement of Principles, based on the Working Papers and the comments received, was prepared by the Executive Secretary and issued to all participants and their sponsoring organizations before the opening of the Conference.

The Conference sessions were devoted mainly to the discussion and amendment of this draft Statement of Principles. After a general discussion of each section of the draft, during which amendments were submitted by delegations, a working group was appointed which, together with members of the enlarged Organizing Committee, considered the amendments and the points made during the general discussion and prepared a revised text of the section, which was submitted to the vote of the Conference at a later session. The final Statement arrived at by this procedure received the support of a large majority of the participants. In addition to the general sessions, which were concerned with this Statement and with general resolutions, a number of special groups met during the Conference and produced reports which will be issued later with a full report of the Conference.

The text of the Statement of Principles, together with other resolutions passed by the Conference, lists of delegations and special groups, and a summary of the votes taken is given below.

RESOLUTIONS

Resolution I

The Conference approves, in accordance with the votes recorded elsewhere, the Statement of Principles set out below.

(1) It requests the official national delegates and the national committees: to arrange for the widest possible publicity for this text among librarians, publishers and booksellers, and the responsible authorities in their respective countries;

(2) to take the necessary action to ensure (a) that cataloguing rules in their countries are established or revised as soon as possible in conformity with the principles laid down by the Conference, and put into practice; (b) that the same principles are taken into account in the compilation of national bibliographies.

It also requests the official delegates of international organizations to bring the text of the Statement of Principles to the notice of the national members of their organizations.

It requests the Secretariat to communicate the text of the Statement to all countries not represented at the Conference, and to any international organizations not represented which may be

SOURCE: Reprinted from I.F.L.A. International Conference on Cataloging Principles, Paris, October 9–18, 1961, "Preliminary Official Report," in *Library Resources and Technical Services*, 6 (Spring, 1962), pp. 161–171, by permission of the publisher, the American Library Association.

deemed to be interested in the problems of cataloging.

STATEMENT OF PRINCIPLES

Adopted by the International Conference on Cataloguing Principles, Paris, October 1961.

1. Scope of Statement

    The principles here stated apply only to the choice and form of headings and entry-words—i.e., to the principal elements determining the order of entries—in catalogs of printed books[1] in which entries under authors' names and, where these are inappropriate or insufficient, under the titles of works are combined in one alphabetical sequence. They are framed with special reference to catalogs enumerating the contents of large general libraries: but their application to the catalogs of other libraries and to other alphabetical lists of books is also recommended, with such modifications as may be required by the purposes of these catalogs and lists.

2. Functions of the Catalog

    The catalog should be an efficient instrument for ascertaining

    2.1 whether the library contains a particular book specified by

    (a) its author and title, or

    (b) if the author is not named in the book, its title alone, or

    (c) if author and title are inappropriate or insufficient for identification, a suitable substitute for the title;

    2.2 (a) which works by a particular author and

    (b) which editions of a particular work are in the library.

3. Structure of the Catalog

    To discharge these functions the catalog should contain

    3.1 at least one entry for each book cataloged, and

    3.2 more than one entry relating to any book, whenever this is necessary in the interests of the user or because of the characteristics of the book—for example:

    3.21 when the author is known by more than one name or form of name, or

    3.22 when the author's name has been ascertained but is not on the title-page of the book, or

    3.23 when several authors or collaborators

have shared in the creation of the book, or

    3.24 when the book is attributed to various authors, or

    3.25 when the book contains a work known by various titles.

4. Kinds of Entry

    Entries may be of the following kinds: main entries, added entries and references.

    4.1 One entry for each book—the main entry—must be a full entry, giving all the particulars necessary for identifying the book. Other entries may be either added entries (i.e. additional entries, based on the main entry and repeating under other headings information given in it) or references (which direct the reader to another place in the catalog).

5. Use of Multiple Entries

    The two functions of the catalog (see 2.1 and 2.2) are most effectively discharged by

    5.1 an entry for each book under a heading derived from the author's name or from the title as printed in the book, and

    5.2 when variant forms of the author's name or of the title occur, an entry for each book under a uniform heading,[2] consisting of one particular form of the author's name or one particular title, or, for books not identified by author or title, a uniform heading consisting of a suitable substitute for the title, and

    5.3 appropriate added entries and/or references.

6. Function of different kinds of Entry

    6.1 The main entry for works entered under authors' names should normally be made under a uniform heading. The main entry for works entered under title may be either under the title as printed in the book, with an added entry under a uniform title, or under a uniform title, with added entries or references under the other titles. The latter practice is recommended for the cataloging of well-known works, especially those known by conventional titles (see 11.3).[3]

    6.2 Entries under other names or forms of name for the same author should normally take the form of references; but added entries may be used in special cases.[4]

    6.3 Entries under other titles for the same work should normally take the form of added entries; but references may be used when a reference can replace a number of added entries under one heading.[5]

6.4 Added entries (or in appropriate cases references) should also be made under the names of joint authors, collaborators, etc., and under the titles of works having their main entry under an author's name, when the title is an important alternative means of identification.

7. Choice of Uniform Heading

The uniform heading should normally be the most frequently used name (or form of name) or title appearing in editions of the works cataloged or in references to them by accepted authorities.

7.1 When editions have appeared in several languages, preference should in general be given to a heading based on editions in the original language; but if this language is not normally used in the catalog, the heading may be derived from editions and references in one of the languages normally used there.

8. Single personal author

8.1 The main entry for every edition of a work ascertained to be by a single personal author should be made under the author's name. An added entry or reference is made under the title of each edition in which the author's name is not stated on the title page.

8.2 The uniform heading should be the name by which the author is most frequently identified in editions of his works,[6] in the fullest form commonly appearing there, *except that*

8.21 another name or form of name should be taken as the uniform heading if it has become established in general usage either in references to the author in biographical, historical and literary works, or in relation to his public activities other than authorship;

8.22 a further identifying characteristic should be added, if necessary, to distinguish the author from others of the same name.

9. Entry under Corporate Bodies

9.1 The main entry for a work should be made under the name of a corporate body (i.e., any institution, organized body or assembly of persons known by a corporate or collective name),

9.11 when the work is by its nature necessarily the expression of the collective thought or activity of the corporate body,[7] even if signed by a person in the capacity of an officer or servant of the corporate body, or

9.12 when the wording of the title or title page, taken in conjunction with the nature of the work, clearly implies that the corporate body is collectively responsible for the content of the work.[8]

9.2 In other cases, when a corporate body has performed a function (such as that of an editor) subsidiary to the function of the author, an added entry should be made under the name of the corporate body.

9.3 In doubtful cases, the main entry may be made either under the name of the corporate body or under the title or the name of the personal author, with an added entry in either case under the alternative not chosen for the main entry.

9.4 The uniform heading for works entered under the name of a corporate body should be the name by which the body is most frequently identified in its publications, *except that*

9.41 if variant forms of the name are frequently found in the publications, the uniform heading should be the official form of the name;

9.42 if there are official names in several languages, the heading should be the name in whichever of these languages is best adapted to the needs of the users of the catalog;

9.43 if the corporate body is generally known by a conventional name, this conventional name (in one of the languages normally used in the catalog) should be the uniform heading;

9.44 for states and other territorial authorities the uniform heading should be the currently used form of the name of the territory concerned in the language best adapted to the needs of the users of the catalog;

9.45 if the corporate body has used in successive periods different names which cannot be regarded as minor variations of one name, the heading for each work should be the name at the time of its publication, the different names being connected by references;[9]

9.46 a further identifying characteristic should be added, if necessary, to distinguish the corporate body from others of the same name.

9.5 Constitutions, laws and treaties, and certain other works having similar characteristics, should be entered under the name of the appropriate state or other territorial authority, with formal or conventional titles indicating the nature of the material. Added entries for the actual titles should be made as needed.

9.6 A work of a corporate body which is subordinate to a superior body should be entered under the name of the subordinate body, *except that*

9.61 if this name itself implies subordination or subordinate function, or is insufficient to identify the subordinate body, the heading should be the name of the superior body with the name of the subordinate body as a subheading;

9.62 if the subordinate body is an administrative, judicial or legislative organ of a government, the heading should be the name of the appropriate state or other territorial authority with the name of the organ as a subheading.

10. Multiple authorship
When two or more authors[10] have shared in the creation of a work:

10.1 if one author is represented in the book as the principal author, the others playing a subordinate or auxiliary role, the main entry for the work should be made under the name of the principal author;

10.2 if no author is represented as the principal author, the main entry should be made under

10.21 the author named first on the title page, if the number of authors is two or three, added entries being made under the name(s) of the other author(s);

10.22 the title of the work, if the number of authors is more than three, added entries being made under the author named first in the book and under as many

other authors as may appear necessary.

10.3 Collections[11]
The main entry for a collection consisting of independent works or parts of works by different authors should be made

10.31 under the title of the collection, if it has a collective title;

10.32 under the name of the author, or under the title, of the first work in the collection, if there is no collective title.

10.33 In both cases, an added entry should be made under the name of the compiler (i.e., the person responsible for assembling from various sources the material in the collection) if known.

10.34 Exception: if the name of the compiler appears prominently on the title page, the main entry may be made under the name of the compiler, with an added entry under the title.

10.4 If successive parts of a work are attributed to different authors, the main entry should be made under the author of the first part.

11. Works entered under Title

11.1 Works having their main entry under the title are:

11.11 works whose authors have not been ascertained,

11.12 works by more than three authors, none of whom is principal author (see 10.22),

11.13 collections of independent works or parts of works, by different authors, published with a collective title,

11.14 works (including serials and periodicals) known primarily or conventionally by title rather than by the name of the author.

11.2 An added entry or reference should be made under the title for:

11.21 anonymous editions of works whose authors have been ascertained,

11.22 works having their main entry under the name of the author, when the title is an important alternative means of identification,

11.23 works whose main entry is made under the name of a corporate body, but which have distinctive titles not including the name of the corporate body,

11.24 collections whose main entry is made exceptionally under the compiler.

11.3 The uniform heading (for main or added entries, see 6.1) for works entered under title should be the original title or the title most frequently used in editions of the work,[12] *except that*

11.31 if the work is generally known by a conventional title, the conventional title should be the uniform heading.

11.4 The uniform heading for works of which successive parts or volumes bear different titles should be the title of the first part, unless the majority of the parts or volumes bear another title.

11.5 When a serial publication is issued successively under different titles, a main entry should be made under each title for the series of issues bearing that title, with indication of at least the immediately preceding and succeeding titles. For each such series of issues, an added entry may be made under one selected title.[13] If, however, the variations in title are only slight, the most frequently used form may be adopted as a uniform heading for all issues.

11.6 Multilateral international treaties and conventions and certain other categories of publications issued with non-distinctive titles may be entered under a uniform conventional heading chosen to reflect the form of the work.[14]

12. Entry Word for Personal Names
When the name of a personal author consists of several words, the choice of entry-word is determined so far as possible by agreed usage in the country of which the author is a citizen, or, if this is not possible, by agreed usage in the language which he generally uses.

Resolution II

The Conference resolves
(1) that its Organizing Committee, as now enlarged, remain in being until the next annual meeting of the I.F.L.A. Council, for the purpose of
(a) making editorial corrections where necessary to the texts adopted by the Conference;
(b) distributing these texts to all delegates and observers and to all national committees and other participating organizations, as well as to the professional press;
(c) editing and publishing the Conference Report;
(d) ensuring the execution of all resolutions of the Conference;
(e) ensuring the continuation of the work undertaken in the course of the Conference by special groups;
(f) preserving and utilising the documentary material accumulated during the preparations for the Conference and during the Conference itself;
(g) submitting to the Bureau of I.F.L.A. a list of further subjects for study in the field of cataloging;
(2) that the Bureau of I.F.L.A. be asked to consider means of continuing the work of the Conference and further subjects for study in the field of cataloging, and to seek financial resources for carrying out the projects approved by the Conference and required by any future programme.

Resolution III

The Conference considers that, in the interests of future international activity, the national bodies created for the purposes of the Conference should remain in existence and continue to cooperate with the Organizing Committee.

Resolution IV

Projects to be undertaken
A. The Conference proposes that the following projects be undertaken under the direction of the Organizing Committee:
(1) The publication with the minimum of delay of a statement of the practice approved in each country for the entry of the personal names of its nationals.
(2) The preparation and publication of the following lists:
(a) a list of approved forms for catalog entries of the names of states and other territorial authorities, in conformity

with the official names used by these authorities themselves, and with equivalents in the principal languages of the world;

(b) a list of uniform titles for the anonymous classics of each country, with approved equivalents in the languages of other countries;

(c) a restricted list of categories of publications which may be entered under a conventional heading reflecting the form of the work.

B. The Conference, noting the desirability of establishing certain lists of uniform headings—e.g., of names of classical Greek and Latin authors; of names of the principal corporate bodies existing in each country and of important international organizations—proposes the compilation of a restricted number of such lists by way of experiment.

Resolution V

The Conference recommends that those countries which share, wholly or in respect of a part of their inhabitants, the use of a common language consult together with a view to unifying their practices relating to the entry-word for personal names in that language.

Resolution VI

The Conference recommends that I.F.L.A., in cooperation with other interested international organizations, should study the possible repercussions on cataloguing rules of the use, especially in large general libraries, of electronic machinery and of mechanical procedures in general.

Resolution VII

The Conference asks that consideration be given to the possibility of supplementing the Statement of Principles by the addition of a certain number of further points on which international agreement may be possible.

Resolution VIII

The Conference welcomes the cooperative spirit reaffirmed by the delegate of I.S.O. and hopes that the closest possible contact will be maintained between I.F.L.A. and I.S.O., particularly with regard to bibliographical references and transliteration.

Resolution IX

The Conference wishes to record that, if it has attained its objective and reached a very wide agreement on cataloging principles, it owes this success to the ample means put at the disposal of I.F.L.A. by the Council on Library Resources. This assistance has made it possible to carry out the preparations for the Conference under excellent conditions and to bring together responsible experts from a large number of countries and international organizations.

The Conference expresses its gratitude to the Council on Library Resources for its generous help.

NOTES

[1] In this Statement, the word "book" should be taken to include other library marerials having similar characteristics.

[2] The term "uniform heading" has been substituted for the term "standard heading" used in the text submitted to the Conference, in view of the objection that the latter term might imply a heading which has received the approval of a standardizing organization.

[3] The principles established for treatment of works entered under title may be followed also in arranging entries under any particular author heading.

[4] e.g., when a particular group of works is associated with a particular name.

[5] e.g., when a particular variant title has been used in a number of editions.

[6] Subject to Section 7.1.

[7] e.g., official reports, rules and regulations, manifestos, programmes and records of the results of collective work.

[8] e.g., serials whose titles consist of a generic term (Bulletin, Transactions, etc.) preceded or followed by the name of a corporate body, and which include some account of the activities of the body.

[9] It is a permissible alternative, when it is certain that the successive names denote the same body, to assemble all the entries under the latest name with references from the other name.

[10] In this section the word "author" is used to include a corporate body under whose name entries are made (see Section 9).

[11] A large minority of the Conference did not accept the text of 10.3 but favoured the following alternative text:

10.3 The main entry for a collection consisting of independent works or parts of works by different authors should be made
    10.31 when the collection has a collective title
        10.311 under the name of the compiler (i.e., the person responsible for assembling from various sources the material in the collection) if he is named on the title page,
        10.312 under the title of the collection, if the compiler is not named on the title page;
    10.32 when the collection has no collective title, under the name of the author, or under the title, of the first work in the collection.
    10.33 An added entry should always be made under the name of the compiler (if known), when not chosen as heading for the main entry; and under the title, if the main entry is under the compiler.
[12] Subject to Section 7.1.
[13] If it is desired to collect information about the serial publication as a whole in one place in the catalog.
[14] If it is desired to group these publications in one place in the catalogue.

APPENDIX I

Delegations

The number of participants was 105, made up of delegations from 53 countries and 12 internation organizations together with the members of the Organizing Committee appointed in London in 1959 and the authors of working papers commissioned by the Committee. One hundred and four observers from 20 countries also attended the Conference.

National delegations were from: Argentina, Australia, Austria, Belgium, Brazil, Bulgaria, Canada, Ceylon, Chile, Republic of China, Colombia, Czechoslovakia, Denmark, Finland, France, Germany (Bundesrepublik), Great Britain, Guatemala, Hungary, India, Indonesia, Iran, Israel, Italy, Jamaica, Japan, Republic of Korea, The Lebanon, Luxembourg, Mexico, Netherlands, New Zealand, Norway, Pakistan, Peru, Poland, Portugal, Federation of Rhodesia & Nyasaland, Rumania, Singapore, South Africa, Spain, Sweden, Switzerland, Thailand, Turkey, U.S.S.R., U.S.A., Uruguay, Democratic Republic of Viet-Nam, Republic of Viet-Nam, West Africa, and Yugoslavia.

International organizations represented were: Association of Libraries of Judaica and Hebraica in Europe, Federation International de Documentation, FAO Library, International Association of Agricultural Librarians and Documentalists, International Association of Law Libraries, International Association of Music Libraries, International Federation of Library Associations, International Standards Organization, International Publishers' Association, United Nations Library, New York, United Nations Library, Geneva, and UNESCO.

The following appointed delegates were unable to attend: Cuba, Germany (D.D.R.), United Arab Republic, and International Community of Booksellers' Associations.

APPENDIX II

Organizing Committee

Appointed at Preliminary Meeting, London, July 1959:
Sir Frank Francis, K.C.B., Director and Principal Librarian, British Museum, London (President)
M. Paul Poindron, Conservateur en chef à la Direction des Bibliothèques de France, Paris (Vice-President)
Dr. Ludwig Sickmann, Dozent, Bibliothekar-Lehrinstitut des Landes Nordrhein-Westfalen, Cologne
Miss N. A. Lavrova, Scientific Secretary and Chief Bibliographer, All-Union Book Chamber, Moscow
Mr. A. H. Chaplin, Keeper, Department of Printed Books, British Museum, London (Executive Secretary)
Members added at the Conference, October 1961:
Sra. Maria Luisa Monteiro da Cunha, Director, Central Library, University of São Paulo, Brazil
Dr. Andrew Osborn, Librarian, University of Sydney, Australia
Shri Benoyendra Sengupta, Assistant Librarian, National Library, Calcutta
Mr. Wyllis E. Wright, Librarian, Williams College, Williamstown, Mass.

AMERICAN ACTION ON THE I.C.C.P.

At its Midwinter meeting, January 27-28, 1962, the ALA Catalog Code Revision Committee approved the adoption of the I.C.C.P. principles as the basis for the rules in a new code, subject to the following modifications in the paragraphs noted:

6. There must be a recognition of the possibility of entry under various names for a single author in approved circumstances.

9.3 In doubtful cases, the main entry should be made under the title or the name of the personal author, with an added entry under the name of the corporate body.

9.12 Footnote 8. Omit the qualification "and which include some account of the activities of the body."

9.12 Note that this should not be understood to include serials having a distinctive title, even though the title page states or implies the collective responsibility of a corporate body.

9.44 Territorial names should follow the forms established by the U. S. Board of Geographic Names.

9.45 There is need to define what is meant by "minor variations of one name."

9.45 Footnote. The alternative should be omitted.

9.5 By "formal or conventional title" is to be understood a title which includes a categorizing word or phrase followed by an individualizing element.

"Appropriate state or other territorial authority" is to be understood to include "state or other territorial authority governed by them."

In considering this paragraph the Committee voted that the conventional titles for constitutions and treaties should be placed on the line below the author line, but that "Laws, statutes, etc.," should continue to be placed on the author line, with the individualizing part of the title on a second line.

10.3 The conference text was accepted in place of the alternative given in the footnote.

10.4 The difference in choice of entry between 10.4 and 11.4 requires further study.

11.11 This should read "anonymous works whose authors have not been ascertained" in order to exclude cases of unresolved pseudonyms.

11.5 Provision should be made for the possibility of cataloging completed serials under a single title.

11.6 Decision is reserved on the possible categories of material which may be included here.

12. The Committee reaffirms its preference for the agreed usage in the language which the author generally uses as the preferred criterion.

Wyllis E. Wright, Chairman
ALA Catalog Code Revision Committee

DESCRIPTIVE CATALOGING

Standards

There is a ditty which sing-songs along to the words "If all the sea were one sea, what a mighty sea it would be." This has been extended into any sort of philosophy conceivable, and it has also been applied to the world of cataloging. Many librarians would agree that "if all the rules were one rule, or all the codes were one code, what a mighty code we would have."

There has been a great deal of activity in the area of standards and codes in recent years. Neglect of nonbook-type materials, of report literature, and a long list of other forms of information have proliferated the ways to describe the record. A direct result of this, too, is a much deeper need to standardize what and how bibliographical (in its broadest sense) data is recorded.

The Need to Standardize Descriptive Cataloging

Stanley D. Truelson, Jr.

"Because there are too many ways to describe a book, its presence may not be discovered in a bibliography or catalog. Standardized descriptive cataloging is needed to solve this problem and also to eliminate wasteful duplication of cataloging."

The biggest problem of descriptive cataloging is that there are too many ways to describe a book. Whether we want to know if a book is in a particular collection or how it is related to other books in a collection, we often are unable to make one another understand which book we are talking about, because we are unable to agree on using the same way of describing that book. This is more of a problem for persons not trained as librarians than for those who are supposed to be experts on such matters, but librarians, too, can be stymied by the inconsistencies of descriptive cataloging.

By "describing a book" and "descriptive cataloging," I am referring primarily to description of the contents rather than the physical construction of a book and particularly to the choice of main entry and the form of entry headings.

Some people say that careful descriptive cataloging is unnecessary. We read about using *Books in Print* as a library's main catalog,[1] and we hear proposals to copy without alteration the words on a title page as a sufficient guide to finding a book when one looks for it later in a catalog. Such shortcuts undoubtedly would work some of the time, but not enough of the time. Moreover, they would do little to show the relationship of one title to another when one is looking, for example, for all volumes in a series or for several editions of a work with varied titles. There is a need for descriptive cataloging, as opposed to mere copying. But it is a major problem that variations in descriptive cataloging sometimes confuse rather than clarify the bibliographic record.

In the January 1968 *Library Trends*, Tate and Wood point out that "the difference between one library's cataloging practices and those of another" is the result of local decisions built up over the years "by analogy with the rules and examples found in the various editions of the cataloging codes." They add that sometimes the cataloging rules "are even tailored to fit the cataloging practices of individual divisions and departments within the same library." This lack of compatibility between systems, they conclude, "is time-consuming and therefore costly. It may even obstruct access to the document."[2]

One can only agree. The great card catalogs of our large libraries, proud products of decades of devoted work, massively complex apparatuses as they are, and amazing tools for finding bibliographic needles in bibliothecal haystacks; all have their omissions and their inaccuracies. Who is to say that the special practices which shaped one catalog were any more successful in serving library users than those which shaped another, when over the years dozens of minds added dozens of different interpretations of the supposed special needs of one library's users compared with another's? While striving for an elusive perfection in their catalogs, librarians have caused problems beyond those they have solved.

The call for standardization is not new, but it is being restated these days with renewed insistence. The journal, *Nature,* in an editorial of December 2, 1967, asserted that "the time . . . has come to deprive librarians of the right to develop independent cataloguing systems in the misguided notion that they thus serve the interests of their readers. No cataloguing system," it continued, "can be ideal, but the advantages of a common system override the virtues of any one of them, especially now that computers have arrived in libraries."[3] And Verner Clapp agreed when he wrote in the July 1967 *Library Trends* that "one lesson has been consistently taught by the experience of the last two centuries, namely, that uniformity of practice—a common standard—is basic."[4]

Hand in hand with the need to eliminate confu-

SOURCE: Reprinted from *Bulletin of the Medical Library Association*, 57 (January, 1969), pp. 21–27, by permission of the publisher. Originally presented as part of a general session on "Current Cataloging Problems" at the Sixty-seventh Annual Meeting of the Medical Library Association, Denver, Colorado, June 13, 1968.

sion by standardizing the way in which we describe a book is the need to eliminate duplication of work by sharing the efforts of our catalogers. Cataloging talent and money are in short supply, and we have long been squandering our limited resources by duplicative cataloging in libraries throughout our land. Librarians have a direct responsibility for seeking a way out of such wasteful overactivity. Fortunately, the time is nearing when we can do better.

CONFLICTING STANDARDS

One might suppose that the publication of a new cataloging code in 1967 would have solved the problem of standardizing, but not so. The new *Anglo-American Cataloging Rules*[5] are a great improvement in cataloging theory and principle[6] over the red and green books which had guided catalogers since 1949.[7,8] Yet, while Seymour Lubetzky's catalytic criticism in 1953 of the earlier rules for entry, which he called "vague in design and weak in structure,"[9] stimulated the many years' planning which led to the new book in blue, the new code does not correct all the logical defects he described, but instead embodies compromises in the face of operating realities; namely, certain long-imbedded practices of large libraries which represent investments too great to change.

Most importantly, the new rules did not result in total agreement on principles. We now have, for example, both the North American Text and the British version of the *Anglo-American Cataloging Rules:* equal, perhaps, but nevertheless separate. And, as if they were not enough, we have for that peculiar breed of document known as the technical report, a peculiar set of special rules published in 1966, called the COSATI Standard.[10]

The COSATI Standard is particularly peculiar in its choice of main entry. Before examining this choice, let us consider the need for a main entry, as did Lubetzky in his 1953 critique.[11] There are those, especially some computer advocates, who say that, since a catalog or a computer file may contain all useful entries for a work, it does not matter which of them is the main entry. But it does. Multiple entries are not always possible: Many finding lists, such as library order files, library union catalogs, or published bibliographies, enter a work only once. In order to search those files successfully to see whether they include a particular work, one must use the same entry that appears or would be apt to appear in the file. So

long as choice of main entry differs, bibliographic access may be prevented.

North, in the October 1967 *Special Libraries,* says that "the Anglo-American Rules, and the COSATI Standard are in remarkable harmony...." Yet she reasserts the divisive assumption of the COSATI Standard that "one of the principle distinctions of report literature is the relative unimportance of the personal author" and that "the organization responsible for the report has been generally recognized as the most useful author citation."[12] Warheit stated in 1952 the main reason for this view. "Many continued research programs, as reflected in a series of progress reports," he said, "do not always have the same personal authors: they do have the same corporate author."[13] This argument, however, overlooks the fact that in the academic community research projects often move from institution to institution right along with the research personnel involved.

As a result of the clash of the main entry rules of the COSATI Standard with those of the *Anglo-American Cataloging Rules,* a scientific paper written by a medical school professor, for example, is entered under personal author, as it should be, when published as a journal article or a monograph, but when published in the format of a technical report with essentially the same scientific content and author responsibilities, it is entered under the name of the author's employing institution. Sometimes the work is published as a journal article, and reprints of that article are cataloged and distributed under the procedures for technical reports with the technical report accession number stamped across the face of the reprint.

There is no more logic to calling a university or its subdivision the author of a faculty member's scientific or scholarly work when it has received a federal grant to support his research and writing than when it pays him from tuition income and gifts. And there is no more logic to creating an artificial corporate authorship when the work is published in near-print, distributed by the Clearinghouse for Federal Scientific and Technical Information, assigned AD, PB, or XYZ accession numbers, and indexed in the *Government-wide Index to Federal Research and Development Reports* and its companion abstracting services, than when it is distributed in hard covers by a commercial publisher and thus listed in the main part of the National Library of Medicine *Current Catalog* instead of the new Technical Report Literature sections.

Worse than the breakdown in logic is the breakdown in producing standard cataloging data. But the National Library of Medicine accepted these illogical distinctions in practice when it announced that "papers which report on research in progress, usually being performed under contract with a U. S. Government agency," would be cataloged under rules adapted from the COSATI Standard and listed separately in the 1968 issues of the *Current Catalog.*[14] As a result of NLM's application of this policy, medical school faculty papers are entered under the names of the schools, whereas, if the same papers were in journal or book format, the schools would be identified only in small print under the authors' names or in a footnote and not at all in the catalog or index entry. Even student theses for the M.S. degree are listed in NLM's *Current Catalog* with the name of the university and its subordinate center as the main entry heading, merely because of the financing and format of the published versions.[15]

These examples, it is true, are exceptions to the typical progress report, which is more ephemeral in content and more efficiently cataloged as an institutional report than as a scientific paper. But a way to distinguish the preliminary laboratory or corporation research report from the true scientific paper or monograph of personal authorship, when either can be clothed in the covers of a technical report, apparently has not been discovered. The COSATI Standard thus may have approached compatibility with the *Anglo-American Cataloging Rules,* but it has not quite offered the ultimate embrace.

VARYING PRACTICES

Such variations in principle are not the only roadblocks to standardization. Once we finally agree on policy, we still must face the differing degrees to which it is accepted and followed. The country's leader in cataloging, the Library of Congress, follows the *Anglo-American Cataloging Rules* only under very special circumstances, an approach which it calls "superimposition."[16] "Superimposition" means that only new titles—and only some of them—are handled under the new rules and that the inconsistencies and poor practices of the past usually must remain untouched. The only real standard possible in this mélange of practice and occasional principle is the standard that "what is shall be": the cataloging description which has any possibility whatsoever of becoming the established version is that which issues from the Library of Congress on its printed cards, com-

puter tapes, or published catalog volumes. Perhaps, however, this situation is not as bad as it might seem.

ESSENTIAL ELEMENTS

Principles or guidelines, in the end, do not guarantee consistent practice; they only encourage it. Beyond cataloging principles stands the product that they lead to, the cataloging record itself. One of the reasons that the experiment several years ago of cataloging in source, where the cataloging record was printed on the verso of a book's title page, offered so much promise even beyond the easy availability to libraries of cataloging copy, was that readers, booksellers, and librarians alike could agree on the standard description of a particular book, because there it was in black and white with even the blessing of the publisher himself. One may hypothesize that the essential elements of standardized cataloging are widespread availability and general acceptance of the data for a specific book and that conformity to any particular cataloging code is less important than these two elements. It may be annoying when, for example, one year's conference proceedings are entered under a main heading radically different from the previous year's, but even this inconsistency would be less serious if everyone agreed to use these variant headings for their respective volumes: at least we could make each other understand which book we were talking about, even if the relation of that book to other volumes in its series remained cloudy.

Shared cataloging thus contains already the potential for becoming standardized cataloging. If access to the cataloging records of the Library of Congress and the National Union Catalog were rapid and easy for all users of books, those records, in spite of their internal inconsistencies, could become universally used cataloging descriptions of the books they cover. They could, that is, provided that a mechanism is created for correcting errors.

LOCAL ADAPTATIONS

Someone may object that it is impossible for all libraries to accept a shared cataloging record without all kinds of local adaptations to fit special circumstances. How do we handle the plethora of local adaptations? Are they merely the result of downright refusal to be satisfied with even the thought of using an established entry?

We cannot sidestep the need for local adaptations by pretending that there is no need. While the needs are probably far fewer than library practice admits, there are instances in which a local library must revise the standard cataloging record in order to give effective service. For example, in the National Library of Medicine *Current Catalog* (2: N-566, Jan.-Sept. 1967) there is an entry as follows:

> Citizens Commission on Graduate Medical Education. The graduate education of physicians. [Chicago, 1966] xii, 114 p. . . . I. Title.

Except for subject entries, no other added entries are traced. While the main entry is proper, this cataloging record poses a problem, because it is incomplete. The work is a report commissioned by the American Medical Association and distributed by its Council on Medical Education, and a reader may look for it under the name of either the AMA or its Council. And like many reports of major interest (for example, the DeBakey Report and the Report of the Warren Commission), this one is popularly known by the name of the chairman of the reporting body; in this case, as the Millis Report. Any library hoping to retrieve this document whenever needed must make at least two added entries not in the established cataloging record. My own library catalog now contains a record for this work much different from the one it, itself, was responsible for establishing in the *National Union Catalog* (Jan.-March 1968, pt. 1, p. 64).

Another situation in which the cataloging record must be altered by the local library is when a data error, such as a misspelling, occurs. The usual percentage of human errors creeps through even on the Library of Congress's MARC tapes. (The computer, it seems, is not much better than the typewriter in helping us to spell. While it is possible for a computer to compare an entry with previously established entries and report similarities so that a human editor can examine them to determine whether an error has been made, the computer cannot do much if the file contains nothing similar to the newly entered name.) When a local library discovers an error of this kind, it is compelled to correct it.

These examples, along with the previous mention of variant headings for congress volumes, should be sufficient to demonstrate that the need for local adaptations in shared cataloging is not merely an illusion of perfectionist members of the library profession; it is sometimes a genuine need, and means must exist to meet it.

Certain notes must be added to cataloging data in local libraries to describe unique features of their copies, such as an inscription or a defect. These can be added to the established record as local option notes. But the examples just given are of basic elements of cataloging records which are inadequate for general use, as well as for the particular local library that revises them. What is required, therefore, is a feedback method whereby essential corrections to the standard record may be proposed by any user, reviewed by a coordinator of some kind, and acted upon when appropriate in order to give all users the benefit of the needed changes. In the national on-line computerized system which we may have in the future, such updating should be fairly painless. But, for the present, it is very difficult to erase the entry in the published catalog or printed card and notify all who used the earlier version of the changes. This is one reason why advances in computer storage and distribution of cataloging data are important—indeed, essential—to the solution of the major problem of descriptive cataloging, our present inability to obtain and use a standard cataloging record which is satisfactory. The fact that computers may soon tackle this storage and distribution job, including updating where needed, is the bright ray of hope ahead in this field.

COMMUNICATION STRUCTURE

The structure for communicating standard cataloging data in the United States today consists of published volumes of the *National Union Catalog;* printed cards, proofsheets, published volumes, and magnetic tapes of the Library of Congress; Library of Congress cataloging published in *Publishers' Weekly* and *American Book Publishing Record;* and sometimes alternate versions of the data in the National Library of Medicine *Current Catalog* and the *Cumulative Book Index*, to name the sources which come foremost to mind. Recent arrangements by the Library of Congress to accept the cataloging done for the national bibliographies of some other countries have increased the speed and comprehensiveness of data available from the present communication structure. But, the structure tomorrow (or more likely, the day after tomorrow) may be a shared computer data bank fed by many libraries, although primarily by the Library of Congress, the National Library, and large university and other research libraries, just as the National Union Catalog is fed now. From this data bank, libraries across the country would be able to obtain instantaneously the established cataloging record for any book by means of an on-line information terminal or, if no record were in the data bank, to enter their own original cataloging for the benefit of all succeeding inquirers of the data bank. The very small libraries, so long as the cost of information terminals continued to be beyond their reach, should be able to arrange for the services of a terminal at another nearby library, perhaps by mailing batches of requests to be searched in the computerized data bank.

CITING IN THE LITERATURE

But even if libraries succeed in standardizing, how can an entire nation ever agree in practice on a particular cataloging entry for a particular work, even if it should agree on the rules for constructing entries? Not everyone can be trained in the rules—certainly not the general public of library users—and lists will continue to be made either in ignorance or in disregard of the rules, let alone with varying results from applying them.

The sad complaint of a book reviewer in a recent issue of *Nature* emphasizes this dilemma: "It is a pity," he writes,

> that this good book is a "conference proceedings." As such, despite the useful and valuable information it contains, the book will be neglected. It will be misplaced in the library, in that it will not be among the current literature; it will be difficult to refer to and it will be tedious to write out the references to the articles which it contains.
>   This seems to be the fate of all conference proceedings now, with the exception of those published in the normal literature such as *Discussions of the Faraday Society*. By being produced sometimes under the name of an editor and sometimes not, they inevitably seem to be filed in the wrong places. Quoting articles from them in papers or in reviews is always difficult: for anyone who does not agree, I suggest that they write out for themselves a short form reference of the article contained in this volume by G. Porter on page 79, working from the full reference to the book shown above. I suggest there will be as many versions as people attempting the problem and many of them will be ambiguous and lengthy.

The reviewer suggests that a solution would be for publishers to make all their conference proceedings numbered parts of series, which could then be cited by series title and volume, like a periodical. "In this way," he states, "our librarians would both wish to obtain them and know where to file them; they would be easy to reference."[17]

It is not likely, of course, that this would be a real solution, even if a consistent form of series title were followed. One of the most ambiguous situations in descriptive cataloging is where there is a choice of either series title entry on the one hand or one of the several kinds of entries for a volume with separate authors, editors, or title, on the other. It is not enough to cite a paper by Egger and Flynn as being in *Progress in Brain Research* 27: 165-182, 1967, when many librarians, contrary to our reviewer's hopes, may have the volume on order with a single entry in their catalogs under "Adey, W. Ross, ed." with the specific title of *Structure and Function of the Limbic System*, even though the order slip may state that this title is volume 27 of *Progress in Brain Research.* On the other hand, there are equal difficulties when libraries cannot afford to catalog series volumes as separate works (the monographic supplements to journals such as the Scandinavian *Acta*, for example) and regretfully are compelled to trust that library users will know the series title and volume and thus find the monograph that the card catalog fails to reveal under its author, editor, or title.

The only apparent way to improve citation practices is to publicize the use of standard cataloging records. The standard record could decide the question, for example, of whether the series volume should be cited as a separate title or as merely part of the series, and even further, could decide the exact entry heading. With the standard record on hand, we would all know enough to cite volume 27 of *Progress in Brain Research*, for example, not under editor Adey, but under "Symposium on the Structure and Function of the Limbic System, Hakone, Japan, 1965." We need to be able to point to a sacred text, a bibliographic bible, as it were, in which the authoritative entry, the specific entry for the specific work in question, is clearly, accurately, and fully established for all to use without question. This suggestion may have repelling overtones of authoritarianism, but it is intended to help bring order out of chaos, perhaps an end that justifies the means.

How do we reach the community of citers—authors who list books and papers as references in their own works? The chaotic world of free-for-all citation practices seems almost beyond reform. We must admit that it can never be expected to reach the state of orderliness which should be possible in library catalogs. But insofar as those catalogs have reasonably complete cataloging data for each book, filed under multiple entries, the brief or erratic citation in the literature, so long as it is not grossly inaccurate, should permit a successful search of a library's holdings' files. It is primarily in the use of single-entry lists where the so-called "dirty" citation causes trouble, and it is because the choice of main entry is crucial to the use of a single-entry file that the advantages of using standard entries must be publicized among authors and other library users. They will never all be persuaded or trained to discover and use standard entries, but it is very possible that many would change their habits as knowledge of the standard entries becomes easier to obtain. Some progress would be better than none, and for this partial improvement I think we should work hard: first, by intensifying our efforts to reach agreement among libraries on using an established description of a particular work, second, by developing a computerized cataloging data bank and a rapid means of sharing it, and, third, by publicizing and encouraging readers' use of the standard data.

SUMMARY

The problem, then, is our failure to agree on a standard way of describing a book so that everyone can refer to it without confusion and libraries can save cataloging time and money. The technological help of computers is gradually making possible a system for rapid sharing of new and old cataloging data among many libraries throughout the country. Libraries unable to maintain their own computers may be able to afford terminals linking with computers and cataloging data banks elsewhere. To distribute standard cataloging data beyond libraries to the wider community of library users is a more difficult matter and one less likely of adequate solution, but the prospects of at least visible improvement are good once librarians get their own houses in order.

NOTES

[1] Daniel Gore, A shortcut to book catalogs? Libr. J. 93: 1110-1113, March 15, 1968.

[2] Fred A. Tate and James L. Wood, Libraries and abstracting and indexing services—a study in interdependency. Libr. Trends 16: 360-361, Jan. 1968.

[3] Where should books be kept? Nature 216: 881, Dec. 2, 1967.

[4] Verner W. Clapp, Retrospect and prospect. Libr. Trends 16: 173-174, July 1967.

[5] American Library Association, et al. Anglo-American Cataloging Rules. North American Text. (Chicago: American Library Association, 1967), xxi.

[6] Bernice F. Field, The new catalog code: The general principles and the major changes. Libr. Res. Tech. Serv. 10: 421-436, Fall 1966.

[7] American Library Association. Division of Cataloging and Classification. A.L.A. Cataloging Rules for Author and Title Entries. Edited by Clara Beetle. 2d ed. (Chicago: American Library Association, 1949), xxi.

[8] Library of Congress. Descriptive Cataloging Division. Rules for Descriptive Cataloging in the Library of Congress. (Adopted by the American Library Association.) Washington, 1949, vi, 141 p.

[9] Seymour Lubetzky, Cataloging Rules and Principles; a Critique of the A.L.A. Rules for Entry and a Proposed Design for Their Revision. (Washington: Processing Department, Library of Congress, 1953), ix, p. 61.

[10] U. S. Federal Council for Science and Technology. Committee on Scientific and Technical Information. Standard for Descriptive Cataloging of Government Scientific and Technical Reports. Revision No. 1. (Washington: Clearinghouse for Federal Scientific and Technical Information, Oct. 1966), iii. (AD 641 092, PB 173 314.)

[11] Lubetzky, Op. cit., pp. 57-60.

[12] Jeanne B. North, A look at the new COSATI Standard. Spec. Libr. 58: 582-584, Oct. 1967.

[13] I. A. Warheit, Bibliographic identification and organization. Amer. Docum. 3: 105-110, Apr. 1952.

[14] Current Catalog to broaden coverage. Nat. Libr. Med. News 22: 3, Dec. 1967.

[15] Lehigh Univ., etc. Cited in: Curr. Cat. 3: 49, Feb. 26, 1968.

[16] Libr. Congr. Inform. Bull. 26: 183-185, March 9, 1967. (Amplified in Libr. Congr. Cat. Serv. Bull. 79-81, 1967.)

[17] Peter Borrell, [Review of] Reactivity of the Photoexcited Organic Molecule. . . . 1967. Nature 216: 900, Dec. 2, 1967.

Convergence Toward Common Standards in Machine-Readable Cataloging

C. D. Gull

"The adoption of the MARC II format for the communication of bibliographic information by the three National Libraries of the U.S.A. makes it possible for those libraries to converge on the remaining necessary common standards for machine-readable cataloging".

The Directors of the three National Libraries of the United States have announced their joint adoption of the Machine-Readable Cataloging (MARC II) format for the communication of bibliographic information . . . "[1] This format provides the identification (tags) for the set of bibliographic data elements required for monographs. Their decision was based on the first recommendation of the National Libraries Task Force on Automation and other Cooperative Services, which was forwarded to them in February 1968.

While this adoption does not commit each library to include all the data elements described, it is the essential step in convergence toward common standards in machine-readable cataloging.

The significance of this format and of its acceptance by the three National Libraries of the United States can be illustrated by comparison with present practice. Just as there has been for many years an accepted standard format for the printing of bibliographic information on the traditional catalog card, including the positioning of the data and the typefaces used, the MARC II format will now make it possible for bibliographic components to be identified uniformly for computer manipulation. Magnetic tapes can be produced in a standard format that will be intelligible to any computer programmed to accept it. Thus, the output of the three libraries may then be utilized in the development of bibliographies, union lists, and other products and services. Furthermore, other libraries will be able to merge their bibliographic contributions with entries on the MARC II tapes.

Agreement on this format is a stimulating demonstration of the three National Libraries' mutual desire to extend the usefulness of their collections and services through the application of new technological capabilities wherever economically feasible, and it opens the way for further development throughout the library and scholarly communities. The adoption of MARC II by the three National Libraries will facilitate the exchange of cataloging data and bring the creation of a national data base of library cataloging information one step nearer reality.

Convergence on common standards for machine-readable cataloging is necessary now because powerful new machinery exists for application to bibliographic purposes, and because compatible communication systems exist for distributing the results of bibliographic processing to libraries, information centers, and individual users of information.

Intersystems compatibility has always been an unnoticed and unappreciated requirement in the use of libraries and their bibliographic apparatus; because of the development of computers, it has become an extremely significant requirement. Human beings meet this requirement in the conventional library; they can adjust to great variety in the format of the bibliographic data they use, which was collected for them in discrete packages by mechanical transport. In creating computerized bibliographic communication systems, electronic transport is substituted for mechanical transport, and the great variety of bibliographic data formats is no longer acceptable. The data must be fitted into a common format to achieve intersystems compatibility for a computerized bibliographic communication system.

In the computer field, compatibility is an intersystem characteristic, defined as "the quality of an [a computer] instruction to be translatable or

SOURCE: Reprinted from *Bulletin of the Medical Library Association*, 57 (January, 1969), pp. 28–35, by permission of the publisher. Originally presented as part of a general session on "Current Cataloging Problems" at the Sixty-seventh Annual Meeting of the Medical Library Association, Denver, Colorado, June 13, 1968.

executable on more than one class of computer."
It is the "characteristic . . . by which one computer may accept and process [programs and] data prepared by another computer without conversion or code modification." In complex systems, components "are often completely compatible electrically, logically, and mechanically with other systems components,"[2] although compatibility does not necessarily require identical machinery, programs, or data formats. Within one manufacturer's series of computers, compatibility may exist only from the smaller to the larger machines, or it may exist in both directions.

In the United States, there is a healthy diversity of computing systems which can be used for bibliographical purposes, and we know that the diversity and the rapid development and improvement of our computers are due to the manufacturers' competition for new customers. Compatibility among these systems is not an outstanding characteristic, however; and, as we at the National Library of Medicine enlarge the decentralized MEDLARS program, we are reminded daily of this fact.

The capability of intersystems convertibility has been developed to overcome the lack of intersystems compatibility among computer models.

Convertibility is the characteristic "of changing information from one form of representation to another; such as, from the language of one type of machine to that of another, or from magnetic tape to the printed page." Convertibility between two computer systems means that data and programs used for one system can be processed by machine for use on the other computer.[3]

THREE LEVELS OF STANDARDS

The standards needed for machine-readable cataloging can be assigned to three levels. The standard for the character set is on the fundamental level. The structure for the communication of bibliographic data is on the intermediate level of standards; this format is MARC II. The standards at the detail level permit the input and output operations to be performed; at this time the detail level standards include main entries, authority files, serials data elements, classification, and subject headings.

Because of its importance as well as its chronological place, MARC, the intermediate standard, is described next.

BRIEF HISTORY OF MARC: THE INTERMEDIATE STANDARD

Mr. Verner Warren Clapp has been a benevolent, forward-looking, and continuous influence on the development of standards for machine-readable cataloging. While he was President of the Council on Library Resources, the Council provided to the Library of Congress the means by which Dr. Gilbert W. King and his colleagues issued the report. "Automation and the Library of Congress." This report described the enormous potentialities for library work possessed by automation, dependent upon the conversion of the bibliographic record to a form in which it could be manipulated by machines. The Council commissioned Mr. Lawrence F. Buckland of Inforonics, Inc., to demonstrate a method employing typewriter-generated perforated paper tape to meet all forseeable bibliographic and typographic applications of cataloging data represented by Library of Congress catalog entries. These events occurred in 1964, when the MEDLARS system at the National Library of Medicine was providing a daily demonstration that a computer could be used for bibliographic purposes—in the preparation and publication of *Index Medicus* and for the retrieval of bibliographic data in response to individual requests.

In order to ascertain the acceptability to the library community of the proposed method of conversion, a meeting was held at the Library of Congress on January 11, 1965, under the joint sponsorship of the Library and the Committee on Automation of the Association of Research Libraries. The discussion elicited no serious obstacle to the adoption of the proposed conversion method, and Mr. Buckland's report was, with a few minor revisions, reproduced for general distribution.

Among the conclusions recorded at the meeting were these: "Most participants favored coding as much data as possible to assure maximum retrieval in the future." "Agreement on form of input is desirable, and standardization should be more nearly attainable in a machine system. If LC makes the decision on the form of all bibliographical information, this could become the best single source of standardization."[4]

Three LC staff members were soon delegated to analyze cataloging data from the machine-processing viewpoint. The leader of this team was Mrs. Henriette D. Avram, who has since secured her place in the history of computerized cataloging by carefully nurturing the original ideas into the present MARC II format, which has been adopted by the three National Libraries, by COSATI (Committee on Scientific and Technical Information), by the International Atomic Energy Agency, by three divisions of the American Library Association, by the United Kingdom MARC Project for the British National Bibliography, and by the United States of America Standards Institute.

The LC staff report was issued in June 1965, as "A Proposed Format for a Standardized Machine-Readable Catalog Record" (5). A "record" was defined there as containing all of the cataloging data pertaining to a particular work. It is analogous in concept to the unit catalog card, and "record" is used to characterize the data transcribed by a cataloger on an input form or the data transcribed onto magnetic tape or some other storage medium. The report outlined the contents of a machine-readable record, described the manner of representing the bibliographic data, and applied the concepts of "tags" and of "fixed" and "variable fields" to the data.

The report identified "a field as a unit of information which is explicitly tagged and named" and identified two kinds of fields; fixed and variable. "A fixed field contains information which is always expressed in the same number of characters thus readily accessible for machine processing." "A variable field contains information the length of which cannot be predetermined because it cannot be controlled." i.e., it reflects the variable information taken from the monograph being cataloged.

The need for tags was recognized in the Inforonics report. 'A Tag is an input label" serving "as a method if defining, specifying, and locating what follows in the record and allowing the flexibility of including or deleting the information following the tag in any display or in any computer processing. Any information in the record that is not tagged is lost in the body of the data for machine processing. Tagging in a machine system is comparable to human recognition in a manual system."[5]

After LC's intensive consideration of Planning Memorandum #3 and discussion with the library community, a Second Conference on Machine-Readable Catalog Copy was held on November 22, 1965, at LC. The discussions concerned the fields to be represented in machine-readable form and possible magnetic tape formats with fixed and variable field data. The great interest shown by the participants strengthened the belief that the Library of Congress should begin an experimental magnetic tape distribution service as soon as possible.

The Library of Congress asked for and, in December 1965, received a grant of $130,000 from the Council on Library Resources to initiate the MARC Pilot Project. The grant supported contracts to develop the required procedures for data conversion and the computer programs for input, file maintenance, distribution of tapes, etc. The United Aircraft Corporation contracted to provide the necessary design and development support, including the computer programs for processing the cataloging data at the Library of Congress and for indexing and printing the bibliographic record for participating libraries. UAC also contracted to provide operating procedures for collecting, editing, transcribing, and distributing the data. Programmed Services, Inc., contracted to assist in the cost evaluation of the project. Sixteen libraries were selected early in 1966 to participate in the project; their representatives met at the Third Conference on Machine-Readable Catalog Copy at the Library of Congress on February 25, 1966. Regular distribution of the tapes was started in October 1966 and extended beyond the planned closing date of June 1967.

In March 1967, the MARC staff began a formal evaluation of the MARC Pilot Project format, resulting in the presentation of a preliminary MARC II format to the library participants during the MARC meeting held at the San Francisco American Library Association Conference in June 1967. At this meeting, LC also announced that a full-scale operational MARC subscription service would be started in 1968 and that the pilot project would continue during fiscal year 1968. A Fourth Conference on Machine-Readable Catalog Copy was held at LC on December 4, 1967, to discuss the MARC II format and a proposed character set for bibliographic data.

MARC II continues to use the definitions of record, fixed and variable fields, and tags as in the MARC Pilot Project. It states that some tags may be used as often as desired and in any order. Although the tags in the pilot project were immediately associated with the texts of the variable fields, in MARC II, the tags are collected in Field 2 of a record as part of the directory which indexes the locations of the variable fields within a record. Each entry in the computer-generated directory contains a tag, the length of the variable field in number of characters, and the starting character position within the record. The use of a directory facilitates the location of variable information within a record for processing and retrieval purposes. An end-of-field symbol (field terminator) has been introduced at the end of the text of each variable field. Delimiters are also used within a variable field to separate data elements within a tagged field; for example, to distinguish pages from illustrations in the collation field.

Although MARC II is limited to monographs, the structure of MARC II is intended to be used in the cataloging of other materials, such as serials, maps, music, etc. The MARC II structure, therefore, provides the basis for current and future agreement on the standard bibliographic access points for other materials.

In order to permit the exchange of bibliographic data among libraries and to permit the development of a network of library and information services, it is essential that the structure of MARC II be a standardized communications format, so that an institution wanting to send or receive data needs only a single translation program to convert from its local format to the communications format. The specifications of MARC II are drawn to meet this requirement.

THE CHARACTER SET: THE FUNDAMENTAL STANDARD

The development of MARC II has included the adoption and modification of some of the standards from the United States of America Standards Institute for the interchange of information on magnetic tape. One of the standards is that the length of a physical record on tape is 2.048 characters. While the majority of bibliographic entries will be shorter than this, some will require two or more physical records. While there will be one leader and one directory for each logical record, a data field may be split between two physical records in MARC II.

The number of characters required for bibliographic purposes, commonly known as the character set, is larger than the 128 provided by the standard seven-bit ASCII code, but most of the additional characters can be accommodated within the capability of an extended code of eight bits providing 256 characters. By dropping some of the standard characters in the seven-bit code, it is possible to introduce a shift-out control character enabling the use of the extra characters afforded by using eight bits. A code will stay in the eight-bit mode until a shift-in control character is

reached. The eight-bit code will permit libraries to use computer-driven photocomposing machines and to transmit information to other libraries with the seven-bit code. A receiving library might reduce this to a six-bit code by removing the eighth bit and the sixth bit and continuing to process and then print the bibliographic information on a conventional line printer limited to the sixty-four characters of the six-bit code. However, the set of sixty-four characters implies a very high degree of intelligibility for a common use among all libraries.

The problem of transliteration is closely bound up with the decisions about the character set. The number of characters available through MARC II and through the communications system represents the upper limit of the number of characters into which various alphabets can be transliterated. Fortunately the problem of transliteration does not appear to be too difficult at this time. The Working Group on Descriptive Cataloging Practices compared the transliteration tables in use by the three National Libraries and found no substantial difference in practice.

The number of characters in the character set is ample to accommodate the needs of all three libraries. Although it appears probable that the three libraries will follow the same practices, it may not be of practical difficulty to users if differences in use were continued, because presumably the source of each catalog entry would be clearly shown, and the source could be compared with a note describing the variations in transliteration practice.

DETAILED STANDARDS

Agreement on Descriptive Cataloging Practices:
The three National Libraries are very close to complete agreement in their descriptive cataloging practices. This situation was the pleasant conclusion of the Working Group on Descriptive Cataloging Practices in the winter of 1967.

Such a conclusion was unexpected after decades of controversy over cataloging rules and the continuing differences in practices of the three libraries. The quick and ready agreement achieved appears to come from two causes:

(1) the realization that uniform practices are inherently desirable and acceptable to accommodate computerized processing, and
(2) the existence of the MARC II tags, which provided a new way of looking at descriptive cataloging practices. It was easier to compare the projected application of the forty tags for fixed and variable fields of MARC II than to compare the practices, rule by rule,

of the three libraries against the *Anglo-American Cataloging Rules.*

The new consideration of uniform practices revealed immediately thirty-five areas of fundamental agreement among the three libraries and six areas of minor disagreement. It was then possible to agree upon recommendations for the resolution of the disagreements. I am happy to report that the National Library of Medicine has already introduced the necessary changes to conform with the practice of the other two libraries in these areas. It is interesting to note that this agreement on recommendations means that MARC is being asked to provide two additional tags and that the American Library Association is being asked to make two changes in the cataloging rules.

The areas of agreement, including the six recommendations, do not require that the National Libraries provide completely identical cataloging, but only that they follow uniform practices where the joint use of computers or the services to the public would be hampered by following different practices.

One of the most recent developments toward standardization appears to be the imminent adoption of standard book numbers as an international or universal book numbering scheme. This is an outgrowth of the plan initiated in 1967 in Great Britain, and it will require the cooperation of publishers and libraries. Each publisher is assigned a prefix and a block of title numbers. The code is expansive enough to allow for a very large number of publishers with few titles and for a small number of publishers with very large publishing lists. Although the Library of Congress intends to include these numbers on its printed catalog cards, they will not supersede nor eliminate the Library of Congress card number.

Codes for Language, Place, and Date: Standardization is also going forward on codes for the representation of language, place, and date. As to dates, a four-digit field can represent any year, and a six-digit code can be used to represent a twentieth century date, allowing two digits for year, month, and day in that order. This code is likely to coincide with the standards of the USASI and the Bureau of the Budget. Since bibliographic dates frequently contain years from two centuries, there will be an eight-digit code, allowing four digits for the year and two each for month and date.

The code for place will probably be a two-digit alphabetic code with an upper limit of 676 codes. Over 300 place names have been accepted and coded for the list. The place names are a mixture of English names for nations, geographic areas, and political subdivisions, such as states of the United States, provinces of Canada, and republics of the Soviet Union, but not names of the principal cities of the world.

The code for languages is similarly selective. Out of the 17,000 known written and spoken languages of the world, a list of some 400 written languages has been further reduced to approximately 140 languages coded in a three-letter mnemonic code.

Main Entry and Authority Files: The effort at standardizing the choice of main entry and in preparing authority records has been assigned to one working group for initial investigation.

The practice of superimposition at LC and NLM was excluded from consideration. In this practice, the libraries may use existing headings for newly received materials even though these headings do not agree with the new *Anglo-American Cataloging Rules.*

Investigation showed six cases in which the libraries vary in the choice of main entry (principally serials) when they establish new headings and six exceptions in determining the form of heading. Five examples of the omission of added entries have also been discussed, since they contribute to the growth of the authority files.

The consequences of pooling authority file information are seriously affected by the size of the files: LC has the largest, approximately 1,400,000 entries; NLM has 150,000; and NAL, 6,300. Although NLM and NAL have both attempted to follow LC main entry practice for many years, variation does exist, and its extent is unknown. A project is underway to explore the problems of pooling the authority files.

Classification: No effort at standardization of classification has been undertaken as yet. The problems of standardization in classification are likely to be minimal, since NAL adopted the LC classification in January 1966, and NLM adopted it in 1946. The principal variation is that NLM developed and uses Classes QS through QZ and Class W, in place of Classes QM, QP, QR, and R, which are used in the other two libraries.

Serials Data Program: At present the Serials Data Program is the largest effort at standardization. A Working Group of the Task Force is overseeing this work, and staff members at LC are working on this in conjunction with a contractor, Nelson Associates.

In contrast to the situation for MARC I and II, in which the bibliographic data for monographs is complete at the time of cataloging, the problem of determining the bibliographic elements for serials is that the data vary over a period of time. This characteristic complicates the coding of the serials data elements.

In developing MARC I and MARC II, the personnel found that the work of collecting the data had been accomplished over a long period of time, and the data was readily available by sampling the printed catalog cards. This situation was not true of serials data elements. Consequently, it was necessary to survey the serials control efforts in nearly two hundred and fifty institutions that were undertaking to automate the control of serial publications. About twenty-five efforts were given careful study, and over two hundred serial data elements were extracted from these efforts. These two hundred data elements formed the basis for the contractual study of consumer needs performed by Nelson Associates and scheduled for release in late May 1968. Using the results of that study, an effort will be made to reduce the two hundred data elements to a smaller number.

One of the most significant of the serial data elements will be that selected for identifying a serial. In parallel with a standard book·number from monographs, a universal numbering scheme for serials has been proposed often in the literature and concretely to the Working Group on the Serials Data Program. It is probable that some arrangement can be established by which the United States of America Standards Institute can become involved in developing the universal numbering scheme for serials.

Subject Headings: Because the three National Library directors place a very high priority on compatibility of subject headings, the Working Group on Subject Headings has been striving towards compatibility very earnestly, but the effort is complicated by differing practices. NLM uses its subject headings for cataloging monographic and serial titles and for very specific indexing of periodical articles. The NAL has developed its Agricultural/Biological Vocabulary experimentally with the same objective, but still uses its separate authority lists. LC uses its authority list for cataloging monographic and serial entries, not for indexing.

The basic possibilities for standardization are:

(1) a single authority list for the three libraries which are consequently identical and self-coding in character, or

(2) separate authority lists.

A single authority list has the possibility of producing the same headings in all printed products, regardless of which library is printing, or by the use of reference tables, the possibility of printing individual headings in the individual libraries from a common list. In the case of separate authority lists, they could be keyed to a single code, or separate codes could be used with conversion tables permitting the effect of using a single code. The concept of a single authority list is being seriously investigated.

The Working Group has been considering the differences in structure of the subject heading authority lists in the three libraries; the use or failure to use the most specific term; frequency of change of headings; the use of subheadings; the order in the arrangement of subheadings such as topical, geographical, language, and form subheadings; the old question of whether to choose place divided by subject or subject divided by place; and whether to use direct or indirect subdivision for geographic headings.

The urgent need for compatible subject headings and the flexibility of the MARC II format are illustrated by the decision of the Library of Congress to make available in magnetic tape form the text of the seventh edition of *Subject Headings Used in the Dictionary Catalog of the Library of Congress*, which at its publication was the largest computer-produced publication of the Library of Congress.

IMPLICATIONS OF CONVERGENCE ON STANDARDS

The present convergence on standards for machine-readable cataloging implies that a Joint Bibliographic Data Bank can be created and operated by the three National Libraries. Although the physical characteristics and geographic location of the Data Bank are as yet undefined, the requirements for using the Data Bank can be predicted. Any use of the data will require a *search* capability to find data, a *consult* capability to allow visual inspection on a CRT screen, and a *print* capability to record what is found or what was processed into useful arrangements.

The basic identification for any monograph or serial becomes the Standard Book Number or the Universal Serial Number respectively.

Any bibliographic data can be contributed to the Joint Data Bank by one, two, or three of the National Libraries. For entries contributed by two or three Libraries, there is always the possibility that variations will occur in the data chosen to fill out the blank for a given tag. Excluding variations which are errors to be corrected, other variations will contribute to the usefulness of the total bibliographic entry without violating cataloging or standardizing rules, such as the inclusion of both R and W class numbers for a medical book or the addition of a specialized subject heading to supplement a more general one. Users will need to have such variations attributed to the libraries providing them. MARC II indicators could be modified to show the source of the variations in a tagged field.

The proposed establishment of a Joint Data Bank implies that the system will thoroughly process each entry before it is added to the Joint Data Bank. This prospect argues that each Library should provide to the Joint Data Bank a full record for each entry, with no specified maximum number of filled-out tags. A full record would enable the updating computer to make more effective searches to prevent the possible duplication within the Joint Data Bank of one original item under two or more forms of entry then would a record limited to a minimum number of tags.

Many cataloging decisions in the past have been based on the necessity of economy in the creation, operation, and maintenance of large dictionary catalogs. The introduction of the computer into cataloging has reduced the need for this kind of economy and will permit greater attention to the needs of users of the catalogs and indexes by allowing an increase in the number of access points with increased depth of indexing.

After studying cataloging rules and directions for the choice of main entries, secondary entries, classification numbers, and subject headings, catalogers are often required to choose among two or more possibilities for one bibliographic element when they are cataloging an individual work.

The two requirements, of choosing among possibilities, and of attempting to be economical in assigning access points, have interacted to seriously reduce the number of catalog entries that catalogers can produce per day, in the past and currently.

The adoption of the MARC tags for bibliographic data elements provides an explicit structure into whose blank spaces a cataloger can place all the readily available information and against which he can see by inspection whether he has sufficient information to form an acceptable entry. Since each MARC tag for a variable field can be used more than once for an entry, there is no requirement that a single choice need be made to fill out one tag. Since two or more easy choices can often be made more speedily than one difficult choice, there can be hope that the use of MARC II will increase the catalogers' daily production.

And now a concluding word on "convergence." While the MLA Program Committee chose the title of this report, it was my mode of travel, the family auto with vacation trailer attached, which demonstrated the nature of the convergence we can anticipate for machine-readable cataloging. We travelled on much of the magnificent Interstate Defense Highway System, which the Bureau of Public Roads is linking together, section by section, all built to standards which are improved over the years. Although the divided lanes of these highways appeared to converge at the endless horizon, they remained apart as we drove ever forward. In a similar fashion the three National Libraries are linking their parts of the national information and bibliographic effort together, but whenever we may pause to contemplate the actual situation from time to time in the future, we will still see at each pause the need for more convergence and for improved standards.

NOTES

[1] U.S. Library of Congress. Information Systems Office. The MARC II Format; A Communications Format for Bibliographic Data, prepared by Henriette D. Arvram, John F. Knapp, and Lucia J. Rather. Washington, Jan. 1968. 167 p. Supplement 1, 7 p.

[2] Charles J. Sippl, Computer Dictionary and Handbook. (Indianapolis: Sams, 1966), p. 65.

[3] Ibid., p. 80.

[4] Buckland, Lawrence F. The Recording of Library of Congress Bibliographical Data in Machine Form. Rev. (Washington, D.C.: Council on Library Resources, 1965), pp. viii-ix.

[5] U.S. Library of Congress. A Proposed Format for a Standardized Machine-Readable Catalog Record; A Preliminary Draft. . . . Washington, D.C., June 1965, pp. 8-12.

DESCRIPTIVE CATALOGING

The Catalog

The catalog whether card, book, sheaf, or film provides the major if not the only key to the mass of materials in a collection. Its functions are directly tied to both the classification system and the descriptive cataloging code adopted. They, in turn, directly influence the type of catalog.

The catalog has remained a mystery to practically every one from the librarian to the patron. Systematic studies are few and far between and their results have been open to considerable question. In the United States the card catalog has proven to be the most popular form to date and none of the others have yet begun to compete. It has kept us wed to the 3 X 5 catalog card.

The form and substance of the catalog has often come under direct attack. Nowhere is this attack more apparent than in the book catalog, now computer-produced and maintained. Characteristics of such catalogs run the gamut from the very detailed to the very simple. The element which has changed the most is the function of the catalog. Should it, as history has dictated, tell not only what the library has, where the library shelves it, but also try to bring together all the works of one author under one name and the works on the same subject together under similar or related headings?

The Function of the Catalog

L. Jolley

> *"The catalog is an instrument of communication. Its function is to communicate information about the books it records."*

The cataloger's art is not in general held in high esteem either by the users of the catalog or by new entrants to the profession of librarianship. Both tend to think of cataloging as an essentially simple process which catalogers render unnecessarily difficult. Many commercial and scientific readers tend to speak of the catalog as "the card index" with the implication that cataloging is merely one form of filing. More informed critics complain that catalogers spend their time in the meticulous study of minor points which are of no practical importance, and in the careful application of elaborate distinctions without question as to their point or use. Such criticism is not entirely without foundation. The work of the cataloger demands great accuracy and a constant attention to many points of detail. It is easy to devote so much attention to the quality of execution of the work that no energy is left for considering the object of the work. The young cataloger is discouraged when every mistake is considered equally culpable and no opening is provided for initiative and imagination. His discouragement is a lamentable and unnecessary waste for there is no aspect of librarianship which has greater need of initiative and imagination and which offers more scope for real scholarship than cataloging.

That this should be so is not surprising for it is the function of the catalog to interpret the library to the reader. It is not necessary to stress the importance of the catalog. No large library can function without an adequate catalog and in almost every library the use which can be made of the library's resources depends very largely on the quality of its catalog. The function of a library is to provide a reader with the books he needs and it is the catalog which makes possible the discharge of this function by bringing the reader's needs into relation with the resources of the library. Other instruments pursue the same end—classification, display, the personal knowledge of members of staff—but the catalog is more important than any of these because it is more permanent, more exhaustive and more precise. It is not surprising that many libraries take steps to ensure that a copy of the catalog will be preserved if disaster should overtake the library. The catalog is the record of what has gone into the building of a library and can, if need arises, be the guide to its reconstruction.

The catalog is an instrument of communication. Its function is to communicate information about the books it records. If it fails to supply information then it fails to discharge its function. This does not necessarily mean that it is an imperfect instrument. Even the best instrument will not function if it is incorrectly used. It does mean that in designing a catalog the cataloger must concern himself primarily with the object of communication. Anything of whatever nature which distracts from the achievement of this object is to be condemned.

It is widely believed that for most of the first half of this century catalogers were distracted from their chief end and became absorbed in the development of the catalog for its own sake. Certainly the cataloger who held that a catalog entry should be so designed as to enable a bibliographer to use it as a substitute for actual examination of the book, or the other cataloger who defended the retention of authors' dates in Library of Congress headings on the ground that these dates were often more accurate than those to be found in reference books, was not thinking of the catalog primarily as a tool for providing the user with the information he needs. But the weakness of the ALA rules springs from other causes than an undue attention to form and style in cataloging, qualities which in moderation are eminently desirable. In part they spring from a failure of nerve. The growth of cooperative cataloging made it seem essential that catalogers in different libraries

SOURCE: Reprinted from L. Jolley, *The Principles of Cataloging* (London: Crosby Lockwood, 1960), p. 1–11, by permission of the publisher.

should select the same heading for the same book. The ALA code tries to secure this by providing specific rules for almost every difficulty which a cataloger may meet. It fails to be exhaustive and what is more important it fails to present an orderly and consistent development of a few leading principles. It is not necessary at this date to enlarge on the deficiencies of the code. There is general agreement that it is cluttered up with overlapping and redundant rules. Its specificity leads to the multiplication of exceptions to rules and even to exceptions to exceptions, whilst the unity of broad categories is obscured. There are two distinct and in part contradictory roots for all the weaknesses. One is the anxiety to possess a "correct" answer to all difficulties and "correct" answers are constantly given without any explanation of the relevance of their correctness to the function of the catalog. The other is the continuance of the tradition stemming from Cutter which permits a valid principle to be abandoned whenever it is thought that its maintenance will result in a heading which will not seem "natural" to a reader.

The ALA code is now being revised. There are two impulses behind its revision. American library administrators have been worried by the constant increase in cataloging costs and the inability of cataloging staffs to keep pace with accessions. High cost is not necessarily an indication of inefficiency. The various electronic information retrieval devices which are being experimented with are a good deal more expensive than a conventional catalog. More important is the growing dissatisfaction of catalogers with their own work. Despite its elaboration the catalog was not functioning as well as it should. It was not merely that the reader sometimes found it a slow and difficult business to extract the information he needed. It was not impossible on occasions for catalogers themselves to have difficulties in answering apparently simple questions from their own catalog. As far as the subsequent move towards "simplified cataloging" was simply an administrative effort to reduce expense it did not necessarily involve any question of principle. It is possible to decide to cut out certain features of a catalog without necessarily altering the concept of the desirable catalog. The catalog may function in its truncated state but if it functions less efficiently the real answer is to increase the funds available for the cataloging department. The cataloger's approach to simplified cataloging is quite different. The cataloger endeavours to define the objects of the catalog and to distinguish the means by which these objects can be most economically achieved. If he rejects parts of existing practice it is because he considers either that they are irrelevant to the attainment of these objects or actually harmful.

The object of the catalog is to serve the needs of the reader. What questions may a reader legitimately put to the catalog? Surely none which is not directly related to the tracing of books. In this sense at least a catalogue is a "finding list." The implications of this position will be developed in the next chapter. But the catalog is not concerned solely with tracing a particular book. It serves to answer the questions: Is this book in the library? What editions of this book are in the library? What books by this author are in the library? Not all these questions are of equal importance and not all can be answered with equal certainty. The second question hides a multitude of snares which will also be considered later. In general, however, it would be agreed that a catalog should answer all these questions and that most of the difficulties of cataloging spring from the fact that the entry which will answer the first question most directly will not always answer the second or third. Books may change titles from edition to edition and authors names.

It is the necessity of answering all these questions that prevents the adoption of one method of disposing of cataloging difficulties which is sometimes urged by interested readers and even by some catalogers. It is admitted that it is often extremely difficult to know which is the correct heading under which to enter a book and still more difficult to know which will be the heading under which the reader will look. Why not then adopt the practice of the annual indexes issued by the book trade and enter under all headings under which a reader could possibly look without worrying too much about the choice of a main entry? If this practice were adopted it would certainly be possible to answer the question "Is this book in the library?" It might, however, be a very tedious business to answer the two remaining questions as different editions of a book might be entered under different forms of title or under editor or author and the same author might be entered under various forms of his name. It would indeed be possible to assemble all the information needed but only by following a multitudinous labyrinth of cross-references. In addition it must be remembered that every nonessential entry adds to the size of the catalog. This is not merely a problem for the library administrator. After a certain point which the catalogs of all large libraries have already passed any increase in the size of the catalog tends to lead to an increase in the difficulty of use. The multiplicity of title entries which American catalogers make use of certainly facilitates the finding of particular books but by so greatly increasing the size of the catalog it possibly does more than counterbalance this service.

Amongst catalogers there are two trends in the approach towards the new ideal of the catalog. All are agreed on the necessity for a catalog code to be drawn up with the function of the catalog constantly in view, and for the new code to possess a simpler more coherent and more logical structure. The divergence arises over the extent to which logic and consistency can be taken as immutable guides. The sharp controversy over "form headings" and Lubetzky's denunciation of the concept of "natural headings" springs from different attitudes to this question. Lubetzky feels that the catalog will be a more efficient instrument if it is based on the consistent development of a few well defined principles. His opponents are prepared when such consistency results in a heading which seems unlikely to be of practical utility to depart from first principles and substitute a "natural heading." This controversy will be considered in more detail in connection with specific examples. It will then be necessary to try to decide how far the "natural heading" is merely a revival of Cutter's practice of deferring to the alleged preferences of the reader. It is clear that in one sense all catalogs must be based on the user's habits. This does not mean that the way to construct a better catalog is to study readers' approach to the present catalog and modify the rules to fit in with what is discovered. Such counting of heads is of little value as it takes no account either of the quality of the heads or of the source of what information they contain. The method a reader adopts for seeking information is determined primarily by the sources of his information although it is often modified by his carelessness or special interests. The cataloger works from the actual book he is describing. His aim is to provide a description which will be related to the other descriptions of the book which the reader is likely to encounter. These sources are very varied and very variable but together they form the whole nexus of bibliographic references of which the catalog is but a part. The catalog is an instrument of communication and all instruments of communication like language itself are social habits. The catalog

use process is a social habit. If the social habit is a simple one it is possible to inculcate a completely new habit in a very short time—a road traffic signal is an obvious example. The catalog is an extremely complex communication system. It must therefore be based on existing habits. This is not to say that it must follow them blindly. The library catalog is the most highly organized section of the whole network of bibliographic references, but it is not an independent section. The task of the cataloger is to select and develop the elements of consistency and logic in the existing habits. He cannot impose completely new habits. To this extent then all headings must be natural headings if they are to serve their purpose. In a closed system any conventional device can be employed to identify a book. The consecutive numbering of reports issued by a research organization or even the systems of coloured signals used by some organizations to indicate the origin of documents are obvious examples. The cataloger in a general library works in an open system where he cannot disregard the habits of publishers or even of compilers of telephone directories. The relevance of this statement is more obvious in a country such as Brazil where it remains often extremely difficult to determine what part of a man's name forms the surname, but it applies to more than names. It is a comparatively recent and European convention to regard the author as the most important distinguishing feature of a book. Most medieval western lists give books under titles and this is still the practice of some twentieth century Arabic catalogers. The starting point of any catalog is contemporary convention. The cataloger codifies existing practice. Codification is the precise and explicit development of principles already imperfectly and uncertainly present. It implies not grouping books according to the most specific peculiarities they may have in common with other books but arranging them in broad classes embodying the same basic principle. A code which encourages the cataloger and the user to treat their material according to its essential characteristics will be easier to apply and to use than one which attempts to deal with every possible form of published matter from spirit communications to reports of cemetery associations and Luther Colleges. It may not ensure that different catalogers will always arrive at the same method of treating the same material, but the ALA code gives plenty of opportunities for catalogers to differ.

The catalog is the codification of practice. It is not the development of first principles. The cataloguer is a social scientist not a philosopher. If a certain practice establishes itself decisively he follows it. There are many possible ways of cataloging periodicals which can be justified by logical argument. The existence of the *World List of Scientific Periodicals* and similar works has rendered these arguments unnecessary. Every scientific reader and many a nonscientific reader now thinks of the journals he needs in terms of their title or an abbreviation of their title. Title entry has always been a possible method but it is the practice of scientific writers which has now made it the almost universally accepted method. It can easily be shown to have many disadvantages in certain instances but when a new habit of reference is developing it is the task of the cataloger to assist and not to hinder. Above all the cataloger must not regard the more satisfactory treatment of a particular instance as being more important than the consistent treatment of a whole class. When a journal changes its name frequently it is more convenient to enter under the body responsible for the journal than under the title. It is much easier to deal with the quick changes of title of what was once the *American Journal of Diseases of Children* if the entry is under American Medical Association. It is not, however, possible to divide journals into those with fixed and variable titles. To enter under American Medical Association is perhaps to deal in the best way with this particular case, but it is to introduce a principle of confusion into the catalogue. It may, however, be possible to define a whole class of periodicals which are best entered under the body issuing them. Annual reports possess two characteristics. They usually contain administrative matter and are always the official pronouncement of the issuing body. In addition they often possess titles which are not permanent. A secretary may without thought change from "Annual report" to "Report for the year" and back again. The *World List* solves the problem of annual reports in a different way the merits of which do not need discussing at this point. The position which is being put forward is not that the cataloger should follow the practice of any authority which has sufficient weight. This would be futile as there is usually another authority to be cited on the other side. It is when some authority has established a bibliographical habit which is both consistent and satisfactory fully justified in using his own judgment in developing or modifying this habit if he can show that his modification is not put forward on purely subjective grounds, but can be made the ba-

sis of a consistent general practice. When an objectively definable class of works is concerned it is perfectly justifiable to divide it off for more satisfactory treatment. It is making an exception for a special case (in the interests of an apparent immediate utility) which weakens the catalog.

A different question which raises issues of fundamental importance is the character of the sources of the catalog entry. The cataloger works first from the book before him. That can never be the sole source of his information. He must always consult his own catalog, otherwise the same author may appear under two distinct forms of name, perhaps in one case with initials and in the other full forenames. The limited cataloging of the Library of Congress permits such a reference to the library's own catalog but lays down that apart from this all the information must be obtained from the book itself. Much information which users have expected to find in catalogs can only be gathered from very varied sources. The book itself will usually contain no indication that the author's name is a pseudonym or that the work has previously been issued under another name. The fact that two societies with quite distinct names are in fact the same society at different stages of its existence may be very difficult to establish. How wide should the cataloger spread his investigations and how much time should he spend on them? Clearly he cannot continue until he has convinced himself that he has exhausted all possibilities of establishing the full facts. A bibliographer may devote a lifetime to the study of one author and still be left with many problems which only chance can solve. The cataloger is not a research worker and indeed to describe his investigations as researches—a common practice—is a misuse of terms. Research is the bringing to light of knowledge which is either new or has been forgotten. This cannot be the cataloger's task because he has not the time in which to carry it out properly. It follows that the catalog can often answer only very imperfectly the two questions "What editions of this book are in the library?" or "What books by this author are in the library?" Unsuspected pseudonyms may be as common as unsuspected murders. The catalog is not a record of original researches but it may perhaps be expected to reproduce in addition to the information contained in the book whatever other relevant facts are readily accessible. "Readily accessible" is a very vague term and indeed must be interpreted according to the character and situation of the library in which the cataloger is working. A cataloger in a large academic library may reasonably be expected to consult the relevant national bibliographies, biographical reference works and catalogs of national libraries. Must he go on and consult specialist author and subject bibliographies? And what if these give contradictory information? No authority is infallible and even the catalogs of the great national libraries all contain a fair sprinkling of sheer misinformation. It is difficult enough to try to bring together all the work of one author. It is far harder to relate all the editions of one work. What is the definition of one work? If the cataloger is not to become a literary historian he must restrict himself to the task, difficult enough in itself, of relating works with exactly the same content which have different titles, or works which have varying contents with the same title, unless a work which varies both in title and content carries in itself an indication of relationship to the other work. Even if the cataloger is personally a historian he must not utilize in the catalog any new discoveries he may make. The cataloger deals not in new facts but in generally accepted data. He therefore restricts his investigations to works which have acquired the status of standard works of reference. This restriction does not of course apply to the cataloger of a special collection. He is in the happy position of creating a standard reference work and may legitimately pursue researches as far as his opportunities allow. But the cataloger in the general library must deny himself all this. He must deal not with things as they are but as they are generally taken to be.

It has been said that the catalog is part of the whole network of bibliographical references. It is part also of the wider network of general reference works and cannot function independently of them. If a reader comes across a reference to "the dev-astating reply composed by the Paymaster General to the Forces" he will need to consult some other reference work before he can discover from the catalog whether this work is in the library. "The learned work of Bishop Williams" will again be hard to find unless some further details are acquired about Bishop Williams. Even an apparently straightforward name may need elucidation. A reference to Chaloner Smith in the standard art reference dictionary omits the essential fact that the full name is John Chaloner Smith. No catalog can function on its own and almost certainly the catalog would carry out its own function more effectively if it left more of its peripheral work to other sources. It is not even certain that the tracing of references from different forms of names is always a task for the catalog. In cases such as some mediaeval or Arabic names either of authors or of books, the possible variants on a name may be very great. Could not the cataloger choose the name which is generally preferred and leave the elucidation of the lesser used forms to the appropriate reference book? Perhaps he would have to add a reference from the actual form used in the book being cataloged. Current catalog codes prescribe entries under almost all recorded forms of names, but since the original texts will be asked for by those who are familiar with the authors and modern translations by those who will know only the accepted modern name the value of these numerous references from variant forms seems doubtful. After all no catalog would attempt to list all recorded sixteenth or seventeenth century spellings of contemporary names. The exact applications of the principle are open to argument but there can be no doubt that catalogers would save much trouble if they ceased to look on the catalog as a reference tool always complete in itself.

The Changing Character of the Catalog in America

David C. Weber

"The character of the American library catalog has not changed in other than minor respects since the beginning of libraries in this country. Some major changes seem certain in the years ahead."

Librarianship is a sociological art. It uses many techniques and faces many intellectual problems found in many other professions. The fundamental responsibility of librarianship is the systematic provision and effective utility of graphic records. Its basic technique for achieving this goal is bibliography, the major instrument of library services.

"Bibliographic control" is the organization of individual works in an order for effective retrieval. The resultant "bibliographic organization" may take the form of shelf arrangement or classification, but the term is generally used with reference to a bibliography or catalog in printed or card form. "Individual works," as used above, may mean word compositions, paintings, vases, and so forth; and "word compositions" refers to any unit whether one poem, a letter, an article, technical report, or a lengthier work. In one method or another libraries must provide bibliographic control over all graphic records in their custody.

One other distinction should be made. Bibliographic control means providing content accessibility as well as physical accessibility. Contents are made accessible by means of indexing and abstracting services and by individual lists and formal bibliographies. Physical access is provided through catalogs of the holdings of a particular library with book numbers by which to locate each item. Analytics in a library catalog serve both these forms of bibliographic control.

ORIGIN OF CATALOGS

Techniques for bibliographic control have progressed over the years. A detailed title page, a table of contents, and an index to a single book were the first steps in improving access. When books were few in number, a reader or librarian could know what was in each and where each was shelved. (It has been said that as a rule of thumb any individual can know well ten thousand documents.) A list of holdings was useful for inventory purposes, and as collections grew the inventory would also be used to assist in locating volumes. The great libraries of several hundred thousand scrolls in such places as Alexandria and Pergamum must have had finding lists; however, the only known specimen is the "list of cases containing the books on great rolls of skins" graven on the House of Papyrus walls at Edfu, not far below the Aswan Dam. An early union list of holdings in English monastic libraries was compiled to improve access toward the end of the thirteenth century. During the nineteenth century, when the publications of journals and magazines increased markedly, libraries had the added problem of achieving subject indexing of articles. As individual American libraries tried to control this sudden increase in individual works, several lists were published, notably the comprehensive general indexes compiled by William F. Poole in 1848, 1853, and 1882. Analysis followed of volumes of essays and other compilations, resulting in *The A.L.A. Index* of 1893. Then five libraries prepared for some 250 learned journals analytics which the American Library Association began publishing on cards in January, 1898. The H. W. Wilson Company later took over these activities for its series of indexes. Similarly each year we find libraries, individuals, or firms compiling such works as an index to *Articles on American Literature, 1900-1950* (Duke University Press, 1954), an index to *Articles on Antiquity in Festschriften* (Harvard University

SOURCE: Reprinted from Ruth French Strout, ed., *Library Catalogs: Changing Dimensions* (Chicago: University of Chicago Press, 1964), pp. 20–33, by permission of the author and the publisher. Copyright © 1964 by the University of Chicago Press.

Press, 1962), and the *Meteorological and Geoastrophysical Abstracts* (American Meteorological Society, 1950————). In this fashion libraries have been increasingly relieved of much of their work on content accessibility.

The analysis of content has always been a concern of libraries, though rarely have individual budgets permitted much to be accomplished. Reliance can be placed on published analysis by others wherever it exists. The control of physical accessibility, on the other hand, must remain a dominant local concern as long as libraries seem impelled to cater to local nuances of classification or have material not part of a national control program.

A catalog should be designed to answer questions as to what books are in the library—questions of physical accessibility. The best catalog answers the greatest variety of questions with the greatest ease for the least expense. For reasons of economy a library may refuse to answer certain types of inquiries and may today rely on published lists, indexes, abstracting services, and bibliographies for considerable support.

The physical form taken by catalogs has varied over the years. Before reviewing the major forms that have been used, it may be well to suggest the objectives which have generally controlled these forms.

The overriding influence has been the desire to provide ease of access for one or more of several requirements:

1. The local need to find books in the collection by author, title, subject, or form.
2. The need to have the catalog available in several local locations.
3. The need to add or change records frequently to keep the listing up to date.
4. The belief that scholars will welcome widespread availability of the catalog as facilitating their work.

A secondary influence is financial. This seems to control most decisions. It may dictate a brief-entry typed on sheets, or it may permit a handsome publication by virtue of a subsidy. Some local requirements can be met together with national interests if the production can be a union list or can otherwise be a sound commercial venture. Library catalogs will have a wide variety of combinations of access requirements and financial strictures.

Lacking regular funds for purchasing books, libraries often relied on gifts for the majority of their acquisitions.[1] It seems evident that catalogs made for inventory purposes were early seen as an effective means of acknowledging and soliciting gifts. In the Colonial period these motivations were dominant; however, as time progressed, the need for an index to the collections came to be the primary motive for catalog preparation.[2]

PATTERN OF EARLY CATALOGS

In order to understand the use made of the catalog in its two major forms, in books and on cards, we shall review the catalogs of the oldest American university library because its records are clear and its method of library administration was quite typical of the best thought of the day.

In 1667, the Overseers of Harvard College drew up laws for the young library providing for a library keeper and for three catalogs: (1) books as they are placed, (2) alphabetical author list, and (3) lists by donors. Here we seem to find motivations of inventory, access, and appreciation. The first printed catalog appeared fifty-six years later. This octavo catalog was compiled by Joshua Gee in 106 pages and published in 300 copies: *Catalogus librorum Bibliothecae Collegij Harvardini quod est Cantabrigiae in Nova Anglia. Bostoni Nov-Anglorum, MDCCXXIII*. Two years later a ten-page supplement was published and, in 1735, another ten-page supplement appeared.

The reason for publication of the first American library catalog seems clearly to have been the opportunity to solicit additional gifts. The Harvard Corporation "Upon the Intimation lately made by Mr. Hollis, and formerly by Mr. Neal, that it may be of great Advantage to the College Library, that a Catalogue of the Books in the sd Library be printed and Sent abroad, Voted, that forthwith the Library-keepr take an exact Catalogue of the Books in the Library, and that the same be printed in Order to transmitt to friends abroad . . . ."[3]

The Harvard laws of 1667 are confirmed in almost identical language by those of 1736, and there is evidence that a manuscript catalog by donors continued to exist. One and possibly two manuscript catalogs of the collection arranged by size were later prepared before the fire of 1764. In November, 1765, the corporation voted that the librarian "be allowed for reducing the Books of the new Library into alphabetic Order, and transcribing several copies of them."[4] In December of 1765, new laws were adopted in which the third regulation for the library read: "A written catalogue of all the Books in each Alcove, shall be hung up therein; And an alphabetic Catalogue of the whole Library, divided into Chapters, according to the Diversity of Subjects, shall be printed and a Copy chain'd in each Window of the Library. There shall also be an Account of the Donors, open to every Ones inspection, to begin with the Donors to the former Library."[5] (The count in June, 1766, was 4,350 volumes.)

The 1765 catalog was folio manuscript, and an early supplement was quarto. In addition, the Librarian "apparently made copies of donations and arranged them in a docket file as a donors' catalogue."[6] Another catalog was begun in 1770 and dropped; another was completed during 1771. In 1781, the library was using the 1779 folio alphabetical manuscript catalog for its books and a separate alphabetical folio manuscript catalog of 1781 for its pamphlets which had not previously been cataloged.

Meanwhile in 1773 a second printed catalog had been published as a result of the 1767 laws, which quoted a still earlier regulation. This stated that certain duplicates should be set aside and cataloged "for the more common use of the College ... & the Librarian shall prepare a Catalogue of such Books."[7] The 1773 catalog had a Latin title page which may be translated as *Catalogue of the Books in the Cambridge Library selected for the more frequent Use of Harvard men who have not yet been invested with the Degree of Bachelor in Arts.* An explanatory note following the title page has been translated as follows:

> Inasmuch as the Catalogue of Books in the College Library is very long, and not to be completely unrolled, when Occasion demands, save at very great expense of time, embracing Books in almost all Tongues and about all Sciences and Arts, most of which are above the Comprehension of Younger Students, it has seemed wise to put together a briefer Catalogue, to wit, of Books which are better adapted to their use ....[8]

The full manuscript catalogs of 1779 and 1781 lasted until 1789 when two men were employed to prepare a new folio manuscript of the 12,000 volumes in alcove (shelf) arrangement and subject divisions. This became the third printed catalog in 1790, *Catalogus Bibliothecae Harvardianae Cantabrigae Nov-Anglorum*, in 362 pages. And doubtless there then was "a Copy chain'd in each Window of the Library." This became crowded in turn and a 1795 manuscript catalog of the alcoves was prepared.

THE NINETEENTH CENTURY

Another alcove catalog was begun in 1817 in twenty-one folios but never finished. During 1821–22, the reclassified collection was listed by Librarian Cogswell in a new alcove catalog of eighteen folios. In the year following, Cogswell introduced an early form of the card catalog as had existed since the turn of the century in various German and Scandinavian libraries.[9] This alphabetical "sheet catalogue" was composed of "seventeen boxes," and books would there be listed by author. A separate subject catalog and a shelf-list (or alcove) catalog remained. However, in 1823, Cogswell's successor copied the "sheet catalogue" into five volumes and tradition was restored.

The next printed catalog at Harvard was the author list published for the Law School Library in 1826, supplemented four times from 1833 to 1846. A fifth catalog, the third general catalog of the University, was issued as *Catalogue of the library of Harvard university* appearing in 1830, an alphabetical author list with a subject index. These two volumes listed nearly 35,000 books, and the "systematic index" was in a small third volume which also included a catalog of maps and charts. In 1834, a supplement of 260 pages was published; in 1835–36, a second was planned but never printed. Meanwhile the 1781 pamphlet catalog was replaced in 1833 by a manuscript which occupied eight large folio volumes at its termination in 1850.

A new manuscript catalog was proposed in 1840. This one foretold a remarkable change in the physical form of the library catalog and was a "slip catalogue" which would list holdings on cards 1½ inches tall and 6½ inches long. By 1847, this alphabetical catalog of additions had been adopted and existed on cards measuring 2 by 9½ inches, an outgrowth of Cogswell's sheet catalog and of the experience with interfiling entries cut from the 1790 printed catalog together with written additions to make copy for the 1830 publication.

Since the creation of this card catalog, the only printed catalogs of substantial portions of the Harvard Library have been the following:

> *Catalogue of Scientific Serials of All Countries ... 1699–1876.* 1 volume, 1879.
> *A Classified Catalog of Chinese Books.* 3 volumes, 1938–1940.
> *The Kress Library of Business and Economics: Catalog.* 2 volumes, 1940–56.

Catalogue of the Lamont Library. 1 volume, 1953.
*Author and Subject Catalogues of the Library of the
Peabody Museum of Archeology and Ethnology.*
53 volumes, 1963.

Let us now turn to one major and early innovation of public libraries which deserves special note. A catalog of different character was proposed in the middle of the nineteenth century: a catalog published in parts, as were many popular novels of the day. Mr. Cogswell, who was then at the Astor Library, proposed "to take up the library by departments, and prepare a classed catalogue, to be printed as each department is completed."[10] The Astor Library issued in 1854 a *Catalogue of Books . . . Relating to the Languages and Literature of Asia, Africa, and the Oceanic Islands.* The Boston Public Library adopted this plan and in 1866 issued three brief subject lists followed by several others in later years. Each of these was reprinted repeatedly.

This method of spreading costs was used for a slightly different purpose by the Boston Library when it began issuing its very popular quarterly bulletin of recent additions in 1867. The bulletin was the "current-awareness" service of its day. This practice was initiated by other libraries such as the Chicago Public (in its *Temporary Finding Lists . . .* which were an immediate success when first issued in 1874). Harvard began its *Bulletin* in 1875 and continued it for a slightly different purpose in its distinguished series of *Bibliographical Contributions,* 1878–1911. Many libraries now issue these bulletins in one form or another. These bulletins lent themselves to being cut and pasted on cards to improve the card catalog appearance, as was reported in 1872 by the Boston Public and the St. Louis Public School Library. (The Harvard Library issued printed catalog cards from 1888–1931, as did various other libraries.)

THE OCCASIONAL BOOK CATALOG

As the above summary indicates, the manuscript catalog was the basic form, with the printed edition a rarity. From 1936 until 1840 the wealthiest university had only three general printed catalogs with three supplements—a total of six times when the printed list was relatively up to date. Meanwhile, at least fourteen fresh manuscript versions were begun, and one or more was used to keep up-to-date the record of the collection. Yale College had issued five catalogs, between 1743

and 1823, with the largest only 122 pages. Ranz has noted that "it would be unfortunate if the impression were left that the usual practice for libraries was to print catalogs of their collections. Indeed, quite the opposite was true, for the great majority of libraries printed no catalogs during this period."[11]

It is correct to state, therefore, that the issuance of a printed book catalog was always an unusual event. One copy of the Harvard 1790 catalog was annotated with new acquisitions, and perhaps the other book catalogs were as well; yet these were in fact single "manuscript" copies. In nearly all libraries, manuscript records were the rule although many of them published one or two catalogs in the middle half of the nineteenth century. Typical of these were the catalogs of the Eastport, Maine, Athenaeum in 1836; of the Portland Athenaeum in 1839 and 1849; of Colby College in 1845; and of Bowdoin College in 1821 and 1863, with a medical list in 1830. (In fact Bowdoin's 1863 catalog with 16,000 volumes was far above average in size.) Library catalogs, with only four or five exceptions, listed less than 40,000 volumes. A few libraries put out annual supplements.

It was natural that the social library and public library felt a particular urgency for issuing printed catalogs because the publication served to attract new members as well as to encourage use and support. The general availability of a catalog increased the circulation of books and is even said at the Boston Public to have "had a marked effect in elevating the character of the circulation."[12]

The only large libraries which were consistent publishers of catalogs were such wealthy institutions as the Astor Library, Boston Athenaeum, the Boston Public Library, the Library of Congress, the New York Mercantile Library, the New York State Library, the Library Company of Philadelphia, and later the United States Surgeon-General's Office. The most universal user of the printed catalog during the period 1850–75 was the state library; the academic library had all but abandoned them.[13]

THE MODERN CARD CATALOG

The use of the manuscript catalog was reserved for librarians. It was apparently never available to the public, yet few justifications of printed catalogs appear to have been based on the resultant saving of librarians' time. One of these is the comment of the Brookline Public Library that the printed catalog "meets an urgent demand from the public, as well as a need *within* the library, and facilitates all the routine work of the circulating department beyond measure."[14]

The historic significance of Harvard's 1862 card catalog seems to have been not only its format but also its open availability to readers. In the summer of 1862, the new catalogs of authors and subjects were first made accessible to all students and "all literary gentlemen" who were "freely admitted."[15] Just one hundred years ago, Ezra Abbot wrote his famed "Statement Respecting the New Catalogues of the College Library."[16] These catalogs set the pattern followed ever since, so some description of this change may be appropriate.

The "slip catalogue" of the 1840's included all additions filed by author on 2 X 9½ cards. These cards were particularly designed for the chief librarian's use. They recorded author, title, classification, binding condition, date of receipt, name and residence of donor, if a gift, and cost and fund if a purchase. The new "Indexes," begun October 22, 1861, on 2 X 5 cards, were particularly designed for use by readers; and they recorded subject, full name of author, title, place and date of publication, size, illustrations, and classification. Included in the catalog were cards for analytics and cross-references. The cards were kept in four cases each holding twenty-eight drawers, 15¼ inches long, in seven tiers. The only major difference from modern card catalog cases was that each drawer was double width to hold two rows of cards, a notable economy before later standards increased the card size and weight by 50 percent.

These improvements and innovations in the catalog were recognized by the Harvard Overseers. The Committee To Visit the Library reported its satisfaction:

> The new Catalogue on cards . . . has been making such progress and has been so constantly in use, during the past year, that experience has dissipated all doubts as to its intrinsic *practical* value. The theoretical soundness and the beauty of its method have never been questioned; and it would seem that the Librarians and the frequenters of the Library must now be congratulated on the possession of the best mode yet devised of summarily answering the questions, 1. "Is the book I want in the Library?" 2. "What books in the Library treat of the subject on which I am seeking information?"[17]

The new Harvard form for the library catalog

was adopted almost universally within the United States during the next decade. Only four or five of the very largest libraries had the financial resources to hope to continue printing a general catalog. Aside from those wealthy libraries, only the small libraries had printed catalogs; very few of those holding above twenty thousand volumes had printed lists. The card catalog more nearly met their requirements. The beauty and permanency of library card catalogs seemed assured when the Library of Congress began issuing its printed catalog cards in November, 1901.

With the increased cost of issuing printed catalogs, with the greatly increased size of public libraries of all types, and with the growth in book publishing and book availability, the urge to print catalogs declined rapidly during the 1880's and 1890's. Further, the growing desire to reveal the subject content of public and academic libraries increased the bulk of catalogs in a way which hastened abandonment of printing plans.[18]

In those years of transition when the published catalog could no longer be the constant goal, there was a clear understanding of the advantages and the disadvantages of the card and book forms, nowhere better summarized than by Charles A. Cutter.[19] Suffice it to point out the obvious currency and economy of the card file and the wide availability and ease of use of the book. The comparative advantages could only be altered as mechanical techniques invalidated the early assumptions of cost and time.

Attempts have occasionally been made to combine the card advantages with the book form. The Rudolph Indexer was widely discussed and tried in a few locations in the mid-1890's.[20] Visible file drawers have found usefulness in such areas as the control of current serial records. The upright visible record is widely used to present cards in a book format.

One other departure was investigated in a card catalog mechanization study undertaken in 1958 by the Operations Research Department of the University of Michigan. This project analyzed the feasibility and costs of using closed-circuit television and a card manipulating device to permit access to a card catalog from a remote location. No application was found where the costs could be justified.[21]

THE NEW ERA

Between the 1870's and the 1950's the growth of library catalogs was not matched by printing techniques economically equal to the reproduction task although photo-offset had helped. Single volumes for special collections continued to be issued. National libraries dutifully obtained funds to continue publishing. Yet when one tries to find an early indication that techniques existed which once again permitted a library to publish a general catalog, it seems to occur in 1951 when the branch catalogs of the King County Public Library in Seattle, Washington, were issued in tabulating-machine format. The author, title, adult subject, and juvenile subject catalogs were updated by fortnightly changes arranged in shelflist order, and the entire catalog was replaced every six weeks. These innovations were forced on Librarian Ella R. McDowell because there were thirty-eight branches and a typical branch annually exchanged 69 percent of its books with the central collection. The use of rented tabulating equipment provided the King County Public Library with an ideal control of physical accessibility for a rapidly changing deployment of its books.[22]

With 114 service outlets and only 25 of these equipped with card catalogs, the Los Angeles County Library adopted the King County system in modified form in 1952 by publishing its *Children's Catalog*. This was followed two years later by the first edition of the *Adult Catalog*. In 1956-60 the New York State Library published three *Checklists* of its books and pamphlets in three large subject areas, a return to the printing of catalogs-in-parts now made possible by the tabulating machine.

In 1958, the twelve-volume *Catalog of The Avery Memorial Architectural Library*, Columbia University, was the first of many G. K. Hall publications employing xerography for reproduction. And a second major new technique had appeared. In 1959, the National Library of Medicine began using the Listomatic camera for production of the *Current List of Medical Literature*. This machine was one of the sequential card cameras—a third major new technique. High-speed computers have qualified as the fourth major new technique which can be exploited in the preparation of library catalogs.

These samples may serve to indicate that printing techniques of the 1950's had brought costs down to a reasonable level. The Avery catalog has long been a major scholarly tool in the arts, and its publication helped the library staff as well as the scholarly world; and the National Library of Medicine could expand its indexing coverage considerably by use of a superb new mechanical

technique. Further, the growing complexity of library organization was a strong reason for using these methods. King County had a fluid collection to serve a wide area with a small staff; record-changing had to be minimized if not eliminated. Los Angeles County had a comparable problem of providing access to its collection with minimized records. The New York State Library was striving to make it as easy to find books as to find telephone numbers, and the state-wide interlibrary lending process was greatly simplified by the issuance of the book catalog.

The quantity of library catalogs published in the past few years constitutes a major event in library history. It is welcomed for its liberating effect, but appreciation is cautious because of the purchase costs and the possible lack of suitable standards in these publications. One result has been the preparation by the ALA Book Catalogs Committee of a statement on "Preferred Practices in the Publication of Book Catalogs."[23] The technological achievements are certainly most heartening to librarians. They are the result of mathematical and chemical advances earlier in this century applied in newly designed machines. Significant improvements are constantly being made.[24]

The access motivations for printing a library catalog referred to earlier in this paper still pertain while the economic controls are not so restricting. The regional and national interdependence among libraries strengthens the old arguments. One new motive is evident: concern over the great space now occupied by card catalogs in the largest libraries.

As far back as 1904, William C. Lane saw this space problem approaching since the catalog "occupies much floor space.... Its bulk gives some cause for uneasiness.... The question of space must be seriously reckoned with by the architect ...."[25] Lane's successor fifty-two years later reported "these catalogues ... are becoming more and more enormous and complex jungles of cards ... and they outgrow the space that is readily available for housing them."[26] There seems to be no library which yet has printed its catalog in order to reduce space. Nevertheless, though it may not be a prime reason, the great saving of space through conversion to book form will provide a substantial dividend and one which the larger libraries may have to achieve later in this century.

It is too early to see what will result from the publication of the huge catalogs of the University of California, Berkeley and Los Angeles. Their printing was prompted by the need to have records for these collections available on the other campuses of the University; and, from the experience of the past century, it seems most doubtful that the card file will soon be discarded at either Berkeley or Los Angeles.[27] Libraries which can afford these sets will simply have two more exceedingly useful catalogs on their shelves for purposes of bibliographic sleuthing, interlibrary borrowing, and photocopy orders.

MICROFORMATS

The card and book forms of the catalog may be miniaturized. It was suggested, in 1938, that microcopies of library catalogs could be manufactured for $30 per million cards given a sizeable market.[28] At the 1940 Graduate Library School Institute, Fremont Rider considered it not unlikely for microphotography "in some one of its forms . . . to go far toward changing completely both catalogs and libraries . . ."[29]

After World War II microphotography was used for bibliography and catalog publication in opaque microprint editions. Microlex Corporation reprinted the *American Law Reports,* the Microcard Foundation published Sabin's *Bibliotheca Americana*, and Readex Microprint reissued the *Catalog of Copyright Entries.* Now, in 1963, Readex is publishing the *Cyrillic Union Catalog,* an original publication. This Cyrillic catalog is first being issued on cards this fall, to be replaced in the early winter by a printing on both sides of thinner sheets which will be bound in volumes for use on an opaque projector or with a twelve-power loupe which will accompany the publication. It is the first major library catalog in this form, and its scholarly reception will be watched with great interest. Photography has created a frenzied state of publishing. Fortunately, it also promises to simplify the printing and reprinting of bibliographic records.[30]

A different use of microphotography is its utility in such index machines as the Filmorex, Flip, Fosdic, Media, Minicard, Rapid Selector, Verac, and Walnut. The size of record- and film-handling procedures varies widely in these machines. The output is visual display of the index record and the document or is hard copy print-out or film duplication. This form of catalog is a radical, and in some ways a highly efficient, departure from tradition. However, its application is restricted because of high cost. The machines are not yet engineered to handle hundreds of thousands of documents; and, even if they were, they would seem suited only to special library situations because in their present design their store is monopolized by a single investigator, programming the query takes time, and browsing is not possible. The same limitations seem to apply to computers when used as stores rather than merely as manipulative and printing machines.

LIMITATIONS

Since these highly sophisticated machines have been said to have only specialized applicability, an explanation may be useful as to why not all library catalogs can be placed in such machines—why they will not universally change the character of the catalog. There have been at least three descriptions of machine limitations for library records. Six years ago it was said that the use of machines for storage and retrieval of information would be desirable only when all the following conditions prevail:

1. A single subject is being covered.
2. There is a high concentration of publications in this subject area.
3. There is a continuing high intake rate of publications.
4. Adequate subject access is unavailable in published form.
5. Use is made by people having several different approaches or uses in mind.
6. There is high urgency in the location of every pertinent publication.[31]

In 1962 it was said that it may become feasible to use computers for the logical processes of searching, given certain combinations of the following requirements:

1. The bibliographical universe to be handled should involve relatively large amounts of material. . . . On the other hand the bibliographical input unit should be small enough so that it is feasible to search units of reasonable size. . . .
2. There should be need for multiple access to any or all entries from differing points of view. . . .
3. The material should need to be recast into different arrangements . . . or different . . . forms. . . .
4. There should be a relatively large amount of change in the basic file. . . .
5. The field covered must be lacking in good bibliographical control in conventional form and must not lend itself readily to such control.
6. The materials should be relatively frequently used.
7. The materials should be needed in multiple physical locations. . . .
8. The field must be important enough to justify a high level of expenditure of a high order of intellectual effort if the coding manipulated by

machine is to be so sophisticated as to justify this level of manipulation.[32]

This year it was stated in a discussion of computer applicability to library systems that such a machine could be used logically and economically if it were applied under these conditions:

1. The application must be to a high volume of documents and must require highly repetitive use.
2. There is need for sterile handling: no errors and the highest quality and security.
3. The job is so complex that no human can reasonably do it once correctly.
4. The response time must be short for payoff, and the penalty for delay is beyond comprehension.
5. Multiple hands are required in the file at the same time.
6. There is need for complete currency.[33]

Choosing appropriate specialized applications for the sophisticated machine demands a rigorous analysis of a host of factors.[34] The major advantage of the machine is its accuracy in storing, moving, and reproducing data. Manual methods can be used for all information systems; but as volume increases, machines may be of advantage as has been proven in the information systems of government, of business, and of libraries.

EFFECT OF NEW TECHNIQUES

At this point one may ask what has been the effect of the newer printing techniques on the ease of access to information. For most applications, the card-form catalog is unsurpassed for use in one location. The book-form catalog is portable and most convenient to scan. A microfilm catalog is probably as rapid to use as the card catalog once one is accustomed to the machine, especially if it is a catalog on microtext cards or sheets. The microform catalog is not portable, is not convenient to scan, is difficult to update, and requires a rather expensive projector. The automatic viewing screen with keyboard control is not portable and is generally very expensive; however, it can be operated rapidly and can be designed to produce the document itself as well as the index reference. This also applies to computers which give libraries a most powerful bibliographic tool once they can afford to use a complete computer and leave the data in its store—as with Medlars—rather than use it only a few moments to arrange and print out a sheet catalog.

Yet in considering the ease of access it is well to remember that by far the greatest aid to access is the existence of a comprehensive collection of publications. Without the literature behind it, no index device can produce satisfaction.

A second point is that the degree of bibliographic analysis of the literature—the number of useful author, title, and subject entries—is also more important than is the form of the catalog. The most sophisticated electronic index is only as good as the entries it has been fed. Given equal collections and equal analysis for entry, then the form of the catalog and its organization and editing will produce different working conditions. The success in information retrieval is not dependent on the form of the instrument, yet the form will have a marked effect on convenience and speed.

This point may be developed through reference to the unique card catalog formed by the Uniterm system of coordinate indexing. In this form of catalog, cards for each major word of the document's chosen subject phrase list the document numbers arranged by the last digit. When cards are matched for the terms used to describe the subject of inquiry, numbers appearing under all the chosen terms will produce relevant documents. This catalog apparatus has gained specialized popularity during the past dozen years. The point here to be noted is that its ability to extract information from a subject approach has been found to be at least equal to three other common cataloging methods using traditional card catalogs.[35]

The choice for a library catalog may be one of the following: the 7.5 × 12.5-cm. card, punched tabulating card, edge-notched card, manuscript book, sheaf, printed book, roll microfilm, microtext sheets or cards, magnetic tape or wire, and other electronic devices such as magnetic drums. Each form may meet certain requirements better than the others. So the degree of convenience and basic utility of each form would depend on the relative importance of such additional factors as a requirement for portability, need for copies in several locations, number of simultaneous users to be accommodated, importance of currency, requirements for flexibility in intercalating new entries, the importance of browsing, and the importance of cost.

There is also the degree to which the cataloged collection changes, for in a stationary collection a card file offers no advantage. Where the list evolves slowly and rather uniformly with copies needed in many locations, a book with pocket supplements and periodic reprinting may be ideal, as with the *Corpus Juris Secundum.* Where changes are of little importance, availability must be widespread, and costs are of prime importance, then a microtext version may provide entirely adequate ease of access. What may provide the best solution for a botanical scholar in a Boston museum may be most awkward for a group of aeronautical engineers in Pasadena laboratories. Each form of catalog may offer suitable ease of access in cases where all requirements are compatible.

CURRENT DEVELOPMENTS

It may seem dubious that any further form of the library catalog will gain wide popularity.[36] Still, the use of electronic devices combining features of microfilm projectors, language laboratories, and teaching machines may still in special library situations lend some novelty to librarianship in this century. In the past three years high-speed computers have been used in a number of experiments with library records. Well known are the processing studies at the University of Illinois, Chicago, the serials catalogs produced by the University of California, San Diego, and the Washington University Medical School, as well as the first regularly published permuted index *Chemical Titles*, the catalog of *Dissertations in Physics*, and the *Index Medicus* plans for the spring of 1964. The brilliant Medlars program for *Index Medicus* at the National Library of Medicine is the first example of a truly automated catalog. The end

result in each case mentioned is a book catalog of traditional appearance.[37]

However, current research is directed toward applying existing computer technology in "systems." A description of a possible library catalog of the future was presented at the Conference on Libraries and Automation of last May. Central to the operation of the mechanized library, as described there by Don Swanson, would be a console machine—an electronic system in lieu of the tangible catalog. The user console would consist of a keyboard for search-and-select action, a cathode-ray-tube display screen with the tube in direct communication with a computer storing a national union catalog, a microfilm viewer with enlarger-printer and an intercom to permit consulting of a reference librarian.[38] Computer technology holds promise to revolutionize many aspects of library operation in the near future.

Bibliography remains basic to librarianship and documentation. Library concern with bibliographic control is not fundamentally different now from what it was in previous centuries. For content accessibility, libraries will rely to the greatest degree possible on published lists and national services; given unstandardized collections, libraries must continue to provide local physical access.

The character of the American library catalog has not changed in other than minor respects since the beginning of libraries in this country. Some major changes seem certain in the years ahead.

NOTES

[1] Louis Shores, *Origins of the American College Library 1638-1800* (Nashville, Tenn.: George Peabody College, 1934), p. 109; the point also seems clear in Jesse Shera, *Foundations of the Public Library* (Chicago: University of Chicago Press, 1949), p. 201.

[2] James Ranz found in his study of early printed catalogs that this motive became dominant as soon as libraries grew to even a modest size ("The History of the Printed Book Catalogue in the United States" [unpublished Ph.D. dissertation, University of Illinois, 1960], pp. 62-63).

[3] Colonial Society of Massachusetts, *Publications,* XVI (1925), 467. In addition, Ranz has noted that "the promotional character of Colonial catalogs was quite evident in their handsome physical appearance" (*op. cit., p. 76*). On the other hand, Yale's first catalog, in 1742, seems to have been motivated by the need to improve access: President Thomas Clap noted that "before this Time there never had been any perfect Catalogue of the Books in the Library; for want of which the Students were deprived of much of the Benefit and Advantage of them" (*The Annals or History of Yale-College* . . . [New Haven, Conn., 1766], p. 43).

[4] Clarence E. Walton, *The Three-Hundredth Anniversary of the Harvard College Library* (Cambridge, 1939), p. 18.

[5] *Ibid.,* p. 25.

[6] *Ibid.,* p. 19.

[7] "The Laws of Harvard College 1767," Chapter vii, Regulation V, The Colonial Society of Massachusetts, *Publications,* XXXI (1935), 369.

[8] Keyes D. Metcalf, "The Undergraduate and the Harvard Library, 1765-1877," *Harvard Library Bulletin*, I (1947), 30.

[9] Ruth French Strout found the first mention of card catalogs in the 1791 "French Instructions"; see "The Development of the Catalog and Cataloging Codes," *Library Quarterly,* XXVI (1956), 30.

[10] Astor Library, *Annual Report of the Trustees . . . 1854* (New York, 1855), p. 30.

[11] *Op. cit.,* p. 81.

[12] U.S. Department of the Interior, Bureau of Education, *Public Libraries in the United States of America* (Washington, D.C., 1876), p. 572.

[13] Ranz, *op. cit.,* p. 145.

[14] U.S. Department of the Interior, *op. cit.,* p. 572.

[15] *Report of the Committee of the Overseers of Harvard College Appointed To Visit the Library for the Year 1863* (Boston, 1864), pp. 11, 31.

[16] *Ibid.,* pp. 35-76.

[17] *Ibid.,* pp. 6-7.

[18] This point is well developed by Ranz, *op. cit.,* p. 146, who also gives a useful discussion of catalog costs from Colonial times through the nineteenth century.

[19] U.S. Department of the Interior, *op. cit.,* pp. 552-54. See also James A. Whitney, "Considerations as to a Printed Catalogue in Book Form," in Boston Public Library, *47th Annual Report* (1898), pp. 49-59.

[20] Editorial, *Library Journal,* XVIII (1893), 277.

[21] University of Michigan Engineering Research Institute, *Final Report: Application of a Telereference System to Divisional Library Card Catalogs–a Feasibility Analysis* (Washington, D.C.: Council on Library Resources, 1958).

[22] Dorothy Alvord, "King County Public Library Does It with IBM," *PNLA Quarterly,* XVI (1952), 123-32.

[23] *ALA Bulletin,* LVI (1962), 836-37.

[24] Among many recent descriptions, Richard H. Shoemaker, "Some American 20th Century Book Catalogs: Their Purposes, Format and Production Techniques," *Library Resources and Technical Services,* IV (1960), 195-207; C. D. Gull, "Mechanization: Implications for the Medium-sized Medical Library," *Bulletin of the Medical Library Association,* LI (1963), 197-210; *The MEDLARS Story at the National Library of Medicine* (1963), esp. chap. iv; and Samuel N. Alexander, *The Current Status of Graphic Storage Techniques: Their Potential Application to Library Mechanization* (Washington, D.C.: Library of Congress for the Conference on Libraries and Automation, 1963).

[25] "Present Tendencies of Catalog Practice," *Library Journal,* XXIX (1904), 140.

[26] Harvard University Library, *Annual Report for the Year 1955-56* (Cambridge, Mass., 1956), p. 6.

[27] For a brief discussion of attendant problems see David C. Weber, "Book Catalogs: Prospects in the Decade Ahead," *College and Research Libraries,* XXIII (1962), 307.

[28] Robert C. Binkley, "Microcopying and Library Catalogs," *American Library Association Bulletin,* XXXII (1938), 241.

[29] "Alternatives for the Present Dictionary Card Catalog," *The Acquisition and Cataloging of Books* (Chicago: University of Chicago Press, 1940), p. 152.

[30] See Peter Scott, "Graphic Aids for Information Retrieval," *Information Retrieval Today* (Minneapolis: University of Minnesota Center for Continuation Study, 1963), pp. 71-87.

[31] David C. Weber, "A Quagmire of Scientific Literature?" *College and Research Libraries,* XVIII (1957), 106.

[32] Ralph R. Shaw, "Electronic Storage and Searching," *Times Literary Supplement,* April 6, 1962, p. 235.

[33] Robert L. Patrick, comments at the Conference on Libraries and Automation, Warrenton, Virginia, May, 1963.

[34] For example, see the parameters of operation in Joseph Becker and Robert M. Hayes, *Information Storage and Retrieval* (New York, 1963), chap. xii.

[35] Cyril W. Cleverdon, *Aslib-Cranfield Research Project; Report on the Testing and Analysis of an Investigation into the Comparative Efficiency Indexing Systems* (Cranfield, England, 1962), esp. chap. ix. Coordinate indexing is also being mechanized in the Termatrex equipment series which speeds the coordinate determination of document numbers.

[36] C. D. Gull found no "trend towards any physical substitute which will replace the card catalog in the near future as the basic record of each library" as reported in his study of "Substitutes for the Card Catalog," *Studies in Coordinate Indexing* (Washington, D.C.: Documentation, Inc., 1953), Vol. LXX, reprinted with slight revisions in *Library Trends,* II (1953), 318.

[37] An informative general survey is John Markus' "State of the Art of Published Indexes," *American Documentation,* XIII (1962), 15-23.

[38] Don R. Swanson, "Dialogues with a Library Machine" (paper delivered at the Conference of Libraries and Automation, Warrenton, Va., May 1963 [35 pages]). (Multilithed.)

The Potential Usefulness of the Catalog Access Points Other Than Author, Title, and Subject

William S. Cooper

"Library patrons who wish to obtain a known document with which they have had prior personal contact often cannot remember the standard author-title-subject information about it with sufficient accuracy to be able to look it up easily in present-day card catalogs. However, they may remember a surprising amount of such 'nonstandard' information as the color of the document's cover or its approximate length".

Most of us have had, at some time or other, the frustrating experience of being able to remember quite vividly the general physical appearance of some book we have read, but of being unable to recall either its author or its exact title. Professors complain that what their students remember best about a textbook is the color of its cover. A book owner is often able to remember what condition one of his books is in, even though its author and title may have for the moment escaped his memory. These commonplace observations suggest that there is often a considerable amount of miscellaneous "nonstandard" information concerning a document which is more memorable to one who has had contact with the document than the "standard" author-title-subject information is. This paper is addressed to the question of whether it might be worthwhile to attempt to make use of such nonstandard information in the design of future library catalogs and retrieval systems.

NONSTANDARD INFORMATION

Let us agree to use the phrase "nonstandard information" as a cover term for all those types of information about documents which could conceivably be helpful in specifying a wanted document, but which cannot be used to look up a document in the catalogs found in present-day libraries. Since present-day libraries normally provide nothing but author, title, and subject catalogs, this includes virtually all types of data about documents except for author-title-subject information. Data such as the date of publication of a document, its length (number of pages), and an indication of the presence or absence of illustrations in it are usually to be found in present-day catalogs; but under our definition these must be regarded as nonstandard types of information, for such data cannot be used for search purposes as long as catalogs are alphabetized only according to author, title, or subject. Of cource, such physical features of a document as its cover color and design are definitely "nonstandard," since they do not appear in today's catalogs in any form.

All nonstandard information represents an as yet untapped resource for aiding the retrieval process. To illustrate the possibilities, suppose that a patron of a library or information center desires a particular document with which he has has previous contact. He may be unable to remember the author or title of his document with the accuracy and completeness needed to look it up in a conventional author-title catalog. He may also be unable to specify the subject area in terms of a heading which would permit a quick search in the subject catalog. But it is quite possible that he can nevertheless state with assurance that the document in question is say, large, green, in good condition, recently published, a translation from the German, and well illustrated. Here is a case where the remembered nonstandard information has the potential for being extremely useful, for surely there could not be very many documents in the collection answering this description. If these few documents (possibly just one) could be retrieved and assembled for the requester's inspection, he would presumably have no trouble in picking out the needed one from among them. Examples could also be given in

SOURCE: Reprinted from the *Journal of the American Society for Information Science*, 21 (March-April, 1970), pp. 112-127, by permission of the publisher. Copyright ©1970 by the American Society for Information Science, 1140 Connecticut Ave., N.W., Washington, D.C. 20036. This work was supported by National Science Foundation Grant GN482 (A Requirement Study for Future Catalogs) to the University of Chicago Graduate Library School.

which the nonstandard information might not be sufficient in and of itself, but would nevertheless become sufficient if it could be combined with whatever shreds of standard information are remembered.

The possibilities inherent in nonstandard information have never been seriously exploited in conventional libraries. There are good reasons for this. It seems to be the nature of nonstandard information to consist of a variety of "weak clues" rather than just one "strong clue." For example, the information that a book has a green cover is a weak clue in the sense that there may be thousands of books in the collection with green covers. It follows that the clue "green-covered" would be by itself quite inadequate for retrieval, and it is only by combining a number of such weak clues that one might hope to narrow down the set of candidate documents to a helpful extent. Now, to construct and maintain a conventional file such as a card catalog for looking up combinations of weak clues would be a difficult task indeed. The file would have to be alphabetized for lookup first on one type of information, say, color, and then within color on, say, size, within size on something else, and so forth through all the various nonstandard clue types. But one file would not be enough; the requestor who has forgotten the color of his book but remembers other nonstandard information would need a different file alphabetized first on some other clue type which he is able to remember. Continuing this line of thinking, it becomes apparent that one would need almost as many different files as there are *permutations* of clue types—a number large enough to raise doubts as to whether there would be any room left for books in the library after all the catalogs were installed. As if this problem were not serious enough, we shall see later that any combination of several weak nonstandard clues reported from memory is likely to contain at least one clue that is in error, a circumstance that complicates the problem of catalog design immeasurably.

For these reasons, it seems impractical to try to exploit nonstandard information by conventional means. However, it does not necessarily follow that it could not be exploited with the help of computers. It is unthinkable that a library user should have to scan all or even a substantial fraction of a complete holdings file to track down his document, but it is not unthinkable that a computer might do so. With an automated catalog or retrieval system, it may well be within the realm of practicality to perform searches for any arbitrary combination of remembered nonstandard clues. Moreover, the problem of partially mistaken information is not necessarily insurmountable if the use of computers is contemplated. Should the wanted document turn out not to be among the retrieved documents fulfilling his description, it must then be among some set of documents which *almost* matches his description, assuming that most of the data in his description are correct. The nearly matching documents most likely to include the wanted document could be retrieved for the requester's inspection, then the next most likely, and so on, until either the requester found what he was looking for, or else the probability of doing so in a reasonable amount of time dropped too low to justify continued searching. This plan would require the computer to make some sophisticated probability computations, it is true, but the retrieval process would not necessarily be significantly slowed down because of this. Numerical computation is just what computers are best at.

It is not our purpose here to describe exactly how a computer could be programmed to perform searches on the basis of possibly mistaken clues, except insofar as we shall have occasion in a later section to set forth for a special case the probability calculations the computer would be required to make. The questions that should claim prior attention to all programming considerations are the following: Assuming that appropriate retrieval mechanisms were somehow made available for exploiting nonstandard clues to the maximum possible extent, how great an improvement in retrieval performance could one expect? Specifically, are there a significant number of potential library patrons who possess nonstandard information about the documents they need and who would make use of whatever future facilities might be provided to exploit this information? Even more important, would these people tend to remember *enough* nonstandard information, and remember it *correctly* enough, to make the potential improvement in retrieval results worth pursuing? These questions will be the focus of attention in what follows.

THE NEED FOR RETRIEVAL FACILITIES EXPLOITING NONSTANDARD INFORMATION

How great is the need for a means of allowing library patrons to use nonstandard information in their search for documents they want? Unfortunately it is impossible to gauge this need by questioning users in present-day libraries. The reason for this is that present-day libraries can do little or nothing to help a potential patron whose only information is of the nonstandard variety, and so such patrons, knowing this, stay at home. The best that can be done with current user surveys is to make some rather oblique inferences about the probable number of potential library users who find themselves in the position of having nonstandard information but no way to exploit it.

In discussing questions of document retrieval it is helpful to distinguish between what is usually called *subject retrieval* and what we shall here call *specific work retrieval*. In the subject retrieval situation, the library user wishes to locate works on a topic or subject area of interest to him, but he does not necessarily have any prior familiarity with the works, nor for that matter even any advance assurance of their existence. The specific work retrieval situation is quite different, in that the requester already knows of the existence of some particular document that he wants. Clearly, nonstandard information about the wanted document will enter the picture chiefly in connection with specific work retrieval, for the user will normally be able to specify physical details only in connection with particular works with which he has had previous contact.

Since nonstandard information has potential value mainly for specific work retrieval, it is pertinent to ask whether specific work retrieval searches form a substantial part of all catalog searches made in present-day libraries. A number of catalog use studies provide evidence that they do. In E. Montague's recent survey of card catalog use studies,[1] a summary is presented, which includes fifteen studies that give clear statements of the proportion of catalog searches observed which were of the specific work type. The 15 percentages for the proportion of specific work searches ranged from 41.8 percent (for a public library system) to 90 percent (for a specialized library), the median figure being 60 percent. Two investigators commented on a tendency for the proportion of specific work searches to be higher in libraries where the educational level of the population was high. The picture that emerges is that the preponderance of catalog usage today has as its purpose the locating of specific known works, and that this is especially true in libraries that serve a highly educated or highly specialized

community of users. Of course, proposed improvements in specific work retrieval facilities such as those considered in this paper would well increase even further the proportion of specific work searches made in future libraries, for the ratio of specific work searches to subject searches reflects not only user needs but also the adequacy of the facilities made available for specific work retrieval and subject retrieval.

Another issue of interest is the number of potential searchers for a specific document who have actually had contact with the document itself. Those who have not are poor prospects as users of future facilities to exploit nonstandard information, for searches based exclusively on a citation or bibliography are likely to be completed on the basis of author-title information alone, assuming that they can be successfully completed at all. A recent survey made by M. Blackburn[2] provides some idea of the percentage of specific work searches whose purpose was to locate documents actually read or at least seen by the searchers. In Blackburn's survey, 126 patrons of the University of Chicago library were stopped and questioned as they reached for a drawer of the main catalog. Of these, one hundred turned out to be attempting to locate a specific work, confirming the previously mentioned findings to the effect that a majority of present-day catalog users seek known items. Of the one hundred seeking a specific work, twenty nine stated that they had previously seen or used the work they were looking for, and an additional thirteen who had never actually seen their document had nevertheless been given a verbal recommendation of it by someone who had. This makes at least 29 percent and possible somewhat more specific work searchers who would have been in a position to supply nonstandard information from their own personal memory or that of their colleagues. This finding is admittedly based on a small sample, and is not necessarily generalizable to other libraries with different user populations, but it serves to suggest at least that the number of searchers who possess nonstandard information is not insignificant. Moreover, the 29 percent figure presumably understates to some unknown extent the number of *potential* patrons in a position to supply nonstandard information, for only those who could supply a sufficiency of standard information in addition to the nonstandard ever reached the library catalog to be interviewed.

The reader is referred to [Blackburn's *Information about Books* . . .[2]] for further details concerning the amount and types of nonstandard information that users of the University of Chicago library catalog tend to remember, as well as the accuracy of their recollections. It appears that a considerable amount and variety of non-standard information, some of it accurate and some inaccurate, is in the users' memories. However, the ultimate significance of findings from user surveys for the design of future catalogs is unclear for the reason already mentioned, which is that what library patrons can remember at today's catalogs is not necessarily indicative of what the potential users of tomorrow's improved catalogs might be able to remember if future catalog facilities were designed to allow use to be made of nonstandard information.

THE UNIVERSITY OF CHICAGO MEMORY EXPERIMENT

In view of the limitations of the user survey method, it was decided to conduct a special experiment to gain insight into what types of information tend to be remembered most often and most accurately about books commonly found on library shelves. In this "memory experiment," as we shall call it, human subjects were to be exposed to books and after a suitable lapse of time were to be questioned to determine what they could remember about the books. A memory experiment can, if properly designed, largely control such problems as variability in the duration of the subjects' exposure to the books and also variability in their browsing or reading environment at the time of exposure. The experimental environment, motivation, time lapse between exposure and questioning, and other conditions of the experiment are truly representative of real-life conditions. Nevertheless, it was felt that the advantages of the experimental approach more than justified it as a complement to user survey techniques, and so the experiment was undertaken.

The experimental design is fully described elsewhere.[3] However, the features of the experiment which are essential for present purposes are easily sketched. Briefly, a large number of subjects were allowed to select and read from books that interested them, but with which they had had no prior acquaintance. Two weeks later, each subject was asked to fill out from memory a mimeographed questionnaire about each book from which he had read. The questionnaire attempted to determine which standard and non-standard features of the books read were remembered best. The subjects were not told the purpose of the experiment, so that what they remembered about the books was presumably fairly close to what they would naturally have remembered in a real-life browsing situation. The "library" from which they were allowed to make their selection consisted of a previously assembled collection of approximately 180 books in the subject area of psychology. No attempt was made to make this experimental collection a random sample of all existing books on psychology; instead, an attempt was made to cover a variety of topics in psychology which were thought to be of interest to the lay reader, as well as to include a wide range of nonstandard features. In all, 104 experimental subjects were tested on up to five books each, and a total of 440 usable questionnaires were obtained.

The findings of the experiment concerning the memorability of standard author-title-subject information are reported elsewhere.[3-8] One finding is of special interest, here, however, since it bears on the need to exploit nonstandard information to as great an extent as possible. It was found that standard author-title-subject information sufficient for looking the document up directly in conventional card catalogs was remembered only 18 percent of the time. Moreover, sufficient information to narrow down the location of the book to within fifty cards was remembered in an additional 37 percent of the cases only. Thus according to this data, if we think of the typical library patron as being unwilling to read through more than fifty catalog cards one by one, the chances are only around 55 percent that present-day catalogs will be of any use to him in locating items on the basis of remembered clues. This makes a strong case for seeking out ways of exploiting nonstandard information, if possible.

In addition to standard author-title-subject data, the questionnaire interrogated the subjects about the following nonstandard features of the books they had read:

1. Color of cover (whether white, gray, orange, etc.);
2. Binding (spiral, cloth, etc.);
3. Approximate height (samples supplied);
4. Approximate number of pages;
5. Condition (new, somewhat used, etc.);
6. Approximate date of publication;
7. Type of work (handbook, textbook, etc.);
8. Level of work (popular, professional, etc.).

The questionnaire also inquired whether or not

the book in question possessed the following features. These will later be referred to as "binary" features because only two answers (feature present or feature absent) are appropriate to such questions.

9. Index;
10. Tables;
11. Figures, charts, diagrams;
12. Chapter titles;
13. Quotations from literary works;
14. Case studies;
15. Graphs;
16. Prefatory material;
17. Footnotes;
18. Bibliography or suggested readings;
19. Dedication;
20. Glossary;
21. Problems at ends of chapters;
22. Single volume (i.e., Is the book a single volume work?);
23. Translation (i.e., Is the book translated?);
24. Reprint or revision (i.e., Is the book a reprint or revised edition?).

This list of twenty-four features is thought to cover most, though not all, of the more obvious kinds of nonstandard information which come to mind as being of possible use. A few other kinds were touched upon in the questionnaire, but they will not be taken up here.

To give a clearer impression of the nature of the questionnaire, the full text of the question on cover color is quoted below as an example of a typical question format:

Color (Check the choice that most accurately describes the book.)

___blue or blue green   ___black, dark gray, dark blue, etc.   ___green
___brown or tan   ___red   ___purple or violet
___orange   ___white   ___yellow
___gray

The ten color categories listed in this question were settled upon more or less arbitrarily by the experimenters. A sheet of special instructions was issued along with the questionnaire, one of which informed the subjects that it was permissible to check two or more color categories if necessary to describe a multicolored book. Most of the questions followed a format similar to the above one, except that some—to be specific, the questions on size, date of publication, and number of pages—did not have the format of a multiple choice question but instead provided a single blank for an approximate figure. Note that no "don't know" blank was provided as part of the question on cover color. The absence of specially provided "don't

know" blanks may have prompted some subjects to guess at many of the questions as best they could, a possibility whose implications will be discussed presently.

The pertinent data obtained from the memory experiment is tabulated in [Cooper's *Data Supplement* . . . .[9]]. It consists of twenty-four tables, with one table corresponding to each nonstandard feature type listed above. Each table constitutes a cross classification of questionnaires by correct answer and by response actually given. Data from single blank questions such as the one asking the approximate date of publication were put into this matrix form by choosing a series of discrete ranges and interpreting the response as though it had been a choice from among such ranges.

PRELIMINARY SURVEY OF EXPERIMENTAL RESULTS

In examining the data compiled from the memory experiment, the two most obvious issues that come to mind are the following. First, what was the proportion of subjects who attempted an answer, as opposed to leaving the question blank? Secondly, of those attempting an answer, what percentage was correct? These two proportions can be readily determined for any nonstandard feature of interest using the tables in [Cooper's *Data Supplement* . . . .[9]]. The proportions of subjects attempting to answer ranged from a low of 29 percent for the question on whether the book contained a dedication, up to 99 percent for the question on the level of readership for which the work was intended. The median response rate for all twenty-four features was 74 percent. The proportions of attempted answers (other than "don't know") that proved to be correct ranged from 24 percent for the inquiry regarding the approximate number of pages (an answer was counted as "correct" if it fell within a hundred pages of being correct) up to 97 percent for the question of whether the book was a single-volume work, with a median accuracy rate for all features of 72 percent. In order to obtain the accuracy rates some rather arbitrary decisions had to be made in some cases as to what constituted a "correct" response. For this and other reasons, it would be unwise to attach much significance to the exact figures just given. They are intended to convey a general impression only, to wit, that the response rate was on the whole rather high but that the accuracy rate among those who responded was for the most part unimpressive.

The high response rate and low accuracy rate observed for many of the questions suggest the possibility that the subjects may have been indulging in a good deal of guesswork. Because a "don't know" blank was not provided for all questions, and because there was no specific directive asking the subjects to indicate "don't know" responses by leaving questions blank, it is possible that there was a tendency for the subjects to make a stab at all questions that had a multiple choice format, whether they really knew the answer or not. Such a tendency would hardly be surprising in subjects who were students accustomed to multiple choice tests of the if-you-don't-know-make-a-guess type. There is no way of knowing just how strong the compulsion to guess was, although some evidence that it was not overwhelming is seen in the fact that almost all subjects left at least a few multiple-choice-format questions blank. The likeliest presumption is that the subjects did not do very much purely random guessing, but that they nevertheless indulged in quite a bit of what might be called "semi-guesswork." That is to say, they probably attempted to give answers to many questions on the basis of exceedingly dim recollections or vague hunches.

If indeed a lot of semi-guesswork took place during the experiment, it was not necessarily a bad thing. In fact, it can be argued that a method of questioning which encouraged semi-guesswork was entirely appropriate for an experiment whose purpose was to gauge the usefulness of nonstandard information for retrieval purposes. Briefly, the argument runs like this: When a retrieval system is unable to retrieve just one document for the patron with certainty that it is the one he wants, the next best thing it could do is, in effect, to determine for him an optimal order in which to search the collection. That is, it would be the task of the retrieval system to retrieve documents for the user's inspection in such an order that documents with the highest probability of being the wanted one would be presented to the user first. Even a vaguely recalled and possibly mistaken feature described by the patron, if exploited in the right way, could be used to improve this search order somewhat; for the feature in question presumably has at least a slightly greater probability of being as the patron describes it than it has of being any other way. Semi-guesswork should therefore actually be encouraged at future automated catalogs, and so it is appropriate that nothing was done to discourage semi-guesswork in the memory experiment. However, care is required that the data

from the experiment be analyzed in such a way as to take the possibility of guesswork properly into account.

THE MEMORABILITY OF NONSTANDARD INFORMATION

The most obvious factor of importance affecting the potential usefulness of a given type of nonstandard information is its memorability. Unfortunately, the "memorability" of a feature is not an easy thing to define. The most obvious suggestions are quickly seen to be inadequate. For example, one might consider measuring the memorability of a feature by the percentage of questionnaires in which the question about that feature was answered correctly; but unfortunately this percentage fails to indicate whether the remaining questionnaires had wrong answers or no answers at all, a matter which is clearly significant in judging memorability.

The basic problem in using the experimental data to determine "memorability" is the unknown amount of guesswork and semi-guesswork that went on in the experiment. This means that any given correct answer may have been merely a lucky guess; it is certainly no proof in and of itself that the subject really remembered anything. To meet this problem, it is essential that the data be analyzed in such a way as to evaluate the subjects' performance through comparison with what their performance would have been had they adopted a strategy of guessing at all times. That is, we must ask: How much *better* did the subjects do by availing themselves of their recollections than they could have been expected to do through random guesswork alone?

For concreteness let us examine the figures found in Table 1 adapted here from [Cooper's *Data Supplement* . . . .[9]]. A reasonable approach would be to compare these figures in some sensible way against what they might have been had subjects used a chance device to determine their answers. The first such device to come to mind is a fair coin. Are the figures in Table 1 consistent with the hypothesis that in all cases where a definite response was given, the subject had merely flipped a coin, answering that the book had an index if it came up heads and that it did not if it came up tails? Under the fair coin flipping hypothesis, one would expect the numbers of "index present" answers and "index absent" answers to be approximately equal, but the results show that the former outnumbered the latter by 212 to 87.

TABLE 1.

Data from Memory Experiment Concerning Indexes
Augmented by Expected Values

| | ACTUAL PROPERTY | | |
REMEMBERED PROPERTY	INDEX PRESENT	INDEX ABSENT	TOTAL
Index present	155 (145.3)	57 (66.7)	212
Index absent	50 (59.7)	37 (27.3)	87
No response	96	45	141
Total	301	139	440

Such a disproportion is extremely unlikely under the fair coin hypothesis and so that hypothesis must be rejected.

The assumption that the random device used was a fair coin was purely arbitrary, and this is an observation that suggests a more enlightening test. Could the subjects have been using a *biased* coin, one weighted in such a way that the expected ratio of heads to tails was 212 to 87? Testing the biased-coin hypothesis is equivalent to testing the hypothesis that the subjects were merely guessing, but doing so with a marked tendency to guess "index present" rather than "index absent," the odds being 212 to 87 in favor of the former. Such a tendency could easily appear without the memory of the book in question being its cause; for example, a tendency to guess "index present" could be occasioned by the general knowledge that most books have indexes, hence the necessity to find out whether the obtained responses were correct more often than would be expected from such guesswork. Now, if a coin biased to produce on the average 212 heads for 87 tails had been used, one would expect that for books with indexes the number of "index present" answers and "index absent" answers would be approximately the ratio of 212 to 87, and the same for books without indexes. On this basis, the cell entries to be expected under the biased coin hypothesis can be calculated. The calculated values are shown in parentheses in the upper four cells of Table 1. The observed numbers in the table are not strikingly different from those in parentheses, indicating that as a group the responding subjects did only slightly better on this nonstandard feature by applying their memories than they could have been expected to do with an appropriate chance device.

In cases where the difference between computed and observed results is small, it is customary to apply a statistical test to see whether the difference might reasonably be accounted for by chance fac-

tors alone. An appropriate test (the two-tailed chi-square test at the .05 significance level with Yates correction for continuity) was applied to the above table, and it indicated that the differences between the observed and computed values could *not* reasonably be attributed wholly to chance factors. Stated more precisely, results as different from expectations as those observed would have less than one chance in twenty of occurring under the biased coin hypothesis, and so the hypothesis may be rejected. This is statistical assurance that at least some of the subjects must have been using their memories rather than their guessing facilities on this question. The same test was made for the remaining six-cell tables[9] with similar results in all cases but one. That case was the question on whether the book had problems at the ends of its chapters, the responses to which turned out not to be significantly more accurate than random guessing.

Comparing the four parenthesized figures in the above table with their unparenthesized counterparts gives some idea of the memorability of the index feature of books. However, it would be desirable to summarize the memorability of indexes in a single figure. As a step in this direction, it is possible to condense the six-cell table down to four cells by combining the "no response" row with the two upper rows. This is done as follows: One assumes that the 141 subjects giving no response had no recollection of the feature whatsoever. Therefore, if they had been forced to make a response, that response would have been a random guess. Suppose that a certain proportion p of the 141 had guessed "index present," and the remaining fraction $(1 - p)$ had guessed "index absent." The results would have been as shown in Table 2. This table shows the quantities from the upper four cells of Table 1 augmented by the expected numbers of additional guesses which would have accrued to these cells if the no-response sub-

TABLE 2.

Data from Memory Experiment Collapsed into Four Cells and Augmented by Expected Values

REMEMBERED PROPERTY	ACTUAL PROPERTY		TOTAL
	INDEX PRESENT	INDEX ABSENT	
Index present	$155 + 96p$ $(145.3 + 96p)$	$57 + 45p$ $(66.7 + 45p)$	$212 + 141p$
Index absent	$50 + 96(1 - p)$ $[59.7 + 96(1 - p)]$	$37 + 45(1 - p)$ $[(27.3 + 45(1 - p)]$	$87 + 141(1 - p)$
Total	301	139	440

jects had been forced to make wild guesses. In effect, collapsing Table 1 into Table 2 changes the rules of the experiment after the fact in such a way as to remove the complicating factor of null responses.

A single figure indicating memorability can be obtained from Table 2 simply by subtracting the expected percentage of correct answers from the observed percentage of correct answers. The observed number of correct answers is $155 + 96p + 37 + 45(1 - p)$ and the number expected if all subjects had guessed is $145.3 + 96p + 27.3 + 45(1 - p)$. Converting to percentages and subtracting, one obtains a difference of 4.4 percent. This figure,

which represents the percentage of correct answers over and above the percentage to be expected from guesswork, we shall call the memorability level" of the feature. It is possible to compute the memorability level in a similar way for all the nonstandard features under consideration, including those whose tables in the appendix consist of more than six cells.

In Table 3, the twenty-four nonstandard features are ranked according to their memorability indexes. From the table it is seen that the approximate number of pages was the most memorable feature of a book to the subjects of this experiment. The color of the cover, which one might

TABLE 3.

Nonstandard Features Ranked in Order of Decreasing Memorability

NONSTANDARD FEATURE	NUMBER OF RESPONSE CATEGORIES	MEMORABILITY LEVEL (%)
Number of pages	6	19
Case studies	2	18
Level of work	6	17
Figures	2	16
Date	10	15
Type of work	13	15
Tables	2	13
Height	7	12
Color of cover	11	11
Quotations from literary works	2	10
Binding	8	9
Condition	5	9
Footnotes	2	8
Graphs	2	7
Translation	2	7
Reprint or revision	2	5
Index	2	4
Bibliography	2	4
Dedication	2	4
Single volume	2	3
Chapter titles	2	3
Preface	2	2
Glossary	2	1
Problems at ends of chapters	2	0.4
Average	4	9

have supposed would be among the most memorable features, ranks only ninth. The least memorable aspect of a work among all those investigated was whether it had problems at the ends of its chapters, which is not surprising in view of the previously mentioned finding that the observed responses did not even show a statistically significant difference from random responses for this feature.

The average feature showed an improvement of only 9 percent in number of correct answers over what would be expected from sheer guesswork, and the most memorable feature an improvement of only 19 percent. This is hardly an impressive showing. However, in fairness to the mental abilities of the subjects, it must be added that not all mistaken responses were necessarily occasioned by faulty memory. Some of what were recorded as mistakes may have been merely a matter of semantics—of terminological differences between experimenters and subjects. As a case in point, there was a strong tendency for subjects to classify as "black, dark gray, dark blue, etc." books which the experimenters had judged to be "blue or blue-green." The experimenters themselves commented on the difficulty of deciding in which of these two classes to put certain moderately dark blue books, so it would hardly be surprising if there had been some differences of judgement on this point between experimenters and subjects. There are indications that where type of work and condition of work were concerned, rather wide differences in judgement arose between the experimenters, who were accustomed to the terminology of librarianship, and the subjects, who were not. The extent to which such differences of judgment contributed to the total number of ostensibly "incorrect" answers obtained in the experiment is not known. Whatever the extent, however, any semantic difficulties affecting the experiment could well affect the success of future retrieval systems also, and so for present purposes they can be viewed as influences tending to make the experiment more realistic.

The measure of memorability level employed in Table 3 has many good aspects. For example, because it involves a comparison with random guessing it is not greatly affected by the arbitrary decision as to how close a subject's recollection of the number of pages in a book must be to the actual number of pages in order that his estimate be considered "correct." On the other hand, it is necessary to bear in mind that this measure of memorability has limitations. Its most serious defect is that it has a tendency to favor features with many

response categories over those with few; at least, this is so under certain plausible interpretations of the work "memorable." In consequence, it is not clear that, for example, a book's color is really more memorable than its footnotes, for the better showing of the former in terms of the memorability level may be due mainly to the color question's larger number of allowable responses on the questionnaire eleven as opposed to two. However, features with the same or nearly the same number of answer categories can be compared with reasonable safety. The number of answer categories for each feature is included in Table 3 to aid in its interpretation. Another limitation of the measure is that it makes no allowance for degrees of mistakenness. For example, an estimate of a book's length which is in error by only a hundred pages is treated as if it were just as mistaken as an estimate which is out by five-hundred.

Conceivably some more elaborate measure of memorability could be constructed to overcome the dependence of the "memorability level" measure on the number of response categories. However, there is some question whether one could ever discover a completely convincing mathematical formulation for such a vague concept as "memorability." In any case, it would seem that efforts to construct a more refined measure would be better directed toward explicating the concept of "retrieval usefulness" instead of "memorability." It is the utility of a book property for retrieval purposes which is of ultimate interest, and it will shortly be seen that memorability is only one factor affecting retrieval usefulness.

EXPECTED SEARCH LENGTH AS A MEASURE OF RETRIEVAL USEFULNESS

How can "retrieval usefulness" be gauged? The measure which will be employed here is based on the concept of *expected search length* and its companion notion, the *reduction factor* in expected search length. These concepts are presented in detail elsewhere[10] in the more general setting of subject retrieval. The basic notions are equally applicable to specific work retrieval however, and in this context they are simple enough to be conveyed by a few examples.

By the "expected search length" of a request is meant the number of unwanted documents the requester could expect to have to search through randomly before finding the wanted one. For example, if the wanted document is known to be in a set of 201 documents, the user could examine the documents in the set one at a time in random order until he came upon and recognized the one he was after. If he did this, the wanted document might turn up early in his search and it might turn up late, but the statistical expectation is that this user would have to look through exactly 100 unwanted documents (i.e., half of the unwanted documents in the set) before coming to the wanted one. A nontechnical interpretation of this statistical expectation is that if he were to repeat his random search for many hypothetical trials, the *average* number of unwanted documents he would be forced to discard in each trial would be approximately 100.

This simple idea contains the germ of a method for the evaluation of nonstandard clues. For the sake of a clear example, let us make some simplifying assumptions. First, let us assume that we wish to evaluate a nonstandard clue type's potential not in combination with other nonstandard information, as it would almost certainly be used in practice, but instead in complete isolation. That is, we imagine a hypothetical library in which a certain type of nonstandard clue is the *only* type of clue, standard or nonstandard, which a requester is allowed to submit. The question of interest is how much the library's retrieval system would be able to do for the requester with this one clue. Secondly, let us assume for simplicity that the clue type in question is of the binary sort. Thirdly, let us put aside for the moment the problem of poor memory and assume that every requester in this library can be counted on to remember, and remember accurately, whether or not the book he wants has this binary property. Finally, let us make up some statistics about this hypothetical library: (1) The size of the collection is only 201 documents; (2) 61 of the documents have the property and the remaining 140 do not; (3) when users submit requests to this library, 40 percent of the time it is a document having the property which is wanted and 60 percent of the time it is not.

Obviously no retrieval system could isolate the wanted book on the basis of this single binary clue, but it could isolate the *set* of all books that answer to the clue, and this will decrease the requester's expected search length. Suppose a requester submits a request consisting of the answer "feature present" to the question of whether the book he wants has the property. The set of 61 documents having the property could be retrieved for his inspection on the basis of this clue. One of the 61 is the book he wants, so if he searches this retrieved set randomly, his expected search length will be one half of 60 or 30 unwanted documents. Similarly, the expected search length for a "feature absent" request is half of 139 or 69.5 unwanted documents. With 40 percent of the incoming requests resulting in an expected search length of 30 and 60 percent in 69.5, the *average* expected search length will be $.4(30) + .6(69.5) = 53.7$. This means that the number of unwanted documents that would have to be searched through should average approximately 54 per request in the long run in this library.

The figure of 54 can be put in perspective by comparing it with what the average expected search length would have been if not even the single binary clue had been utilized. As previously calculated, a totally random search would have an expected search length of 100. Exploiting the clue reduced this by $100 - 54 = 46$; that is, the expected search length was reduced by a factor of 46 percent as against what it would have been if the retrieval process had made no use of the clue. The figure of 46 percent we call the *expected search length reduction factor* associated with the binary property. It can be interpreted to mean that using the binary property as a clue for retrieval would save the average user 46 percent of the search effort he would otherwise have had to expend to search out his book randomly. Speaking more generally, it can be viewed as a measure of the potential utility of the nonstandard feature in question.

Some of the simplifying assumptions made for the sake of the above example are inessential. The calculation of the expected search length reduction factor for nonbinary features is a direct extension of the binary case. The assumption of a definite collection size is not really needed, since the reduction factor is virtually independent of collection size except for very small collections. Hence statistic (1) could have been dispensed with and (2) restated in terms of percentages. It will be shown later how the possibility of mistaken information can also be taken into account.

THE ROLE OF COLLECTION STATISTICS

Although the exact relationship may not be immediately apparent, it seems clear that the relative abundance or paucity of books having a certain property must have something to do with how useful that property would be as a retrieval clue. To take a colorful example, there is reputed to be a rare edition of a book on reptiles, the binding of which contains a rattlesnake's rattle, which is activated whenever the book is opened. Now, the property of containing such a rattle is presumably a highly memorable property. However, it is such a rare property that it would hardly be worthwhile to ask the *average* library patron whether his book rattles when opened, because the chances are so remote that it does. In practical terms, one would not wish to use up questionnaire space and the user's patience by making every patron answer the yes-or-no question, "Does the book you are after have a rattlesnake's rattle in the binding?" And similarly it would be a waste of computer memory space to assign a special data field to indicate the answer to this question as a binary property for every book in the collection. Evidently then, the memorableness of the property is not the only consideration; the "collection statistics" also affect utility.

The example in the last section showed that the collection statistics that enter the question are of two distinct types. One is what could be called *holdings statistics*, and pertains to how the documents on the library shelves are distributed among the possible categories of a feature. The other type may be called *use statistics*; and pertain to the distribution of a feature's categories observed among incoming specific work requests. To give insight into how collection statistics affect retrieval utility, let us once again consider the hypothetical example of a binary feature that is always remembered accurately. Assuming for the moment that there is no noticeable difference between the holdings and use statistics for a given property, it is possible to compute the expected search length reduction factor for any statistics of interest by the method of the last section. For example, if 30 percent of the documents held in a collection have the property and likewise for documents requested, the expected search length reduction factor turns out to be .42. (Actually the figure is only approximately .42, although it will approximate it more and more closely as larger and larger collection sizes are assumed.) By generalizing this calculation, the reduction factor associated with any given proportion x as the assumed collection statistic can be shown to be $2x(1 - x)$.

The dependence of potential usefulness on collection statistics raises a problem. It is impossible to gauge a feature's potential usefulness for retrieval, either absolutely or relative to that of other features, without making assumptions about the collection for which its use in retrieval is contemplated. What assumptions should be made? No library collection is exactly like any other, so that if the nonstandard features are evaluated relative to one particular library, the evaluations obtained will not be entirely valid for any other library. The best that can be done here is to make the evaluations with respect to some more or less typical library collection, so that at least a gross impression can be gained of what their value would be in other collections. Then, if a reader has special need of a more precise evaluation relative to some other collection, it should be possible for him to repeat our calculations using the statistics of that particular collection.

The collection statistics we shall adopt here are estimates obtained from two random samples of the collection of the main library at the University of Chicago. The first sample, which provided the holdings statistics, consisted of 125 documents drawn with the help of random number tables from the main holdings list. The second, which yielded use statistics consisted of 106 documents drawn randomly from those returned to the circulation desk by the library patrons. These seemingly small samples were in fact sufficiently large so that all estimates of proportions could be made with .95 confidence intervals whose width ranged between ±3 percent and ±9 percent. This was felt to be sufficient accuracy in view of the fact that the expected search length measure of utility for which the data are required is less sensitive to collection statistics than to statistics pertaining to memorability. There is also an argument against the need for large samples arising from the circumstance just discussed, namely, that the statistics of other library collections are not necessarily identical with those of the University of Chicago library anyway.

The raw data obtained from the samples is tabulated in Tables 1b through 24b of [Cooper's *Data Supplement . . . .*[9]]. As one would expect, some features showed collection statistics that were much more favorable for retrieval purposes than others. Among the binary features, the following seven were distributed in the library holdings in the most favorable way: index, bibliography, footnotes, tables, figures, preface, and quotes; each of these occupied a proportion of the library between .3 and .7. Three features—glossary, problems, and single-volume works—showed extremely unfavorable distributions, lying outside the range .04 to .96. There were no truly striking differences found between the holdings statistics and the corresponding use statistics, although for some features there was a difference large enough to be statistically significant (at the .05 significance using the chi-square test) in spite of the smallish sample sizes. These included the type of work, level of work, type of binding, condition, chapter titles, index, and presence of literary quotations.

EXPECTED SEARCH LENGTH FOR A POSSIBLY MISTAKEN REQUEST CLUE

The hypothetical one-clue-library method of evaluation illustrated earlier is easily extended to apply to nonbinary features. We shall show next how it can be generalized to apply as well to information that may be mistaken. Consider a patron who submits to the retrieval system the information that the book he wants is red. Because his memory may be faulty, there is no subset of the collection which can be said with certainty to contain the book he is really after. By the same token, no book or set of books can be eliminated from consideration entirely. The most that can be said is that the books in a certain set—probably but not necessarily the set of all red books—have a higher probability of being what is wanted than do any of the remaining books. Thus all inferences drawn from the patron's stated clue must be probabilistic in nature; they must be inferences to the effect that certain books are *more likely* to be the one wanted than are others.

Suppose now that a retrieval system uses an appropriately programmed computer or is in some other way able actually to compute for each book in the collection the probability that it is in reality the wanted one, given that the requester believes his book to be red. The highest probability figure will be assigned to the members of a certain color class, presumably the class of red books. The next highest probability will be assigned to members of some other class—the orange books, perhaps, if a strong tendency has been observed among requesters to confuse red and orange in their memories. The third highest probability will go to each member of still another class, and so on until each of the eleven color classes has been assigned a number which is the probability that any given member book is the required one. The obvious retrieval strategy is the following: Retrieve for the requester's examination the books with highest probability first. If he fails to find his book by searching randomly through these but is willing to search further, retrieve next books with second highest probability, and so on.

The assumption involved here is essentially that the retrieval system is able to respond to a requester's nonstandard clue by ranking all documents in the collection according to their probability of being wanted. This assumption will allow a calculation of the potential utility of that clue expressed in terms of an expected search length reduction factor. The calculation will show the *maximum* utility of the clue which would be realizable in isolation from other clues, for it seems clear that to rank the documents by probability is the best that could be done for the requester on the basis of a possibly mistaken clue. The remainder of this section presents the details of how the probabilities can be calculated and how the expected search length reduction factor can in turn be computed from the probabilities. Readers willing to accept the mathematics on faith may wish to proceed directly to the next section.

The first task is to deduce, for any given search request having the form of an isolated nonstandard book property, that ranking of the collection by probability which an ideal retrieval system would present to the requester as a response to his request. For the sake of concreteness, let us continue to speak in terms of a color clue. Let the symbol "Black" denote the event that the request consists of the clue that the book has a black or very dark cover. That is, "Black" names the event that the library patron *thinks* the book he wants is black, and that he has so stated, say by checking the appropriate blank on the request card. similarly, let "Blue" denote the event that he thinks his book to be blue, and so forth through the eleven color categories. The symbol "No response" can be added to denote the event that the requester does not remember the color at all and so leaves the request form blank. Further, let "BLACK" denote the event that the book which our requester wants is *really* black, let "BLUE" denote that it is actually blue, and so forth for the remaining color categories. As a preliminary step toward deducing the wanted ranking, we calculate conditional probabilities of the form typified by $pr(\text{BLUE/Black})$, which is the probability that our patron is really after a blue book, given that he says the book he wants is black.

The calculation proceeds using Bayes' theorem:

$$pr(\text{BLUE/Black}) = \frac{pr(\text{Black/BLUE})pr(\text{BLUE})}{pr(\text{Black/BLUE})pr(\text{BLUE}) + \ldots + pr(\text{Black/BLACK})pr(\text{BLACK})}.$$

The right-hand side of the identity involves conditional probabilities such as $pr(\text{Black/BLUE})$. By Table 1a of [Cooper's *Data Supplement* ....[9]], there are ninety cases in which subjects were questioned about books that were really blue, and in twenty of these ninety the subjects mistakenly remembered their book as being black, so the experiment indicated that pr(Black/BLUE) is approximately twenty/ninety. A slightly better estimate of the true probability is obtained by adding one to the numerator and the number of possible responses (including no response) to the denominator, yielding $(20 + 1)/(90 + 12) = .206$ as the desired probability. (This correction is a generalization of the formula of Laplace.[11 (pp. 133-135)] Although controversial, it is nevertheless preferable to the uncorrected ratio, which would lead to such absurd estimates as a probability of zero for small samples when the numerator happens to be zero.) The remaining eleven conditional probabilities on the right-hand side are calculated similarly. The right-hand side involves also quantities such as pr(BLUE), the probability prior to receiving his request that the patron's desired book is blue. According to Table 1b of [Cooper's *Data Supplement* . . . .[9]] 28 of the random sample of 106 books withdrawn from the University of Chicago library were blue. Making a Laplacian correction as before, we take $(28 + 1)/(106 + 11) = .248$ as the estimate of the proportion of users who desire blue books. The other ten colors are treated analogously. Upon substituting all these estimates into the Bayesian equation, one obtains the estimate pr(BLUE/Black) = .330. This figure can be interpreted as meaning that when a library patron states that the book he wishes to locate is black, the chances are about one in three that it is really blue. Such an interpretation assumes of course that the patron is encouraged to use guesswork to the same extent as were the experimental subjects, and also that the semantic difficulties associated with the color category labels are as they were in the experiment. The remaining ten conditional probabilities pr(RED/Black), pr(BLACK/Black), etc., are calculated in a similar way.

It may be asked why a probability such as pr(BLUE/Black) cannot be obtained directly from Table 1a of [*Data Supplement* . . . .[9]], instead of indirectly via Bayes' identity. The reason is that the book collection used in the memory experiment was not a random sample of any real library collection, and the estimate of pr(BLUE/Black) so obtained would be contaminated by any accidental bias toward or away from blue books in experimental collections. In contrast, the conditional probability pr(Black/BLUE) can be safely obtained from Table 1a and is not affected by any such bias the experimental collection might have had. It might also be asked whether the use of

Bayes' theorem is not objectionable. In spite of the controversy surrounding Bayes' theorem and the notorious misapplications of it that have been perpetrated in the past, its application in the present situation is felt to be legitimate, especially since the prior probabilities used are not mysterious assumptions but empirically obtained estimates.

With the foregoing calculations completed, the assignment of probabilities to individual documents is easy. We wish to assign to each document in the entire collection its probability of being the one truly wanted. Suppose the collection contains a total of N documents. Then the number of, say, blue documents it can be assumed to contain is obtained from the holdings sample findings of Table 1b in the [*Data Supplement* . . . .[9]]. According to the table, 26 of the 125 books sampled were blue, which leads to the assumption that the number of blue books in the hypothetical library equals the proportion $(26 + 1)/(125 + 11)$ times N, or $.199 N$. We have already determined that when a user thinks his book is black, the probability of its really being blue is .330. In the absence of information to the contrary, each blue book can be considered equally likely to be the one in question. It follows that each blue book has probability $.330/.199N = 1.66/N$ of being the wanted book. Treating all 11 colors in this way, one can determine the ideal ranking in response the request "Black." It has 11 ranks or "levels" in the following order:

.081 N	black books each having probability	2.22/N
.199 N	blue books each having probability	1.66/N
.029 N	gray books each having probability	1.60/N
.103 N	brown books each having probability	.95/N
.007 N	purple books each having probability	.79/N
.015 N	yellow books each having probability	.78/N
.015 N	orange books each having probability	.66/N
.154 N	multicolored books each having probability	.65/N
.007 N	white books each having probability	.63/N
.118 N	green books each having probability	.60/N
.272 N	red books each having probability	.52/N

This list describes the best possible ranking with which a retrieval system could respond to the isolated request clue "Black." To illustrate the meaning of the list, in a 1,000 document collection constituted like the University of Chicago library, there would be about 81 black books, and these, having a relatively high probability of about .002 each, should be retrieved first. If the patron does not find his book among these but still wished to continue his search, the 199 blue books should be presented next; and so forth. The rankings that would be required by some other clue that a requester might give, such as his statement that his book is blue, or even his statement that he does not remember its color, can be constructed in a completely analogous fashion.

Let us turn now to the problem of evaluating the average usefulness of these rankings. A formula for the expected search length of a request in any arbitrary collection ranking is derived in [Cooper's *Expected Search Length ....*[10]]. When specialized to the case of specific work retrieval, it becomes

$$esl\,(q) = j + \frac{i}{2}\,,$$

where q is the query or search request in question, j is the total number of documents in all levels of the ranking which precede the level containing the wanted document, and i is the number of unwanted documents in the level containing the wanted document. This formula merely states that a requester determined to find his book would have to search through all the books in all the levels preceding the level in which he will eventually find his wanted book, plus an expected total of half the unwanted books in that level. For example, the expected search length for a user who submits the request clue "Black" when the book he wants is really blue would be

$$esl_{\text{BLUE}}\,(\text{Black}) = .081N + \frac{.199N - 1}{2}\,.$$

If N is assumed to be large, this expression can be simplified by deleting the minus one.

The special case where the wanted book is really blue is of no particular interest in itself, but the value of esl_{BLUE} (Black), esl_{GREY} (Black), etc., using the formula

$$esl(\text{Black}) = pr(\text{BLUE/Black})\,esl_{\text{BLUE}}\,(\text{Black}) + \ldots$$
$$+ pr(\text{BLACK/Black})\,esl_{\text{BLACK}}(\text{Black}).$$

This formula weights each special case's expected search length by the probability that that special case will arise from the request "Black." The resulting value is an expected search length free of special assumptions about where the wanted document really is in the weak ordering. Substituting previously obtained figures for the probabilities, one obtains $esl(\text{Black}) = .353N$. To illustrate the meaning of this figure, in a library of 1,000 documents, a user submitting the lone clue "Black" could expect to have to search through 353 documents, on the average, before finding the wanted one.

Even the value of $esl(\text{Black})$ is of little interest in and of itself, since "Black" is merely one of twelve possible responses to interrogation about color. What will the expected search length be *on the average* after a patron has been asked the color of the book he desires? This average can be obtained by weighting the expected search lengths for particular colors by the probabilities of those colors being given as clues. In symbols,

$$esl = pr(\text{Black})\,esl(\text{Black}) + \ldots$$
$$+ pr(\text{Blue})\,esl(\text{Blue})$$
$$+ pr(\text{No response})\,esl(\text{No response}),$$

where esl denotes the expected search length averaged over all users of the system. The probabilities on the right-hand side can be expanded using identities of the form

$$pr(\text{Black}) = pr(\text{Black/BLUE})pr(\text{BLUE}) + \ldots$$
$$+ pr(\text{Black/BLACK})pr(\text{BLACK}).$$

The conditional probabilities in this latter expression have already been estimated from Table 1a of [Data *Supplement ....*[9]], and its remaining probabilities we have already estimated as use statistics from Table 1b. Substitution of these values yields the estimate $pr(\text{Black}) = .155$, and the other probabilities are similarly obtainable. With all the necessary ingredients now available, esl can be computed and turns out to be $.353N$.

We conclude that by exploiting nonstandard cover color information it would be possible to attain an expected search length of around $.353N$ documents for the average user of a library of N books. An average expected search length of $.5N$ is achievable by totally random searching. The expected search length reduction factor is therefore $(.5N - .353N)/.5N$, or $.294$. In other words, the use of a patron's color memory could be expected to cut down the length of his search by about 29 percent on the average. This percentage can of course be computed for any of the nonstandard features, not just cover color, and provides a convenient basis for comparing the retrieval utility to be expected from one type of feature with that of others.

THE RELATIVE USEFULNESS OF THE VARIOUS CLUE TYPES IN ISOLATION

The first two columns of Table 4 constitute a list of all twenty-four clue types together with their corresponding expected search length reduction factors in descending order of the latter. As previously explained, a reduction factor represents the percentage by which a library user's search effort for his book would (on the average) be cut down if he were given an opportunity to state his recollection of the feature in question as an input request to an appropriate retrieval system. It is seen from the table that a properly used nonstandard clue could be expected to reduce the length of a patron's search by as much as 57 percent or as little as 3 percent, depending on the clue type. The reduction factors of the various clue types are spread fairly evenly between these extremes, and average 21 percent.

The first observation to be made about Table 4 is that none of the reduction factors are impressively large. One might have hoped, for example, that by exploiting a library patron's knowledge of a book's color it would be possible to reduce the amount of searching he would have to do to find the book by 80 or 90 percent—that is, by a factor of five or ten. Instead, the experimental results indicate that not even a factor of two would be achieved. This makes it clearer than ever that no single clue type would be of much use in isolation. A second and related observation is that there are some clue types, such as the presence in a book of a dedication, a glossary, or problem sets, which show so little promise of retrieval usefulness that it is questionable whether it would be worthwhile to make use of them at all. Thirdly, there is a tendency in Table 4 as there was in Table 3 for clue types with many answer categories to appear near the top of the ranking, while those with few or only two answer categories appear lower down. Apart from this, it is difficult to discern any very striking pattern in the ranking. There is, for example, no noticeable tendency for the "intellectual" attributes of a book such as its level and type to ,ank either much higher or much lower than "physical" attributes with a similar number of answer categories.

The tendency for features with many response categories to appear high in the list has a straightforward explanation. When a patron is questioned

TABLE 4.

Nonstandard Features Ranked in Order of Decreasing Potential Usefulness

NON-STANDARD FEATURE	EXPECTED SEARCH LENGTH REDUCTION FACTOR (%)	NUMBER OF RESPONSE CATE-GORIES	EXPECTED SEARCH LENGTH REDUCTION FACTOR PER STORED BIT (COL. 2 ÷ LOG$_2$ COL. 3) (%)
Date	57	10	17
Type of work	49	13	13
Number of pages	43	6	17
Binding	32	8	11
Color	29	11	9
Level	27	6	11
Height	27	7	9
Quotes	26	2	26
Condition	26	5	11
Index	23	2	23
Figures	21	2	21
Tables	21	2	21
Chapter titles	20	2	20
Graphs	18	2	18
Footnotes	18	2	18
Case studies	16	2	16
Translation	15	2	15
Preface	14	2	14
Bibliography	8	2	8
Single volume	7	2	7
Reprint or revision	7	2	7
Dedication	5	2	5
Glossary	3	2	3
Problems	3	2	3
Average	21.4	4.0	13.5

about a many-category feature such as color, his reply contains more information (in the information-theoretic sense) than would his answer to a question about, say, a binary feature, such as the inclusion of an index. This is true because a multiple choice question offering many choices is by nature capable of eliciting more information than one offering only two choices. The same point can be made in terms of partitions of the document collection: A binary feature can only divide the collection into two subsets, whereas nonbinary features can partition it further and so permit a better focusing of the requester's search efforts. The ranking in Table 4 is "unfair" insofar as it fails to correct for the natural advantage enjoyed by the features with many response categories.

These admittedly vague remarks can be made more concrete by considering the amount of computer storage space that would be taken up by the various types of document descriptions. A binary feature would require only a single binary digit of storage per document, with, say, a "1" to signify the presence of the feature in the document and a "0" to indicate its absence. A four-category feature would require two bits, an eight-category property three, and so on, with each n-category feature requiring approximately $\log_2 n$ bits of storage space. In an automated catalog where computer storage space was a crucial consideration, the utility of a feature would have to be considered in relation to its price, namely, the storage space needed to record it. In such circumstances the critical quantity to be examined would be the expected search length reduction factor *per stored bit*, obtained by dividing the reduction factor for a feature by the logarithm to the base two of the number of categories subsumed by the feature. The storage problem is a real one, but even aside from any practical storage considerations, this quantity probably achieves as good a correction for the above mentioned "unfairness" as could be hoped for. In the last column of Table 4, the expected search length reduction factors are given on a per-stored-bit basis. Column 4 would be consulted in lieu of column 2 if it is desired to gauge potential usefulness relative to a given amount of stored catalog information rather than to a given number of questions to be answered by the library user.

Table 4 ranks clue types according to what we have called "potential usefulness," but to avoid confusion it must be remembered that the ranking does not necessarily indicate which clue types it would be most *practical* to exploit. For example,

librarians will be quick to point out that color of cover, though shown by Table 4 to be a moderately high-ranking clue-type in terms of memorability and collection statistics, would nevertheless be difficult to exploit in existing libraries because when books are rebound, the new cover is usually of a different color, and also because different copies of the same document often have different cover colors. Other librarians may see a special practical potential in those nonstandard clue-types which happen to be available on MARC tapes of the Library of Congress catalog. We have not touched on any of the practical problems of implementation here, for the reason that the logical first step would seem to be to investigate potential usefulness in principle only. If this theoretical potential turns out to be great enough, it will then become appropriate to explore questions of practical feasibility.

THE USEFULNESS OF NONSTANDARD CLUES IN COMBINATION

The assumption in force up until now that only a single nonstandard clue would be used to effect retrieval was a highly artificial one. It was imposed only in order to obtain separate usefulness ratings for the different clue types. In actual practice, a large number of clues would have to be solicited from the library patron and used in combination in order for him to derive any substantial benefit from their use.

Let us review in more detail how nonstandard clues could be used in combination. Suppose that a library patron cannot remember enough standard information about a book to be able to locate it using conventional library resources, but can nevertheless remember some nonstandard information about it. In a future library equipped to cope with his problem, he might well be asked to fill out a search request card consisting of multiple-choice questions much like the twenty-four questions with which we have been concerned in this study. His completed request card would be submitted as input to a computer programmed especially to compute, for any combination of nonstandard properties, the probability that a book having that combination of properties is the book wanted by the requester. The computations would be based on statistics pertaining to the memorability of the properties—statistics obtainable either from memory experiments such as the one reported here or from the recorded past experience of the system—and also on collection statistics. The results of the computations would be that books having such and such a combination of properties are the likeliest candidates, books with some other combination are next likeliest, and so on. The file of library holdings would then be searched automatically for documents belonging in the high-likelihood classes. The final output given to the user would be a bibliographic list of documents (or possibly the physical documents themselves) grouped in such a way that he could conveniently scan the documents with the highest likelihoods first. If the computed probabilities were very low even for documents in the highest likelihood group (this would be the case, if, for example, the user had left most of the questions on the request card blank), he might wish to abandon his search at the start. Otherwise, he would scan the list until he had recognized the book he was after, although he might at any time give up either from lack of patience or lack of further documents having a sufficiently high probability to justify continued searching. No doubt there are many possible variations on this outlined procedure for exploiting nonstandard clues, but the essential element in all of them must be some means of obtaining for the user's inspection at least the first few levels of a ranking by probability of the document collection.

The computations necessary to associate probabilities with property combinations are fairly involved. The complicating factor is that the nonstandard features of interest are in general not distributed in the document collection in such a way as to be statistically independent of one another. There is also no assurance of statistical independence between what a library user tends to remember concerning one type of feature and what he tends to remember about another. The generalization of the previous probability calculations in such a way as to take proper account of the troublesome dependencies, though not impossible, will not be carried out here. Instead, we shall merely present an extremely rough indication of how effective a retrieval system that could compute the proper probability rankings would be.

One can readily obtain a crude estimate of the effectiveness of a given combination of clue types simply by ignoring the problem of statistical dependencies. To illustrate this, consider the case of a retrieval system that will accept both data and type of work clues. By Table 4, the use of information as to approximate data will (roughly speaking) cut down by 57 percent the number of books to be searched, leaving 43 percent. The type-of-

work information will cut this down by a further 49 percent leaving only 43 percent—.49(43 percent) = 21 percent of the original body of documents. The reduction factor for the combination of these two leading clue types is therefore 100 percent—21 percent = 79 percent. A first approximation to the reduction factor for any clue-type combination of interest may be obtained in the same way.

Using this crude method of estimation, one finds that the expected search length reduction factor achievable from the simultaneous use of all twenty four types investigated is approximately 99.8 percent. This estimate is on the high side; it would probably have to be lowered substantially if the statistical dependencies were taken into account. On the other hand, if refinements were made in the use of the twenty four clue types, and if, in addition, clue types not among the twenty four were used, the additional retrieval power so achieved would help to make up for this to some unknown extent. Perhaps the best that can be done at present is to take the 99.8 percent figure as it stands as an order-of-magnitude guess as to the combined potential retrieval usefulness of "all" nonstandard types of information. To the extent that the conditions of the memory experiment can be assumed to reflect future retrieval conditions, and to the extent that the statistics of the University of Chicago library are typical of document collections in general, it can be said that optimal use of all nonstandard information possessed by a library patron about a document with which he has had previous contact would result in reducing by a ratio of something like five hundred to one the expected search effort necessary for him to locate the document in a large collection.

Some tentative conclusions can now be drawn. An expected search length reduction factor of around 99.8 percent would be very useful in a small library of, say, ten thousand documents, for if the typical user has his expected search length reduced from the five thousand documents to be expected from a random search down to only ten documents, his search efforts will usually meet with early success. On the other hand, in a large collection of, say, one million documents, it is questionable whether a reduction factor of only 99.8 percent would be worth striving for. Even if optimal use were made of all nonstandard clues, there would still be an expected search length in the neighborhood of one thousand documents—a formidable number except for the more patient or desperate of library patrons. This is not to say that *all* requesters would have so large an expected search length. Those of them who were able to supply an above-average amount of nonstandard information with above-average confidence in its accuracy could expect better retrieval results. However, a minority would find the special facilities to be of real value. One is led to the tentative conclusion that the nonstandard information that could be supplied by a patron who has had previous contact with a document would by itself usually be adequate in small collections, but inadequate in large collections, for the location of the document with a modicum of search effort on the patron's part.

If the patron can remember some fragment of standard information in addition to the nonstandard information, the picture changes. Suppose, for example, that he is able to remember that the work he wants comes under the subject heading "Psychology," but he can remember neither author nor title, nor can he supply more specific subject headings. A library of one million documents might have, say, ten thousand documents under this heading, in which case his single piece of standard information would by itself be hopelessly inadequate for retrieval purposes. Retrieval could nevertheless be effected in most such instances if the patron were able to supplement this subject heading information with nonstandard information; for his subject heading information in effect makes it a small collection to be searched instead of a large one. The same would hold true of any other fragment of standard information that could be used to "narrow down" a large collection prior to a search using nonstandard information. Nonstandard information that is by itself inadequate for retrieval may become adequate when supplemented by whatever fragments of standard information are available, and this observation tempers somewhat the pessimism of the previous conclusion stating that nonstandard information would usually be useless for retrieval in very large collections.

SUMMARY

The two most significant findings of the research were the following:

1. *The relative usefulness for purposes of specific work retrieval of the various types of nonstandard book information which were investigated are likely to be approximately as indicated by the ranking in Table 4.* (This ranking assumes a collection makeup similar to that of the University of Chicago library.)
2. *The amount by which the average specific work requester's expected search effort could be reduced by providing him with an appropriate retrieval system to exploit his nonstandard information is a ratio on the order of five hundred to one.* (This very approximate figure assumes that the nonstandard information to be elicited from the user is somewhat more extensive than that investigated in the experiment. It is understood that the figure has relevance only to the requester of a specific work who is already acquainted with the physical document but cannot remember enough standard author-title-subject information about it to look it up on this basis alone.) *Such a ratio would normally be adequate for convenient retrieval in small document collections, but inadequate in large collections except in cases where the nonstandard information can be supplemented by some fragment of standard information.*

It is interesting to speculate whether the retrieval usefulness of nonstandard information could be enhanced by allowing each reported piece of nonstandard information to be accompanied by an indication of the degree of confidence which the person reporting it has in its accuracy. This could be done, for example, by means of a three-choice supplementary question asking him whether he is "certain," "fairly sure," or "not at all sure" of the accuracy of the answer he has given to a main question about a nonstandard feature. This supplementary information would introduce another level of complexity into all probability calculations, but it might increase retrieval effectiveness considerably. There are also other additions and refinements that would probably improve the list of twenty-four questions considered in this paper; for example, one could add questions on loan status (e.g., "Is the book a two-day book or a two-week book?"), on past circulation data (e.g., "Have you taken the book out before?" "If not, can you name anyone who has?"), and on a number of other physical characteristics such as weight or thickness. A few additional questions beside the twenty-four were in fact asked in the experiment; the results are reported in [Vaughn's *Memorability of Book Characteristics. . . .*[3]]. A final possibility for improving the retrieval effectiveness of nonstandard information would be to bring circulation data into play to further improve the prior probability estimates used in the document ranking presented as final output to the user. A simple rule for so doing would be: Within each rank of the ranking established on the basis of the nonstandard information, order the individual documents according to the number of times each has been withdrawn from the library within the past year. More sophisticated rules of greater potential value could obviously be formulated, and there is hope that a very substantial further deduction in expected search length could be achieved through such methods. It is especially recommended that this last possibility be investigated in any future research on the subject.

ACKNOWLEDGMENTS

The findings reported here were obtained as a result of the combined efforts of the entire University of Chicago Graduate Library School catalog research group. They are by no means attributable solely or even largely to the present writer, whose contribution was, in fact, restricted to the development of methods for analyzing and evaluation the experimental data. The conception, design, and execution of the memory experiment, as well as most of the actual numerical computations involved in analyzing its results, were carried out by the other members of the groups. The group members include Don R. Swanson (co-principal investigator), F. Schlipf, R. Carnovsky, D. Vaughn (project leader), M. Blackburn, D. Day, V. Harris, W. Hinkley, E. Montague, N. Radford, H. Schmierer, R. Spaith, and C. Woolpy. Professor George A. Miller and Dr. Jerome Cohen have served as consultants. I am indebted also to Robert K. Tsutakawa, Peter Burns, and Jim Landwehr for individual assistance with some of the more detailed statistical work.

NOTES

[1] E. Montague., Card Catalog Use Studies, 1949-1965. Unpublished Master's dissertation, Graduate Library School, University of Chicago, 1967.

[2] M. Blackburn, Information about Books Known by Users of the Catalog Who Are Looking for a Particular Work. Unpublished Master's dissertation, Graduate Library School, University of Chicago, 1968.

[3] D. Vaughn, Memorability of Book Characteristics: An Experimental Study, in *Requirements Study for Future Catalogs, Progress Report No. 2* (NSF Grant GN 432), University of Chicago Graduate Library School, March 1968, pp. 1-41.

[4] H. Schmierer, Evaluation of Variations in Response Patterns of Psychology and Non-Psychology Students for All Characteristics, in *Requirements Study for Future Catalogs, Progress Report No. 2* (NSF Grant GN 432), University of Chicago Graduate Library School, March 1968, pp. 42-44.

[5] D. Vaughn, Effectiveness of Book-Memory Data for Conventional Catalog Retrieval, in *Requirements Study for Future Catalogs, Progress Report No. 2* (NSF Grant GN 432), University of Chicago Graduate Library School, March, 1968, pp. 45-54.

[6] D. Day, Accuracy and Utility of Subject-Related Responses, in *Requirements Study for Future Catalogs, Progress Report No. 2* (NSF Grant GN 432), University of Chicago Graduate Library School, March 1968, pp. 55-63.

[7] W. Hinkley, An Analysis of Non-Exact Data, in *Requirements Study for Future Catalogs, Progress Report No. 2* (NSF Grant GN 432), University of Chicago Graduate Library School, March 1968, pp. 64-72.

[8] N. Radford, Title, Subtitle and Table of Contents as Sources of Index Words, in *Requirements Study for Future Catalogs, Progress Report No. 2* (NSF Grant GN 432), University of Chicago Graduate Library School, March 1968, pp. 73-80.

[9] W. Cooper, Data Supplement to "The Potential Usefulness of Catalog Access Points other than Author, Title, and Subject, in *Requirements Study for Future Catalogs, Progress Report No. 2* (NSF Grant GN 432), University of Chicago Graduate Library School, March 1968, pp. 221-248.

[10] W. Cooper, Expected Search Length: A Single Measure of Retrieval Effectiveness Based on the Weak Ordering Action of Retrieval Systems, *American Documentation 19* (No. 1): 30-41 (1968).

[11] H. Jeffreys, *Theory of Probability,* 3d ed. (Oxford: Clarendon, 1961).

DESCRIPTIVE CATALOGING

Application and Automation

It is perhaps presumptous to assume that any selection of readings could reflect current trends in the application of descriptive cataloging, but this particular area is of vital importance to the whole library and information community from the point of view of communication. It has offered the greatest promise for cooperative effort between libraries of all types, and nations all over the world. The world of universal bibliography has long since ceased to exist, if it ever existed at all, but continual effort, as reflected through cooperation and centralization, manipulated and maintained by the nonhuman hands of the computer may very well achieve what man could not.

Centralized Cataloging at the National and International Level

John W. Cronin, John M. Dawson, William S. Dix, and James E. Skipper

"For many years librarians had longed for the coming of centralized cataloging, but it remained only a dream until the passage of the Higher Education Act."

INTRODUCTION

When President Johnson signed on May 13 of this year [1966] the Second Supplemental Appropriation Act for Fiscal Year 1966, the earth did not shake nor did the seas open up. I have not heard that there was even dancing in the streets of Lake Placid. But a notable event in the history of libraries had occurred. For in that bill was $300,000 to fund in part, for the next six weeks, Part C of Title II of the Higher Education Act of 1965. This simple piece of legislation reads as follows:

> Sec. 231. There are hereby authorized to be appropriated $5,000,000 for the fiscal year ending June 30, 1966, $6,315,000 for the fiscal year ending June 30, 1967, and $7,770,000 for the fiscal year ending June 30, 1968, to enable the Commissioner to transfer funds to the Librarian of Congress for the purpose of—
>
> (1) acquiring, so far as possible, all library materials currently published throughout the world which are of value to scholarship; and
>
> (2) providing catalog information for these materials promptly after receipt, and distributing bibliographic information by printing catalog cards and by other means, and enabling the Library of Congress to use for exchange and other purposes such of these materials as are not needed for its own collections.

In other words, the Federal Government, after more than one hundred years of hoping and planning by librarians, has accepted a responsibility for the cataloging of books for non-Federal libraries, as a part of its support for higher education, and has provided funds to begin meeting this responsibility.

Title II of the Higher Education Act also provides funds for another notable first, direct money grants to colleges and universities for acquisitions— what I think of as the Edmon Low Bill—, but that it is not the subject . . . . We have been asked to tell the story of nationally-centralized cataloging— of its history, of what has been achieved, and of what its future prospects may be. The latter part of this story has not been told until now to any public audience, although the members of the ARL, and the Executive Committee of the ALA cataloging and Classification Section have been kept informed, for those involved in it have not wanted to report until they had something to say. They now have progress to report.

Let us begin with the early history of centralized cataloging. Mr. Dawson's article, in the *Library Quarterly* for January, 1957, was influential in calling renewed attention to the unnecessary waste of effort in the repeated original cataloging of the same work by individual libraries.

A History of Centralized Cataloging

John M. Dawson

The first documented proposal for centralized cataloging in America was suggested 119 years ago when Charles Coffin Jewett, then Librarian of Brown University and later Librarian of the Smith-

SOURCE: Reprinted from *Library Resources and Technical Services*, 11 (Winter, 1967), pp. 27-49, by permission of the publisher, the American Library Association. Except for Mr. Cronin's paper, this is a verbatim report of a program at the New York Conference of ALA on July 11, 1966, sponsored jointly by the University Libraries Section of ACRL and the Resources and Technical Services Division. The program was organized by William S. Dix, Librarian of Princeton University and Chairman of the ARL Committee on Shared Cataloging, who served as moderator of the panel.

273

sonian Institution, wrote to his English friend, Harry Stevens, asking him to discuss with "gentlemen connected with the British Museum" his plan to make stereotype blocks for individual titles that could be used for later reprintings. Jewett's plan, published a year later, was for the printing and updating of book catalogs. Together with this simple technique for keeping catalogs up to date, Jewett envisioned a uniform system of cataloging with the Smithsonian serving as the agency for centralized cataloging. This proposal is well known to every librarian, and it would be foolish to elaborate on it here. Unfortunately, the scheme foundered and failed because of administrative shortsightedness in the Smithsonian, lack of funds, and the technological inadequacy of the time.

The year 1876 is a landmark in the history of American librarianship and in the history of centralized cataloging. For the Philadelphia Centennial Exposition of that year the United States Bureau of Education published a survey of the public libraries of the country in which Otis H. Robinson advocated centralized cataloging for college libraries, and F. M. Muller, Orientalist and former Librarian of the Bodleian Library, suggested national centralized cataloging, with the British Museum cataloging English books, the Bibliothèque Nationale cataloging French books, and so on, with the cataloging available to all. It is interesting to note that in January of this year (1966) a conference was held at the British Museum to discuss the proposal of the Library of Congress to accept for cataloging purposes the description of publications listed in the national bibliographies of some 18 countries, and that this program is now being implemented by the Library of Congress for books listed in the *British National Bibliography.* One cannot avoid the wry comment that the mills of librarians grind exceeding slow—let us pray that they grind exceeding fine!

In the convention of librarians held in Philadelphia in that same year—the convention which led to the founding of the American Library Association—cooperative cataloging was one of the principal topics. The committee to which this was referred had its hands full with Poole's index so that a year later a new committee was formed to forward cooperative cataloging. (This organizational hassle is not unfamiliar to us today.) Little emerged from this second committee other than proposals to standardize library supplies, and they made no suggestions for centralized or cooperative cataloging.

However, Melvil Dewey, who had raised the question of cooperative cataloging at the 1876 meeting, used the pages of the *Library Journal* to ask, "Shall we try to establish a central cataloging bureau supported by the Association? Can the publishers be induced to prepare suitable titles and furnish them with books? Is it practicable for the Library of Congress to catalog for the whole country." He concluded that centralized cataloging was practical, and, like Jewett, saw the need for uniform cataloging and went so far as to present rules for the preparation of cooperative copy. So a committee on Uniform Title Entries was set up. Impatient with the proliferation of committees (another modern note?) Dewey was equally impatient with the paucity of results. "While we have so much with which to be satisfied, there has been no progress in what seemed the main question—cooperative cataloging." Proposals similar to Dewey's were made by Justin Winsor and C. A. Nelson.

The enthusiasm and demand for joint action in cataloging that flourished in these years bore but little fruit. *Publishers' Weekly* did begin publishing "title-slips" prepared under the supervision of librarians, but this plan was abandoned after operating at a loss for a year. Still, the concept was not forgotten. In 1882 W. K. Stetson (in an article aptly titled "Cooperation Again") advocated centralized cataloging and gave the result of what may well be the first study of duplication between libraries.

In 1887, the ALA Publishing Section attempted the printing of catalog cards from electrotypes set for the *American Catalog,* but the lack of subscriptions brought this venture to an early demise. Not until late in 1893 were concrete plans for printing and distributing catalog cards again discussed. The Rudolph Indexer Company proposed to issue cards for use with its ingenious catalog cabinet, and the Library Bureau announced its own plans for printing cards. The Rudolph Indexer program was short lived, but the Library Bureau continued its activities until, in 1897, the Publishing Section of the ALA took it over. About sixty libraries subscribed; many publishers sent their books for cataloging and, by selling the books as well as the cards for some 1,350 titles per year, the project maintained an uncertain self-sustaining position. To this in 1898 was added the printing of cards for analytics for a selected list of periodicals, the copy furnished by a few major research libraries. This combination of centralized and cooperative cataloging seems to have been the first really successful endeavor in the field.

At the end of the nineteenth century, librarians had been discussing cooperative and centralized cataloging for some fifty years. Of the many schemes proposed, a few had been tried, and one had been operating with some success for seven years. It was centralized cataloging on a small scale, to be sure, but it had demonstrated, for the first time, that such a scheme was practical. It was a monument to faith and persistence. But there were other developments since Jewett's day: the card catalog had been generally accepted; the catalog card had been standardized; the need for uniform rules of cataloging had been recognized, and a beginning had been made in the formulation of the necessary codes; and, perhaps more important, a climate of opinion favorable to the development of cooperative and centralized cataloging had been created. The stage, then, had been set for the progress of the twentieth century.

At the Montreal Conference of the ALA in 1900, Ernest Cushing Richardson reported that the Co-operation Committee had unanimously recommended the formation of a bureau under the Publishing Section for the cooperative cataloging and printing of cards, the cooperating libraries to guarantee the costs. Arrangements were made for the Library of Congress to sell to the Publishing Board cards for current American titles. Dewey favored the plan but thought that a better solution would be for the Library of Congress to print and distribute its cards.

Dewey's hopes were soon to be fulfilled. Herbert Putnam, recently appointed Librarian of Congress, announced that the Library of Congress was prepared to distribute copies of its cards directly to libraries desiring them, and on October 28, 1901, issued a circular describing its plan. This had been urged as early as 1876, and at last the Library of Congress had accepted at least a part of this responsibility. In addition, the depository catalog system was established so that scholars throughout the country might be aware of the resources of the Library of Congress. In the first full year of service 212 libraries ordered cards, cash sales had been made to the amount of $3,785.19, and deposit accounts of $6,451.53 had been received. The success of the enterprise was assured.

A few years later other government agencies agreed to furnish copy to the Library of Congress for printing and distribution, and in 1905 the Washington Public Library began supplying copy. At the end of 1902 cards were available for about 90,000 titles; six years later cards were available for some 347,000 titles. Then, in 1910, deposi-

tory libraries were asked if they would supply copy for titles which the Library of Congress did not expect to catalog; about one-third agreed to do so, but the number supplying copy increased as the number of libraries using LC cards increased. And in 1930, through subscriptions, a section was established at the Library of Congress to add Dewey Decimal numbers to these cards.

This program was eminently successful and might have been expected to answer the needs of the libraries of the country. It soon developed that the needs of research libraries were not adequately served, and in 1923 ALA appointed a Committee on Bibliography with the expansion of centralized cataloging as its objective. Little came of it. In 1927 the Catalog Section held a symposium which culminated in the appointment of another committee. This committee reported that from 20 to 75 percent of the annual accessions of college and university libraries were not covered by LC cards, and asked that Council appoint a permanent committee to work on the problem. This committee, with Keyes Metcalf as chairman, was appointed and a grant secured to finance its investigations.

The Metcalf committee studied duplication of original cataloging (again!) and other aspects of the problem, and worked out a scheme for an office at the Library of Congress to solicit and revise copy to be distributed by the Library of Congress, with an initial support grant. The Richardson Committee felt that this new committee was infringing on its territory, and a bitter internecine quarrel resulted.

In 1932 the office began its work; in 1934 it was reorganized as a department of the Library of Congress and eventually absorbed the earlier contributions of cooperative copy. This continued until 1940 when, in the general reorganization of the Library of Congress, it severed its connection with the Cooperative Cataloging Committee and was reorganized as the Cooperative Cataloging Section of the Library of Congress. For years cooperative copy was a significant proportion of the number of LC cards in print; in recent years this proportion has been declining.

The Library of Congress card service is the largest and most successful centralized cataloging agency in the world. In 1965 it sold over 61 million cards at a gross revenue of over $3,700,000 to some 17,000 subscribers. Yet so extensive a service has not completely met the needs of the larger libraries. In 1937 a study was made of some 65 university, college, and public libraries; it found that the range of use of LC cards was from 15 to 82.5 percent, with a median of 66.6 percent. In a survey made of 11 large libraries in 1947/48 of the cost of cataloging, 6 reported their use of LC cards as ranging from 51 to 75 percent. In 1956 an intensive study of the use of LC cards by nine major academic libraries showed that they were available for from 30 to 65 percent of the titles acquired by those libraries.

The constant need for more centralized cataloging than has been available has led to many proposals. In 1941 the Colorado College and Head Librarians Conference appointed a committee to study centralization of technical processes which produced an extensive program of research in the field that excited national interest. As a result of their proposals, in 1943 a "Joint Committee for the Study of Basic Problems in Technical Processes" was appointed. Unfortunately, war and other circumstances prevented the development of this committee's activities. When the Midwest Inter-Library Center was in its planning stage, centralized purchasing and cataloging were urged as important elements of its program, but this suggestion came to naught. In 1948 Ralph Ellsworth, at the invitation of the Library of Congress, studied the existing system and recommended the establishment of a Centralized Cataloging Service to which participating libraries would send copies of their order slips so that if the Library of Congress had not already acquired the book, it would do so and catalog it promptly. Libraries were to pay for this by paying not the cost of printing and distribution alone, but what it would have cost them to catalog the book themselves.

The concept of "cataloging-in-source" was implicit in a number of very early proposals for centralized cataloging and persisted down through the years. Finally, in 1958 the Council on Library Resources, Inc., made a grant to the Library of Congress to explore the possibilities of such a plan, and Andrew D. Osborn, then Assistant Librarian of Harvard University, undertook the study. He recommended the project. The Council on Library Resources made a grant to the Library of Congress to finance a pilot operation. The work began; publishers were solicited to cooperate by sending copy before publication so that facsimiles of LC cards could be incorporated as an integral part of the published book. Some 1200 titles were so cataloged, and a panel of experts made a study of "consumer reaction." It is fruitless to delve into the project too deeply. The conclusion of the Library of Congress was "that neither a full nor a partial Cataloging-in-Source program is desirable. . . .There should be no further experiments with Cataloging-in-Source. . . ." On the other hand, the principal recommendation of the Cataloging Policy and Research Committee on the consumer reaction survey was "that a national program of Cataloging-in-Source be undertaken immediately by the Library of Congress, with as complete publisher cooperation as possible." The Librarian of Congress stated, "I am compelled to the conclusion that a modified Cataloging-in-Source program could not be justified in terms of utility versus cost and that the Library of Congress should not seek funds for a further experiment along those lines." One of our professional wits quoted, "They came to bury Caesar, not to praise him." Cataloging-in-Source died, but it died hard, and one still runs across lamentations in current library literature.

And so we come to the next phase—the concern of the Association of Research Libraries with centralized cataloging which led to the "Shared Cataloging Project."

Recent Developments in Centralized Cataloging

William S. Dix

It is hard to know where to pick up the story of which John Dawson has sketched in the background. Perhaps this phase begins with Ralph Ellsworth's characteristically forthright editorial in the Fall, 1963, *Colorado Academic Library,* in which he picked up an old theme of his and pointed out forcefully the absurdity of each individual library laboriously and independently cataloging the same books at the same time. Perhaps it begins with a letter which Richard Logsdon, as Chairman of ARL, wrote to Ellsworth on October 29, 1963, saying, in part, "Since writing to you a few days ago I have pretty much come to the conclusion that ARL could do nothing more important in the next year or two than improve the situation with respect to coordinated and centralized cataloguing."

At any rate, in the fall of 1963 various members of the Association of Research Libraries began informal discussions looking toward some solution of a problem which was becoming intolerable. From a very general survey it appeared that the seventy-four ARL libraries were spending about 16 percent of their total budgets on cataloging. This amounted to about $16,000,000 a year for this small group of libraries alone. Yet they still had to do about 45 percent of original cataloging, without benefit of copy from the Library of Congress, even though LC had been since 1901 making available copies of the cards prepared for its own use and had last year sold 46 million cards to some 17,000 individual libraries. Backlogs of uncataloged material were mounting sharply in many libraries, having increased 160 percent in the previous decade.

Against this background the members of the ARL, upon recommendation of the Executive Board, voted unanimously at the Sixty-third Meeting in January, 1964, to make some solution to the cataloging problem its principal priority and to appoint a committee to attack the problem. The Committee, which immediately named itself the Committee on Shared Cataloging, was composed of Ralph Ellsworth, Richard Logsdon, Stephen McCarthy, James Skipper, and, later, Edmon Low, with William Dix as Chairman.

There is time here to trace only in the barest outline the development of the Committee's thinking. It decided first of all that it needed more facts and, like all committees, proposed a series of studies. Only one of these was in fact undertaken, a study of the characteristics of original cataloging being done in a sample group of libraries, an updating of the study made by John Dawson in 1952 and published in the *Library Quarterly* in 1957. This study, financed by a grant from the Council on Library Resources, was valuable in confirming original impressions that centralized copy was particularly needed for current Western European monographs and in general for indicating the nature of the problem.

It soon became clear, though, that no one was in a mood to wait for long studies, and during the next year in a number of meetings the Committee concluded, more or less in this sequence, that a way must be found to reduce the percentage of original cataloging of current monographs, concentrating first on Western Europe; that copy must be available very promptly to be useful; that some single, centralized agency would probably be more feasible than any system of cooperative cataloging by a number of libraries; and that the Library of Congress, already meeting 55 percent of our needs, was the logical agency.

A meeting was held with the Librarian of Congress and his staff, at which Mr. Mumford stated that he believed the specifications of the Committee could be met under certain conditions, but that he could not initiate budget proposals for solving the problem without legislation specifically authorizing and directing the Library of Congress, as the national library, to extend its current program to meet the national cataloging need.

All through this period there was a feeling, in the absence of hard cost analysis, that it might be possible for the libraries themselves to finance a central agency; but a strong and vocal element insisted that there was strong justification and at least a dim possibility of obtaining government support. This brings us down to February of 1965.

About this time, the Higher Education Act appeared, with various forms of library assistance in Title II, and the idea dawned that the centralized cataloging concept might be added. Along with other library witnesses on other aspects of Title II, the Committee presented testimony before Congresswoman Edith Green's House subcommittee on March 10, 1965, and Senator Morse's subcommittee on May 19, 1965, proposing to each the amendment of the pending legislation to provide funds for the Library of Congress to increase its acquisitions, to catalog the books promptly, and to distribute copy to other libraries. In introducing the House testimony on the cataloging proposal, Mrs. Green generously said, "While it is not something that, to the best of my knowledge, is covered in this particular bill, I do think it is perhaps more significant than any part covered in the bill." Senator Morse was even more dramatic. He interrupted me half-way through my prepared statement to say: "I think you have proved your case. I want to announce that I am willing to introduce this as an amendment." And he did, that afternoon.

Now, all of this did not happen by accident. We had a sound idea, but we would not have had the right hearing for it without the skilled and careful advance work by Germaine Krettek, Director of the ALA Washington Office; by James Skipper, Executive Secretary of the ARL; and particularly by a new friend, Professor Julian Levy of the University of Chicago, an old Washington hand.

What happened then and later would have been impossible without the help at critical moments of dozens of others, particularly Edward Freehafer of the New York Public Library, then Chairman of the ARL.

There followed a year in which both congressional committees reported out bills with the cataloging provision intact; it survived the conference committee in spite of a considerable hassle over other aspects of the legislation; and the Higher Education Act was finally passed on November 8, 1965, at the very end of the session. But the appropriations bill, which was approved almost simultaneously, omitted Title II completely, for reasons too complicated to recount. There began again work with the Office of Education, the Bureau of the Budget, and the Congress to get an appropriation the next time around, ceasing, temporarily, only with the signing of the appropriations bill which I cited at the beginning of this program as a rather significant event.

I hope that from all of this I have left an impression of an orderly, well-planned march toward an objective—for I would like to deceive you. Actually, I must confess that there was quite a bit of barking up the wrong tree, of running off down the wrong lane, and in general of thrashing around in the Washington underbrush. It must be said though, that the Committee did keep its collective eye clearly fixed on a single objective, the providing somehow from a central agency of a considerably-greater amount of cataloging copy. The prospects for reaching this objective look brighter than they have for a good many decades.

Through all of this the Library of Congress, once the will of the Congress was clear, has acted with energy and imagination.

Remarks on LC Plans for Implementation of New Centralized Acquisitions and Cataloging Program Under Title IIC, Higher Education Act

John W. Cronin

The general purpose of my part in this program discussion is to report to you on the new program of centralized acquisitions and cataloging to be undertaken by the Library of Congress under authorization granted under Title IIC of the Higher Education Act of 1965. By this action, the Congress took two most important steps to aid libraries of higher education in the United States: (1) it fully recognized for the first time, the importance of granting Federal aid and assistance toward solving the problem of cataloging in this country; and (2) it gave the Library of Congress a clear mandate to provide new and unparalleled services for the benefit of academic and research libraries of this country.

For many years librarians had longed for the coming of centralized cataloging, but it remained only a dream until the passage of the Higher Education Act. The impetus for this legislation originated first in discussions of the Subcommittee on the National Union Catalog of the ALA/RTSD Resources Committee at its meeting held at the Library of Congress in November 1963. The Committee, at that time, requested the Library of Congress to prepare alternative agenda proposals for a centralized cataloging program to be considered at the 1964 Midwinter meeting of the Association of Research Libraries in Chicago. These proposals were as follows: the first concerned a shared cataloging program based on a decentralized plan of having the Library of Congress distribute catalog entries for current publications supplied by cooperating libraries to the National Union Catalog; and the second was on the basis of establishing a centralized cataloging control for current publications at the Library of Congress. In December 1963 both the above draft proposals were reviewed by LC staff with the Cataloging Policy and Research Committee of RTSD at a meeting held at the Library of Congress. Representatives of the ARL, the National Library of Medicine, and the National Agricultural Library were in attendance. It was the unanimous opinion of the Cataloging Policy and Research Committee that a centralized cataloging program based at the Library of Congress was to be preferred since such a program would insure a standardized product and would be of maximum benefit to all libraries concerned.

The proposals were then considered at the ARL Midwinter meeting at Chicago in 1964, and it was decided to establish a Committee on Shared

Cataloging to plan the implementation of a centralized cataloging program and to report definitive recommendations to ARL for necessary action. The matter was further discussed by the ARL at its St. Louis meeting in June 1964, and the Committee met also with the Librarian of Congress and his staff in the late Fall of 1964. Formal approval was given by ARL at the 1965 Midwinter meeting to the Committee's recommendation that Federal funds be sought for the purpose of establishing a centralized acquisitions and cataloging program to be administered by the Library of Congress. This action was also endorsed and approved by RTSD and the ALA at the same meeting. Congressional hearings in both the Senate and House followed, with final passage of the Act in October 1965. Great credit is indeed due to the Washington Office of ALA, the ARL, and others for their diligent efforts in securing necessary amendments to the Higher Education Bill, resulting in Title IIC of the Higher Education Act.

At the hearings on the Bill before the Committees of the House and Senate the testimony of the ALA and ARL spokesmen, and others, stressed the need for the new program. The highlights can be summarized as follows:

1. College and university libraries of the country face a critical situation in attempting to gain prompt and effective cataloging control of ever-increasing quantities of important materials being published throughout the world. Until they have been fully cataloged, these materials are of little value to potential users ranging from students to advanced researchers.

2. Cataloging the types of materials which are required for college and university libraries involves technical skill and intellectual competence of a high order.

3. To cope with all library materials currently published throughout the world requires, therefore, a cataloging staff to deal with the whole range of human knowledge and with the entire span of languages in which materials are published.

4. There has been and continues to be a severe shortage of qualified catalogers.

5. It is wasteful of this limited manpower to require duplicative cataloging of the same titles in a number of libraries across the country.

6. Centralized cataloging of these books at the Library of Congress would eliminate wasteful duplication of effort, would provide the most efficient use of the limited cataloging resources available, and would result in much improved cataloging control.

7. The original cataloging of a book, if it is done in a consistent and standard pattern, need not be repeated when the second library gets the same book—if it can also get a copy of the first library's catalog card promptly. University libraries of the country

can obtain Library of Congress catalog cards when they need them for only a little over *half of the books they acquire each year.*

8. The reduction of this nearly 50 percent of original cataloging which is now required, much of it duplicated in libraries across the nation, will result in substantial savings. The obvious central agency to perform this service is the Library of Congress, which has already established the mechanisms of information and distribution and is essentially a national bibliographic center. The Library of Congress should be authorized and directed (a) to acquire on the most comprehensive basis currently-published library materials of scholarly value; and (b) to provide catalog copy for these accessions promptly after receipt, generally within three to four weeks.

It must be noted that the funding for the new program was delayed by the Congress. During the last fiscal year ending June 30, 1966, a small supplemental appropriation of $300,000 was approved which made it possible for the Library of Congress to make a small start toward implementing the program. For the fiscal year beginning July 1, 1966, an appropriation of $300,000 was made for the new program operations during the year. This amount is less than half the authorized amount included in the 1965 Act. Consequently, it will be necessary to limit the scope of coverage for the program. In addition, the effect of this late funding will be to limit the original authorization to a four-year period in so far as active operations are concerned.

It should also be noted that, based on the testimony of ALA and ARL representatives and others on the Bill at hearings before committees of the House and Senate, it is obvious and can be considered that the funds are made available to the Library of Congress for two main purposes:

(1) To accelerate its present acquisitions and cataloging operations for the materials it ordinarily acquires; and

(2) To acquire and catalog promptly all other titles that are added to libraries of higher education in the country.

In planning the implementation of the program, the Library of Congress has, from the beginning, consulted with the ARL Shared Cataloging Committee in determining the general policy guidelines to be followed by the Library of Congress in the development of the new program. (Messrs. Dix, Ellsworth, Logsdon, McCarthy, Skipper, and Low). It will continue to do so in the future. The following is a summary of the various issues and points of consideration discussed between the Library of Congress and the Committee.

Three basic issues were discussed by the ARL Shared Cataloging Committee and the Library of Congress at a joint meeting on October 25, 1965. They were:

(1) Is the program intended primarily to build up the collections of the Library of Congress or to provide "on order" cataloging for other libraries?

(2) Should the program be entirely centralized at the Library of Congress or should supplementary arrangements be made for the "dispersal" of the cataloging workload?

(3) Should the catalog copy be distributed in the form of catalog cards or in machine-readable form?

The ARL Shared Cataloging Committee and the Library of Congress were in agreement that:

(1) The program should have the dual purpose of building up the collections of the Library of Congress, as the national library, thereby benefiting libraries as a whole, and of providing catalog information to meet the needs of other libraries. The two purposes are inseparable.

(2) The program should be centralized at the Library of Congress, but the Library of Congress should work out arrangements, as prove feasible, for sharing the cataloging workload with the National Agricultural Library and the National Library of Medicine.

(3) Initially, catalog copy should be provided in the form of catalog cards, but provision should be made for conversion to machine-readable copy when this becomes feasible.

As to scope of coverage it was agreed:

(1) All titles published with imprint date 1966 and later and all titles listed in current foreign national bibliographies regardless of imprint date will be eligible for acquisition and cataloging under the program.

(2) Earlier imprints will not be acquired, but the Library of Congress will attempt to catalog and print cards for its holdings of earlier imprints now under preliminary control, on request of cooperating libraries.

(3) The program will cover both trade and non-trade monographic publications, including titles in numbered and unnumbered series, annuals (reports, yearbooks, proceedings, transactions), individual foreign dissertations selected for their collections by cooperating libraries, and atlases.

(4) Periodicals and non-book-format materials will not be covered at the beginning of the program. Off-prints will not be covered.

The present acquisition policies of the seventy-four ARL libraries (including the Library of Congress, the National Agricultural Library and the National Library of Medicine) are necessarily selective though comprehensive and also representative in scope. Materials in various subject fields are selected in order to meet the general as well as the special research interest requirements of their individual institutions. Considering the time element involved in the selection and ordering of different titles by each library, it is necessary to institute coordinated acquisition controls between the Library of Congress and all cooperating libraries in the new shared cataloging program if the centralized cataloging objectives are to be achieved.

Even if the Library of Congress could acquire all items currently published throughout the world, it would not be able to supply promptly catalog cards for the titles acquired by other libraries to meet their service requirements if it did not know specifically what material was being currently collected by them. Priorities in a centralized cataloging operation are a necessary requirement to successful operation in meeting the current cataloging needs of cooperating libraries.

The processing operations will be accelerated as follows:

(1) LC will use air freight for its current foreign acquisition operations. The prompt acquisition of all current foreign material needed for the program is of primary importance in making the program effective for overall control purposes both in LC and cooperating libraries.

(2) For purposes of the earliest possible selection of titles currently published throughout the world LC will establish close working arrangements with the authorities in each country who are responsible for publication of national bibliographies. LC will attempt to secure in advance of publication in national bibliographies all entries that are to be listed. LC will also endeavor to improve its present arrangements for acquiring domestic material.

(3) LC policy for its recommending officers will be to continue to select and recommend, as at present, on a selective, comprehensive but representative basis within the limits of LC appropriations for the purchase of books.

(4) Where cooperating libraries have established broad blanket order arrangements with foreign book dealers, the Library of Congress will place similar orders with these dealers to assure complete coverage for cataloging purposes.

(5) LC will make arrangements to receive a second copy of all titles supplied by Farmington Plan dealers.

(6) LC will place orders for all series now under standing continuation order or ordered in the future by cooperating libraries. Arrangements for the purpose will be made with cooperating libraries. It is also planned to prepare a list of all series for checking and control purposes.

(7) LC will accelerate and expand its purchasing

arrangements in such areas as Latin America, Africa, Southeast Asia, etc., where the book trade is not well organized and where there are no national bibliographies.

(8) Cooperating libraries will be expected to send copies of all their orders for both current domestic and foreign acquisitions for which no catalog card is found in their depository control file of LC cards or the published *National Union Catalog.* This applies also to all items received on an automatic basis unless already provided for as a result of coordination of blanket order arrangements.

(9) LC will provide a copy of each card printed for current imprints (1956 to date) to each cooperating library for its cataloging control purposes. This file will serve the following purposes:

(a) Provide full bibliographical information about the title to be ordered;

(b) Provide catalog copy which can be used for card reproduction needs of the cooperating library or for ordering LC cards by number.

These cards will be sent on a weekly basis and will be in filing order.

(10) LC will request the Government Printing Office to accelerate and improve all card printing operations. To this end, the Government Printing Office has already established a second shift in its Library Branch Printing Office.

The Government Printing Office will also be requested to provide a faster schedule for the printing of issues of the *National Union Catalog* (monthlies, quarterlies, and annuals).

(11) LC will institute a special recruiting program for catalogers. The lack of qualified cataloging staff is the most serious problem facing LC in implementing the new program. The efficient implementation of the new program is dependent on LC's ability to recruit and train sufficient staff for the purpose. Accordingly, it can be expected that full performance cannot be realized until staffing has been accomplished. LC expects that it will take about three years to meet fully the objectives envisioned.

(12) As noted in (2) above, LC will make arrangements with foreign national libraries or other national authorities responsible for publication of national bibliographies to accelerate their acquisition and cataloging operations. It will also make arrangements to use the cataloging information in these bibliographies for its own cataloging purposes. LC and ARL recommend acceptance of the description of the publication (i.e. title tran-

scription, imprint, collation, and notes) given in the national bibliography as "standard" for the purposes of the new program. Choice and form of main entry as well as corresponding secondary entries will be adjusted according to ALA-LC *Cataloging Rules for Author and Title Entries.* It is to be noted that the title description used in national bibliographies is equivalent to, or fuller than, the present LC standard as established in the *LC Rules for Descriptive Cataloging.* Adoption of this proposal will result in a most important step toward international cooperation in cataloging.

(13) Where LC is unsuccessful in acquiring through its own acquisitions channels material for which cataloging copy is known to be needed by a cooperating library, LC will borrow this material from the cooperating library and catalog it.

(14) LC will arrange regional meetings with technical processing staffs of ARL and other academic libraries to explain the plans for the new program and to insure coordination between LC and cooperating libraries.

At its 67th meeting, in Chicago on January 23, 1966, the ARL considered the detailed proposals listed above and approved them in principle.

Meanwhile the Library of Congress had been engaged in a further exploration of the possibility of international cooperation in cataloging under the Higher Education Act. This has been mentioned briefly above, but some further details may be of interest.

Anticipating increases in the acquisition of foreign publications, the shortage of trained catalogers, and the accelerated procedures required under the Act, LC's Processing Department investigated the feasibility of using as cataloging aids the entries in national bibliographies from countries in which the book trade is sufficiently organized for adequate bibliographies to exist. After its study, the Department proposed that LC accept for cataloging purposes the descriptions of publications listed in the national bibliographies of eighteen countries: Austria, Belgium, Czechoslovakia, Denmark, France, Germany, Great Britain, Hungary, Italy, the Netherlands, Norway, Poland, the Soviet Union, Spain, Sweden, Switzerland, Turkey, and Yugoslavia. It was understood that the form and choice of the main and secondary entries would be adjusted, as necessary, to conform to the pattern of the Library of Congress catalogs and to the ALA *Cataloging Rules for Author and Title Entries.* At its recent meeting the ARL accepted this feature of the Library's overall proposal.

Since international acceptance of the principle of "shared cataloging" would be a first but most important step toward international cooperation among national libraries, the Director and Principal Librarian of the British Museum, Sir Frank Francis, arranged for a small international conference to discuss the Library of Congress proposal. The meeting, with Sir Frank Francis as Chairman, took place in the Trustee Room of the British Museum on January 13. It was attended by Peter Brown, A. Hugh Chaplin, and R. A. Wilson, all of the British Museum; A. J. Wells and Joel Clarke Downing, both of the *British National Bibliography;* Etienne Dennery, Director of the Bibliothèque Nationale, and Roger Pierrot of the cataloging staff; Harold L. Tveteras, Director of the Oslo University Library; Kurt Köester, Director of the Deutsche Bibliothek, Frankfurt; Gustav Hofmann, Director of the Bavarian State Library: and, from LC, L. Quincy Mumford, Librarian of Congress; John W. Cronin and William J. Welsh, Director and Associate Director, respectively, of the Processing Department; and Johannes L. Dewton, Assistant Chief of the Union Catalog Division.

A working paper prepared by the Processing Department, with a large number of sample entries from national bibliographies and adjustments to Library of Congress form was the basis of the discussions. The discussions led to complete agreement in principle for standardizing descriptions based on the listings in the national bibliography of the country in which the publications originate.

The acceptance and implementation of the principle of "shared cataloging" should result in a more uniform international description of each publication, identified by a reference to the listing in the national bibliography of the home country. As advance listings are made available, they are expected to speed up ordering and cataloging procedures, to result in faster bibliographical control in the home country and abroad, to reduce the cost of cataloging in libraries all over the world, and to contribute toward the increased sale of publications on an international scale, with resulting benefits to libraries, scholars, publishers, and book dealers alike.

In order to provide a testing of the shared cataloging concept in cooperation with national bibliographies, the Library of Congress, since January 1966, has operated a prototype shared cataloging program in cooperation with the *British National Bibliography*. Under this program, advance print-

er's copy for entries to be published in the *BNB* has been received two to three weeks in advance of publication in the *BNB*, and LC has accelerated its own acquisitions of current British imprints by a combination of dealer blanket-order selection and LC selection by its own recommending officers. In addition, LC has used the *BNB* descriptive entry listing as the base for its own cataloging. In order to test the efficiency of the new program operations, a number of large research libraries were requested to send to the Library of Congress copies of their current purchase order requests for British titles with imprint date 1956 to date. It is to be noted that all titles with 1966 imprint date were automatically ordered if they had not been selected for LC collections in the first place. The results indicate that acceleration of LC recommendations for its collections plus the additional recommendations for titles not selected in the first place by LC give satisfactory evidence that the shared cataloging program based on the British prototype controls should meet the requirements of the shared cataloging program.

Analysis of the statistics of searching 4,873 orders for 1966 British imprints received from 29 selected libraries for the period April 25 to July 1, 1966, show that 3,823 (78.4 percent) of the titles either had printed cards available, were already received and in process of cataloging and card printing, or had already been ordered by LC. During the period, LC placed 1,050 orders (21.6 percent) for titles not originally selected by the Library of Congress.

In addition, during late April and May, exploratory discussions were held with national bibliography authorities and dealers in the following countries: Great Britain, Norway, Austria, Germany, and France. Another visit was made to London in late June to establish the shared cataloging program in cooperation with the *British National Bibliography* on a fully-operational basis, beginning July 1, 1966. Discussions in each country visited were concerned with the following general arrangements:

1. Securing of final printer's copy for new titles in advance of printing in the national bibliography.
2. Preparation of LC preliminary cataloging entries from this copy.
3. LC blanket order purchase acquisition arrangements, plus additional LC selection of new titles with dealer cooperation on basis of LC re-

quirements, with inclusion of preliminary cataloging copy.

4. Listing of published titles not yet received by the national bibliography authorities and the preparation of preliminary cataloging copy.
5. Regular checking of book trade listings, dealer catalogs, etc., against master control files to assure completeness of coverage of all new titles published or to be published.

As a result of these discussions, it is expected that shared cataloging program arrangements will be operational in the centers noted below on the following time schedule:

1. London. *British National Bibliography* and dealer–Stevens & Brown. Operational July 1, 1966.
2. Oslo. Royal University Library and dealer–Tanum. Operational in October, 1966.
3. Vienna. Austrian National Library, the Oesterreichisches Institut für Bibliotheksforschung and dealer–Prachner. Operational in September, 1966.
4. West Germany. The Deutsche Bibliothek (Frankfurt) and dealer–Otto Harrassowitz (Wiesbaden). Operational in September, 1966.
5. France. Limited cooperation between the Bibliothèque Nationale and the Library of Congress, for the present as follows: LC will receive on a weekly basis copies of entries for new titles currently deposited in the Depôt Legal and final corrected page proof for current issues of the *Bibliographe de la France*. In addition, LC will select currently-announced publications listed in the *Livres de la Semaine*. Tentative arrangements have been made with a dealer–Stechert-Hafner–to establish a processing center for current French titles in Paris in fiscal 1967.

Other arrangements are as follows:

1. Eastern Europe. Exploration has been made of the feasibility of an informal conference of Eastern European librarians in the fall of 1966 in Vienna with a view to establishing processing centers in Munich and Paris for East European publications.
2. Africa. In May, LC staff visited countries in East Africa and Central Africa, and a director for field operations has been appointed to begin acquisition operations on July 25, 1966.
3. Latin America. During June, LC staff visited Rio de Janeiro and Buenos Aires, and it is hoped to establish acquisitions centers in both places during fiscal 1967.

In closing, I would like to note that great credit is due ARL and its Shared Cataloging Committee, ALA and especially the Washington Office, and many others for their efforts in securing the necessary legislative authorization to enable the Library of Congress to provide a centralized cataloging service to American libraries.

Future Implications of Title IIC, Higher Education Act of 1965

James E. Skipper

The most significant future implications of Title IIC of the Higher Education Act of 1965 are based on the expectation that the Library of Congress will become the world center for bibliographic control. For the first time in modern history we will have a library capable of global comprehensiveness in collecting currently-published material of scholarly value and providing bibliographic information for these titles quickly enough to be used by all libraries in cataloging their own acquisitions.

All future implications flow from this fact.

Perhaps the most exciting prospect of the program concerns the possibility of international cooperative action. We have long dreamed of being able to communicate in an international bibliographic language. Mr. Cronin's article describes the bold and imaginative planning being done by the Library of Congress to utilize to the fullest the bibliographic information produced in foreign national bibliographies. This is a tremendously significant development. It involves the use of an operating program to achieve international cooperation. Such a vehicle is essential to move us beyond international agreements, resolutions, and other manifestations of good will. This program will not only reduce costs and improve efficiency at the Library of Congress, but it has the potential pragmatic effect of drawing the international bibliographic centers together in an operating situation. It has the possibility of becoming a two-way street. If we admit that it is economically and socially wasteful to catalog the same book more than once in the United States, it would seem to follow that the same principle could be accepted by other countries, provided, of course, that catalog copy of high standards is readily available.

Without doing violence to reality, it is possible to speculate that the expanded and accelerated bibliographic information being generated at the Library of Congress would be of more than passing interest to foreign libraries. Many of these institutions lack adequate bibliographic control for their collections, and it is conceivable that increasing numbers of libraries would take advantage of the LC product, to be used without modification, or by altering elements to suit local needs and customs.

A careful reading of Part C, Title II of the Higher Education Act will reveal three elements: (1) the Library of Congress is authorized to become globally comprehensive in acquiring currently-published naterials of scholarly interest; (2) a bibliographic record is to be created for these titles shortly after receipt, that is, within three to four weeks; and (3) this bibliographic record is to be distributed by printed catalog cards *and by other means.*

The ARL Shared Cataloging Committee was convinced that the quality of the total program would depend on the comprehensiveness of the materials being collected and the availability of intellectual manpower required to identify, or catalog, these titles. These two elements are essential whether the catalog information is to be distributed by printing on a piece of pasteboard or by digital form on magnetic tape.

Thus, the program developed was conceived as the requisite base for an automated system to make the access to this bibliographic information more efficient. The Committee was well aware that an effective system for distribution catalog copy was an essential element. This factor has been demonstrated by several studies which reveal that LC catalog copy has been available, but not used for 8 to 9 percent of the books cataloged originally in research libraries, and it was assumed that inefficiencies in our present system of file maintenance and bibliographic "matching" were largely responsible for this lack of utilization. It is hoped that automation will have an effect in resolving some of the difficulties which have been experienced in the past. Future implications for automation reach beyond the area of bibliographic identification and suggest possibilities for some type of information retrieval.

The topic of bibliographic automation should also be related to future international cooperation. Experience gained at the recent Anglo-American Conference on the Mechanization of Library Services held at Brasenose College, Oxford University, suggests the possibility that automation itself may be the catalytic agent that will draw the international library community together under common systems of bibliographic controls which have eluded us in the past. For centuries, musicians and mathematicians have been able to communicate internationally by a standard language of symbol and notation. One of the most significant future implications of the present program is the possibility of achieving greater bibliographic compatibility.

It is certainly true that the local library will experience a considerable impact from Title IIC. In fact, the entire program started in an effort to increase the availability of cataloging copy to individual libraries. The higher degree of reliability of Library of Congress copy could result in a larger number of libraries shifting to LC cataloging standards. As one example, Stanford University has decided to change to LC cataloging with only selective recataloging of its retrospective collection.

A cynic has suggested that no technological displacement of manpower should be anticipated under this program as the increased number of LC cards available will require an ever-larger local staff to modify the standard bibliographic information. A more optimistic view of the future would suggest that the increased availability of copy would tend to discourage local modification and that cataloging information from the Library of Congress would be accepted without change just as libraries accept entries in the *Reader's Guide*, the *New York Times Index,* and *Chemical Abstracts* without local modification.

At present, the absence of a sufficient amount of LC copy requires large, linguistically-competent staffs in research libraries to catalog materials in foreign languages. The increasing availability of LC copy—especially for materials in non-Western languages—could relieve libraries of a currently-serious manpower problem.

It is admitted that a standard bibliographic product cannot be all things to all types of libraries. Theological libraries, for example, may require modifications of main or added entries to provide adequate access to their collections. One can visualize a future cataloging network through which the LC product will pass to be "re-packaged" by a national sub-system and made available to all special libraries of a type. The basic cataloging information from LC would be used to the fullest extent with required modifications being done but once on the national level.

Title IIC concerns expanding bibliographic control over currently-published material. It is obvious that, over the years, what is current now will become retrospective. In addition, the forthcoming publications of the *National Union Catalog* should provide an invaluable bibliographic tool for cataloging older titles.

It is anticipated that the Library of Congress will indicate the price of the title on each catalog entry when this information is readily available. As these entries should reach local libraries in advance of foreign bibliographies, it is possible that this record could be used for book selection purposes with the attendant advantage of having reproducible catalog copy immediately available.

The Association of Research Libraries looks upon the Title II program at the Library of Congress as the logical extension of two earlier efforts which the Association supported to obtain greater coverage of currently-published materials of scholarly interest. The first of these programs was the Farmington Plan, implemented by ARL in 1949. The second was the Public Law 480 amendment, which authorized the use of excess counter-part funds in designated foreign countries to acquire library materials. The latter program, ably administered by the Library of Congress, channels materials to twenty or twenty-five of our research libraries. It seems logical that IIC should afford the possibility of not only obtaining one copy for the Library of Congress, but also acquiring multiple copies for distribution to additional libraries thus providing adequate national access to these titles. One copy will not, in most instances, be sufficient. ARL is presently developing this phase of the program with the cooperation of LC.

Up to this point, the IIC program has been related to cataloging. With the demonstrated need for indexes to the periodicals of Latin America, Africa, and the Orient, it is reasonable to anticipate a future program under an expanded Title IIC which would authorize this type of bibliographic activity at the Library of Congress. This effort would be directly related to the strong subject divisions now existing at LC and the fact that the present program would bring to these collections the most comprehensive group of serial titles in the world.

While it is easy to speculate on the future implications of Title IIC, we must be very careful to structure extensions of this program so that they are logically ordered and interrelated. Funding and manpower problems must be fully considered. Thus, while our motto is "Ad Astra Cum LC," we must exercise patience, demonstrate common sense, and, most important, cooperate to the fullest extent with the institution which has accepted responsibility for the most exciting bibliographic venture of our time—the Library of Congress.

International Implications of the Shared Cataloging Program: Planning for Resource Development

Robert Vosper

> *". . . it is clear that this impressive undertaking developed logically out of the long-standing efforts on behalf of those same libraries to perfect a national resource development program."*

Although the instrumentality we discuss today is called the "Shared Cataloging Program," and although central to the enabling Federal legislation (Title II-C of the Higher Education Act of 1965)[1] was the desire of research library officials in the United States to reduce the increasing amount of duplicative cataloging all have been engaged in, nonetheless it is clear that this impressive undertaking developed logically out of the long-standing efforts on behalf of those same libraries to perfect a national resource development program. We are, in point of fact, concerned here with a new "National Program for Acquisitions and Cataloging" (NPAC), as the overall effort at the Library of Congress is officially designated. Title II-C is indeed an essential handmaiden of resource planning in the United States and we expect increasingly, as I will indicate, to call on her services to that important end.

The "Shared Cataloging Program," in which many other countries are already so helpfully participating, is a major cataloging instrumentality, especially as we envision the total bibliographical implications which are discussed in other papers at this session. But the dynamic end product, for research libraries in the United States at least, is an extension of our continuing resource development efforts. As to whether a similar advantage will be feasible and useful for libraries in other countries, I am of course in no position to judge. However, other countries may wish to consider an analog to the American experience, so I will in due course raise a few questions with that international possibility in mind.

Under the epochal Title II-C legislation, which was drafted by the Association of Research Libraries in consultation with officials of the Library of Congress, that Library is provided authorization for: (1) acquiring, so far as possible, all library materials currently published throughout the world which are of value to scholarship; and (2) providing catalog information for these materials promptly after receipt and distributing bibliographic information by printing cards and by other means.

It is no accident that this statement parallels the basic objectives of the Farmington Plan which, following upon discussions instituted in 1942 by the Librarian of Congress, was launched in 1947 by the Association of Research Libraries. The Farmington purpose, still maintained, is: to make sure that at least one copy of each new foreign book and pamphlet that might reasonably be expected to interest a research worker in the United States will be acquired by an American library, promptly listed in the Union Catalog at the Library of Congress, and made available by interlibrary loan or photographic reproduction.

There is no need here to recount the twenty-year evolving history of the Farmington Plan,[2] but a glance at some aspects of its mechanism is essential to understanding the dynamic relationship of the "Shared Cataloging Program" to national resource planning in the United States.

To be noted from the outset is the vital and voluntary collaboration, in the national interest, between the Library of Congress and the country's major university and other research libraries, operating through the agency of the Association of Research Libraries, of which the Library of Congress is one constituent member.

From the inception of the Farmington Plan there were differences of opinion about two primary functions: centralized vs. decentralized

SOURCE: Reprinted from *Libri*, 17 (1967), pp. 285-293, by permission of the publisher, the University of California at Los Angeles.

housing of the incoming publications, and centralized vs. decentralized cataloging. At the time, the arguments for decentralization seemed most impressive, but experience and more recent developments suggest that the weight of argument may have shifted somewhat.

Under the Farmington pattern, let me remind you, a large number of American libraries, including the Library of Congress, undertook individual responsibility for receiving, and paying for, all currently published books in certain subject fields or from certain countries, the latter approach being operative particularly in countries with less well developed bibliographical apparatus. In this decentralized distribution pattern the Farmington Plan has some similarity to the Scandia Plan and the German Sondersammelgebiets-plan. But in addition, the recipient libraries under the Farmington Plan were to catalog their own receipts and forward cataloging copy to the National Union Catalog. Thus the deposit of incoming material, its cataloging, and the costs of the program were decentralized. The only Federal contribution to the program was the participation, as individual libraries, of the Library of Congress and the National Libraries of Agriculture and Medicine.

In the 1940's and 1950's there seemed no likelihood that the Federal government would financially support the entirety of such a program, and the totality of incoming publications was considered quite beyond the scope of the Library of Congress' own canons of selection. Moreover, because the Second World War was so close in our memories, there was some worry about the insecurity of a single, central repository serving the whole nation. Thus a decentralized, cost-sharing mechanism seemed requisite. Moreover, at that time there seemed no acceptable procedure for all incoming books to be routed through the Library of Congress, en route to other libraries, in order to be centrally cataloged. The Library of Congress was already in arrearage with its own cataloging, so such a procedure would only seem to produce intolerable delays in actual local access to incoming books.

It will be evident, then, that the intervening twenty years have witnessed some impressive changes in the climate of opinion as well as in the state of knowledge about large-scale inter-library cooperation in the United States.

During those intervening years the American academic community and American public opinion in general, discovered the world outside Europe, as it were. Intensive research and teaching concerned with the economics, linguistics, political science, and general culture of the countries of Africa, the Middle East, South Asia, and Latin America have become a standard part of American academic life, to an extent not envisioned in the mid-1940's.

The consequent problems for individual libraries—problems linguistic, bibliographical, and logistical—became very large indeed, and the impact on the Farmington Plan mechanism and concept was a major theme of the Survey of the Plan that was called for in 1957 by the Association of Research Libraries and thereupon undertaken by the writer of this paper. On the one hand, it was obvious that in response to national needs American research libraries must undertake a far better job of acquiring current books comprehensively from all parts of the world and speedily making them available. On the other hand, it became increasingly clear that the procurement and cataloging tasks were beyond the capacity of individual libraries to finance or to staff. The need for Federal participation became clear.

At about this same time the Federal government for the first time became sufficiently aware of national library needs to begin participating in the planning and the costs of general library service. The Library Services Act of 1956, which provides Federal support for local public libraries, marks in fact a major turning point in American library history. The significant library implications of the Higher Education Act of 1965, which we are discussing today, proceed inevitably from this shift in 1956 to a sense of Federal responsibility for the state of libraries across the nation.

An intervening development is relevant to our discussions today. In 1958 an amendment to Public Law 480 authorized the Library of Congress to use United States credits in certain foreign countries for the purchase and cataloging of books and other library materials for selected American libraries. In 1962 the program became operative in India, Pakistan, and the United Arab Republic. Subsequently it was extended into Israel, Indonesia, Ceylon, and Nepal. Most recently negotiations were instituted with Poland and Yugoslavia. Thus for the first time in our history the Federal government is in the position of enhancing the resources of individual research libraries. Moreover, this development has in fact brought the Federal government directly into the business of the Farmington Plan, at least for a few countries, namely the business of comprehensive current book procurement.

Under the Farmington Plan, as originally instituted in Western Europe, experienced book dealers were commissioned, within defined schedules, to gather in the newly published scholarly books and ship them automatically and quickly to the participating American libraries. Outside Western Europe, in countries with an immature book trade, the responsible American libraries tested a variety of procedures for securing comprehensive publishing intake. In most cases a personal mission, often on a recurrent basis, has seemed the only effective device for assuring anything like a consistent coverage of newly issued publications. In a few cases a group of libraries have been able to dispatch a joint book buying mission.

The Public Law 480 program has produced a fruitful new kind of procurement experience. In each country involved the Library of Congress has established a local staff which arranges through government offices and commercial dealers to identify, select, and ship to selected American libraries all current publications of presumed scholarly utility. Thus, in these selected countries, at a level of Farmington requirement, the Library of Congress has become in very fact a procurement agent for American libraries, and the cost of the books themselves is covered by Federal funds.

The Public Law 480 program, however, has been frustrating in two ways. It has been limited to a very few countries where appropriate funds are available. Thus it could by no means support the global emphasis of the Farmington Plan. Moreover, although the legislation permits the Library of Congress to undertake cataloging as well as procurement services, available funds have never been fully adequate to the complex cataloging job. Thus the recipient libraries have been obliged to contribute funds to the Library of Congress in order to support this difficult and expensive cataloging task. This latter experience was a primary factor in leading the Association of Research Libraries to design the Title II-C legislation with its specific emphasis on centralized cataloging.

As these various forces leading toward a more centralized effort involving Federal support came into play, all concerned became increasingly aware of the gap between, on the one hand, the foreign book intake and cataloging output of the Library of Congress; and, on the other hand, the comparable requirements of American academic libraries and the scholarly community they serve. Estimates in 1965, when the new legislation was being forwarded, indicated that the academic libraries were currently acquiring from abroad about 100,000 current volumes not received at the Library of Congress, and that the Library of Congress was providing catalog copy for only about 55 percent of the academic library requirement. It seemed imperative then, in the interests of efficiency and economy, to close the gap. This is the thrust of the "National Program for Acquisitions and Cataloging" under Title II-C.

As we all know, officials of the Library of Congress have moved forward with remarkable speed and with forceful imagination. In order to insure the rapid selection and receipt of books to be cataloged under this global project, the Library of Congress has drawn on the selection and procurement experience of both the Farmington Plan and Public Law 480, with precise efforts to increase both speed and efficiency.

Library of Congress offices abroad were established first in London, then in Wiesbaden, Oslo and other European centers, and more recently in Kenya and Rio de Janeiro. Others, of course, are being established as rapidly as feasible. In Great Britain and Western Europe procedures were coordinated with book dealers who have had long experience with the Farmington Plan mechanism, and the Library of Congress specifically makes certain that one copy of every Farmington publication comes through the Library of Congress for cataloging purposes. In addition, all participating American libraries (over ninety at this time) are encouraged to notify the Library of Congress of any individual blanket order arrangements, so that those books, too, can be integrated into Library of Congress receipts. In addition, a procedure has been developed so that the participating libraries can notify the Library of Congress of individual books not caught in the net. In other procurement centers—Rio and Kenya, and Yugoslavia and Poland when established—the Public Law 480 experience and mechanism provide a solid basis for early action. On the home front a neatly dovetailed program has been established with the National Libraries of Agriculture and Medicine.

A word should be inserted here about what types of material are covered by the National Program for Acquisitions and Cataloging. At this point it involves both trade and nontrade monographic publications, including titles in numbered and unnumbered series, annuals (reports, yearbooks, proceedings, transactions), atlases, and certain individual foreign dissertations. Up to now periodi-

NPAC offices abroad, June, 1967:
(from NPAC Progress Report No. 4)

Shared Cataloging Offices

Location	*Source of bibliographic data*	*Source of books*
1. London	British National Bibliography	Stevens & Brown
2. Vienna	Osterreichische Bibliographie	exchange arrangements with Österreichische Nationalbibliothek
3. Wiesbaden	Deutsche Bibliographie	Harrassowitz
	Deutsche Nationalbibliographie	
	Das Schweizer Buch	Helbing & Lichtenhahn
4. Oslo	Norsk bokhandler tidende	Tanum
	Svensk bokhandel	
	Det danske bogmarked	
5. Paris	Bibliographie de la France	Stechert-Hafner
6. Belgrade	Bibliografija Yugoslavije	Mladost (Croatian books)
		Cankarjeva Zalozba (Slovenian books)
		Prosveta (others)
7. The Hague	Nieuwsblad voor de boekhandel	Martinus Nijhoff
	Brinkman's Cumulatieve Catalogues	
	Bibliographie de Belgique	Office International de Librairie

Regional Acquisitions Offices

Location	*Countries*	
8. Rio de Janeiro	Brazil	
9. Nairobi	Kenya	Malagasy Republic
	Uganda	Somali Republic
	Malawi	Seychelles Islands
	Zambia	Ruanda
	Tanzania	Burundi
		Ethiopia

cals and nonbook format materials are not covered, but we all agree that the aim is to cover all forms of library materials.

Thus it is evident that through the National Program for Acquisitions and Cataloging the Library of Congress in both procurement and cataloging fully expects to match the requirements, in speed of access and in comprehensiveness of coverage, of the American research library community. Although it is too soon for much analysis, it has been estimated that already the Library of Congress had doubled its intake of French books, for example. Thereby, it is evident that the concept of the Farmington Plan will come far closer to realization than we could have assumed a decade ago. In fact, it is recognized that Title II-C developments will continue to have influence on Farmington Plan activities in ways which we cannot now fully foresee.

This brings us logically to the point of further developments now underway. The Association of Research Libraries, again with the support of the Librarian of Congress, has proposed amendments to the Title II-C legislation, with two important resource development ends in view. It is proposed, first of all, that the Library of Congress procurement offices, especially in those countries where the bibliography and book trade are inadequately developed, be authorized to act also in behalf of individual American libraries which may wish to call on their services. The recipient libraries would pay the cost of the books themselves, but the Library of Congress operation would be stepped up to secure multiple copies as required. This would benefit a number of libraries and reduce a great deal of complex and duplicative procurement effort.

The second amending proposal is equally impressive. The increasing number of colleges and universities in the United States and the persistent rise in academic population have resulted in an unendurably heavy traffic in book use, both within local institutions and through interlibrary loan demands. Thus the original Farmington ideal of "at least one copy" has become somewhat obsolete. Therefore, the proposal is to establish outside the Library of Congress, which already faces a tremendous service load of its own, the beginnings of a national lending library which will receive by free deposit a second copy of certain items brought in through the National Program for Acquisitions and Cataloging and other mechanisms. The initial emphasis will be on materials difficult to obtain through normal trade channels, African materials for example. Specifically we have in mind the Center for Research Libraries (formerly MILC) in Chicago. The Center, as this audience will recall, is a nonprofit corporation, a sort of library's library, operated, now on a national basis, by a number of participating institutions. The Center's ties with the Association of Research Libraries are, in fact, becoming closer and closer. With this proposal for a national lending library we of course modify in an interesting way the Farmington Plan consideration of centralized *vs.* decentralized deposit of incoming books. The complexity and size of the American scholarly community require a multiplicity of library solutions. It should be made clear that under this proposal individual academic libraries will continue to develop their own collections as richly as may be locally requisite. Only experience will reveal the extent to which the Center collection will relieve the service load on other libraries and the extent to which its current foreign collections should be further extended beyond present plans. It does become an additional important national resource center, and this development will certainly permit other libraries to reassess local needs. It is also worth noting that in this instance we have watched with profit the British experience with their National Lending Library for Science and Technology and the All-Union Library for Foreign Literature in Moscow.

With this exposition before us of the implications of the National Program for Acquisitions and Cataloging for planned resource development within the United States, one can now reasonably ask what the implications may be internationally and thus for libraries in other countries.

At an initial level, it would seem useful and reasonable for individual libraries in any country, including the United States, to test the Shared Cataloging Program as a selection mechanism for foreign books. If the bibliographical information, including book prices, produced for and emanating from the Program is sufficiently rapid and complete, conceivably it can provide an effective current book selection tool as well as cataloging tool. This possibility was suggested in discussions a year ago at Scheveningen. Full or selective depository sets of Library of Congress cards are now going to several countries, and it would seem desirable to explore the fullest possible use of this information. Eventual access to automated information might even enhance these values.

Beyond this, we might ask whether parallel or coordinate procurement arrangements to those established by the Library of Congress, in Kenya and Rio for example, might be useful in behalf of other countries or groups of countries? The fiscal, management, and political problems in such an international enterprise are not minor, but the possible advantages should be considered, especially in those areas where book procurement is a difficult task for any library.

And beyond this, one might ask whether the concept of a deposit and central lending facility envisioned for the Center for Research Libraries might have utility elsewhere. The British for some time have wondered about the possibility of a national lending library for humanities and social sciences. Would such an institution now have validity, particularly for non-European books, working in parallel with the Library of Congress procurement pattern?

If valid in the United States or in Great Britain, would one or more central, multi-national deposit and lending libraries of this type, especially for non-European books, be meaningful in Europe itself? The problems of course mount rapidly, and it would be presumptuous for an American librarian to do more than raise the question. We can recall that the IFLA/UNESCO Symposium on National Libraries in Europe (Vienna, 1958) concluded: "It is recommended that a national plan for the acquisitions of foreign materials should be established in countries where no such plan exists; however, a general European plan should not be contemplated until the national plans are more fully developed." Since then the multi-national Scandia Plan, which we all so much admire, has flourished. Thus Harald Tveterås in the 1960 *UNESCO Bulletin for Libraries*, discussing the Scandia Plan, raised our sights even higher: "Even a system of close cooperative acquisition for European libraries may in time be feasible. Perhaps we librarians for once should give proof of boldness, and take the necessary steps to achieve this aim."

Can we hope then that the widespread cooperation centering on the Shared Cataloging Program provides us now with the mechanism and the right timing to take this next bold step forward on the international scene?

NOTES

[1] L. Quincy Mumford, "International Breakthrough", *Library Journal*, January 1, 1967, pp. 79–82. See also James E. Skipper, "Future Implications of Title II-C, Higher Education Act of 1965", *Library Resources and Technical Services*, Winter 1967, pp. 46–49.
[2] Edwin E. Williams, *Farmington Plan Handbook*, Harvard 1953, and revised 1961. See also Vosper, Robert, *The Farmington Plan Survey: A Summary . . .* , Illinois 1965.

Cooperative Cataloging in North America—Problems and Possibilities

David Hudson Haykin

"The problem of cooperative and centralized cataloging is an economic one above all else. The quality of the product of cooperation in cataloging is a secondary consideration. Centralized cataloging can be achieved only after the libraries of North America find it possible to pool financial resources for cooperative acquisition."

This paper proposes to set down some of the basic problems and limitations of cooperative cataloging in the United States and Canada and the possible lines of development in the future. Since the major details of our American experience in cooperative cataloging are fairly generally known, it will not be necessary to go into them beyond an occasional reference to procedures, difficulties, results, and the lessons to be drawn from them.

For the purposes of this paper it is necessary to begin with certain definitions, draw certain distinctions, and state certain axioms. After the ground is cleared in this manner, it will be possible to consider problems and possibilities.

What is cooperative cataloging anyway? In its broadest sense, it is the production of catalog entries through the joint action of several libraries. It is possible for several libraries to underwrite an enterprise for the cataloging, in a given place by a selected group of catalogers, of books in the possession of one or more of these libraries. An enterprise of this sort is cooperative, since it is maintained at the joint expense of the libraries concerned. For the sake of clearness, however, we shall refer to this mode of cooperation as centralized cataloging. Centralized cataloging is to be understood here as cataloging *maintained* by several independent libraries but not performed by them. It should not be confused with central cataloging in a library system such as a central public library with its branches or of a university library with its departmental libraries, where the cataloging is done at headquarters. In nearly all essentials the problem of cataloging in such libraries is no different from that of a large library housed under one roof and in many essentials it is like that of a medium-sized library.

The term "cooperative cataloging" has of late been used (and understood) in a narrower sense, that of the joint participation in the actual work of preparing catalog entries by several libraries under a compact which defines and allots, expressly or tacitly, to each library its share of the work. The work is done by each library in its own quarters, the product being available on equal terms to all.

The enterprise being now carried on through the Cooperative Cataloging Committee of the American Library Association is according to this definition of a work of cooperative cataloging. Approximately thirty-five libraries are associated in this compact. The scope of their joint work is closely defined. The cataloging is limited to recent books in foreign languages (books bearing imprint dates not more than two years old) and monographs and articles in serial and periodical publications which have not been and are not now being "analyzed" by the Library of Congress. On the basis of the number of orders for cards for books in the first category, the Card Division of the Library of Congress determines whether a given book should be cataloged by one of the cooperating libraries and the library is then requested to do it. The serials are allocated to each of the cooperators on the basis mainly of their willingness to undertake the work. It should be noted here that the cooperators in this undertaking are among the largest and most important libraries in the United States and may at least be presumed to have cataloging staffs and reference and bibliographic tools adequate to the task. The catalog cards produced as a result of this enterprise are

SOURCE: Reprinted from *The A.L.A. Catalogers Yearbook*, 6 (1937), pp. 26-35, by permission of the publisher, the American Library Association. Originally presented as a paper read before the Large Libraries Round Table of the Catalog Section, A.L.A. Conference, Richmond, 1936.

available not merely to the cooperators, but to all libraries. The Cooperative Cataloging Committee realized that to initiate a project like this a revolving fund would be necessary. It, therefore, secured a grant from the General Education Board for the purpose. The cost of producing and distributing the catalog card, it was thought, would in time be in large part covered from the income from sales. There would become available to all libraries through this effort, catalog cards for titles in foreign languages which the Library of Congress did not have or did not analyze.

Librarians in general and catalogers in particular are not always aware of the underlying motives of the cooperative and simplified cataloging movement. At any rate they do not always consider these motives in the order of their actual importance in the whole economy of librarianship. They think, for instance, that the outstanding reason for engaging in a cooperative cataloging enterprise is the need for securing catalog cards which are not otherwise available. As a matter of fact, most libraries, perhaps nearly all of them, are competent to do cataloging of a quality sufficient for their needs. It is not merely the question of the availability of printed cards as such that is involved. It is primarily the difference in the cost of cataloging by each library individually and the cost of collective cataloging. The primary motive is certainly economic. One of the sources of this motive is, of course, the fact that cataloging is a relatively expensive process and takes a substantial part of the library's appropriation. This fact has undoubtedly made a very strong impression on library administrators and the public and university authorities to whom they are responsible. It should be noted here by a cataloger that the true measure of the cost of cataloging is not the outlay of money for the preparation of a set of entries for a given book but rather that cost in relation to the use and usefulness of those entries to members of the reference staff and the library's public. The cost of cataloging a given book is high if the cataloging does not aid the user of the catalog in getting the information he seeks as expeditiously as possible. Nevertheless the absolute cost of cataloging is a real factor in cooperative cataloging, perhaps the most important. To be sure, there are other factors of some importance. For example, where a given task of cataloging can best (and most cheaply) be performed by a given library, it had better be done by that library for all others rather than by each library for itself.

To continue the consideration of what might be called the economic factor, the desire to secure catalog cards for titles for which printed catalog cards are not available rests definitely on the question of cost. For over thirty-five years the Library of Congress has made available to all libraries the results of its cataloging in the form of printed cards. In view of the fact that the Library of Congress is a very large library and secures through the operation of the copyright law and otherwise a large number of the titles acquired by other libraries, it is able to supply catalog cards to other libraries for a substantial proportion of the books acquired by them. It is not always remembered that the price of the catalog cards distributed by the Library of Congress does not cover the cost of cataloging or even of typesetting. The Library of Congress, would, of course, have to bear this cost itself if it did not distribute any of its cards. In any case, the price of Library of Congress catalog cards covers merely the relatively insignificant cost of presswork and card distribution. In enlarging the stock of available catalog cards through cooperative means these facts should very definitely be borne in mind. Comparisons between the cost of Library of Congress cards and those produced by cooperative effort which do not take account of them are futile. It is the cataloging which is the principal item of cost and not the printing or typing of cards. And enlarging the stock of available cards must mean no less than making available to libraries the results of *cataloging* at a lower cost than if each library had to do the work for itself alone.

The experience of the cooperative cataloging enterprise sponsored by the Cooperative Cataloging Committee has already established certain facts which must be taken into consideration in the future. One of them is that it and similar enterprises in the future will have to concern themselves with relatively non-lucrative cataloging. The Library of Congress already prints cards for practically all of the titles which are in the grestest demand in American libraries. Cooperating libraries are thus forced to limit themselves to less popular books, the analysis of serial publications of unusual cataloging difficulty, etc. It is doubtful, therefore, whether cooperative cataloging enterprises similar to the present one can ever really pay as they go by comparison with Library of Congress cards. Nevertheless, they should be engaged in on some basis, since they produce catalog entries more cheaply than they can be produced by an individual library for its own use, even if that library's cataloging staff is in every way adequate. In the long run the expense to the library in cataloging the entries allotted to it will be more than counterbalanced by the savings of entries prepared by the other libraries which this library may secure at a nominal cost. In view of the "rugged individualism," voluntary or enforced, of American librarians, it is more than likely that cooperative enterprises will have to depend on subventions from philanthropic foundations rather than the prorata assessment of costs on the beneficiaries.

Let it not be thought that the inability, or unwillingness, of American libraries to share the costs as well as the benefits of cooperation is the only problem before cooperative cataloging. The quality of the cataloging is a factor of paramount importance. Before embarking upon a cooperative cataloging enterprise it is necessary to establish certain norms and secure checks on the general adherence of the libraries concerned to these norms. In North America we are very fortunate in having secured imperceptibly through the years general agreement on all major elements of the technique of cataloging. The Anglo-American code, together with the Library of Congress supplementary rules, has found general acceptance among libraries. The dictionary catalog being master of the field now, it is fortunate, too, that a single code of subject cataloging is followed by libraries almost without exception. The principles of subject cataloging have nowhere been fully stated as yet, but they have nevertheless been fairly faithfully and consistently followed by all libraries. In the present cooperative cataloging undertaking it was therefore very easy to get the libraries concerned to agree that the Library of Congress practice be the sole guide and criterion. The check on adherence to this guide and criterion is secured by a staff of revisers in the Library of Congress itself. Proof is not lacking that the work of these revisers has brought a large measure of consistency and uniformity to the varied product of the approximately thirty-five cooperating libraries scattered over the whole area of the United States and embracing public libraries, reference libraries, university libraries, and special libraries. Nevertheless, the work of these revisers constitutes cataloging, or the revision of cataloging, at long range without the benefit in many cases of having the books in hand. Due to the fact that the Library of Congress sometimes acquires books after cards for them produced cooperatively have become available, it has been possible to gauge the correctness and adequacy of the cooperative cataloging product. This has led to the conclusion that at best, in spite of all checks and counterchecks, long range cataloging falls short of the usual requirements of accuracy and completeness. This constitutes the weakness of cooperative cataloging from the point of view of technique. The consoling element in the situation is that on the whole practically all entries produced cooperatively have apparently proved adequate and that the number and seriousness of the errors reported by the users of the cards have been slight.

It is the paradox of cooperative and centralized cooperative cataloging in North America that the Library of Congress catalog cards are both an advantage and a hindrance. Part of this advantage lies in the fact that for a large proportion of books American libraries can secure Library of Congress cards at the mere cost of printing and distributing. Another is that these cards, because of their high standard of accuracy and completeness, have been found adequate to the needs of librarians, bibliographers and users of libraries, thus establishing an acceptable norm in cataloging which all catalogers may follow. The disadvantage which stands out above all is that the selling price of Library of Congress cards has somehow been set up as a criterion of cost whereas it cannot be considered such with any reason. Furthermore, because Library of Congress cards are available for the books of greatest incidence in American libraries, cooperative and centralized cataloging enterprises are brought to the necessity of limiting themselves to cataloging which is costlier and for which they are least likely to be reimbursed from the sale of cards. This situation does not, of course, invalidate the fact that in the long run cooperative cataloging or centralized cataloging applied to books found in a relatively small number of libraries still results in a real saving to the libraries concerned and may, if properly managed, give each of the libraries a higher quality of cataloging than it can secure for itself. By proper management is meant the assignment of tasks in cataloging on the basis of the competence of a library in personnel and bibliographic aids to do them better than anyone else. By way of example, it can be pointed out that some libraries are so fortunate as to have specialists of unusual equipment in certain fields of knowledge, in certain languages, in the ability to secure and weigh evidence and the like.

Very little has been said in regard to the advantages and shortcomings of centralized cataloging. It is more than likely that the reasons for the failure to give sufficient consideration to centralized cataloging are the "rugged individualism" of American librarians mentioned above and the Library of Congress catalog cards. In Europe centralized cataloging has made great strides as Mr. Russell's paper has shown. One reason for that is doubtless the fact that the central governmental authorities there had the discretion and power to initiate it and maintain it by using public funds. In North America we are faced with the situation where, in the first place, we have 48 sovereign states in the United States, nine provinces in Canada, territories and other possessions possessing varying degrees of autonomy, and, in the second place, libraries are subject only, or largely, to either local authorities or privately maintained institutions. In a certain sense centralized cataloging may be said to be carried on by the Library of Congress. Strictly speaking, however, the Library of Congress carries on its cataloging for its own use. Since it prints its catalog cards, it is able and willing to offer to other libraries the product of its cataloging. It is under no obligation, however, to satisfy the cataloging needs of other libraries beyond this.

Let us see what a centralized cataloging project would involve. In the first place, it would be necessary to bring together a staff of competent catalogers qualified to deal with a wide variety of subject matter and the most difficult cataloging problems. This staff would have to have available a large and well selected collection of books on all subjects as well as an adequate collection of bibliographic aids. It may be assumed that technical norms acceptable to all libraries are already available. Methods for reproducing catalog entries would have to be studied and determined and means for storing and distributing a stock of cards provided. Since, as has been stated above, the cataloging of the Library of Congress already covers a large proportion of the titles required and since these titles are among those of the greatest incidence in American libraries, the field of cataloging available to either a centralized project or a cooperative project in the stricter sense would be limited to collections of books in libraries acquired many years ago but which have remained uncataloged, collections acquired by them more recently *en bloc*, new foreign books and the analysis of monographic series and possibly articles in a selection of periodical publications. It is perhaps unfair to assume that the cost of the cataloging produced in such a setup would be lower than that of the average cooperating library. It is probably true, nevertheless, that for books in the above categories which are to be found in two or more libraries centralized cataloging would be cheaper. It has been contended that the printing of fewer than a certain number of copies of a catalog card does not pay. There is at least a suspicion that such a contention is based on the consideration merely of the cost of printing and distributing the cards and not on the cost of cataloging proper. In a centralized enterprise, there would probably be no saving (there would perhaps be a loss) in the printing and distribution of the cards. There would, however, be a net gain in that the proportionate cost of cataloging to each library would be lower.

The great advantage of centralized over cooperative cataloging is that the catalogers in a centralized cooperative undertaking have the books before them and the revision can be carried out with books in hand. Furthermore, with unity of supervision, cataloging policy would tend to be uniform and consistent. Under cooperative cataloging, the work is scattered over a number of libraries, each with its own cataloging policy and its own point of view. Furthermore, the individual library may be guided in the choice of catalogers to be assigned to the cooperative work by considerations, which, however laudable in themselves, would not be advantageous to the cooperative undertaking. Revision of entries prepared cooperatively is doubtless more costly and the product is of uneven quality. The cost of cataloging a given book is borne by the library doing the work, to be sure, but it is unlikely that it is less than it would be under a centralized project where the cost would be distributed among the cooperators.

What are the practical obstacles in the way of centralized cataloging? In the first place, perhaps, is the method of financial support and control prevalent in American libraries. As noted above in this paper, no central state, provincial, and territorial authority over libraries exists in English-speaking North America. Financial support is derived mainly from local sources and control is local and immediate. Under such circumstances it is obvious that legal and other restrictions on the use of library funds would impede their use for a project not under the immediate supervision of and not directly responsible to the library. This is, of course, the obstacle to other forms of library cooperation as well. Because the cost of setting in motion a project of centralized cataloging would require an initial outlay of a considerable sum of money, this obstacle is particularly serious here. In the second place centralized cataloging would have a tendency to slow up the supply of catalog cards, unless a central office for recording accessions, perhaps a central office for acquisition, were in existence which would make it possible to determine at once for which catalog cards there would be a sufficient demand to warrant cataloging and to begin cataloging as soon as a book is received. With cataloging activities centering so largely in Washington, with agreement on cataloging principles and procedure so general, with the example for efficient card distribution which the Card Division of the Library of Congress offers us, the problem of centralized cataloging is not so formidable as it might be. It is, nevertheless, obvious that until the millennium of library cooperation arrives, centralized cataloging is a thing to be hoped for and little more. Cooperative cataloging in its more restricted sense, however, is within narrow limits a reality. If some way can be found to finance it—and to many it is obvious that the libraries themselves ought to—it can be continued indefinitely as an adjunct of the service offered by the Library of Congress.

In recent years two other factors have entered the field of library service which may or may not have a part in advancing or limiting cooperation in cataloging. The first of them is the movement for the division of responsibility for the acquisition of books and other research materials on a regional basis. It is a concomitant of the movement for a planned library economy in the United States and Canada and is expected to aid in building up the total available book resources by eliminating useless duplication. The other factor is the development of photographic means for reproducing catalogs and individual catalog cards. The division of the responsibility for acquisition can be expected to have the effect of reducing the total number of copies of a given book available in American libraries. On the other hand it would make it necessary to develop union catalogs of varying scope and proportions, which would require copies of the catalog entries produced. The new methods of reproduction, such as photographing on film and enlarging, would on the whole tend to reduce the unit cost. It has recently been shown that the cost of reproducing on film a single card in a series of some proportions is a fraction of a cent. Printing an enlargement of it can be reduced to as little as one cent. This will affect the cost of catalog cards. The cost of cataloging proper, however, is still to be expressed largely in terms of the cost of catalogers. This cost cannot be reduced with profit to the libraries and, as stated at the beginning of this paper, is not so large as it appears, if measured not on the basis of the original outlay, but on the effectiveness of the cataloging product in meeting the requirement of library users.

To recapitulate, the problem of cooperative and centralized cataloging is an economic one above all else. The quality of the product of cooperation in cataloging is a secondary consideration. Cooperation should continue on the grounds of quality as well as economy. Centralized cataloging has distinct advantages over cooperative cataloging properly so-called. The feasibility of maintaining a cooperative cataloging project on as small a scale as desired gives it a practical advantage over centralized cataloging. Centralized cataloging can be achieved only after the libraries of North America find it possible to pool their financial resources for cooperative acquisiton. Either type of cooperation in cataloging, however, is economically superior to "rugged individualism." If it were not for the card distribution service of the Library of Congress, librarians would probably be able to look at cataloging costs more realistically and would not attempt comparison between what is practically nothing more than the cost of catalog card making and the cost of cataloging proper.

Cooperation in Cataloging

C. D. Batty

"In spite of an unfortunate reputation for parochialism and idiosyncratic practice in individual libraries, librarians have always exhibited a general urge towards cooperation. It is clear that cooperation in cataloging never occurred satisfactorily in period after period because in each case analysis of the problem suggested an adequate and satisfactory solution that could not be matched by technical capability at the time, either in the provision of source material or in the organization and reproduction of the bibliographic data."

Librarianship itself is inherently an act of cooperation. We are communications specialists bridging the gap between information and ignorance, by organizing information so that we can use it, and by organizing ignorance so that we can find information to match it. A part of this effort is the exploitation of the total resource of recorded knowledge, and the catalog is one of the most valuable tools that we use in this exploitation, provided that, as with all tools, we keep it in good order, and know how and when to use it. In recent years and even in recent weeks, much has happened both directly and indirectly to promote cooperation in the field of cataloging; sometimes these developments have occurred because catalogers have recognized a need and they sometimes form part of a larger movement for professional cooperation. I should like to concentrate on an important aspect of the whole problem of cooperation in cataloging, and that is the nature of the relationship between the problem itself and its practical solution. I intend to offer a summary of the way in which the problem has developed and the way in which different kinds of solutions have been proposed, since perhaps one of the most important things we can do as librarians to ensure effective cooperation in the future is to examine the very peculiar nature of the situation that faces us. We may then confirm the developments that are now taking place, or we may begin to wonder if some of them are not likely to suffer the same fate that has overtaken attempts at cooperation in the past.

For well over one hundred years our profession has seen many attempts to join libraries in a bibliographic unity, in particular in the field of what we might call cooperative cataloging and what the nineteenth century called universal bibliography: the control and announcement in an integrated way of the world's literature. As far back as the 1840s Charles Coffin Jewett urged the cause of universal bibliography and even attempted a single-handed effort, and his proposal was based on three conditions that have become almost classic for cooperative ventures.

Jewett described two necessary conditions that must be met before an effective cooperative venture could be attempted. The first was improved copyright legislation; at that time the law on copyright in the United States was notoriously weak and largely ignored. The second was agreement on cataloging rules, and in this Jewett echoed a general professional demand also expressed very forcefully by Panizzi in the British Museum; this demand was itself another aspect in the move towards cooperation: in this case the adoption of uniform practice in different libraries. There was a third unstated condition: the availability of a technology capable of handling the physical quantity of material and reproducing it. It was unstated because for Jewett it must have been, as it has been since, a *sine qua non* of large-scale cooperation. Jewett's efforts failed and the reasons for his failure only confirm his theories: copyright legislation was so weak that the supply of material was unreliable, the administrative aspects of cooperation between libraries were not easy to handle, and, flexible though Jewett's store of stereotypes may have seemed at the time, they remained a clumsy method of handling data. But at least Jewett provoked active discussion, notably on copyright legislation and on the provision of union catalogs, and his suggestions for a code of generally applicable cataloging rules were taken

SOURCE: Reprinted from *ASLIB Proceedings*, 21 (December, 1969), pp. 488-497, by permission of ASLIB.

up by Panizzi, who owed a great deal to Jewett's ideas, as did Cutter later in the century. It is remarkable that in this first and now quite remote period of attempts at cooperation the problem should have been seen as clearly as it was and the aspirations should have been as farsighted and as realistic as they turned out to be.

Towards the end of this period, in 1877 at the first International Conference on Librarianship, a Central Bibliographic Bureau was proposed by Henry Stevens. Its independent nature differed from Jewett's assumptions of reliance on existing large libraries, but otherwise it follows very closely the suggestions of Jewett for the provision of authoritative entries on cards or slips and indeed it is difficult to imagine a better description of the British National Bibliography than these words written in 1877 (apart from the unfortunate last phrase) '. . . [a bureau] where librarians . . . may buy descriptive slips or card titles of books. . . . Such a bureau . . . might be made self-supporting or even remunerative, like the Post Office'. Stevens' proposals were typical of an age that saw the first conference of the American Library Association; the publication of the Dewey Decimal Classification; Cutter's *Rules for a dictionary catalog*; the US Bureau of Education report on public libraries of which those rules were a part; Dewey's report on cooperative cataloging and his recommendations for a cooperative system; and the recommendations of Rogers of the Philadelphia Mercantile Library for national catalogs. The emergence of the dictionary catalog and the controversy about dictionary and classified catalogs had led to a fundamental examination of cataloging theory and practice. Laws on copyright and legal deposit had been improved. Probably most importantly, technical processes had improved almost out of recognition; where Jewett had to rely on the physical manipulation of stereotypes, Stevens could propose photo-bibliography. But what Stevens was proposing and what Jewett had spent much of his life trying to organize looked increasingly doubtful of achievement.

Unfortunately by 1880 the rapidly increasing production of material made the problem much more complex. In the second half of the nineteenth century book production doubled and periodical production quadrupled, and it was clear that this was a rising figure. In 1879, the *Library Journal* attempted a cataloging service for current titles that would have gone at least some way to answer Henry Stevens' call. But within a year the experiment had failed because it satisfied neither the librarians for whom it was neither comprehensive nor fast enough, nor the publishers who had to supply advanced copies of the material to be cataloged. In the 1840s Jewett's analysis and proposals had been sufficient for the problems that he then faced, but now the problem itself had changed, at the very moment when the technology and general context which made a major contribution to Jewett's failure had improved sufficiently to achieve what he had set out to do.

The next twenty-five or thirty years were years of experiment and lasted until just before the first world war. A new assessment of the problem that faced librarians in the control of world literature led to two separate lines of development which took bibliographers and catalogers in different directions. The awareness of the need for complete current coverage forced subject bibliographers to turn their attention away from books alone and realize the importance of other sources, and realize also the importance of the access to the material rather than its description. They began to concern themselves with works like Poole's *Index to periodical literature* of 1882 and the *Concilium Bibliographicum*.

The traditional cataloger concentrated on a different kind of detail altogether concerned almost entirely with the world of books. Publications like the *ALA Catalog* of *1893* and the services of the Library Bureau (founded partly by Dewey for the supply of library equipment but which in 1893 began to issue printed catalog cards) show that librarians now limited their aspirations in the field of cooperative cataloging to either select lists or lists of current titles. Probably the most intensive and noticeable effort in this period was the work on an internationally agreed code of cataloging rules, published in 1908 as the Anglo-American Code. This was the culmination of three quarters of a century of cataloging theory but, like many major efforts of this kind, it came about only because of formative discussion in the past and was therefore the final solution to the problems that had been so long discussed; it looked backwards and not forwards. In many ways it was an elegant and economical solution to the problems defined first by Jewett and Panizzi and further explored by Cutter. Its rules concerning personal authors concentrated on what version of the name to use, while the rules concerning corporate authors concentrated on identifying the kind of corporate body involved rather than on how to write its name down. What had been problems to Jewett and Panizzi were problems no longer and problems that had never existed in their day or had seemed slight were now becoming major problems. Cause or effect or manifestation, the 1908 code of cataloging rules suggests that much of cataloging thinking at that time lay in the past rather than in the future. Curiously enough the achievements in the field of subject bibliography and documentation towards international cooperation show a clear recognition of the conditions defined by Jewett: the need for an agreed language of control (in this case the Universal Decimal Classification); a certain source of material (in this case cooperation through an international agency—the newly founded Institut International de Bibliographie); and improved technical processes.

These separate developments, culminating on the one hand with the agreed code of cataloging rules looked for by Jewett, and on the other hand in the establishment of an international organization already at work on practical schemes for the international control of literature, might well have been expected to promote effective cooperation. But the split was too great, and catalogers continued to look inwards and to put their own house in order; the publication of the A.A. code of 1908, instead of acting as a spur to further and wider action on an international front, led only to further self-examination and revision of the cataloging rules themselves. It was left to another profession entirely to achieve results.

A third period, this time of the realization of practical limitations, extended to the middle of this century. In the middle of the 1920s the IIB failed to collaborate with the League of Nations and the United States withdrew financial support from this international project, and there began the commercially produced national current booklists like Whitakers and the Russian *Letopis' Zhurnalnykh Statei*. This seemed the end of universal bibliography as it had been envisaged in the nineteenth century, and it was confirmed within a few years by the depression, the need for stringent economy and growing international political suspicion. But the need for self-examination in the interests of economy revealed yet again the advantages of centralization and cooperation, and in America and in Britain the first really practical steps were taken by the profession itself to achieve at least national coverage: The establishment in America of the National Union Catalogue, and in this country of the National Central Library and the first of the

Regional Library Bureaux, paradoxically facilitated the need to provide 'made' work for the workless. The self-examination also revealed how much time was wasted in routine copying and duplication of effort among libraries; it served ultimately to reduce the gap between the cataloger and the bibliographer, between those insistent on full entry and those who saw abbreviated entry sufficient for their purposes.

In the foundation of the British National Bibliography in 1950 we find the nearest expression in real terms to the aspirations and plans of men like Jewett and Stevens. It satisfied the conditions laid down by Jewett and unchanged since then: a basis of legal deposit, agreed standards in cataloging, and the use of up-to-date technical resources. Basically, however, the BNB never was and fundamentally is not now a cooperative cataloging venture; it began as a national bibliography and in its plans for the future it is likely to expand its activities far beyond the range of normal cataloging in the traditional sense. It was not for some years after the initiation of BNB that the printed card service was started and although it is likely to continue in the future the development of a machine-readable record does not necessarily have the production of catalog cards as its prime objective. BNB's philosophy is at once a return to the nineteenth century association of cooperative cataloging schemes with the idea of universal bibliography and also a reflection of the modern ideas consequent upon automation: of abandoning separate and self-contained routines. Perhaps this and the continual search for more and more efficient and flexible technical capability has ensured the survival of BNB beyond a point at which it might have failed by providing a solution to a particular and past analysis of the problem.

To some extent this kind of failure had already occurred with the cataloging-in-source experiment in the Library of Congress. The Library of Congress has sold printed cards for over half a century and for much of that time the printed cards have represented entries not only in the catalogs of the Library of Congress but also in the National Union Catalogue, and they may therefore be held to be part of a cooperative cataloging system that satisfies the conditions laid down by Jewett. But it remains the general dissemination of a single library's catalog and in the past has proved to be in some respects both idiosyncratic and slow. In 1958 the Library of Congress tried to put a specimen catalog entry on the back of the title page of the book itself. This was an engaging idea and similar to some ideas proposed in the nineteenth century but it was really only a refurbishing of the existing printed card service with the same design and methods. The changes involved a reliance on the publishers and on external lines of communication, and both publisher and the post office, directly or indirectly, demonstrated the unworkability of the scheme. It is interesting to speculate on the effect of the printed card service: would cataloging-in-source have had a better chance of success if the service had not existed to affect the design of the experiment, or even the judgement of those who had to pronounce it so complete a failure? Yet again, a solution valid for the problem as it had existed in the past (but when the technical facilities were not available) proved to be the wrong solution, or a solution to the wrong problem, when it was finally put into effect.

Belonging to this fourth age of achievement is the computer-based system that handles machine-readable bibliographic records, beginning historically with computerized union catalogs and leading ultimately to the provision of machine-readable bibliographic data in the MARC system. Computers were seen for some time and still are seen by some as the latest means to the provision of conventional catalogs, but offering a better service through the use of national libraries or bibliographic agencies and the enormously powerful technical capability of the machine. Even at this level of thinking it seems that for once the problem might be analyzed and a solution might be suggested simultaneously with the provision of a technology powerful enough to meet its demands. But it very soon became apparent that much more was possible with this new technology, and co-operative cataloging moved out of its age of achievement into an age of automation in which it can no longer be considered by itself but must be considered as a part of a larger system involving all the provision, manipulation, and use of bibliographic data within the library, and indeed outside it, wherever that bibliographic data may occur.

I should like now to begin to form a question on the basis of the historical outline that I have tried to give you. It is clear that cooperation in cataloging never occurred satisfactorily in period after period because in each case analysis of the problem suggested an adequate and satisfactory solution that could not be matched by technical capability at the time, either in the provision of source material or in the organization and reproduction of the bibliographic data. And by the time that either of these conditions could be satisfied the

problem itself had changed so that the solution for which the technological capabilities were designed was no longer valid and a fresh analysis had become necessary. Now apparently we find ourselves with a technology powerful enough to answer the needs of almost any theoretical solution; we have just passed through a period of reassessment, certainly of cataloging and to some extent of the library as a total system; and we are in the process of reassessing the library as an element in the social structure, trying to define its role and possible effectiveness. For once we seem to have brought the two sides of the solution closer together. But have we really achieved a match of theoretical and practical solution, or are we deluding ourselves and will the old pattern of leapfrogging continue unless we take particular account of this phenomenon?

The introduction of computers into libraries for anything but the purely administrative use that exists in business and industry began in the area of cataloging and indexing, and even now this is felt to be one of the most profitable areas for computer deployment. In the United States, county and regional systems realized that the computer could offer easier up-dating, sorting and reproducing techniques for the supply of catalogs and particularly of union catalogs. In Britain with the reorganization of the London boroughs, when heavily duplicated bookstocks from different libraries controlled through widely different kinds of catalogs had to be amalgamated in the formation of a new borough, the computer offered an easy means of processing the information. Simple though they were, it is doubtful if any large-scale national experiment such as the MARC experiment could have been envisaged without *ad hoc* projects that were in effect pilot projects run independently and individually by libraries roughly between 1955 and 1965. But although technical capability of handling and reproducing bibliographic data is certainly essential and although its absence has been one of the causes of failure in the past, it is not the only essential factor; it is also essential to secure sources of supply, and also to have a context of demand in which the profession recognizes its need in the long-term view in spite of short-term disadvantages of a new system. Recent developments have involved not only computers but also the other two factors.

Arising from the critique by Seymour Lubetzky of the American Library Association *Cataloguing Rules* of 1949 and driven onwards by the enthusiasm of a number of perceptive and energetic librarians, the International Conference on Cataloguing Principles held in Paris in 1961 offered an opportunity for a fundamental reappraisal not only of the detail of cataloging practice but also of its philosophy. For the first time in many years the profession had the opportunity of planning ahead and offering itself a code of practice flexible enough to adapt to rapidly changing times. The ICCP brought together librarians from all over the world, intent on taking positive action to standardize access to information through bibliographical description and the catalogs of their libraries. It acted as a focus for aspirations and intentions, since, unlike many international conferences, it was not content simply to hear different points of view, but to work out and offer an agreed set of principles that would form a basis for international cataloging practice. This meant that it also focused attention on the problem itself, and thus reawakened the consciousness of the pressing need for international provision. By offering a solution to a problem clearly perceived by a few members of the profession it defined a context of demand that the rest of the profession could understand and endorse. So at one stroke the ICCP satisfied two of the conditions recognized in the nineteenth century as essential for cooperative cataloging, particularly on an international scale: it promoted the realization of the need and the desire for its satisfaction and it offered the basis for an agreed code of practice.

Partially consequent on the ICCP the British and American committees jointly produced the new code of cataloging rules that are now called the AACR. This provides for the intellectual analysis and representation of the names of documents and the names of their authors and could well have provided us with exactly the vehicle needed for the future. As Michael Gorman of the British National Bibliography said in reviewing the code, 'this is not only the best cataloguing code we have, it is also the best we are likely to have for a very long time'. But under the pressures of what we might call practical necessity large libraries and the associations that guard their interests encouraged the modification of the rules to conform with existing practice so that libraries adopting the rules should not find themselves in grave economic difficulties because of too much revision. We might in passing observe the irony that one of the large libraries principally concerned in encouraging the modifications then decided not to use the rules at all. In spite of the fact that this code is based more firmly than any

preceding code on principles rather than on cases and might therefore be expected to be more adaptable in changing circumstances, we must ask the question: On what basis were the principles formulated and do we have yet again a code which is the culmination of preceding theoretical analysis rather than one that anticipates problems for the future?

One of the problems faced by all cooperative cataloging ventures has been to ensure the source of supply. Jewett's call for improved copyright legislation was the first step towards ensuring that the library or agent principally concerned would receive the necessary material. In the succeeding century national libraries could rely increasingly confidently on copyright legislation to the point where the British National Bibliography could base its activities without question on the British Museum's receipt of copyright books. It is significant that the decision to separate BNB from the copyright office of the BM, and to rely instead on the copyright agent, caused the BNB more problems of speed and coverage than any other decision in its history. But the world of literature is international; if either the Library of Congress or the British National Bibliography were to feel confident that some kind of international coverage might be achieved it would be necessary to think on a broader front. Logically there are two ways to do this: by the exchange of national bibliographical data, or by the acquisition by one agency of material on an international basis, and the subsequent issue by that agency of bibliographical data on an international scale.

Curiously enough, the second of these alternatives, which might just have been possible in the first half of the nineteenth century, was never attempted until recently and it came closest to being realized in the Title II-C program of the Library of Congress. This ambitious program sought to collect literature on the widest scale the profession has yet seen, and for some time, with the full weight and capability of the Library of Congress behind it, the signs were promising. But, perhaps inevitably, the program is running into financial difficulties; earlier this year the budget was cut by about a third, and consequently special services have been eliminated, plans to include more developing and underdeveloped countries have been scrapped, and a lower price limit has been placed on automatic purchase (thus ironically making it difficult to obtain just those scholarly works whose inclusion justifies such a program). As we might have expected logically, it is the first alternative that is likely to yield the best results, although in all fairness we should remember that decentralization and the acceptance of records from different institutions do not necessarily provide the right answer. The Farmington Plan showed the damaging effect of insufficient technical resources. Now, however, a solution based on decentralization is offered by the development that also satisfies the last of the conditions for successful cooperative cataloging: a powerful technology for handling and disseminating bibliographical data.

Against a background of the failure of the cataloging-in-source experiment, and the King report on the automation of the Library of Congress, that library established an experimental project to produce a machine-readable cataloging format. In 1966 what is now known as the MARC I pilot project began to develop the format and supply tapes to a group of sixteen participating libraries. The intention was to allow these libraries to develop their own systems for handling machine-readable bibliographic data, and to use their experiences in building the operational stage to be called MARC II. It is hardly necessary now to describe the format or the results of that pilot project, but I would like to emphasize one or two points that seem to me of significance for the future of cooperative cataloging.

The Library of Congress seems to have begun by thinking of the MARC format as a cataloging format, based originally on LC cataloging practice and intended to produce authoritative card or book catalogs as output from a computer. Many librarians still think like this. Only a year ago one of the members of the MARC team stated publicly that he saw catalog production as the chief use of the format for many years to come. And recently in the *Library Association Record* there was an eloquent doubt of the values of a machine-readable tape that might contain only two-thirds of the library's accessions, that cannot be relied upon to announce them within a week or so of the arrival of the book in the library, and that may have a different cataloging style, based possibly on the shifting sands of the latest version of a cataloging code. But this is to forget that there must always be a residue of local cataloging in any library, that it is possible to function with a temporary, abbreviated catalog entry (or even without one at all for a time), that no library's cataloging style is perfect, and certainly very few libraries can honestly claim that it is consistent and correct throughout their catalogs and that it is only by

adopting a standard that it becomes tried and accepted as a standard. It is also to continue to assume that these machine-readable tapes are there simply to produce human readable catalogs; but it is obvious from even a cursory study of automation in other fields and by an examination of what actually happened in several of the libraries participating in the MARC I project that the provision of a machine-readable unit record can be used more economically by seeing the catalog as just another manifestation of processes that organize and handle bibliographic data.

When the Library of Congress began to develop the MARC II format in 1967 it called the format a *communications* format, and this is the name used on the manual first published in 1968. In other words, the designers themselves encourage a wider use of machine-readable bibliographic data, and the work at the Fondren Library of Rice University in Texas and at the Atomic Weapons Research Establishment in Aldermaston shows that it can support all stages of processing, from selection to dissemination. Indeed, Hillis Griffin, who helped to set up the MARC distribution service, has suggested that in time the catalog itself may disappear in favour of an information network using MARC tapes as a data base.

Arguments about the nature and purpose of MARC will long continue, but I suggest that there is a more fundamental problem. We have now a recognition among the profession of the need for cooperation, hopefully on an international scale, but it is in danger of stopping short at catalog production and catalog exchange. We have an agreed standard of practice for bibliographical description, and in its basic principles it looks ahead, although in its expression it was compelled to amend its views in order to deal with present problems based inevitably on past tradition—and in some senses it looks backwards instead of forwards. We have a powerful tool in the computer, that can handle, store and disseminate information in greater quantity and at greater speed than ever before, but it is not designed basically to handle bibliographic data, which needs immediate and simultaneous access to large files consisting of alphabetical information, and we are therefore in constant danger of accepting machine constraints that are irrelevant and even damaging to our interests.

We are in danger of allowing theory and technology to leapfrog again. If we accept the theoretical assumption that the computer is just a bigger typewriter-cum-filing drawer, and if we base our design on a standard code of practice that solves yesterday's problems, then we shall ignore the capability that the computer now offers us, and cooperative cataloging will briefly be realized, only to fail, and to fail us paradoxically in its realization, because if we insist on cooperation only in the production of catalogs then we shall inhibit the early realization of cooperation in other spheres, and by the time we have solved the theoretical problem all over again we shall have to seek a new technology.

Fortunately the signs are hopeful: More and more librarians are realizing the importance of the systems approach to the library; there are indications that the Library of Congress will adopt AACR at least for MARC; there are also indica-

tions that full international agreement will be given to a revised AACR that will emerge soon, and will be very like AACR (British text) in which any changes will be towards a reliance on principle rather than on cases. We have a chance, perhaps the first, to match our theoretical solutions to the technology now available. I hope we do not throw away that chance through ignorance, prejudice or suspicion. Individual costs and effort cannot always be matched by individual benefits. It is clear that in the context of automation it is no longer a question of *whether* or *why* but of *how* and *when*. The same is true of cooperation. The general benefit is undeniable; what we must do is to accept the principle and work as forcefully and sensibly as we can towards its realization.

The Effective Use of Bibliographic Information and the Role of Automation in This Process

Paul R. Reimers

"Bibliographic information is not only the most reduced data form for a large number of disciplines but is also, of necessity, one of the most organized bodies of information. Automation provides more powerful methods for organizing bibliographic data because machines work cheaply, tirelessly, and very accurately."

The information necessary for any continuing endeavor exists in a number of forms: as raw data, as reduced information, and as organized information . . . . The purpose of bibliographic files has been the retrieval of books and other materials and beyond this the retrieval of the information contained in them.

Automation promises more powerful methods for organizing and handling bibliographic data because machines work cheaply, tirelessly, and very accurately. Norbert Wiener, one of the great modern pioneers in computer technology, was one of the first to see the computer's proper role in regard to man's work.[1] His thesis was that the computer was a servant which would free men by allotting human work to human beings. He advocated that creative tasks be reserved to people and that the dull, the routine, the repetitive be consigned to machines. Wiener was mainly considering the work of the mathematician, but the principle holds as well for other kinds of intellectual work. Computer technology has now been applied to business systems to tool and process control, and even to tasks of scholarship. When computers are used with respect to bibliography the same precept holds: Do with machines those things machines can best do and reserve to men those things men can best do.

It is especially timely that we should be discussing now the effective utilization of automation for the control of bibliographic information. The Library of Congress has just completed an experiment to test how bibliographic data can be distributed in machine-readable form and how it can be used at receiving libraries. The experiment is called MARC, a convenient form for *MA*chine *R*eadable *C*atalog. Other schemes have distributed bibliographic information, but they have been limited in subject, in coverage, in number of records, or in clientele. MARC is conceived as an open-ended system designed to serve all functions now served by the man-readable catalog card.

In order to engage in a concrete discussion of automation, MARC will be described, its results will be discussed, and certain projections will be derived. Because MARC is even now just finishing the experimental stage of its life, no final conclusion can be stated. Sufficient evidence, is available, however, so that the next stages are not expected to produce surprises.

THE EXPERIMENT

There were two necessary parts to the MARC experiment. One was conducted at the Library of Congress and the other at other cooperating libraries. The experiment at the Library consisted of devising and testing the means to put bibliographic data into a machineable medium. A basic method was developed and tested; the method was then improved to increase accuracy and to reduce time and effort. The experiment at the cooperating libraries consisted of using this machineable record for local needs and reporting usage to the Library of Congress. Before the process is described it will be useful to consider the operating constraints at the central production point and at the outlying user points.

At the Library of Congress where the machineable record was created, the experiment was designed to minimize disruption of the normal flow of work. To be a real test, however, MARC had to use real bibliographic information as it was being produced. It was therefore decided to borrow the

SOURCE: Reprinted from *Libri*, 17 (1967), pp. 305–317, by permission of the author. Originally presented at the Thirty-third Session of the IFLA General Council, Toronto, Canada, August, 1967.

manuscript catalog card and reproduce it just before it went to the printer. MARC had to use available equipment. This meant that the computer programs had to be less sophisticated than they could have been and that the means of input to the computer had to use tested tape-punching typewriters. MARC had to produce results in a relatively short period of time because the results of the experiment were needed to guide developmental work going on at the same time. The consequence was that computer programs prepared by an outside group were not so well designed or tested as they could have been. A limitation on funds as well as a rigid deadline controlled how much could be done. It will become clear how these constraints influenced the design of the central experiment.

Other considerations governed the selection of and the cooperation with the libraries which were to receive the tapes in the MARC experiment. The number of libraries had to be limited because time at the Library of Congress was limited, and the experiment had to be within manageable limits. Sixteen participants were therefore selected from a larger number of volunteer libraries. They included libraries of different kinds located in different parts of the country. Research libraries, school libraries, and public libraries were represented among those chosen. Interests varied from the limited area of specialized researchers to the broad one of the general public. Each participating library further agreed to report to the Library of Congress the use made of the tapes and the degree of success attained.

The first test tapes were distributed to participants in October of 1966. The first regular distribution of the tapes was made in November of 1966 and has been continued to the present time. Each weekly tape contains a selected portion of the records of those English monographs cataloged by the Library of Congress during the preceding week. Forty-three computer programs were written of which thirty were required for the central operation. The details of the programs are expressed in some four thousand pages of documentation. Cataloging information is now being added for approximately eight hundred titles a week, and the tape contained approximately 16,000 records by July 1, 1967, the end of the test period.

THE PROCESS

The process followed in MARC will be described in non-technical terms. A description of this kind

runs the risks of offending both librarians and computer technicians because it does not do justice to the subtleties of either profession. But descriptions are needed which can be understood by all those interested so that all can help in judging how far and in what direction automation should go. Because computers have been used to accomplish more and more complex tasks, it is no longer clear where the role of the machine must end and that of man begin.

The normal operation at the Library of Congress had been to complete the essential steps of cataloging and then to have the LC card printed and distributed. All of the bibliographic information is included on a manuscript card which is sent to the printer. The MARC process interrupts this normal flow in order to reproduce the manuscript card on an input worksheet. The manuscript card itself is then returned to its place in the normal flow of processing and MARC processing continues as a separate stream.

The reproduced worksheet is passed to a MARC editor, who tags each item of information and codes certain of them. Tagging is the process of marking the kind of information, such as the author's name, by prefixing to it a number group which will identify this to the machine as an author's name. Coding is the step by which certain information is expressed by a group always of the same length. Place of publication, for example, is always expressed by means of a four-letter group taken from a list prepared for MARC.

The edited sheet then goes to a typist, who types the information on a typewriter which simultaneously produces a punched paper tape. The paper tape is read into a computer, and the information is stored in computer memory. Each record is subjected to a number of tests for accuracy and conformity, and a daily tape is prepared with all correct records entered that day. Once a week a tape is prepared which contains all records processed in that period. The weekly tape is reproduced and a copy of it is sent to each of the libraries participating in the experiment.

When a library receives a magnetic tape, it processes the tape through its own computer and uses the data for its own requirements. The most common requirement was the production of catalog cards; computer programs were therefore provided so that all libraries could perform this basic function. One of the results of the experiment was to find to what extent computer programs written tend to indicate which functions the participants found to be the most valuable uses for a machine-able bibliographic record.

Before the MARC system can be considered an acceptable way to operate, certain changes in the procedure will be required. In some cases less than optimum procedures have been accepted because the effort was known to be experimental, and in other cases improvements have been identified in the course of the pilot project. For example, typing of the data—keyboarding as it is called by data processors—duplicates other identical operations. At the beginning of the cataloging process this same information was typed onto a manuscript card. It will be handled again as the manuscript card is prepared for printing. An efficient operation must find ways of preserving and correcting recorded information so that only one keyboarding will be required.

More important than changes in the production of the bibliographic tape are changes which must be made in order to make it a better bibliographic tool. As the experiment drew to a close, the chief concern of the designers was to improve the format so that it would be most useful to the greatest number of libraries. The MARC format had been adopted in order to satisfy a large number of needs expressed by libraries. As the format was used, some of these needs were found to have changed, and others were found to be more pressing than those originally included. A new format evolved which was designed to be an efficient means for transmitting information.

THE FINDS

The most important and most overlooked result of the pilot project is a MARC system in being—a network that is distributing bibliographic data on a regular basis to a limited number of libraries, which, in turn, may take the data tapes available to other libraries not selected as active participants in the experiment. The pilot project provided a base upon which a continuing system could be built. The lessons learned from the pilot concerned procedures, organization, and format. Current and projected uses made clear the fact that the form of material and its treatment had to be changed if it was to be most useful to libraries.

Improvements in the process have developed from the operation itself. A character set, early established by a cooperative effort, provided an input keyboard for punching as well as a computer print train. The number of characters was limited to that which could be handled by the machine.

The character set has been studied to determine its coverage of the Roman alphabet languages. As MARC is extended, the set may be modified and should become widely used in American libraries. Inefficiencies have been eliminated. Many of these were procedures which had been allowed initially to insure that no errors could enter the record. For example, logs had been set up to insure that no record was lost or misplaced. Training of operators was documented and developed to allow them to reach accepted levels of performance in the least possible time.

To a great extent the design of programs affects the efficiency of the operation not only of the computer itself but also of the people who support it. In many cases programs had been written in a way that was easiest for the programmer. This meant that the staff had to provide input and accept outputs which were convenient to the machine rather than to the man. It also meant that programs could be improved only with difficulty because they had been hastily written by people who were not completely aware of the power of the equipment complex or of the necessity for program flexibility.

Lessons learned about organization are closely related to those learned about procedures. These are based on intuition for the most part because it was not possible to vary the method in order to find the "best" organization. In some cases it was possible to compare results with participating libraries or with other libraries which had undertaken similar developments. A limiting but very necessary condition for the experiment was that the normal operation not be disrupted, as previously pointed out. The project was managed by a group with no operating responsibilities so that the new operation could react to deadlines rather than to operational crises. There is no way to tell absolutely what might have happened if the experiment had been part of current operations, but in this case separation of functions worked well.

The experience among participating libraries confirmed the fact that better programming will result when programs are written under the control of libraries. In cases where librarians had to request support from a data-processing organization, even within the same institution, a longer time elapsed from specification to operation and programs tended to be less well suited to the operation. The ideal situation is obtained when the librarian is also a programmer or when the two work together very closely.

Since Project MARC was built around a format

by which bibliographic data is distributed to user libraries, it is natural that the most important results should relate to the kind of record best suited to this purpose. The original format was designed to convey bibliographic data in a form which was efficient for the machine. This format was modified so that processing at user libraries could be efficiently accomplished. Local requirements are not, however, all the same. Different kinds of libraries and different library functions demand that the same material be expressed in different forms. A new format has been evolved from the recommendations of MARC participants and other potential users. The new MARC format will emphasize the transmission rather than the processing role. It will thus aim at convertibility rather than compatibility. This will probably mean that a library upon receipt of a tape will have to convert to a local processing format. The conversion will be made without human intervention and will be required only once as the library "speaks" to all other libraries. Processing in the new format will be possible for those libraries which elect to process directly. The new format will be universal enough to accommodate a large variety of material.

The content of the distributed tape will also change as a result of participant experience. MARC was originally accumulated at the Library of Congress so that each weekly tape included all titles which had been recorded up to the time of issuance. Although it was realized that future accumulated tapes would become very large and that some change would be necessary, it was felt that accumulating records once at the Library of Congress would save processing at individual libraries. Experience has shown that many recipients look at new accessions rather than at the complete list. Processing time in the cooperating libraries is not really saved because the tape must be passed through the local computer in order that the material may be locally useful.

CONCLUSIONS

MARC can be considered a scientific experiment in that certain parts of the environment were varied while other parts were held as constant as possible. The method by which a book is cataloged at the Library was not changed. The means by which the catalog record was distributed, on the other hand, were automated. Improvements noted by recipient libraries, therefore, can be attributed to automation except for minor induced effects.

The results of the experiment have the validity of a controlled case study rather than that of a replicated experiment. Statistics are available on the number of records processed, on costs accrued, and on resources expended, but the substance of the experiment is not statistical. This is not a severe limitation when one considers that each library is maintained to serve a given clientele or discipline. Results will therefore be applied to individual cases which are similar in function rather than to large populations which can be described by a statistical profile. With these reservations in mind, it will be useful to draw conclusions from the findings.

One of the most striking conclusions has also been observed in other attempts to automate. In this case it is clear that the organization of the Library staff *vis-a-vis* the computer staff greatly influenced the success of automation in the early stages. Librarians and computer specialists had to be able to cooperate, and each profession had to be willing to learn the basic language of the other.

Sufficient time had to be allowed for administrative as well as technical delays. Institutions differed in their review and budget cycles, and it was not fair to some to begin the operation and to expect that they would be operative in the same time frame as others. Because of the variation between institutions, time must be allowed for all participants to reach proficiency.

Project MARC addresses the critical problem of how to move bibliographic information efficiently and without loss from one library center to another. It was found in the process industries that the first parts of the process to be automated involved movement of materials between work stations. Only in highly automated processes was the operation itself under control of the machine. In the process industries as well as in other information systems, the greatest progress from automation has come from improving existing procedures. None of these improvements, by themselves, seemed to change the process radically but as new procedures were added and as they were combined in the same chain of production, results became apparent. Methods were improved and allowed to interact until the process seemed quite different from that which started the cycle.

Librarians have been understandably reticent to alter prior decisions because each change entailed a very large expenditure of clerical effort. If the clerical effort was not possible, a decision to change could not be made, no matter how much it was justified by theory. Automation will make possible changes in procedures and policies which are hitherto considered impossible. The result will be that methods and files can change with new developments in retrieval and can keep pace with advances in the taxonomy of information. From this ability to change and to progress, a whole new attitude will emerge in regard to files and processes. In an automated system, major changes can be contemplated and publications can be updated as often as necessary.

The same ability that allows bibliographic files to be changed also allows records to be changed to meet local conditions. Each library is unique in regard to size of collection, clientele served, and catalog characteristics. The MARC format dedicates to local libraries certain positions in the record in which local bibliographic material can be entered.

It is clear from the examples given that automation need not and should not cause bibliography to become rigid. Although computers require that data be presented to them in a prescribed format, the speed and flexibility of the machine allow records to be changed. In a manual system, the human technician can recognize data in changed position or even explicitly, but methods must be carefully explained in order to assure that the same decisions are made. A prescribed form allows functions to be less prescribed than they are with manual operations.

An example of change made possible by automation occurred in Project MARC itself. The MARC format was developed in a relatively short time and was not fully accepted by all who might have had to use it. It was decided to proceed with a tentative format in order to gain experience. After eight months of use and a number of consultations, the format is being changed.

The ability to correct a record or a part of it allows records to be released without the intensive and time-consuming controls required by a manual procedure. This does not mean that a lower quality of product should be allowed because it is always more efficient to complete a transaction in a single pass through the system. It does mean, however, that libraries can be using the great majority of correct records much more quickly and that errors which would be found in proofreading will still be found and will be corrected.

The effective use of automation in regard to bibliographic information demands a very close scrutiny of the functions to be performed by records. This scrutiny will enable librarians to direct and to control the kinds of systems they will be using. Functions are important because some changes will be brought about by automation and some anomalies must be accepted. A greater control of the format is required to produce greater flexibility of use. A short term acceptance of some imperfections is required to produce greater timeliness of product. To understand what concessions must be made and what are proposed only for the convenience of the machine, a continuing dialogue must be carried on and from this dialogue will come better understanding and more effective systems.

NOTE

[1] Norbert Wiener, *The Human Use of Human Beings; Cybernetics and Society*. Boston, 1950

ADDITIONAL REFERENCES

U. S. *Library of Congress. Information Systems Office.* Planning memorandum number 3. A proposed format for a standardized machine-readable catalog record. A preliminary draft prepared by Henriette D. Avram, Ruth S. Freitag, and Kay D. Guiles. Washington, 1965.

U. S. *Library of Congress. Information Systems Office.* A preliminary report on the MARC (*MA*-chine *R*eadable *C*atalog) Pilot Project. Washington, 1966. 101 p.

King, Gilbert W., *and others*. Automation and the Library of Congress. (Washington: Library of Congress, 1963).

Markuson, Barbara Evans. A system development study for the Library of Congress automation program. *Library quarterly*, 36:197–273, July 1966.

Buckland, Lawrence F. The recording of Library of Congress bibliographical data in machine form; a report prepared for the Council on Library Resources, Inc. Rev. (Washington: Council on Library Resources, 1965).

Snyder, Samuel S. Automation at LC: philosophy, plans, progress, *Library journal*, **90**:466–471, Nov. 1, 1965.

Avram, Henriette D., Kay D. Guiles, *and* Guthrie T. Meade. Fields of information on Library of Congress catalog cards: analysis of a random sample, 1950–1964. *Library quarterly*, **37**: 180–192, Apr. 1967.

Library Automation and Project MARC

Henriette D. Avram[1] and Barbara E. Markuson[2]

"A small system, Project MARC is an experiment in the centralized production and distribution of a standardized machine-readable catalog record."

GENERAL SYSTEMS CONSIDERATIONS

Among the difficult and time-consuming operations associated with the utilization of computers in library applications are the analysis of requirements and the conversion of data to machine-readable form. A number of articles—ranging from the elementary to the highly theoretical—has been written about this problem.[3] It has been pointed out to the librarian that, due to the constraints of machine operations, data must be specified in much more precise detail than before.

Standardization of cataloging practices has made centralized cataloging possible, and conversely, centralized cataloging has made standardization more necessary, if only for economic reasons. It has become more and more obvious that the efficient modern library buys as much cataloging as it can obtain. The increasing interest in the computer gives rise again to the spectre of everyone preparing data locally, eliminating many of the benefits gained by centralized cataloging. It is obvious that means must be sought to distribute centralized cataloging in machine-readable form widely and economically.

The use of the computer allows the capability of manipulating bibliographical data for a variety of uses providing that the elements of information are tagged or identified properly. The difficulty lies in knowing in advance the way in which specific items of bibliographic data actually will be used in searching, retrieval, comparing, and filing. This lack of predictability gives rise to decisions based on judgment or emotion; we can in many cases only imagine how certain uses could be facilitated by the computer.

However, solution of bibliographic problems is not enough. If librarians are to utilize computers in more than a trivial way, a number of rather complex system problems must be faced. For example, an automated library might include both manual and automated subsystems. The automated subsystem might encompass elements such as man/machine operations and procedures; hardware, including computers, input devices, and printers; and software (computer programs) for on-line processing, multi-programming, and file maintenance.

The library problem is essentially a system problem—it has always been so. The computer is merely a tool, but its constraints are such that its use requires much more careful attention to even the minutiae in a system. It could be said that the computer forces attention on the interfaces between operations to a greater extent than any other tool. One would like to develop a system which allows efficient processing of bibliographical data through the entire acquisitions, cataloging, circulation, reference, and printing cycle. Our primary focus has been on catalog card data because the catalog constitutes, in a very real way, the heart of the system and because decisions concerning this file affect all other operations. Library systems will require decisions about bibliographical data, procedures, policies, and hardware, and these elements must be fused in a manner which results in an organization which is not only efficient, but economical and reliable as well.

What are some problem areas which librarians face in developing completely or partially automated systems? The following lists are provided to provoke thought and discussion.

The bibliographical decisions to be made include the following:

1. Does the formatting of entries for efficient machine processing affect the bibliographic function of the entry?
2. Should certain data, now implicitly stated in the bibliographic entry, be made specific? For example, should the language of the title and

---

SOURCE: Reprinted from J. Harrison and P. Laslett, eds., *Brasenose Conference on the Automation of Libraries* (London: Mansell, 1967), pp. 97–123, by permission of the authors and the publisher.

the text, the kind of author (corporate, personal, etc), and other attributes of a particular work be described explicitly?

3. To what extent do certain filing practices need to be retained in machine systems?

4. How many access points to the bibliographic data should be provided in a machine system? Should these include increased depth of subject indexing, more name entries, chapter headings, place of publication, etc? Which items could be reduced to codes for efficient searching, and how shall these codes be structured and maintained?

5. What diversity of cataloging practice actually exists throughout the world? What impact does this diversity have on the development of a standard for international data interchange? What classes of practices present the most difficult areas for analysis and agreement and how might fruitful attempts to study and solve these problems be undertaken?

6. To what extent could a standardized format be developed which would be hospitable to description of materials in different media—monographs, serials, slides, motion pictures, phonograph records, maps, etc?

7. To what extent could a standardized format be developed which would be useful for a variety of library operations such as acquisitions, cataloging, circulation, bibliographical work, etc. To what extent would the development of such a format permit the creation of a complete bibliographic record of an item as a result of collecting data input from many separate library operations?

Machine problems are many and complex; the following examples illustrate their range and variety.

1. How can a multiplicity of languages be efficiently encoded for machine processing and how can they be transferred back to the original language for output printing?

2. How should bibliographical data be structured for efficient storage and retrieval? To date most work has been done on the problem of formatting for machine production of traditional library products such as book catalogs, printed catalog cards, and lists. The problems of file design for actual machine search and retrieval on special elements of bibliographic data will need intensive study if large-scale automated library systems are to be achieved.

3. What coding schemes most efficiently permit the machine identification of data elements in the record? That is, can data be so structured that the computer can recognize, by the configuration of codes, a particular item of data and process it in a variety of ways?

4. What are the trade-offs between frequency of use of data, the organization of the machine files, the configuration of the particular equipment available, and the use of minimal coding techniques for storage of the data? By minimal coding one attempts to store the most data in the least space, but in some cases one has the concomitant problem of processing the data upon request back to their original form. There is some point at which a balance has to be reached for the sake of system efficiency.

5. What relationships exist between the manner in which bibliographical data are formatted and encoded and the terminal devices (display consoles, typewriters, teletypewriters, etc.) which one might wish to use?

Systems problems are concerned with the effective configuration of men and machines to create and utilize data efficiently. Those of interest to librarians include the following:

1. A basic ground rule is to ensure that the system permits men to create and utilize data in a manner suitable for human processing and machines to manipulate data in a manner most suitable for machine processing.

2. When is it most efficient to have centralized rather than decentralized computer operations in a library system? For example, in a large system would specific operations, e.g., serial record control, or specific media, e.g., maps or manuscripts, utilize separate computer systems?

3. In a library system what part of the operation is batched or on-line? For example, do some files have to be updated immediately or can they be updated in a batched operation?

4. To what extent is it possible to design an operational library system which eliminates redundancy among the various files?

5. How can the system designer identify the diversity of user needs and response times and assign priorities to these?

6. How can the system designer maximize the probability that the library system can incorporate new techniques, provide new services, and also remain stable under normal expansion?

7. What monitoring techniques should be incorporated in the system design to insure that library managers receive information about

system overloads or underloads, error rates, cost, use, and efficiency?

8. How will direct man-machine dialogue be utilized in the library system? Will the dialogue be standardized throughout the system, or will there be a requirement for some specialized dialogues to interrogate certain files or to perform certain operations? What techniques would be used to insure that the dialogue could be expanded as the system develops?

9. What problems will result when the library system interfaces via communications links to other library systems and to other information systems? Does the hardware selected permit an efficient interface with other systems and have standards been used which permit data to be utilized with a minimum of reformatting?

The questions raised above should make it obvious to librarians who are neophytes to the computer field that data, hardware, and operational elements are almost inextricably interwoven. Once any system element is fixed, there must be a resulting accommodation elsewhere in the system.

A small system, Project MARC, which is an experiment in the centralized production and distribution of a standardized machine-readable catalog record, will be described in some detail in the next section of this paper. It has been selected as an example for two reasons. First, its size permits system elements to be more readily understood and, second, it will be an actual system operating in a research library environment. The decisions made in Project MARC were responsive to system objectives and constraints; they illustrate those problems which will have to be solved in the design of large, complex automated library systems.

PROJECT MARC

Objectives: Project MARC (Machine-Readable Cataloging) is an experiment based on the hypothesis that it is feasible to produce a standardized machine-readable catalog record that can be manipulated and reformatted in local installations to serve local practices and needs. The Project will provide information on a number of topics of interest to librarians. For example, there will be an evaluation of the cost of distribution, the timeliness, and the use of the data. A study will be made of the cost of including certain additional data elements in the record and the actual use of these elements. Since the MARC pilot operation is the first distribution service for current machine-readable data based on a standardized format which was widely discussed throughout the library community, the results should be of significance in the development of larger projects. One specific result should be the identification of those local uses which cannot be served by centrally produced data and the extent to which the central agency must be concerned with actual local operating practices.

Background: During 1965 the Library of Congress requested support from the Council on Library Resources for the development of a pilot operation for the distribution of machine-readable catalog data to a representative segment of the library community.[4] The Council responded in December 1965 with a grant of $130,000 of which $100,000 was to be used to develop and plan the pilot project.[5] The actual operation of the project was to be funded by the Library of Congress and was to be implemented in September 1966 with a proposed termination date of March 1967.

In June 1965, a preliminary report on problems associated with converting catalog data to a standardized machine-readable form was prepared in the Information Systems Office (see item 7 in the bibliography). In the process of writing this report, the authors reviewed the pertinent literature and consulted with experts in the library and data processing field. The report was submitted to intensive review both in the Library of Congress and the library community. There seemed to be a consensus that a standard was possible, but that additional work needed to be done. The MARC project would serve as a vehicle to gather additional data before even a tentative national standard could be suggested.

The format used in MARC was based on this preliminary report, the comments received during the discussions, the results of two conferences (see items 8 and 9 in the bibliography), and some system constraints to be described later. The important thing to note is that, to the extent possible, a format was developed which had the consensus of a wide user group. Of equal importance is the inclusion of some data elements (for example, a publisher code and the height of the book), the uses of which were strongly advanced by certain individuals and strongly questioned by others. Since objective criteria about the actual use of these elements were unavailable, it seemed wise to subject them to actual testing.

System Constraints: Any experimental test is bounded by the test facility to be utilized, the data selected, the available funds and staff, and the time allowed for making observations and evaluating results. These boundaries influence the design of experiments; similar constraints, which, as we shall see, influence certain factors of Project MARC, would also have to be reckoned with in the design of larger library systems.

In Project MARC there were two kinds of constraints. First, there were aspects of the Project outside the control of the system analysts, such as the money available, the time for implementation of the Project, and the time for evaluation of the results. The second group of constraints were largely based on the first and, in turn, further influenced design considerations. These constraints included equipment selected for the test, the procedures to be followed, and the data to be tested.

Basic Constraints: The most important constraints in system design are those factors outside the influence of the system analysts. In Project MARC these included the money to be allocated and the Project schedule.

Funds: The budget for Project MARC comes from two sources: $100,000 granted from CLR and a matching amount from Library of Congress appropriated funds. An agreement was made to use the Council's grant entirely for system planning and preparing computer programs and Library funds for the actual operation of the Project.

Time for Implementation: The Project was to operate on an accelerated time schedule for several reasons. The Library wanted to gather as much information as it could on the creation and use of machine-readable data in order to have information which would be useful in work on a system development study for the design of an automated central bibliographic system which would begin at the Library in the summer of 1966 and continue for fifteen months. The Library also wanted to obtain a data base for research in areas such as computer typesetting, file organization studies, retrieval modes, man-machine dialogues, filing, etc. Finally, there were so many uncoordinated efforts in the use of machine-readable data that it was obvious that an immediate program, even on a limited scale, would be of great benefit. Less than nine months was allowed for the entire planning for Project MARC, from initial design to full-scale operation. This time-frame made it mandatory to restrict the system in ways to be described later.

Time for Evaluation: One objective of the Project

was to get immediate answers to certain questions about the creation and utilization of machine-readable cataloging data. Results were wanted so that modifications could be made, both to the data and the system procedures, to aid the Library of Congress and the library community to begin making plans, should the test be a success, for further projects on a larger scale. This decision also greatly influenced the system because it became apparent that user libraries could only make meaningful evaluations if they were able to use the data promptly and efficiently. To achieve this it was decided to supply the user with both the bibliographical data and a limited set of computer programs. Obviously a significant amount of effort and money had to go into computer programming and the equipment available at the user libraries became an important part of the experiment.

Secondary Constraints: In view of the basic constraints the system analysts made certain decisions which tended to 'freeze' the system. Once these decisions were made, the system planning could begin in detail and during the weeks devoted to planning, the analysts gradually worked the system design to the level of extremely precise and specific details concerning data, programs, and manual operations. The secondary constraints included the actual operating site, procedures to be followed in obtaining and converting data, and the data to be selected.

Operating Site: It was decided that in order to learn about the actual problems in centralized production of machine-readable data, the Library of Congress staff should manage the Project directly rather than contract the work to a service bureau. This decision brought up the problem of equipment. Should the Library rent new equipment, augment existing equipment, or use its present computer with minor modifications? The Project Director elected to use the existing computer installation[6] because there were so many unknowns and variables and because the Project was an experimental rather than a permanent operation. Changing the equipment configuration would therefore prove expensive and difficult to justify. This decision immediately influenced the kinds of programs which could be operated efficiently, the amount of data which could be handled, and, in effect, fixed the hardware elements of the system.

Procedures: In view of the time constraints and

the experimental nature of the Project, it seemed wise not to disturb the actual internal operations of the Library. A group would be set up to receive cataloging data and edit and prepare it for conversion without any interruption of normal cataloging procedures. This influenced the kinds of work sheets devised and the operational procedures and routines to be followed. Furthermore, it meant that evaluation and projections might prove more difficult because the system does not test how actual cataloging operations would be influenced. However, there will be mechanisms set up to gather data on the problems raised in the editing procedures and the difficulties editors and typists have with respect to the data sheet, interpretation of manuals, and application of procedures.

Data: In order to meet the time constraints and to ensure that there would be a high probability that the pilot libraries could use the MARC data, it was decided to limit the initial operation to current, English-language monographs. All the English-language materials (excluding certain documents, rare book materials, and all serial titles) catalogued each day (an estimated 125 titles) will be entered into Project MARC. The data will be sent to the participants on magnetic tapes on a weekly basis in order to approximate as nearly as possible an optimum distribution service.

Operational Details: A brief review of some of the operational details of Project MARC is provided to enable the reader to understand what the system will accomplish, how it will operate and the extent to which it falls short of an ideal distribution service. Since the system is still under development, some operational details are as yet uncertain.

The Project MARC system includes the following elements:

1. A method for capturing English-language catalog data, for monographs, together with any pertinent new name or subject cross references, at the earliest possible time when the catalog record is complete.
2. A method for editing and transcribing catalog cards into a format for subsequent conversion to machine-readable form. The data so edited include both traditional catalog information and additional data to allow more sophisticated machine searching and processing.

3. A method for converting data to punched paper tape form.
4. Computer equipment and programs for conversion of punched paper tape data to magnetic tape.
5. A tape format which provides for three different kinds of records: the full catalog record, the cross references for names and subject, and an abbreviated author/title record.
6. Computer printout of printed copy for proofreading.
7. Error correction routines.
8. Computer programs to provide file maintenance routines and print routines to produce a limited number of traditional library products, e.g. a complete set of catalog cards with overprinted headings.
9. Distribution routines for sending new tapes to users and recirculating old tapes back into the system.
10. Methods for evaluating the effectiveness of MARC operational procedures and the utility of the MARC data.

MARC Tape Record Format: The MARC record is divided into two sections: fixed fields and variable fields. Variable fields, in general, contain the same data that are presently on printed Library of Congress catalog cards. Fixed fields, in general contain information about the characteristics of the work being described, for example, the language in which it is written and whether the work is intended for juvenile readers.

Fixed Fields: The fixed field contains information which can be described with a constant number of characters and which is located in the same position in every record.

1. The Library of Congress catalog card number (serves as a unique control number).
2. Supplement number. (Supplements, indexes, and other dashed-on-entries are carried as independent records. The supplements are assigned the same Library of Congress catalog card number as the major work and therefore it is necessary to identify each supplement.)
3. Type of main entry, subdivided as follows:
   (a) Personal Author
   (b) Government Body
   (c) Society or Institution
   (d) Religious Society or Institution
   (e) Miscellaneous Corporate Body
   (f) Uniform
   (g) Title

4. Form of work. (For the MARC experiment, provision is made for identification of monographs and serials only.)
5. Bibliography indicator. (If a work contains a bibliography or is itself a bibliography, this field will be checked.)
6. Illustration indicator. (If the work contains any illustrations other than maps, this field will be checked.)
7. Map indicator. (If the work contains maps this field will be checked.)
8. Conference indicator. (If the work is a report or the proceedings of a conference, symposium, etc, this fixed field will be checked.)
9. Annotated card indicator. (Annotated cards have been designed by the Library of Congress for a card catalog of children's literature. If the work is included in the annotated card program, this field will be checked.)
10. Language field. (This field can contain up to two language codes and an indicator to describe their relationship. Indicators and their uses are listed below.)

INDICATOR USE

S   Work is in one language. Field 1 contains language code; Field 2 is blank.

T   Work is a translation. Field 1 is language of text; Field 2 is language of the original.

M   Work contains more than one language. Field 1 is principal language; Field 2 is the second language. If more than two languages are used, Field 2 is identified as Polyglot.

D   The work is a dictionary of more than one language. The Fields will contain the languages as described in M above.

G   Work is a grammar or reader. Native language of student is in Field 1; the language being studied is in Field 2.

11. Date field. (A date indicator is used to describe the relationship of the two date fields.)

INDICATOR USE

S   A single volume with a known date of publication is recorded as Date 1. The copyright date, if known, is Date 2.

R   A reproduction. The date of the reproduction is Date 1; the original publication date is Date 2.

N   Date of publication not known. Both Date fields are blank.

M   A multivolume work. The initial date is Date 1; the terminal date, if known, is Date 2. If the terminal date is not known, Date 2 will be set to 9999 to indicate that the date is open-ended.

Q   A questionable publication date is described as follows:

	Date 1	Date 2
18—	1800	1899
189—	1890	1899
189–?	1890	1899
1965?	1965	1965

12. Place of publication (expressed as a four-character code).
13. Publisher (expressed as a four-character code).
14. Height of volume (in centimeters).
15. Types of secondary entries. (In processing the variable fields, the computer program will set a unique character for each of the types of entry described in a-g of 3 above, for which there is one or more added entries. A unique character will also indicate the presence of one or more subject headings.)
16. Series indicator. (If a series note is present in a variable field, the computer program will set a series indicator.)
17. Local use. (Characters which are reserved for use by participating libraries.)
18. Control indicator. (Information about incoming records for local participants.)
   N = Record new this week
   O = Record new last week
   R = Record revised this week
   Blank = Record more than 2 weeks old
19. Length of record. (The total number of characters in the record.)

Variable Fields: Each variable field will be preceded by a six-character field, three characters of which identify the name of the field and three the length of the field.
1. Library of Congress call number.
2. Dewey Decimal Classification number.
3. Main entry. (All main entries except title main entry which will be recorded in (5) below.)
4. Filing title.

5. Title statement. (Includes the title and all information up to but not including the edition. A special delimiter will be used to define end of title and end of short title.)
6. Edition statement.
7. Imprint. (Including price when given.)
8. Collation.
9. (a) Series note (No added entry is to be made.)
   (b) Series note (Added entry to be made. A special delimiter will be used to define that portion of the note to be used as the added entry.)
10. Notes.
11. Tracings.
    (a) Subject headings
    (b) Personal author tracing
    (c) Government body tracing
    (d) Society or institution tracing
    (e) Religious society or institution tracing
    (f) Miscellaneous corporate body tracing
    (g) Title tracing (If the added entry is defined as the short title or full title in the title statement, this fact will be indicated in the tracing as T.)
    (h) Uniform heading tracing
12. Series tracing. (If the added entry is defined in the series note, this fact will be indicated in the tracing as S.)
13. Copy statement. (Library of Congress local information.)
14. National Bibliography number (National Bibliography citation number.)

MARC Worksheet and Input Device: Since normal cataloging procedures were not to be disturbed during the experiment, a worksheet had to be devised to capture data at the end of the cataloging process. When the cycle is complete, the finished catalog card (called a 'manuscript' card) is duplicated, by photographic means, on a MARC worksheet just before it is delivered to the typesetter.

The MARC editors then indicate on the worksheet the relevant variable fields and fill out the fixed fields as required. The form requires a minimum of work by the editors, is designed to facilitate the subsequent retyping, and has certain built-in error detection controls.

The data for the MARC record will be punched on a Dura Mach 10 automatic typewriter which produces both typewritten copy and an 8-level punched paper tape. A pre-punched program tape will allow automatic typing and punching of repetitive information. The program tape will also permit the names of each variable field to be typed automatically. These names will not be punched on the paper tape since they serve only as a guide to the typist as she transcribes each field.

The character set and keyboard design for the Project MARC typewriter was based on the model keyboard for standard library typewriters which reflects the current thinking of the Typewriter Keyboard Committee, Resource and Technical Services Division of the American Library Association. The intent was to achieve maximum compatibility between the punched paper tape typewriter and the standard manual typewriter.

MARC Printout Products: The computer programs for Project MARC will enable the following to be printed. (Where applicable, the programs will enable print-out in upper and lower case or upper case only, depending on equipment available at local installations.)
1. Diagnostic printouts for proofreading at LC.
2. Listings to be sent, with the magnetic tapes, to participants.
3. Printed products to be produced at local installations.

Diagnostic Printouts: For each record, whether new or corrected, there will be a diagnostic print-out of the machine-readable record reformatted for ease in proofreading. Certain notes may be printed to alert the proofer to errors in the data noted by the computer while making validity checks.

In the Project, to check for both human and machine errors, it was decided that all records would be proofed after computer processing. The cost and efficiency of this technique, as compared to proofing the typewritten copy before input to the computer, will be evaluated.

Printed Listings: Two printed lists will be mailed to the participants along with the magnetic tape. The first is a cumulative list of the LC card numbers in numerical order for which there are records contained on the tape. The first two weeks a record appears on a tape, the card number is marked with an asterisk, a blank indicates an old record. The second listing provides an access for those who don't know the LC card number since it is an abbreviated (120 characters) author/title list in alphabetical order with the LC card number.

Printing Capability: Participating libraries will receive computer programs which will enable them to print the following:

1. The contents of the entire record (either all the records on the entire tape or selectively by LC card number).
2. The name and subject cross references either in a list form or on 3 × 5 cards.
3. An entire set of 3 × 5 catalog cards with over-printed added and subject entries. Obviously the use of the computer printer does not allow the typographical niceties of typeset cards and compromises had to be made. The maximum amount of data which can be placed on the card is seventeen lines of print with forty-nine characters per line. No facility exists for either hyphenation or horizontal justification of the right margins. No words will be broken at the end of the line, therefore the right-hand margin may have noticeable variation from line to line. (The programs permit upper and lower case printing where such a print chain is available.)

MARC Staff: Project MARC is a co-operative experiment utilizing staff drawn from a number of administrative units throughout the Library. The Processing Department is responsible for getting the catalog data into the MARC system and for editing. The Data Processing Office staff will punch the data and perform all computer and control functions. The Office of the Secretary will undertake the duplication of listings and the mailing of lists and magnetic tapes to the participants. The Information Systems Office will monitor and co-ordinate the entire project, assume responsibility for any modification of MARC programs, and evaluate the results of the experiment.

The full-time staff will include an editor drawn from the Library's senior cataloging staff, two assistant editors, four typists for data conversion, one operation control clerk, and one operation supervisor. In addition, there are many part-time participants including supervisors, computer room staff, secretarial support, etc.

Operating Routines: When the MARC work-sheets, with the photocopied manuscript catalog card, are forwarded to the MARC editor, they are completed and sent daily for typing. There are elaborate control routines to ensure that each record is processed through the entire routine including proofing, correction, revision, and actual dissemination of the participants. The data are processed by the computer on a daily basis and are cumulated weekly. Routines have been devised to allow this processing to be done either when

there are small units of free time on the computer or all at one time.

Participating libraries will receive the tapes and select information as required for local needs. Tapes are to be returned to the Library of Congress for re-use. It is expected that allowing three tapes per library will enable one to be available for the weekly distribution at all times.

During the entire six-month test period about 18,000 records will be generated. At some point the records will exceed the capacity of a single tape. The Library would simply start a new tape to avoid the problems of distributing two or more tapes to a library; participants may set up routines to merge data locally at this time.

MARC Evaluation and Findings: The actual results of the experiment are, of course, unknown at this time. However, several libraries have indicated a number of specific uses to which they plan to put the MARC data. A sampling of proposed uses is listed below. (Uses related to traditional library products, e.g. catalog cards, are excluded.)

1. Search of incoming MARC tapes against machine-readable faculty interest profiles to test feasibility of selective dissemination service on a university campus.
2. Selection of juvenile titles to prepare listings for use in library school courses in children's literature.
3. Book catalog studies.
4. Test suitability of data for university book union catalog.
5. Preparation of machine-readable book cards.
6. Use MARC data for local on-line testing.
7. Experiments with bibliographical projects in reference department.
8. Correlation of subject headings and main entries.
9. Use of data for acquisitions routines.
10. Create list of publishers who publish books about Latin America.
11. Test concept of development of regional distribution centers for machine-readable data.
12. Study authority file problems in a mechanized system.

MARC should provide information on the actual cost of converting and distributing data; on the use of specific data elements in the record; on the suitability of the record for modification and manipulation at local libraries; identification of problem areas in editing for machine processing;

and the identification of problem areas in maintaining codes, authority files, etc.

Participating libraries will be requested to submit reports during the Project. In spring 1967 these reports, together with Library of Congress evaluations, and other independent comments, will be given intensive study. A final report on the entire project, including a detailed analysis of user comments, will be prepared for distribution.

MARC EXTENSIONS AND THE LIBRARY OF CONGRESS SYSTEM DEVELOPMENT STUDY

When Project MARC was announced and the early discussion meetings were held, it became obvious that there was a tremendous interest in this experiment in the library and information community. The general feeling was that such a project should not be terminated without permitting the user group to make a serious attempt to effect its continuation. On the other hand, the Library of Congress had been advised by the survey team, whose recommendations have been made public in *Automation and the Library of Congress*[7], that it should concentrate on a total systems approach to its central bibliographic processing and control operations. Thus any extension of Project MARC would have to enhance and be compatible with the long-range goal of a large-scale computer-based bibliographic system, to be implemented in full or in part by 1972. In addition, since it might, in fact, be replaced by the new system, costs for such extension might have to be amortized over a much shorter period.

It would be feasible to design a series of extensions for Project MARC which could gradually approach the 1972 system and be phased into, or replaced by it. Such extensions might include one or all of the following features:

1. Increase of MARC data to include other than monographic materials.
2. Increase of MARC data to encompass an ever-expanding number of foreign languages.
3. Increase number of libraries to whom service can be offered.
4. Utilization of more sophisticated equipment for encoding and dissemination of data.
5. Selection of individual items of some sub-set of data, i.e., providing a 'tailor-made' tape for an individual customer or for a group of customers with like requirements.
6. Capability of utilizing electronic photocomposi-

tion devices for printing catalog cards and other printed materials.

Such MARC extensions depend on so many variables that at this time plans are extremely tenuous. However, the first modification of the existing pilot operation will probably be in the data conversion operation. It would be desirable to bypass the complex and error-prone routines associated with either the keypunch or punched paper tape typewriter as an input device. One possibility is direct, on-line input to the computer. This method could not be used in Project MARC because of problems of equipment delivery and the time required to prepare the more complex computer programs which such an input system requires.

System Development: The first stages in the development of long-range system planning began in December of 1965 when a request for proposals[8] for a functional description of an automated central bibliographic system for the Library was mailed to potential contractors. A contract will be awarded in June 1966 and work is expected to begin in late summer. The contractor will begin by reviewing the detailed analysis of present Library operations which has been prepared by the Information Systems Office staff. Understanding the basic problem of what librarians are trying to accomplish, how data are created and manipulated, and identification of problem areas and areas for potential improvement will account for a large part of the contract effort. A statement of system requirements will be drawn up and, finally, a recommended system will be presented along with alternative systems for consideration by the Library.

In this study all of the central data files of the Library will be analyzed in depth. The nature of the requirements for file organization in the system eventually designed cannot even be predicted now; therefore, a system such as MARC can only be regarded as an interim stage in the development of new techniques. The benefit stems from the actual experience which can be gained from operating and participating in Project MARC and from the creation of a machine-readable data base available to libraries for testing of complex computer-based techniques.

SELECTED REFERENCES ON MACHINE-READABLE CATALOGING

1. Atherton, Pauline. Is compatibility of authority files practicable? *in* Newman,

Simon N., ed. Information Systems Compatibility. Washington, Spartan Books, 1965. (American University, Washington, D.C. Technology of Management Series, v. 1) p. 69-81. (In press)

2. Bregzis, Ritvars. The Ontario New Universities Library Project—an automated bibliographic data control system. *College and Research Libraries*, v. 26, Nov. 1965: 495-508.

3. Buckland, Lawrence F. The recording of Library of Congress bibliographical data in machine form; a report prepared for the Council on Library Resources, Inc., by Lawrence F. Buckland. Revised. Washington, Council on Library Resources, Inc., 1965. 54 p.

4. Fasana, Paul J. Automating cataloging functions in conventional libraries. *Library Resources and Technical Services*, v. 7, Fall 1963: 350-65.

5. Hines, Theodore C. and Jessica L. Harris. Computer filing of index, bibliographic, and catalog entries. New York, School of Library Service, Columbia University, 1965. 1 v., various paging.

6. Perrault, Jean M. The computerized book catalog at Florida Atlantic University. *College and Research Libraries*, v. 25, May 1964: 185-97.

7. U.S. *Library of Congress. Information Systems Office.* Planning memorandum number 3: A proposed format for a standardized machine-readable catalog record. A preliminary draft prepared by Henriette D. Avram, Ruth S. Freitag, and Kay D. Guiles, Office of the Information Systems Specialist. Washington, June 1965. 110 p.

8. —— Proceedings of the second conference on machine-readable catalog copy; [held at the] Library of Congress, November 22, 1965. Washington, 1965. 35 p.

9. —— Proceedings of the third conference on machine-readable catalog copy (Discussion of MARC Pilot Project); [held at the] Library of Congress, February 25, 1966. Washington, 1966. 30 p.

10. —— MARC Pilot Project, report no. 1. Magnetic tape format of the machine-readable catalog record. Washington, April 1966. 11 p.

11. —— MARC Pilot Project, report no. 2. Progress report. Washington, April 1966. 15 p.

12. —— MARC Pilot Project, report no. 3. Interim technical report describing the MARC pilot system. Washington, April 1966. 28 p.

NOTES

[1] Project Director for Project MARC.
[2] Project Director, Phase I, Library of Congress System Development Study.
[3] See bibliography at the end of this article.
[4] Participants were selected from a roster of thirty-seven libraries who wanted to take part in the Project. The selection was based on the following factors: computer equipment available, assigned staff, proposed uses of the MARC data, geographic location, type of library, expressed willingness to utilize data and provide reports and user evaluations. Sixteen libraries were selected: Argonne National Laboratory, Chicago, Illinois; Georgia Institute of Technology; Harvard University; Indiana University; Montgomery County Public Schools, Maryland; Nassau (County) Library System, New York; National Agricultural Library; Redstone Scientific Information Center, Alabama; Rice University; University of California at Los Angeles, Institute of Library Research; University of Chicago; University of Florida; University of Missouri; University of Toronto; Washington State Library, Olympia; Yale University.
[5] The remaining $30,000 of the grant will be used for studies to determine the demand which exists for catalog data in machine-readable form and to plan methods for meeting that demand on a permanent basis.
[6] The Library of Congress computer system presently consists of an IBM 360 computer with the following configuration including necessary control units:
1 Model 30D Central Processing Unit
4 9 Track, 800 b.p.i. Magnetic Tape Drives
1 Card Reader/Punch 2540
1 Printer with 48 character set 1403 MOD 3
1 Multiplexer Channel
1 Console Typewriter 1052
For purposes of the MARC Pilot Project, this system will be augmented with the following equipment, together with necessary control units:
1 7 Track, 556 b.p.i. Magnetic Tape Drive
1 7 Track Magnetic Tape Compatibility Unit
1 Paper Tape Reader 2671
2 Selector Channels

1 9 Track, 800 b.p.i. Magnetic Tape Drive
1120 Character Print Train
[7] Gilbert W. King, Automation and the Library of Congress. [A report] submitted by Gilbert W. King [and others].
(Washington: Library of Congress, 1963.)
[8] B. E. See Markuson, 'A System Development Study for the Library of Congress Automation Program,' *Library Quarterly.* **36:** 197-233, No. 3, July 1966. This article includes a reprint of the request for proposals.